INTRODUCTION TO CORRECTIONS

INTRODUCTION TO CORRECTIONS

SECOND EDITION

Clemens Bartollas
The University of Northern Iowa
John P. Conrad

Foreword by Simon Dinitz
The Ohio State University

HarperCollins*Publishers*

To Linda Dippold Bartollas and Charlotte Conrad

Sponsoring Editor: Alan McClare
Project Editor: Robert Ginsberg
Design Supervisor: Jaye Zimet
Cover Design: Jaye Zimet
Cover Photo: COMSTOCK, Inc./Jack Elness
Photo Researcher: Mira Schachne
Production Assistant: Linda Murray
Compositor: American–Stratford Graphic Services, Inc.
Printer and Binder: R. R. Donnelley & Sons Company
Cover Printer: New England Book Components, Inc.

Introduction to Corrections, Second Edition

Library of Congress Cataloging-in-Publication Data

Bartollas, Clemens.
Introduction to corrections / Clemens Bartollas, John P. Conrad; foreword by Simon Dinitz.—2nd ed.
p. cm.
Includes index.
ISBN 0-06-040527-9
1. Corrections—United States. I. Conrad, John Phillips, 1913–. II. Title.
HV9304.B37 1992
364.6′0973—dc20 91-23187
CIP

92 93 94 95 9 8 7 6 5 4 3 2 1

Contents

Foreword

The U.S. penal system has never been in worse shape. It is cursed with massive overcrowding, at a level not even imaginable a decade earlier (the prison population has doubled since 1980 and quadrupled since 1970), and there is no respite in sight. The system has inadequate resources to build new jails and prisons and upgrade or replace those long since antiquated. There is a shortage of staff and especially of adequately trained correctional line personnel. The inmate population is racially and ethnically polarized, and relationships among these communities is often strained—communal warfare is just a spark away. Correctional administrators also face the problems of prison gangs, drug and alcohol abuse, and an increasing population of AIDS-afflicted prisoners as well as inmates with extensive histories of violence and mental-health and mental-retardation problems (these so-called special offender groups also include sex violators, a growing geriatric and physically impaired population, and the fastest growing group of all, that of female prisoners).

Lacking a supportive political or public constituency of any significance or size, penologists are rethinking the correctional mission, ideology, practices, and programs. It is still too early to offer a blueprint of the emerging system in the next century, but it is a fair presumption that emphasis on treatment and rehabilitation will continue to decline, as will court involvement in prisoners' rights issues, while more attention will be given to the efficient and cost-effective management of the prison system. Community-based treatment innovations such as house arrest, intensive probation supervision, and restitution centers will expand (and widen the net of offenders under penal supervision). "Boot camps" will become even more the rage, and the transportation of convicted felons to distant locations to serve time in medium and minimum security facilities is more than likely. Although it is difficult to predict the exact shape of the correctional future, it is not too early to dismiss recent correctional history as a painful stage in the evolution of punishment in the United States.

Nevertheless, despite grave problems, the criminal justice and penal systems have made important strides in the past 25 years in ensuring greater fairness and equity in sentencing policy and in providing a more humane and less cruel prison environment for those in penal confinement. Under the First, Eighth, and Fourteenth Amendments to the Constitution, among others, institutions now usually meet basic minimum standards, such as those of health and safety, of sanitation and recreation, of visitation, of access to a law library—as well as myriad other rights not expressly denied prisoners by virtue of their confinement. The "total," closed institution has become more open. The criteria that together define legally acceptable confinement now center on the "totality of prison conditions" and on "evolving standards of decency." Although many individual prisons are still far out of compliance, by necessity and less often by choice, the trend is toward meeting court-imposed minimum standards with all deliberate speed.

The correctional enterprise has many detractors and few defenders. Humanitarians and human service advocates decry the lack of emphasis on rehabilitation and, conversely, the current passion for incapacitation. There are complaints about the warehousing of inmates without much attention, if any at all, to their presenting problems such as that of addictive drug use. There are complaints about idleness, about inadequate job training programs, about absent or inferior counseling and guidance programs, and about a lack of focus on coping with serious personal failings and incapacities. Not much that now passes for treatment deserves to be taken as serious behavioral, social and psychological intervention. Institutions are sorely pressed to house, feed, and attend to the basic needs of the masses of inmates, let alone cope with organic and functional disabilities. In the past 25 years, the formerly unspoken has become correctional dogma: With regard to treatment, "nothing works"—at least, not very well or for very many. As a result, far too little is done, or even attempted (with the exception of educational and voluntary self-improvement programs), to return to the community prisoners who are better prepared for independent living than they were when they were received from the courts. Under these circumstances, the high post-incarceration failure rate is not unexpected. Nor is much being done to transform the criminogenic streets and neighborhoods that dump huge numbers of males into the juvenile training school and prison streams. Prisoners can hardly be faulted for the fact that some underclass communities send more age-eligible males to the correctional system, including probation and parole, than to college.

Correctional administrators commonly complain about their inability to manage. The bureaucratization of the system forces them to cope with the central office officials' demands, which may be tangential to their pressing concerns of creating and maintaining a safe, secure, peaceful environment. In addition, management is confronted with unionized staff who are no longer beholden to the superintendent for their employment. Officers seek to control the conditions of their everyday lives, including shift assignment, location in the institution, fringe benefits, and wages.

And officers are likely to grieve over contract provisions and sometimes even over things like the dress code—petty grievances that drive administrators to distraction. Line officers have a frightful "burnout" rate as well as high job turnover, and many suffer debilitating stress-related physical and psychological problems. They often feel impotent and angry that they cannot carry out their tasks without second-guessing by the administration and attorneys for the prisoners who routinely challenge their actions. They feel that they they have been deserted by administrators and by the legislature and the executive and, most of all, by a judiciary that cares more about the rights of inmates than the rights of staff. In an already tense, high-stress environment, these feelings and perceptions add to the alienation of those who are confined or get paid to work behind the walls or fences.

Inevitably, inmates are the most embittered of all. Regardless of the justice of their confinement and despite access to due process procedures and the exercise of legal rights, historically foreign to the convict state, prisoners are keenly aware that they live in a society of captives and suffer its "pains of punishment." The traditional bonds that united them in their opposition to the administration have loosened. They are more divided by race, religion, ethnicity, and geographic region than united by their state of confinement. The influence of the outer world (the importation of street values) has made confinement much more dangerous than in the past. There is much to fear from the psychologically unstable, from gang members contesting for turf, from sexual exploiters, and from drug-dependent inmates involved in the contraband trade. Surviving in this setting is an adventure of sorts and, for all but the most committed to the inmate life, an unhappy interlude. Understandably, institutions have exploded with great frequency and ferocity. Sometimes these disturbances make media headlines, as in the deadly Attica and New Mexico riots, but most of the time the several dozen annual disturbances receive little or no notice or attention. Institutional instability also yields a considerable number of murders and suicides (69 and 140, respectively, in 1988) and many times more rapes and assaults.

This second edition of *Introduction to Corrections*, like its predecessor, tries to make sense of the anarchic and discouraging state of the criminal justice system, especially the corrections subsystem which is its tail end. In this comprehensive and well-researched book, Clemens Bartollas and John Conrad—who together have more than 75 years' experience in the system as professors, researchers, administrators, practitioners in institutions and in the community, and as expert witnesses in correctional cases before the courts—combine their considerable talents and writing skills to describe and analyze what was, what is, and what is likely to be. An accomplished essayist, Conrad assesses in Chapter 1 the state of corrections and the changing correctional landscape. In setting the table, the chapter focuses on eight aspects, covered elsewhere in greater detail, that reflect the changed character of the field. Earlier in this foreword I referred to some of these changes: the centralization of administration, the collapse of the rehabilitative ideal, the professionalization of the practitioners in the field, the population explosion, the prison facility building boom, court-reform litigation, the growing incidence of prison violence, and the almost total domination of the prison by the underclass. Societal response may already be late in coming.

Three remarkably good chapters trace and highlight the events and innovations that have transformed our ideas about penal sanction and its implementation. The text begins its analysis in the most ancient period of recorded history and moves us forward step by step, highlighting the process of change and its specific products: death, torture, corporal punishment, exile, enslavement, the discovery of institutionalization, the emergence of the "total institution," the differentiation of institutions in everything from architecture to programming, the search for alternatives to confinement, and the development of the smorgasbord of options currently available. Underpinning all of this material is the question to which the authors return frequently: What is the purpose of punishment? In the end, two competing goals emerge: the goal of "just deserts" (in earlier times, simple and proportionate vengeance) and the utilitarian ends of prevention and deterrence (including rehabilitation). There is also a balanced and timely chapter on the death penalty, which, after a period of non-use, has returned forcefully to the American scene. In some sense, the death penalty debate sets limits on the field. With more than 2200 inmates on death rows, the death penalty conflict is joined and rejoined with predictable regularity. The chapter takes the format of a debate between John Conrad and Ernest van den Haag, a philosopher, psychoanalyst, and thoughtful advocate of retention.

Part Three of the book details the history, development and recent innovations in community corrections, including privately run community-based correctional programs. This overview is followed by chapters on the ever-controversial but necessary alternatives of probation and parole as well as various reentry programs such as prerelease, work and educational release, and halfway house release. The number of men and women in these community options is growing apace with the institutional population. Far from disappearing from the correctional scene, we can expect continued growth in the number and variety of such programs and their increased importance in managing convicted felons as an alternative to or after institutionalization. The most obvious example of the proliferation of alternatives to jail and prison confinement is the use of various electronic monitoring devices or programs.

The most overlooked aspect of institutionalization is the county and municipal jail. There are well over 3000 such facilities, and they receive about 10 million cases a year. About half of these are awaiting trial, and the other half are serving short sentences for misdemeanors and lesser felonies. There is no way the jails, mostly old and mostly quite deteriorated, can cope with this many charges a year. The transient nature of the detainees and their many problems, principally substance abuse and drunk driving, as well as mental, emotional, and social deficits, makes treatment, however necessary, difficult to provide. In this chapter on the jails and workhouses, the authors do full justice to this institution and to efforts to bring it into conformity with the minimum standards of decency and services that the courts have mandated.

The chapter on state and federal prisons focuses on institutional administration and styles of management, on security concerns, and on prison violence. Bartollas and Conrad present insightful and cutting-edge data on and analyses of virtually all aspects of prison life from the standpoint not only of the inmate but also of the correctional and treatment staffs and the administration, from the warden on down. This material is instructive, current, and well written. It should engage everyone with an interest in prison life.

Few things about corrections irritate the public as much as concern over the rights of wrongdoers. And nothing has had a more profound or lasting impact on prison life—indeed, the entire criminal justice process—as court-determined prisoner rights. These rights can be summed up as follows: Prisoners have the same rights as those guaranteed to all of us by the Constitution and the Bill of Rights except those expressly denied them by virtue of their confinement. Chapter 16 contains a detailed review and discussion of the controversial issue of prisoners' rights. It is up to date and focuses on the implications of various court decisions regarding speech (censorship), assembly, religion, search and seizure (contraband), security, and legal representation on life behind bars.

The number of women at all points in the criminal justice system pipelines has never been greater. State and federal facilities are virtually bulging with numbers of women thought improbable even a decade (or less) ago, before the impact of drugs on the system. Women present special problems in confinement—problems inherent in their roles as mothers and the primary caregivers of children. The chapter on women in prisons contains an overview of the special characteristics of the female prison population; their special needs and attempts to provide education, work, and job training; parenting; health needs and practices; and preparation for reentry into the community for this rapidly growing segment of inmates.

There follows a chapter on research, and a final one that looks to the future. The chapter on research in the field is a welcome departure from conventional corrections textbooks. The material is current, important, and a factor in policy debates on such issues as selective incapacitation and the outcome of treatment programs. Mainly, however, the thrust of the chapter is that research must be an integral part of theory and practice and that there is no substitute for well-conceived and well-executed studies, both qualitative and quantitative. Both these topics are unique to this text and round out an excellent introduction to corrections past and present.

SIMON DINITZ
THE OHIO STATE UNIVERSITY

Preface

Our purpose in this book is to provide a comprehensive introduction to corrections. American prisons, jails, and youth facilities have been widely and severely criticized. Many of these criticisms have been deserved. There are horror stories, though fewer now than in an ugly past. A visit to any maximum security prison will dishearten the humane reformer. Violence is endemic and lethal. Lives are lost, and only rigorous coercion maintains control.

The past century has been cluttered with panaceas, most of which have blossomed briefly only to wither into failure. The wheel has been reinvented again and again. It is a parochial history; only in the past three decades have wardens and parole boards been receptive to the ideas of professional men and women in related fields. Change is slow. Obstacles to improvement are real and supported by substantial public opinion. The hard line prevails today, and it is politically popular to "get tough" with felons of all descriptions.

In spite of a discouraging past, these are exciting times in which to study corrections. A new generation of leaders has been trained and is expected to abide by professional standards. Crime rates are high, and prison populations have risen dramatically. The cost of corrections is now a major and growing burden in the budget for every state in the union as well as for the federal government. It is generally recognized that prison space is an expensive resource and becoming more so every year; it is not to be squandered on men and women who can be kept under control in the community. Mere benevolence no longer motivates community-based correctional programs; the need for them is pressing and inescapable. The day is past when probation and parole were nominal services carried out by overworked men and women with unmanageable caseloads.

To meet these needs, this newly professionalized field has adopted standards of management, control, and programming that are widely accepted and implemented. All levels of staff come to work with at least a complete high school education and are encouraged to continue their education and training throughout their careers. The federal courts once kept their distance from corrections but for the past twenty years have mandated humane standards of treatment. Corrections has emerged from a dismal past. It now offers challenging careers to men and women who wish to be of service to their communities.

Textbook writers should make their subjects come alive. Every student, every teacher has had enough of droning textbooks that inspire the reader to count the pages until the reading assignment is finished. We have tried to reflect the vitality of modern corrections. The real world of corrections is to be found in the cellblocks, the halfway houses, and the probation officers' rounds of clients' homes and work places. With descriptions of that real world, with interviews of correctional leaders and practitioners, with case studies and photographs, we have tried to show what reality in corrections is like.

A number of themes unify this text. First, a knowledge of the past is essential to understanding corrections in the present. Second, the wider social context, or environment, shapes what takes place within corrections. Third, American society is committed to the preservation of the prison. Fourth, the hopelessness of the underclass is resulting in higher rates of violent and property offenses, drug trafficking, and alienation from traditional values. Fifth, correctional bureaucracies tend to be top heavy, resistant to change, and inefficient. Sixth, crowding dramatically affects the quality of residential programs in the community and confinement in jails and prisons. Seventh, the intervention of the courts has contributed much to conventional reform. Finally, good people make a difference in the management, supervision, and control of offenders.

It is this final theme that good people make a difference wherein we see the hope of corrections. The present period of repression will eventually pass, and a new day of reform will come, as has taken place throughout the history of corrections. We believe that these good people are already laying the groundwork for a new age of reform, and, therefore, we give special attention to their characteristics, to how they see their jobs, and to what they believe should be done to effect change.

New features of this second edition include a more extensive examination of the history of corrections, the justification of punishment, community corrections acts, and the controversy over the death penalty. Innovations that are changing the face of criminal justice are also featured, including intensive probation supervision, electronic monitoring of offenders in the community, the use of house arrest, boot camp confinement, and the New Generation jail. We place a special emphasis on new wardens of the 1990s, as we examine the new style of prison management, with systematic classification, high technology in maintaining security, and better use of human resources in understanding and controlling prisoners. Both the old curse of violence and the new curse of prison gangs are discussed. Finally, unique to corrections texts, we include a chapter on correctional research.

Chapter 1 provides the background for the study of corrections and invites students to study this changing field in depth. Chapters 2, 3, and 4 recount the history of corrections from ancient times to the present; Chapters 3 and 4 focus on the development of the uniquely American version of corrections. Chapter 5 examines in some detail the justification and administration of punishment. Chapter 6 reviews the sentencing process and considers the changes the changes introduced in new sentencing legislation. In Chapter 7 we trace the history of capital punishment and its present status, together with the continuing controversy about its propriety and its value as a deterrent. Chapters 8 through 10 take the reader through the gamut of community corrections, including probation and parole and the new demands made on practitioners. Chapters 11 and 12 describe the changing structure and programs of jails and prisons. The next four chapters, 13 through 16, deal with prison administration: management, security, violence, and the rights of prisoners. Chapters 17 and 18 examine women's and men's prisons. Chapter 19 describes the present status of research and considers what students and practitioners need to understand about research in order to facilitate it and make use of its findings. Chapter 20 peers into an uncertain future.

Neither of us is value-free, but we have tried to make a fair and balanced presentation of a field that is beset with controversy, much of it passionate and emotional. Everyone agrees that corrections should be just and humane. If that end is to be achieved, present policies and practices must be objectively examined. We have tried to assemble the information upon which a basis for that examination can be constructed.

ACKNOWLEDGMENTS

Many friends and colleagues—more than we can acknowledge here—have made invaluable contributions to this second edition. Our wives, Linda Dippold Bartollas and Charlotte Conrad, have always been tolerant and supportive. A number of corrections practitioners kindly consented to be interviewed for this book, including Orville Pung, commissioner of the Minnesota Department of Corrections; Chase Riveland, secretary of the Washington Department of Corrections; Morris L. Thigpen, director of the Alabama Department of Corrections; J. Michael Quinlan, director of the U.S. Bureau of Prisons; George Beto, former director of the Texas Department of Corrections; Janet A. Leban, director of the Pennsylvania Prison Society; JoAnne Page, director of the Fortune Society, New York City; Louise Wolfgramm, director of Amicus, St. Paul, Minnesota; Vincent Nathan, Special Master; Frank Wood, warden of the Oak Park Heights Prison in Minnesota; W. H. Dallman, warden of the Lebanon Correctional Institution in Ohio; Dennis Schrantz, executive director of the Office of Community Corrections; and Jeff Martin, coordinator of the Community Corrections Act in Minnesota.

The year's sabbatical that Clemens Bartollas received from the graduate school of the University of Northern Iowa was crucial to the completion of this project. We thank Rosemarie Skaine for all that she and her staff did to keep the manuscript moving into final form. Heidi Anderegg, Trina Cherrie, Annemarie Stilwell, Cynthia Betterton, Esther Bishop, Dixie Smith, Reygan Howard, and Lisa Gioimo were indispensable. Finally, we are grateful to Alan McClare, editor, to Robert Ginsberg, the project editor, and to Eric Newman, our copy editor.

CLEMENS BARTOLLAS
JOHN P. CONRAD

PART ONE

History and Development of Corrections

Chapter 1

Invitation to Corrections

CHAPTER OUTLINE

EIGHT EMPHASES TO GUIDE STUDY
- *Importance of History*
- *Influence of the Wider Social Context*
- *Society's Belief in the Preservation of the Prison*
- *Prevalence of Overcrowding*
- *Hopelessness of the Underclass*
- *Bureaucratic Resistance to Change*
- *Court Intervention and Reform*
- *Good People Make a Difference*

IDEALISTIC LIP SERVICE AND STAGNANT REALITY
- *Condemned to Hard Labor*
- *From "Kin See" to "Kain't See"*
- *The Secret World of Wardens and Guards*
- *The Realism of Practical Men and Women*

THE CHANGING CORRECTIONAL LANDSCAPE
- *The Centralization of Administration*
- *The Rehabilitative Ideal*
- *A Get-Tough Stance on Crime*
- *The Population Explosion*
- *The Building Boom*
- *Reform Litigation*
- *The Growing Incidence of Violence*

POINTING THE WAY TO A BETTER FUTURE

CONCLUSIONS

This is a textbook written to inform students about the institutions and methods that society now uses to punish, control, and change the behavior of convicted offenders. The preservation of order requires that people conform to society's rules. But devising the proper methods for dealing with those who do not has been a perplexing problem since the dawn of history. Striking out vengefully against wrongdoers was one of the first methods used to deal with criminals. At various times and in various societies, criminals have been fined, forced to pay restitution for the harm they have committed, banished, tortured, and even executed. In the past two centuries, punishment in the form of imprisonment has been a popular way of dealing with the criminal. More recently, it was thought that it made more sense to reform than to punish the offender, thereby preparing him or her for a useful and productive role in society. Finally, in the United States during the 1970s and 1980s there was a return to old solutions—punishment and incarceration. A tough stance with criminals has resulted in crowded prisons and jails, a return to determinate and mandatory sentencing, and the reinstatement of the death penalty.

We have prepared this book during a period when corrections is in a daunting crisis. No one can be sure that successful remedies can be found for obvious shortcomings in a dangerously overloaded system. We intend to describe the crisis in detail; it will not be a glowing picture. The times call for able, courageous, and wise public servants who can bring purpose and vitality to a confused and stagnant system. The challenge is formidable. The opportunities for service are great. To borrow Charles Dickens's famous statement about the French Revolution, in corrections, these are the best of times and the worst of times.

EIGHT EMPHASES TO GUIDE STUDY

We call our readers' attention to the major emphases of our approach to the study of corrections. Throughout this book, we will touch on each of them many times. An understanding of their significance in past, present, and future developments will be essential to an understanding of corrections in the 1990s.

Importance of History

We have stressed the historical aspects of corrections throughout this book. The history of corrections reveals the events, individuals, and trends of the past and examines why particular beliefs and trends appeared at the time. A knowledge of the past is essential to an understanding of the present and for planning the future: You cannot know where to go without knowing where you have been.

Influence of the Wider Social Context

The administration of justice reflects the attitudes of the wider society toward persons convicted of serious offenses. Fundamental influences on the philosophy of punishment, the mission of corrections, and correctional programs are found in what the public and its policymakers want.

Society's Belief in the Preservation of the Prison

American society has been historically committed to the prison as the ultimate form of social control. Although there is much dissatisfaction with its performance, there is little disagreement as to its necessity in dealing with serious offenders.

Prevalence of Overcrowding

More people are sent to prison, put on probation, and released to parole than ever before. Not only are the nation's correctional services burdened with too many men, women, and children to correct, but there is also mounting uncertainty about what to do with them and for them.

Hopelessness of the Underclass

The most threatening problem confronting the criminal justice system as a whole and the correctional agencies in particular is the continuing existence of a large underclass in the inner cities of our metropolitan centers. Because of the lack of access to legitimate employment opportunities, there is an abnormally large incidence of crime and use of narcotics in this segment of the community. This state of affairs has yet to be successfully resolved by criminal justice and other agencies of social control.

Bureaucratic Resistance to Change

Like all large public and private organizations, correctional agencies must be administered through bureaucracies. Correctional bureaucracies tend to be top heavy, resistant to change, and inefficient. Efforts to reform corrections must take into account the obstinacy of established correctional staff and provide for ways to assure their cooperation.

Court Intervention and Reform

The reform of corrections during recent years has depended heavily on litigation to establish prisoners' constitutional rights. The failure to grant such rights have resulted in prisons in thirty-six states being declared unconstitutional.

Good People Make a Difference

The maintenance of reforms requires not only the vigilant interest of staff committed to effective and humane services but also the persistent concern of a responsible public. We believe that good people managing and working in short- and long-term correctional institutions, supervising probation, parole, and residential services, and providing support networks in a variety of correctional contexts have made a difference.

Before describing briefly the correctional landscape as we begin the final decade of the twentieth century and examining what is needed to point the way to a better future, we present the grim picture of where corrections was prior to World War II. As perplexing as the correctional landscape may be today, an examination of the recent past reveals how far corrections has come in this century.

IDEALISTIC LIP SERVICE AND STAGNANT REALITY

During the 1930s, California's maximum security prison at Folsom was ruled by a succession of wardens chosen for their loyal political service rather than for their penological expertise, a specialty that was neither well established nor generally recognized. In those times wardens throughout the nation were like feudal barons, lords of all they surveyed, not to be held accountable as to specifics of management. Wardens were judged by their peers: "He's a good prison man" or "He just can't handle it." Riots, escapes, and exposés of scandalous corruption might shake or even end their tenure, but if no such events came to public attention, they could expect to remain in office for as long as their political parties could elect the governor. A credible legend about one such warden at the Folsom prison appears in Box 1-1. That anecdote is characteristic of a simpler time. One famous warden allowed himself to be photographed in the act of flogging a misbehaving prisoner, explaining to the watching press that "these men aren't here for playing hooky from Sunday School." Discipline in American prisons was rough and physical, though public flogging was not routine everywhere. Until 1966, when the federal courts outlawed the practice, prisoners in Mississippi and Arkansas were punished by the strap, out of public sight. The strap was made of leather, 3½ to 5½ feet in length, about 4 inches wide and with a wooden handle 8 to 12 inches long. Arkansas had an informal requirement that strapping be limited to 10 blows on the buttocks at a time for any single offense. Sometimes, though not always, the prisoner's posterior might be bare. There is some reason to believe that this limit was not always observed.

Southern prisons employed convict guards for perimeter security and to maintain order in the fields and in the cellblocks. Their methods were straightforward and rough. They were not supposed to administer the strap, but the federal courts found that this rule was sometimes breached.[1] The unsightly spectacle of chain gangs on the roads created a national controversy. The men were in convict stripes, chained to one another and under guard by correctional officers with shotguns. After years of denunciation in the press and from the pulpits, and a sensational movie, "I Am a

Box 1-1 A Legend from the Past

The scene is the warden's enormous office during a morning meeting of the senior staff. Behind his uncluttered desk sits the warden. Surrounding the desk are his cronies, comfortably seated in green leather upholstered easy chairs: the associate warden, the captain, the business manager, and others of a favored few. Cigars and coffee keep the discussion genial. The topic is not on record, but it may or may not have concerned prison operations.

The tranquil gathering is interrupted when a young lieutenant bursts into the office.

"Warden, sir," he says, "I have to report that there's been a serious fight out on the yard. Prisoner Smith stabbed Prisoner Jones. I have rushed Jones to the hospital, but he is not expected to live. Prisoner Smith has been taken to isolation. We have ordered all the men on the yard back to their cells while we investigate."

The warden contemplates his cigar.

"Thank you, lieutenant. If it weren't for things like this happening from time to time, it would be a shame to draw our salaries."

Fugitive from a Chain Gang," this demeaning category of hard prison labor was abandoned.[2]

Condemned to Hard Labor

Throughout the nation, prison industry was mostly out of sight but consisted of work that was miserable and punitive. If there was pay at all, it was in pennies. Some states had coal mines in which prisoners were required to labor regardless of their skill or experience in mining. The danger of work in such conditions was great, but concern for the safety of convicts was not a priority. Depending on demand, most prisons had some sort of hard labor for convicts to do. A long-standing example of hard and unpleasant labor was the jute mill at California's largest prison, San Quentin (see Box 1-2).

Box 1-2 The San Quentin Jute Mill: A Long Story with a Fiery Ending

At San Quentin all able-bodied prisoners were required to work for a year in an antiquated jute mill, making burlap sacks for sale to California farmers, whose demand for burlap always exceeded the capacity of the mill to produce. The looms and spinners were so old that replacements for worn-out parts had to be fabricated at the prison (the manufacturer, a Scottish concern, had long since ceased production of that type of mill equipment). The mill was dark and crowded. The noise of spinners and looms was deafening. The air was thick with dust and jute fiber. The danger from the rickety machinery was considerable. In this gloomy atmosphere it was easy for a convict to hurl objects at an adversary, or sometimes at a guard, without detection.

Assignment to the mill was for a year, during which time prisoners had to complete a daily task—so many spools of yarn, so many yards of burlap sacking—to the satisfaction of the foreman, or the day didn't count toward the fulfillment of the required year. With heavy irony, the assignment lieutenant would explain to prisoners that it was for their benefit to learn to work in an industry in which measured performance made it possible for them to qualify for the demands of industrial employment in free society. At the end of the mandatory year, convicts could be assigned to other and more constructive activities, to school, to vocational training, or to less miserable work than the mill, such as the manufacture of spare parts for the looms. Return to the mill was a dreaded sanction for prisoners who had been found guilty of serious disciplinary infractions.

In 1953, after the mill had been in service for eighty years, a mysterious conflagration destroyed the plant. Arson must have been the cause, but no arsonist was ever found. The wonder was that it took eighty years for the demolition of this firetrap to be accomplished. It was replaced by a cotton mill with modern machinery with which fabrics were produced for manufacture of clothing for inmates in all state institutions. Employment there was not the most prized assignment for San Quentin prisoners, but veterans of the jute mill saw little reason to complain.

From "Kin See" to "Kain't See"

In Texas all prisoners did their first 6 months "on the line" breaking soil, planting cotton, hoeing weeds, and gathering cotton. The state's prison system was endowed with 100,000 acres of arable land, nearly all of which was put to productive agricultural use. Men working for nothing made it possible for the Texas Department of Corrections to be self-supporting, or almost.[3]

The "line" was long and manned by scores of convicts, all dressed in white, working from "kin see" to "kain't see" (from dawn to dusk). Keeping them in an orderly row were guards on horseback who were not reluctant to administer summary physical discipline on recalcitrant or backward workers. The men were paid in time rather than in money (so many days of good time for so many days on the line). When the allotted introductory period was over, convicts might be reassigned to other and less exhausting work, usually paid at higher rates of "good time," but still not in dollars or cents. As at San Quentin, men who ran afoul of prison discipline were subject to reassignment to the line.

Bruce Jackson aptly describes the line at Ellis Prison in Texas:

> Squad by squad, 25 or 30 men at a time, the members of the Line are counted out the sally port gate. The field major counts them and turns them over to their field officers. As each squad is counted out and runs to the waiting wagons, another mounted guard peels away from the row aligned by the sally port. In five or ten minutes, the wagons are filled with convicts in their white suits and the wagon train is bracketed by the guards on their well-kept horses. The tractors do not move quickly. Each chugs off along the hard-packed dirt roads toward whatever section the men are to work that morning or afternoon. Thirty minutes or an hour later the tractor stops and shuts down. The men jump off, line up, are told where to go and what to do, pick up their hoes or sacks, and begin working.
>
> The Line does manual farm labor. It picks cotton, cleans the banks of the turnrows, weeds, chops. The pace isn't very difficult, but the work is dull. Every so often, the boss calls a water break and the members of the Line walk to the water wagon, take a quick drink, and then go back to the field. The sun moves across the sky, the boss calls out orders, the convicts ask for and get permission to roll a cigarette, to urinate, to ask a question.[4]

The Secret World of Wardens and Guards

Throughout the nation, prisons were governed by men who were seldom qualified by education or experience. Formal training of guards was unknown. In many states the occupation was regarded as so distasteful that it was chosen only by persons who could qualify for no other work. Many guards were illiterate. Most of them worked under conditions that were little better than the regimen they were hired to impose on prisoners. When off duty they were allowed to leave the reservation where they were required to live, but only with the captain's permission. Except to issue orders, direct communication with prisoners was discouraged, if not forbidden. There was an understandable concern that these unsophisticated men, poorly paid, with few prospects for improvement of their lot, would be induced by skillful "con" artists to bring in contraband, or to engage in other, even more subversive activities. Some guards scrambled up the few echelons of the prison hierarchy to become sergeants, lieutenants, captains, or even wardens. They brought with them a dutiful respect for the

Texas inmates on wagon on the way to the Line. (*Source:* Texas Department of Corrections.)

way their prison had always been administered. Innovation shocked them. As they saw it, the only way to run the prison was the old way, the way they had learned so well from the beginning of their service.

Prisons received little attention in the press. A few colorful wardens published memoirs of their service. Their accounts of prison life held the same fascination for the reading public as reports of travelers to strange and exotic lands, inaccessible to ordinary people.[5] The similarity was striking. This inside world was sealed off. Access to prisons was not encouraged; tours by the public of prison yards and cellblocks were almost never allowed. Intrusions by the press were unobtrusively but effectively prevented. The reality of prison life was left to the speculations of those in the public who chose to exercise their imaginations. Some thought of country clubs in which convicts were coddled, still the verb favored by hardliners. Others conjured up visions of medieval dungeons. Both images were far wide of the mark.

The Realism of Practical Men and Women

The notion that corrections should be a subject of study and that men and women engaged in correctional service should have professional preparation was not taken seriously. People engaged in those services, untrained themselves, could not see that training might help them to do better work. They saw themselves as doing as well as could be expected in their thankless occupation.

True, the famous 1870 Declaration of Principles of the American Prison Association called explicitly for training of prison personnel.[6] Practical prison officials knew

Texas inmates working on the Line. (*Source:* Texas Department of Corrections.)

this to be a reformers' ideal that was best carried out by old-timers taking greenhorns under their wings. Everyone knew that the old ways were the best ways. Outside interference by impractical reformers, none of whom had any experience in running a prison, could only make matters worse.

Stagnation prevailed in the secret world of prisons and penitentiaries. It took a world at war to shake the prison world into the twentieth century. It was no easy matter to introduce modern management principles into that secret world. The task is still far from complete, and it has been immensely complicated by unforeseen and unforeseeable changes in the larger society that the criminal justice system serves.

THE CHANGING CORRECTIONAL LANDSCAPE

Our brief sketch of the way things were is a preface to an overview of the way things became in the postwar years. The landscape in the 1930s and before consisted of a scattering of virtually independent prisons, supplemented by probation and parole, which were mostly administered at a nominal level.

The Centralization of Administration

In 1930 Congress enacted legislation creating a central Bureau of Prisons to administer the expanding network of federal penitentiaries and reformatories. The states were slow to follow. Depending on their size, some states had always managed without any centralized coordination, while others functioned under boards, sometimes with nominal responsibilities, sometimes operating with a modicum of authority.

Since World War II the administration of state correctional systems has been centralized. Most states assign the prisons to departments of corrections in which a director or commissioner is responsible for budgets, policy, and personnel selection. In five small states the prisons are administered under "umbrella" departments of human services, including juvenile institutions, mental health, and public health.

In Chapter 13 we shall trace the causes of these structural changes and discuss their significance. Here it must suffice to say that their importance to the understanding of corrections cannot be overstated. Prison budgets are consolidated. Central staff services make possible the coordination of functions such as the recruitment of personnel, the supervision of technical operations, and the classification of prisoners. Most important of all, the creation of single-headed administration has made possible accountability and coherent policy. Rules and regulations, manuals of standards, and uniform enforcement of laws and policy have replaced the individual decisions of wardens that usually had been delivered off the cuff.

Correctional leadership is vested in the directors or commissioners of corrections. In states in which the occupants of these offices do not lead, no one else can or will. If besetting problems are to be solved, the solutions must be found in the offices of the directors or commissioners, who must also be the primary advocates for their adoption.

The Rehabilitative Ideal

Along with an easygoing national perspective on crime went a belief in the ability of professional educators and psychologists to bring about the reform of most offenders. Many of the new correctional professionals had arrived at the hope, and sometimes the conviction, that prisons and reformatories should be rather like hospitals.[7] A man or woman convicted of a crime was thought to be sick, and the task of corrections was to diagnose the illness and then to prescribe and carry out treatment. The early postwar decade was the heyday of psychiatry. It seemed reasonable to believe that if psychotherapy could relieve the anxieties of the prosperous, surely it could modify the undesirable behavior of the criminal offender. Group therapy flourished in many prisons, and where professional psychologists were unavailable in sufficient numbers, teachers, works foremen, and correctional officers were pressed into service as group counselors.

It was generally recognized that psychotherapy could not be enough in itself. Obviously most of these men and women would not have been in the trouble in which they found themselves if they had been able to follow a legitimate vocation. Many of them were illiterate or, at best, semiliterate. Clearly they could not be trained for steady and remunerative employment if their educational deficiencies were not recognized, addressed, and remedied. In addition to various kinds of psychotherapy, treatment also had to include education and vocational training. The prescription might also include experience in industry or agriculture.

In this way the model of the rehabilitative prison was defined. It was generally thought to be a **medical model*** in which scientific diagnosis would be followed with a prescription for treatment, as in the physician–patient relationship. It followed that the convict/patient should remain in the prison/hospital until "cured" of criminality. That called for an indeterminate sentence in which the duration of time in the prison/hospital would be determined by the progress of the "patient" toward recovery, rather than by the seriousness of the convict's crime.[8]

Of course it was never quite that simple. First-degree murderers might respond very well to treatment, but they would serve a life sentence anyway. Petty thieves might be very recalcitrant, but they would be released as soon as the law would allow. In between were robbers, burglars, forgers, and sex offenders whose real or apparent progress in their assigned programs would determine—at least in part—the length of time they would serve.

The "medical model" dominated sentencing policy for the first two decades after the war. Throughout most of the country, efforts were made to turn it into a reality. As we shall see, disappointment became widespread. What had been a bright hope for transforming criminals into citizens collapsed into discredit from which the rehabilitative ideal has not recovered.

A Get-Tough Stance on Crime

The United States has had to face more extensive social disorder in the twentieth century than at any previous time in its history. First, a world war was fought and won. The era of prohibition showed the tendency of Americans to disobey the law if it did not permit what they wanted. A depression settled in that continued to plague the nation until the outbreak of World War II. Then, the United States became involved in two wars, in Korea and Vietnam, that it did not win. In the 1960s, the order of the American society seemed to be in grave jeopardy. The civil rights movement; urban, college, and prison riots; the expressions of antiwar sentiments by American youth in reaction to the Vietnam War; and the rise of a drug-using counterculture among young people were sobering reminders to political leaders and their constituents that unrest had gone far enough. Conservatives, who promised the return of order, were elected to all levels of government.

In the 1970s and 1980s, mirroring the social disorder of the larger society, the rates of crime appeared to rise dramatically. Underlying the increased rates of crime in American society has been the hopelessness endemic in the inner-city underclass (see Box 1-3).[9] The actual increases in crime, as well as the sometimes exaggerated coverage by the media, brought fear to urban dwellers. Politicians found that the public responded strongly to "get tough" crime proposals. "Law and order" became the theme of the political right, but even the mainstream found that it could not stray far from this theme. Crime became symbolic of all that was wrong in American life, and the public was promised that proper doses of punishment would reaffirm communal values and restore the ordered society of the past.[10]

In the 1990s, crime continues to be acknowledged, both in public opinion polls and in many other indicators, as a major impediment to achieving an ordered society.

---

* Key terms are highlighted by boldface type on first significant use throughout the text.

Box 1-3 Hopelessness of the Underclass

Contributing to the hopelessness among minority males is the realization that they are several times more likely to be victims of homicide than any other demographic group and the fact that they finish last in nearly every socioeconomic category, from the high school dropout rate to unemployment. Moreover, a 1990 study found that more college-age black men—nearly one in four—are in prison or on parole than are in college.

Men and women arrive in prison from urban cultures that receive nothing and have learned to expect nothing from the conventional economy. Society's response is to shunt such individuals aside, to give up on them. Institutionalization holds no terror for them. They have no stake in the system and are not easily amenable to measures designed to rehabilitate them by making them employable or to other measures intended to deter them from criminal conduct. Or to express this in another way, they have given up hope that they can play a meaningful role in American society. Obviously, instead of correctional intervention, the solution lies in the removal of the conditions that give rise to such unsocialized individuals: the lack of opportunities for legitimate lifestyles, the violent values and norms of disorganized communities, the breakdown of the family support systems, and the failure of education to reach hard-core children.

Source: Isabel Wilkerson, "Facing Grim Data on Young Males, Blacks Grope for Ways to End Blight," *The New York Times,* July 17, 1990, p. A14; Thomas J. Bernard, "Angry Aggression Among the 'Truly Disadvantaged,' " *Criminology* 28 (February 1990), pp. 73–96; and Tom Joe, "Economic Inequality: The Picture in Black and White," *Crime and Delinquency* 33 (April 1987), pp. 287–299.

Disorder connotes a threatening lack of predictability in the behavior of others in one's social environment, and crime, especially violent crime and hard-drug use, is seen by many citizens as the final blow to the quality of life. Current political sentiment, in fact, focuses more on the wars on crime and drugs than on the breakup of the family, the failures of the schools, the growing economic needs of the underclass, or the decay of the cities.

The Population Explosion

The crisis that we have suggested in the preceding paragraphs is best demonstrated in Figure 1.1.

The dizzying rise in population and incarceration rates displayed in this illustration reflects the growing public impatience with and fear of crime. For generations, the American public's tolerance of street crime had been such that the national prison population was small and manageable by the unskilled staffs in charge.

We now have a **population crisis** that occupies the attention of most administrators almost to the exclusion of other problems. Between 1970 and 1990 the population of the nation's prisons nearly tripled, and the rate of incarceration more than

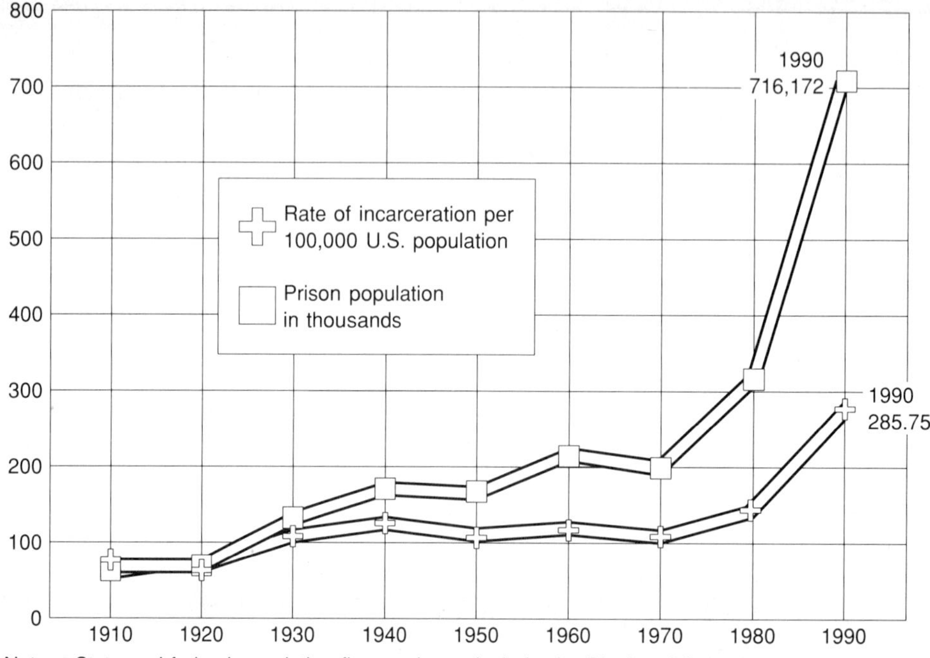

Figure 1.1 Prison population and rate of incarceration in state and federal facilities (as of June 20, 1990). (*Source:* American Correctional Association, *ACA Directory, 1991* (Laurel, Md.: American Correctional Association, 1991), p. xi.)

doubled. Changes of this magnitude do not occur in any system of public services without wrenching distortions of operations. The fundamental doctrines and expectations of the system receive less attention and sometimes are ignored. Throughout this book our discussion of principles and practices will be carried on with one eye fixed on what ought to be done in normal times, if times will ever again be normal, and the other eye on what has had to be done under the stress of overcrowding for the system to operate at all.

We must begin with the practical problems of finding room for prisoners within existing facilities. Two or more prisoners must be crammed into cells designed for single occupancy. Double bunks are installed in dormitories so that one hundred prisoners can be accommodated in a space intended for fifty. Bad as these expedients are, worse adjustments must sometimes be adopted. Dayrooms and industrial facilities are vacated to convert the floors into dormitories. If that is not enough, some prisoners may find themselves sleeping on mattresses spread out in corridors.

The obvious problems of control that such crowding presents have been brought to the attention of the federal courts, which have intervened to mandate strict population ceilings for individual prisons and, in some cases, for entire state systems. These decrees have been observed too often by overcrowding the county jails, which must accommodate convicted felons waiting for vacant cells in a state prison.

Probation and parole agencies have not been immune from the explosion. The conventional caseloads have been enlarged by new probationers and parolees.[11]

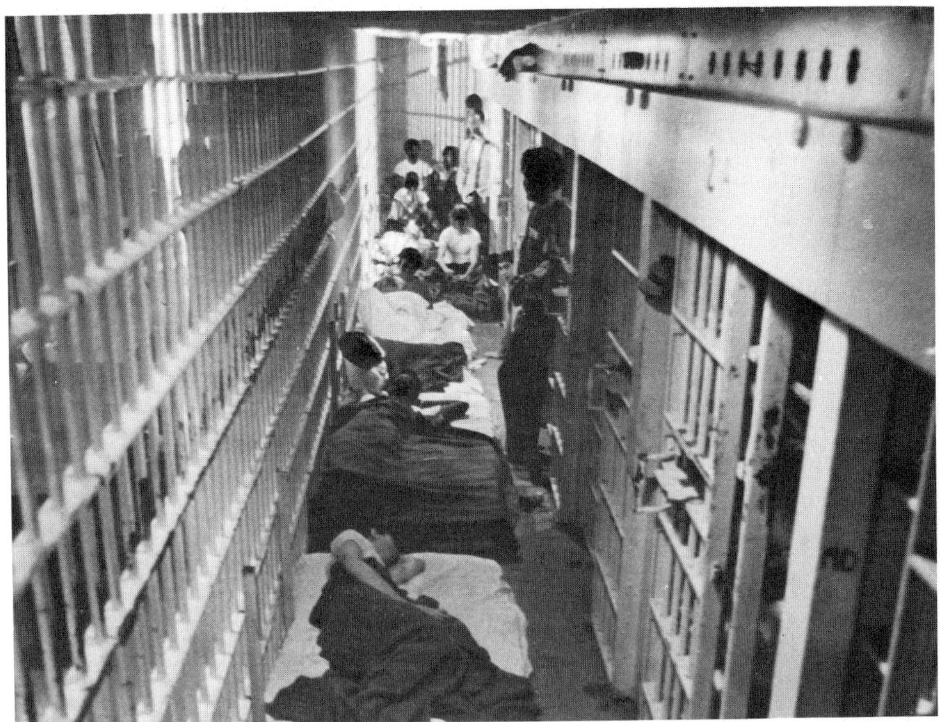

Overcrowding in a South Carolina prison. (*Source:* South Carolina Department of Corrections.)

Community corrections has become increasingly committed to surveillance. The traditional services that such agencies had been expected to provide—job finding, counseling, problem solving—have given way to surveillance so as to ensure that clients are not drifting back into crime and former addicts are not reverting to drugs. The indulgence of so many offenders in marijuana, heroin, and cocaine has turned the work of many probation and parole officers into the regular collection of urine samples and the drafting of violation reports on those whose samples do not meet the required standard of purity.

In a few states, probation and parole have been used to make modest reductions of prison intake. Nonviolent offenders have been offered places on caseloads small enough to allow the officers in charge to make daily contacts. So far, this intensive supervision has been provided on a voluntary basis, leaving the offender with the choice of doing his or her time under these conditions or doing it in prison—a choice that most offenders find easy to make. Surveillance is intensive, but services also become possible. The statistics of recidivism are not as yet conclusive. So far there is no evidence that the public safety has been compromised.

As we begin the last decade of the century, the population crisis shows no signs of abating. Its long-range effects are unpredictable. No one can be sure what normal operations will be like when the intake of offenders is in balance with the outgo of releases. The challenge to professionals will be to reconstruct the essentials of a system that has been severely compromised by necessities over which it could exercise no control.

The Building Boom

The first responses to the population explosion were the hasty erection of tent cities within prison compounds, or the installation of jerry-built shacks into which trusted old convicts could be shunted so that newly arriving felons could be housed in secure cellblocks. Clearly these expedients were not enough or even desirable—though many old-timers liked the small-group atmosphere in their improvised accommodations much better than the cheek-by-jowl anonymity of the main prison.

The answer to the bloated intake had to be new prisons, the costs of which have been enormous. The nation's total capital expenditure budgets for the fiscal year of 1988 were $5,357,747,681. That sum contrasts with a modest outlay of $908,116,000 for 1977.[12] For reasons that we will examine closely in later chapters, the cost of a prison cell begins to approach the cost of modest housing in an average American suburb. In 1987, the average cost of a maximum security cell was $68,978, the average cost of new facilities $28,518,046.[13]

These figures contrast with those of the bad old days. In 1932 the federal penitentiary at Lewisburg, Pennsylvania, was built at a cost of $3,000,000 for 1,300 prisoners—a cost per bed of slightly more than $2,300. That was admittedly cheap. State prisons sometimes were built for as much as $6,000,000, or about $5,000 to $6,000 per prison bed.[14]

The end is not remotely in sight. In 1988 there were 140 new facilities under construction in 34 states, at a total cost of $4,357,747,681. An additional 71,581 beds were planned in 38 states and the federal system, at costs that have not yet been firmly estimated. Once a bed is occupied, the occupant costs the system from $21 a day in Mississippi to $71.93 per day in Alaska.[15]

New construction is financed mainly by large bond issues, which will be burdens on state taxpayers for many years to come. Although these huge expenditures erode appropriations for universities, schools, and other state services, they are generally approved at special elections with surprisingly little controversy or complaint.

For those engaged in correctional operations, the proliferation of new prisons is not at all unwelcome. Most jurisdictions have had to keep in service ancient bastilles dating back to the mid–nineteenth century, in some places even earlier. These old prisons are difficult to adapt to modern needs and even more difficult to maintain in safe and sanitary condition. In contrast, the new prisons almost always have incorporated labor-saving technology and design intended to increase security. The fortresslike prisons inherited from nineteenth-century architects contain dismal cellblocks that cannot be modernized. Numerous guard towers must be manned at enormous expense; around-the-clock personnel costs on pay scales of the 1990s will exceed $120,000 per tower, at a minimum. The helter-skelter placement of buildings within the compound presents serious problems in security and population control. If correctional populations are ever stabilized, these dangerous relics of a simpler penology, most of them designed for impractically large numbers of prisoners, can be demolished in favor of smaller and safer new facilities.

Reform Litigation

Until the mid-1960s, federal and state courts kept to a **"hands off" policy** as to the conditions of confinement and the rights of prisoners. In many states, the statutes provided in so many words that a convict was "civilly dead," with no rights at all, except those that a court or board might allow him or her by exception.[16] Prisoners were vigorously discouraged from initiating litigation. "Writ-writers" who attempted to take their complaints to court were as likely as not to find themselves worse off than ever.[17] Usually they were hustled into segregated confinement from which communication with the courts was entirely blocked off.

That changed with a series of cases, eventually leading to *Holt* v. *Sarver* (1970) in Arkansas, the decision that opened the flood gates.[18] The "hands off" doctrine was thrown out, and the federal courts and some state courts took active hands in establishing standards of care. Their authority for intervention was the Eighth Amendment to the Constitution, which, among other things, prohibits the infliction of "cruel and unusual punishment." In doing so, it was found necessary to place entire prison systems under court orders mandating specific changes in operations, fairness in the administration of discipline, limits on the numbers of prisoners to be housed, and many other details of management and care. To ensure that compliance would be complete, the courts appointed "special masters" to monitor the changes in operations and report on the progress toward full compliance. Because so many prison systems were found to be so far from achieving acceptable conditions of confinement, progress toward compliance has usually been measured in years. Thirty-six prison systems have one or more institutions under court order, and in ten states the entire system is under orders. The body of case law that has thus been created points toward practical standards for corrections.

The correctional profession has also taken an interest in setting standards. As early as 1954 a committee of the American Correctional Association published a volume cautiously entitled *A Manual of Suggested Standards.*[19] In the 1980s, the Association boldly published its manual of standards for adult correctional institutions.[20] Prison administrators were encouraged to meet these standards by a Commission on Accreditation that appointed inspectors to determine whether a particular prison was in compliance with the standards. Undoubtedly this process has prompted wardens and their superiors to improve management and the conditions of confinement.

The Growing Incidence of Violence

The easy days, when lordly wardens assisted by semiliterate guards could manage prisons by the thousands in fortresslike "mega-prisons," has long since gone. Sociologists have pointed out that in those more relaxed years they had a lot of help from their convict charges, most of whom were motivated to do "easy time." In those times, convicts disliked disorder at least as much as their keepers did. Prisoners who rebelled too vociferously against the restrictions imposed upon them or who engaged in violent conduct were ostracized by their fellows as well as disciplined by the authorities.

The new racial mixture in prisons has brought on conflict and confrontations unheard of during the old regime and resolved with difficulty, if at all, in the new order of control. Formerly, prison populations in the northern states were predominantly white. Black and Hispanic prison populations were relatively small and docile minorities. The influx of offenders from these minorities began in the 1960s. In those turbulent years it was possible for revolutionary ideologues to preach that black offenders had become political prisoners and that oppression of blacks in prisons was intended to intimidate blacks in the community. Many black prisoners responded violently to these messages with tragic results to them and to many officials and bystanders.[21]

The would-be revolutionary wave has subsided, but the influx of minority offenders has not. In states with large inner-city populations, white convicts are in a distinct minority in the prison community. In many maximum security prisons, interracial violence has brought about the virtual collapse of the old live-and-let-live accommodations among convicts.[22] In their place, wardens have had to expand their facilities for the segregation of the violent and the protection of the vulnerable. Much more will be said on this subject in later chapters.

The **inmate gangs** that are found in prisons in thirty-two states and the Federal Bureau of Prisons are violent, often lethally violent.[23] Their power has been such that it sometimes rivals the authority of the prison staff. By controlling the distribution of narcotics, these gangs maintain a powerful influence on the prison community. Their power is manifest in measures of extreme violence imposed on informers, delinquent debtors, and gang adversaries. Much time and ingenuity have been spent on neutralizing their influence and frustrating their activities. So far, the gangs survive and even thrive in prison settings.[24] Only the most vigorous measures of custodial intervention, such as the assignment of all identified gang members to segregated units, have had any effect in controlling their activities. As a gang leader in Illinois stated to one of the authors, "We're in control around here. If we wanted to, we would take the prison apart, but we choose not to. We've too much to lose."[25]

In sum, men and women accustomed to violence in their communities and even in their homes have used life-threatening violence on fellow prisoners and on the prison staff. In many prisons, convicts live in constant fear of one another. It is often said that guards dread going to work in the morning and that when they return to their homes after their shift is done, they are relieved to have survived another day without harm.[26]

POINTING THE WAY TO A BETTER FUTURE

In each period since colonial times, reform and reaction have alternated. Each reform cycle has followed long periods of public indifference and has been characterized by brief outbursts of public indignation and by the emergence of new ideas, leading to a period of institution building. But then the cycle shifts again to stagnation, disillusionment, and decline.[27] The pendulum always seems to swing from one extreme to the other. The public goes overboard one generation on reform and then with equal fanfare in the next generation goes overboard on repressive answers.

An eternal optimism that appears to be part of the American spirit continually gives birth to ideas of reform. Americans are convinced that any problem can be solved if only the right approach is used, and this belief has led to a relentless search for panaceas to correct criminal behavior. Yet the American spirit is also a pragmatic one, and when the reform ideas do not work, the public's mood shifts to an acceptance of repressive solutions. Reform measures are also frequently more expensive, and the needs of people who lack economic and political power appear less urgent when fiscal strictures are tightened.

In the mid-1970s, a period of reaction, or repression, replaced a cycle of reform that had existed since the 1960s. Nobody knows when a cycle of reform will replace that of repression. The basic challenge that confronts American corrections is how to make the best of an overcrowded system and, at the same time, to determine what needs to be done to point the way to a better future.

Fortunately, throughout the history of corrections, there have always been admirable men and women who have led the way to a better future. They have eliminated abuses, made useful innovations, and stood fast against pressures to allow the punishment of offenders to sink into corruption and brutality. Richard A. McGee changed the nature of corrections in California by upgrading the physical plants and staffing patterns, by instituting research, and by developing alternatives to imprisonment. Kenneth Stoneman closed Vermont's only maximum security prison. Lloyd McCorkle, instead of building more prisons, developed a network of satellites at other human services institutions. Kenneth F. Schoen was instrumental in laying out the principles of Minnesota's Community Corrections Act. James V. Bennett closed Alcatraz, opened Marion, planned Morgantown, and created a professional bureaucracy at the U.S. Bureau of Prisons. George Beto led Texas away from a plantation-type penal servitude into a less violent and more productive agro-business industrial farm. Elayn Hunt, before her death, was leading Louisiana corrections out of its dark ages. Their work has been celebrated in the narrow community of criminal justice, but they are virtually unknown to the world beyond. Their enlightenment does them honor and deserves the gratitude of civilized people everywhere.

Today, as in the past, corrections needs such individuals to bridge the gap between the present and the future. Corrections is not a career to be chosen by the faint of heart; as the great American jurist Benjamin Cardozo put it, "The timorous may stay at home."[28] But there are certainly reasons to think of a career in corrections as work on the frontier. Correctional systems are under great strain, and standards of performance are frayed. Major changes in methods of control, in services to be offered and carried out, in prison architecture, and in administrative structure are needed and will take place. To have a hand in improvements and prevent relapse are the prospects for correctional recruits. Their effectiveness depends on their preparation for these difficult assignments.

Correctional administration is a profession calling for advanced education and years of preparation. The classification of prisoners, the maintenance of responsible control, the administration of humane but effective discipline of prisoners, and the training and organization of personnel call for a wide spectrum of skills that cannot be fully developed without exposure to the relevant academic disciplines as well as serious immersion in correctional operations. Beyond these specialized skills, administrators must be generalists who understand the principles of organization, the processes required for responsible budgeting, and the technology for effective control of operations. The growing recognition of these requirements has led to the **professionalization** of the field. The new professionals are better educated and more dedicated to careers of service than those who preceded them. They expect more of themselves and their colleagues.

In Box 1-4, while presenting the characteristics that are needed to become an effective warden, Frank Wood offers an exciting invitation for those who want to make a difference in corrections today and to prepare the way for corrections tomorrow.

Box 1-4 Interview with Warden Frank Wood

Question: How can you prepare yourself to be the warden of a maximum security institution?

Wood: I don't know if I can speak for all wardens, but I can go back and search my memory for things that I think were helpful to me. Ideally, I would say it would be nice to have the good fortune of growing up poor. This is to ensure your exposure to good and bad people of all religions and ethnic backgrounds, because you're going to be working with those persons later in life. This helps you to understand the perspective from which those people come. When I analyze why it is that I have a reasonably good rapport with both staff and inmates, I attribute it to growing up in circumstances similar to that of many of our clientele. On the other hand, coming from a local blue-collar working-class background and starting as an officer gave me an appreciation for the struggles that are faced by many of the uniform and entry-level staff.

A very important aspect of my background was the experience as an entry-level uniformed officer. This helps you to understand from the very ground level what is going on in the institution. You learn to recognize the informal and formal organizations and all of the nuances of those structures. You experience and grow in your understanding of the unique dynamics of both the staff and inmate cultures.

I also believe it is helpful for anyone who is planning a professional career in corrections as a supervisor, manager, administrator, or warden to get involved in the union movement when they're line officers. I think it's important to have this experience so that you can appreciate and understand the unique aspects of organized labor. There is a distinct advantage in having experience on both sides of the table. You will learn from firsthand experience that the goals and objectives that people want to accomplish in the union are not significantly different from what management wants to accomplish. I truly believe that honest, hard-working officers, supervisors, managers, and administration all want the same things. It's a matter of putting things out on the table for all to see, so that everyone can recognize and appreciate that we truly do want the same things. We all want fair and equitable compensation for our work; recognition for good performance; to be supervised and led by honest, competent, sensitive and reasonable people; and that performance standards, career advancement, and accountability are applied to staff at all levels equally. Good labor/management relations are enhanced and maintained when there is clear and convincing evidence that this philosophy is practiced and not just given lip service. It has to be apparent to all employees at all levels. It is apparent as management decisions reflect these principles.

College-level academic education is important. I would caution anyone who is planning on being a correctional administrator not to get caught up in making their academic education so focused that he or she narrows it to social work, sociology, and the behavioral sciences, and ignores some of the other essential aspects of the well-balanced academic education that you need: business, administration, fiscal management, leadership, and management techniques. I advocate having a broad-based and generalized college education that can be supplemented periodically in your career with specific course work that will enhance your competence, effectiveness, and leadership skills, and ultimately your promotability.

I would also advise people not to be tempted to stay in a comfortable position, just because there are good working hours and good days off. When I look back and see people retiring today as correctional sergeants who started with me over thirty years ago as correctional officers, some of them found a comfortable spot and were unwilling to give it up. They didn't take calculated risks, and they didn't try to expand their horizons by searching out and accepting real challenges in the workplace. Some people clearly focused on other aspects of their personal life, and their fulfillment came from contributions to their community, church, or social organization that enhanced the quality of life for their children and community. It's very difficult to do both as you work your way up the organization from an entry-level position. At the management level, you are able to bring a healthier balance to your personal and professional life. In most of my experience, but not always, promotions appear to go to those who have made and are prepared to make personal sacrifices. I do not know a competent, long-tenured warden who did not and does not continue to make some personal sacrifices. It is also wise to be alert and look around for tough assignments, where people have failed and where there is a high staff turnover. These opportunities offer excellent challenges and recognition and exposure for taking on tough assignments, exceeding expectations, and making significant contributions to improve the system.

It is also important to avoid thinking that the world revolves around corrections. A lot of people in corrections are so narrowed in their friendships and relationships that most of their associates are corrections people. They start to think that the center of the universe is corrections, but in reality we are a very peripheral part of our society's institutions. If you maintain a wide circle of friends who are not in corrections, you'll have sounding boards and can hear what is being said by other people with other perspectives on what we do in our profession. It is important also to continue your education through a broad range of reading on a wide variety of topics—history, philosophy, psychology, logic, ethics, treatment modalities, and, of equal importance, religion and theology. We must also maintain an informed perspective on the full range of issues, local, state and national. You will always be at a disadvantage if you are not informed on how your work meshes with the changing and dynamic society we live in.

I would advise that anyone aspiring to be a warden or director of corrections exercise caution in their interactions with politicians. The closer you get to politics, there is an increasing temptation and potential that you could find yourself compromising your values, principles, and integrity in an attempt to avoid telling a governor, legislator, or other politician things they may not want to hear. Many politicians appear to have focused their priorities on perpetuating themselves in office and positioning themselves for higher office. They latch on to what appears to be popular, simplistic solutions to society's problems and exploit those issues to the detriment of the country, the state, and their constituents for personal gain. Many ignore the evidence that sound and enlightened public policy is not always popular. Very few directors of corrections are prepared to stand firm in opposition to politically popular, simplistic solutions advocated by their bosses—[the governor]. Advising politicians they are wrong when you serve at their pleasure, or legislators who decide the appropriations and level of funding for the department for the next biennium, has the potential of shortening your career or hurting your department or institution financially.

We operate on the philosophy that there should be no surprises. I don't want to be surprised; my supervisors don't want to be surprised; staff and inmates don't want to be surprised. In that vein we owe it to the politicians and the citizens to tell them the predictable outcome of poor public policy before it becomes law. We need to have enough integrity, confidence, and conviction to tell public policy decision makers in a tactful, respectful, and diplomatic way things they may not want to hear. Corrections professionals and criminal justice experts must speak out. That's the only way we may be able to reduce the amount of wasted resources spent on more prisons and locking up an increasing number of our people for longer sentences on the theory it will lower the crime rates or the level of fear in our society. Instead we have burdened our children and our grandchildren with spending money after the fact on prisons, attempting to build ourselves out of overcrowding driven by poor public policy, and attempting to solve in our prisons society's problems that should be addressed at the front end of the system. Strengthening families, child care, literacy initiatives, education, improved medical and mental-health care, chemical dependency initiatives for the disadvantaged, and early identification and intervention with children who need special attention such as impulse and anger control and other character disorders have the greatest potential for reducing crime and fear in our society.

Finally, in order to develop effective, unique leadership and management skills needed to be a prison CEO [chief executive officer], it is helpful and important to have supervisory and managerial experience in a prison. We need to examine how people do things, what they do right, and how we can acquire these skills and enhance our communications expertise. By being astute observers, we can learn a lot about what not to do by watching what people do that is counterproductive or alienates staff, inmates, or others. Learning from other people's mistakes is extremely important. It will help us avoid the same mistakes when we are in positions of authority. Also important in developing your managerial expertise is adopting your own management style rather than attempting to adopt somebody else's style whose personal characteristics and areas of strengths are very different from yours. It's unlikely that his or her style will work as well for you as it does for him or her.

I believe in shouting praises of deserving staff from the roof, and documenting the achievements and accomplishments of competent staff with letters of commendation that have wide circulation. On the other hand, constructive criticism should be handled in supervisory conferences privately. Only when you reach the point that you think you may have to remove that person should you start documenting negatives in written evaluations. Written evaluations are not the place to make obscure constructive suggestions. They can be verbalized.

Attention to detail cannot be overemphasized. Attention to detail is the best insurance policy against surprises and failure. Ultimately, to manage others well, you need to have a sense of commitment and purpose, a calling, and a proprietary intensity about you.

In summary, it's important to understand that in order to be an attractive candidate for an appointment as a warden, you have to be prepared experientially and academically. Your character strength, credibility, and integrity should be a matter of record. If you are not prepared, it is unlikely you will be asked to administer an institution. Having said that, we all know that a lot of people are excellent performers, well prepared and very competent, but are not selected to be wardens. The elements of timing and chance of being in the right place at the right time are very important. Prepare yourself in the event that you are in the right place and the right time in the future. I would encourage all those people who aspire to be a warden to remember that there are hundreds of important, influential, and high-impact positions in the corrections profession from which you can get a lot of personal and professional satisfaction, make lasting contributions, and grow to your full personal and professional potential without being a warden.

Source: Frank Wood has been a warden in the Minnesota Department of Corrections for the past fifteen years and has been the warden of the Oak Park Heights Correctional Center in Stillwater, Minnesota, since it was built in the early 1980s. Interviewed in July 1990 and used with permission.

CONCLUSIONS

The world changed radically after World War II, and with it society's assumptions about crime and criminals and its expectations of prison management. The nation had suffered through the Great Depression, but its morale had been restored by victory in a long and dangerous war. Optimism about all problems prevailed. If a war could be won by the application of science, modern principles of organization, and determined leadership, surely the human problems confronting the nation would respond to a similar mobilization of resources. One such problem was the administration of criminal justice. Political leaders and judges began to listen to the ideas of reformers. Able administrators were chosen to manage the Federal Bureau of Prisons and the correctional agencies of a few states. Returning veterans who found employment in corrections were impatient with the tried-and-true ways left over from bygone years, and as soon as they got their bearings they began to demand changes.

In Chapter 4 we will have much more to say about the transformation of corrections. It was slow work. Leaders had to know what they wanted to do and had to have the means to do it. That called for a drastic improvement of the human resources of the system. Even the most gifted leaders knew that they had much to learn and that the personnel on whom they relied had to be trained to accomplish old tasks in new ways. The learning process continues to this day and will go on far into the foreseeable future. Corrections is no longer an occupation for unskilled men and women who have been rejected by other professions.

In these times, students need a textbook on all the facets of adult corrections to understand the field as well as to prepare themselves for a correctional career. That is a demonstration of the magnitude of the transformation of corrections. Formerly it was a haphazard mixture of indifference, incompetence, and much outright brutality, coated with protestations of idealism. In the place of this mixture, professionals in corrections can claim a purposeful commitment to the achievement of sound management and the reformation of as many offenders as possible. In the chapters to follow, we will study the extent to which this commitment has been and can be met. The soaring idealism of correctional oratory of the early years of the century was unrelated to the stagnant reality. New perceptions of new realities have sobered penologists and practitioners. Practice has been enlightened by systematically examined experience. Nothing is done as well as possible, but those working in corrections believe they have an accurate notion of what could be done—with better facilities, better personnel, and, as one old captain at San Quentin was fond of remarking, a better class of convicts.

KEY TERMS

"hands off" policy

hopelessness of the underclass

inmate gangs

medical model

population crisis

professionalization

DISCUSSION TOPICS

1.1 How can we account for the stagnation of corrections before the 1930s?

1.2 What forces brought about the changes since the 1930s?

1.3 What distinguishes Warden Wood's concept of his job from that of the warden mentioned in Box 1-1?

1.4 Why is corrections not a career for the faint of heart?

ANNOTATED REFERENCES

Barnes, Harry Elmer, and Negley K. Tetters. *New Horizons in Criminology*, 2nd ed. New York: Prentice-Hall, 1951. *A classic criminology text that is particularly helpful in understanding the history of corrections in the first several decades of the twentieth century.*

Camp, George M., and Camille Graham Camp. *Prison Gangs: Their Extent, Nature, and Impact on Prisons.* Washington, D.C.: Government Printing Office, 1985. *The most comprehensive examination of prison gangs.*

Jacobs, James B. *Stateville: The Penitentiary in Mass Society.* Chicago: University of Chicago Press, 1977. *Jacobs's highly regarded study examines the period prior to and following World War II at the Stateville Correctional Center in Joliet, Illinois.*

Joe, Tom. "Economic Inequality: The Picture in Black and White." *Crime and Delinquency* 33, April 1987: 287–299. *An article that graphically describes the growing hopelessness of the black underclass.*

Martin, Steve J., and Sheldon Ekland-Olson. *Texas Prisons.* Austin: Texas Monthly Press, 1987. *A helpful introduction to the development and demise of the Texas model of confinement described in this chapter.*

Wilson, William Julius. *The Truly Disadvantaged: The Inner-City, the Underclass, and Public Policy.* Chicago: University of Chicago Press, 1987. *One of the most perceptive statements on the plight of the urban underclass today.*

NOTES

1. *Jackson* v. *Bishop*, 404 F.2d 571 (8th Cir. 1968).
2. This movie was adapted from Robert E. Burns' *I Am a Fugitive from a Georgia Chain Gang* (New York: Grosset Dunlap, 1932).
3. For a description of this Texas model, see Steve J. Martin and Sheldon Ekland-Olson, *Texas Prisons* (Austin: Texas Monthly Press, 1987).
4. Bruce Jackson, "Ellis" (unpublished manuscript).
5. One of the best known of these memoirs was Joseph Ragen and Charles Finstone, *Inside the World's Toughest Prison* (Springfield, Ill.: C. C. Thomas, 1962).
6. See Chapter 4, where the Declaration of Principles is presented and discussed.
7. See John P. Conrad, "We Should Have Never Promised a Hospital," *Federal Probation* 49 (December 1974), pp. 3–9.
8. Ibid.
9. See William Julius Wilson, *The Truly Disadvantaged: The Inner-City, the Underclass, and Public Policy* (Chicago: University of Chicago Press, 1987).
10. See James Q. Wilson, *Thinking About Crime*, rev. ed. (New York: Basic Books, 1983).
11. See Bureau of Justice Statistics, *Probation and Parole 1989* (Washington, D.C.: U.S. Department of Justice, 1990).
12. Data compiled by Diana Travisno, editor, *ACA Directory* (College Park, Md.: American Correctional Association, 1989).
13. These figures are from the *1988 Corrections Yearbook* (College Park, Md.: American Correctional Association, 1989).
14. H. E. Barnes and N. K. Teeters, *New Horizons in Criminology*, 2nd ed. (New York: Prentice-Hall, 1951), p. 677.
15. Data supplied by Diane Travisno.
16. See *Ruffin* v. *Commonwealth*, 62 Va. (21 Gratt.) 790, 796 (1871).
17. To show how autocratic wardens like Joe Ragen responded to "writ writers," see James B. Jacobs, *Stateville: The Penitentiary in Mass Society* (Chicago: University of Chicago Press, 1977).
18. *Holt* v. *Sarver* (309 F. supp 362, E.D. Ark. 1970).
19. American Correctional Association, *A Manual of Suggested Standards* (College Park, Md.: American Correctional Association, 1954).
20. American Correctional Association, *Guidelines for the Development of Policies and Procedures for Adult Correctional Institutions and Adult Local Detention Facilities* (College Park, Md.: American Correctional Association, 1987).
21. See John Irwin, *Prisons in Turmoil* (Boston: Little, Brown, 1980).
22. For a discussion of racial conflict in prison, see Leo Carroll, *Hacks, Blacks, and Cons* (Lexington, Mass.: Heath, 1974).
23. George M. Camp and Camille Graham Camp, *Prison Gangs: Their Extent, Nature, and Impact on Prisons* (Washington, D.C.: Government Printing Office, 1985).
24. Ibid.
25. Interviewed in May 1981.
26. See Jacobs, *Stateville*.
27. Samual Walker, *Popular Justice: A History of American Criminal Justice* (New York: Oxford University Press, 1983), p. 83.
28. 259 N.Y. 479.

Chapter 2

From Vengeance to Deterrence

CHAPTER OUTLINE

PREHISTORICAL CRIME AND PUNISHMENT
THE EARLY CODES
- *Hammurabi, King of Babylon*
- *The Hittites*
- *Deuteronomy*
- *The Greeks*
- *The Code of Drakon*
- *The Laws of Solon*
- *Rome and the Criminal Law*
- *The Laws of Islam*

PUNISHMENT IN THE MIDDLE AGES
THE CRIMINAL LAW AND DETERRENCE
- *The Galleys*
- *England and the Gallows*
- *The Conscience of John Howard*
- *Banishment and Transportation*
- *Captain Maconochie's Reforms*

CONCLUSIONS

Throughout prehistory and recorded history, the response of society to crime has had one common element: the punishment of the offender, sometimes administered with horrifying brutality, sometimes with indulgent leniency. As the centuries passed, the purposes of punishment—or what rulers, legislatures, and judges claimed were the purposes—have changed. Depending on the era and the culture, offenders when found guilty were hanged or decapitated, tortured, mutilated, incarcerated, ostracized, publicly humiliated, or otherwise restrained from the enjoyment of life and freedom. Neither punishment nor any other response has succeeded in ending crime.

From the study of primitive peoples, anthropologists have pieced together a general notion of the customs by which our earliest ancestors probably dealt with killers, thieves, and adulterers—the offenders of most concern in a simple society. As clan and tribal societies were superseded by states, kingdoms, and empires, written laws supplanted custom, but the codes embodied the customs by which organized societies had dealt with violators of the norms of conduct.

The kings and prophets who were the early lawgivers intended that the state replace the individual in exacting revenge on the offender. To this day, the state assumes the exclusive right to respond to criminals; it denies the victims of crime the liberty of taking the law into their own hands. Society has become more complex, but the state's basic response to crime continues to be retribution, which has replaced private vengeance.

However, mere vengeance inflicted by the state was thought to be insufficient. Punishment of the individual offender, it was felt, should deter others from committing the same crime or other crimes. With the execution or incarceration of offenders, they were prevented from committing further offenses. The final and most recent stage added the kinder expectation—or hope—that by changing offenders' attitudes, by educating them, or by improving them in other ways they would no longer be apt to commit crimes. Despite society's optimistic expectation that offenders will be better men and women when they are returned to the community, the experience of imprisonment or community corrections is still punishment. No offender misses that point.

The history of punishment is roughly divided into three phases. In this chapter, we shall study the first phase—from the beginnings as we understand them, to the intent to deter and incapacitate offenders. In Chapter 3, we shall trace the development of strategies to make punishment serve the purposes of deterrence and incapacitation. In Chapter 4, we shall see how reformers sought to make punishment serve the positive purpose of reforming offenders. Throughout, the common thread is punishment, always explicit and too often horrifyingly brutal, but in later years subtle and very often merely nominal.

In this brief review of a history spread over thousands of years, our generalizations must be sweeping. To understand the law's present responses to crime, we must understand humanity's experience in responding to crime. We cannot be certain of the motives or thinking of ancient lawgivers like Hammurabi or Moses or Drakon or Solon, to whom we shall refer in these pages. We do know that their influence has been immense as it passed on from legislators to succeeding legislators. We can be sure that in their time they were influenced by predecessors who are nameless to history.

PREHISTORICAL CRIME AND PUNISHMENT

Anthropologists have studied the social controls that the most primitive contemporary tribes exercised over the behavior of their members. We assume that our most distant ancestors lived in small bands much like the African Bushmen or the Negrito tribes of the Philippine Islands and New Guinea. These people still live at the simplest level, gathering food from plants and hunting animals with bow and arrow. To distinguish them from more "advanced" peoples, anthropologists call them "food gatherers"—that is, they are not equipped to plant crops or store food; to survive, they move from forest to forest. Observers report that these most primitive of peoples live in bands of 15 or 20 persons, all related to one another by blood or marriage. Bands rarely spend more than two or three days in the same place, moving on when the food supply dwindles to other locations within a well-defined territory of perhaps 150 square miles.[1] By kinship and language they will have relations with similar bands, but mostly they live in isolated groups. Their contact with similar groups only a few miles away is never close, and they avoid the outside world as best they can.

In a small group such as the food-gathering band, crime and deviant behavior are not pressing problems. Some kinds of behavior offend the entire band—for example, incest and homosexuality—and may be punished by ostracism or ridicule. Such punishment may make it impossible for the offender to remain in the band—a consequence that will endanger his or her survival. Expulsion will make the offender unwelcome in any other group, and he or she cannot live long as an isolated individual.

It is usually expected that homicide and adultery will be avenged by the person harmed. A killer may have to escape the family of the victim by leaving the band. In some tribes, a murderer is thought to be unclean and to have polluted the group to which he or she belongs; that requires the offender's expulsion and the band's purification with ritual and magic. We know that more advanced societies—those of the early Greeks and Romans, for two—also believed that certain crimes polluted the city or the village and required ceremonial purification to appease the offended gods, as well as the expulsion or execution of the offending man or woman.

Adultery may be punished by the aggrieved husband, who may kill the adulterer and his own offending wife. The customs and laws of most early societies criminalized adultery, whether by consent or not, and subjected the offenders to severe punishment. Even in the present time in very advanced societies many people believe that an adulterous pair when caught in the act have provoked justifiable homicide.

No one can say for sure how often the few norms and taboos of primitive food gatherers are violated. It is clear that certain standards of conduct are expected, but the means of enforcement are limited to group disapproval or, when individual harm takes place, to revenge by the victim or the victim's relatives. In the absence of writing, criminal laws could not be codified, nor are they needed. The power of custom is all that these societies require to maintain conformity.

We cannot be sure that our first ancestors lived like today's Bushmen or the Negritos. Many lived in climates or on soil that made food gathering much more difficult than in the tropics, where today's food gatherers are found. We can only guess at the details of social control among northern primitives. However, wherever early men and women lived before the invention of writing, custom must have dictated the response to whatever crimes were defined. Custom still profoundly influences our behavior and determines the foundations of the criminal laws.

THE EARLY CODES

Agriculture changed forever the simple life of food-gathering peoples. Their nomadic existence ended with the discovery that crops could be planted and a food supply could be assured by their settling on the land. The few became many as the sources of life support became reliable. The bands where work was not specialized were supplanted by tribes in which some were farmers, some were merchants who stored and distributed the produce of the land, some were soldiers protecting the territory of the tribe from marauders, and an elite few were kings, prophets, and priests. Farmers became property owners and in time gained property interests not only in their land but in slaves who worked the land. Those interests had to be protected, and the enactment of laws enabled property owners to depend on the community to protect them instead of their having to rely on themselves to defend boundaries and harvests. Later in this chapter, we shall see that property interests have been defended by laws calling for punishments just as severe as the most serious crimes of murder, rape, and assault.

A community of a few food gatherers needed little or no organization. A tribe consisting of peasants, merchants, and soldiers needed a simple organization and authority to maintain it. Prophets and priests formulated the religious support for the laws, and kings codified and enforced the laws. As the centuries went by, society became more complex, and so did the laws required to protect public safety and private interests.

Hammurabi, King of Babylon

The first codifier of whom we have records was Hammurabi, who reigned for 43 years as king of Babylon during the eighteenth century B.C.[2] He began his reign by expanding the authority of Babylon throughout Mesopotamia through military conquest. We can only guess what made him decide to be a lawgiver as well as a conqueror. Perhaps he was far-seeing enough to believe that written laws would stabilize his kingdom; perhaps he was only putting in written form the laws that his predecessors had enforced by custom and tradition. Whatever was the case, the **Code of Hammurabi** (see Box 2-1) provides us with the first comprehensive view of the laws as they stood in the earliest days of the nation state.

Like all kings in his day, Hammurabi combined in his person the functions of unchallengeable executive, sole legislator, and supreme judge. His famous code was issued late in his reign, probably in 1752 B.C. Its influence throughout the Middle East was enormous. Fragments of later codes in other kingdoms have been found that clearly derive from Hammurabi's laws. We know little about the predecessors of his code, although archaeologists have found clay tablets containing some of the earlier laws of the Sumerians and other peoples in that part of the world.

An unusual feature of the code called for compensation to the victim of a robbery by the authorities of the city in which the robbery occurred, if the thief were not caught. In such a case, the victim "shall declare his loss in the presence of a god" to the mayor of the city and certify the amount of his loss. Thereupon the authorities were required to make compensation upon the presumption that they had failed to maintain law and order. There is no way of knowing how often this enlightened principle was invoked.

With all its cruelty, the Babylonian law reduced, if it did not eliminate, the occasion of individual revenge. Before Hammurabi the family of a victim of murder would be expected to revenge itself on the killer, and then an endless blood feud would usually follow. The law of Hammurabi required that the killer be answerable

Box 2-1 Hammurabi's Code

Hammurabi is especially memorable because his code was carved on stone rather than clay, and it is believed that we have it nearly in its entirety. When discovered by French archaeologists in 1901, the slab on which the code was inscribed was taken to the Louvre in Paris, where it remains.

Hammurabi's code may be broken down into 282 clauses, most of them having to do with matters that modern jurisprudence assigns to the civil laws. More than 50 sections deal with crimes and the punishments for committing them. The punishments prescribed are severe. As would be the case up to just a few centuries ago, there were no alternatives to capital punishment other than fines, which were considered inappropriate for the serious crimes. Death was the penalty for robbery, theft, false witness, building a house that falls on its owner, and many other offenses. (A curious feature of this provision of the law required that if the house should collapse and kill the owner's son, the son of the builder—not the builder himself—would be executed.)

The **law of talion**, or the principle of "tit for tat," makes its appearance throughout the sections on the punishment of criminals. (Under this principle, the punishment should be the same as the harm inflicted on the victim, as for example the Biblical precept that offenders should be punished "eye for eye, tooth for tooth." We shall see that this principle survives to the present, though not as pervasively as in ancient law.) For the offense of knocking out a free man's tooth, the offender would have his tooth knocked out. For striking the cheek of a ranking free man, the assaulter would be scourged in the city's assembly. A son who struck his father would suffer the amputation of a hand. If in an assault a victim's bone was broken, the same bone of the assailant would be broken. Differentiations were made as to the penalties to be inflicted in the cases of victims of different ranks. For fatally injuring a free man a payment of ½ *maneh* of silver would be exacted, but for the same injury to a slave the penalty would be only ⅓ *maneh* of silver. Today, these payments would be the equivalent of civil damages payable to the victim or his or her family in addition to the criminal punishment imposed.

not to the family of the victim but to the king. Once the killer had been executed, justice was satisfied, and peace between the families must ensue. This expectation has become common to all criminal codes ever since Hammurabi.

The Hittites

Comparisons of the laws of neighboring cultures with the Babylonian laws suggest that values at that stage of history differed widely. The Hittites flourished about two centuries after Hammurabi and eventually conquered Babylon.[3] Their codes have been discovered, and with great difficulty they have been deciphered. As with the Babylonians, capital punishment was used for many offenses, but these did not include homicide or robbery. Rape, sexual intercourse with animals, defiance of the authority of the state, and sorcery were all punishable by death. The law of homicide provided for restitution to the victim's heirs. To quote one such section,

The Code of Hammurabi. (*Source:* Granger.)

> If anyone kills a man or a woman in a quarrel, he buries him and gives four persons (slaves), men or women, and he (the victim's heir) lets him go home.

The Hittite criminal laws contain many such provisions that cover other kinds of homicide, assaults, arson, and theft. Restitution for each offense is specified, and it is provided that where a slave is convicted he or she will pay compensation at half the amount required of a free man.

Law enforcement and judicial functions were placed in the hands of commanders of military garrisons for the various cities the Hittites conquered and controlled. An order from the king to his commanders contained this instruction:

> Into whatever city you return, summon forth all the people of the city. Whoever has a suit, decide it for him and satisfy him. If the slave of a man, or the maidservant of a man . . . has a suit, decide it for them and satisfy them. Do not make the better case the worse or the worse case the better. Do what is just.

Could a modern chief magistrate put it better?

Deuteronomy

The book of Deuteronomy, the fifth in the Bible, contains the basis of Jewish laws. Its origin is mysterious, but the prevailing theory is that Moses composed it shortly before his death in the thirteenth century before Christ. The laws are found in chapters xii through xxviii. Unlike the Code of Hammurabi, these laws were in the form of a covenant between God and the people of Israel, given to Moses on the mountaintop. They begin with the Ten Commandments and go on to statutes and ordinances that God commanded Moses to teach the people. The law of talion appears in chapter xix:21,

> Your eye shall not pity; it shall be life for life, eye for eye, tooth for tooth, hand for hand, foot for foot.

As we have seen in other ancient codes, adultery is severely punished. If a betrothed virgin lies with a man within a city, both are to be brought to the gates of the city and stoned to death—the virgin because she did not cry for help and the man because he violated his neighbor's wife.

The survival of the law of talion has served to remind lawmakers of the necessity of finding some basis for punishment that will be proportional to the crime for which the offender is punished. We shall see as we go along that making the punishment fit the crime is an elusive goal.

The Greeks

Greek philosophers had a great deal to say about the nature of justice, and one, Plato, wrote extensively on the punishment of criminals.[4] The influence of Greek legislators and judges on the subsequent history of the treatment of offenders has been less significant, although the development of their penal codes, so far as we know them, is of considerable interest. Unfortunately, the two most famous codes, those of **Drakon** and **Solon,** have come down to us in fragmentary form.

Before the Greeks got around to codifying their laws and putting together a system of justice, they relied on custom to deal with wrongs done. Even murder and rape were dealt with by the victim's family. Sometimes negotiations between the offender and the victim's family would culminate in compensation; the bargain would be that the killer or rapist would pay the aggrieved family a sum of money in return for an agreement that the family would not demand further vengeance.

As Greek society became organized into city-states, judgment in criminal matters fell into the hands of kings and elders. There were no lawyers representing clients. It was up to victims or their families to prosecute, and defendants had to depend on their own resourcefulness to present their cases. In early Athens a king might decide what should be done, but a special peculiarity was that interested bystanders could influence the judgment. The disputing parties would state their cases, and the interested public was free to cheer or deride them as they found the speakers convincing or unconvincing.[5] It is a long distance in time from the Greek marketplace (the *agora*), where trials were conducted, to the modern courtroom, but the participation of the public foretold the jury system in wide use for centuries throughout the West. Accounts of these proceedings suggest that many Greeks found them a source of entertainment.

The Code of Drakon

Even now, we speak of "draconian" laws as being the ultimate in severity, referring to Drakon, the Athenian lawgiver of the seventh century before Christ. Historians agree that it is likely that he was a tough-minded legislator, but perhaps not as indiscriminately harsh as the historian Plutarch made him out to be:

> . . . death was the punishment for almost every offence, so that even men convicted of idleness were executed, and those who stole pot-herbs or fruits suffered just like sacrilegious robbers and murderers. . . . it is said that Drakon himself, when asked why he had fixed the punishment of death for most offences, answered that he considered these lesser crimes to deserve it, and he had no greater punishment for more important ones.[6]

No one can be certain of the accuracy of Plutarch's account. He wrote nearly 700 years after Drakon and may well have been misguided by exaggerations. What is certain is that 27 years after his laws were promulgated, the archon Solon repealed all Drakon's criminal laws except for the law on homicide, the exact details of which are uncertain.[7] In 1843 a stone slab was discovered on which part of the Draconian law on homicide was inscribed. The slab was badly deteriorated, but eventually most of the inscription was deciphered.[8] The law sets forth the cases of unintentional or unpremeditated killing for which the killer would not be punished. Nothing is written about the penalties for the various kinds of homicide that were punishable or how they were to be punished. Murderers might avoid execution by going into exile. They would be automatically convicted; their choice of exile would be taken as an admission of guilt. If they were to return to Athens, the law explicitly provided, it was no crime to kill them. Their lives in exile must have been hard. Cast out of Athens, they were unwelcome elsewhere, and their very survival was in jeopardy.

From other sources, we know that the death penalty as inflicted in ancient Greece was administered with great brutality. The convicted offender—not necessarily a murderer—might be cast over a deep precipice, or fastened with metal restraints to a board and left to die of exposure, starvation, or both. A third method of execution, poisoning by a draught of hemlock, was administered to the great philosopher Socrates.

Early Athenians regarded homicide as a pollution of the city. Ceremonies of purification had to take place to remove the curse of the gods. Before trial accused murderers were forbidden to approach the temple or public buildings lest they enrage the gods by polluting sacred places. The trial itself had to take place in the open *agora* to assure that no building would be contaminated with the presence of murderers. Because of the danger of pollution, even persons charged with unintentional homicide were exiled unless they could obtain a pardon from the victim's family.

We know that the 27 years following the issue of Drakon's code were years of great discontent and economic hardship. The Athenian aristocracy was enriching itself at the expense of the city's merchants and the farmers in the surrounding countryside. The appointment of Solon, an aristocrat and a respected merchant, as archon was not occasioned by the harshness of Drakon's code, but rather by the imminence of revolution if measures were not taken to relieve the misery of the poor. Solon's vigorous administration did much to correct economic inequity; but for the evolution of criminal justice, his thorough revision of the criminal laws of Athens deserves a special place in history.

The Laws of Solon

Like Drakon's, Solon's name is embedded in our language. Newspaper headlines refer to legislators as "solons," mainly for the convenience of a short word to fit a narrow space. Baseball teams located in capital cities sometimes are nicknamed "the Solons." That would have mystified the original solon, who was a poet, merchant, military commander, world traveler of his small world, and philosopher as well as an immortal legislator. There is no record of his athletic prowess, if any.

He deserves to be remembered. When appointed archon, he was given legislative powers primarily to reconcile the nobility with the peasants, most of whom had fallen deeply into debt. It does not appear that he had any special charge to do anything about Drakon's criminal laws, but he repealed all but the law on homicide. Tradition has it that he was a man who abhorred killing and on that account substituted fines and banishment wherever such lesser penalties could be substituted for capital punishment. Disfranchisement—the denial of civil rights for the offender and, sometimes, the offender's family—was often imposed. A disfranchised person could neither vote in the *agora* nor enter the temples or public buildings.

A thief was required to return stolen property and pay the prosecutor-victim a sum equal to twice its value. The thief could also be placed in the public stocks for five days and nights. For the crime of temple robbery the penalty was death. For rape of a free woman, the penalty was a fine of 100 *drachmas*. Seduction was considered a more heinous offense because it constituted the corruption of a woman's mind as well as her body. In such a case the aggrieved husband could propose any punishment short of bloodshed. The woman seduced was excluded from religious ceremonies and could be sold as a slave.[9]

Reviewing his accomplishments, Solon said, "Laws I wrote, alike for nobleman and commoner, awarding straight justice to everybody."[10] For his time, Solon was one of the first to see that a lawgiver had to make laws that applied equally to all citizens. He also saw that the law of punishment had to maintain proportionality to the crimes of which offenders were convicted. As a moderate man, Solon built a structure of laws that survived in Athens for centuries. It is little wonder that he is still remembered as a wise lawgiver, if not for the laws he gave.

Rome and the Criminal Law

Roman law began with the **Twelve Tables**, which were written in the middle of the sixth century B.C. when Rome was in a difficult transition from a kingdom to a republic. Before they were legislated by a special commission comprising ten members, some from the patrician nobility and some from the plebeian common people, all law was unwritten custom, administered by the patricians and kept secret from the plebeians and slaves. The demand of the common people for more fairness in the administration of justice seems to have brought about the translation of unwritten custom into written law. So far as can be determined, both the civil and the criminal laws were Roman, not influenced by Greek precedent or practice. The Twelve Tables do not seem to have been innovative; most historians believe that they merely put custom into writing.

Throughout the history of Rome the Twelve Tables were the foundation of all law. They were never repealed. Some statutes remained in force until the end of the Roman Empire, more than a thousand years after they were drafted by the "Decemvirs," the special commission of patricians. The original tablets of bronze were lost, but the tables themselves were considered an essential feature of the education of young men. Romans were proud of their laws. Cicero, the great Roman statesman, wrote:

> [T]hey inculcate the soundest principles of government and morals; and I am not afraid to affirm that the brief composition of the Decemvirs surpasses in value the libraries of Grecian philosophy. How admirable is the wisdom of our ancestors! We alone are the masters of civil prudence, and our superiority is the more conspicuous if we deign to cast our eyes on the rude and almost ridiculous jurisprudence of Draco, of Solon, and of Lycurgus.[11]

It is hard to believe that Cicero, a learned and sophisticated lawyer and philosopher, meant literally what he wrote. Most likely he was playing to a patriotic and chauvinist audience.

The tables setting forth the laws of property and contract were the beginning of the evolution of Roman law into a sophisticated system of administering justice, an evolution that has had traceable continuity in continental European law to this day. Historians and jurists regard the civil law as one of the most significant legacies of Rome.

The criminal law is viewed much less favorably. Most of the original law relating to crime was set forth in 27 sections of Table VIII. The law of talion was applied to a few offenses: For example, "if a man break another's limb and does not compensate the injury he shall be liable to retaliation." For several offenses a fine would be imposed, but the death penalty is required in 9 of the 27 sections. These included a provision that "whoever shall publish a libel—that is to say, shall write verses imputing crime or immorality to anyone—shall be beaten to death with clubs." Arson of a house or a stack of corn was punishable with the utmost severity: "He shall be bound, scourged, and burned alive." Nocturnal meetings for any purpose were prohibited under pain of death. Judges who accepted bribes as well as those who bribed them were subject to execution. Any act of treason was punishable by scourging and crucifixion.[12]

Throughout the history of Rome, the death penalty was inflicted with terrible brutality. A man who killed a relation was guilty of parricide and was subjected to a punishment that began with scourging and concluded with his being "sewn into a leather sack with a dog, a cock, a viper, and an ape, and then to be thrown into the sea." A person guilty of false witness was "hurled from the Tarpeian rock."[13] A vestal virgin who violated her vow of chastity was buried alive.[14]

In later years, executions of any kind were not as frequent as one might expect. According to H. F. Jolowicz, a leading authority on Roman law, the accused might leave Rome after being found guilty but before sentence was pronounced, and magistrates were forbidden to arrest those accused without giving them time to get out of town. All death penalties could be appealed to an assembly of the people, which might reverse the court's sentence.[15]

The authorities do not tell us what effect these harsh laws had in deterring Roman citizens from the commission of crimes, nor are we informed concerning any movements to change or at least to reduce the harsh penalties they imposed. They continued in effect for centuries.

In A.D. 527 the Emperor Justinian succeeded to the throne of a declining empire, now situated in Constantinople rather than Rome. Anxious to restore the empire to its ancient glory, Justinian took many measures to bring it under his firm control. Among these was a restatement of the old Roman law, which by this time had fallen into a state of confusion and public indifference. In *The Decline and Fall of the Roman Empire*, Gibbon tells us that

> [T]he reformation of the Roman jurisprudence was an arduous but indispensable task. In the space of ten centuries the infinite variety of laws and legal opinions had filled many thousand volumes, which no fortune could purchase and no capacity could digest. Books could not easily be found; and thus judges, poor in the midst of riches, were reduced to the exercise of their illiterate discretion.[16]

A commission of twelve experts was appointed to review the laws of Rome and to organize them into a new Digest, known as the **Institutes of Justinian.** This enormous task was accomplished in three years, and the result became the necessary text of legal education. As the Dark Ages came on and went by, the Institutes were lost, only to be rediscovered in the twelfth century at the University of Bologna in Italy. It was recognized that the times required the restoration of this systematic set of laws. Scholars from all over Europe flocked to Bologna to learn the Roman law. Until recent times, the Institutes of Justinian were the law of the land throughout most of Europe. Their principles still profoundly influence continental law.

Curiously enough, the Institutes restated the ancient criminal laws without significant amendment. Parricide was still punishable by shrouding the offender in a sack with a cock, a dog, a viper, and an ape and flinging the entire package into the ocean. We have no record of how often this sentence was pronounced and carried out, nor do we have information about its effect, if any, on deterrence.

Gibbon concluded his review of the Institutes with this comment:

> The penal statutes form a very small proportion of the sixty-two books of the Code. . . . [A]nd in all judicial proceeding the life or death of a citizen is determined with less caution and display than the most ordinary question of covenant or inheritance.[17]

It is for experts in civil law to comment on the place of the Institutes of Justinian in the development of a civilized administration of the law of torts, contracts, and inheritance. Modern readers can only be appalled at the continued support the Institutes gave to the application of the most brutal forms of punishment. The succeeding centuries saw the legitimation of even more brutality in the punishment of common criminals as well as of religious and political dissidents. As historians have observed in their study of Roman law, the horrors imposed by the courts on ordinary criminals contained their own corrective. In the long run, the public could not countenance these extremes of punishment regardless of the authority of the laws that allowed them. This is a pattern that has been repeated many times in the history of punishment. In this chapter we shall see how this reversal occurred during one of the harshest periods in the history of criminal law.

The Laws of Islam

The culture of Islamic countries has many points of parallel custom with Christian and Jewish cultures. As to the laws in general, Islam holds that like the law of Deuteronomy, the laws set forth in the Koran are of divine origin, given by Allah to the prophet Mohammed. As such, they may not be changed. Because many Islamic countries have been subjected to Western imperialism and the laws brought with them by English and French administrations, many adjustments have had to be made.

The Koran is specific about three kinds of offense: homicide, theft, and adultery.[18] As to homicide, the penalties vary with the status of the killer and the victim as believers. Commentators also agree that the punishment to be inflicted depended on the circumstances of the case. In the case of unusually brutal or heinous crimes, offenders might be crucified and left on the cross to deter others. Other verses allow the killer to negotiate with the family of the victim for compensation.

The Prophet seems to be harsher with thieves:

> And as for the man or woman addicted to theft, cut off their hands as a punishment for what they have earned, an exemplary punishment from Allah. And Allah is Mighty, Wise.
>
> But whoever repents after his wrongdoing and reforms, Allah will turn to him mercifully. Surely Allah is Forgiving, Merciful.[19]

Islamic commentators interpret these passages as "metaphorical," but open to literal implementation in appropriate cases. According to some contemporary interpreters, it is possible to think of the phrase "cutting off his hands" as meaning that the thief should be restrained by imprisonment. This interpretation does not rule out the actual amputation of a thief's hand, and this is still done in some conservative Islamic countries.

The Koran calls for equal punishment for adulterers of both genders. Both participants are to be flogged with a hundred stripes, "and let not pity for them detain you from obedience to Allah. . . . [A]nd let a party of believers witness the chastisement." Conviction of adultery requires the affirmative testimony of four witnesses. Some commentators point out that the Koran mercifully does not allow stoning offenders to death, as was the law in Deuteronomy, and the flogging may be done with a stick or even a hand.

The Koran allows for mitigation of some punishments for those who repent or reform, and where that option is not specifically authorized, interpretations are allowed in some but not all countries to evade the extreme harshness of some of the penalties. Although the laws set forth in the Koran are divine, their interpretation is left to the discretion of mortals. What is unusual about the Islamic law is its consistent provision for remission of severity where the judge finds that the offender has repented.

PUNISHMENT IN THE MIDDLE AGES

After the fall of Rome, law and order were left mostly in the hands of nobles and bishops who ruled the towns and small feudal principalities into which the empire had been fragmented. The Twelve Tables and the Institutes of Justinian were unknown. Rulers decided the fates of offenders according to what seemed best to them. The record is one of appalling cruelty. The contrast between the riches of the few and the miseries of the many has never been more stark. One historian remarks, "We . . . can hardly understand the keenness with which a fur coat, a good fire on the hearth, a soft bed, a glass of wine were formerly enjoyed."[20] And enjoyed by the few, who also knew how the cold of winter and the afflictions of incurable illness weighed down on the many. Crime was another misery, and criminals were seen as menaces to the community and as insults to God.

It was believed that criminals deserved severe punishment, and most of the punishments provided for torture as well. Executions were public, with large throngs gathered to enjoy the proceedings. At Mons in what is now Belgium, the citizens actually bought a brigand for the pleasure of seeing him quartered—that is, pulled apart by horses drawing on his arms and legs, "at which the people rejoiced more than if a new holy body had risen from the dead."[21]

Those were violent centuries during which life was insecure, justice was uncertain, and danger was everywhere. Small wonder, then, that those who increased misery by their criminal acts were punished with severity unknown to the ancients. The difference between right and wrong was sharp. No one hesitated over such questions as whether guilt might be mitigated by the poverty of offenders, or the possibility that they might be innocent, or the prospect that they could be reformed if good influences were brought to bear. Brigands were brigands, and that was enough to justify their extermination by horrible means.

THE CRIMINAL LAW AND DETERRENCE

The foundations of the criminal law that were laid by the Romans were forgotten during the Dark Ages. Slowly they were revived during the Renaissance and Reformation and on into the eighteenth and nineteenth centuries. We cannot point to landmark legislation that established the severity of the law and authorized the increasing use of painful and public executions of offenders who might have committed much less serious crimes than murder or treason. During the 38-year reign of Henry VIII in England, more than 72,000 thieves were hanged; under his daughter, Elizabeth I, "vagabonds were strung up in rows, as many as three or four hundred at a time."[22] By the mid–eighteenth century more than 200 distinct offenses, ranging from sheep stealing to murder, and including forgery and poaching, were punishable by hanging in England.

The callousness of the law of those times may be most strikingly exemplified by the famous execution of Robert François Damiens in Paris in 1757. Damiens had been convicted of the attempted murder of Louis XV, of whose dissolute conduct the straitlaced Damiens disapproved. He managed to stab the king, inflicting a slight wound. For that attempt he paid a terrible price, as related in a contemporary news story (see Box 2-2).

Box 2-2 The Execution of Damiens

On 2 March 1757 Damiens the regicide was condemned to "make the *amende honorable* before the main door of the Church of Paris," where he was to be "taken and conveyed in a cart, wearing nothing but a shirt, holding a torch of burning wax weighing two pounds"; then "in the said cart, to the Place de Grève, where, on a scaffold that will be erected there, the flesh will be torn from his breasts, arms, thighs and calves with red-hot pincers, his right hand, holding the knife with which he committed the said parricide, burnt with sulphur, and, on those places where the flesh will be torn away, poured molten lead, boiling oil, burning resin, wax and sulphur melted together and then his body drawn and quartered by four horses and his limbs and body consumed by fire, reduced to ashes and his ashes thrown to the winds.

"Finally, he was quartered," recounts the *Gazette d'Amsterdam* of 1 April 1757. "This operation was very long, because the horses used were not accustomed to drawing; consequently, instead of four, six were needed, and when that did not suffice, they were forced, in order to cut off the wretch's thighs, to sever the sinews and hack at the joints.

"It is said that, although he was always a great swearer, no blasphemy escaped his lips, but the excessive pain made him utter horrible cries, and he often repeated: 'My God, have pity on me! Jesus, help me!' The spectators were all edified by the solicitude of the parish priest of St. Paul's who despite his great age did not spare himself in offering consolation to the patient."

Source: Michel Foucault, *Discipline and Punish*, trans. Alan Sheridan (New York: Pantheon, 1977), pp. 3–6, quoting an article in the *Gazette d'Amsterdam*, 1 April 1757.

How can such a terrible execution be explained? Although Louis XV was one of the least admirable of monarchs, he ruled by the divine right of kings. An attempt on his life not only shook the safety of the state but was also an affront to God, who was believed to have appointed Louis to rule over France. Undoubtedly Damiens' fate was intended to be a deterrent example to the restive populace—an example that did not deter that populace from guillotining Louis' grandson, Louis XVI, 36 years later, as well as thousands of the French nobility.

The Galleys

Naval vessels in the sixteenth century required galley slaves to row them. The conditions of their service were harsh and severe. They were chained to their benches, 4 to an oar, and as many as 200 might be required to propel a ship. In England and France, the **galley** oarsmen were criminals convicted of less-than-capital crimes. Elizabeth I proclaimed in 1602 that prisoners "except when convicted of willful Murther, Rape and Burglarye," might be reprieved from execution and sent to the galleys "where in, as in all things, our desire is that justice may be tempered with clemency & mercy . . . and the offenders to be in such sort corrected and punished that even in their punishments they may yeld some proffitable service to the Commonwealth." In France the courts were instructed to refrain from executing, torturing, or even fining criminals so that the king's galleys would be filled with oarsmen. At this distance in time it is difficult to determine how much better off the galley oarsman was as a result of this clemency and mercy. Usually it was a lifetime assignment, and there was little concern about the oarsmen's well-being—there were always more recruits in the jails. The development of men-of-war under sail gradually put an end to the galley by the end of the seventeenth century.[23]

England and the Gallows

In the eighteenth century about 200 crimes, perhaps more—nobody is sure—were lawfully punishable by death. These crimes ranged from murder down to stealing from a shopkeeper objects valued at 5 shillings or more. The deterrent effect of these seemingly ferocious statutes was eroded by the disinclination of judges, prosecutors, and juries to impose capital punishment on men and women who were correctly seen as petty offenders. Juries would convict thieves of larceny of goods valued at less than 1 shilling, regardless of the true value as set forth in the prosecution's charge. This was known as "pious perjury." It was tolerated and sometimes encouraged by prosecutors with no stomach for demanding death for petty thieves. No leniency was allowed to forgers, who regularly were sentenced to the gallows. About 70 percent of all sentences in the London criminal court in the 1760s were for transportation to America. Later, as we shall discuss at length in this chapter, thousands of felons were shipped to Australia. Some would be sentenced to brief imprisonment in houses of correction. Some would be publicly whipped or placed in a pillory in the marketplace.

All hangings were public and usually conducted like theatrical performances, with critical attention given to the enactment of their roles by the hangman, the chaplain, and the condemned individual. The hangman's part was played without words but had to be done deftly and without mistakes. The chaplain had a sermon to preach to the man who was about to meet his Maker, and to the attending crowd, to impress on all who could hear the wages of crime. The condemned man was at liberty to say anything he pleased, including a protestation of innocence. If his demeanor at this awful time was marked by contrite manliness he would be applauded, but he would swing anyway.

Thoughtful Englishmen came to doubt the usefulness of these ritual hangings and whippings before crowds who were certainly not viewing them with the awed solemnity that such occasions should call for. One such observer, the satirist Bernard Mandeville, commented that the riotous behavior of the crowds led the poor "to believe that there was nothing to a hanging but an awry neck and a wet pair of breeches." Nevertheless it was well into the nineteenth century before public hangings were stopped, and far into the twentieth century before the end of capital punishment.

Minor offenders were sent to local prisons managed by county sheriffs. **Bridewells,** or "houses of correction," were established under local authorities to teach habits of industry to vagrants and idlers. There were also debtors' prisons, to which those who were unable or unwilling to pay their creditors were sent. There were laws that established the standards of treatment of prisoners that sheriffs and magistrates were supposed to observe. Those laws were universally ignored by the local authorities with impunity. The conditions in these places of detention called for radical reform, and the process began with a pious county sheriff.

The Conscience of John Howard

In 1773, John Howard (1726–1790) was appointed High Sheriff of Bedfordshire. He was a well-to-do country squire of an especially pious religious background. As a young man he had traveled to Europe hoping to help in the relief of Lisbon after the disastrous earthquake of 1755. On the way, he was captured by the French, with whom England was at war, and held prisoner for two months in conditions of great barbarity. He was returned to England on a prisoner exchange. His biographers do not tell us to what extent his experiences as a prisoner of war influenced his later single-minded determination to reform all the prisons of Europe.

His book *The State of the Prisons in England and Wales*, published after his initial survey, made him a celebrity. His name is still associated with prison reform in Britain and the United States, where Howard Leagues have long been established to maintain vigilance over the standards set for prison operations.

When Howard became a sheriff—then a ceremonial office with nominal responsibility for the county's jails and bridewells—he took the post seriously, as practically no other holder of the office ever had. He inspected the jail that was under his control. It was an intrusion that had never before happened. He was shocked to discover several penniless prisoners who had been acquitted of the offenses with which they had been charged, were eligible for release, but were being detained until they paid "sundry fees" to the jailer and the clerk of the court. This practice was not countenanced by the law, but the officials' only source of income was the fees paid by their prisoners.

Howard proposed to the magistrates of his county that these officers be paid salaries. The magistrates agreed that something ought to be done but asked the sheriff first to find out what other counties were doing to pay jail personnel. Sheriff Howard proceeded to a methodical county-by-county survey and found that not only no other county paid jailers and clerks a salary, but also that conditions were uniformly horrifying. He decided to devote the rest of his life to the reform of prisons and jails. Explaining his motives, he wrote:

> I was prompted by the sorrows of the sufferers and love to my country. The work grew on me insensibly: I could not enjoy my ease and leisure in the neglect of any opportunity, offered me by Providence, of attempting the relief of the miserable.[24]

His inspections were hazardous in a sense that modern prison reformers have been spared. Jail fever, or typhus, was endemic in most prisons, spread by rats and lice, and then from prisoner to prisoner. Numerous prisoners, as well as jailers, judges, and court functionaries, died of it. In addition to typhus, many prisoners suffered from active cases of smallpox. One early result of Howard's exposure of the dangerously unsanitary conditions in English prisons was attention to cleaning them up and providing for proper ventilation. In his report to Parliament, Howard remarked:

> It was not, I own, without some apprehensions of danger that I first visited prisons; and I guarded myself by smelling to vinegar, while I was in those places, and changing my apparel afterwards. This I did constantly and carefully when I began: but by degrees I

> grew less attentive to these precautions, and have long since omitted them. On account of the alteration made by the act for preserving the health of prisoners, one may now look into many a prison without gaining an idea of the condition it was in a few years ago.[25]

Although the condition of British prisons improved, there was much to do in other countries. Howard died of typhus after inspecting a prison in Kherson in southern Russia.

Howard's survey of English prisons was published in 1774 in the first of four editions (the last was published two years after his death). It immediately attracted the attention of Parliament, before which Howard appeared to present his proposals for reform. What he recommended can be found in the first pages of his report, and most of his ideas are just as relevant today as they were in his time. To summarize:

1. Prisoners should be classified according to their offenses. Men and women should occupy separate quarters. Young prisoners should not associate with old and hardened offenders.
2. Prisoners awaiting trial should not be required to work, but those convicted of felonies should have a full day of work to do.
3. Jailers should be honest and sober. Howard noted that most of the men he encountered in charge of jails added to their income by "promoting drunkenness and midnight revels so that most of our jails are riotous alehouses and brothels." Jailers should live near the prison premises and should make daily inspections. They should not demand fees but should receive salaries.
4. Conscientious chaplains and surgeons should be employed at each jail. Howard noted that some physicians insisted on a clause in their contract of employment that they not be required to enter the cells of prisoners suffering from the "jail distemper" (fever or typhus).
5. Prisoners should be regularly bathed, and the jails should be properly ventilated.
6. There should be a daily allowance of wholesome food.
7. Inspectors should be appointed to ensure compliance with standards required by law. The inspector "should make his visit once a week, changing his days. . . . He should look into every room to see if it be clean, &c. He should speak with every prisoner; hear all complaints; and immediately correct what he finds is manifestly wrong."
8. Instead of congregate housing, each prisoner should sleep alone in a cell to himself, but they should not be in the rooms in which they sleep during the daytime.[26]

Between 1774 and 1791 Parliament enacted a series of statutes embodying Howard's recommendations. Unfortunately, the legislation was permissive and not mandatory. It was up to the local magistrates to enforce them. There was no little reluctance by local authorities to raise taxes to make life healthier for prisoners. Change for the better was slow. In 1818, 28 years after Howard's death, an inmate in the debtors' prison of London died of starvation, and two female prisoners were found with only a rug to hide their nakedness. When these conditions came to light, the aldermen of the city of London responded to charges that they had not complied with the laws by saying that "their prisoners had all that they ought to have, unless gentlemen thought they should be indulged with Turkey carpets." The notion that prisons are luxury hotels where criminals are coddled goes back a long way.

John Howard's truly astonishing career demonstrates the achievements made possible by a tireless reformer determined to collect the facts and make them speak for themselves. It also demonstrates the impermanence of reform. Down to the present time in England and the United States, reformers have found that neglect and abuse still result in grotesquely inhumane conditions in our prisons. Their complaints have too often received the same kind of response that the aldermen of the city of London gave to inspectors who thought that prisoners should be clothed decently and should not die of starvation.

Banishment and Transportation

Throughout the eighteenth century and far into the nineteenth century, England sent convicted criminals to colonies abroad, first to America and then, after the American Revolution, to Australia. The experience of **transportation** was miserable for those transported, but out of the miseries came a significant new departure in penology that has special importance in understanding today's correctional policy. First, it is necessary to review the general background.

Those men and women who were sent to America were indentured to planters and tradesmen, usually for five but often for nine or ten years. Their condition was little better than slavery. They were forbidden to return to England before the expiration of their sentences, and they were hanged if caught in the attempt. Transportation to America having ended in 1776, and the supply of convicted offenders continuing to be plentiful, work projects, such as clearing gravel from the riverbed of the Thames, were found in and around London. The prisoners lived in "hulks," decommissioned naval vessels. Conditions were notoriously unhealthy; prisoners were ill fed and kept in unsanitary and overcrowded quarters. Something had to be done to relieve a miserable situation that was in plain sight of the general public. The jails of England, hitherto mostly used for the detention of accused offenders before trial, received unprecedented numbers of men and women who could not be accommodated in the hulks. The atrocious conditions in which these unfortunates lived were documented in the massive surveys conducted by John Howard, and they led to the first serious prison reform movement. Practical politicans knew that the gallows, hulks, and antiquated jails did not add up to a solution to the crime problem. A better way had to be found.

The discovery of Australia provided the answer. From 1787 to 1857, when the British Parliament abolished the transportation system, more than 130,000, perhaps as many as 160,000—no one is sure of the exact number—men, women, boys, and girls were transported to various locations in Australia. The first shipment from England across the world to New South Wales carried 983 prisoners on embarkation, 273 of whom died during the 10-month voyage and 486 of whom were too sick to disembark on their own power. Accounts of conditions on the first convict transports lead a modern reader to wonder how anyone could have survived the experience.

Convicts who survived the voyage to Australia and lived inoffensively under the harsh regimen of the military and naval officers who managed the settlements could work under reasonable conditions. Skilled and semi-skilled men and women could obtain paid employment either from the settlement or from employment by free immigrants. Unskilled men would work in chain gangs. Good behavior would eventually entitle a convict to a "ticket of leave," giving him freedom to seek paid employment anywhere in the colony, subject to severe restrictions and to revocation for cause. This was a precursor of the modern system of parole. Beyond that, a man could hope for full liberty to go anywhere he pleased. Many, when their sentences ended, became settlers with farms or shops of their own. Discipline was severe and began with flogging—as many as a thousand lashes administered with the cat-'o-nine-tails. For more serious offenders, reassignment to one of four penal settlements was the dreaded punishment.

The most infamous of these settlements was maintained on Norfolk Island, 930 miles out in the ocean northeast of Sydney. It is 5 miles long and 2½ miles wide. It has no harbor, and landings are difficult except in very calm water. About 2000 convicts were settled there, under the government's order that ". . . the felon who is sent there is forever excluded from hope of return."[27] They were "doubly convicted" first of felonies committed in England, and then of new crimes committed in Australia. The contemporary accounts of the treatment of Norfolk Island prisoners describe conditions of depravity and brutality that have seldom been matched in the long course of humans' inhumanity to their fellows. A chaplain reported that so terrible were the conditions of existence that when he went into a cell in which condemned men were awaiting execution to announce the results of the governor's review of their sentences, the men who were reprieved "wept bitterly, and each man who heard of his condemnation to death went down on his knees and thanked God."[28]

Captain Maconochie's Reforms

In 1840 one of the most remarkable men in the history of punishment was assigned to superintend this hellhole. Captain Alexander Maconochie (1787–1860) was a retired naval officer brought to Australia by Sir John Franklin, a fellow naval officer and a friend who had been appointed lieutenant governor of Van Diemen's Land, now known as Tasmania.[29] Van Diemen's Land was a separate colony populated mostly by transported convicts. Maconochie, a strict Scotch Presbyterian, was shocked by the treatment of the convicts. He was so articulate about his disapproval of the brutality of the system that he developed proposals for drastic changes. Despite his friendship with Maconochie, Franklin was so disturbed by the criticisms that he dismissed him.

Maconochie's proposals were indeed startling for those times, when the need for the utmost severity in the administration of sentences was doctrine. A famous English clergyman, Sydney Smith, a man who was otherwise noted for wisdom and altruism, wrote,

> [A prison] should be a place of punishment, from which men recoil with horror—a place of real suffering painful to the memory, terrible to the imagination . . . a place of sorrow and wailing, which should be entered with horror and quitted with earnest resolution never to return to such misery; with that impression, in short, of the evil which breaks out in perpetual warning and exhortation to others.[30]

Despite the temper of the times, the proposals advanced by Maconochie in several long memoranda to the Colonial Office in London received a sympathetic review which ended with the recommendation that he be appointed to superintend a penal settlement where he could try out his ideas. Maconochie's proposals were based on two beliefs. First, "brutality and cruelty debase not only the person subjected to them, but also the society which deliberately uses them or tolerates them for purposes of social control." Second, "the treatment of the wrongdoer during his sentence of imprisonment should be designed to make him fit to be released into society again, purged of the tendencies that led to his offense, and strengthened in his ability to withstand temptation to offend again."[31]

Sir George Gipps, the governor of New South Wales, decided that Norfolk Island would be a good place for the experiment. About 800 ordinary convicts—as distinguished from the "doubly convicted"—would be sent to the island. Sir George's idea was that the new convicts would be kept separate from the old, an obviously impractical plan in view of the size of the island and the limited facilities for housing more prisoners. From the first, Maconochie expressed his reservations about the feasibility of the plan but went ahead with the hope that something positive would emerge.

On arrival at the island, he told the prisoners what he intended to do and why. A mark system would be installed whereby prisoners would receive a fixed number of "marks of commendation" for completing assigned tasks. The marks could be used to purchase food and clothing and could accumulate to a total that would entitle the prisoner to a ticket of leave.[32] Those who earned 6000 marks would discharge a 7-year sentence; 8000 marks would free a man from a life sentence. Instead of flogging, prisoners guilty of disciplinary infractions would be fined a certain number of marks. Maconochie decided that the doubly convicted and the new men had to be treated alike, a decision that got him into trouble with Sir George Gipps. That distant official rebuked Maconochie, pointing out that this plan

> disregarded equally the effects which so great a change of discipline was calculated to produce on the large convict population of this Colony, and the feelings of . . . alarm with which the colonists would contemplate the speedy return to the colony of more than a thousand persons of the most reckless character, who had been sent from it for the commission of crimes for the most part of the deepest dye.[33]

From that time on, Maconochie operated under constraints, and his system of marks was limited to offenders with sentences of three years or less. Upon personal inspection, Sir George Gipps admitted that the system might have been working well on the island, but that its impact on convicts on the mainland would be to lessen deterrence. Worse, settlers, urgently needed by the colony and who are beginning to arrive in some numbers from England, were concerned about their safety. It all ended in 1844 with Maconochie's recall to England.

That he lasted so long was at least in part due to the difficulty of finding a replacement. Two superintendents followed him with instructions to restore the old system of discipline by terror. The results were predictable. There was a succession of bloody riots in the course of which many of the island staff were killed. Inspections of Norfolk Island eventually convinced the colonial office of the necessity of closing down this element of the convict system in 1853.

We have dwelt on Captain Maconochie's experiment at some length because of its long-run significance. Maconochie returned to England and engaged in a long and seemingly unsuccessful campaign to reform the British prison system. He wrote and published pamphlets on his ideas and how they could not only humanize penology but also save the taxpayers a great deal of money. Captain Maconochie's campaign, to which he devoted the rest of his life, attracted many disciples as well as the skepticism and derision of contemporary hardliners. His most important follower was Walter Crofton, of whom more will be said in the next chapter.

His pamphlets contained much good sense that received little attention in his lifetime. For example,

> I think governors [of jails and prisons] ought to belong to a profession; I think it is very wrong to allow magistrates to elect their own governor; it should be a department of the State, and men should enter the department early, and rise gradually through successive stages, with a regular practical and scientific education for the purpose, and then you would be quite sure that a man would not be either a blockhead or a capricious person, capriciously lenient or capriciously severe; he would be like a surgeon trained in his profession. In like manner, if you change the type in the jail, you must improve partly the status of the inferior officers.[34]

Decades passed before this wise advice took hold in the penal services of Britain and the United States. But not long after Maconochie's return to England a group of citizens in Birmingham gathered to make a presentation to him. A prominent judge spoke in testimonial:

> Years must elapse, and many trials must be made before a perfect system can be devised; but we feel assured that no future explorer will act wisely, who does not make himself acquainted with the charts you have laid down before he sails on his voyage of discovery.[35]

Captain Alexander Maconochie certainly qualifies as one of the heroes in the history of penology.

CONCLUSIONS

We have rushed through thousand of years of history, touching too briefly on the landmarks of change. We have seen that inhuman punishments have been administered to men, women, and children by states and communities where fear of crime prevails. No matter how horrible the punishment, there have always been legislators to authorize it, and preachers and philosophers who, in the security of ignorance, have found principles for its justification. Ordinary men and women—in later chapters female reformers will make their appearance—who have been directly exposed to the reality of deterrence by terror have forced the changes that made humane punishment possible. In spite of the work of men like John Howard and Alexander Maconochie, the nature of punishment is such that without the vigilance of good and wise men the system relapses. Good people pass on, leaving the system in the hands of indifferent bureaucrats and, too often, men and women who enjoy the administration of needless misery on others. The horrors of the twentieth-century holocausts and gulags remind us that the courage and zeal of Howard and Maconochie are still needed—perhaps as never before.

KEY TERMS

Bridewells

Code of Hammurabi

Drakon

galley

Institutes of Justinian

law of talion

Solon

transportation

Twelve Tables

DISCUSSION TOPICS

2.1 Does Hammurabi's law of talion survive in our times? If so, for what crimes and in what form? What justification, if any, exists for this law?

2.2 The Greek lawgiver Solon is still remembered today. What were his distinctive contributions to criminal justice and why are they still important?

2.3 Over 200 offenses were punishable on the gallows in eighteenth-century England—from sheep stealing to murder. How can this be explained? What were the effects on the administration of justice?

2.4 What were the advantages and disadvantages of public executions of offenders? Would you favor televised public executions of offenders? If not, why not?

2.5 Captain Maconochie thought that prison governors or wardens should belong to a profession. If so, how should the warden qualify as a professional? What training and experience would be needed?

ANNOTATED REFERENCES

Beccaria, Cesare. *On Crimes and Punishments.* Trans. Kenelm Foster and Jane Grigson. London: Oxford University Press, 1964. *We prefer this translation to the more commonly cited version by Henry Paolucci (Indianapolis: Bobs-Merrill, 1963). The Foster-Grigson translation is the first part of a volume devoted to Beccaria's life and accomplishments by his grandson, Alessandro Manzoni, entitled* The Column of Infamy.

Drapkin, Israel. *Crime and Punishment in the Ancient World.* Lexington, Mass.: Lexington Books, 1989. *A scholarly and comprehensive account of crime and justice, so far as the subject is known to history, in all of the ancient societies, including those of China and the Orient, India, Persia, Islam, and Ethiopia, as well as Greece and Rome. Highly recommended.*

Howard, John. *Prisons and Lazarettos.* Montclair, N.J.: Patterson Smith, 1973, two volumes. *The first volume is limited to the state of the prisons in England and Wales and constitutes the report that Howard made to Parliament on his survey of English prisons. The second volume covers the* lazarettos *(hospitals for the diseased poor) and the prisons in foreign countries that Howard surveyed after his earlier report on English prisons had made him a celebrity.*

Radzinowicz, Leon. *A History of the English Criminal Law.* London: Stevens, 1948–1968, four volumes. *A massive history covering the development of the criminal law from the eighteenth century to the present. An indispensable work of reference, readable even though voluminous.*

Rusche, Georg, and Otto Kirchheimer. *Punishment and Social Structure.* New York: Columbia University Press, 1939, reissued 1968, Russell and Russell. *A Marxist interpretation of the history of punishment. There is an emphasis on the function of criminal justice to protect the values of the dominant classes in society. In his foreword, Thorsten Sellin remarks that the "authors . . . have shown the close interrelationships between punishment and the culture which has produced them." The book contains much historical information not elsewhere available in English.*

NOTES

1. A. S. Diamond, *Primitive Law, Past and Present* (London: Methuen, 1971).
2. We have drawn on the definitive study of the Code of Hammurabi in G. Driver and John C. Miles, *The Babylonian Laws* (London: Oxford University Press, 1952, 2 vols.). See also, C. H. W. Johns, *The Oldest Code of Laws in the World* (Edinburgh: T. & T. Clark, 1905) for a full translation.
3. Our brief review of Hittite laws relies on O. R. Gurney, *The Hittites* (London: Penguin Books, 1952).
4. See Chapter 5 for full discussion of the philosophical justifications of punishment.
5. See Douglas M. MacDowell, *The Law in Classical Athens* (Ithaca, N.Y.: The Cornell University Press, 1978), pp. 10–23.
6. Plutarch, *Plutarch's Lives* § XVII, trans. Aubrey Stewart and George Long (London: Bell, 1906), vol. I, pp. 144–145.
7. The archon of Athens was an elective office that was held for one year. He acted as a chief magistrate. As an archon, Solon was specially empowered to repeal old laws and make new ones.
8. Ronald S. Stroud, *Drakon's Law on Homicide* (Berkeley: University of California Press, 1968).
9. MacDowell, *The Law in Classical Athens*, pp. 120–132 contains an adequate summary of what is known about punishment in Athens.
10. Victor Ehrenberg, *From Solon to Socrates* (London: Methuen, 1968), p. 70.
11. Cicero, *De Legibus*, ii. 23. Quoted by Edward Gibbon in *The Decline and Fall of the Roman Empire* (New York: Modern Library, 1932), chap. XLIV. Lycurgus was the lawgiver of Sparta, of whom nothing is known for sure—even whether he actually lived. The translation is presumably Gibbon's.
12. Ibid.
13. The Tarpeian rock was a steep rock face on one of the Roman hills. Thrown from its height, no one could possibly survive.
14. For a text of the Twelve Tables, see W. A. Hunter, *A Systematic and Historical Exposition of Roman Law* (London: Sweet and Maxwell, 1897), pp. 16–24. There is an excellent discussion of the criminal law in the Roman Republic in H. F. Jolowicz, *Historical Introduction to the Study of Roman Law* (Cambridge: Cambridge University Press, 1954), pp. 321–331.
15. Jolowicz, *Study of Roman Law*, p. 373.
16. Gibbon, *The Decline and Fall of the Roman Empire*, p. 341.

17. Ibid.
18. *The Holy Qu'ran*, trans. Maulana Muhammad Ali (Lahore, Pakistan: Ahmadiyyah Anjuman Isha'at Islam, 1973), pp. 250–251.
19. Ibid., p. 252.
20. Johan Huizinga, *The Waning of the Middle Ages* (London: Edward Arnold, 1924), p. 1.
21. Ibid., p. 15.
22. Georg Rusche and Otto Kirchheimer, *Punishment and Social Structure* (New York: Russell and Russell, 1968), pp. 19–20.
23. George Ives, *A History of Penal Methods* (London: Stanley Paul, 1914), pp. 101–107.
24. John Howard, *Prisons and Lazarettos*, Vol. 1, *The State of the Prisons in England and Wales* (Montclair, N.J.: Patterson Smith, 1973), p. 1
25. Ibid., p. 3.
26. Ibid.
27. Ibid.
28. Ibid., p. 165.
29. At that time the title of lieutenant governor was assigned to the chief executive of the smaller colony, whose lieutenancy signified his subordinate status to the governor—in this case, of New South Wales.
30. John Vincent Barry, *Alexander Maconochie of Norfolk Island* (Melbourne: Oxford University Press, 1958), p. 178; quoting from Sydney Smith, *On the Management of Prisons* (London: Warde Locke & Co., n.d.), pp. 226, 232. It is not on record that Sydney Smith had ever set foot in a prison. He was neither the first nor the last to give an opinion about the treatment of criminals from a standpoint of obvious ignorance.
31. Ibid., p. 72.
32. Maconochie's system was complex; we have sketched only the essential ideas. For a complete account, see Barry, *Alexander Maconochie*, p. 75.
33. Ibid., p. 103.
34. Ibid., p. 128.
35. Ibid., p. 1. The judge was Matthew Davenport Hill, Q.C., Recorder of Birmingham.

Chapter 3

From Deterrence to Reform

CHAPTER OUTLINE

The seeds of modern corrections were sown during the eighteenth and nineteenth centuries. Indeed, most of the ideas that make up modern penology can be traced to three European philosophers: Baron de Montesquieu, Cesare Bonesana Beccaria, and Jeremy Bentham. Deterrence, rather than revenge, was the dominant theme of their writings. The American experience with corrections was of course shaped by what had transpired before. Excluding the Quaker-inspired "Great Law" of Pennsylvania, brutal punishment derived from methods used to punish criminals in Europe was common throughout the colonies. The belief that offenders were responsible for their behavior and should be punished was derived from Beccaria and Bentham. But these antecedents were combined with the idealism and reform orientation found in the Colonies to result in the early American practices toward the criminal.

MONTESQUIEU'S APPEAL FOR MODERATION IN PUNISHMENT

In Chapter 2 we saw how John Howard, an unlettered sheriff, exposed the horrors of the jails that disfigured England and most European countries. His was the practical approach of a puritanically religious man of affairs who believed that the New Testament meant what it said. In his version of Christianity, the laws of any Christian country had to be consistent with the compassion taught by Christ.

From an entirely different moral standpoint, continental European philosophers—the men of the **Enlightenment**—called for moderation in punishment. It is far beyond the scope of this book to present a history of the Enlightenment and the many concepts by which it changed the outlook of humanity toward itself and the values that govern, or should govern, society. The immense influence of French, English, and Italian philosophers of the eighteenth century on the criminal laws and the application of punishment continues to this day. Their influence on the founding fathers of the United States, the framers of our Constitution, was explicitly acknowledged by men such as John Adams, Thomas Jefferson, and James Madison.

All three of these great statesmen had read the works of Charles de Secondat, Baron de Montesquieu (1689–1755), one of the founders of political science. His *On the Spirit of the Laws*, published in 1748, was a literary success from the first, selling 22 editions in less than 2 years.[1] It was almost immediately translated into English. In 1760 John Adams, who was to become our second president, was studying it with admiration. Thomas Jefferson copied extracts in his commonplace book, and James Madison wrote that Montesquieu "had lifted the veil from the venerable errors which enslaved opinion." The Constitution of the United States obviously followed Montesquieu's precept that the powers of government should be separated among the executive, the legislature, and the judiciary in order to preserve the liberties of the people.

Montesquieu's concern with the proper roles of government included the punishment of criminals. As he considered the problem, he argued that

> The severity of punishments is fitter for despotic governments whose principle is terror, than for a monarchy or a republic whose strength is honor and virtue. In moderate governments the love of one's country, shame and the fear of blame, are restraining motives, capable of preventing a great multitude of crimes. Here the greatest punishment of a bad action is conviction. The civil laws have therefore a softer way of correcting, and do not require so much force and severity.
>
> In those states a good legislator is less bent upon punishing than preventing crimes; he is more concerned to inspire good morals than to inflict punishments. . . .
>
> Whatever we observe among particular men, is equally observable in different nations. In countries inhabited by savages who lead a very hard life, and in despotic governments, where there is only one person on whom fortune has lavished her favours, while the miserable subjects lie exposed to her insults, people are equally cruel. Leniency reigns in moderate governments.[2]

To a modern reader there is nothing radical in these ideas, but imagine their impact on men and women accustomed to the horrors inflicted on Robert Damiens, as described in Chapter 2, or to the ghastly punishments inflicted in England and her colonies for relatively minor offenses. To the rulers of the Old World, *On the Spirit of the Laws* was nothing less than sedition. Montesquieu could not publish it in France but had it printed in Switzerland. The Vatican immediately placed it on its Index of Prohibited Books. It is no wonder that for men like Adams, Jefferson, and Madison the works of Montesquieu were like a great light pointing the way to a new world.

BECCARIA'S AGENDA FOR PENAL REFORM

The second great influence propelling the movement to reform the savage criminal laws of the eighteenth century was the short treatise *On Crimes and Punishments*, published in 1766 by the Marchese Cesare Bonesana Beccaria (1738–1794), a young Milanese aristocrat.[3] It was written under unusual circumstances. Recently qualified as a lawyer, Beccaria found himself at loose ends with nothing urgent to do. He was invited to join a reading club, the Academy of Fists, so named because the intellectual disputes aroused by the reading were intended to be vigorous, with no holds barred short of fisticuffs. It was a small group, consisting of not more than a dozen young men, meeting nightly to read and discuss the famous French and English authors of the Enlightenment.

At the time, the government of Milan was undergoing a fiscal crisis having to do with the exchange rates for the various currencies circulating in the province of Lombardy, of which Milan was the capital. Beccaria wrote a pamphlet outlining remedies for this state of affairs and suggesting monetary reforms that were eventually adopted.

Impressed with how Beccaria had disposed of a serious economic problem, Pietro Verri, the organizer of the Academy of Fists, suggested that he look into the state of criminal justice. The work of Montesquieu had been widely read in Italy, and the terrible execution of Robert Damiens had been discussed and condemned as unacceptably barbarous. The time had come for a serious consideration of criminal justice reform, and it was an appropriate topic for the Academy of Fists. Accepting the assignment, Beccaria amassed a great deal of information about how crimes were punished both in Italy and in other countries. There was much discussion within the academy about his ideas, and, after a year of research and discourse, his book *On Crimes and Punishments* was published in 1764.[4]

It was a short treatise, not a hundred pages long. It was terse and clear, and its brevity may partly account for its immense influence. It has become a classic of criminological literature, a landmark still read by scholars and jurists.

Success was immediate. Copies were sent to Paris, where they were received by the leading philosophers of the time. Voltaire, Diderot, and d'Alembert read it and sent admiring compliments to the author. A distinguished scholar translated it into French, and it was published in 1766.[5] Beccaria was invited to come to Paris, where he was lionized by some of the most famous men of the time. Homesick and shy, he found the experience uncomfortable and cut it short after ten weeks, although he had intended to stay for as long as six months.

He returned to Milan and out of the blue received an offer from Catherine the Great to come to St. Petersburg to overhaul the criminal laws of Russia. The empress had been particularly impressed by Beccaria's arguments against the use of torture and the death penalty. He considered the invitation carefully; his wife, excited by the prospect of foreign travel, urged him to accept, but friends pointed out that the weather in Italy was far superior to that which he would find in Russia. He decided to remain in Milan, where, on the strength of the Russian invitation, he was appointed a professor of public economy and commerce.

From that time on, his work was almost exclusively in economics, where he made contributions to theory and was a member of the Economic Council of Milan.

His work in this entirely different discipline is often credited as anticipating the thought of Adam Smith, the great Scottish economist. Toward the end of his life he was appointed a member of a commission to reform the criminal laws of Lombardy, then a province of the Austrian empire. He was a leading member of the commission, and its final product incorporated most of his ideas. The important exception was his opposition to capital punishment. He was unable to persuade his colleagues that the death penalty should be abolished. One of them gave as his opinion that if this were done, Lombardy would attract criminals from all over who would know that if caught they would be safe from the executioner. This must have been one of the first of a long line of entirely speculative—and highly dubious—arguments for the retention of capital punishment.

Despite its surprising success, Beccaria's slim treatise was met by some vehement opposition. Within weeks of its publication, Father Ferdinando Facchinei, a monk, wrote a tract denouncing the book, charging its author with 6 counts of sedition and 23 of irreligion. A year later Beccaria's book joined Montesquieu's *On the Spirit of the Laws* on the Vatican's Index of Prohibited Books, where it remained until 1962, when a wiser pope, John XXIII, abolished the Index. Two French jurists attacked Beccaria as advocating "new ideas which, if they were adopted, would simply overthrow the laws accepted up to now by the best governed states and would endanger religion, morality, and the most sacred rules of government."[6] Another writer took issue with his arguments against torture, pointing out that torture had proved its usefulness over many centuries in most civilized nations. We shall see that resistance to change in the administration of justice is a chronic impediment to reform, regardless of the nature of the changes proposed.

For students of criminal justice, *On Crimes and Punishments* is the object of our attention. It was translated into many languages, and its principles were praised and sometimes observed in countries not otherwise noted for a humane and liberal administration of justice. Its influence in England and America is of the most significance for our survey of the history of penal reform.

English jurists, scholars, and politicians took Beccaria seriously. His work attracted the interest of William Blackstone, whose *Commentaries on the Laws of England* became an essential authority on the common law. His praise of Beccaria was restrained, but he conceded that the treatise suggested improvements that could be made in the administration of English criminal justice.

Much more significant was the response of Jeremy Bentham, about whom we shall have much more to say later in this chapter. Bentham allowed in rather extravagant language that he was a disciple of Beccaria:

> Oh, my master, first evangelist of reason . . . you who have made so many useful excursions into the path of utility, what is there left for us to do?—Never to turn aside from that path.[7]

Beccaria's influence crossed the Atlantic, where his writing attracted the interest of John Adams, Thomas Jefferson, and James Madison. Adams quoted Beccaria in his successful defense of the British soldiers charged with the Boston Massacre, and he later mentioned Beccaria's work in his diary:

> I have received such blessing, and enjoyed such tears of transport; and there is no greater pleasure or consolation.[8]

Jefferson was also a lawyer with much background in the criminal law. The Revolutionary War was over, and change was in the air. Dissatisfied with the brutalities inherited from England and built into the Virginia statutes, he accepted an assignment from the legislature to membership in the Committee of Revisors charged with the reform of the legal system. He drafted a "Bill for Proportioning Crimes and Punishments in Cases Heretofore Capital," annotated with several references to Beccaria. It was introduced in the legislature in 1785, where it was defeated by one vote. It was presented again in 1796 and then passed into law. Jefferson commented on the statute's legislative history in his autobiography:

> Beccaria, and other writers on crimes and punishments, had satisfied the reasonable world of the unrightfulness and inefficacy of the punishment of crimes by death; and hard labor on roads, canals and other public works had been suggested as a proper substitute. The Revisors adopted these opinions; but the general idea of our country had not yet advanced to that point. The bill, therefore, for proportioning crimes and punishments was lost in the House of Delegates by a majority of a single vote. . . . In the meanwhile, the public opinion was ripening, by time, by reflection, and by the example of Pennsylvania, where labor on the highways had been tried, without approbation, from 1786 to '89, and had been followed by their Penitentiary system on the principle of confinement and labor, which was proceeding auspiciously. In 1796 our legislature resumed the subject, and passed the law for amending the penal laws of the Commonwealth. They adopted solitary instead of public labor, established a gradation in the duration of confinement, [and] approximated the style of the law more to the modern usage.[9]

We summarize Beccaria's treatise at some length (see Box 3-1) because it represents the dividing line between the terrible, unreasoning past of criminal justice as he found it when he wrote, and a new commitment to humanity and reason in dealing with criminals. Gone were the justifications of torture, the indiscriminate application of capital punishment to hundreds of crimes, many of them petty, and the emphasis on retribution rather than prevention. To this day the American criminal justice system has been unable to comply with Beccaria's admonition that punishment be swift and certain as well as mild, but everyone agrees on the validity of the principle—except those who profit from confusion and delay.

On the whole, Beccaria's work represents an astonishing performance by a young man in his twenties.

JEREMY BENTHAM AND THE GREATEST HAPPINESS PRINCIPLE

Jeremy Bentham (1748–1832) is chiefly remembered by American penologists for the Panopticon,[10] a design for a prison that he invented and almost persuaded the British government to adopt. He was enormously proud of the general idea, spent thousands of pounds of his own money on the purchase of land to build it, and was obsessively angry with King George III (who, he thought, was personally to blame) and his ministers for rejecting it after long and sometimes tentatively favorable consideration. After he had made a pest of himself for many years, Parliament granted him £23,000, at that time a very large sum of money, to recoup his investment. The Millbank Prison was built on the land that he had purchased, and the Panopticon was forgotten so far as England was concerned.[11]

Box 3-1 Summary of *On Crimes and Punishments*

We must now summarize the principles that Beccaria proposed as the foundations of a just criminal law. While we can present the most important elements of *On Crimes and Punishments,* the reader is urged to review the original for a full understanding of the author's ideas and the logic of their development. The most salient points are these:

> . . . [I]f by upholding the rights of man and the rights of invincible truth, I should help also rescue from the pains and anguish of death some hapless victim of tyranny and ignorance, which are equally fateful, then the thanks and tears of that one innocent man, in the transports of joy, would console me for the contempt of all men.[a] (Section 1)

In forming a human society, men and women sacrifice a portion of their liberty so as to enjoy peace and security. (Section 2)

Punishments which go beyond the need of preserving the public safety are in their nature unjust. (Section 2)

Criminal laws must be clear and certain. Judges may not interpret the law; they must make uniform judgements in similar crimes. When they sentence offenders they must not be influenced by caprice or by the state of their digestion. (Section 4)

The law must specify the degree of evidence that will justify the detention of an accused offender prior to his trial. (Section 6)

Accusations must be public. A secret accusation cannot be justified. They cause distrust among citizens. False accusations should be severely punished. (Section 9)

Suspected offenders must respond to interrogation and should be punished if they refuse. However, if it is beyond doubt that the accused committed the crime with which he is charged, there is no point in proceeding with interrogation. (Section 10)

To torture accused offenders to obtain a confession is absurd and inadmissible. An advantage is gained by the sturdy but guilty rogue who can withstand the stretching of muscles and the dislocation of bones. In contrast, the innocent but weak man will be forced to confess to crimes he did not commit.[b] (Section 12)

The promptitude of punishment is one of the most effective curbs on crime. However, a reasonable time must be allowed the accused to prepare his defense. (Section 13)

[a] This was the sentence quoted by John Adams in his summation to the jury in his defense of the soldiers charged in the Boston Massacre.

[b] Beccaria's argument against torture for any reason is well worth study for its eloquent but rigorously logical demolition of all arguments in favor of the practice.

Although treachery is implicitly authorized thereby, an offer of impunity to accomplices willing to testify against crime partners is legitimate and should be allowed by statute. (Section 14)

The aim of punishment can only be to prevent the criminal committing new crimes against his countrymen, and to keep others from doing likewise. Punishments, therefore, and the method of inflicting them, should be chosen in due proportion to the crime, so as to make the most lasting impression on the minds of men, and the least painful of impressions on the body of the criminal. . . . For a punishment to be efficacious, it is enough that the disadvantage of the punishment should exceed the advantage anticipated from the crime, in which excess should be calculated the certainty of punishment and the loss of the expected benefit. (Section 15)

Capital punishment is inefficacious and in its place should be substituted life imprisonment. . . . [T]here is no one who, on reflection, would choose the total, permanent loss of his individual liberty, no matter what advantages a crime might bring him. It follows that the severity of a sentence to imprisonment for life, substituted for the penalty of death, would be as likely to deflect the most determined spirit—indeed I should think it more likely to do so.[c] (Section 16)

One of the greatest checks upon crime is not the cruelty of punishment but its inevitability. . . . [T]he vigilance of magistrates and the inexorable severity of a judge . . . must go hand in hand with a mild system of laws. (Section 20)

There must be proportionality between crimes and punishments. Whoever sees that the same penalty of death is laid down, for example, for the man who kills a pheasant, the man who murders another man, or the man who falsified an important document, will draw no distinction between these crimes; this destroys those moral sentiments . . . which have been produced so slowly and painfully in the human mind. . . . (Section 23)

It is better to prevent crimes than to punish them. That is the chief purpose of all good legislation, which is the art of leading men—if one may apply the language of mathematics to the blessings and evils of life—toward the maximum of possible happiness and the minimum of possible misery. We want crimes to be prevented? Then we must see to it that laws are clear and simple, and that the whole strength of the nation is concentrated upon their defense. . . . We must see to it that the law favors individual men more than classes of men, that men fear the law and nothing but the law. Fear of the laws is salutary, but fear between man and man is dangerous and productive of crime. (Section 41)

CONCLUSION: From all I have written a very useful theorem may be deduced, little though it conforms to custom, that common lawgiver of the nations. It is this: *In order that punishment should never be an act of violence committed*

[c] Beccaria's position on capital punishment is uncompromising; he does not allow it for murder or treason. As to the death penalty for murder, even Voltaire and Diderot, otherwise his enthusiastic admirers, differed with him.

by one or many against a private citizen, it is essential that it be public, speedy, and necessary, as little as the circumstances will allow, proportionate to the crime, and established by law. (Section 42)

Source: Alessandro Manzoni, *The Column of Infamy,* tran. Jane Grigson (London: Oxford University Press, 1964). Reprinted by permission of Oxford University Press.

We shall return to the Panopticon and its long-range significance for penology. However, Bentham must be understood in the context of an enormously influential political philosopher, with profound impact on the criminal law as well as on other institutions of government. We shall turn now to a presentation of his ideas on criminal justice, the significance of which far exceeds the absurd story of the Panopticon.

> Never have [the laws] been dictated by a dispassionate student of human nature who might, by bringing the actions of a multitude of men into focus, consider them from this single point of view: *the greatest happiness shared by the greatest number.* (Section 1)

This sentence from Beccaria's Introduction to *On Crimes and Punishments* stands out as the foundation for his argument for a reform of punishment as it was administered in the eighteenth century. When Jeremy Bentham read it, he took it over, literally, as the basic principle—to which he referred in his articles and books as **The Greatest Happiness Principle**—on which his theory of government was built. It was, he wrote, "the foundation of morals and legislation."[12] From The Greatest Happiness Principle (which he usually capitalized), Bentham spun out the theory that established the "subordinate" principles that should govern the administration of justice. For him, The Greatest Happiness Principle was like an axiom in mathematics. It could not be proved, but "it is used to prove everything else," and "a chain of proofs must have their commencement somewhere."[13]

This theory, **utilitarianism,** for better or worse, became the framework for change, not only of criminal justice but also of education, welfare, and nearly every other social program for which governments have assumed responsibility. It is far beyond the scope of this book to review the full impact of Bentham's utilitarianism, as further elaborated by John Stuart Mill and other disciples, on the role of government in Western nations. What concerns us here is the effect of his ideas on criminal justice and penology, topics on which he had plenty to say in the course of a long and productive life.

He was the son of a prosperous London lawyer. A child prodigy who was reading history and studying Latin at the age of 3, he entered Oxford University at 13, finished at 16, and went on to study law, completing that phase of his education at 18, too young to be admitted to the bar. He never practiced as a barrister.

He assumed the role of "censor" of the laws of England, which he considered to be crude, mystifying, needlessly complex, and requiring codification rather than reliance on ancient case law. As a "censor" of the laws, he insisted that his role was in contrast to that of Sir William Blackstone (1723–1780), the author of *Commentaries on the Laws of England,* who was the "expositor" of the laws as they were and had been, but not as they ought to be. As the "censor," Bentham wrote indefatigably. His published work runs to 6 million words, comprising 11 volumes. There exists a vast number of manuscripts that have never been printed.

Working from The Greatest Happiness Principle, Bentham arrived at the corollary that as all laws ought to "augment the total happiness of the community," therefore they should exclude "as far as may be, everything that tends to subtract from that happiness: in other words to exclude mischief." He went on to say that "all punishment is mischief. . . . to be admitted in as far as it promises to exclude some greater evil." That statement required that punishment be logically and reasonably justified. His paragraph of justification is written in typical Benthamese,[14] but it has been the cornerstone of our thinking about the punishment of criminals ever since. Because of its importance for all subsequent writing about the subject, we quote it at length:

> The immediate principal end of punishment is to controul action. This action is either that of the offender, or of others: that of the offender it controuls by its influence, either on his will, in which case it is said to operate in the way of *reformation;* or on his physical power, in which case it is said to operate by *disablement:* that of others it can influence no otherwise than by its influence over their wills; in which case it is said to operate in the way of *example.* A kind of collateral end, which it has a natural tendency to answer, is that of affording pleasure or satisfaction to the party injured, where there is one, and, in general, to parties whose ill-will, whether on a self-regarding account, or on the account of sympathy or antipathy, has been excited by the offence. This purpose . . . is a beneficial one. But no punishment ought to be allotted merely to this purpose, because . . . no such pleasure is ever produced by punishment as can be equivalent to the pain.[15]

Methodically, Bentham went on to discuss the four situations in which punishment should not be inflicted: (1) Where there is not mischief to prevent, the act not being mischievous; (2) where punishment cannot act so as to prevent mischief; (3) where the mischief of the punishment would be greater than the mischief to be prevented; and (4) where the mischief may cease or be prevented without the mischief of punishment. The trend of these rules is to limit punishment to the minimum necessary and to exclude the use of punishment where it cannot accomplish the reduction of "mischief."

One of the basic ideas in Bentham's thought was that human beings are governed by "twin masters": pleasure and pain. If we are to punish an offender, the pain inflicted should exceed the pleasure of the crime,[16] but the differential must not be more than absolutely necessary under the circumstances. Bentham believed in a **"hedonic calculus,"** by which the amount of pleasure and the amount of pain could be calculated, compared, and adjusted so that punishment would be no more than sufficient and always just. The idea is easier for a theorist to grasp than for a judge or legislator to implement.

Bentham went on to propose four subordinate aims for the administration of punishment that would, he argued, achieve "the general object of all laws: . . . to prevent mischief." In his design, a legislator should aim to prevent all crimes. If a citizen decided to commit an offense, the law should motivate him to commit the least mischievous of two or more offenses he might be considering. When the decision was made to proceed with an offense, the law should dispose him to do as little mischief as possible. Finally, whatever the mischief committed or to be committed, the punishment should be no more than required to prevent further crimes of the same kind, or to prevent crime "at as *cheap* a rate as possible." There followed 13 specific rules "by which the proportion of punishments to offenses is to be governed.[17]

Bentham had written only 32 years after the grotesque execution of Robert Damiens in Paris, described in Chapter 2, and at a time when more than 200 offenses on the books called for the death penalty. During the decades ahead, thousands of men and women were to be transported to Botany Bay, in Australia, at the other end of the Earth, many of them for crimes as trivial as the theft of a spool of thread from a dry-goods store. The impact of his radical ideas on the conservative establishment was slow to be realized, but in the end his program won out, not only in England but also across the Atlantic in the new United States and in many countries of continental Europe.

The year of publication, 1789, was bad luck for Bentham. The French Revolution was in full progress. The attention of legislators, jurists, and the public was riveted on the epochal events taking place in France. It took the British Parliament 19 years to abolish capital punishment for theft from the person. Legislation passed in 1834 reduced the number of crimes punishable by death to 15, and by 1861 there were only 4. Leading the attack on the "bloody code" was Sir Samuel Romilly (1757–1818), a member of Parliament and a close friend of Bentham's. Arrayed against him was the judiciary, one of whose members had told a sheep thief, "You are to be hanged not because you have stolen a sheep, but in order that others may not steal sheep." Later, responding to Romilly's bill to remove the death penalty for stealing 5 shillings or more from a shop, Lord Ellenborough, the lord chief justice of England, cautioned the House of Lords as follows:

> Your Lordships will pause before you assent to a measure so pregnant with danger for the security of property. The learned judges are unanimously agreed that the expediency of justice and public security require that there should not be a remission of capital punishment in this part of the criminal law.[18]

In the short run, Bentham's stand-pat adversaries won the day. In the long run they are remembered chiefly as his reactionary opponents, defeated by common sense and common humanity.

Bentham was a strange man, convinced of his genius, impatient with those who disagreed with him—especially King George III—and for most of his life surrounded by disciples who were as persuaded as he was of his genius. When he died, his body was dissected, as he had requested in his will, for medical enlightenment. Then his corpse was embalmed, dressed in his usual clothes, and placed in a glass case in the library of the University of London, where he can still be seen.

THE PANOPTICON

The war between Jeremy Bentham and King George III was fought over the **Panopticon.**[19] It lasted for 23 years and ended with the defeat of Bentham's idea, but Bentham received the consolation of his reimbursement for the considerable investment of his personal funds that he had made.

It began with a visit in 1786 to his brother, Samuel Bentham, an engineer who had traveled to Russia to assist in the industrialization of that nation. For his principal employer, Prince Potemkin, a favorite of Catherine the Great, he had designed an innovative factory in which managers would work in a central unit of a circular, walled building. From the central unit spokes would radiate to the walls; between the spokes, workers for the factory would carry on their specialized labors, always under the direct observation of the managers stationed in the central unit.

Bentham seized on his brother's invention as the solution to the crime problem, the care of the insane, the education of the young, and the rehabilitation of paupers. Returning to England, he modified the factory design to provide for the panopticon prison. This would be a circular building around the circumference of which tiers of prison cells would rise, holding 1000 or as many as 2000 offenders, serving terms varying from a few months to many years. From a towerlike structure in the middle, prison inspectors could observe, unseen, through venetian blinds the behavior of the inmates who would be in their cells throughout the day, working on various hard-labor projects. The inmates' lives would be austere. At first, Bentham thought they should sleep on straw mattresses, but after further consideration he decided that hammocks would be cheaper and less likely to be infested with vermin. Attention to this kind of detail is characteristic of Bentham; if genius is the infinite capacity for taking pains, Bentham's genius must have been second to none. The prisoners would work at least 12 hours a day, perhaps 14 if need be to get the work done. He pointed out that that was not an excessive work day for sedentary workers.

Bentham would manage the Panopticon under contract with the government. The profits from the factories that would be established in the Panopticon would be shared by the contractor with the prisoner-workers, who would divide among them one-sixth of the proceeds, the remaining five-sixths going to the manager. In addition to their work, the prisoners would learn trades. In their leisure hours they would be afforded the benefits of education. Although Bentham had no experience whatsoever in the management of factories or prisons, he confidently volunteered to manage the Panopticons personally and even engaged to insure the lives of the inmates, to provide for annuities for their old age, and to pay the government a sum for each escape. After all, he was a genius and knew it.

Bentham's enthusiasm for his idea was boundless. In his proposal he presented it as nothing less than the panacea for all the ills of the land:

> Morals reformed—health preserved—industry invigorated—instruction diffused—public burthens lightened—Economy seated, as it were, upon rock—the gordian knot of the Poor-Laws not cut, but untied—all by a simple idea in Architecture.[20]

The "war" came to an end in 1810, when Parliament made its final rejection. One of the most telling arguments against the Panopticon was made by Sir George Onesiphorus Paul, a well-to-do country magistrate. Troubled by the suspension of transportation to the American colonies after 1776, he had persuaded the county authorities of Gloucester to build five new penitentiaries to house felons who crowded the old jail. Testifying before a committee of the House of Commons, Paul warned that "the reformation of the offender" would be a "secondary concern" in a prison "where all the power and influence . . . are lodged in the hands of persons contracting for the manual labour of prisoners." He concluded his argument by observing that the contract system of management would create opportunities for corruption and excesses of discretion.[21] The historian Michael Ignatieff, in reviewing Paul's arguments against the Panopticon, observes that Parliament's rejection "was a major event in the history of imprisonment. . . . He also noted that "[P]unishment was too delicate a social function to be left to private entrepreneurs."[22]

The French philosopher and historian Michel Foucault, however, is impressed that the

> Panopticon is a marvelous machine which, whatever use one may wish to put it to, produces homogeneous effects of power. . . . It is not necessary to use force to constrain the convict to good behavior . . . there were no more bars, no more chains, no more heavy locks. All that was needed was that separations [of the convicts from one another] should be clear and the openings [of the inspection tower and the cells] well arranged.[23]

Astutely, Foucault observes that in contrast to the old ways of punishment, in which the body was the object, the Panopticon focused on the personality of the prisoner. The power of the Panopticon depended on the achievement of its object: the knowledge of the prisoner as an individual man. He is observed so that the warden will know him and can with knowledge control his mind and actions.

It is not relevant to Foucault's argument that the Panopticon was adopted so infrequently, and never in the country for which it was designed. Panopticism, to use Foucault's adaptation of Bentham's word, is the essence of modern penology. The warden in the twentieth-century prison exercises control by organizing information about each convict. Prisoners are classified and assigned to housing and programs in which the information assembled can be used and augmented by further observation. In the United States, only in the Stateville penitentiary in Illinois does the Panopticon itself survive.

To the end of his days, Bentham lamented his defeat, never realizing that his emphasis on the utilitarian objectives of reformation, disablement, and example would be the regularly stated goals of corrections, replacing the ancient commitment of the law to retribution.

The Illinois Stateville Correctional Center. (*Source:* Courtesy of Illinois Department of Corrections.)

He was not comforted by his friend Romilly's explanation that Parliament could hardly have acted favorably: "The public does not care tuppence for prisons and prisoners at any time, but during these years of critical emergency, during the French Wars, they care nothing at all."[24] Bentham was not the last correctional reformer to face public indifference to innovation in a field about which the public doesn't "care tuppence."

We close this account of Bentham's scheme with his lamentation, written in his memoirs toward the end of his life:

> I do not like to look among the Panopticon papers. It is like opening a drawer where devils are locked up—it is breaking into a haunted house.[25]

AMERICAN COLONISTS AND THE BLOODY CODE OF ENGLAND

The colonists who settled in America during the seventeenth century brought with them the bloody criminal code of England as described in Chapter 2. Most of the colonies enforced it, sometimes more rigorously than in the mother country. "Pious perjury," mentioned in Chapter 2, does not seem to have been exported along with the ferocious laws.

Some repulsive touches were added by slave-owning colonies where the legislatures wished to reinforce the absolute powers of masters over their human chattels. In Virginia, the death penalty was ordered and carried out with dispatch on any slave who attacked his owner. Secret plots or conspiracies among slaves could be punished by castration.[26] Under the law, a slave who gave false testimony at a trial was punishable by "[having] one ear nailed to the pillory, and there to stand for the space of an hour, and then the said ear to be cut off, and thereafter the other ear nailed in like manner, and cut off at the expiration of one other hour; and, moreover . . . thirty-nine lashes, well laid on, on his or her bare back at the common whipping post.[27]

Alone among the colonies, the Quaker provinces of Pennsylvania and West Jersey rejected the English criminal law. Legislation enacted in 1682 by the first assembly in Pennsylvania provided that only murderers were subject to the gallows.[28] The rest of the traditional felonies were punishable by hard labor. William Penn, the founder of the colony, drafted these comparatively mild statutes expressing the Quaker aversion to cruelty and bloodshed. To a greater extent than any criminal justice system of those times, Pennsylvania substituted imprisonment for the gallows and the whipping post.

In 1718 a crisis was created by the Quaker insistence on affirmations[29] rather than oaths in legal procedures. In 1715 the British Parliament had enacted a law that ruled out affirmation in criminal trials and made it applicable to all British colonies. An impasse followed. No trials took place. Judges refused to sit in their courts, and accused offenders were kept in jail awaiting trial until the conflict could be resolved. It took three years before a compromise was reached. Affirmations would be allowed after all, and in return the Pennsylvania legislature repealed the Quaker criminal code and adopted the criminal laws of England. In addition to murder, twelve other crimes—manslaughter by stabbing, treason, maiming, highway robbery, burglary, arson, sodomy, buggery, rape, concealing the death of an illegitimate child, advising the killing of such a child, and witchcraft—became capital offenses.[30]

Larceny and the less serious crimes, especially fornication and giving birth to an illegitimate child, became punishable by whipping, branding, or mutilation. The pillory and the stocks were much used to make examples of petty offenders such as drunkards, swearers, and public gamblers. The pillory was a device that clamped the head and arms of the offender while he stood in a public place. The stocks clamped arms and legs while he sat. Exposed to the insults, abuse, and occasional stone throwing of censorious citizens, the offender suffered an unpleasant and humiliating penalty at best, and sometimes serious injuries.[31]

Until the Revolutionary War, Pennsylvania's criminal code was as bloody and barbarous as that of England and the other colonies, with an unusually obsessive concern over offenses of intemperance, blasphemy, and sexual irregularity. It is difficult for modern men and women to understand the severities of our forefathers' criminal laws. Thousand of years of tradition and moral philosophy had crystallized a belief that those who committed crimes were inherently different from ordinary law-abiding people. For English dissenters who had left home because of their disapproval of the permissiveness of the established church, this belief had special significance.

It was clear to lawmakers and preachers that those who committed serious felonies should be exterminated in the interest of public safety. As condemned men stood on the scaffold awaiting the noose, clergymen preached sermons to the witnessing crowds, holding forth on the wickedness of the man about to be hanged and the righteousness of ending his life. Those who swung on the gallows were examples to those who shared their defective moral outlook but who had not so far committed similar crimes.

Those who blasphemed, drank intemperately, or fornicated might profit from a whipping or a session in the stocks that would tell them what good folks thought of their behavior.[32] Eternal damnation awaited them if they did not mend their ways. Their public humiliation reminded passersby of the wages of unrighteousness.

REPLACING THE GALLOWS

The Quakers had made the first solid steps toward ending the promiscuous use of the gallows. Dungeons, stockades, and jails had been used from remote antiquity for the detention of political offenders and those awaiting trial for criminal offenses. It was left to the Quakers to adopt incarceration as the alternative punishment to hanging. Although William Penn's criminal code continued the death penalty for murder, all other crimes were subject to milder penalties, including relatively brief periods of imprisonment as well as the pillory and the stocks. The law of 1682 required the first prison in these clauses:

> All prisons shall be workhouses for felons, thiefs, vagrants, and loose, abusive, and idle persons, whereof one shall be in every county.
>
> Gaolers [jailers] shall not oppress their prisoners, and all prisons shall be free as to room, and all prisoners shall have liberty to provide themselves bedding, food and other necessaries, during their imprisonment, except those whose punishment by law, will not admit of that liberty.[33]

That changed in 1718, when Penn's laws were repealed and the old laws of England were adopted. The county prisons no longer housed felons doing time instead of mounting the scaffold to meet the hangman. The prisons became workhouses for "the keeping, correcting and setting to work of all rogues, vagabonds, or sturdy beggars, and other idle and disorderly persons, who, by the laws and usage of Great Britain or by the laws of this province, are to be kept, corrected, or set to work, in such houses and backsides."

The prison for the sentenced felon came to an abrupt end in 1718, but the county jail ("gaol") for the detention of accused offenders awaiting trial survived in degradation. A memoir written in 1826 by a reform advocate eloquently sums up the dreadful situation of those jailed under the old law:

> What a spectacle must this abode of guilt and wretchedness have presented, when in one common herd were kept by day and night prisoners of all ages, colors and sexes! No separation was made of the most flagrant offender and convict, from the prisoner who might, perhaps, be falsely suspected of some trifling misdemeanor; none of the old and hardened culprits from the youthful, trembling novice in crime; . . . and when intermingled with all these, in one corrupt and corrupting assemblage were to be found the disgusting object of popular contempt, be smeared with filth from the pillory—the unhappy victim of the lash, streaming with blood from the whipping post—the half naked vagrant—the loathsome drunkard—the sick, suffering from various bodily pains, and too often the unaneled[34] malefactor, whose precious hours of probation had been numbered by his earthly judge.[35]

This was the state of penal affairs as the years drew on to 1776 and the outbreak of the Revolutionary War. The management of the jails and the use of the gallows and the whipping posts of Pennsylvania were better and more humane, respectively, than in some of the other colonies and certainly no worse than the rest. All had inherited the bloody code of England, and, with independence, all had the occasion to revise those laws. In doing so, the influence of the French Enlightenment and of the British reformers was crucial in bringing to an end the ghastly treatment of offenders.

This was an age of intellectual ferment. The old ideas about the state and its powers and citizens and their rights were subjected to rigorous question. Criminal justice received attention without precedent in all history. Did capital punishment really stay the hands of potential criminals? Did the torture, the beatings, the mutilations and branding, the public humiliation of minor offenders serve any useful purpose at all? For perhaps the first time in the history of Western society, civilized men and women were asked to consider whether the way justice had always been administered was the right way.

The answers of the philosophers forthrightly rejected the traditional approaches to punishment and its justifications. European rulers and parliaments listened, and so did thoughtful American politicans.

In the new United States, the death penalty has never been entirely replaced, and the whipping post survived well into the twentieth century. The penitentiary—a Pennsylvania invention—took the place of the long-established barbarism of mutilation and branding. There were high hopes that penitence, pastoral counseling, and reasonable discipline would reform criminals instead of killing, flogging, and humiliating them as had been done under the old law.

Those high hopes were in the end disappointed, as would be the case with many penological innovations in the decades that followed. Modern reformers think of penitentiaries, prisons, and reformatories as necessary evils of which little good can be expected except the segregation of serious lawbreakers from society. For the Pennsylvania Quakers and for enlightened citizens in the other colonies the incarceration of offenders was a necessary step toward civic decency. To replace the gallows was to reject the old laws of England from which most of the colonists and the colonists' ancestors had fled. At the same time European reformers were demanding that the indiscriminate punishment of death for a long catalogue of crimes come to an end.

INNOVATION IN PENNSYLVANIA

Earlier in this chapter we mentioned the replacement of the mild penal laws of the early Pennsylvania Quakers with the "bloody code" of England. As soon as possible after the adoption of the Declaration of Independence, the Pennsylvania legislature set about the task of repealing the British laws that the colony had been forced to enact. A series of statutes abolished capital punishment for all crimes other than first-degree murder.[36] For the major felonies, terms of imprisonment were provided. Fines or jail terms replaced the whipping post, the pillory, and the stocks. A system of state prisons was established to accommodate the felons escaping the gallows under the terms of the new laws. To separate juvenile delinquents from their elders in crime, the Philadelphia **House of Refuge** was created in 1827. It was no exaggeration when later prison reformers reviewed this series of developments and claimed that

> . . . a more thorough transformation in the character of a penal code, by peaceful legislation, is not recorded in the world's history than that which took place in Pennsylvania during the eighteen years immediately succeeding the Declaration of Independence.[37]

To bring about this transformation in a community accustomed to much more stringent penalties for criminals required an unusual climate of opinion. First among the former colonies, Pennsylvania undertook a purposeful new overhaul of its criminal laws aimed at the reformation of offenders rather than retribution. At least three major influences moved change so rapidly. First was the Quaker morality that found punishment inflicted on the bodies of offenders thoroughly repellent, and the hope for their reform so consistent with the ethics of the Society of Friends. Second was the unusually sophisticated intellectual leadership of such men as Benjamin Franklin, Dr. Benjamin Rush, and other political and professional figures in Philadelphia. They were well-read men who were familiar with the works of Montesquieu, Beccaria, and Bentham as well as the observations of John Howard. Franklin had lived in France for many years and was well versed in the ideas brewed by the French Enlightenment. In their receptive Quaker community, they were more successful in translating concepts into programs than Thomas Jefferson and James Madison had been in Virginia.

Third was the organization, in 1787, of the Philadephia Society for Alleviating the Miseries of Public Prisons (hereinafter the "Society").[38] This was by many years the first prison reform organization in the United States. With a far-sighted vision of its role, its leaders proclaimed in the eloquent preamble of its constitution that

> [T]he obligations of benevolence, which are founded on the precepts and example of the Author of Christianity, are not cancelled by the follies or crimes of our fellow creatures; and when we reflect upon the miseries which penury, hunger, cold, unnecessary severity, unwholesome apartments and guilt . . . involve with them: it becomes us to extend our compassion to that part of mankind, who are the subjects of these miseries. By the aides of humanity, their undue and illegal sufferings may be prevented; the links which should bind the whole family of mankind together . . . be unbroken; and such degrees and modes of punishment may be discovered and suggested, as may, instead of continuing habits of vice, become the means of restoring our fellow creatures to virtue and happiness. . . .[39]

The founders of this remarkable Society knew that fine words were not enough. They remembered the horrors of the pre-Revolutionary jails and knew that rhetoric would not prevent their return. The constitution went on to establish an Acting Committee of the Society's officers that was required to "visit the Prisons at least once a month, inquire into the circumstances of the Prisoners, and report such abuses as they shall discover, to the proper officers appointed to remedy them. They shall examine the influence of confinement or punishment on the morals of the Prisoners."[40]

There was much to examine. The penal law of 1786 directed that certain classes of convicts be put to work cleaning the streets of Philadelphia. Their heads were to be shaved, and they were to be attired in "infamous" dress. To prevent them from retaliating against tormentors, they were

> encumbered with iron collars and chains, to which bomb-shells were attached, to be dragged along while they performed their degrading service. . . . These measures begot in the minds of the criminals and those who witnessed them, disrespect for the laws executed with so much cruelty, and did not fail to excite the early notice of the society.[41]

In 1788 the Society petitioned the General Assembly for a statute providing for solitary confinement at hard labor in the privacy of the penitentiary. The legislature adopted the society's recommendations and went on to request its consultation on the revision of the criminal code and further improvements in the prison system.

The Society's report urged that the existing Walnut Street Jail, completed in 1790, be no longer used for long-term prisoners and that a new penitentiary be constructed following John Howard's ideas for a model jail. In 1803, the legislature authorized a new prison, which was used for the detention of debtors. That solved one problem—the mingling of debtors with felons—but it was not until 1818 that the legislature authorized the construction of two new penitentiaries: the Western penitentiary near Pittsburgh, and the Eastern State Penitentiary in Philadelphia. The Western prison was so badly designed that no industry of any kind could be provided for the convicts. In 1833, four years after it was completed, the legislature passed a statute to demolish and rebuild it.

The **Eastern State Penitentiary** was finished in 1829 and still stands, although unoccupied. It became a model, but not in the United States. Word of its unique structure and program soon reached England, where replicas were built that are still in use. Penologists in several European countries were so impressed by its seeming advantages that the architecture and the programs that the Eastern penitentiary was designed to accommodate were adopted in their entirety.

As originally designed and built, it comprised 7 wings, each containing 76 cells, radiating from a central hub where control personnel were stationed. (See Figure

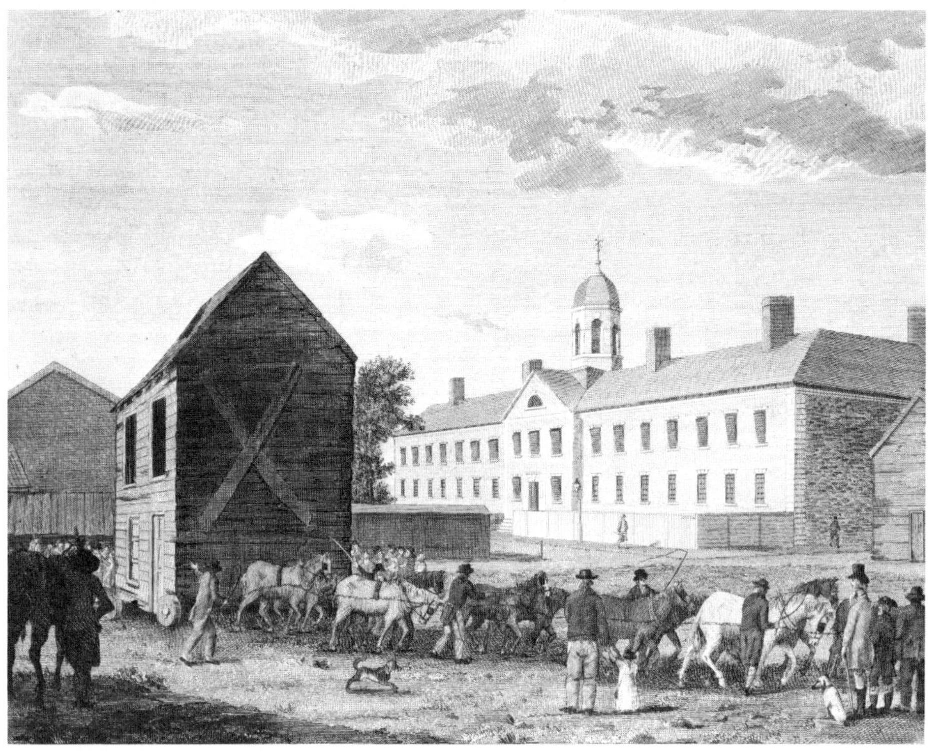

The Walnut Street Jail in Philadelphia. (*Source:* Granger.)

3.1.) Each cell was 12 feet long, 8 feet wide, and 10 feet high, designed for single occupancy.[42] A separate exercise yard, in which the prisoner was allowed to refresh himself in the open air for one hour a day, was provided adjacent to the cell. The cells were separated by stone partitions 18 inches thick, which effectively prevented communication from prisoner to prisoner. Solitude was the goal, and prisoners spent their days alone. Even at compulsory chapel services they could not see one another, as they were seated in chairs resembling upended coffins.

The building itself, said to be the largest structure of any kind in the United States at that time, was a massive fortress, resembling a medieval castle, intended to impress on all who passed by and all who lived in it the grave penalties of misdeeds. As the years passed, additional units were built, and the regimen was modified to allow double occupancy of the cells, so that by the end of the Civil War the penitentiary's population had reached 1117 prisoners. Until 1913, when the legislature formally abolished the system, the 1829 plan was the official basis for Pennsylvania penology, although most of the original concepts had been abandoned as impracticable.

Although the **Pennsylvania system** has not survived, its main features occupy a prominent part in penal history. The principles on which it was designed are significant because of their emphasis on the reformation of the offender and the belief that a system could be devised that would assure that most prisoners would benefit from the experience of incarceration at the Eastern State Penitentiary. Like Jeremy Bentham and his hopes for the Panopticon, the founders of the penitentiary were

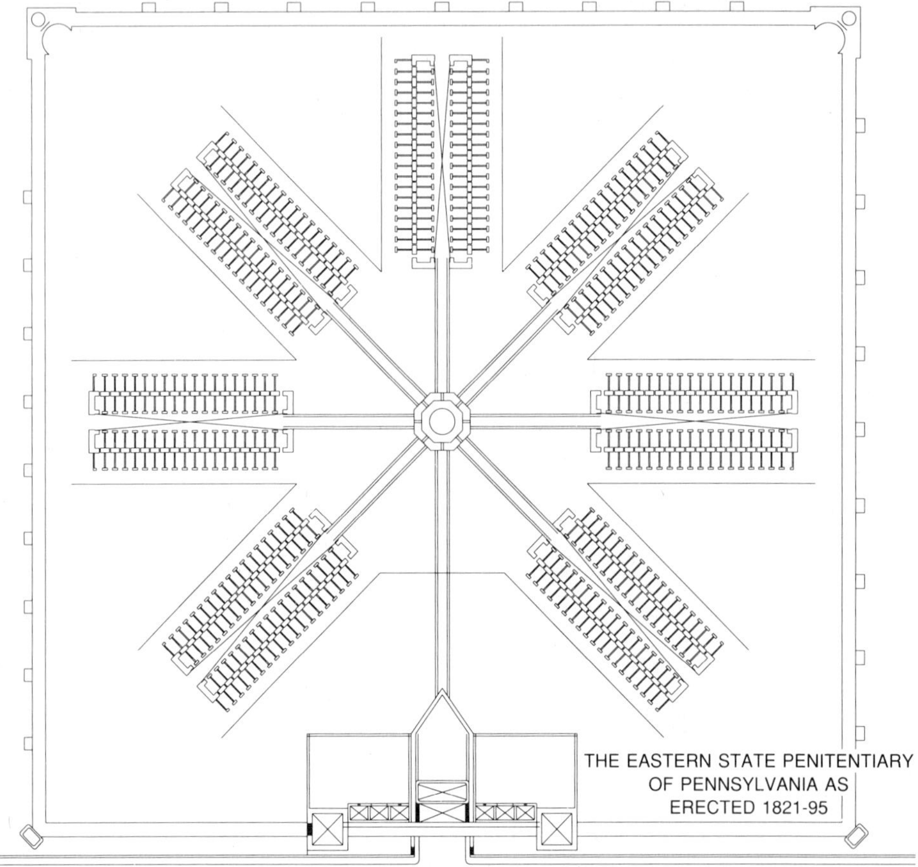

Figure 3.1 Ground plan of the Eastern State Penitentiary, 1829.

certain that their program, a judicious mixture of industry and religious instruction, administered to prisoners in solitary confinement, would transform offenders into solid citizens. Here the first warden, Samuel Wood, describes the essence of his program:

> When a convict first arrives, he is placed in a cell, and left alone, without any work and without any book. His mind can only operate on itself; generally but a few hours pass before he petitions for something to do and for a Bible. No instance has occurred in which such a petition has been delayed beyond a day or two. If the prisoner have [*sic*] a trade that can be pursued in his cell, he is put to work as a favour; as a reward for good behaviour, and as a favour, a Bible is allowed him. If he has no trade, or one that cannot be pursued in his cell, he is allowed to choose one that can, and he is instructed by one of the overseers, all of whom are master workmen in the trades they respectively superintend and teach. Thus work and moral and religious books are regarded and received as favours, and are withheld as punishment.[43]

This was the program. It was administered in solitary confinement, and the intention was that no prisoner see or communicate with another. The work was designed for solitude; prisoners had their choice of shoe making or weaving cloth. From time to time members of the Society visited prisoners, offering religious counseling and, sometimes, genuine friendship. These were the only human contacts allowed.

We do not know the consequences of such a program for the individual or for the community. Data on recidivism, now normally accessible in great detail, were not collected. The early reports from the warden and the Society were favorable:

> So long as the Pennsylvania system has been in operation, it has fully satisfied its authors and advocates. It continues to convince unbiased examination; it is superseding rival and opposite modes of punishment; and it will, at last, by the force of facts and experimental operation . . . paralyze the efforts of interested opposition, and take bread from the mouths of mercenary scribblers. . . . The Board entertains a hope that . . . the separate confinement of prisoners will become, not the Pennsylvania, but the American System of Prison Discipline.[44]

It was not to be. The system was costly to run. The problem of crowding overtook the capacity of the prison in a very few years after it was first occupied. Double celling had to be accepted, and that ended the principle of solitude. There was growing skepticism about the underlying value of solitary confinement. The great English novelist Charles Dickens visited the penitentiary in 1842 and had this to say about what he saw:

> In its intention I am well convinced that it is kind, humane, and meant for reformation; but I am persuaded that those who devised this system of Prison Discipline, and those benevolent gentlemen who carry it into execution, do not know what it is that they are doing. I believe that very few men are capable of estimating the immense amount of torture and agony which this dreadful punishment, prolonged for years, inflicts upon the sufferers; and in guessing at it myself, and in reasoning from what I have seen written on their faces . . . I am only the more convinced that there is a depth of terrible endurance in it which none but the sufferers themselves can fathom, and which no man has the right to inflict on his fellow-creature.[45]

Eastern State Penitentiary, Philadelphia. (*Source:* Wide World.)

Dickens talked to several prisoners and was impressed with their haggard appearance. Most of them were serving long sentences and seemed resigned to their unnatural, solitary life. His account of their surroundings and the routine of the prison is brief but contains enough detail for an appreciation of the reality of the Eastern Penitentiary. Harry Elmer Barnes, the historian of Pennsylvania penology, concluded his review of the system with the remark that

> A successful prison system can scarcely be tested by its ability to turn out Robinson Crusoes, and such was, at the best, all that the Pennsylvania system could make any serious pretention of doing.[46]

The New York prison reformer Thomas Mott Osborne, about whom we shall have more to say in the next chapter, summed up the system's weaknesses in a sentence: "It showed a touching faith in human nature, although a precious little knowledge of it."[47]

That the Pennsylvania system survived, in principle if not in practice, for so long and was imitated so widely in other countries indicates the power of a concept, however misguided. For all its obvious faults it had the attractive advantage of good intentions and a naïve belief in the reformation of offenders by a regimen of solitude, work, and religious instruction. Not nearly so much can be said in behalf of its victorious rival, the Auburn Silent System, which became American's standard throughout the nineteenth and much of the twentieth centuries.

NEW YORK AND THE AUBURN SILENT SYSTEM

It was no contest. Pennsylvania clung to the principles of the system that bore its name but had to compromise it, eventually out of all recognition. New York began with its own adaptation of the Pennsylvania system under the leadership of Thomas Eddy (1758–1827), a Quaker merchant who had been raised in Philadelphia. A Tory during the Revolutionary War, he had experienced the wretched conditions in pre-Revolutionary American jails. As a Quaker convinced that an "inner light" could be found in everyone, even in criminals, he believed that society had an obligation to reform offenders while punishing them.

His first accomplishment was a successful agitation for the abolition of the bloody code of England. Following the example of Pennsylvania, in 1796 New York enacted legislation abolishing capital punishment for all offenses other than first-degree murder and treason. To accommodate felons who would now do time rather than be subjected to flogging or the gallows, Newgate prison was built in 1797 in what is now Greenwich Village in Manhattan. It was abandoned in 1828. It was so small that to avoid overcrowding prisoners had to be pardoned so that new commitments could be admitted. Eddy himself, apparently an incurable optimist, had designed it for a population of 432 inmates living in eight-man cells, 12 by 18 feet in dimension. He served as its warden until 1804, when political changes forced his resignation.

The design of Newgate was a tragic mistake. Years later, long after he had resigned, and after watching successions of frequent and destructive disorders, he acknowledged that his plan had been crucially wrong. In a memorandum to the governor, he said that he should have provided for 500 solitary cells. To an English correspondent he wrote, "*No* benefit, as it regards *reformation,* ever has been, *nor ever will be* produced unless our prisons are calculated to have separate rooms . . . so that each man can be lodged by *himself*."[48]

The prison housed the whole gamut of criminals and delinquents: adult male felons; female felons; juvenile delinquents of both sexes, many of them very young; and the criminally insane. In the overcrowded and unsanitary conditions that prevailed from the start and steadily worsened, there was constant concern about the danger of epidemic disease. By 1821 there were 817 convicts at Newgate, with a capacity of little more than half that number. It was estimated that if there had been no resort to clemency, the population would have exceeded 2000.

As in the Pennsylvania penitentiaries, Newgate convicts were put to work at making shoes, nails, and cloth. There was always the hope that the production of commodities would turn a profit, but with an inefficient and unpaid workforce, prone to sabotage, profits from prison industries never supported Newgate as Eddy had hoped. In 1817 the legislature provided that convicts be employed on public works.

Riots and mutinies were frequent. Eddy had limited punishment for infractions—solitary confinement on bread and water. The virtual collapse of discipline became so alarming that in 1817 the legislature authorized capital punishment for arson and assaults on prison officers. Two years later, a statute legalized flogging—but no more than 39 strokes at any one time—and the pillory and stocks.

The New York State Prison at Auburn. (*Source:* Wide World.)

A crime wave had followed the end of the War of 1812. There was no abatement of the overcrowding that had crammed Newgate to the bursting point from the beginning. The inadequacy of the prison was obvious and becoming more so with the passing years. In 1816 the legislature authorized a new prison at the western New York town of **Auburn.** It became famous as the model for maximum custody prisons throughout the United States. It is still occupied, and replicas are in service in many states to this day. It was not intended to be an archetype; its original design copied that of Philadelphia's Walnut Street Jail.

Two years after its completion, a new wing was built that became famous as the Auburn cellblock. In its center was an island of cells 5 tiers high and 20 cells long, surrounded by 11 feet of vacant space on all four sides. It was built for long-term solitary confinement, from which inmates would not emerge until the end of their terms. The cells were 7 feet long, 3½ feet wide—24½ square feet. Each tier consisted of two rows of cells, back to back. A convict who could manage to get out of his cell without permission would then have to break out of the building and then somehow negotiate the prison wall—altogether so nearly impossible a feat that it seems never to have been successfully attempted.

Prisoners assigned to this block, first occupied on Christmas Day, 1821, were not allowed to work, nor were they permitted to lie down during the daylight hours.[49] The rationale for this austere program was simple:

> One who would expect gentle means, with advice and admonition, to produce a change of moral character in convicts, should not forget that such means have been tried in vain upon them in society, and he will find that no radical change can be effected until their stubborn spirits are subdued, and their depraved hearts softened by mental suffering. . . . [The penitentiary system could not be preserved] unless the convicts are made to endure great suffering, and that applied, as much as possible, to the mind.[50]

Suicides, attempted suicides, and various mental and physical infirmities attributed to the requirement that men be on their feet all day became so prevalent under this regimen that it was ended in 1825. The cellblock remained a model for prison architects for generations to come. In the opinion of many a contemporary warden and guard captain, the Auburn model is the essential tool of penology. Only since World War II have alternative designs for close custody been designed.

The officials were still persuaded that solitude was essential to prison discipline. A manufacturing industry required congregate movement of prisoners. The problem was to maintain solitude while large numbers of prisoners were eating together, working together, and moving through the prison together. An ingenious deputy warden, one John D. Cray, found the solution and with it initiated the Auburn Silent System. It was the successful answer to the Pennsylvania system and, like the Auburn cellblock, was the basis of practical penology throughout the nineteenth century and well into the twentieth.

The system demanded from all convicts silence at all times. They marched in lockstep from the cellblock to the mess hall and to the factory. His right hand on the right shoulder of the man immediately ahead, face turned toward the watching guards, each convict in this platoon of mute offenders was scrutinized for signs of attempted communication.

Presiding over the Silent System was Captain Elam Lynds (1784–1855), certainly one of the most memorable figures in American penological history. An army captain in the War of 1812, he returned to Auburn, his home town, when he was demobilized. In 1817 he joined the staff of the new prison, and when the first warden, William Brittin, died in 1821, he was appointed warden—or, to use the terminology of the time, the "agent" and principal keeper.

Lynds would not stand for individual treatment of convicts. Each man was to be treated exactly like all the others. Prisoners were known by number, and their names were blanked out for the duration of their sentences. Good behavior was not to be rewarded in any way, neither by privileges nor by remission of time. In Lynds's opinion and in the opinion of the Auburn Board of Inspectors, justice was mocked by executive clemency or pardons. According to Lynds, a prisoner's good behavior was no sign of a change of character: "Men of the most artful, desperate, and dangerous character are the most orderly, submissive, and industrious when confined."[51] No one should be offered an incentive to behave according to penitentiary rules, he believed.

Every effort was consciously made to divest prisoners of self-respect and personality. They were dressed in black-and-white-striped uniforms. No visitors were permitted. They were not allowed to send or receive letters. They could read nothing but the Bible. To add to the prisoner's systematic humiliation, citizens who paid admission could come into the prison to look them over, as if the prison were a zoo. Punishment for rule infractions was immediate and administered with the lash on the spot.

There was no little criticism of the severity of Captain Lynds's discipline. His defenders pointed out that flogging was the standard discipline of enlisted personnel in the army and navy, and prisoners were certainly not entitled to better treatment than the defenders of the nation.

What accounted for the nationwide success of the Silent System? Economics was a large part of the answer. Louis Dwight (1793–1854), the founder and leading figure of the Boston Prison Discipline Society, was a tireless enthusiast. Most prisons, he found, were "sink-holes of abuses and corruption." Not Auburn. Said he: "It is not possible to describe the pleasure we feel in contemplating this noble institution after wading through the fraud, and material and moral filth of many prisons. We regarded it as a model worthy of the world's imitation."[52] Perhaps unconsciously echoing Jeremy Bentham's enthusiasm for the Panopticon, he thought that the Auburn Silent System might well be adopted by schools for the young. Fathers of American families would do well, he thought, to copy it to maintain discipline in their homes.

The clinching argument was economic. Regardless of the system's success in reforming criminals, it was cheap. A prison built on the Auburn plan would cost $91 per cell, whereas the Pennsylvania system, which required round-the-clock solitary confinement, would cost $1650 per cell. That convinced the legislatures of most states—that and the fact that prisoners paid part of the costs with their labor. It was even conceivable that, with good administration by the officials, prisoners might pay for their entire upkeep. By 1833 Auburn had replicas in 11 states, the District of Columbia, and one Canadian province.

In 1825, Auburn was full. The legislature authorized a new prison at Ossining on the Hudson River. The state gladly accepted Lynds's offer to build the new facility with convict labor. He organized a detail of 100 Auburn convicts, transported them in two barges on the Erie Canal—surely a remarkable logistical feat—to the building site, built barracks to house them, and put them to work quarrying marble for building the new prison. The building project was completed in three years. Lynds employed only three civilians—a master carpenter, a blacksmith, and a mason.

During the three years of construction of Sing Sing, the convicts lived in makeshift barracks. There were only two attempted escapes, one of which succeeded. Guards armed with muskets patrolled the area, and within the construction site the keepers could flog recalcitrant workers at their own discretion.

The prison, designed for 800 prisoners, almost immediately expanded to 1,000. It remained in use for more than a century, housing more than 100,000 inmates during that time. Lynds continued as warden until 1830, ruling with untrammeled authority. He made up his own rules and enforced them as he saw fit. Staff were hired and fired at his discretion. As time went on, his impregnable tenure of office lured him into availing himself of highly questionable perquisites of office. He was charged with starving the convicts, defrauding the state on contracts, appropriating penitentiary supplies for his own use, and making personal trips at state expense.

There was a legislative investigation, but as the only possible witnesses were his subordinates, none of whom were inclined to testify against him, Lynds was cleared of wrongdoing. His honor restored, he decided to rest from his labors and resigned.

He retired, and his deputy, Robert Wiltse, took over as warden, faithfully continuing Lynds's regimen for the next decade. In 1840 his administration was discredited by the exposure of serious abuses and brutality culminating in the deaths of two prisoners. Wiltse was dismissed, and a new warden, David Seymour, took over with an explicit commitment to rehabilitate, not to punish. Prisoners were allowed to read books, and the use of the lash became infrequent. Their families could visit them, and correspondence was permitted. A convict poet wrote,

> Give us Christians like David Semore
> And this prison is like heven above
> He is one that used kindness
> And he has the prisners luv.[53]

The Whigs lost to the Democrats in the 1842 state elections, and the new commissioners set about reversing the policies of Warden Seymour. They appointed a new warden, who seems to have been a figurehead for Captain Lynds—who returned as chief disciplinary officer. He brought with him his dedication to the lash, which he administered in person and so liberally that the Board of Inspectors restricted him to 25 blows for any one rule violation. He lasted for two years. Charged with drinking while on duty and misuse of state property, he was fired for good.[54]

During his first tenure at Sing Sing, Lynds attracted many foreign visitors, the most notable of whom were Gustave de Beaumont and Alexis de Tocqueville, two young French magistrates charged with surveying American methods of dealing with criminals and considering their suitability for adoption in France. Their report, *On the Penitentiary System in the United States and its Application in France*,[55] devoted a great deal of attention to Sing Sing and the policies of its warden, Captain Lynds, with whom they were deeply impressed. They noted his remarkable achievement in bringing convicts from Auburn to build Sing Sing but also found the atmosphere of the prison dangerously oppressive:

> It is impossible to see the prison at Sing Sing, and the system of working there, without being struck with surprise and fear. Though the order is perfectly kept, it is apparent that it rests on a fragile basis: it is owing to a power always active, but which must be reproduced every day, if the whole discipline is not to be endangered. The safety of the keepers is incessantly menaced. In presence of such dangers, avoided so skillfully, but with so much difficulty, it seems impossible to us not to apprehend some future catastrophe. For the rest, the dangers to which the officers are exposed form, for the present, one of the surest guarantees of order; every one of them sees that the preservation of his life depends on it.[56]

They interviewed Lynds at some length. Asked if he thought flogging might be dispensed with, he was forthright: "I consider chastisement by the whip the most efficient, and at the same time, the most humane that exists. . . . I consider it impossible to govern a large prison without a whip. Those who know human nature from books only, may say the contrary." In conclusion, Lynds insisted that "it was necessary to begin with curbing the spirit of the prisoner, and convincing him of his weakness. This point attained, everything becomes easy, whatever may be the construction of the prison or the place of labor."[57]

The Auburn Silent System became the model for the nineteenth-century prison. Unfortunately, too many wardens thought of Lynds's methods as their proper model, too. (One of the authors of this textbook vividly recalls seeing inmates of California's Preston School of Industry marching in lockstep as recently as 1946.) Captain Lynds's whip has been retired, but his belief in severity as the only safe method of governance lingered almost to the present.

CONCLUSIONS

Most of the ideas that make up modern penology can be traced to Montesquieu, Beccaria, and Bentham. They powerfully influenced the changes that took place in the administration of criminal justice in England and in this country. What they could not prepare for, in spite of their confidence that they could, was a humane alternative to the whipping post and the gallows. They prescribed the penitentiary, an innovation in concept and architecture.

No one knew how to run a penitentiary, but the penitentiary was the only alternative that anyone could imagine. Both the Pennsylvania and the Auburn systems must be seen as attempts to meet the urgent requirements of justice. Though sadly misguided by a rigid ideology, the Pennsylvania system had the merit of adopting Bentham's goals of the reformation and deterrence of the offender.

The Auburn system was a pragmatic effort to administer the processes of punishment as thriftily as possible. The pragmatism of the times called for measures that we would now see as unacceptably brutal but that were tolerable in an age when criminals were thought to be uniformly defective in mind and morals. In the next chapter we will trace the influences that brought about milder methods and a commitment to penological goals that would have been approved by the Pennsylvania Quakers but scorned by Captain Lynds and the hard men who thought it their duty to emulate him.

KEY TERMS

Auburn Silent System

Eastern State Penitentiary

Enlightenment

The Greatest Happiness Principle

hedonic calculus

House of Refuge

Panopticon

Pennsylvania system

utilitarianism

DISCUSSION TOPICS

3.1 What accounts for the immediate spread of Beccaria's ideas for criminal justice reform?

3.2 The British practice of transporting felons to Australia certainly had inhumane aspects. From the felon's point of view, were there any advantages?

3.3 What did the Greatest Happiness Principle have to do with the administration of criminal justice?

3.4 Were there any positive aspects to the Pennsylvania penitentiary system?

3.5 Why did European prison planners reject the Auburn Silent System?

ANNOTATED REFERENCES

Barnes, Harry E., and Negley K. Teeters. *New Horizons in Criminology: The American Crime Problem*, 2nd ed. New York: Prentice-Hall, 1951. *These authors were effective critics as well as comprehensive historians. For students of corrections, parts IV through VIII are particularly valuable.*

Beaumont, de Gustave, and Alexis de Tocqueville. *On the Penitentiary System in the United States and its Application in France*. Philadelphia: Carey, Lea, and Blanchard, 1833. Trans. Francis Lieber. Original edition in English published in 1833. *In this volume the Philadelphia system and the Auburn Silent System are described as observed by two young French visitors, one of whom, de Tocqueville, was to become famous for his study of democracy in America. Most of the work in this book was by de Beaumont, who was understandably tentative in his conclusions about the merits of the two systems.*

Bentham, Jeremy. *A Bentham Reader*, ed. Mary Peter Mack. New York: Pegasus, 1969. *A serviceable anthology of Bentham's essential writings. Much more accessible than in the complete Jeremy Bentham edition,* The Works of Jeremy Bentham, published under the superintendence of his executor, John Bowring (Edinburgh: W. Tait, 1843, 11 volumes). *See particularly pages 189–208, "The Panopticon Papers."*

Hughes, Robert. *The Fatal Shore*. New York, N.Y.: Random House, 1986. *This is a definitive history of the transportation of English convicts to Australia. The personalities of the men who administered the penal colonies are vividly described, as well as particulars* concerning the unfortunates who were transported to the fatal shore. The author minces no words about the ineffectiveness of the transportation system or the deterrence of crime in the English cities.

Lewis, W. David. *From Newgate to Dannemora; The Rise of the Penitentiary in New York, 1796–1848.* Ithaca, N.Y.: Cornell University Press, 1965. *A detailed and authoritative account of the development of the New York prison system up to the time of major revisions of the Auburn Silent System. Particularly good on the contributions of Captain Elam Lynds.*

McKelvey, Blake. *American Prisons: A History of Good Intentions.* Montclair, N.J.: Patterson Smith, 1977. *The standard history of American prisons is still a reliable source on the development of penological practice. Readers should judge for themselves the goodness of the intentions exhibited by the putable and disreputable figures reported in McKelvey's history.*

NOTES

1. Montesquieu, *On the Spirit of the Laws,* book VI, chap. 9, trans. Thomas Nugent, 1750, David W. Carrithers, editor (Berkeley: University of California Press, 1977).
2. Ibid., p 158.
3. For an informative biography of a complicated man see Marcello Maestro, *Cesare Beccaria and the Origins of Penal Reform* (Philadelphia: Temple University Press, 1973).
4. There have been several translations into English. The most readily available is by Henry Paolucci (Indianapolis: Bobbs-Merrill, 1963). A somewhat more fluent version is contained in Alessandro Manzoni, *The Column of Infamy,* trans. Jane Grigson (London: Oxford University Press, 1964), from which our quotations are drawn.
5. An English translation was published in 1767, but Beccaria never visited England.
6. Quoted by Maestro, *Cesare Beccaria,* from Daniel Jousse, *Traité de la Justice Criminelle de France,* not translated (Paris: Chez Debure Pere, 1771).
7. Quoted by Maestro, from an unpublished manuscript in the University College Collection, London.
8. Ibid., from *The Works of John Adams* (Boston: Little, Brown, 1856), vol. 2, pp. 238–239.
9. *The Writings of Thomas Jefferson* (Washington: The Monticello edition, 1904), vol. 1, p. 67.
10. From the Greek, "all visible."
11. A faithful Panopticon was built and is still in use in Breda, The Netherlands. The general idea of the Panopticon was put into effect at Stateville in Illinois, where it is being phased out.
12. Quoted by H. L. A. Hart in *Essays on Bentham: Studies in Jurisprudence and Political Theory* (Oxford: The Clarendon Press, 1982), p. 40.
13. For a brief but reasonably comprehensive account of The Great Happiness Principle, see the article on Bentham by D. H. Monro in the *Encyclopedia of Philosophy* (New York: Macmillan & The Free Press, 1967).
14. One reader, Augustine Birrell, a British statesman and essayist, remarked that when reading Bentham, he felt "as though [he] had been asked to masticate an ichthyosaurus." Compared with his later writings, the sample quoted here is relatively easy to chew.
15. Excerpted from *An Introduction to the Principles of Morals and Legislation,* chap. XIII. See Mary Peter Mack, *A Bentham Reader* (New York: Pegasus, 1969), p. 120.
16. Bentham did not think of crime as bringing about pleasure for the criminal as we would understand pleasure. In our vocabulary we would refer to the *benefits* of a crime, but the principle is the same.

17. See Mack, *Bentham Reader*, note 26, pp. 121–122. The "rules" specified by Bentham are illustrative of his characteristic determination to leave no detail unspecified or open to the reader's erroneous interpretation.
18. Quoted by Lionel W. Fox, *The English Prison and Borstal Systems* (London: Routledge and Kegan Paul, 1952), p. 11.
19. In 1830, Bentham published a pamphlet entitled *History of the War Between Jeremy Bentham and George the Third, by One of the Belligerents.* As excerpted by the editor, it contains as full an account of Bentham's plan as the modern reader will want.
20. Quoted by Mary Peter Mack, *Jeremy Bentham: An Odyssey of Ideas, 1748–1792* (New York: Columbia University Press, 1963), p. 403.
21. Michael Ignatieff, *A Just Measure of Pain: The Penitentiary in the Industrial Revolution, 1750–1850* (New York: Pantheon, 1978), p. 112.
22. Ibid., pp. 112–113. Paul's arguments anticipated by nearly two centuries the contemporary discourse on the privatization of corrections, a topic to which we shall return in later chapters.
23. Michel Foucault, *Discipline and Punish*, trans. Alan Sheridan (New York: Pantheon, 1977), p. 202. French original: *Surveiller et Punir; Naissance de la Prison* (Paris: Gallimard, 1975).
24. Mack, *A Bentham Reader*, note 28, p. 192.
25. Gertrude Himmelfarb, *Victorian Minds* (New York: Knopf, 1968), p. 132.
26. Paul W. Keve, *The History of Corrections in Virginia* (Charlottesville: University of Virginia Press, 1986), p. 12.
27. Ibid., p. 12, quoting William Waller Hening, *The Statutes at Large of Virginia*, vol. 4 (Richmond, Va.: W. W. Hening, 1809), p. 127.
28. In West Jersey the death penalty applied only to first-degree murder and treason.
29. An affirmation, in Quaker usage, is distinguished from an oath by omitting the invocation of the Deity—for example, "so help me God."
30. For a full account of this preposterous tradeoff see Harry Elmer Barnes, *The Evolution of Penology in Pennsylvania* (Indianapolis: Bobbs-Merrill, 1927), pp. 31–48. Barnes quotes at length contemporary narratives describing the brutal corporal punishments administered to petty thieves and fornicators.
31. Occasionally the offender might enjoy the encouragement of passersby who might think that he—or sometimes she—had been unjustly convicted.
32. There was a consistent sexual discrimination in the punishment of fornication. Women were whipped or subjected to the ducking stool. Men were fined or, at the worst, committed to a session in the pillory or the stocks.
33. From the *Charter and Laws of Pennsylvania, 1682–1700*, p. 121, as quoted by Barnes, *Evolution of Penology*, p. 56.
34. *Unaneled:* Not having received the last rites of the church.
35. From Roberts Vaux, *Notices of the Original and Successive Attempts to Improve the Discipline of the Prison at Philadelphia . . .* (Philadelphia, 1826), Quoted by Barnes, *Evolution of Penology*, p. 64.
36. One reformer, the famous Dr. Benjamin Rush, the leading physician of Philadelphia, argued vigorously but unsuccessfully against the death penalty even in cases of murder.
37. Barnes, *Evolution of Penology*, p. 73, quoting from the Pennsylvania Prison Society, *A Sketch of the Principal Transactions of the Philadelphia Society for Alleviating the Miseries of Public Prisons* (Philadelphia: Merrihew and Thompson, 1859), p. 5.
38. Still thriving, but under the more prosaic title of The Pennsylvania Prison Society.
39. Barnes, *Evolution of Penology*, p. 82.
40. Ibid., p. 83.
41. Ibid., p. 86.

42. Note that at 96 square feet, these cells far exceeded the 60 square feet called for in the present Standards of the American Correctional Association.
43. Ibid., pp. 159–160.
44. Ibid., p. 294, quoting from *The Report of the Inspectors of the Eastern Penitentiary* (1842). By 1842, the Auburn Silent System, its rival, had been established in most of the states and could claim to be the American system of prison discipline.
45. Charles Dickens, *American Notes* (Gloucester, Mass.: Peter Smith, 1968), p. 120. Original publication in 1842.
46. Barnes, *Evolution of Penology,* p. 291.
47. Ibid., p. 291.
48. W. David Lewis, *From Newgate to Dannemora: The Rise of the Penitentiary in New York, 1796–1848* (Ithaca, N.Y.: Cornell University Press, 1965), p. 51.
49. As we shall see, the Auburn officials were an unsentimental lot.
50. Lewis, *From Newgate to Dannemora,* p. 68, quoting from the Journal of the State Assembly, 1822, p. 218.
51. Ibid.
52. Ibid.
53. Ibid., p. 211, quoting from the Tenth Report of the New York Prison Association (1855).
54. For a more comprehensive account of Lynds's remarkable career, see Lewis, *From Newgate to Dannemora,* pp. 86–90, 136–138, 206–209, 215–218, and *passim.*
55. Published in France in 1832. Translated by Francis Lieber and published in Philadelphia in 1833. See the republication by the Southern Illinois University Press (Carbondale, 1964). Tocqueville's participation in the survey enabled him to write his classic study *Democracy in America.*
56. Beaumont and Tocqueville, *The Penitentiary System in the United States,* p. 200.
57. Ibid., pp. 161–165.

Chapter

4

From the Age of the Reformatory to the Age of Models

CHAPTER OUTLINE

Until late in the nineteenth century, penology in America and Britain stagnated. The Auburn Silent System prevailed throughout the United States with the nominal exception of Pennsylvania, where the commitment to the separate system still held sway in principle, but not in the harsh reality of prison life. There were riots and insurrections, but the formidable Auburn System was resilient enough to contain its problems without conceding changes.

THE TRANSFORMATION OF AMERICAN CORRECTIONS

The actual transformation of American penology began in 1870 and continues to this day. At first, the innovators were sure they knew where they were going and why.

A century later, we have become more and more uncertain of directions, although nearly everybody recognizes that further changes are urgently needed. To understand the present controversies it is necessary to know how the transformation began. In this chapter we will trace the course of change and outline the divergences from the original principles.

It has been a slow process, hindered by the resistance of the penal establishment to changing the old ways, thought to be tried and true, pioneered by Captain Elam Lynds. There were—and still are—many Auburn cellblocks still in use. Before the great changes began, a number of wardens were groping for more humane methods, but success had been slow in coming.

A roundabout circulation of ideas from Australia to England to Ireland eventually reached the United States. In 1870, a group of reforming zealots—some of them clergymen and other outsiders, some of them wardens unhappy with the hidebound methods made standard by the Auburn system—convened the leading figures in penology for an exhilarating conclave in Cincinnati to hear their proposals for changes in the management of prisons. The hardboiled wardens of the old school who attended the session were exhorted to accept the principle that the rehabilitation of offenders must be their goal. No longer should they be satisfied with repression by whips, shackles, and lockstep.

NEW PRINCIPLES AND OLD PRACTICES

It is a strange story. It began with a small cast of characters, men who were certain that Captain Lynds's model of prison management had to be abandoned in favor of innovations unprecedented in the United States. These idealists brought together the tough-minded wardens and keepers of America's prisons and induced them to sign off on a radically new **Declaration of Principles** to guide the reformation of the nation's prisons.

The meeting was carefully planned. Speakers from abroad were invited to present new and progressive ideas. Eloquent American reformers denounced repression and urged that prisoners have educational opportunities and religious instruction. No one was prepared to speak up for the traditions of the Auburn Silent System or Pennsylvania's Eastern State Penitentiary. Powerful support was given the meeting's presiding officer, Ohio's Governor Rutherford B. Hayes, who was later to become the nineteenth president of the United States.[1]

Blake McKelvey, the historian of American corrections, described it as a "mountain-top experience," more of a religious revival than a professional conference. Because the reformers knew exactly what they wanted and, more important, what they did not want, a memorable document emerged from their exalted deliberations. Practical prison men from 22 states, Canada, and Latin American nations enthusiastically

> . . . rose above the monotony of four gray walls, men in stripes shuffling in lock-step, sullen faces staring through the bars, coarse mush and coffee made of bread crusts, armed sentries stalking the walls. They forgot it all and voted for their remarkable declaration of principles.[2]

There were 37 principles in all. Ever since their resounding acceptance in 1870, they have been admired, respectfully quoted, and often ruefully dismissed as visionary. In actuality, most of them have had a profound impact on the practice of corrections. Here are 22, the most relevant to the subsequent history of criminal justice:

1. Reformation, not vindictive suffering, should be the purpose of penal treatment of prisoners.
2. Classification should be made on the basis of a mark system, patterned after the Irish system.
3. Rewards should be provided for good conduct.
4. Prisoners should be made to realize that their destiny is in their own hands.
5. The chief obstacles to prison reform are the political appointment of prison officials and the instability of management.
6. Prison officials should be trained for their jobs.
7. Indeterminate sentences should be substituted for fixed sentences, and the gross disparities and inequities in prison sentences should be eliminated. Repeated short sentences are futile.
8. Religion and education are the most important agencies of reformation.
9. Prison discipline should be such as to gain the will of the prisoner and to conserve his self-respect.
10. The aim of the prison should be to make industrious free men rather than orderly and obedient prisoners.
11. There should be full provision for industrial training.
12. The system of contract labor in prisons should be abolished.
13. Prisons should be small, and there should be separate institutions for different types of offenders.
14. The law should strike against the so-called "higher-ups" in crime, as well as against the lesser operatives.
15. There should be indemnification for prisoners who are later discovered to be innocent.
16. There should be revision of the laws relating to the treatment of insane criminals.
17. There should be a more judicious exercise of the pardoning power.
18. There should be established a system for the collection of uniform penal statistics.
19. A more adequate architecture should be developed, providing sufficiently for air and sunlight, as well as for prison hospitals, schoolrooms, and so on.
20. Within each state, prison management should be centralized.
21. The social training of prisoners should be facilitated through proper association, and abolition of the silence rules.
22. Society at large should be made to realize its responsibility for crime conditions.

FROM AUSTRALIA TO IRELAND TO CINCINNATI

The origin of these influential principles deserves our attention. We must return to Captain Alexander Maconochie, about whom we wrote with admiration in Chapter 2. His system of governance was unappreciated by his superiors in Australia. As with his mark system at Norfolk Island, his attempts to install it in England at the Birmingham prison met with the disapproval of the Home Office—so mild a prison regimen was considered insufficient to deter crime. Terror was required, and Maconochie's plan would not deliver it.

In 1850, legislation began the centralization of the "convict-prisons" (or penitentiaries) for the incarceration of felons, as distinguished from "local prisons," under the jurisdiction of county Justices of the Peace. Traces of Captain Maconochie's "mark system" can be found in the general plan for the administration of the convict-prisons.[3]

In 1857, Parliament passed the second Penal Servitude Act authorizing regulations for a "Progressive Stage System" in the penitentiaries.[4] This system allowed for nine months in separate confinement, with the remainder of the sentence to be divided in three stages. Increased pay and privileges were awarded to prisoners as they succeeded in passing from stage to stage.

It fell to Maconochie's younger colleague Walter Crofton (1815–1897) to make the mark system famous by putting it into effect in the Irish prisons. His influence spread throughout Europe. To American reformers, the Irish Mark System seemed to be just what the prisons of their country needed. Ireland, in its history so often one of the unluckiest of nations, became for a time an international leader in progressive penology. Although mid-nineteenth-century Ireland is long ago and far away, the story of Crofton and the Irish Mark System must be told to understand the reformatory system as it burst into being in the United States.

THE LUCK OF THE IRISH

In England, the transportation of convicts continued until January 1868, when the last shipment was landed in Fremantle, Western Australia, where they were still welcome in an underpopulated and remote land that was badly in need of working hands. The other Australian states had successfully campaigned to end their status as the "receptacles for England's felons." Transportation to Botany Bay and Tasmania had ended in 1858. Gold had been discovered in the state of Victoria. Convicts from Tasmania were no longer welcome as cheap labor but rather were seen as threats to property in a newly prospering community.

In England, the economics of convict transportation ended the shipments. Prisons had been built. It cost £15 a year to keep a convict in Dartmoor, the maximum security prison, and £100 to keep him in Tasmania for the duration of his sentence. No unpopular policy could survive such a comparison of costs. Further, to the hardliners of those days, transportation from the crowded cities and miserable wages of the mother country to the green and sunny land of Australia was anything but the punishment a wrongdoer deserved. Even if the Australians had not objected to the influx of convicts, transportation could not have continued for much longer.

Penitentiaries were built, most of them faithfully adapting the Pennsylvania plan. The first of them, London's Pentonville, was built in 1842 to hold convicts for a disciplinary 18 months before their shipment to Botany Bay as "ticket of leave" men.[5] Pentonville was a replica of the Eastern State Penitentiary and subsequently copied in England and in most of northern Europe. The planners had compared the Auburn and the Pennsylvania systems and chosen Pennsylvania. They surmised that the Auburn plan stimulated vindictive feelings among the prisoners, whereas the Pennsylvania system induced habitual submission. The Auburn Silent System never caught on in Europe.

In the 1850s the British Parliament passed a succession of Penal Servitude Acts, anticipating the gradual end of the transportation system. Under Sir Joshua Jebb (1793–1863), the first chairman of the Board of Directors, a "Progressive Stage System" of convict management was developed. From the beginning the influence of Captain Maconochie's mark system can be seen. After some experimentation, in the Act of 1857 it was settled that convicts would serve nine months in solitary confinement for the first stage of their sentences. That would be followed by a second stage in which there would be some pay for work done and privileges of movement and association with other prisoners. The third stage was release on license for the rest of the sentence to be served.

This system, intended to seek reform of convicts while they were undergoing punishment, was not universally popular. Advocates of a hard line in the administration of justice were positive that criminals were not entitled to privileges of any kind. If they worked, they should be put to useless or demeaning labor. Not much thought was given to regulating the provision of productive labor for prisoners. Without a central administration of the prisons, local authorities were free to assign convicts to any kind of work or none. In the opinion of some British magistrates, "labor, to be fully deterrent, should be not only monotonous and severe but quite useless, this being more likely to 'plague the prisoner.' Employment in useful and interesting work, on the other hand, seemed to be positively encouraging crime."[6] For years, prison rules in many countries called for convicts to be put on treadmills for a full work day, or to turn a heavy crank for months before being allowed assignment to public works.[7]

In the central system of penitentiaries, the Progressive Stage System survived, in spite of much public opposition to its apparent leniency. Successive acts of Parliament tightened up the rules, lengthened sentences, and provided for stricter supervision of convicts released on license.

Walter Crofton, a retired army officer, had worked with Jebb in the prison administration. The terrible famine of the late 1840s in Ireland had led to a serious increase in crime and a resultant explosion of the prison population. Jebb built a new Pentonville-style prison at Mountjoy, near Dublin. In 1854 Crofton was sent to introduce the progressive stage system. The basic plan with which he began was Jebb's, but he soon developed innovations, the propriety of which Jebb was dubious. The complete program became known as the Irish Mark System and made Crofton a celebrity in international penology. Because the mark system was the inspiration of the Declaration of Principles and the American reformatory movement that followed its adoption in that 1870 conference in Cincinnati, we must devote a few paragraphs to its description.

The system applied to convicts serving terms of three years or more. The first stage was for eight or nine months, depending on the man's conduct. It was a rough introduction to prison life. The first three months were spent in solitary confinement (no work) and on reduced rations (no meat). The thought was that three months so spent would inspire the most indolent convict to ask for work. He would be weakened by the meager diet, and less resistant to the requirements of the prison authorities. He would be put on full rations and set to picking oakum[8] or other sedentary but unskilled labor. Services and instruction would expose him to religion and literacy classes to make sure that he would not leave prison without knowing how to read and write.

When finally eligible for the second stage, the prisoner would be moved to Spike

Island, off the southern coast of Ireland, or, if he happened to be skilled at a craft, to a construction site at Philipstown where convicts were building a new prison. The second stage included four classes: third, second, first, and the "Advanced" class. In each class, a prisoner had to earn marks for a maximum of 9 a month: 3 for good conduct, 3 for good work on an assigned job, and 3 for diligence in school. A prisoner moved from the third class to the second class in a minimum of two months—that is, after accumulating 18 marks. Progressing from second to first class required 54 marks, or at least six months. From first to Advanced took at least 12 months, or 108 marks.

Prisoners were punished for rule violations by the loss of marks. While all classes worked together, they were distinguished from one another by badges, gratuities that increased from class to class, and progress toward the third stage. Time in the Advanced class was determined by the length of the sentence to be served and the number of marks awarded. With a maximum number of marks, a sentence of 15 years could be served in 10 years.[9]

The third or Intermediate stage was spent at Lusk Common, 15 miles from Dublin, where convicts were housed in dormitories, worked at land reclamation, and were given vocational training to fit them for employment when finally released. This was a truly minimum custody situation. There were 6 unarmed guards for 100 prisoners. Crofton was specific about the intention of this part of the program:

> First, you have to show to the convict that you really trust him, and give him credit for the amendment he has illustrated by his marks.
>
> Second, you have to show to the public that the convict, who will soon be restored to liberty for weal or woe, may upon reasonable grounds be considered as capable of being safely employed.[10]

He argued that his system induced the convict to cooperate in his own "amendment," or rehabilitation.

> He cannot ignore the conviction . . . that the system, however penal in its development, is intended for his benefit; and that moreover, it has by its stringent regulations and arrangements after the liberation of the convict . . . made the vocation of crime very unprofitable and hazardous to follow.[11]

Crofton was clear about the penal objectives his system was designed to achieve. In his terminology there were three elements: *application*, *incapacitation*, and *reformation*. There was no confusion in his mind about the importance of punishment. Application was the suffering and indignities that the convict experienced by being incarcerated. Both the convict and the public should learn "that the profits of crime are overbalanced by its losses." The incapacitation of the prisoner meant that during incarceration he would be incapable of further harm to the public. For Crofton, reformation was as essential an element of the system as application and incapacitation. Prisoners should be so changed in attitudes and behavior that when released they would be unlikely to return to crime. Just to be sure, when they were finally released on license (or "ticket of leave") from Lusk Common, they were required to report periodically to the police. The license expired at the conclusion of the sentence. They were made to understand that if there were signs of a relapse into criminal ways, they would be hustled back to Mountjoy in ignominy.

Because of illness, Crofton retired from the Irish prison service in 1862, after eight years. The system had come under attack from many influential quarters. The

Lord Chief Justice disapproved of using the police to monitor the behavior of convicts on license. Sir Joshua Jebb, the architect of the Progressive Stage System, was upset about the deviations that Crofton had introduced.[12] There was a lot of pamphleteering on both sides, and Crofton held up his side of the conflict well enough to be returned to Ireland in 1877. He retired again the following year, and, aided by widespread foreign interest, his system became the standard in England.

In 1863, Gaylord Hubbell, warden of Sing Sing, visited Ireland and returned to New York a convert to the mark system. Hearing Hubbell's report, Franklin Sanborn (1831–1917), the secretary of the Massachusetts Board of State Charities, became the untiring "apostle" of Crofton's system. Long dissatisfied with both the Auburn and the Pennsylvania systems, Sanborn, Hubbell, and two other associates, Enoch Wines (1806–1879) and Zebulon Brockway (1827–1920), formed a movement to introduce the Irish system as a humane and progressive alternative. None of the elements of the system was exactly new to the United States, but Crofton had combined them into a system that seemed to work. He was invited to speak at the Cincinnati meeting of the National Prison Association, and from his mark system the American **reformatory movement** got under way. It gathered a remarkable momentum.

THE ELMIRA REFORMATORY AND THE SAD STORY OF ZEBULON BROCKWAY

Zebulon Brockway began his correctional career at the age of 21 and spent 50 years managing prisons in Albany, New York; in Detroit; and finally at the new Elmira Reformatory in Elmira, New York, where he served as warden from 1876 to 1900. His innovations at Elmira won him praise as the greatest warden ever produced in the United States.[13]

To the Cincinnati conference of 1870 Brockway came as the warden of the Detroit House of Correction. He read a paper, "The Ideal Prison System for a State," which was acclaimed as the outstanding contribution to those memorable proceedings.[14] Because of Brockway's influence on the assembled penologists of 1870 and his later administration of the Elmira Reformatory, we will summarize the views expressed in this enthusiastic advocacy of the reformatory ideal.

He began by contrasting the two incompatible opinions about crime. The traditional administrators of justice held that men and women are free to do what they will. If they do wrong they must be punished with "anguish and pain for their wickedness, and [to] strike with terror those who know of their fate." He then went on to contrast the views of reformers who were urging a new and different penology:

> On the other hand, . . . our individual liberty of action is limited by the bias with which we are born, or by that arising from the circumstances of our early life . . . [and] society should not punish the criminal, but impose upon him such restraint and treatment as shall secure protection to itself and conduce to the further and higher development of the wrong-doer himself. The advocates of this latter view hold that vengeance has no place in a true prison system. . . . They further affirm that, in the history of jurisprudence, the deterrent force of punishment is found practically a failure. . . . They espouse no sickly sentimentalism. . . . They urge upon society the obligation to treat the great company of criminals . . . in such a manner that they shall either be cured, or kept

> under such continued restraint as gives guarantee of safety from continued depredations.[15]

Brockway went on to give his attention to the organization, the necessary legislation, and the proper administration of a prison system established to pursue the goal of reformation. In passing he urged that the very word *prison* be stricken from the statutes: "The true attitude of government is that of guardian; its true function to shelter, shield, help, heal."

The system he proposed called for

- *Primary schools* for the education of children from the alms-houses, who are three years of age and upward, "away from the contamination and taint of these miserable places, where they shall be . . . trained for good citizens, instead of criminals as now; also *schools of a compulsory character* . . . for the control and culture of the incorrigible, who are now expelled from the public schools or brutalized by corporal punishment."
- *Reform schools* for juveniles, "older and more advanced in wrong development."
- *District reformatories* for [adult] misdemeanants. "The whole vile system of common jails for the imprisonment of convicted persons must be uprooted and blotted from existence . . . [T]he structures for detaining alleged offenders [should] be made suitable . . . with large, well-lighted, cheerful apartments, strong and secure against escape, entirely isolating the occupants from each other."
- *A Graduated Series of Reformatory Institutions for Adults.* These should consist of:
  (a) The House of Reception. "Here all prisoners should be received and retained until reliable information is obtained as to their ancestral history, their early social condition and its . . . influence in forming their character . . . upon which basis a plan of treatment may be outlined. Here the incorrigible must be detained in solitary or safe custody, and experimental treatment applied to all, for the purpose of finding those who can be properly transferred to the next grade."
  (b) The Industrial Reformatory. For prisoners in "good physical health" to be trained for productive employment. "Their perseverance and self-command will be developed and subjected to appropriate tests. Such of the prisoners as thrive under this training may be removed, with great hope and confident security to the last of the series for male prisoners, *viz.*:"
  (c) The Intermediate Reformatory. At this stage Brockway's imagination outstripped his expository powers. This was to be an "enclosure, secure in and of itself," which would contain separate rooms for prisoners, a dining hall, "upon the plan of a well regulated restaurant for work people, where, within due limits, any desired edible may be supplied," a library and a "public hall suitable for reading rooms, religious services, scientific and other intellectual exercises of a public nature. . . ." All this would be combined with industrial and agricultural enterprises to be "organized substantially upon the cooperative plan." The records do not disclose what the assembled penologists made of this burst of correctional utopianism.

- *Separate Reformatories for Women.* "These should be under the immediate management of women, and that exclusively. . . . Wayward women must be won to virtue by their own sex if they are to be won at all." The program proposed for women offenders emphasized "womanly affection" but recognized their need to be prepared to "earn an honest and sufficient support."[16]

Modern readers may smile at some of the ingenuous simplicities embodied in Brockway's ideal system. Nothing like it had been heard before in the United States, where only two schools of penology—Pennsylvania and Auburn—had been conceivable. This humane new vision contrasted with the harsh and brutalizing penology of the mid–nineteenth century. Brockway had offered his colleagues a system that may have been impractical. For many, if not all, of them, it had a significant attraction. It would relieve them of the onus of work in occupations that coerced fellow human beings at the cost of the threats and violence that coercion required. For generations of correctional workers ever since Brockway's uplifting address, the rehabilitative ideal, even if given lip service only, has served to gild their careers with the appearance of respectability and professionalism rather than the unpleasant stigma associated with the exercise of naked coercion.

Brockway went on to urge the indeterminate sentence:

> No man, be he judge, lawyer, or layman, can determine beforehand the date when imprisonment shall work reformation . . . and it is an outrage upon society to return to the privileges of citizenship those who have proved themselves dangerous and bad by the commission of a crime, until a cure is wrought and reformation reached.[17]

Brockway felt strongly about the merits of the indeterminate sentence and advanced in its favor 15 arguments, with which we will not trouble the reader. He concluded that "a reformatory system cannot exist without it, and that it is quite indispensable to the ideal of a true prison system."

Most of Brockway's ideas as voiced in this address found their way into the Declaration of Principles summarized earlier in this chapter. They also were given an opportunity for practical application when he was appointed the superintendent of the new Elmira Reformatory in 1876.

The ground for this institution, soon to become famous, was broken in 1866, but construction had been much slower than at Sing Sing 40 years earlier. It was modeled on Lynds's design, which was certainly not intended for the application of Brockway's benign ideas.[18] It was originally designed for 500 prisoners, but later additions increased its capacity to 1700. Brockway's proposals for a model reformatory were to have full rein.

The limits were established from the beginning. Admission was restricted to first offenders between the ages of 16 and 30. All would receive an indeterminate sentence—no minimum, but a statutory maximum. The program would aim at changing the prisoners's character. The superintendent would decide when the change in the convict's character justified release. All releases were conditional, and discharge would depend on conduct while under supervision in the community over a period of six months.

The program itself was arduous. As originally planned by Brockway, it consisted of these elements:

1. There was a point system by which industry, good behavior, and diligence at school earned points, whereas indolence and bad behavior lost them. The

assumption was the prisoners would want to earn points as fast as possible so as to qualify for release as soon as possible.

2. Convicts with good grades would be rewarded with privileges and better living conditions.
3. All convicts would be required to attend school, regardless of their previous educational status.
4. Daily military drill would be required, just as in the military academies so popular in nineteenth-century private education. Convicts could advance to become sergeants, lieutenants, and captains of their units. The stated advantage to military drill in nineteenth-century reformatories was that it gave the inmate an "erect and graceful bearing, made him obedient to commands, and taught him responsibility. It allows the use of a large number as inmate officers, which allies them with the administration and makes the institution largely self-governing. . . ."[19]
5. Realistic vocational training would be provided to ensure that each convict leaving Elmira would be able to earn an honest living.
6. There was a regular program of physical education under the guidance of trained instructors using a gymnasium planned for the purpose.
7. There was occupational therapy for retarded or handicapped persons.
8. Good nutrition designed to "strengthen the nerves and produce states of mind and characteristics conducive to industry and endurance" was provided.
9. Convicts were exposed to active moral and religious influences.

One visitor remarked that Elmira's success depended on this principle: "Tire out the man with a strict daily routine to the point that he longs to go to bed early."

Elmira was the first correctional institution to pay wages to prisoners according to diligence and productivity. From their wages they paid for room and board, clothing and other necessities, and medical care. The economics of the system were arranged so that at the time of discharge there would be some money to the prisoners's credit.

Brockway's prestige as a correctional innovator and the plausible claims made for the effectiveness of the Elmira program led to its being emulated in 12 other states by the turn of the century and 11 more by 1933, despite growing doubts about the success of the system.

One of the doubters was Brockway himself. In a retrospective address at the annual meeting of the National Prison Association in 1887, he recalled that at the 1870 meeting he had experienced an uplifting inspiration like that of the disciples at the Mount of Transfiguration. He had felt himself strengthened by

> a mysterious, almighty, Spiritual force. . . . I was going to have a grand success . . . but it did not work. . . . I found that there was a commonplace work of education to do with these persons whom I hoped to inspire. . . . That did not suffice. The industrial training of prisoners was taken up, and that is drudgery. Getting down to drudgery, and even lower than that. . . ."[20]

What he meant was that he had had to resort to corporal punishment and solitary confinement of refractory prisoners. He disliked the use of straps and paddles and insisted that he be the only person at Elmira to administer this ultimate sanction.[21]

The difficulties confronting Brockway in carrying out the beneficent program he had intended were increased in 1888 by legislation in New York—and other states as well—outlawing prison industry. His solution was compulsory military drill for several hours a day, followed by calisthenics and vocational training.

The **Elmira Plan** borrowed from the Irish Mark System the notion of assigning convicts to grades. A man was to begin in the second grade, with minimum privileges, and rise through the second to the first. Well-behaved prisoners would stay in the first grade. New prisoners entered in the second grade, where they were to remain until their behavior and diligence qualified them for the first grade. The third grade was occupied by prisoners demoted for disciplinary infractions. They occupied starkly austere cells, marched to and from work in the demeaning lockstep, and could neither correspond with family and friends nor receive visitors. The plan somehow broke down. As time went on, everybody was in the first grade except those in the third and the fresh arrivals in the second grade, who were soon promoted. It is not clear at this distance in time that the loss of this pattern of incentives made any difference one way or another.

Word of the Elmira innovations got around fast. European penologists made the pilgrimage and returned home with generally enthusiastic accounts. One exception was William Tallack, the secretary of the Howard League in England, who objected that even though 80 percent of the Elmira convicts were said to be reformed, the Elmira system was so mild that it could have no deterrent effect—people would no longer be afraid to commit crimes.[22] In spite of Tallack, the influence of Elmira in England was momentous. In 1897 Sir Evelyn Ruggles-Brise, who had the year before been appointed the chairman of the British Prison Commission, traveled to Elmira. He had been concerned with the number of young men under the age of 21 who were confined in local prisons and penitentiaries. Seeing the program in Elmira, he was impressed:

A class in the School of Letters, Elmira Reformatory. (*Source:* Brown.)

> The elaborate system of moral, physical, and industrial training of these prisoners, the enthusiasm which dominated the work, the elaborate machinery for supervision of parole, all these things, if stripped of their extravagance, satisfied me that a real, human effort was being made . . . for the rehabilitation of the youthful criminal.[23]

Based in part on his observations at Elmira and other reformatories, Ruggles-Brise created the English Borstal system. (See Box 4-1.)

What was the real significance of Elmira? It is hard to believe that all the admiring visitors, as well as experienced penologists, who came, saw, and praised were entirely deceived. As we have seen, Brockway's zeal, so eloquently expressed in Cincinnati, was brought down to earth. As time went on, criticism became increasingly severe. Brockway was investigated for brutality in the administration of discipline. Although he was cleared of the charges, he was saddened and made resentful by the experience. In their text on criminology, Harry Elmer Barnes and Negley K. Teeters summed up the realities of Elmira and the many similar facilities it inspired:

> . . . the Elmira system had serious defects. . . . The system of discipline was repressive, varying from benevolent despotism to tyrannical cruelty. . . . There was practically no grasp of the fundamental fact, basic in the newer penology, that a prisoner can be fitted for a life of freedom only by training in a social environment that resembles, in point of liberty and responsibility, what he must enter after his release. . . . In fact, the reformatory is just another prison. But it made two contributions to penal science. It broke the stupid impasse between the two rival systems which bogged down institutional treatment. . . . [I]ts greatest contribution was the realistic introduction of the indeterminate sentence. . . .[24]

In spite of these strictures it was a step ahead, well beyond the unrelieved harshness of Auburn and the Eastern State Penitentiary. At the end of his career, Brockway was a sad old man doing many things that he had hoped never would be necessary in his brave new system. Other wardens in other reformatories were not so sensitive. The traditional punishments were freely inflicted: Offending convicts were shackled to the walls of their cells, and the strap and the cat-o'-nine-tails were in liberal use.

It remained for two Harvard researchers, Sheldon and Eleanor Glueck, to complete the disillusion with the reformatory ideal. In their landmark study *500 Criminal Careers*,[25] they showed that of the men released from the Massachusetts State Reformatory between 1911 and 1922, 72.7 percent committed recorded crimes during the period of their parole; only 21.1 percent made a reasonably adequate adjustment. Five years after the expiration of their parole, 9.2 percent of these men could not be found. Of the remaining 90.8 percent, 18.4 percent were in correctional institutions, 6.7 percent were fugitives from justice, 6.9 percent were either hospitalized or in military service or otherwise innocuously occupied, and 11.9 percent were dead. However, 46.7 percent had been in the community for the entire 60-month period of the study. Almost 80 percent of the men whose conduct could be traced for the full period had committed some kind of offense during this period. The Gluecks commented that "the estimates . . . in almost all of the follow-up studies, annual reports of reformatories and prisons . . . that some seventy-five to eighty percent of parolees are 'successes'[26] . . . are so fallacious as to suggest a condition practically the reverse of that reported."[27]

Box 4-1 The Borstal System

We have mentioned the memorable visit of Sir Evelyn Ruggles-Brise (1857–1935) to Elmira in 1897. He returned to England convinced that the reformatory ideas should be tried on young English offenders. As chairman of the British Prison Commission, he was in a position to initiate major changes in a system that had long stagnated. His superiors in the government were sympathetic to his view that the prisons were in great need of renovation. After his observations at Elmira, Ruggles-Brise concluded that the American concern for the 21-to-30 age group caught the young offender too late; the reformatory idea should be applied to youths between 16 and 21. To test this idea, he converted an old convict-prison at the village of Borstal in southeastern England into an experimental reformatory. A London Prison Visitors' Association was formed to interview youths in the 16-to-21 age group in the London prisons. They were removed to Borstal, as the new reformatory became known, and members of the Visitors' Association, now known as the Borstal Association, took responsibility for developing release plans for the inmates, who were—and still are—known in the Borstal vocabulary as "lads."

Ruggles-Brise was specific about the distinctions he wanted to make. The lads were not juvenile delinquents, nor were they adult criminals. "Our object was to deal with a far different material, the young hooligan advanced in crime, *perhaps with many previous convictions*, and who appeared to be inevitably doomed to a life of habitual crime. The American reformatory ideas provided the concept of individualization, so novel in both countries that a good deal of experimental programming was needed to make it a reality. To Ruggles-Brise, the objective was a system leading to a constructive assignment for the Borstal lad when released.

In 1908 Parliament passed legislation authorizing the system along the lines that Ruggles-Brise recommended. The principles of the system are important to outline because they became influential in setting up similar programs in the United States and in the British overseas dominions. Briefly, the Borstal system called for the lad's reform by " *'individualization'* mentally, morally and physically." There would be physical drill, gymnastics, and technical and literacy training. Good conduct would be rewarded. The staff was selected for characteristics that were likely to influence youths of the kind that Borstal had to work with. Soon after the beginning of the program, it was decided that the minimum period of exposure to Borstal should be at least a year.

The **Borstal system** proceeded on this fairly austere plan until 1921, when the remarkable personality of Alexander Paterson (1884–1947) was added to the Prison Commission. He was one of a kind. The son of an affluent family, he attended a public school and went on to Oxford University like hundreds of others headed for conventional careers in the civil service or politics. At the age of 21, he was graduated from Oxford and settled in Bermondsey, one of London's worst slums, as a member of the staff of the Oxford Medical Mission. He lived in Bermondsey for 20 years, organizing boys' clubs and recruiting Oxford students to work with him in the clubs and, later, when he became a prison commissioner, to take on assignments in the Borstal system.

Paterson's work in the Borstal system was notable for at least four achievements. First, so far as possible, he removed the appearances and the procedures of the British prisons from the Borstals. The governor was still called the governor, but the assistant governors were housemasters serving, so far as possible, the roles of housemasters in an English public school. The prison officers were taken out of uniform, and so were the lads, who were allowed to wear civilian clothes instead of the convict's demeaning uniform.

Second, having removed as many of the earmarks of prison as he could, he went on to bring in young university men to fill the posts of governors and housemasters. To induce scions of the upper and middle classes to choose a career in penology was an astonishing innovation. As in the United States, prison work in England did not enjoy even a modest occupational prestige. Paterson's peculiar magnetism changed that. The governor of one of the largest prisons in England tells how he was recruited. He had worked in Paterson's settlement house in Bermondsey during a university vacation. Shortly after his return to Oxford, there was a knock on the door of his college room, and there was Paterson. He said, "I need you as a housemaster at a new Borstal. I want you to report to my office in London next Monday." The startled young student protested that he was only in his second year at Oxford but perhaps could come during the next vacation. "That's not soon enough," Paterson replied. "I need you full time, beginning next Monday." To the mystification of the college authorities and the dismay of his parents, he left Oxford, reported the following Monday, and continued in the Borstal system and later in the Prison Commission for the succeeding 40 years.

Paterson's third innovation was a training school for prison and Borstal staff at Wakefield in the north of England. For years there had been much discussion of whether training of prison staff was needed, and, if so, exactly what training was to be required. The prison staff college was opened in 1935 to train likely candidates for promotion—not a popular new departure among prison officers accustomed to promotion by seniority. Eventually, the training program was expanded to include a six-week curriculum for all new recruits for prisons and Borstals and a six-month course for new assistant governors and housemasters. It was still the time of the British Empire, and colonial prison personnel were invited to attend and did.

Paterson's fourth and surely his most significant contribution was the Borstal mystique. He had a flair for aphorisms: "You cannot train a man for freedom in conditions of captivity." He added:

> The Borstal System has no merit apart from the Borstal Staff. It is men and not buildings who will change the hearts and ways of misguided lads. Better an institution that consists of two log huts in swamp or desert, with a staff devoted to their task, than a model block of buildings . . . whose staff is solely concerned with thoughts of pay and promotion.

American prison reformers took a considerable interest in the Borstal model. In 1940 the American Law Institute made a long and comprehensive study of the problem of youthful delinquency that culminated in a model Youth Correction Authority Act, recommended for adoption by each state; it also called specifically for new institutions patterned on the Borstal system. The system was adopted in California and in modified form by several other states. Experience since thenindicates that the system is not easily transplanted from culture to culture, nor does it survive the tests of time in the country of its origin. Nevertheless, the Borstal stress on the individualization of the offender and his or her treatment as a man or woman with problems that he or she must solve, rather than as a lump to be beaten or squeezed into shape, is an accepted basic principle of penology. For that and his example as a leader, Alexander Paterson deserves to be remembered as one of our great reformers.

Source: Sir Evelyn Ruggles-Brise, *The English Prison System* (London: Macmillan, 1921). Our account of the Borstal origins is drawn from his chapter on the Borstal system, pp. 85–100.

The Gluecks were pessimistic about the future of the reformatory:

> The American reformatory, a device intended and designed to rebuild human character, has gradually been transformed into a well-oiled machine for avoiding friction; and this even at the cost of abandoning the very object of the reformatory, while clinging to its name and outward form. This stage has not yet been completely reached by the Massachusetts institution. But it has come to pass in a number of other so-called reformatories, a few of which are in reality prisons of the worst type.[28]

The influence of the Gluecks was profound. Many administrators actually read their book, and it is still one of the most frequently cited studies in the literature of criminology. It is not too much to say that its publication was as important in the history of penology as the reforms of Brockway and his contemporaries. The truth was painful to face, but the Gluecks said what had to be said, and many urgently needed impovements resulted from their remarkable study.

JOHN AUGUSTUS, FATHER OF PROBATION

Our account of criminal justice change and reform has taken note of many unusual, unconventional men. Space and the reader's patience do not allow us to include all who have diverted the course of corrections from indifference and brutality to more enlightened and purposeful means of dealing with offenders.

We would be remiss in omitting an account of one of the most unusual of reformers, John Augustus. Augustus (1784–1859) was a Boston shoemaker, prosperous enough to have a shop with several employees. He is remembered by name as the First Probation Officer, although his admirers and successors have only the vaguest notions of how he came to be a prototype. Information about his motives and the means he chose to gain his ends comes chiefly from his artless account of himself, *A Report of the Labors of John Augustus*,[29] which he published late in life at the request of his friends. It is full of detail about his hapless clientele, an apparently careful account of people helped and the outcome, and a strenuous emphasis on how much money his work saved the commonwealth of Massachusetts.

Augustus was in court one morning in August 1841 when a door opened and a "ragged and wretched looking man" entered and took his seat upon the bench allotted to prisoners. The poor fellow was charged with being a common drunkard. Before sentence was passed, Augustus "conversed with him for a few moments, and found that he was not yet past all hope of reformation, although his appearance and his looks precluded a belief that he would ever be a *man* again." To make a short story shorter, Augustus provided bail, subject to the man's appearing in court three weeks later. The "wretched" drunkard signed a pledge to never again drink spirits and returned to court at the appointed time as a completely changed man. He was fined one cent and costs, amounting in all to $3.76. Augustus reports that his first client continued industrious and sober and without doubt was saved from a drunkard's grave.[30]

Augustus does not tell his readers how he happened to be in court on that fateful morning, but from that time until his death 18 years later, he was a regular attendant. For some time he was treated as a crank who wouldn't mind his own business,[31] but eventually he gained the confidence of the court and the district attorney. Most of the people for whom he provided bail were drunkards and prostitutes, and if his follow-up accounting is correct, the majority of them gave the courts and the police no further trouble. The general picture of life among the poorer classes in Boston is depressing. Mothers were arrested for drunkenness and sent to jail without any provision for the care of their children—until Augustus came along. Three months in the House of Correction was the fate of streetwalkers—and after their release they were free to resume their profession. Augustus and his wife at first made room for them in their own home; later, they established a House of Refuge where the prostitutes could live while reestablishing themselves as honest women. Augustus's accounting shows that from 1841 through 1851 he provided bail for 1102 males and females, some of them as young as 8 years old. Accustomed to a caseload of 125 to 150 probationers at a time, he had to give up shoemaking and seems to have depended on the contributions of friends and admirers for funds to put up bail.

This was the beginning of probation; the word itself was Augustus's invention. In 1879 the Massachusetts legislature passed a law institutionalizing probation, and the city of Boston appointed the first full-time, publicly paid probation officer. In 1891, Massachusetts law required the criminal courts to appoint probation officers. When Sheldon Glueck wrote his foreword to the 1939 edition of Augustus's *Report*, it was possible for him to say that while the Emperor Augustus was the founder of the Roman Empire, John Augustus was "the founder of an empire of social service that has rapidly spread its wholesome influence not only in America but in other quarters of the globe.[32] As we will see in chapters to come, the practice of probation has become almost universal in the Western world.

In Chapter 9 we will have much more to say about the present state of probation and the influences that have made it what it now is. We conclude this brief account of its founder by reminding the reader that the reform of criminal justice has always depended on unusual men and women who have seen with their own eyes how things were and also saw how they might be changed for the better.

A CHARISMATIC VOLUNTEER TAKES OVER AT AUBURN

It took an Auburn citizen to begin the end of the Auburn Silent System. Thomas Mott Osborne (1859–1926) was the son of an affluent businessman, the inventor of the Osborne reaper and other farm machinery. Educated at Harvard University, he became president of the family business upon the sudden death of his father, not long after his graduation. He continued for nine years, when upon the death of his wife, he decided that a business career was not for him. After a fling in politics, during which he became the mayor of Auburn, he was persuaded to join the board of trustees of the George Junior Republic.

The George Junior Republic was founded by William Reuben George (1866–

1936), a New York City policeman, who conceived the idea of a self-governing community of slum children in which they could prepare for citizenship by taking on the duties of good citizens in a model republic consisting of their peers. These included the roles of executives, legislators in the republic's town meeting, and judges. It was a successful enterprise from the first. Osborne, an enthusiast, soon became the president of the board of trustees. He was a zealous promoter of the Junior Republic idea, which eventually had many replicas throughout the country. He continued as the leader of the board of trustees until 1913, when a trivial quarrel with George burst into a conflict that caused Osborne to resign.

In earlier discussions of the Junior Republic idea with George, Osborne had conceived the notion that self-government might also work in prisons. As a citizen of Auburn he had always been conscious of the prison as a brooding presence in the middle of town. He was generally aware of the way it was governed but had not taken an active role in prison work. No longer immersed in the Junior Republic, he tried to obtain appointment as the state Superintendent of Prisons. His candidacy was unsuccessful, but as consolation the governor appointed him chairman of a new Commission on Prison Reform. From that time on, Osborne's name was nationally synonymous with prison reform. To penological conservatives he was anathema. To the reform community he was a hero who finally fell in battle with superior but reactionary forces. Though he was humiliated and turned out of Sing Sing, where he served as warden for two years, his influence has survived, even though many of his ideas have proved to be impractical.

He began his service on the Commission on Prison Reform by arranging with the warden of the Auburn prison to serve for a week as a volunteer prisoner. Although the prison staff, the guards, and the prisoners themselves knew what he was doing, he went through the standard routines of reception and assignments to cell and work, and he submitted to the rigors of Auburn discipline without deviation. He even violated a rule, by refusing to work as assigned, so that he could spend his last night in the "cooler," a dark and wretched place in which some convicts had spent not weeks but many months as punishment for infractions. So far as we know, he was the first person to submit himself voluntarily to a stretch of prison life. Many others have tried it since, sometimes with motives like Osborne's, sometimes for reasons more morbid.[33] In the case of Osborne, that week was a necessary prelude to his stormy career as a warden and reformer.

The warden of Auburn had been appointed with Osborne's support. He was well aware that reform of the oppressive Silent System was long overdue. He cooperated with Osborne's proposal for an experiment in prisoner self-government.

The structure for the experiment was the **Mutual Welfare League**, an organization open to membership by all convicts that almost all joined. In a town meeting, 49 were elected to serve on a committee of delegates that was responsible for making rules, judging infractions, and assessing penalties for those found guilty. Excluded from the committee's jurisdiction were those convicted of the offenses of murder, assault, and escape. The League's authority was extended to the industries. Formerly the shops were under the firm supervision of guards. When the League took over the responsibilities of supervision, productivity soared.

It was a success story. Throughout the country there was interest and controversy. Inevitably the conservatives in corrections and the media denounced Osborne and his reform ideas as nothing more than "mollycoddling" criminals who deserved no more than the Silent System had to offer. In the increasingly liberal political environment of the times, though, Osborne's success was convincing to many influential people who shared his belief that whatever prisons do, they should not make prisoners worse when they came out than they were when they went in.

OSBORNE AT SING SING

In 1914 a liberal governor consented to Thomas Osborne's appointment as warden of Sing Sing. He had less than two years to preside over the house that Elam Lynds built, and those years were stormy, even though he successfully installed the Mutual Welfare League and cleaned up a prison that was filthy in management as well as in the most literal sense.

Osborne lived in rough times. His superior, the Superintendent of Prisons, charged him, for reasons that had more to do with politics than with penology, with various derelictions of professional duty, including homosexual affairs with prisoners, for which he was indicted. Outraged, Osborne stood trial and was vindicated. He returned to his duties at Sing Sing—from which he had been relieved while under indictment—served for three months, and then resigned. Two years later, he was appointed superintendent of the naval prison at Portsmouth, New Hampshire, where he installed the Mutual Welfare League with success. The naval establishment, accustomed to a more rigorous penology, was by no means pleased with his innovations, but with the support of Franklin D. Roosevelt, then the Assistant Secretary of the Navy, he was allowed to persevere. Because nearly all of the naval offenders were restored to duty without further incident, criticism abated. It was war time, and the navy needed all the able-bodied enlisted men that it could get.

At Portsmouth, Osborne was assisted by Austin McCormick, who was later to go on to a long and illustrious career as a prison administrator, scholar, and reformer. For many years he was the director of the Osborne Association, named after his patron, and engaged in "professionalizing" the prison management. His influence on prison administration was profound. Many of his disciples went on to distinguished careers of their own, thus continuing the optimistic Osborne tradition.

Prisoner self-government is an idea that has come and gone. With the leadership of a charismatic and determined personality like Osborne, it undoubtedly was effective in maintaining a climate of optimism and relative tranquility. Unfortunately, few men and women with Osborne's vigor and qualities of insight and empathy find their way into correctional facilities. The Mutual Welfare League does not lend itself to bureaucratic oversight. Remnants of the concept are found here and there in Inmate Advisory Councils, elective groups set up by wardens who use them as sounding boards through which to assess the fluctuations of attitudes within the prison community. They are seldom allowed a fraction of the authority Osborne conferred on his Mutual Welfare League.[34]

Far from the "mollycoddling" of which Osborne was so often accused, the regimen at Auburn was aimed at order through responsibility. Taking a phrase from the English statesman William Gladstone, he adopted as his maxim, "It is liberty alone that fits men for liberty."[35] It followed then that the principles on which criminal justice should be based were these:

> First—The law must decree not punishment, but temporary exile from society until the offender has proven by his conduct that he is fit to return.
> Second—Society must brand no man as a criminal; but aim solely to reform the mental conditions under which a criminal act has been committed.
> Third—The prison must be an institution where every inmate must have the largest practicable amount of individual freedom because "it is liberty alone that fits men for liberty."[36]

Like that Declaration of Principles of the National Prison Association in 1870, these were brave words, but impossible for the inheritors of the Elam Lynds tradition to follow. Nevertheless, the seeds had been planted, and what came to be known as the **rehabilitative ideal** can be traced to Osborne's thought, eloquence, and example.

THE MEDICAL MODEL OF CORRECTIONS: ORIGINS AND CONTRADICTIONS

Throughout the middle years of the twentieth century, progressive rhetoric about corrections stressed a "**medical model**" of prison management. The contrast between the treatment-oriented prison and the "warehouse for convicts" regularly entered into penological oratory with little concern for a strict definition of terms. Many correctional authorities foresaw a time when the diagnosis and treatment of criminals would match the successes of modern medicine. The prison would become an analogue to the hospital. Cures would be found for most if not all forms of criminal behavior.

It is impossible to trace these notions to a single source. One of the earliest pioneers of the treatment-prison was Howard B. Gill (1889–1989), whose sad story contains several lessons that might have been foreseen by the distinguished criminologists who flocked to his side during his brief heyday but failed to advise him on the probable outcome of his experiments.

In 1927 the Massachusetts legislature appropriated funds to build a new prison to supplement the ancient and crowded facility at Charlestown. To economize on construction, convict labor was used. Gill had unusual credentials to supervise the project. He was a graduate of Harvard and the Harvard School of Business. Although young, he had already acquired a reputation as an efficiency expert while working for Herbert Hoover in the federal Department of Commerce. He had also written a well-regarded study of prison industries.

The first task was to build a wall around a collection of old buildings that was to serve as the nucleus of the new prison—to become famous as the Norfolk Prison Colony. The wall was to be formidable—19 feet high and, to discourage tunnelers, embedded 4 to 18 feet deep.[37] The work went well. Gill had not intended an unconventional innovation in penology, but as the project continued, he was impressed with the diligence and effectiveness of the convict laborers. He became convinced that he could take steps to divert the course of corrections from the traditions of the Silent System still prevailing in Massachusetts.

He proposed that the Norfolk Prison Colony be committed to the rehabilitation of offenders by creating a prison community in which convicts would lead as nearly normal lives as possible given the conditions of confinement. The Commissioner of Corrections was supportive, foundation grants were solicited and obtained to supplement the state's budget for the institution, and Gill was on his way. Because of the great interest in the potential of the project to produce criminological research, Gill agreed to keep a "diary" of the institution in which he and his senior staff recorded major events and their ideas about the progress of the program. It has proved to be a unique mine of information about initial successes and the eventual collapse of Norfolk as a "treatment-prison."

Gill published an *Official Manual of the State Prison Colony*, which opened with a "Statement of Fundamental Policies":

> Norfolk seeks not only to guard securely the men committed to its safekeeping, but as a fundamental policy to assume its responsibility for returning them to society . . . as better men capable of leading useful, law-abiding lives.[38]

Who could object to such a goal? Gill seems to have recognized that there were problems in reconciling custody and rehabilitation, but he was confident that it could be done. Each man was to be regarded as an individual with problems of his own with which he needed help from both staff and his fellow prisoners. He was explicit about the prison's function to cure criminals.

> Sometimes I liken a prison to a great social hospital in which there are men with all manner of diseases—the seriously sick, the men with minor ailments, the men who will get well in a short time, the men who will never get well. . . . The things which the hospital considers elementary we look upon as revolutionary.[39]

He carried the hospital metaphor much farther. Hospitals had to diagnose before treatment could be initiated, so he devised a classification system for sorting out the "diseases" from which his inmates suffered. This was the "**SCAMP**" system, which was to become briefly famous. It was an acronym for five categories of convicts:

> *Situational:* . . . the man whose circumstances and situation are at the bottom of his difficulties. . . . Clear up the situation and he no longer tends to be a criminal.
>
> *Custodial:* They are the subnormal, the very abnormal, the old, the senile, the unfit . . . beyond treatment who will always need supervision. . . .
>
> *Asocial Cases:* They have a philosophy which is anti-social. . . . That group of criminals who need to develop a new philosophy . . . those in which . . . gangster activities, racketeering, professional criminal practices seem to be the chief factors. . . .
>
> *Medical Cases:* Men who are primarily criminals because they are physically unable to make the grade. . . . These are handicapped, deformed, tubercular . . . who have become criminals mainly by reason of their afflictions.
>
> *Personality Cases:* In this class come the psychotics, neurotics, peculiar personalities, who have fallen into crime. . . . [A]ll cases where personality difficulties play the major part in leading the man into crime . . . in which the man's personal problem had ended to get him crosswise with other people.[40]

Gill thought that rehabilitation would be the goal of all these categories except the custodial. The hitch was that treatment modalities had yet to be formulated for the four classes for whom social restoration would be the goal. He was convinced that with social casework methods of diagnosis and therapy, most of them could be helped. Physicians would treat the medical cases, psychiatrists would administer therapy to the personality cases, teachers would be responsible for the asocials, situationals would be the responsibility of the social workers, and the custodials would be for the police and "caretakers" to control.

Just as trial and error in the practice of medicine determined the effectiveness of treatment of disease, experience in the treatment-prison would eventually create a body of knowledge about successful approaches to the rehabilitation of the four categories of offenders. Gill thought he knew where to start and expected that as the years went on the Norfolk Prison Colony would be a fountain of correctional expertise.

The commitment to casework led to an innovative organization of staff. Within the walls, "house officers" were responsible for institutional operations. They would counsel the prisoners, live with them, and be responsible for all aspects of the program except the security of the institution. They would not wear uniforms, and neither would the inmates themselves.

Security was assigned to uniformed guards who would have no contact with prisoners except in the prevention of escapes, the control of contraband, and intervention in disturbances. They would occupy towers on the prison wall and man a formidable arsenal of machine guns, rifles, and tear gas. On top of the wall were four strands of electrified barbed wire. Gill was convinced that only the utmost security would ensure that freedom within the walls could be maintained—"places without a wall have to maintain such a stringent, strict system that psychological conditions are worse than with a wall." How he came to this conclusion is not in the record.

The SCAMP classification system was supplemented by a security classification. The men were grouped according to "their attitude and cooperation in carrying out their *individual programs*, and to the extent to which they can be relied upon to take active part in the *community program*."[41] A lucky few were graded A-1 because they were "entirely cooperative and trustworthy." Next were the A-2's, "who were getting something out of Norfolk and supporting the community program." The Class A men were afforded the greatest privileges. The B class consisted of B-1's "who did not give full cooperation" and B-2's who were "not carrying out and not supporting the program and who cannot be trusted in the dormitory units, or for whom there is no room in the dormitory units." The bottom of the barrel was occupied by the C's, who were disciplinary problems requiring custodial supervision. They were confined to steel cells in the Receiving Unit, through which all newcomers were processed and where rule violators were retained in "jail."

This system was rationalized as facilitating treatment. There would be incentives to move from the less eligible classes to those that enjoyed maximum privileges. The reality was that necessity required reversion to traditional classification. The SCAMP scheme was subordinate to security. Regardless of their need for treatment, some men were dangerous to others, some were more of a nuisance, some were not acceptable to other inmates. As it was impossible to overlook these contradictions, the ABC system protected "the safety and security of the institution." The months went by, and security became more and more the prime concern. The director of social work noted in the institution diary that "the criterion is not so much 'What is the man doing in his program?' as 'How much of a risk is he to the security of the institution?' "

Few of the house officers had any background in social casework. This deficiency was compounded by the role conflict that their assignment called for. They were supposed to be confidants and advisers to the men in their caseloads, all of whom were well aware that detailed jackets (records) were kept on their cases. The information they divulged to their caseworkers would inevitably make its way to the decision-making staff and eventually to the parole board.[42] A-1 inmates might disclose attitudes that would demote them to less privileged ranks and thus delay paroles. In effect, the caseworkers were supposed to be double agents with divided loyalties. It was an impossible role to play, as correctional counselors and probation and parole officers have subsequently found to their discomfiture.

Gill became disillusioned. After a year of difficulties and disappointments, Gill wrote in the institutional "diary":

> It seems impossible that prisons will ever serve as an adequate means of handling the problems of crime. We think of them now as places in which criminals should be confined for reformation. . . . I wonder if we shall not come to another concept. . . . Reliance will be had upon supervision within the community itself as the real corrective. . . . The thought that we can build a community prison which approximates the normal is faint hope.[43]

And that came from a man who a year before had held that Norfolk would be as close an approximation as possible to a real community in the free world. A few days after that diary entry, a team of inmates was discovered in a nearly successful attempt to escape by tunneling under the wall. Three months later two other inmates managed to complete an escape by scaling the supposedly insuperable wall.

Matters went from bad to worse. Severe punishment was imposed on the tunnelers, the number of cells for class C prisoners was increased, and disorders became increasingly frequent. Somehow there was a drunken Christmas Eve party in 1934 followed by a food strike. Gill was dismissed. A new superintendent took charge. At first he tried to maintain the commitment to rehabilitation, but in 1936 the attempt was abandoned. Norfolk became just another prison in the Massachusetts system. See Box 4-2 for an evaluation of the Norfolk experiment in prison reform.

MODERN MANAGEMENT AND CORRECTIONS

While the novelties introduced by Osborne and Gill were attracting the attention of optimistic reformers and academics and then flickering out, most American prisons were continuing the practice of heavy-handed restraint. The lockstep shuffle, the strap, and solitary confinement were characteristic legacies of Elam Lynds. It was the federal government which slowly led the way to standards of penal care that eventually outlawed the hideous practices of the nineteenth century. Along with humanizing corrections, reforms of the federal prisons were accompanied by an administrative style compatible with the standards of other agencies of government. That was a necessary change from the past haphazard management of federal prisons. It also made possible the important changes in practice that have taken place from the 1930s to the present time.

In the mid-1920s, James V. Bennett, a World War I veteran and a fledgling lawyer, took a generalist civil service examination, passed, and was assigned to the Bureau of Efficiency. This was an independent agency, a forerunner of the Office of Management and Budget, that was created to make sense of the jumbled federal bureaucracy. Eventually Bennett was assigned to the Department of Justice to study

Box 4-2 The Norfolk Story

At the beginning, Norfolk was a magnet for criminologists not only in the United States but also from Europe. Expectations ran high, particularly because of Gill's explicit commitment to the rehabilitation of offenders. His dismissal and the gradual demise of the system were attributed by many to politics and the opposition of correctional traditionalists. Nevertheless, hindsight discovers faults in his design and subsequent operations that presage the failure of many later innovations. The Norfolk story is worth examination for an understanding of the fundamental practical dilemmas of penology.

First, Gill was a bright and attractive person with a record of youthful successes that gave him and many others confidence that his abilities as a manager would compensate for his inexperience in dealing with convicts and his lack of training in psychology or social work. Throughout the record of his administration at Norfolk, his honesty and candor are evident. So was his blindness to the effects of coercion on those he hoped to rehabilitate.

Second, low salaries, political influence on appointments, and uncertainty about the qualifications needed for work as the house officers prevented Gill from making suitable appointments to these positions that were so crucial to his plan.

Third, the criteria for admission to Norfolk excluded nobody. From the first, unmanageable "asocials" were mixed in with situational, custodial, medical, and personality cases. So much time and attention had to be devoted to security that the sense of a more or less democratic community declined into a repressive and explicitly coercive state of affairs.

Some of the conditions that led to Norfolk's failure were preventable. A more experienced administrator with more money to spend on staff could have avoided many mistakes. If Gill had had more background in psychology and in the management of prisons, he surely would have been more selective in his intake policies.

Nevertheless, the Norfolk story vividly exposes the contradictions between the necessities of coercion and the requirements of rehabilitation that have bedeviled correctional workers in all their efforts to live up to the rehabilitative ideal. As we will see in chapters to come, there have been some modest successes in resolving this conflict. It is a conflict that must still be faced. Some administrators have understood it and have devised ways to minimize the damage, thereby giving the field some reason to believe that a firm but humane system can prevail. Until then, the history of Norfolk deserves attention for the lessons it has to impart.

the federal prisons. It was thought that the government could save money by putting idle prisoners to work. Bennett had no previous experience in criminal justice, but he took care to learn as much as he could about what was being done in prisons and why. He concluded that "'what progress had been achieved was the work of men of action."[44] He familiarized himself with the achievements of John Howard, the ideas of Cesare Beccaria, the reforms of Alexander Maconochie, and the innovations of Zebulon Brockway and Thomas Osborne. In short, he became a well-informed penologist. Then he set to work to see how the federal prisons were run.

There were three: McNeil Island in Washington state, Leavenworth in Kansas, and Atlanta. There was a superintendent of prisons in the Department of Justice, with a supporting staff of a dozen or so bookkeepers, clerks, and inspectors. The wardens, however, were political appointees, more accountable to the senators of the states in which their prisons were located than to the superintendent in Washington and, in fact, feudal princes like their counterparts in most of the state prisons.

In due course Bennett submitted a series of reports. In his first report he outlined the outrageous conditions he had found in the nation's prisons and jails. He went on to recommend that Congress create a prison bureau with full powers to administer the federal prisons. Three new penitentiaries should be built, as well as "narcotics farms" in which addicts could be treated separately from convicts.

He stressed that the objectives of the bureau should be to humanize prison management and programs and to set an example to the prison reform movement. The new system should be aimed at the rehabilitation of offenders. He ended with the hope that his report would "afford a basis for crystallizing thought, and cause at least a few to devote passing attention to the human scrap heap."[45]

In a second report, he urged that prisoners be put to work in prison industries. Convicts would work full time and would be offered vocational and academic education in their spare hours.

Those were times when a very young man, still in his early thirties, could move rapidly up the civil service ladder. As a result of his survey, Bennett was invited to draft bills for Congress to enact and put his recommendations into effect. This was completed in 1930. Sanford Bates, then the commissioner of corrections in Massachusetts, was appointed the director of the new bureau, and Bennett was assigned as his assistant.

With the advent of the Franklin D. Roosevelt administration in 1933, the Bureau of Prisons was authorized to proceed with a long-range program of development. Although Bates was a Republican, he was retained as director by the Democratic administration. Austin McCormick, who had been Thomas Osborne's understudy at the Portsmouth naval prison, became the assistant director for the program, and Bennett was assistant director for prison industry.

With the resignation of Bates in 1937, Bennett became the director of the Bureau, a position that he held until his retirement in 1967. A self-confident executive, a man with the political skill to translate his convictions into realities, he began by making the Bureau of Prisons a system. In the first place, he held, not all convicts should be confined in maximum security prisons. Medium and minimum security facilities were constructed. It also had to be recognized that the federal prison population included some unusually difficult and notorious prisoners, such as Scarface Al Capone and Machine Gun Kelly, whose presence in ordinary prisons distracted convicts from self-improvement: Instead of concentrating on their programs, they tried to curry favor with these and other famous gangsters for future preferment in organized crime after their release. To reduce such men to ordinary size, the Bureau had acquired Alcatraz Island, formerly an army disciplinary barracks, in 1934. It remained until 1963 as the repository for the men considered most dangerous in the system. Because it was an anachronism in a prison system intended to be humane, Bennett had long wanted to close it down. At long last, because of the enormous cost of maintaining it for the confinement of fewer than 300 convicts, it was closed down, and its function as a super–maximum security facility was taken over by a new prison at Marion, Illinois.

From the first, Bennett was convinced that prisoners needed work to do. Idle convicts were likely to be disorderly and were certainly not going to be better men when released. To put prisoners to work in industries at a time when millions were unemployed during the Great Depression was not a popular goal. Legislation was passed by Congress to prohibit interstate shipment of prison-made goods. Bennett conceived of a way around these statutory obstacles—a government corporation, with its own capital and operating funds to manage prison industries manufacturing products for use by the federal government. The Federal Prison Industries has been a profitable corporation from the start, turning a share of its profits over to the Treasury every year while paying substantial wages to the convicts it employs. Unfortunately, state prison systems have so far been unable to emulate the federal example.

One of the original intentions of the legislation establishing the Bureau was to create an example of systematic control and management for state prison systems to follow. To a considerable extent that objective has been met. The line-and-staff organizational model of the Bureau's management is in place in most of the state prison systems. The classification of prisoners and their assignment according to custodial risk is generally practiced, sometimes well, sometimes through lip service. The commitment to rehabilitation, fundamental in Bennett's view, has been weakened by developments that will be discussed in succeeding chapters, but most of the programs of academic and vocational education are available in most state prisons. Hardly any state enjoys the benefit of a prospering prison industry, but there are few administrators who do not hope for the day when convicts can be put to realistic work on an eight-hour day and paid in real cash instead of in cigarette money or "good time." It will be seen in later chapters that several state systems have been responsible for innovations that have been widely copied. Their institutionalization as standard practice are due to the existence of administrative systems capable of recruiting personnel to carry them out and to control the setting in which they are undertaken. For the example of such a system, the Bureau of Prisons has served corrections well.

CONCLUSIONS

In this chapter we have raced through a history of the complete overhaul of penology. From the heritage of Captain Lynds to the mountaintop at Cincinnati in 1870 was a magnificent leap from the human scrap heap maintained in prisons throughout the nation to the high hopes of Zebulon Brockway and his associates. We have seen that the vision of the 1870 zealots was disappointed by attempts to put it into daily practice. In large part these programs were frustrated by the lack of supporting systems to lend stability to corrections. The advent of the Bureau of Prisons and the state systems modeled on the Bureau have made realities out of most of the ideals of 1870. At the same time, the Bureau profited from the disappointed hopes of men like Brockway, Osborne, and Gill. The model of corrections that we now have in place throughout the country makes it possible for reformers to work within a system rather than as lonely outsiders.

There will never be a correctional utopia, and humanitarians, academics, and cost–benefit analysts will always find many things wrong in any prison system. What we have learned in the decades since 1870 is that prisons can be managed humanely and efficiently—if the American public will allow the essential requirements for policy and practice.

KEY TERMS

Borstal system

Declaration of Principles

Elmira Plan

medical model

Mutual Welfare League

prisoner self-government

reformatory movement

rehabilitative ideal

SCAMP

DISCUSSION TOPICS

4.1 Did the 1870 Declaration of Principles bring about any immediate improvements in correctional administration? What was their significance in the long run?

4.2 From all accounts, Crofton's Irish plan was an outstanding success. Brockway, who tried to emulate him, had to confess failure. What did he do wrong?

4.3 If John Augustus's claims of success with his probationers were valid, what factors might have contributed to his part in rehabilitating such unpromising offenders?

4.4 Nobody but Thomas Molt Osborne seems to have succeeded with inmate self-government. What accounts for his unique success?

4.5 What are the essential elements of the "medical model" of corrections? Do you see any serious flaws in the concept?

4.6 As described in Box 4-1, the Borstal system in England was a remarkable success. Could it have been transplanted to this country? If so, what modifications would have been necessary?

ANNOTATED REFERENCES

Eriksson, Torsten. *The Reformers.* Trans. Catherine Djurklou. New York: Elsevier, 1976. *Eriksson was for many years the director of the Swedish prison system. A reformer himself, he was interested in the movement for prison reform throughout the world. His sketches of the major reformers were thumbnail size, but his judgments were well stated and liberal.*

Fox, Lionel W. *The English Prison and Borstal Systems.* London: Routledge & Kegan Paul, 1952. *Fox was an administrator who wrote in his spare time about the system he administered. He was also a historian with an eye for what in the past was relevant to an understanding of the present.*

McConville, Seán. *A History of English Prison Administration.* London: Routledge & Kegan Paul, 1981. *This is the first volume of a history that will carry its topic down to the present time. McConville begins with the antecedents in the Middle Ages and carries his subject through the development of modern administrative control of the English prison system. Future volumes will cover the various innovations that have been tried in the late nineteenth and the twentieth centuries.*

McGee, Richard A. *Prisons and Politics.* Lexington, Mass.: Lexington Books, 1981. *These are the observations of a prison administrator looking back over a long career in which he was director of the prison systems of New York City, Washington state, and California. Valuable for a perspective from a reflective manager, it contains particularly useful accounts of the realities of corrections in the 1930s and 1940s.*

McKelvey, Blake. *American Prisons: A Study in American Social History Prior to 1915.* University of Chicago Press, 1936. *McKelvey is a valuable source on the first National Prison Congress of 1870.*

Rothman, David. *The Discovery of the Asylum Social Order and Disorder in the New Republic.* Boston: Little, Brown, 1971.

———. *Conscience and Convenience: The Asylum and Its Alternatives in Progressive America.* Boston: Little, Brown, 1980. *In these two volumes Rothman, a historian, explores the history of the institutionalization of social deviants, including criminal offenders. Most of the work in these volumes is concerned with almshouses for the poor and asylums for the insane, but there are excellent chapters on the invention of the penitentiary and on Howard Gill's attempted innovations at Norfolk.*

NOTES

1. Hayes's interest was much more than nominal. When he retired from the White House, he accepted the presidency of the National Prison Association and continued in that role for ten years—the rest of his life.
2. Blake McKelvey, *American Prisons: A Study in American Social History Prior to 1915* (University of Chicago Press, 1936), p. 71.
3. Throughout the nineteenth century, British penal terminology referred to prisons for felons as "convict-prisons," as distinguished from "local prisons" for misdemeanants that were under the jurisdiction of county officials until 1877, when they were transferred to the Home Office.
4. The first Penal Servitude Act was passed in 1853, substituting penal servitude for transportation, and providing that four years in prison was equivalent to seven at Botany Bay or Tasmania.
5. Sir Evelyn Ruggles-Brise, *The English Prison System* (London: Macmillan, 1921), pp. 26–27.
6. Sir Lionel W. Fox, *The English Prison and Borstal Systems* (London: Routledge & Kegan Paul, 1952), p. 36. Fox, the humane and progressive chairman of the British Prison Commission for many years, was writing as a historian, not advocating a principle.
7. For appalling particulars concerning the use of the treadmill and the crank in English prisons, see George Ives, *A History of Penal Methods* (London: Stanley Paul, 1914), pp. 188–194.
8. This task was commonly assigned in nineteenth-century English prisons and workhouses. It consisted of disentangling discarded rope to make caulking of ships' seams, stoppers for

leaks, and sometimes for bandages for wounds. It was said to be tedious work, requiring endless patience.

9. For details of little interest to anyone but a penological antiquarian, see Mary Carpenter, *Reformatory Prison Discipline, as Developed by the Rt. Hon. Sir Walter Crofton* (London: Longmans, Green, Reader and Dyer, 1872), pp. 5–22. A briefer account will be found in Torsten Eriksson, *The Reformers*, trans. Catherine Djurklou (New York: Elsevier, 1976), pp. 91–97.
10. Carpenter, *Reformatory Prison Discipline*, p. 11, quoting from Crofton's pamphlet "Convict Systems and Transportation," published in 1863.
11. Ibid.
12. For an account of Jebb's criticisms of the Irish system, see Seán McConville, *A History of English Prison Administration* (London: Routledge & Kegan Paul, 1981), vol. I, pp. 441–443. From McConville's account, Jebb felt personally affronted by the favorable reports of the Irish system, but his objections were never specific.
13. McKelvey, *American Prisons*, p. 144. See also Eriksson, *The Reformers*, for a clear and coherent account of the Elmira regimen. See also Brockway's autobiography, *Fifty Years of Prison Service* (Montclair, N.J.: Patterson Smith, 1969; reprint of the original edition of 1912). These are the rambling memoirs of a very old man, with many anecdotes but few data.
14. For a condensed version of this landmark speech see Brockway, *Fifty Years*, pp. 389–408.
15. Ibid., p. 391.
16. The account of Brockway's proposed system is abridged from his speech and can be found on pp. 396–399 of his autobiography, *Fifty Years of Prison Service.*
17. Ibid., p. 400.
18. Readers will recall from Chapter 3 that it took Elam Lynds only three years, employing a complement of 100 prisoners and 3 craftsmen, to build Sing Sing.
19. C. R. Henderson, *Penal and Reformatory Institutions* (New York: Charities Publication Committee, 1910), p. 102.
20. McKelvey, *American Prisons*, p. 71, quoting from the *Proceedings* of the National Prison Association, 1887.
21. To ensure that the least possible pain would result from a flogging, he soaked the strap to be used in water so that it would not cut the miscreant young man.
22. Erikkson, *The Reformers*, p. 104.
23. Ruggles-Brise, *The English Prison System*, p. 91.
24. Harry Elmer Barnes and Negley K. Teeters, *New Horizons in Criminology* (New York: Prentice-Hall, 1942; revised edition 1945), pp. 555–556.
25. Sheldon Glueck and Eleanor T. Glueck, *500 Criminal Careers* (New York: Knopf, 1930). The results of their study will be found in chaps. X, XI, and XV, pp. 165–203 and 224–238.
26. See James A. Leonard, "Reformatory Methods and Results," in Henderson, p. 127: ". . . at least three out of four young men discharged from reformatory institutions refrain from crime and become helpful members of society." Leonard was at the time the superintendent of Ohio's Mansfield State Reformatory.
27. Glueck and Glueck, *500 Criminal Careers*, p. 184.
28. Ibid., p. 315.
29. First published in 1852. Now available in a bicentennial edition, published by the American Probation and Parole Association, 1984, with a preface by Milton G. Rector and a foreword, to a 1939 edition, by Sheldon Glueck.
30. Ibid., pp. 4–5.
31. Augustus inserted into his "Report" some hostile letters accusing him of somehow enriching himself from the proceeds of his philanthropy, though the writers hadn't explained how he might have profited.

32. Ibid., pp. xxxiv–xxxv.
33. For Osborne's own account of that memorable week, see his *Within Prison Walls* (New York: Appleton, 1914; republished by Patterson Smith, 1969). The book is summarized in Rudolph W. Chamberlain's *There Is No Truce* (New York: Macmillan, 1935), pp. 241–260. We have drawn from this biography for most of the information presented here on Osborne's life and achievements.
34. For an admiring though mildly critical view of Osborne's achievements at Sing Sing, written by a successor as warden, see Lewis E. Lawes, *Twenty Thousand Years at Sing Sing* (New York: Long & Smith, 1932), pp. 105–107. Lawes credits Osborne with having "introduced the prison to the public" by his books and lectures.
35. Gladstone was referring to home rule for Ireland. Osborne held that what was true for a nation was also true for individuals.
36. Quoted by Chamberlain, *There Is No Truce*, p. 237, from Osborne's address to the 1906 Congress of the National Prison Association.
37. Nonetheless, there were two tunneling adventures during Gill's administration of the Norfolk Colony.
38. As quoted in David J. Rothman, *Conscience and Convenience: The Asylum and Its Alternatives in Progressive America* (Boston: Little, Brown, 1980), p. 385. We have drawn from Rothman's account of the Norfolk experiment for much of this discussion. Rothman's extensive quotations, some of which we use here, were extracted from the 700-page institutional "diary" that Gill and his senior staff kept. Although Rothman is severely critical of Gill and his program, he is scrupulous to document his criticisms by references to the diary.
39. Ibid., pp. 386–387.
40. Ibid., pp. 391–392.
41. Ibid., pp. 395–396.
42. Actually, the parole board members were too busy or too indolent to thumb through the pages of progress reports contained in the inmate files.
43. Ibid., p. 413.
44. James V. Bennett, *I Chose Prison* (New York: Knopf, 1970), p. 61. Bennett's memoirs ramble over a long and distinguished career as director of the Bureau of Prisons and constitute an invaluable account of the development of contemporary penology.
45. Ibid., p. 84.

Chapter

5

The Goals of Punishment

CHAPTER OUTLINE

The tasks of a nation-state, even a repressive or corrupt state, are to serve its people, not to harm them. States defend citizens against foreign enemies, educate their children, provide for their health, and perform such beneficial services as the people or their rulers decide may be needed. Because of ideology, poverty, or other factors, some states provide very few of these services. Others are committed to providing for their citizens "from the cradle to the grave." Of the agencies of the state, only the criminal justice system is designed to do harm to a class of citizens, men and women who have committed acts that their rulers or the citizens themselves have defined, by the laws they enact, as criminal. The harm that is done to criminals is punishment, of course, and few law-abiding citizens question its propriety. Even criminals, for the most part, concede that punishment is necessary and usually just. Punishment is the task of correctional systems. Its justification calls for close attention by all who are concerned with the fair and humane treatment of offenders.

The nature and extent of the harm inflicted on offenders is a matter of indifference to rulers in countries where services are minimal. Where the welfare of the people is the first consideration of social policy, not only is harm minimized but there are efforts to make the experience of punishment as beneficial as possible. As we shall see in later chapters, whether these efforts have succeeded has been much questioned in recent years.

In this chapter we will introduce our readers to a discourse that is many centuries old. The basic question in this discourse is: Is the goal of punishment to provide retribution for past offenses or to prevent the commission of new crimes? This basic question has several additional questions contained within it: Why do we punish? How can we justify punishment? What crimes call for punishment? How severely should we punish? Box 5-1 shows that the reasons for the answers we give, as well as the answers themselves, are not as simple as the questions.

Many sages have influenced both thought and action. Change has been slow, but most of the ancient horrors have been expunged. A common thread remains: Those who offend against others or against society must be punished. To this day, some hold that all punishment must be so severe as to deter both the individual and society at large from the commission of crime. Others are certain that the severities of criminal justice serve only to increase criminality.

From remote antiquity, the state has been responsible for the punishment of criminals. In the beginning the object was to prevent the disorder, violence, and terrible injustices of revenge carried out by victims of crimes and their clan. Early religious prophets and leaders defined crimes as offenses against God and ordained severe punishments—more severe than modern codes allow—for violations of divine laws.[1] Blasphemy, heresy, and impiety were proscribed, but so were many of the offenses that men and women of our time accept as crimes.

Down to recent times, even in the United States, family feuds arising from ancient wrongs have resulted in murders of tribal enemies whose responsibility for whatever wrong was done many decades before was limited to having the wrong family name. The now-legendary Hatfields and McCoys fired their last shots at one another in the second decade of the twentieth century, persisting in an Appalachian feud that had begun shortly after the Civil War. No one really knows what set these two families and their supporters into lethal conflict. In this bloody and foolish history, it is clear that the states of West Virginia and Kentucky could not enforce the law in these out-of-the-way localities for many decades. Right and wrong depended on which family had more firepower. To this day, tribal warfare of this kind, based on forgotten incidents from the distant past, cause death and destruction in remote lands to which the state's authority does not extend.[2]

Justice must be done, not by an aggrieved clan, but by the impersonal state. One of the earliest characteristics of a civilized state was the recognition that justice could not be done by people carrying out vengeance for wrongs committed against them, no matter how grievous those wrongs were. As many commentators on nineteenth-century criminology remarked, it is salutary that criminals should be hated, and not only by their victims.[3] That hatred must be expressed in the criminal procedure, not by victims taking the law into their own hands nor by mobs exercising lynch justice. Wrongdoers must be accused, must have their day in court, and must be formally found guilty and subjected to punishment by the state.

Box 5-1 Billy and the Goals of Justice

On the blackboard the differing goals of criminal justice are easy to comprehend, if not always easy to reconcile. In the courtroom as a conscientious judge struggles to make a reasoned disposition of a tormented youth, too often there seems to be no good answer available. Consider the case of Billy, a real defendant whose plight is narrated in an unpublished paper by John P. Conrad.

> Last year, the Franklin County [Ohio] public defender asked me to testify in a juvenile court hearing to determine whether a 17-year-old whom I shall call Billy should be bound over to an adult criminal court for trial. Billy stood accused of the robbery and murder of a 72-year-old man, an offense that, on the face of it, was guaranteed to mobilize a maximum of antipathy for the defendant. It transpired that there was more to the story than met the eye.
>
> Billy was one of a fairly large family of Appalachian antecedents living on the margins of the economy. His parents had been more often on welfare than not. Poor managers, they had been unable to provide their children with more than subsistence. Love and harmony were rarely manifest in a home chiefly remarkable for violence. Billy recalled having been beaten with electric cords, straps, belts, sticks, broom handles, and boards from early childhood. This kind of discipline went on until one day, when he was 14, his mother came at him in a fury, armed with a plank with which she was going to beat him. He knocked her out. From that time on he was mostly on his own.
>
> School had been an arena of defeat. He had great difficulty in reading and was eventually found to be dyslexic—neurologically impaired so that letters did not arrive in his brain in intelligible order for words to be made out of them. He learned to think of himself as a dummy, the word that other kids applied to him. School records noted that by the time he was 9, he had taken to sniffing glue, which certainly did not improve his nervous system. When he was 14, he dropped out, perhaps because of his unrelieved scholastic failures, perhaps because of his assault on his mother.
>
> He took to hanging around, sometimes in the company of an uncle 14 years older who introduced him to homosexual practices. It was not long before he was earning 20 dollars a trick as a prostitute. A large portion of his earnings was spent on various uppers and downers and marijuana. He does not seem to have used "heavy stuff."
>
> One of his customers was the old man who was the victim in this offense. It is hard to be sure about the events that took place on the Fourth of July weekend last summer. Billy and his uncle spent the holiday at the old man's apartment. They drank heavily and smoked pot. As they became more and more drunk, conviviality turned into acrimony. They ran out of beer, and the old man told Billy to go out and get some more, calling him a dummy and a punk as he issued the order. The police account alleged that in a rage Billy attacked him with his fists, knocked him flat, and then stomped him until the old man succumbed. The pathologist's report showed that the alcoholic content of his blood was so high that death must have been imminent anyway.

Juvenile court jurisdiction in Ohio ends at 18. Billy was 17 and 3 months. The public defender thought the circumstances did not warrant the death penalty, which the county prosecutor was inclined to demand. He was impressed with Billy's vulnerability and concerned about what would probably happen to him in prison. So was I when I interviewed him. He was a slight youth with chestnut blond hair, neatly styled, blue eyes, and a fair, beardless complexion. He spoke haltingly, as though unsure of himself with strangers. A psychologist had elicited an IQ well above average on a nonverbal intelligence test, but he seemed painfully childish. I asked him what he would like to do if he got out of his trouble. He said he wanted to join the army and serve his country. After he had served out his enlistment he would go to Florida and find work as a deep-sea fisherman. He could earn $30,000 a year at that. Last spring a friend had taken him to Florida, and he had liked the climate and the sea. He did not think of himself as a homosexual. He had had lots of girlfriends, but he could make so much money turning tricks with men who fancied boys that he didn't see why he shouldn't.

His dreams about a fisherman's life were based on the hope that he would not be bound over to the Court of Common Pleas as an adult. Committed to the Ohio Youth Commission, he could have been placed in a private facility for treatment if the commission would take the risk.

Such a facility was available. The public defender had interested an entrepreneur of altruism, a man who had accepted the gospel of community-based corrections and had founded a halfway house that he called "Betterway." He had interviewed Billy twice and had convinced himself that Betterway could help him. He testified to that effect at the juvenile court hearing.

The court had three options. If Billy were to be bound over to the Court of Common Pleas and found guilty, he would be committed to prison for life or for a very long term. If jurisdiction were retained in the juvenile court, he would be committed to the Youth Commission if found guilty. The Youth Commission could assign him to one of its more secure facilities. With the approval of the court, the commission could assign him to Betterway.

Ohio prisons in 1979 were overcrowded and underprogrammed. Naturally an effort would be made to protect Billy, but the necessary measures would limit his participation in the educational and remedial programs he needed. In the dense throngs of prisoners, people would get lost. A careful warden would try to keep a pretty youth like Billy out of harm's way, if only to prevent rivals for his favors from doing mortal battle or to prevent him from turning tricks for a prison pimp. Billy would not have been a welcome prisoner. It is inconceivable that he would benefit from incarceration.

The Youth Commission facilities were smaller. Programs relevant to Billy's serious educational and psychological problems were theoretically available. His appearance and immaturity would require a responsible superintendent to take measures to protect him. The willingness of the staff at Betterway to take him on would have struck a responsive chord.

We didn't find out whether Betterway could do as well as we had hoped. The court decided to bind Billy over for trial as an adult. I am certain that the decision was made with regret and concern. The cruel choice was between the child's best interests and the protection of society. Billy stood accused of the most serious of crimes. His background and his personal situation inspired no confidence at all in his ability to change. To argue that he was not dangerous was to dismiss the horrible affair on the Fourth of July, a record of violent family relations, and a life without adult control for the previous three years. If he were to escape from custody, especially if he were to leave Betterway, the court would be subjected to charges of undue leniency and disregard of its duty to protect society. We cannot blame the troubled judge, but we could wish that our powers of social invention could have provided him with a better way to dispose of this pathetic youth. To commit anyone, even the "hardened old repeater," to a long term of years in prison is a hard decision for a conscientious judge. To commit a naïve and beardless boy to such a maelstrom was distressing, no matter how justifiable it might have been.

Three weeks after the juvenile court's decision, Billy hanged himself with a sheet in his cell.

Source: John P. Conrad, "The Hoodlum in the Helpless Society." Unpublished paper delivered at the North Carolina Conference on Juvenile Justice, 1979.

Every modern citizen knows the process, and most of us know what a travesty it can be when the administration of justice falls into the wrong hands. Wrongful accusations can be made by vengeful men and women. Confessions can be extorted by intimidation and torture. Courts have been corrupted by bribery and alliances with antisocial elements in the community. The jails and prisons in which punishment is carried out have too often been theaters of sadism and brutality.

All that conceded, the centuries have gradually transformed criminal justice into a process disciplined by standards. In the nations of the West these standards are too often breached, but more often honored. Their aim is to assure that no innocent person will be punished by mistake, and guilt will be established beyond reasonable doubt before any punishment is inflicted. That is a modest goal, but its achievement is relatively recent in human history. We have seen in our historical chapters that the standards of corrections have gradually emerged from the mindless destructiveness that was universal until late in the nineteenth century. Philosophers and thoughtful jurists have been instrumental in civilizing the prison. This chapter will show how their influence has made a difference.

LOOKING AHEAD OR LOOKING BACK?

The major controversy in justifying punishment is the apparent opposition between society's demand for retribution for past offenses and the goal of prevention of new crimes.

Looking Ahead: Prevention

The most ancient contributor to this debate was the Athenian philosopher Plato (427–347 B.C.), who composed a dialogue in which the main characters were Socrates (470–399 B.C.) and Protagoras (481–411 B.C.), a widely respected sage. In this discourse, Plato laid down this justification for punishment in words attributed to Protagoras:

> Just consider the function of punishment, Socrates, in relation to the wrongdoer. That will be enough to show you that men believe it possible to impart goodness. In punishing wrongdoers, no one concentrates on the fact that a man has done wrong in the past, or punishes him on that account, unless taking blind vengeance like a beast. No, punishment is not inflicted by a rational man for the sake of the crime he has committed—after all, one cannot undo what is past—but for the sake of the future, to prevent either the same man or, by the spectacle of his punishment, someone else, from doing wrong again. But to hold such a view amounts to holding that virtue can be instilled by education; at all events the punishment is inflicted as a deterrent.[4]

In an earlier dialogue, *Gorgias*, Plato had gone so far as to hold that punishment must be inflicted in such a way as to benefit the wrongdoer. Gorgias (483–375 B.C.), a venerable teacher of rhetoric, thought that the happiest man must be the all-powerful tyrant. Socrates disposed of that idea, but one of Gorgias' disciples, Polus, defended his aged master. In the course of the dialogue, this exchange occurs:

> SOCRATES: Where and to whom do we take the sick in body?
> POLUS: To the doctors, Socrates.
> SOCRATES: And the unjust and intemperate?
> POLUS: To the judges, do you mean?
> SOCRATES: To suffer punishment?
> POLUS: Yes.
> SOCRATES: And do not those who punish rightly do so with aid of certain justice?
> POLUS: Obviously.
> SOCRATES: Then money-making rids us of poverty, medicine rids us of sickness, and justice of intemperance and injustice. . . . [O]f two who suffer evil either in body or soul, which is the more wretched, the man who submits to treatment, or he who is not treated but still retains it?
> POLUS: Evidently the man who was not treated.
> SOCRATES: And was not punishment admitted to be a release from the greatest of evils, namely wickedness?
> POLUS: It was.
> SOCRATES: Yes, because a just penalty disciplines us and makes us just and cures us of evil.

The parallels between medicine and justice seem far-fetched to the modern mind, but the point is clear and relevant in our times. A just penalty is still believed to be a wise discipline not only for the offender but also for society as a whole. Socrates does not consider the nature of a just punishment in any of Plato's dialogues. Later, he concludes that

> [If a man] or anyone of those for whom he cares has done wrong, he ought to go on his own accord where he will most speedily be punished, to the judge as though a doctor, in his eagerness to prevent the distemper of evil from being ingrained and producing a festering and incurable ulcer in his soul.[5]

Neither in *Protagoras* nor in *Gorgias* does Plato tell us what kind of treatment the state should administer for the "distemper of evil." The punishment imposed by the judge, whatever it may be, must be accepted to relieve the wrongdoer of guilt. We have seen in Chapter 2 that ancient Greek punishments were severe and callous. They were hardly intended to impart virtue to a wicked offender. The important consideration for Plato is that the consciousness of having done wrong is misery, and the misery is greater when the wrongdoer is not punished.

Many years after these dialogues were written, Plato prepared a long treatise on the laws of a well-conducted city. The *Laws* are the work of an old man, far into his seventies, disillusioned by the train of events in his city but still hopeful that the cultural traditions of Athens and the influence of the wise leaders could overcome the disturbing trends of the times.

In the *Laws* Plato included several statements about punishment that have been influential throughout Western history. Like most later believers in authoritarian government, he held that impiety and heresy were serious crimes, serving to undermine the stability of the city.[6] "Impiety" is not clearly defined but certainly includes blasphemy against the gods, as well as the crimes of predatory and violent persons. Unlike his argument in the earlier dialogues, he was specific about the punishments that should be imposed. They are hardly experiences that such offenders would eagerly seek in order to purge themselves of the "distemper of evil":

> Whosoever shall be taken in sacrilege shall, if slave or alien, have his misfortune branded on hands and forehead, be scourged with such numbers of stripes the court shall think proper, and be cast forth naked beyond the borders. For if he suffer that judgement, he may perchance be made a better man by his correction. For truly judgement by sentence of law is never inflicted for harm's sake. Its normal effect is one of two; it makes him that suffers it a better man, of failing this, less of a wretch. If ever a citizen be detected in gross and horrible crime against the gods, parents, or society, the judge shall treat him as one whose case is already desperate, in view of the education and nurture he has enjoyed from childhood and the depth of shame to which he has sunk. Whence his sentence shall be death, the lightest of ills for him, and he shall serve as an example for the profit of others.[7]

Citizens with the advantages of social position and proper education should be punished more severely than slaves or foreigners—not an unreasonable concept, but one that has never found legislative favor in the real world. Note that the concept of **general deterrence**—the prevention of crime by the example to others—is explicit in this excerpt. Plato does not make it clear how an offender may become better by being branded, scourged, and cast forth naked from the city, but that is the explicit expectation. The offenders' good requires that they be purged by punishment proportional to their crimes. Certainly the citizens observing the consequences of crime as envisaged by Plato would avoid offending if they knew what was good for them.

As for the correctional system itself, Plato proposed one in which there would be three types of facilities. There would be a common jail situated in the marketplace for most offenders. Those whose graver offenses were due to folly rather than viciousness would be sent to a "house of correction" for a term of not less than five years. During that time they would be counseled by senior magistrates "who shall visit them with a view to admonition and their souls' salvation." If at the end of the term the prisoner was "deemed to have returned to his right mind, he shall dwell with the right-minded, but if not and he be condemned a second time on the same charge, he shall suffer the penalty of death." The recidivism of offenders would present no options to the city's judges.

The third class of penal facility was the central prison, to be "in the heart of the country, in the most solitary and wildest situation available and called by some designation suggestive of punishment." The offenders to be confined there would be men who were "beasts of prey" who "do their best to ruin individuals, whole families, and communities." Such culprits would be locked up for the rest of their lives. No free citizen whatsoever would have access to them. Upon their deaths, their corpses would be cast out beyond the borders without burial.[8] Plato does not explain how this treatment would make so vicious an offender "a better man or less of a wretch."

We have dwelt on Plato's thought about punishment for three reasons. First, Plato clearly endorsed the principle that the state must reserve to itself the responsibility of determining guilt and imposing sanctions on offenders. Second, he made it clear that punishment not only had to be justified but also had to be specified. In spite of his vagueness about who should be punished by what means, he insisted that different categories of crime required different levels of "treatment," and that the level should correspond to the seriousness of the offender's condition. Offenders were to be restored to their "right minds," not for the hazy goal of "anul[ing] the wrong they had done." And finally, Plato's view that punishment should serve the objective of prevention rather than "blind vengeance" is the first philosophical contribution to the **utilitarianism** of Jeremy Bentham.

Jeremy Bentham, as we discussed in Chapter 3, was the founding father of the utilitarian school for political philosophy. Moral philosophers have found serious flaws in The Greatest Happiness Principle on which Benthamite utilitarianism is based. The influence of his ideas has survived criticism, although no one now invokes The Greatest Happiness Principle as the basis for social policy. The underlying criterion of utilitarianism, as it has been understood since Bentham, is that acts and laws should be judged by their consequence. In other words, the utilitarian philosophy requires that public policy be useful. Punishment of an offender should bring about consequences that are beneficial to the community he or she has offended, and to the offender, too—by deterrence, incapacitation, or reform.

Bentham's aim in penal jurisprudence was clear: The object of the criminal laws should be to prevent crime, not administer retribution. Criminal justice would prevent crime by three means: Some offenders could be reformed while under the control of the state and would be returned to the community as law-abiding citizens; all offenders would be prevented from committing new offenses while under the restrictions of confinement; and the general public would be deterred by the example of the "mischief"—Bentham's word—administered to the offender. Bentham thought that deterrence might be heightened by the forbidding outward appearance of the prison. He was not averse to conveying the idea of terror in the exterior architecture of the Panopticon, although within this fortress some amenities might relieve the miseries of incarceration.

As we have seen, the Panopticon was not a winning idea, but the utilitarian concept took hold and still stands as the ruling justification of punishment. The prevention of crime is a nobler goal than the administration of vengeance. The limited success of criminal justice in achieving this aim has brought about an uneasy resurgence of retributivism in the interests of justice to the offender whose reform by punishment has not been widely successful.

Looking Back: Retributivism

Retribution was the dominant motive in punishing criminals in Athens, the city in which Plato and Socrates lived. Plato's view that the law should look forward so as to prevent crime was at variance with the idea of punishment as understood by the common man in Athens and everywhere else in those times. The law looked back on what criminals had done and punished them severely and disproportionately. The principle that the punishment should balance the offense is an innovation of later centuries.

Centuries passed. Philosophers in Rome and in the nations that succeeded the Roman Empire devoted much attention to theology and to how reality may be understood but gave little or no thought to what should be done to criminals. The Romans contributed an efficient and durable structure for administering the law but did not bother with the reasons for punishing offenders. The Twelve Tables of republican Rome were adopted without much modification in the Code of Justinian, the sixth-century compilation of civil and criminal law. Even the outlandish punishments that the early Roman legislators prescribed were faithfully included. The *jus talionis*, the law of retaliation, was supposedly the basis for deterring punishment. The state should kill murderers. Other offenders were to be punished with severity comparable to the gravity of their crimes, but the proper severity was difficult to gauge. The *jus talionis* was an uncertain guide.

Throughout the Middle Ages, the Renaissance, the Reformation, and well into the nineteenth century, there was general cultural acceptance of **retribution** as the proper response to crime. It is not easy to account for the savagery of the punishments administered. Grotesque tortures were devised and accepted as necessary to the public safety. Ingenious instruments for the infliction of slow and painful death aroused no serious objection from religious leaders.

To understand how reasonable and humane men and women could accept the severity of the punishments administered for all those centuries, it is necessary to consider the context of the times. Society was divided between a small ruling aristocracy and a vastly larger class of peasants and artisans. For both classes life was precarious. The state could provide the rulers little protection for their lives and property beyond the intimidation of the laws and the force to make intimidation real.

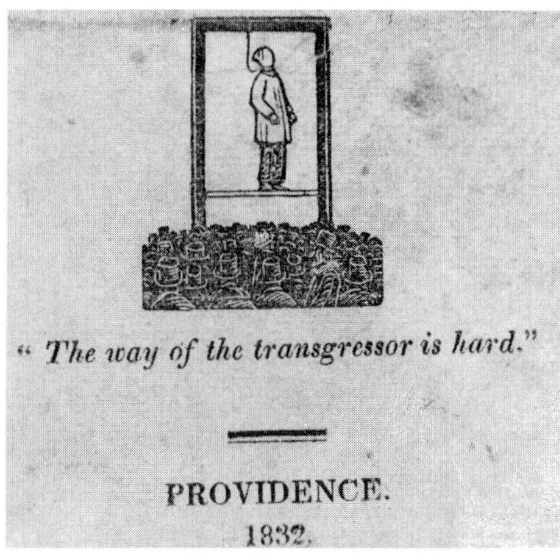

"The way of the transgressor is hard."
PROVIDENCE.
1832.

Punishment and the criminal offender. (*Source:* Warshaw Collection/Archive Center, Smithsonian Institution.)

Even in good times the peasantry and urban workers led lives in which misery was never distant; in bad times they might often starve. The desperation of the poor was obvious to the comfortable rich. Brigands and bandits were common. The terror of the criminal law protected the aristocracy and its property. The governing class viewed the "inferior" classes as made up of truly inferior people who required great severity if they were not to endanger the state. Sympathy for their suffering would be wasted.

For the state, intimidation was a necessary means of social control. There was no organized police. Malefactors were many, and punishments had to be either capital or corporal, sometimes both. There were no prisons in the modern sense. Confinement in the Tower of London or the Bastille in Paris was reserved for defeated rivals for the throne, for those who had incurred royal displeasure, and for political malcontents. Common criminals, when caught and convicted, would be expeditiously sent to the gallows. A humane philosopher might find the necessities of justice distasteful, but as a practical matter, no likely alternatives suggested themselves. The hangman was the bulwark of the state.[9]

The great German philosopher Immanuel Kant (1724–1804) was firm on the moral obligation to punish:

> Judicial punishment can never be used merely as a means to promote some other good for the criminal himself or for civil society, but instead it must in all cases be imposed on him only on the ground that he has committed a crime; for a human being can never be manipulated merely as a means to the purposes of someone else and can never be confused with the objects of the Law of Things [i.e., good or property]. His innate personality, his right as a person, protects him against such treatment, even though he may indeed be condemned to lose his civil personality. He must first be found to be deserving of punishment before any consideration is given to the utility of this punishment for himself or his fellow citizens. The law concerning punishment is a categorical imperative, and woe to him who rummages around in the winding paths of a theory of happiness looking for some advantage to be gained by releasing the criminal from punishment or reducing the amount of it—in keeping with the Pharisaic motto: "It is better that one man should die than that the whole people should perish." If legal justice perishes then it is no longer worthwhile for men to remain alive on this earth.[10]

Kant's reference to the "winding paths of a theory of happiness" was obviously aimed at Jeremy Bentham, whose *Introduction to the Principles of Morals and Legislation*, in which The Greatest Happiness Principle was expounded, had appeared in 1789, eight years before the publication of Kant's *Metaphysics of Morals*.

Kant's view of the human condition required that social policy should never allow for men and women to be used as a means toward an end, unless they were also ends. He stressed that the offender "must first be found guilty and punishable before there can be any thought of drawing from his punishment any benefit for himself or his fellow citizens." To a newcomer to ethics, this position may seem too subtle to be significant. It is more than justified by the abuses of humanity in totalitarian states where dictators justify punishment of dissidents in the interest of removing obstructions on the ideological road to utopia. The contemporary English legal philosopher H. L. A. Hart explains:

> This meant that we are justified in requiring sacrifices from some men for the good of others only in a social system which also recognizes their rights and their interests. In the case of punishment, the right in question is the right of men to be left free and not

> punished for the good of others, unless they have broken the law when they had the capacity and a fair opportunity to conform to its requirements.[11]

Bentham's justifying aim of punishment was the prevention of crime by the reformation, incapacitation, and deterrence of the offender—all very reasonable, but conferring on the state enormous power over the offender. Until the offender can show that he or she is indeed reformed, the state may keep him or her under its control to assure incapacitation for further crime. This reservation did not occur to Bentham or any of his critics, but it has become a formidable argument against the application of utilitarian justice in the late twentieth century. Injustice to the individual is the consequence of treating him or her as a means to the achievement of a social good.

CONTEMPORARY DEBATE

Ever since the 1870 Declaration of Principles, American corrections has been formally committed to the rehabilitation of offenders. After World War II, the commitment was reinforced by the optimism of medical and social scientists. Experience led most correctional officials to conclude that the rehabilitation of any offenders is difficult to achieve, and impossible for many. In the 1970s, reviews of evaluative research confirmed this pessimistic assessment. The result has led to the elimination of many programs, and the commitment of many correctional agencies to policies of retribution and control. In this section we examine the events that brought about the rejection of the rehabilitative ideal and the renewal of the age-old debate between retributive and utilitarian punishment philosophies.

The Rehabilitative Ideal Under Attack

Rehabilitative philosophy had its heyday in the 1940s and the 1950s. In the national euphoria that followed the victorious end of World War II, all things looked possible, even the rehabilitation of convicted felons. To carry out rehabilitative programs, forward-looking correctional systems hired teachers, psychologists, social workers, and psychiatrists. There were plenty of diagnosticians, and in such systems no prisoner was without a diagnosis in his record. Cures were less certain.

Correctional officials seriously composed orations in which they likened the prison of the future to a hospital in which crimes would be regarded as symptoms of psychological and social malfunctions that could be diagnosed and cured. The prisons of the past were deplored as warehouses in which criminals were kept and returned at the end of their sentences to states no better than they were in upon arrival, and probably worse.

Elaborate intake procedures were installed at reception centers providing for detailed social histories, the most sensitive psychological testing, a review of the newly arrived convict's educational needs, and, in the case of the most serious offenders and those who seemed mentally disturbed, a full-scale psychiatric interview. From all this information a treatment plan could be recommended. Whether the system could carry out the plan was usually in doubt, but the plan itself documented the need for specific programs that, if they did not exist, should be installed.

Whatever was happening or not happening to the convict was dutifully recorded: school performance, job assignments, disciplinary record, and visitors.

Commitment to the "rehabilitative ideal," as the new correctional objective came to be known, began to lag in the 1960s. The indeterminate sentence was openly challenged by some as ineffectual in controlling the behavior of released offenders. Others claimed that it was an oppressive system based on an inappropriate "medical model."

What went wrong?

The data on recidivism stubbornly refused to fulfill the promises of the medical model. Many plausible reasons for this discrepancy were advanced: There were not enough trained professionals to carry out the programs that offenders needed. It was difficult to interest psychiatrists and physicians in the treatment of offenders. Professionals new to corrections had not been properly oriented to the problems of offenders. Custodial officials, concerned about traditional prison routines, interfered with educational and therapeutic activities prescribed for the convicts. There was not enough attention given to the transition between prison and freedom. Good jobs were hard to find for ex-convicts. Parole officers carried large caseloads and could not possibly offer the intensive assistance and supervision that a parolee needed. And so on. Whatever the explanation, the recidivism data showed that released, and presumably rehabilitated, offenders seemed to commit offenses at about the same rates as in the old days when convicts were warehoused. If recidivism rates were the test of the rehabilitative ideal, it seemed clear that rehabilitation was not effective in protecting people from crimes committed by criminals who were hardened during incarceration.

In an essay written in 1974 for *The Public Interest*, a quarterly devoted to articles on public policy, Robert Martinson pronounced his verdict on prison rehabilitation programs. The crucial sentence was repeated again and again in the media:

> With few and isolated exceptions, the rehabilitative efforts that have been so far reported have had no appreciable effect on recidivism.[12]

This was the essence of his article, "What Works?—Questions and Answers About Prison Reform." The quoted sentence seemed to answer the question in the author's title. It was reduced to two words: *nothing works* and that became the conventional wisdom on the reform of offenders. Those two words were all that anti-reform advocates needed to hear. For many politicians it followed that if nothing worked, then the only purposes that prisons could serve were punishment, deterrence, and incapacitation. Rehabilitation programs, especially counseling, were a waste of effort, and what was more important, a waste of money.

Martinson's article was a summary and interpretation of a survey of treatment evaluations of 231 correctional programs that he, with two colleagues, had conducted. It was intended to be a comprehensive review of rehabilitative projects that had been competently evaluated, including probation and parole, counseling, skill development, group and individual psychotherapy, and even "leisure time activities."[13] The competence of some of the evaluations was at least open to question.

The programs considered were under way and evaluated from 1945 through 1967. Almost none showed a consistent and significant positive finding. A few seemed to show tentatively favorable results, but the authors cautioned that much more research was needed to confirm the outcomes.

It is hard to estimate the full impact of the Lipton-Martinson-Wilks survey. The complexity of the volume discouraged all but academic readers, but Martinson's article was widely read and even more widely quoted. Support for counseling and casework programs in prisons and youth training schools declined sharply. Probation departments, never adequately funded, lost so much credibility that some agencies were limited to the preparation of pre-sentence investigations. Some states went so far as to abolish parole.

The most vigorous and comprehensive response to Martinson's survey was published by Palmer in 1978.[14] Palmer had been the research analyst for programs conducted by the California Youth Authority, most of which Martinson had dismissed as ineffective. In his detailed review of Martinson's "What Works?" article, Palmer argued that many of the evaluations included in the survey had shown a reduced rate of recidivism for some subjects. Further, in Martinson's evaluation a rehabilitation program had to reduce the recidivism of the total population exposed to it to be considered effective. Most of the programs evaluated did not differentiate among offenders according to the problems they presented in achieving rehabilitation. Some offenders were of average or better intelligence, others were dull normal or less. Some were relatively well educated, most were not. Some had occupational skills, others had none. Some completed the program to which they were exposed, but others did not. None of these factors was taken into consideration in most of the original evaluations or by Martinson in his review. As a social scientist actively engaged in the evaluation of correctional programs, Palmer urged that the research enterprise should be far more precise, or meticulous, in its methodology.

In 1979 Martinson took stock of his previous work and of a large collection of evaluation research projects that had accumulated since the publication of the "What Works?" article. The new evidence caused him to recant his earlier conclusion:

> The conclusion I derived from *The Effectiveness of Correctional Treatment* [ECT] is supplied in ["What Works?"]. However, new evidence from our current study leads me to reject my original conclusion and suggest an alternative more adequate to the facts at hand. I have hesitated up to now, but the evidence is too overwhelming to ignore. . . . In brief, ECT focused on summarizing evaluation research which purported to uncover causality. In our current study we reject this perspective as premature and focus on uncovering patterns which can be of use to policymakers in choosing among available treatment programs. These patterns are sufficiently consistent to oblige me to modify my previous conclusion. . . . No treatment program now used in criminal justice is inherently either substantially helpful or harmful. The critical fact seems to be the condition under which the program is delivered. . . . Parole supervision should be extended to those misdemeanor and felony offenders who are currently released "max-out" as part of a definite sentence, so that parole will be properly limited both in duration and function, which is to reduce crime through surveillance and quick action when danger threatens.[15]

Martinson's gallant retraction of the conclusion that had made him famous has attracted little attention. Unfortunately, his death occurred before he could complete the study to which he referred in the Hofstra article. His finding is uncertain in that reference is not made to particular studies and their outcomes.

What we must conclude is that some programs in probation and parole are in fact effective. Halfway houses and group homes, popular alternatives to incarceration in the 1970s, Martinson found to be uniformly ineffective. Some prison programs, mostly educational, seemed to be useful in reducing recidivism. The upshot of the article is that it was far from true that nothing worked; indeed there were many programs that were effective.

Louis Genevie and his associates completed Martinson's review of experimental and quasi-experimental research on criminal recidivism.[16] Their findings suggested that short-term, resource-oriented programs for adults produced favorable results. Such projects included financial aid, job placement, and "contract programming." Offenders who were released from prison at the expiration of their sentences without supervision tended to have a much higher rate of recidivism than offenders placed under any form of supervision. It seemed to be futile to aim at the long-term rehabilitation of adult offenders.

Paul Gendreau and Robert R. Ross reported on their review of the literature on offender rehabilitation published during the period 1981–1987. While attempts at rehabilitation strategies using biomedical procedures were unproductive, they found a number of diversion projects that found significant reductions in recidivism when tracked for periods of 24 months. Some programs for the rehabilitation of sex offenders have shown very high rates of success. The unrelieved skepticism of Martinson's early work is replaced with a mixed perspective. From their close examination of the projects under review, the authors noted that many were unenlightened by any theoretical guidance, that is, they attempted interventions that were unrelated to the causes of the crimes the subjects had committed or to their personalities and social circumstances. Worse was the frequent absence of quality control: Many projects were well intended but not monitored at all. It was not surprising that structure without substance led to the conclusion that "nothing works."[17]

None of these studies takes account of the environment to which a prisoner will return or in which the probationer must prove his or her intentions. While the restoration of an offender with middle-class assets and values is uncertain and the task will often end in failure, there is some logic to programs that stress work, education, and casework. Though a middle-class offender may return to a supportive family and a paying job, many underclass offenders will return to surroundings in which nobody has steady work at a legitimate job, and in which his or her family and associates have been accustomed to drugs, prostitution, and thievery. For the underclass offender, restoration to the inner-city milieu too often means resumption of the lifestyle that got him or her into trouble in the first place. It cannot be said that research has yet pointed the way to even modest successes with this unfortunate class of offenders.

The value of rehabilitation is still to be properly assessed. The methods used by Martinson raised serious questions for both correctional staffs and for social scientists. Extravagant claims of success were exploded, as they should have been, but the gross deficiencies of early evaluation methodology have received less attention from the general public. Program evaluation research is still in a rudimentary stage. The questions that now call for answers are

- Who benefits from what program?
- How can these benefits be identified and measured?

- What programs can be designed for the benefit of those who fail in existing programs?
- How shall system costs be offset by reduction of prison population and offender recidivism?

All these questions and many more urgently call for study. The corrections systems of the nation are under increasing stresses that can only be relieved by major changes in the types of sanctions imposed on offenders. Such changes should be cautiously introduced and subjected to rigorous evaluation to assure that they are worth the cost and do not adversely affect public safety.

The Return to Retributivism

Until the 1970s there was little overt dissension on the utilitarian goals of punishment. The Benthamite triad—deterrence, incapacitation, and rehabilitation—was assumed by both theoreticians and practitioners to contain the governing justifications for the administration of the various sanctions against the criminal embodied in our criminal laws. The 1970 Declaration of Principles of the American Prison Association was explicit in its support of the indeterminate sentence as the criterion for sentencing required by the "rehabilitative ideal." It continued to be the firm policy of correctional practitioners, in spite of increasing skepticism about the feasibility of rehabilitation.

Two American academics reopened the debate. In an aggressively forthright tract, ". . . *We Are the Living Proof* . . . ," David Fogel, a correctional administrator who transferred to academia as a professor of criminal justice, challenged the very foundations of the "rehabilitative ideal."[18] He attacked the administration of the indeterminate sentence, arguing that the rehabilitation of offenders or their failure to achieve it should be irrelevant to the sentencing decision. The wide disparity of sentences for the same crimes depended more on the personal values of judges than on any consideration of fairness. Therefore, Fogel proposed that criminal codes should be revised to provide for uniformity in sentencing, making some allowances for mitigating or aggravating factors involved in the offense. In place of the "medical model" of sentencing, so long enshrined in correctional ideology, Fogel urged that his proposed reforms should be known as the **Justice Model.**

The concept of **just deserts,** is the pivotal philosophical basis of the justice model. Fogel contends that offenders are volitional and responsible human beings and, therefore, deserve to be punished if they violate the law. This punishment shows offenders that they are responsbile for their behavior. Decisions concerning offenders, then, should be based not on their needs, but on the penalties they deserve for their acts. This nonutilitarian position is not intended to achieve social benefits or advantages, such as deterrence or rehabilitation, but instead is designed to punish offenders because they deserve it; it is their "just deserts" for the social harm they have inflicted upon society.

The punishment given offenders must be proportionate to the social harm they have done. Fogel believes that the just deserts approach offers a more rational ground for the construction of correctional policies and offers a "set of principles for the rehabilitation of the system itself" (see Chapter 6 for Fogel's sentencing recommendations):

> The retributive position, in contrast (to rehabilitation), is essentially nonutilitarian, holding that punitive sanctions should be imposed on the offender simply for the sake of justice. Punishment is deserved; the form and severity of the punishment must, however, be proportionate to the criminal act. The right of the state to impose treatment of one sort or another on the offender holds no place in this approach.[19]

In 1976, Andrew von Hirsch, as executive director of the Committee for the Study of Incarceration, drafted the report of the committee's study, which was published under the title, *Doing Justice: The Choice of Punishments.* The committee's orientation calls for sentences administered on the basis of just deserts, very much like Fogel's justice model. The fundamental principle is that the *severity of punishment should be commensurate with the seriousness of the wrong.*[20] Neither deterrence, nor incapacitation, nor rehabilitation should enter into the sentencing decision. The principle was clearly stated and explained but, unlike Fogel's Justice Model, the proposed sentence structure was not related to past sentencing practice (see Chapter 6 for the proposed sentencing structure of *Doing Justice*).

The commensurate deserts proposal found in *Doing Justice* was later developed by Von Hirsch and Kathleen Hanrahan into a modified desert model.[21] This new retributionist rationale for punishment attempted to put into practice the moral bases of retributionism. Some of the salient recommendations in these proposals were the following:

- weighting the punishments for a crime to fit the degree of seriousness of the offense;
- the time spent in prison should be reduced for all crimes in keeping with the relative weights of seriousness . . . ;
- determinate or fixed-time sentences should be imposed upon conviction . . . ;
- parole be abolished or at least radically modified to reduce discretion;
- prison conditions should be modified to produce a fair and just environment in which to serve flat-time sentences . . . ;
- incarceration should not be used to achieve other goals: crime prevention, rehabilitation, or general deterrence.[22]

The flat terms that result from the movement toward retributivism have been fairly inflexible compared to the policies of indeterminate sentencing. The public perception of crime and drugs on the streets has put pressure on legislators and judges to increase the length of sentences with serious consequences for the country's overcrowded prisons.[23] Both liberals and hardline conservatives welcomed an end to the inequitable indeterminate sentence. As the crime wave continued without abatement, the conservative preference for longer terms gained sway. An unprecedented increase of prison populations has been the predictable result.

In the 1980s and 1990s, the Justice Model continues to have its supporters and its critics. The critics charge that the concept of just deserts or "just punishment" is a fatal weakness, because making retribution the ultimate aim of the correctional process breeds a policy of despair rather than one of hope.[24] In this regard, it is argued that while the idea of just deserts has been around for centuries, it has never totally dominated the penal policy of any advanced society.[25] Critics also state that while the justice model may have broad support in theory, there is little evidence that it is producing a more humane system. They point out that determinate sentencing has even been used by state legislatures to create more punitive and prolonged sentences. Furthermore, the criticism is made that prisons are worse today than in 1975, when Fogel began to gain the ear of politicians and correctional administrators. Fogel agrees that the Justice Model has fallen short of its intended objectives: "I am encouraged by the rhetoric of the nationwide acceptance of the Justice Model, but there are precious few places that have accepted it as a mission."[26]

The Utilitarian Punishment Model

In the mid-1970s, the United States returned to the philosophy of utilitarian punishment to deal with serious juvenile as well as adult crime. The utilitarian punishment philosophy is grounded on the assumption that punishment is necessary to deter offenders and to protect society from crime. Thus, punishment is justified because of its presumed social advantages. Proponents of this approach, the correctional right, make the argument that if we are unable to improve offenders through rehabilitative programs, we can at least assure that they are confined and that potential lawbreakers are deterred by the consequences incurred by those who do break the law.[27]

James Q. Wilson and Ernest van den Haag, leading spokespersons for utilitarian punishment philosophy, have described the main points of this hardline approach.[28] First, proponents of utilitarian punishment philosophy resent losses in the quality of American life caused by the problem of crime. They feel that a paramount duty of government is to provide the necessary social controls so that citizens are secure in their lives, liberties, and pursuit of happiness. Because the duty of the government is to protect the rights and liberties of its citizens, punishment should be used against those who violate the laws of the state.[29]

Second, punishment is an effective deterrent against crime. Van den Haag is particularly convinced of the deterrent effects of sanctions, believing that the "first line of social defense is the cost imposed for criminal activity."[30] The higher the cost, the more likely that it will deter crime.

> If a given offender's offenses are rational in the situation in which he lives—if what he can gain exceeds the likely cost to him by more than the gain from legitimate activities he does—there is little that can be "corrected" in the offender. Reform will fail. It often fails for this reason. What has to be changed is not the personality of the offender, but the cost–benefit ratio which makes his offense rational. That ratio can be changed by improving and multiplying his opportunities for legitimate activity and the benefits they yield, or by decreasing his opportunity for illegitimate activities, or by increasing their cost to him, including punishment.[31]

Third, proponents of utilitarian punishment philosophy believe in free will—that is, that offenders can reason and have freely chosen to violate the law. Such offenders are not controlled by any past or present forces, and, therefore, they deserve punishment for the social harm they have inflicted on society.

Fourth, criminals are deterred from crime only through the awareness that unlawful behavior will result in a period of isolation from society. Hardliners dismiss the community-based movement, because they claim that offenders do not take the justice process seriously until they "do some prison time" (see Box 5-2).

In sum, hardliners today are informing policymakers that a panacea is available: That is, the simple solution to the crime problem is to increase the cost, especially

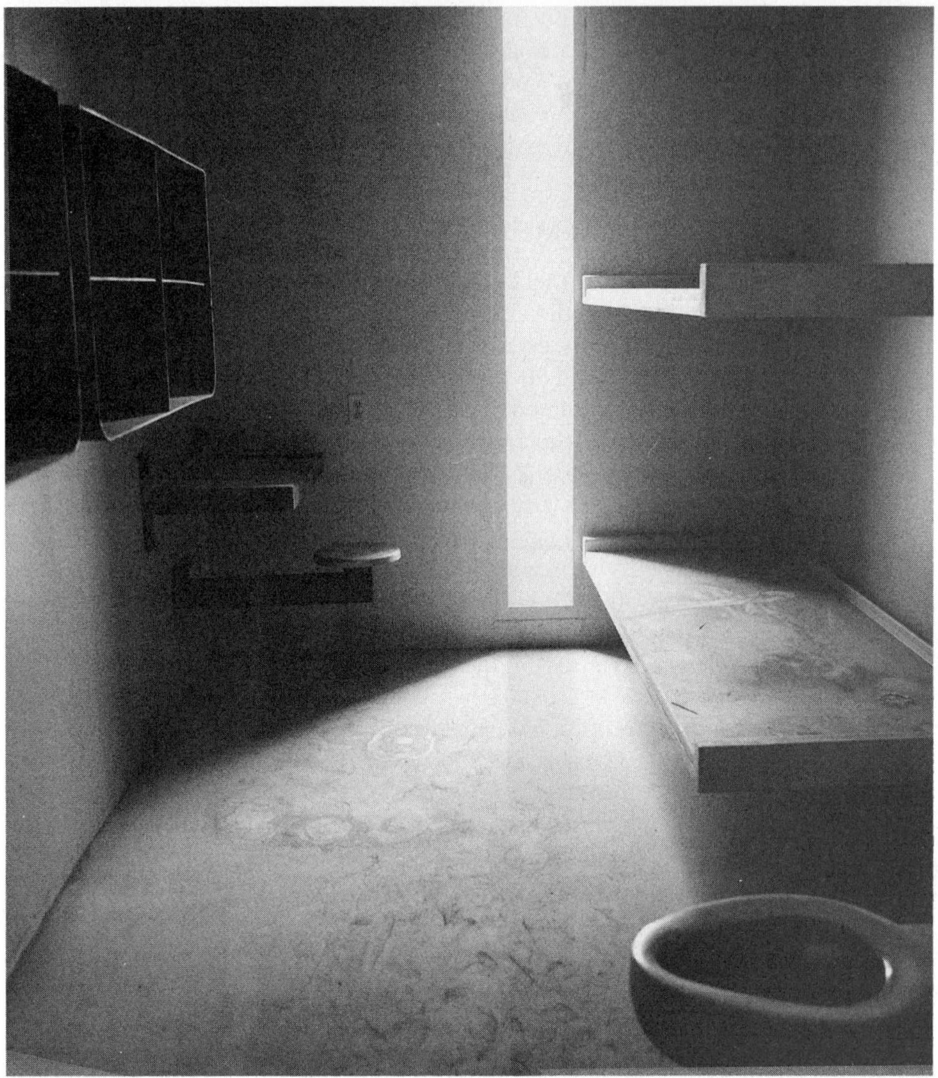

Modern prison cell. (*Source:* California Department of Corrections.)

for street offenders. Wilson and van den Haag, chief high priests of this "get tough" approach, promise that such a strategy will protect the community and deter would-be offenders.[32]

The basic problem with implementing a crime-control policy based on the principles of utilitarian punishment philosophy is that the celerity and certainty of punishment cannot at present be attained by the criminal justice system. No one involved seems to know how the time lag between the commission of the crime and the punishment for the crime can be significantly shortened. Nor does anyone appear to know how the certainty of arrest and conviction can be raised to an acceptable level. But because the celerity and the certainty of punishment cannot be attained, policymakers are being urged by some to become more severe in punishing criminals.

Box 5-2 "Get Tough" with Crime

Campaigning successfully for governor of California in the summer of 1990, Senator Pete Wilson announced that if he were elected his policy on crime would be severe. According to a newspaper account of a speech to the state Sheriff's Association, he called for "an end to the practice of giving prison inmates time off their sentences for good behavior and for working or studying while behind bars." He will "support bonds to construct as many prisons as necessary to keep the state's growing prison population behind bars." The news account explained that "current California law permits most of the state's 90,000 inmates to trim off as much as half their sentences if they take part in work or educational programs and do not make trouble. . . . Even conservative Republicans acknowledge that it would require a major construction program that would dwarf the expansion plan now under way."

Not many correctional authorities or jurists would go so far as Governor Wilson. James Q. Wilson, a leading political scientist and conservative writer on criminology, comes closest to Wilson's program for criminal justice. The concluding paragraph in *Thinking About Crime*, his influential commentary on the state of American justice, reads as follows:

> Wicked people exist. Nothing avails except to set them apart from innocent people. And many people, neither wicked nor innocent, but watchful, dissembling, and calculating of their chances, ponder our reaction to wickedness as a clue to what they might profitably do. Our actions speak louder than our words. When we profess to believe in deterrence and to value justice, but refuse to spend the energy and money required to produce either, we are sending a clear signal that we think safe streets, unlike all other great public goods, can be had on the cheap. We thereby trifle with the wicked, make sport of the innocent, and encourage the calculators. Justice suffers, and so do we all.

Many criminologists dispute James Q. Wilson's bleak outlook. The data of crime do not support the hypothesis that punishment is a strong deterrent of potential criminals. To separate the wicked from the rest of us requires more specifics than Wilson offers: Who is "wicked"? How shall we distinguish the wicked from the misguided, the impulsive, and the opportunistic? Is wickedness a lifelong condition requiring lifelong separation from the innocent, or can it be expected to atrophy with the age of the individual? These questions, and others, are not addressed by either Pete Wilson, the politician, or James Q. Wilson, the political scientist.

Source: *San Francisco Chronicle*, 12 June 1990; and James Q. Wilson, *Thinking About Crime*, rev. ed. (New York: Basic Books, 1983), p. 260.

Critics also claim that a crime-control policy based on utilitarian punishment philosophy focuses almost entirely on street crime and is blind to the more serious violation of trust inherent in economic or white-collar crime. Furthermore, advocates of this crime-control model are accused of neglecting the social and structural conditions—such as poverty, unemployment, and social injustice—that may lead to crime. Marxist criminologists add that this crime-control position solidifies the power of the middle class, thereby preventing the structural transformation of an exploitative economic system.

LOOKING IN BOTH DIRECTIONS

As a debate, the opposition between retributivism and utilitarianism has been useful but endless. The utilitarians have shown us that retribution must be limited in the interests of humane justice but that no guiding principle is available to settle how retributivism should be applied to individual offenders. The German philosopher G. W. F. Hegel (1770–1831) demonstrated the difficulty in what was for him an unusual fit of clarity:

> Reason cannot determine, nor can the concept provide any principle whose application could decide, whether justice requires for an offense (i) a corporal punishment of forty lashes or thirty-nine, or (ii) a fine of five dollars or four dollars and ninety-three, four &c. cents or (iii) imprisonment of a year or three hundred and sixty-four, three, &c, days or a year and one, two, or three days. And yet injustice is done at once if there is one lash too many, or one dollar or one cent, one week in prison or one day too many or too few. [T]he matter [must] be decided somehow, no matter how (within a certain limit).[33]

Hegel's impatience is clear, but his point was well taken even if he never got around to specifying the "certain limits" within which punishment might be legitimately imposed. In recent years the movement to specify guidelines for sentencing has attempted to standardize sentencing policy in the interest of eliminating disparities. We shall discuss this movement in Chapter 6. It summarily meets head-on Hegel's paradox and even settles the "certain limits" that he conceded were necessary. From the point of view of ethical principle, we are no further toward a solution. If the standard sentence for a "strong-arm" robbery is two years, we still cannot say why two years and no more or no less is just. All we can say is that that is what the courts are now required to do, and that that requirement is firmly based on the past sentencing policies of the judges who sat in those courts. As practical penologists we can say that at least this sentence is fair because it applies to all first-offending strong-arm robbers.

The retributivist's case against utilitarian sentencing stresses disparities. Two men commit a robbery together. For each it is a first offense. Both are convicted and sent to prison. One resists treatment, won't attend group counseling, doesn't learn a trade, and engages in rule violations that are duly recorded. The other faithfully does what the classification committee recommends and becomes a "model prisoner." The first will do more time, sometimes years more time, than his crime partner. This outcome is good Benthamism, but questionable justice. The policy places enormous power in the hands of wardens and parole boards. Whether prisoners are serious about their reformation—and many are—the ineffectiveness of coerced treatment and its irrelevance to parole outcome has been too often demonstrated to be easily reconciled to fairness in the administration of justice.

C. S. Lewis (1898–1963), an English academic and essayist with a flair for colorful imagery, makes this point well:

> To be taken without consent from my home and friends; to lose my liberty; to undergo all those assaults on my personality which modern psychotherapy knows how to deliver; to be remade after some pattern of "normality" hatched in a Viennese laboratory to which I never professed allegiance; to know that this process will never end until my captors have succeeded or I grow wise enough to cheat them with apparent success—who cares whether this is called Punishment or not? . . . This means that you state being "kind" to people before you have considered their rights, and then force on them supposed kindnesses which no one but you will recognize as kindnesses and which the recipient will feel as abominable cruelties. You have overshot the mark. Mercy, detached from Justice, becomes unmerciful.[34]

Mercy and Justice are at even worse loggerheads in the case of two judges sitting in the same jurisdiction, one of whom firmly believes it to be her duty to impose the most rigorous sentences the law allows in order to deter crime, the other sure that long terms in prison are counterproductive and preferring to assign offenders to probation when he can, or to sentence to minimum terms when he can't. Both can justify their sentencing policies as soundly utilitarian, but a crafty defense lawyer will do everything possible to keep clients out of the first judge's court and before the second judge's bench.

The critique of retributivism draws on incidents of callous brutality, and on the indifference of a retribution-oriented correctional system to the maintenance of standards of decency. Federal courts have been consistent in their requirement that although prison officials cannot be obliged to rehabilitate the offenders committed to them, they may not administer their institutions in such a way that inmates have no opportunities to improve themselves. Modern criminal justice looks back on what the offender has done and mandates a punishment that fits the crime, not the criminal. It also looks forward and demands that punishment must make it possible for the criminal to become, in Plato's formulation, "a better man, or, failing this, at least less of a wretch."

PUNISHMENT AND THE SOCIAL SYSTEM

To understand the philosophy of punishment at a particular time, it is necessary to locate this philosophy in time and place. Emile Durkheim wrote at a particular time of social crises, as did Karl Marx. Their interpretation of the role of punishment is related to the particular social contexts in which they were a part. Similarly, Michel Foucault has examined the role of power and its relationship to punishment in the late twentieth century.

Emile Durkheim and Punishment in Support of Social Solidarity

The development of sociology brought about a new perspective on the justification for punishment. One of its founders, the French sociologist Emile Durkheim (1858–

1917), saw the object of the social sciences to be the explanation of the social milieu. He insisted that this had to be done in terms of what he referred to as "**social facts**." What is relevant for the criminologist is Durkheim's position that the causes of crime must be traced through the varied impacts of the society on the individual. These social constraints on men and women—which Durkheim defined as social facts—account for much of our behavior, along with biological and psychological facts. Thus a poorly educated child of subnormal intelligence living in an underclass community will be limited in his or her choices by the social facts of poverty and incompetent education as well as the psychological fact of limited intelligence.

Analysis of the social facts involved in crime causation leads to hypotheses that, when validated by experience, become contributions to theory. Durkheim was a persevering theoretician. His work was done at a time when biology and psychology were believed to explain the whole range of human behavior. In his insistence on the primacy of social facts, Durkheim was one of the pioneers of sociology as we know it today. His influence on the development of the discipline has been immense.

As he saw the world at the end of the nineteenth century, society was in a state of crisis. The solidarity that held nations and communities together was slowly falling apart, with a loss of the consensus of citizens on values and norms. Durkheim thought that punishment of the criminal was one of the essentials in maintaining the solidarity of the community:

> Although [punishment] proceeds from a quite mechanical reaction [to crime], from movements which are passionate and in great part non-reflective, it does play a useful role. It does not serve, or else serves only quite secondarily, in correcting the culpable or in intimidating possible followers. From this point of view, its efficacy is doubtful and, in any case, mediocre. Its true function is to maintain social cohesion intact, while maintaining all its vitality in the common conscience.[35]

Durkheim's theory of punishment returns its justification to the idea of retribution. When criminals are not caught and punished, the social consensus about values is eroded. Indeed, for Durkheim crime is normal, necessary, and, in a way, desirable. When a criminal is found guilty, the public is reminded of the importance of the value that has been violated by the offender. In Durkheim's view, both crime and punishment build the solidarity of the community:

> Crime, then is necessary; it is bound up with the fundamental conditions of all social life, and by that very fact it is useful, because these conditions of which it is part are themselves indispensable to the normal evolution of morality and law.[36]

This is far from saying that the sequence of the crime committed and the criminal duly punished are all that is needed to maintain **social solidarity**. Durkheim held that even in a society of saints there would be social deviance, and much of the deviance would be defined as punishable. To assure that norms of conduct are respected, any society must be organized to make them effective. Honest work must be rewarded, and opportunities for work must be real and visible. When crime goes unpunished, when men and women perceive that the desire for employment will not be satisfied and hopes for the future are unrealistic, the condition of normlessness spreads. Durkheim referred to that state of affairs as **anomie**. Those sectors of society that are affected by anomie will manifest various kinds of social deviance—crime, alcohol and drug addiction, prostitution, and dependency. It is this condition that Durkheim foresaw when he wrote of a crisis slowly developing in Western society. Much more than efficient law enforcement is required to correct this bleak outlook, but certainly that is a requirement for the restoration of standards and values in the community.

Karl Marx and Conflict Criminology

Karl Marx (1818–1883) had much to say about the historical forces that created bourgeois capitalism, about the economics of surplus value, and about the coming empowerment of the proletariat through revolutionary means. He had rather little to say about crime and punishment. In his view, crime was one of the consequences of the capitalist system and would doubtless play a much less significant part in the socialist system of the future. Perhaps his most significant remark about the problem of crime in nineteenth-century society was contained in an article written for the *New York Daily Tribune* on the topic of capital punishment:

> [I]s there not a necessity for deeply reflecting upon the alteration of a system that breeds these crimes, instead of glorifying the hangman who executes a lot of criminals to make room only for the supply of new ones?[37]

For Marx, most criminals came from a class lodged in the lowest "sediment of relative surplus population," the casualties of capitalism. He dismissed them as "the tatterdemalion or slum proletariat," consisting of vagrants, criminals, and prostitutes. So long as capitalism exists, he thought, this "sediment" would accumulate; the production of paupers "is an inevitable outcome of the production of relative surplus population, which is one of the developments of wealth."[38]

Marx held that the miseries of the proletariat, of which the "tatterdemalion" segment is only the most miserable, would continue until capitalism is overthrown and the nations of the world become classless societies. Hence there is no reason to suppose that crime will diminish while capitalism survives.

From this sketchy account of crime, Marxist criminologists have moved on to a theory that crime is the natural and inevitable result of the conflict of classes. If society is engaged in a class war, then the criminals are casualties of the war. The vogue for Marxist criminology reached its heyday in the 1960s and the 1970s. The explanation of crime lies in the economics of capitalism, which, as Marx pointed out, will inevitably create a **tatterdemalion proletariat**, concentrated in high-density areas of the inner cities.[39] It follows that prisoners are the victims of oppression, their crimes motivated by hardship, and their status is analogous to that of political prisoners in totalitarian countries. Indeed, some amateur Marxists claimed that criminals were really the "vanguard of the revolutionary forces of the proletariat." This notion is not regarded favorably by more thoughtful Marxists.

The consequences for prison administration in the decades of the 1960s and 1970s were serious. Black prisoners, particularly, learned to think of themselves as the helpless victims of a racist society whose plight would be relieved by the revolution to come. Few white prisoners joined in solidarity with their black fellows, but many of them, too, accepted and acted on the notion of victimization by an oppressive ruling class.[40] In California, particularly, the revolutionary mystique was influential, resulting in many disturbances and a spate of homicides in which a judge, some correctional officers, and George Jackson, a leading prisoner exponent of Marxism, were victims.

The influence of Marxist criminology has waned with the decline of Marxist socialism in eastern Europe. Prisoners are no longer as politicized as they were in the decade of turmoil. There have been some lasting effects, foremost among them the conviction among many critics of the criminal justice system as it stands now that there is indeed a "tatterdemalion proletariat," now best known as an underclass. From the underclass, the "sediment of the surplus population," as Marx referred to them, comes the supply of convicts who overcrowd American prisons.

Marx's impractical solution was a revolution creating a classless society. Penologists must hope that social policy will bring about a peaceful integration of the underclass into the society of opportunity.

Michel Foucault and the Power of Panopticism

The publication in 1975 of Michel Foucault's *Surveiller et Punir; La Naissance de la Prison* and its English translation in 1975 under the title *Discipline and Punish; The Birth of the Prison* amplified an ongoing debate as to the uses of the prison in a modern society.[41] Foucault stood at the pinnacle of French academia and his weighty book has received wide attention from liberal criminologists. Radical critics in western Europe and the United States had long contended that the prison served only to oppress the poor and ethnic minorities. The power of the ruling classes was maintained by a severe criminal law that intimidated the working proletariat and served no other purpose.

Foucault was interested in the apparatus of power that has been constructed in modern society and the uses of knowledge in reinforcing that apparatus. He noted that until the arrival of Jeremy Bentham and the general acceptance of utilitarian political philosophy, the small ruling classes had maintained power by the use of physical punishments, including such horrifying examples as the execution of the unfortunate Damiens in mid–eighteenth-century Paris. Although Bentham's Panopticon never was a standard model of prison architecture, its underlying idea was the germ of "panopticism," or the application of a technology of control by systematic observation and the accumulation of information. The prison replaced the gallows and guillotine. It has been no more effective than its predecessors in controlling and eliminating crime. Foucault explained its acquisition and maintenance of power in this paragraph:

> [P]enal justice defined in the eighteenth century by the reformers traced two possible but divergent lines of objectification of the criminal: the first was a series of "monsters," moral or political, who had fallen outside the social pact; the second was that of the juridical subject rehabilitated by punishment. Now the "delinquent" makes it possible to join the two lines and to constitute under the authority of medicine, psychology, and criminology, an individual in whom the offender of the law and the object of a scientific technique are superimposed—or almost—one upon the other. That the grip of the prison on the penal system should not have led to a violent . . . rejection is no doubt due to many reasons. One of these is that in fabricating delinquency, it gave to criminal justice a unitary field of objects, authenticated by the "sciences," and this enabled it to function on a general horizon of "truth."[42]

Foucault's argument has a superficial appearance of veracity. Modern society has certainly expanded the information that the state accumulates about the individual—as, for example, the records of social security and the revenue services. It is not clear that the power that the state exercises over the "delinquent" does more than maintain control while the individual is in custody. With electronic monitoring and other means of intensive surveillance, control can be greatly enhanced. Foucault would no doubt claim that modern technology has proved his point.

CONCLUSIONS

At the beginning of this chapter, we posed the hard questions about punishment that have perplexed conscientious men and women since the time of Plato. As we have seen, the answers oscillate between retributivist justice and utilitarianism. Following the media and the oratory of political leaders, it is clear that American political pragmatists firmly believe that the main justification of incarceration is the incapacitation of offenders. This belief is anchored in the perception that the American public, angry about the hazards of the streets, wants drug dealers and muggers locked up for as long as possible. It is distressingly clear that criminal justice cannot be had "on the cheap." To house hundreds of thousands of felons in state and federal prisons is now a social burden costing billions of dollars a year, and the bill increases annually.

Is there any answer to our hard questions addressed in this chapter? Let us consider the suggestions of the English criminologist Nigel Walker. Looking at what a conscientious judge must keep in mind when pronouncing sentence on guilty offenders, Walker concludes that there are different justifications for different circumstances, resulting in different approaches to the penalties to be inflicted. Thus, in sentencing for a crime that is ***mala in se*** (e.g., a crime of violence or against property), the judge will argue that punishment should be retributive, to denounce the crime and the criminal. For an offense that is ***mala prohibita*** (e.g., speeding in traffic, antitrust law violations), the penalty should be utilitarian, to deter the individual and like-minded others from commission of this or similar offenses. Walker refers to this position as eclecticism in sentencing.

> There is nothing inherently illogical in this argument so long as one can offer an explicit and plausible distinction between the situations in which each justification is appropriate, and so long as one is not using the argument to allow one to justify what one really wants to do for other reasons (e.g., personal dislike of, or sympathy for, the offender).[35]

Walker will not simplify further. His final words on the topic are

> There are occasions on which a sentence has a valuable expressive function, as there are occasions on which it is obviously necessary to protect or deter. The eclectic can even argue that now and again he has to deal with a degree of wickedness which calls for retributive punishment, provided that he can define the degree. Most of the time, however, he can be no more than a fairly pessimistic reducer, trying at the same time to avoid inconsistency, discrimination, useless stigma, misdiagnoses of dangerousness and the penalising of the excusable.[44]

Walker's prescription calls for legislators and judges to make important distinctions among various kinds of offenses and offenders. For correctional personnel these distinctions are equally relevant. Neither retributivism nor utilitarianism can be fairly applied across the board to all offenders. Criminal justice must look backward and forward to justify punishment.

KEY TERMS

anomie

general deterrence

just deserts

Justice Model

mala in se

mala prohibita

retribution

social facts

social solidarity

tatterdemalion proletariat

utilitarianism

DISCUSSION TOPICS

5.1 If the administration of punishment must be reserved to the state, does that mean that crime victims should have no voice in recommending the penalty for those who committed offenses against them?

5.2 Is the principle of retributive justice incompatible with the utilitarian objectives of incapacitation, deterrence, and rehabilitation?

5.3 Durkheim's idea that crime is necessary grates on our common sense. What useful purpose could crime possibly serve?

5.4 Karl Marx thought that the "tatterdemalion proletariat" was responsible for much if not most of the crime problem. His solution was proletarian revolution. What solution is there for a capitalist society?

5.5 Jeremy Bentham wrote that all punishment is "mischief." If he was right, how shall we distinguish between humane and inhumane "mischief"?

ANNOTATED REFERENCES

Fogel, David, and Joe Hudson, eds. *Justice as Fairness: Perspectives on the Justice Model.* Cincinnati: Anderson Publishing, 1981. *A collection of essays that provides a good background to the theory and application of the Justice Model.*

Hart, H. L. A. *Punishment and Responsibility.* Oxford: Clarendon Press, 1968. *One of the classic examinations of punishment by a highly respected English legal theorist.*

van den Haag, Ernest. *Punishing Criminals: Concerning a Very Old and Painful Question.* New York: Basic Books, 1975. *In this book van den Haag, a spokesman for the "get tough" position, challenges nearly every premise of liberal criminology.*

Walzer, Michael. *Spheres of Justice.* New York: Basic Books, 1983. *Walzer examines the impact and stigma of punishment. He states: "Punishment is a powerful stigma; it* dishonors its victim. . . . There is no way of punishing that doesn't mask and stigmatize those who are punished."

Wilson, James Q. *Thinking About Crime*, rev. ed. New York: Basic Books, 1983. *Wilson's book is the widely related statement on utilitarian punishment philosophy.*

NOTES

1. For an outstanding example of the severity of early religious law, consult Leviticus and Deuteronomy in the Bible. See also Emile Durkheim, *The Division of Labor in Society*, trans. George Simpson (New York: Free Press, 1964), p. 92.
2. For an account of an African feud of the present time illustrating the lethal effects of traditional hostilities when the state is impotent or indifferent, see Rian Malan, "Msinga," *Granta* 29, Winter 1989: 43–111.
3. *Hatred* is no longer a word in common use in jurisprudential discourse, but in the nineteenth century this word was frequently found. On the moral rectitude of hating criminals, see James Fitzjames Stephen, *A History of the Criminal Law in England* (London: Macmillan, 1883), p. 383.
4. *Protagoras*, 324b. This citation uses the Estienne pagination, common to all editions of Plato's dialogues. Readers new to Plato should know that he composed his dialogues using the names of real people, attributing to them views that they may or may not have actually held. In *Protagoras*, the distinguished philosopher whose name is the title of the dialogue held that virtue and goodness could be taught, a position with which Plato disagreed, using the persona of Socrates to express his views.
5. *Gorgias*, 478, a–d, 485.0, b.
6. As, for example, in Marxist states, where "slander of the state" was severely punished, and "subversive" activities were crimes in the penal codes.
7. *Laws*, 854d. Although Plato's sanctions for the crimes of impiety are little short of draconian, for crimes that he thought less grievous expiation would be possible by the payment of a fine. Failure to pay would result in long terms of imprisonment or pillorying. Note also that in Athens a citizen was a member of the privileged classes—as contrasted with the slaves, who worked and had limited civil rights. Therefore, thought Plato, slaves should be punished less severely than free men for the same kinds of crime.
8. Ibid., pp. 908–909.
9. The executioner's indispensability to a well-ordered state was explicitly and vigorously argued by the French anti-Enlightenment philosopher Joseph de Maistre (1753–1821) in a panegyric to be found in the posthumously published *Les Soirees de Saint* (Petersbourg and Paris: Garnier, 1821), vol. 1, pp. 29–33; vol. 2, pp. 4–5.
10. Immanuel Kant, *The Metaphysics of Morals*, trans. John Ladd (Indianapolis: Bobbs-Merrill, 1965), p. 100. Original published in 1797 as *Metaphysische Antangsgrunde der Rechtslehre*. The reference to the "categorical imperative" is an important Kantian usage: In this context, the law concerning punishment is an absolute and unconditional requirement for organized society.
11. H. L. A. Hart, *Punishment and Responsibility* (Oxford: Clarendon Press, 1968), p. 244.
12. Robert Martinson, "What Works?—Questions and Answers About Prison Reform," *The Public Interest* 35, Spring 1964: 22–54.
13. Douglas Lipton, Robert Martinson, and Judith Wilks, *The Effectiveness of Correctional Treatment* (New York: Praeger, 1975), p. 8.
14. Ted Palmer, *Correctional Intervention and Research* (Lexington, Mass.: D.C. Heath/Lexington Books, 1978).
15. Robert Martinson, "New Findings, New Views: A Note of Caution Regarding Sentencing Reform," *Hofstra Law Review* 7, 1979: 243–258. In this article, Martinson made much of

the need to differentiate among kinds of recidivism by the nature of the actions taken by criminal justice. To make his point he urged that the word recidivism be abandoned in favor of "re-processing." This suggestion has not caught on.

16. Louis Genevie, Eva Margolies, and Gregory L. Muhlin, "How Effective Is Correctional Intervention?" *Social Policy* 17, Winter 1986: 52–57.
17. Paul Gendreau and Robert R. Ross, "Revivication of Rehabilitation: Evidence from the 1980s," *Justice Quarterly* 4, September 1987: 349–407. This article is supplemented with an exhaustive bibliography of recent correctional evaluation.
18. David Fogel, ". . . *We Are The Living Proof* . . ." (Cincinnati: Anderson, 1975).
19. Ibid.
20. Andrew von Hirsch, *Doing Justice: The Choice of Punishments* (New York: Hill & Wang, 1976), pp. 132–140. This chapter contains a full discussion of the proposed scale of punishments which has never taken hold in any American jurisdiction, although it deserves serious reflection by policymakers.
21. Andrew von Hirsch and Kathleen Hanrahan, *The Question of Parole* (Cambridge: Ballinger, 1979).
22. Richard Hawkins and Geoffrey P. Alpert, *American Prison Systems: Punishment and Justice* (Englewood Cliffs, N.J.: Prentice-Hall, 1989), p. 85.
23. For a thorough discussion of the complex issues involved in the transition from the indeterminate sentence to the flat term, see *Determinate Sentencing: Reform or Regression? The Proceedings of a Special Conference at the University of California* (Washington, D.C., The National Institute of Law Enforcement and Criminal Justice, March 1978).
24. Willard Gaylin and David J. Rothman, "Introduction," in Andrew von Hirsch, ed., *Doing Justice: The Choice of Punishment* (New York: Hill & Wang, 1976).
25. Francis Allen, *Decline of the Rehabilitation Ideal* (New Haven: Yale University Press, 1981), p. 69.
26. Quoted in Clemens Bartollas, *Correctional Treatment: Theory and Practice* (Englewood Cliffs, N.J.: Prentice-Hall, 1985), p. 44.
27. John P. Conrad, *Justice and Consequences* (Lexington, Mass.: Lexington Books, 1981), p. 157.
28. Ernest van den Haag, *Punishing Criminals: Concerning a Very Old and Painful Question* (New York: Basic Books, 1975); James Q. Wilson, *Thinking About Crime*, rev. ed. (New York: Basic Books, 1975).
29. van den Haag, *Punishing Criminals*, pp. 1–5.
30. Ibid., p. 57.
31. Ibid., p. 59.
32. Wilson, *Thinking About Crime*; van den Haag, *Punishing Criminals*.
33. Georg Wilhelm Friedrich Hegel, *The Philosophy of Right*, trans. T. M. Knox (Oxford: Clarendon Press, 1942), p. 101. Original German edition, 1821, p. 71.
34. C. S. Lewis, "The Humanitarian Theory of Punishment," in Rudolph J. Gerber and Patrick D. McAnanu, eds. *Contemporary Punishment: Views, Explanations and Justification* (Notre Dame, Ind.: University of Notre Dame Press, 1972), pp. 198–199. See also K. G. Armstrong, "The Retributivist Hits Back," *Mind* 70, October 1961: 471–490, reprinted in H. B. Acton, editor, *The Philosophy of Punishment* (London: Macmillan, 1969), pp. 138–158.
35. Emile Durkheim, *The Division of Labor in Society* (Glencoe, Ill.: Free Press, 1933), p. 108.
36. Emile Durkheim, *The Rules of Sociological Method*, trans. Sarah A. Solavay and John H. Mueller (New York: Free Press, 1964). Original French edition, 1895, p. 70. Durkheim's thought on crime and punishment has been given a helpful commentary by Robert Nisbet in *The Sociology of Emile Durkheim* (New York: Oxford University Press, 1974), pp. 209–237.

37. "On Capital Punishment," *New York Daily Tribune*, 18 February 1853. Reprinted in David F. Greenberg, ed., *Crime and Capitalism* (Palo Alto, Cal.: Mayfield, 1981), pp. 55–56.
38. Karl Marx, *Capital: A Critique of Political Economy*, trans. Eden and Cedar Paul (London: J. M. Dent, 1930), pp. 711–712. Original German edition, 1867. The usage "tatterdemalion proletariat" is the choice of the translators. The German word Marx used for this class was the *Lumpenproletariat* (*Lumpen*: "ragged"). This is the common usage by contemporary Marxist writers.
39. Ibid.
40. The anger and hatred engendered by this version of Marxist ideology was forcefully voiced in George Jackson, *Soledad Brother: The Prison Letters of George Jackson* (New York: Bantam Books, 1970).
41. Michel Foucault, *Discipline and Punish; The Birth of the Prison*, trans. Alan Sheridan (New York: Pantheon Books, 1977).
42. Ibid., p. 256.
43. Nigel Walker, *Punishment, Danger and Stigma* (Totowa, N.J.: Barnes and Noble Books, 1980), pp. 30–31.
44. Ibid., pp. 190–191.

PART TWO

Criminal Courts, Sentencing, and the Death Penalty

Chapter

6

The Criminal Courts and Sentencing

CHAPTER OUTLINE

We have seen in our historical review that it has been less than 200 years since capital punishment was the prevailing, almost exclusive punishment administered to convicted felons. We have come a long way from the days when a man could swing for the theft of a sheep, or a small boy could be strung up for shoplifting.[1] Although criminal justice has changed in many ways since the bloody code of England and its variants in the United States became horrors of the past, there have been two constants in its administration. First, the guilt and the punishment of the offender have been pronounced by the courts in accordance with the laws, however terrible the laws may have been. Second, punishment has been administered by the state in accordance with the court's decrees. An understanding of the processes by which a criminal is brought to justice and then to corrections is essential for the student of corrections.

In this chapter we shall briefly describe the structure and functions of the criminal courts, the factors influencing sentencing, the changing principles of sentencing, and the development of new laws governing the process.[2] It will be seen that the intention is that justice be done in all procedures from the beginning to the end. The execution of these intentions often falls short, sometimes because of human fallibility, and sometimes because of downright mean, contemptible actions. Sentencing is now in a stage when remedies for its shortcomings are actively sought by practitioners and scholars. In an institution that deals with gross human imperfections, the approach to perfection will never be close.

STRUCTURE AND FUNCTIONS OF THE CRIMINAL COURTS

Most states divide their criminal court systems into three tiers: courts of limited jurisdiction, courts of general jurisdiction, and courts of appellate jurisdiction. The lower or inferior courts are at the bottom of the judicial hierarchy; they are frequently called municipal or magistrates' courts. The second tier consists of trial courts, which may be called county courts, district courts, superior courts, and courts of common pleas. The third tier consists of appellate courts, which include both the state and federal forums that hear all challenges to the decisions of the lower courts. Appellate courts are further divided into intermediate and final appellate courts.

The federal government has also established a three-tiered court system, consisting of the U.S. District Courts, the U.S. Courts of Appeals, and the U.S. Supreme Court (see Figure 6.1). There are 92 federal district courts; each state has at least one. The 11 federal courts of appeals hear all appeals from federal district courts as well as the appeals of the decisions of certain administrative and regulatory agencies. The U.S. Supreme Court is the final appellate court for both the state and federal court systems, and its justices hear only cases that they have decided involve a new or important point of constitutional law. The Supreme Court hears only about 200 cases a year, a small fraction of those brought to its attention.

The main functions of the courts are to dispose of criminal cases and to supervise juvenile probation and some adult probation departments. The courts of limited jurisdiction generally handle all cases as they move from arrest to the adjudicative stages of the criminal justice process. These courts are charged to deal with all of the less serious cases, the misdemeanors, petty offenses, and local ordinance violations. They also handle the more serious cases that require bail and appointment of counsel for indigents before transfer to the trial court. The courts of general jurisdiction, or the trial courts, dispose of serious cases through dismissal, guilty pleas, or trials. Dismissals and guilty pleas are the most frequent outcomes, for only 5 to 10 percent of all defendants arrested eventually go to trial. The state and federal appellate courts are primarily concerned with issues of law, and only when new evidence is uncovered do they deal with the issues of fact that are significant to the trial court.

The court is both a participant in the criminal justice system and the supervisor of its practices. As participant, the court determines guilt or innocence and imposes sanctions. The court also administers juvenile probation and in some jurisdictions adult probation. Probation officers become officers of the court who are expected to see the probationers obey the law and comply with the conditions of probation. Prisons are repositories of the results of court decisions, and institutional staff are

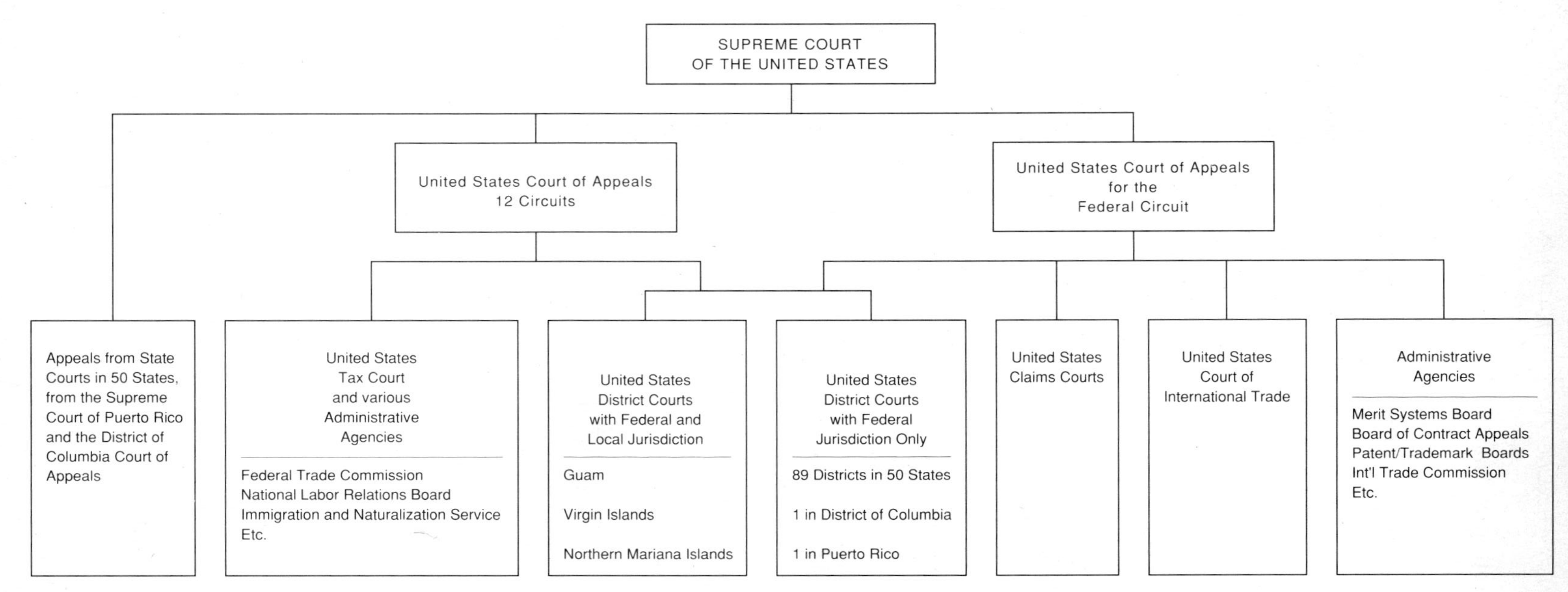

Figure 6.1 The United States Court system. (*Source*: Federal Judicial Center, Washington, 1987.)

charged with providing meaningful programs for incarcerated misdemeanants and felons.

The court recently has also become a supervisor of correctional practices. Federal court decisions on probation, parole, and institutional practices have had a dramatic effect upon corrections. In response to the suits filed each year by prisoners, the courts have frequently ruled that the values found in the Constitution take precedence over the efficient administration of correctional institutions. Indeed, 9 entire correctional systems and prisons in 36 states have been ruled unconstitutional because their prison conditions were found to represent cruel and unusual punishment.

The courts affect the daily operations of corrections in a number of ways. The rights of probationers and parolees have been enlarged, and these rights must be respected in revocation procedures. Institutional staff must make room for more offenders in already overcrowded prisons and jails. This places considerable pressure on staff: It is not easy to assimilate criminally violent offenders into an overloaded and tension-filled prison system. Nor is it easy to protect the young, first-time offenders sent by the courts. Furthermore, limitations on disciplinary methods have made it more difficult to handle the recalcitrant prisoner; no longer can a prisoner be rapped on the head or be thrown into the "hole" (segregated) without adequate food, clothing, and medical care. Finally, correctional staff must deal with the effects of disparity: A prisoner who is serving a 20-year sentence for the same act for which a fellow prisoner is serving 5 years is not likely to be receptive to correctional programs.

The relationship between the courts and corrections, however, is not just a one-way street. The courts, like the police, must deal with corrections' failures, which further bog down the court system. Most judges have become aware of the criminogenic nature of adult prisons and therefore view the prison as a last resort. Federal judges must also deal with the ever-increasing number of civil suits filed by prisoners. If departments of corrections refuse to comply with the court orders that result from these suits, the judges must decide what has to be done to implement their decisions.

FACTORS INFLUENCING SENTENCING

Societal, criminal justice system, and individual factors influence the length and nature of sentences.

Societal Factors

The law-and-order mood current in American society has motivated state legislators to revise criminal codes in a more punitive direction. For example, this "get tough" mentality has encouraged due process liberals and moderate conservatives to pass determinate sentencing acts. Yet Jonathan Casper, David Brereton, and David Neal concluded that liberals soon regretted going along with the California Determinate Sentencing Law:

> Due process liberals who supported this bill with reservations have found one of their fears borne out: Once legislators get into the business of setting prison terms there is

> little stopping them from raising them substantially. Terms have been raised several times already, and many new probation disqualifiers have been introduced since the 1979 passage of the DSL (determinate sentencing law).[3]

The political environment of a local community also frequently influences the way judges sentence defendants. Martin Levin's examination of the criminal courts in Minneapolis and Pittsburgh revealed that sentencing reflects the prevailing political style of a city.[4] James Eisenstein and Herbert Jacobs's study of the criminal courts in Baltimore and Chicago found that as the political values of a city change, the policies pursued in criminal courts also change.[5]

Moreover, judges are political creatures. Their sentencing decisions are very much influenced by the messages they receive from their various publics. That the public wants the criminal off the streets is clear. The skyrocketing prison population is an indication that judges hear the demands for a hard line in sentencing. Sentences in the United States are already the longest in Western society, but the law-and-order mood of today is persuading judges to hand down more and more punitive decisions. In short, the mood of society is persuading judges to create a harsher system.

Finally, economies cannot be divorced from the sentencing decision. Judges decide the proper judicial disposition on a cost-benefit basis: Who will benefit? What will it cost? Who will pay? Do the expected costs outweigh the potential benefits? How do the costs and benefits of one sentence compare with those of another? Will an overall savings result from substituting one decision for another?

Criminal Justice System Factors

Legal and systemic factors influence the sentencing decision. Judges generally are influenced more by the seriousness of the crime and the defendant's previous record than by any other factors when they impose sentence. Indeed, many states forbid the disposition of probation to offenders who have committed violent offenses.[6]

Plea bargaining, pre-sentence investigation reports, the system's capacity, and the courthouse team are systemic factors influencing judicial decision making. Plea bargaining is so widely used because it reduces judicial backlog, and judges, therefore, are likely to give more severe sentences to those defendants who refuse to "cop a plea."[7] The pre-sentence investigation report also typically influences the sentencing decision; for example, studies have reported that judges follow the recommendation in the pre-sentence report about 95 percent of the time.[8]

Furthermore, the capacity of the system can have an effect on sentencing. If a federal court orders a state to reduce its prison population, judges in that jurisdiction know it is imperative to avoid imposing as many prison sentences as possible. Finally, the courtroom team plays in important role in the sentencing decision. Sentences, rather than being arbitrarily handed down by the judge, flow from the continuous interaction among courtroom personnel.[9]

Individual Factors

Personal factors cannot be overlooked in understanding the sentences pronounced by judges. Their socioeconomic backgrounds, the law schools they attended, their experiences in the courtroom, the number of offenders they have defended earlier in their careers, their biases toward various crimes, their emotional reactions to defen-

Judge confers with defense attorney and prosecutor during criminal trial. (*Source:* Michael O'Brien/Archive Pictures, Inc.)

dants, and their personalities all blend to shape the decisions judges make. John Hogarth's study of judges in Ontario, Canada, concluded that sentencing is a human process: "Sentencing is not a rational, mechanical process. It is a human process and is subject to all the frailties of the human mind."[10]

What is disturbing about these extralegal influences is that they can lead to prejudice and favoritism in sentencing defendants. Although the importance of race as a significant factor in the sentencing decision appears to have decreased, it is a serious miscarriage of justice when race or sex influences the decision that a judge makes about a defendant.[11]

SENTENCING: FROM THE GALLOWS TO THE GUIDELINES

For the correctional official, the critical step in the long series from the arrest to conviction is the sentence of the court. This decision determines the intake of the prison system and the duration of stay for prisoners. A correctional system has no control over the number of offenders it receives and the numbers it can release. It is like a hotel that must find room for all who come but that can evict no one. This obvious fact is often ignored by reformers who are shocked by the overcrowding of prisons. Prison officials ought to do something, they say, about prisoners' sleeping on the floor in a jam-packed dormitory. They are right—something ought to be done, but the prison officials can only complain, and too often their complaints reach only deaf ears in the legislature.

Indeterminate Sentencing

The prison reform movement of the nineteenth century was based on the generous presumption that the function of the prison was to reform the offender. If that was the case, then it defeated the purpose of punishment to keep a convict locked up when he was reformed. Therefore, the thinking went, it should be up to the prison authorities, not the sentencing court, to decide when a prisoner should be released. A judge would have no way of estimating the time it would take to achieve the needed rehabilitation. From that reasoning it followed that sentences should be indeterminate, allowing the prison authorities to release a felon when he was ready for the outside world, no sooner and no later.

We have seen in Chapter 4 that this concept was enshrined in the 1870 Declaration of Principles adopted by the National Prison Association. From that point on, the indeterminate sentence became a standard to which all states were urged to adhere, and eventually most did. Boards of Prison Terms and Pardons were appointed to make decisions about the duration of sentences based on evidence of the prisoner's personal reform. Later, as the concept of parole was added to the correctional structure, parole boards took on this responsibility as well as that of prescribing the length and conditions of parole.

The law never allowed the **indeterminate sentence** to be completely indeterminate. For the minor felonies—auto theft, for example—a sentence ranging from between one and five years would be prescribed in a typical penal code. More serious felonies would carry a longer minimum sentence and sometimes would allow a maximum sentence of life imprisonment. For first-degree murder, when the convicted person was not to be executed, the sentence would always be for life.

None of these sentences meant exactly what they said. A parole board might establish a policy allowing for a minimum time to be served for eligibility for parole, with the remainder of the sentence fixed to be served in the community under parole supervision. Thus, a sentence for auto theft might be fixed at three years, with eligibility for parole set at two-thirds of the sentence and the remaining year on parole. A life sentence would be open to release on parole for life after some minimum number of years established in the penal code.

This system was considered to be humane and reasonable by reformers like Zebulon Brockway and Enoch Wines, who proposed it to the 1870 National Prison Association. When they got used to it, wardens and prison officials became very fond of it. This was a system that encouraged convicts to behave themselves in order to accumulate evidence of their reform. Those who violated prison rules would have their misbehavior brought to the attention of the parole board, which would view such reports as evidence that they were unready for the streets outside. The system also provided powerful incentives to engage in the self-improvement programs offered by the prison. A record of school attendance and diligence in prison industries could not fail to be viewed with approval, if not as justification for immediate release.

Determinate Sentencing

A consideration of the criteria used by parole boards in making their decisions led some critics to argue that a large element of caprice decided parole's application and denial. This point was vigorously expounded by Kenneth Culp Davis in a brief but searching study of the procedures and assumptions of the United States Parole

Board, generally thought to be one of the more enlightened paroling authorities.[12] Pointing to the lack of rules governing procedures or decision making, the lack of precedents, the closed hearings, and the refusal of the Board to explain its decisions to the prisoners denied favorable consideration, Davis argued that disparity in sentences for similar offenses, even for crime partners in the same offense, discredited the concept of the indeterminate sentence by leading to such obvious injustice.[13]

Two years later, a "working party" of the American Friends Service Committee published a polemic, *Struggle for Justice,* calling into question all the reigning assumptions about criminal justice, extending from the behavior of the police to the discretion allowed to decision makers in the courts and on the parole boards.

While *Struggle for Justice* was short on data and not much longer on anecdote, its argument was vigorous: Whatever could be said in favor of the indeterminate sentence system in theory and principle, the results were clearly unjust. The slim volume caught the attention of the prison reform movement.[14] It was followed in the ensuing five years by three compatible critiques, each leading away from the rehabilitative ideal and indeterminate sentencing.

In 1975, David Fogel, a professor of criminal justice at the University of Illinois and formerly the commissioner of corrections in Minnesota, published "*We Are the Living Proof": The Justice Model for Corrections.*[15] The "Justice Model" which Fogel advanced was summarized in the proposition that the lengthening or shortening of sentences should not be based on unreliable professional claims. Instead, the legislature should prescribe flat terms for each crime listed in the penal code, and these flat terms should be proportional to the gravity of the offense for which one is being punished.

Fogel proposed an elaborate **flat-time system**, incorporating three "types" of sentences. Type A sentences would be imposed on offenders who were convicted but who would not be imprisoned. In this model, 11 "factors in mitigation" are specified that would justify this leniency.[16] Type B sentences would be the "ordinary" terms to be imposed on convicts sent to prison. Type C sentences would be "enhanced" for "especially dangerous or repeat offenders." Table 6.1 presents the sentence structure proposed for Type B.

In 1976 two more tracts urging a **retributivist model of sentencing** appeared. *Doing Justice* is the Report of the Committee for the Study of Incarceration, organized by Charles Goodell, a former U.S. senator, and funded by two major foundations. The book was published over the name of Andrew von Hirsch as the author, but it seems to have been distilled from the combined thought of 15 committee members. In an appendix, 4 members presented dissenting views of considerable vigor, although all asserted that they were in general support of the conclusions.[17]

Rejecting the "Rehabilitative Ideal" and its implications as unworkable and unjust, the Committee concluded that a criminal's sentence should "depend on the seriousness of the defendant's crime or crimes—on what he did rather than on what the sentencer expects he will do if treated in a certain fashion."[18]

The concepts underlying the Committee's program do not merely jettison the "Rehabilitative Ideal." They also reject the objectives of Jeremy Bentham's utilitarian criminology. The Committee could find no reason to suppose that incarceration resulted in a reduction of crime rates by incapacitating, intimidating, or reforming offenders or that it had any discernible deterrent effects on the general population.

Table 6.1 TYPE B SENTENCE STRUCTURE

Offense	Flat-time sentence	Range in aggravation or mitigation	Range of allowable sentences
Murder A	Death or life imprisonment	——	Death or life imprisonment
Murder	Life imprisonment or 25 years	Up to 5 years	Life imprisonment or any fixed term from 20 to 30 years
Class 1	8 years	Up to 2 years	Any fixed term from 6 to 10 years
Class 2	5 years	Up to 2 years	Any fixed term from 3 to 7 years
Class 3	3 years	Up to 1 year	Any fixed term from 2 to 4 years
Class 4	2 years	Up to 1 year	Any fixed term from 1 to 3 years

Source: David Fogel, *"We Are the Living Proof": The Justice Model for Corrections* (Cincinnati: Anderson, 1975), pp. 254–255.

Therefore these long-accepted goals of criminal justice could no longer be accepted. Instead, desert would be the justification for punishment. If an offender is convicted of a crime, the punishment will be his or her just desert. Crimes could be arrayed in five categories on a scale of seriousness—"minor, lower intermediate, upper intermediate, lower-range serious, and upper-range serious."[19] There would be no incarceration for the "minor" and "intermediate" offenders. Repeated "lower-range serious" offenders would be incarcerated; first-timers in that category would get "intermittent confinement" (weekends or evenings). All "upper-range serious" offenders would be incarcerated; their sentences would range from 18 months to 3 years for first offenders. Repeaters might serve 5 years. Longer terms would be meted out to some murderers—for example, "unprovoked murders of strangers, political assassinations, and especially heinous murders such as those involving torture or multiple victims."[20] Just how much longer, the Committee left unsettled.

A decade and a half later, the punishments prescribed in this model are archaic. The generous inclinations of liberal criminology have been sternly rejected by legislatures in the face of the realities of urban street crime, the wave of narcotics sales and addiction, and the increasing violence of American society. Instead, the trend toward longer and longer sentences is well established and obviously accepted. The enormous costs of the incarceration that this committee sought to reduce so drastically are assumed by an anxious public to be necessary for protection against crime.

The most recent contribution to the discourse on sentencing was published in 1976 under the auspices of the Twentieth Century Fund. *Fair and Certain Punishment* was also the work of a prestigious committee.[21] The Task Force on Criminal Sentencing was chaired by Edmund G. Brown Sr., a former governor of California, and its report was drafted by Professor Alan Dershowitz of the Harvard Law School, who was also a member of the Committee for the Study of Incarceration. Andrew von Hirsch, the director of that Committee, was a member of the Task Force.

The Task Force was initially motivated by a concern about the "grotesque" disparity in sentencing practice in the United States and the idiosyncratic principles that guided individual judges. It was stressed that this unfairness surely breeds disrespect for the law.

To remedy the unfairness of the present administration of justice, the Task Force recommended the legislative creation of a guidelines structure to be drafted, implemented, and periodically reviewed by a commission composed of representatives of the judiciary, correctional officials, the police, ex-convict groups, and the general public.[22] The guidelines that this commission would produce and, from time to time, amend, would be a system of **presumptive sentencing**. By that term the Task Force meant that when an offender was found guilty of a crime, he or she would predictably "incur a particular sentence unless specific mitigating or aggravating factors are established." For example, a first-offending armed robber might be sentenced to 2 years as the presumptive sentence, but if he fired his gun with intent to injure the victim, the sentence would be increased to 5 years. If this crime were repeated after the expiration of his first sentence, he would incur a 50 percent increase in the sentence. The Task Force offered several examples of the operation of its general principles, as well as a brisk and informative background paper by Alan Dershowitz that described the existing criminal justice system and the foibles it permits and even encourages.

What was particularly significant about the Task Force's report was the rationale and specific design of the concept of guidelines. Unlike *Doing Justice*, the authors of *Fair and Certain Punishment* did not agonize over the justifications of punishment or the distinctions to be made between the hypocrisy of the medical model and the harshness of sentencing by just deserts. As the title of the report forthrightly states, the Task Force's interest was in establishing a system of fair and certain punishment without worrying about the philosophical justifications for punishing at all. Throughout, its stress on fairness and certainty as the prime essentials in the administration of justice are valuable contributions to thought and practice.

Determinate-sentencing reform has been implemented in a dozen states: Alaska, Arizona, California, Connecticut, Colorado, Illinois, Indiana, Maine, Minnesota, North Carolina, Pennsylvania, and Washington. A number of other legislatures and the federal government currently are considering determinate-sentencing acts. Moreover, parole practices and policies have undergone significant reform in Oregon, Minnesota, and the federal government, to cite several jurisdictions.[23]

Dissatisfaction with the indeterminate sentence was general in California by the mid-1970s. Conservatives disliked the apparent leniency of the paroling "Adult Authority," which seemed to link short sentences to good grades in school and satisfactory reports from work supervisors. Liberals thought that the charade of coerced rehabilitation performed by prisoners in their appearances before the Adult Authority resulted in terms that were inconsistent with the justice model. Both sides of the political spectrum agreed that sweeping changes in the penal code were in order. What was difficult to decide was the direction of change—toward a harder line or toward shorter but better-defined sentences. Nevertheless, in 1977 they combined their usually incompatible forces to produce a Determinate Sentencing Law (DSL), referred to for convenience as Senate Bill 42 (SB 42).[24]

The provisions of SB 42 were much simpler than the elaborate matrices of the federal and Minnesota guidelines. Under the indeterminate-sentence laws, the Adult Authority fixed prison terms within a wide range of choice at any time the Authority chose within that range. SB 42 changed all that. Judges were required to fix sentences at the time of the offender's conviction, and within a very narrow range of choice. Terms could be increased, at the request of the prosecutor, for prior terms of imprisonment, the use of a weapon, the infliction of great bodily injury, or for property losses above a certain amount, if such facts were proved. "Good time" was awarded on the basis of 4 months for 8 months served with participation in an educational or therapeutic program. Prisoners convicted of first-degree murder would serve life sentences[25] but would be required to serve 3 years on parole. Other prisoners would get only 1 year of parole. Parolees who violated the conditions of parole (without committing a new crime) would be returned to prison for no more than 6 months.

With the increasing rates of serious crimes, the structure of the DSL remained intact but its provisions were toughened. In 1981 sentences were lengthened. Terms for minor felonies began with a choice of 16 months / 2 years / 3 years and went up to 5 years / 7 years / 11 years, with stages in between. The three steps at each stage allowed for mitigation or aggravation of the middle choice. Counsel for the prosecution or the defense could move to mitigate or aggravate the middle sentence for documented cause. Aggravation might be moved and allowed for the defendant's role as the leader of a group of crime partners, mitigation for a minor role, such as merely being present and not interfering or, sometimes, for cooperation with the police.

Murder sentences were also toughened. Murder in the first degree called for life without possibility of parole, while second-degree murderers would be sentenced to prison for life, with parole eligibility after 25 years.

But that was not all. Enhancement (lengthening) of a sentence might be moved by the prosecution's proving the possession of a weapon at the time of the offense (one year), use of the weapon (two years), and the infliction of great bodily injury (three years). If the victim's loss was between $25,000 and $100,000, another year would be added. A loss exceeding $100,000 would be worth two more years. Further, each prior felony conviction with a prison term on the offender's record would add three years to the sentence. For each additional count on the current conviction one-third of the middle term plus the enhancement would be added. Under the 1981 amendments to DSL, a man or woman convicted of a felony could serve a great deal of time and thereby add significantly to the prison population. Parole terms were also hardened. Those not serving life sentences now serve three years on parole; "lifers" serve five years.

As many feared at the time of the 1976 DSL enactment, the original guidelines, which called for comparatively milder sentences, could easily be moved toward a much harder line. The consequences have been dramatic. California's prison population has escalated from 37,000 in 1983 to 78,000 in 1988. The projection for 1992 is for 102,000; for 1994, 136,000.

The DSL is not solely responsible for this dizzying increase. Because of the use of narcotics by parolees, about one-third of the male and female parolees return to prison for a six-month stretch. The DSL, however, has been structured to require that more than one-third of all those with felony convictions get prison sentences, many of them very long. (See Box 6-1 for the effect of the determinate-sentencing law in the state of Washington.)

Box 6-1 Interview with Chase Riveland, Secretary of the Department of Corrections, Washington

Question: Let's talk about the determinate-sentencing law. What effects has it had on corrections?

Answer: Actually, it has met a couple of its objectives. One, its original objective was intended to put violent offenders in for a longer period of time and to divert nonviolent offenders from the system. For the most part, that has occurred. Our violent offenders are incarcerated at a higher rate than they were in the indeterminate law, and they do longer time. The sentences may not look longer, but the time they do is longer. Concurrently, there have been larger numbers of nonviolent offenders diverted from incarceration, [and] the time served by even repeat property offenders has generally gone down.

Second, the new law has served the purpose of improving at least the parity and equity issues of sentences across the state, in ethnicity, gender, as well as geographic analysis. I would say that the consistency in which people receive the same sentence for the same crime with similar criminal backgrounds has been improved drastically. Also, from a practitioner's perspective, it is very attractive that its finiteness allows us to do very accurate population projections. I think for planning purposes and for keeping a corrections system stable and matching the resources to the need, that's very important. I would guess we probably have one of the more accurate projection capacities in the country.

This particular law also has a couple of other things that are really unique. We don't have parole violators anymore because parole was eliminated. That has a lot of meaning when you look at California, for example, in which some 40 percent of prison admissions are parole violators. Another unique thing is that probation was significantly modified. In this state, the term *probation* no longer exists. It's called community supervision. But if you violate community supervision, you go to the county jail for up to 60 days; you don't go to prison. In contrast, look at Texas, where 40 percent of prison admissions are probation violators. I'm using some very general kinds of statistics here, but what I am saying is that we do not have technical violators going into our prison system unless they commit an offense.

Source: Interviewed in June 1990.

THE GUIDELINES IN PRACTICE

Fascinated by demonstrations of the computer's power to store, recall, and compare the results of decision making, members of the United States Parole Commission[26] arranged for studies leading, they hoped, to the creation of actuarial tables informing them of the risks of recidivism for any given offender as shown by experience with offenders with similar records. A grant was obtained in 1972, and a team of criminologists was commissioned to produce such an instrument. The team was composed of Don M. Gottfredson, the director of research of the National Council on Crime and Delinquency; Leslie T. Wilkins, professor of criminal justice at the State University of New York at Albany; and Peter B. Hoffman, a research associate at the National Council on Crime and Delinquency.[27]

It was decided after a year or so of experimentation that the actuarial tables would be impractical to produce and of no great use in decision making. Instead, the researchers recommended that guidelines be developed using the unwritten standards that the commission members had used over the years. Data on these decisions were collected and analyzed.

The analysis found that decisions were ordinarily the result of a consideration of the severity of the crime for which the offender was serving a sentence and the "salient factors" in his or her personal history that predicted the risk of his or her committing new offenses after release. After a study of the predictive power of 66 variables that could be found in the case records maintained by the Bureau of Prisons, 9 were chosen as powerful enough to be used in combination for prediction. These were scored with positive values for the presence of the factor, and a zero value for its absence. With experience in their use, the number of factors was reduced to 8, which seemed to predict as well as the 9 originally selected. Table 6.2 shows the 8-factor scoring, resulting in a line-up of scores from 0 to 10.

The second element for the construction of the guidelines was the severity of the crime. Here each member of the Commission was asked to grade the severity of each of a list of 51 federal offenses in relative severity, ranking them in severity in six classes: "low severity," "low/moderate severity," "moderate severity," "high severity," "very high severity," "greatest severity I." Later a seventh category, "greatest severity II," was added to distinguish murder, aircraft hijacking, and treason from somewhat less grievous crimes, such as armed robbery and the sale or distribution of narcotics. There was close agreement among the members in this ranking exercise.

From the risk / severity ratings it became possible to construct a grid on which the risk rating of the offender was the horizontal axis and the severity rating of the crime was the vertical axis. This is shown in Table 6.3. Following are some examples of the severity ratings:

Low: Theft of property valued at less than $2,000.
Low moderate: Possession of very small quantities (less than 200 doses) of drugs with intent to sell.
Moderate: Property offenses, values from $2,000 to $19,000.
High: Involuntary manslaughter. Property offenses, values from $20,000 to $100,000.
Very high: Robbery, 1 or 2 counts. Property offenses, values from $100,000 to $500,000.
Greatest I: Voluntary manslaughter. Possession of more than 200,000 doses of narcotics with intent to sell. Forcible rape.
Greatest II: Murder. Aggravated felony with serious injury to victim. Espionage. Treason.[28]

These guidelines have been criticized on several scores. The use of a history of recidivism is seen as unfair. That offenders have committed previous crimes should be irrelevant to their punishment; retributivist doctrine calls for persons guilty of the same offense to be punished alike. The influence of the salient factors on the sentence imposed seems excessive to some. A prisoner serving a sentence for a "very high severity" offense who is scored as "very good" on his salient factors will serve about the same term as a prisoner serving time for a "moderate severity" offense who is scored as "poor" on her salient factors.

Table 6.2 SALIENT FACTOR SCORES, U.S. PAROLE COMMISSION

ITEM A: Prior convictions / adjudications (adult or juvenile)	
None	3
One	2
Two or three	1
Four or more	0
ITEM B: Prior commitments of more than 30 days (adult or juvenile)	
None	2
One or two	1
Three or more	0
ITEM C: Age at current offense / prior commitments	
26 years of age or more	2
20–25 years of age	1
19 years of age or less	0
ITEM D: Recent commitment-free period (three years)	
No prior commitment of more than 30 days (adult or juvenile) or released to the community from last such commitment at least three years prior to the commencement of the current offense	1
Otherwise	0
ITEM E: Probation / parole / confinement or escape status violator this time	
Neither a probation, parole, confinement nor escape status at the time of the current offense, nor committed as a probation, parole confinement or escape status violator this time	1
Otherwise	0
ITEM F: Heroin / opiate dependence	
No history of heroin / opiate dependence	1
Otherwise	0

Source: Federal Register, volume 46, no. 1 (10 July 1981), pp. 35,638–35,639.

In spite of criticism, the Parole Commission has been guided by this sentencing model since 1978 and will continue to use it until the last prisoner received before November 1, 1987, has been discharged from the system.

Guidelines for Sentencing Judges

In October 1984 Congress passed the Comprehensive Crime Control Act, which, among other things, abolished parole, effective November 1987.[29] The United States Sentencing Commission was created in a companion **Sentencing Reform Act** of 1984. The Commission consisted of seven members, its chairman and two others are sitting federal judges. Its first function was to design a new set of guidelines to establish flat terms for all federal prisoners. After two years of research and discourse, an extraordinarily elaborate sentencing structure was produced. It is far too intricate to summarize in this text in any but the broadest terms, but some of its assumptions and unusual procedures are important to understand. It can be expected that in time it will influence sentencing structures in state criminal justice systems.[30]

Table 6.3 U.S. PAROLE GUIDELINES
Recommended Months of Incarceration Before Release on Parole for Adults

	Offender characteristics			
Offense severity	Very good 10–8	Good 7–6	Fair 5–4	Poor 3–0
Low	0–6	6–9	9–12	12–16
Low moderate	0–8	8–12	12–16	16–22
Moderate	10–14	14–18	18–24	24–32
High	14–20	20–26	26–34	34–44
Very high	24–36	36–48	48–60	60–72
Greatest I	40–52	52–64	64–78	78–100
Greatest II	52+	64+	78+	100+

Source: Adapted from National Research Council, *Research on Sentencing: The Search for Reform* (Washington: National Academy Press, 1983), vol. I, p. 171. Reprinted from "Research on Sentencing," 1983, with permission from the National Academy Press, Washington, D.C.

The Sentencing Reform Act established three objectives for the Commission. First, it was to "reduce crime through an effective, fair sentencing system." To accomplish this goal, the system had to be *honest*—that is, there was to be no more reduction of terms in prison by grants of parole. The sentence in months or years, whatever it was, would be served.[31] Second, there should be *uniformity* in sentencing so that persons committing similar crimes would serve similar terms. Third, there should be *proportionality* by imposing "appropriately different sentences for criminal conduct of different severity."[32]

The Commission made no bones about the relevance of a criminal history in achieving the purposes of the Comprehensive Crime Control Act. It prepared the guidelines on the premise that a defendant with a prior criminal history is surely more culpable than a first offender. Six criminal-history categories were established. Points are assigned to each of five different indications of a pattern of career criminal behavior. For example, 3 points are added to the basic offense category for each prior sentence of imprisonment exceeding 13 months, up to a maximum of 13 points, which would land the defendant in Criminal History Category VI, which would substantially increase the time to be served in Category I for the same offenses—at some levels more than doubling the time.

Forty-three levels of offenses are specified, and most of the federal crimes are assigned to a defined level. Petty offenses are not included, and the Commission did not get around to assigning levels for some rarely committed felonies. Departures by the sentencing judges from the guidelines are discouraged, and where the judge believes he or she must commit a departure, the judge must justify that reason in writing and expect that it will be appealed. Several adjustments to the basic offense level are allowed for aggravating or mitigating circumstances. For example, in the case of a bank robbery causing a loss of $1 million where one defendant was the leader of the group, his or her offense level would be increased from level 18 (27 to 33 months) to level 24 (51 to 63 months). If somebody were shot and suffered a permanent injury, the offense level would be increased to level 29 (87 to 108 months). In the same group offense, a crime partner who was minimally involved might have her offense level decreased from level 18 to level 14 (15 to 21 months).

The basic principles and their application have been sketched here. They seem very simple. When sentencing an offender, all that a judge has to do is to refer to the *Guidelines Manual*, find the offense of which the defendant has been found guilty, check for aggravating or mitigating circumstances, add or subtract the number of levels indicated, refer to the sentencing table in S5.2, run a finger down to the indicated level, and then add up the points that will establish the criminal-history category. The judge will then find the range of months from which can be drawn the sentence that he or she thinks appropriate. All the defendant has to do is to serve that appropriate time.

Simple, but a lot of judges didn't like it. Some refused to use the guidelines at all until the Supreme Court ruled on its constitutionality. The Court considered this challenge in *Mistretta* v. *United States*, and, in an 8-to-1 decision, Justice Antonin Scalia vigorously dissenting, ruled that the guidelines were indeed constitutional.[33]

The Sentencing Commission is a permanent feature in the criminal justice landscape. It will monitor the application of the guidelines, hear suggestions for change, and conduct further research on their effectiveness in achieving Congress's objectives. It must revise the guidelines as needed and submit an annual report of its operations to Congress.

In its studies leading to the formulation of the guidelines, the Commission gave only secondary attention to the impact of this new sentencing structure on the population of the Bureau of Prisons. The Commission has made a rough estimate of an increase of about 10 percent a year. With a substantial increase in the number of criminal offenders passing through the federal courts, this guess must be on the conservative side. Just how conservative remains to be seen.

Guidelines and Minnesota

Many states have adopted some kind of **sentencing guidelines.** A good many others have rejected the idea as an improper interference with the role of the judiciary, or because respected judges have been vocal in their opposition to the idea.

Probably the guidelines that are most admired by criminal justice scholars are those that have been in force in Minnesota since 1978. Like the two federal guidelines that we have reviewed, the Minnesota guidelines are based on a grid—the vertical axis with 10 levels of severity, and the horizontal axis providing for 6 scores for criminal history (see Figure 6.2).

The scoring system for criminal histories was developed by the Minnesota Sentencing Commission and is weighted for various factors in roughly the same way as the federal system. The figures shown in each square of this matrix show the range of months for a sentence to be imposed on a convicted offender whose crime falls into that specific cell in the grid. Judges may depart from the range shown in the applicable cell only if they find substantial and compelling circumstances justifying the adjustment. The guideline rules list factors of aggravation or mitigation that justify a departure. Every departure is subject to review by the Sentencing Commission. If the Commission rejects the reasons submitted by the judge, the state supreme court will review and decide whether the sentence should be overruled.

The heavy zigzag line on the Minnesota matrix is the "in–out" line. Cells below the line require a prison sentence; cells above require a sentence other than prison—probation, intermittent jail confinement, or a county jail term. The in–out line makes a lot of difference. On line 5, for simple robbery, one crime partner who is a first

Presumptive Sentence Lengths in Months

Italicized numbers within the grid denote the range within which a judge may sentence without the sentence being deemed a departure.

Offenders with nonimprisonment felony sentences are subject to jail time according to law.

SEVERITY LEVELS OF CONVICTION OFFENSE		CRIMINAL HISTORY SCORE 0	1	2	3	4	5	6 or more
Unauthorized Use of Motor Vehicle Possession of Marijuana	I	12*	12*	12*	13	15	17	19 *18 – 20*
Theft Related Crimes ($250 – $2500) Aggravated Forgery ($250 – $2500)	II	12*	12*	13	15	17	19	21 *20 – 22*
Theft Crimes ($250–$2500)	III	12*	13	15	17	19 *18 – 20*	22 *21 – 23*	25 *24 – 26*
Nonresidential Burglary Theft Crimes (over $2500)	IV	12*	15	18	21	25 *24 – 26*	32 *30 – 34*	41 *37 – 45*
Residential Burglary Simple Robbery	V	18	23	27	30 *29 – 31*	38 *36 – 40*	46 *43 – 49*	54 *50 – 58*
Criminal Sexual Conduct, 2nd Degree (a) & (b) Intrafamilial Sexual Abuse, 2nd Degree subd. 1(1)	VI	21	26	30	34 *33 – 35*	44 *42 – 46*	54 *50 – 58*	65 *60 – 70*
Aggravated Robbery	VII	24 *23 – 25*	32 *30 – 34*	41 *38 – 44*	49 *45 – 53*	65 *60 – 70*	81 *75 – 87*	97 *90 – 104*
Criminal Sexual Conduct, 1st Degree Assault, 1st Degree	VIII	43 *41 – 45*	54 *50 – 58*	65 *60 – 70*	76 *71 – 81*	95 *89 – 101*	113 *106 – 120*	132 *124 – 140*
Murder, 3rd Degree Murder, 2nd Degree (felony murder)	IX	105 *102 – 108*	119 *116 – 122*	127 *124 – 130*	149 *143 – 155*	176 *168 – 184*	205 *195 – 215*	230 *218 – 242*
Murder, 2nd Degree (with intent)	X	120 *116 – 124*	140 *133 – 147*	162 *153 – 171*	203 *192 – 214*	243 *231 – 255*	284 *270 – 298*	324 *309 – 339*

1st Degree Murder is excluded from the guidelines by law and continues to have a mandatory life sentence.

[shaded box] At the discretion of the judge, up to a year in jail and/or other non-jail sanctions can be imposed as conditions of probation.

[unshaded box] Presumptive commitment to state imprisonment.

Figure 6.2 Sentencing guidelines grid. (*Source*: Minnesota Sentencing Guidelines Commission.)

Box 6-2 Interview with Commissioner Orville Pung

Question: How have the sentencing guidelines influenced corrections?

Answer: There are pluses and minuses. On the plus side, they've allowed for better planning for both the inmate as well as for our population planning. You have a much better idea of when people are going to get out, and inmates know when they are going to get out. When they know they're going to get out, the level of anxiety created by the uncertainty of the indeterminate sentence and the fear that the board might change its mind or get new board members are relieved.

One of the negatives is that people have the notion that the state is pushing people that used to come to the state level back into the local level. They always stayed in a community, but because of the short memories of the public, it is thought that these people used to go to the state, and now the guidelines make them stay in the county. Well, that's foolish because these people used to get probation. The first-time property offender in Minnesota ten years ago got probation.

I think there's another problem with the guidelines. For example, when a man commits second-degree murder, he used to get a 1- to 40-year sentence. The paper would say that he got 40 years. The public, press, and politicians never followed it that closely. The public was probably simply unaware that the average sentence in prison was anywhere from 18 to 24 months. I think we now sentence people at the front end, as I put it, when the blood is still wet, when the victims are still crying, and when the media headlines are still screaming. So, it is easy to double sentences; it is easy to feel a high degree of vengeance publicly and privately. Thus, dropping a 30-year sentence on a person is not hard to do.

In the old indeterminate sentence, the parole board would review a case and say, "That happened 15 years ago. Look what he's done for the first 15 or 10 years." It might have been a little easier to say we're not going to give him another 15 years because the victim's family may have moved, or the judge may have died. I think I'm seeing that longer and longer sentences are being handed down. That's going to continue, and I don't know where that's going to lead us because we have sex offenders in prison now who have a longer sentence than if they'd killed the victim and got first-degree murder. You play an elevation game and continue to increase the thing proportionately.

Source: Interviewed in June 1990.

offender will get 27 months in jail or probation. His or her crime partner with aprevious felony conviction will fall into column 3 and will have to do 29 to 31 months in a state prison. Fortunately, Minnesota prisons are among the best in the country, so the disparity of sentences will not fall so heavily on the recidivist, as would be the case in many other states.

One special feature of the Minnesota guidelines is that the sentencing commission is legally required to adjust the application of the guidelines in order to avoid prison crowding. In the decade since the guidelines were first applied, the Commission has on one occasion modified the matrix to reduce prison sentences so that population would not exceed capacity. This provision creates an anomaly: If rising crime rates increase the number of convictions so that sentences must be reduced to keep prison populations down, general deterrence is compromised at a time when, in principle, more rather than less deterrence is required. It does not appear that Minnesota's crime rates were particularly affected. (See Box 6-2 for Commissioner Orville Pung's evaluation of these guidelines.)

CONCLUSIONS

The purpose of corrections is the punishment of the offender. To carry out this purpose in a humane society requires that sentences be administered fairly and proportionately to the gravity of the offense. Similar crimes should be similarly punished. These objectives are complicated by pragmatic exceptions. The existence of prior offenses "enhances" (increases) the punishment to be imposed. Some persons will be convicted of an offense in which in fact they were only marginally involved; they will receive mitigated terms. There are many other exceptions to the rule of uniformity in sentencing. That demonstrates the impossibility of strict adherence to a penal philosophy.

Whether flat-time sentencing will be general throughout the nation remains to be seen. One of the major difficulties is the impossibility of adjusting the application of the law to accommodate increases in prison population; this has already occurred in California, in the Bureau of Prisons, and elsewhere. Under the indeterminate sentence, judges and paroling authorities could usually—but not always—see their way clear to adjust their sentencing practice to the realities of prison overcrowding. Although penal philosophy may be the underlying foundation of penology, experience steers it. The experience of decades of violent street crime and almost uncontrollable narcotics traffic has forced dramatic changes on the entire criminal justice system. There may be a recognition among well-informed people that criminal justice can do little to prevent crime, but the consequences of crime fall heavily on every element of the system—especially corrections.

KEY TERMS

determinate sentencing

flat-time system

indeterminate sentence

presumptive sentencing

retributivist model of sentencing

sentencing guidelines

Sentencing Reform Act

DISCUSSION TOPICS

6.1 What are the main factors influencing sentencing?

6.2 Describe the retributivist model of sentencing.

6.3 Compare the indeterminate and determinate sentencing structures.

6.4 What is your evaluation of guidelines?

ANNOTATED REFERENCES

American Friends Service Committee. *Struggle for Justice.* New York: Hill & Wang, 1971. *A widely read critique of indeterminate sentencing.*

Fogel, David. *"We Are the Living Proof": The Justice Model for Corrections.* Cincinnati: Anderson, 1975. *Presents Fogel's justification for determinate sentencing as well as the basic concepts of the Justice Model.*

Gottfredson, Don M., Leslie T. Wilkins, and Peter B. Hoffman. *Guidelines for Parole and Sentencing.* Lexington, Mass.: Lexington Books, 1978. *Summarizes the background and research leading to the Parole Commission's guidelines.*

Kamisar, Yale, Wayne R. LaFave, and Jerald H. Israel. *Modern Criminal Procedure,* 6th ed. St. Paul, Minn.: West Publishing Company, 1986. *Provides a more extensive discussion of the process of sentencing briefly discussed in this chapter.*

McGee, Richard A. "California's New Determinate Sentencing Act." *Federal Probation,* March 1978: 3–10. *Provides a good overview of California's determinate-sentencing law.*

Moore, Mark H. *Dangerous Offenders: The Elusive Target of Justice.* Cambridge, Mass.: Harvard University Press, 1984. *Presents the critique that determinate- and mandatory-sentencing practices are needed to provide sufficient punishment for violent and serious offenders.*

NOTES

1. We refer the incredulous to Leon Radzinowicz, *A History of English Criminal Law,* vol. 1 (London: Stevens, 1948), p. 523. It was argued in the case in point that the court should make an example of a 10-year-old boy to discourage parents from sending their children out to steal in the belief that the law would not punish a small child for a crime for which an adult would be hanged.
2. Our review will be compressed to the point of encompassing only the most prominent essentials. Readers who desire more thorough coverage will find abundant material for thought and reflection in Yale Kamisar, Wayne R. LaFave, and Jerald H. Israel, *Modern Criminal Procedure,* 6th ed. (St. Paul, Minn.: West, 1986).
3. Quoted in Stuart A. Scheingold, *The Politics of Law and Order: Street Crime and Public Policy* (New York and London: Longman, 1984) p. 187.
4. Martin A. Levin, *Urban Politics and the Criminal Courts* (Chicago: University of Chicago Press, 1977), p. 5.
5. James Eisenstein and Herbert Jacobs, *Felony Justice: An Organizational Analysis of Criminal Courts* (Boston: Little, Brown and Company, 1979), p. 122.
6. Ibid., p. 162.
7. Conrad G. Brunk, "The Problem of Voluntariness and Coercion in the Negotiated Plea," *Law and Society Review* 13, Winter 1979: 527–553.
8. Eugene H. Czajkoski, "Exposing the Quasi-Judicial Role of the Probation Officer," *Federal Probation* 37, September 1973: 9–10.
9. Eisenstein and Jacobs, *Felony Justice,* p. 286.

10. John Hogarth, *Sentencing as a Human Process* (Toronto: University of Toronto Press, 1971), p. 356.
11. Eisenstein and Jacobs, *Felony Justice*, p. 284.
12. Kenneth Culp Davis, *Discretionary Justice: A Preliminary Inquiry* (Baton Rouge: Louisiana State University Press, 1969), pp. 126–132.
13. It is fair to say that after the publication of Davis's book the procedures of the United States Parole Board were much improved, perhaps partially in response to Davis's brief critique.
14. The American Friends Service Committee, *Struggle for Justice* (New York: Hill & Wang, 1971), pp. 145–146.
15. David Fogel, *"We Are the Living Proof": The Justice Model for Corrections* (Cincinnati: Anderson, 1975). See also David Fogel and Joe Hudson, *Justice as Fairness: Perspectives on the Justice Model* (Cincinnati: Anderson, 1981).
16. See *"We Are the Living Proof,"* pp. 250–252, where they are listed and discussed.
17. Andrew von Hirsch, *Doing Justice* (New York: Hill & Wang, 1976).
18. Ibid., Goodell's preface, p. xvii.
19. Ibid., p. 133.
20. Ibid., p. 139.
21. Report of the Twentieth Century Fund Task Force on Criminal Sentencing, *Fair and Certain Punishment* (New York: McGraw-Hill, 1976).
22. Ibid., p. 25.
23. Albert Blumstein, "Sentencing Reform: Impacts and Implications," *Judicature* 68, October–November 1984: 129–139.
24. A full account of this legislation and the preceding debates will be found in *Determinate Sentencing: Reform or Regression? The Proceedings of a Special Conference on Determinate Sentencing* 2–3, June 1977 (Washington: Government Printing Office, March 1978).
25. In later amendments, the court was given the option of committing for life without possibility of parole.
26. This agency has gone through changes of nomenclature over its lifetime. It was originally known as the United States Board of Parole. From 1976 and until its eventual demise, caused by the abolition of parole for offenders convicted after November 1, 1987, it has been known as the United States Parole Commission. Until all offenders received before November 1987 are released, the Commission will remain in existence.
27. For a full account of the research leading to the Parole Commission's guidelines, see Don M. Gottfredson, Leslie T. Wilkins, and Peter B. Hoffman, *Guidelines for Parole and Sentencing* (Lexington, Mass.: Lexington Books, 1978).
28. A full distribution of the crimes among the seven severity levels can be found in the *Code of Federal Regulations*, volume 28, S 2.20 (1 July 1980).
29. Under S 5.15 of the *Guidelines Manual*, the court must order a period of supervised release for any prisoner serving a term exceeding one year.
30. The reader may find the details in United States Sentencing Commission, *Guidelines Manual* (Washington: Government Printing Office, 1988).
31. One concession to the old ways was allowed. Good time could be earned and vested in the amount of 54 days for each year served in compliance with the rules of the Bureau of Prisons. Those prisoners who did not behave accordingly would lose the good time for the year in which their misbehavior occurred. Good time accumulated in previous years could not be canceled.
32. Ibid., p. 3. This is the Commission's policy statement. It discusses in some detail the difficulties of reaching these objectives and goes on to review the need for "subcategories" of crime—for example, robbery, which may be almost nonviolent and minimally remunerative, to planned, violent, and involving millions of dollars.
33. *Mistretta* v. *United States*, 109 Sup. Ct. 647, January 1989.

Chapter 7

The Death Penalty

CHAPTER OUTLINE

Until Cesare Beccaria made it an issue,[1] jurists, philosophers, and theologians did not seriously question the propriety of the death penalty. It has been debated ever since. The debate has ended in Western Europe and Canada, where capital punishment has been abolished. The debate has not begun in Iran or Saudi Arabia, where capital punishment is the natural retribution to be imposed not only on murderers but also on many other varieties of offenders, especially narcotics traffickers and adulterers. Capital punishment is retained in all the Marxist states and in South Africa to protect citizens from murder and various other crimes and the state from political challenge.[2]

American public opinion on this emotional subject is volatile. As recently as 1978 a Roper poll found that 66 percent of the population opposed the death penalty. The relentless increase in violent street crime has reversed public opinion.[3] Polls taken in the late 1980s find that as many as 80 percent of Americans now favor it. Because legislators find that advocacy of capital punishment sends an unmistakable signal of the will to be "tough on crime," they find it expedient to express their implacable support. It is unlikely that this pendulum will swing toward abolition in the foreseeable future.

THE EARLY ARGUMENTS

The survival of capital punishment in the United States has been debated since the earliest days of the republic. In 1787 Dr. Benjamin Rush (1745–1813) of Philadelphia, the most famous physician of his time and a signer of the Declaration of Independence, delivered an oration on the subject that set forth a position taken by religious liberals, especially Quakers, throughout American history. His rationale rests on suppositions that must have been improbable in his time and that would not be taken seriously in ours:

> The punishment of murder by death is contrary to reason and to the order and happiness of society.
>
> 1. It lessens the horror of taking away human life and thereby tends to multiply murders.
> 2. It produces murder by its influence on people who are tired of life, and who, from a supposition that murder is less a crime than suicide, destroy a life (and often that of a near connection) and afterwards deliver themselves up to justice, that they may escape from their misery by means of a halter [hangman's noose].
> 3. The punishment of murder by death multiplies murders from the difficulty it creates of convicting persons who are guilty of it. Humanity, revolting at the idea of the severity and certainty of a capital punishment, often steps in and collects such evidence in favour of a murderer as screens him from justice altogether, or palliates his crime into manslaughter. . . .[4]

Famous and revered though Rush was, he could not persuade the Commonwealth of Pennsylvania to outlaw the death penalty for homicide. He did succeed, however, in eliminating capital punishment as a sanction for the lesser felonies.

As eminent as Dr. Rush in his time was the New York lawyer Edward Livingston (1764–1836), who abruptly left New York in 1803 as a result of a scandal in his law office for which he felt responsible. He settled in New Orleans and in 1820 was elected to the Louisiana Assembly. Because of his influential advocacy of criminal justice law reform, he was commissioned by the legislature to draft a revision of the state's criminal code. When he presented his draft to the legislators, he accompanied it with an essay entitled "The Crime of Employing the Punishment of Death."[5] His argument depended less on religious and moral precepts than on his view that capital punishment was an ineffectual and needless deterrent to crime and that imprisonment could better serve the aims of justice.

Livingston's argument was reasoned and eloquent, but it failed to move the Louisiana legislators. The code that he drafted was reprinted in England, France, and Germany, where he was acclaimed as "'the first legal genius of modern times." The death penalty survived in all three countries until well into the twentieth century. It is still administered in Louisiana. Livingston's essay was widely quoted by nineteenth-century abolitionists. His arguments are still relevant to the abolitionists' cause.

Rush and Livingston were among the first in a long line of famous Americans who vigorously opposed the death penalty. The arguments favoring its retention have never been so articulate. Perhaps the most powerful rhetoric favoring the death penalty came from England, where Sir James Fitzjames Stephen (1829–1894), a lawyer and judge, propounded uncompromising views on the need for severe punishment of all criminals:

> No other punishment deters men so effectually from committing crimes as the punishment of death. . . . [T]his is one of those propositions which it is difficult to prove, simply because they are in themselves more obvious than any proof can make them. It

is possible to display ingenuity in arguing against it, but that is all. The whole experience of mankind is in the other direction. The threat of instant death is one to which resort has always been made when there was an absolute necessity for producing some result. . . . "All that a man has he will give for his life." In any secondary punishment however terrible, there is hope; but death is death; its terrors cannot be described more forcibly.[6]

Sir James was a lawyer and judge much respected for his learning and industry. His contact with murderers was frequent, but only in the courtroom. His assumption that the terror of death could be a factor in a killer's calculations when deciding whether to engage in homicide must have been drawn from an estimate of his own probable behavior in the unlikely event that he would be faced with such a decision. It seems never to have entered his mind that criminals acting on the spur of the moment and with imperfect powers to calculate the risk might behave differently from an upper-class judge. If capital punishment did not deter potential criminals, at least he believed it satisfied society's justifiable demand for vengeance. He put it this way, "The criminal law stands to the passion of revenge in much the same relation as marriage to the sexual appetite."[7]

Table 7.1 METHOD OF EXECUTION, BY STATE, 1989

Lethal injection	Electrocution	Lethal gas	Hanging	Firing squad
Arkansas[a,b]	Alabama	Arizona	Montana[a]	Idaho[a]
Colorado	Arkansas[a,b]	California	New Hampshire[a,d]	Utah[a]
Delaware	Connecticut	Maryland	Washington[a]	
Idaho[a]	Florida	Mississippi[a,c]		
Illinois	Georgia	Missouri[a]		
Mississippi[a,c]	Indiana	North Carolina[a]		
Missouri[a]	Kentucky			
Montana[a]	Louisiana			
Nevada	Nebraska			
New Hampshire[a,d]	Ohio[e]			
New Jersey	Pennsylvania			
New Mexico	South Carolina			
North Carolina[a]	Tennessee			
Oklahoma	Virginia			
Oregon				
South Dakota				
Texas				
Utah[a]				
Washington[a]				
Wyoming				

Note: Federal executions are to be carried out according to the method of the state in which they are performed.

[a]Authorizes two methods of execution.

[b]Arkansas authorizes lethal injection for those whose capital offense occurred after 7/4/83; for those whose offense occurred before that date, the condemned prisoner may elect lethal injection or electrocution.

[c]Mississippi authorizes lethal injection for those convicted after 7/1/84; execution of those convicted prior to that date is to be carried out with lethal gas.

[d]New Hampshire authorizes hanging only if lethal injection could not be given.

[e]On 6/13/89 the Ohio Legislature passed a bill to adopt lethal injection as the method of execution. This bill was vetoed by the governor on 7/3/89. Action to override the veto was pending in the legislature at year end.

Source: Lawrence A. Greenfield, *Capital Punishment 1989* (Washington: Bureau of Justice Statistics, 1990), p. 5.

THE DEATH PENALTY TODAY

Twelve states do not keep the death penalty in their statutes for any crime. The remaining thirty-eight and the federal statutes retain it for first-degree murder and treason.[8] After a moratorium on executions declared by the Supreme Court in 1972[9] and ending in 1976,[10] some states have resumed executions; others have kept the death penalty on the books but have not put it to use. (See Table 7.1 for methods of executions; see Box 7.1 for insight into those who carry out the executions.)

Lawyers have debated in the federal courts whether capital punishment is cruel and unusual within the meaning of the Eighth Amendment of the Constitution. Whether it is cruel or not depends on one's perspective, but it certainly is unusual. During 1988 there were 20,675 homicides in the United States, an increase of 2.9 percent over the total for 1987. Not all were first-degree murders, by any means. Data on the number of first-degree convictions throughout the country are not collected. The percentage of reported homicides that are cleared with an arrest is high—more than 70 percent. The percentage of death sentences pronounced is minute: during the late 1970s, 25 percent of the "death-eligible" cases in Georgia and 11 percent of the death-eligibles in Cook County, Illinois.[11] There has been a clear-cut decline in the annual numbers of executions. In 1933 there were 199 executions, a peak that has not been matched in any subsequent year.

As of January 1, 1990, 2,250 men and women were technically awaiting execution on the nation's condemned rows, where many of them have waited for many years. Since 1976, when the Supreme Court allowed the resumption of capital punishment, only 135 people have been executed. (See Table 7.2.)

At that rate, it would be more than a century before the present backlog could be cleared away, not allowing for the hundreds who will be condemned during the coming decades if the death penalty is not abolished. Death will come for most of the prisoners from natural causes rather than at the hands of an executioner.

Box 7-1 The Execution Team

The literature on capital punishment is vast and varied. It includes little on the executioner, how the work of killing is carried out, and the attitudes of the men—no women, up to the present time—who carry out the sentence of the court. This lack has been filled by Robert Johnson in an eloquent study of the work of executioners. We quote:

> The execution process starts with the prisoner's commitment and doesn't end until the prisoner has been killed. In today's world this means that death work starts on death row, the bleak and oppressive "prison within a prison" where the condemned are housed for years awaiting execution. Death work culminates in the death watch, a brief period, usually twenty-four to forty-eight hours long, that ends when the prisoner has been executed. . . .

In many states it is a member of the death watch or execution team, acting under the warden's authority, who in fact plays the formal role of the executioner. Though this officer may technically work alone, his teammates are apt to view the execution as a shared responsibility. As one member of deathwatch team told me in no uncertain terms,

> We're all as a team . . . together. We all take a part of the killing, the execution. So, this guy that pulled the switch shouldn't have more responsibility than the guy that cut his hair or the guy that fed him or the guy that watched him. We all play a part in it; we all play 100 percent in it, too. That takes the load off this one individual [who pulls the switch].

The formal executioner concurred. "Everyone on the team can do it," he said, "and nobody will tell you I do it. I know my team." . . .

The tone of this enterprise is set by the team leader, a man who takes a hard-boiled, no nonsense approach to correctional work in general and death work in particular. . . . He seeks out kindred spirits, men who see killing as a job—a dirty job one does reluctantly, perhaps, but above all a job one does dispassionately. In his words.

> I wouldn't want to put a man on the team that would like it. I don't want nobody who would like to do it. I'd rather have a person not want to do it than to have a person who wants to do it. And if I suspected or thought that anybody on the team really's getting a kick out of it, I would take him off the team. . . . I would like to think that every one of them is doing it in the line of duty, you know, carryin' out their duties.

. . . The execution process has been broken down into simple, discrete tasks and practiced repeatedly. The team leader described the division of labor in the following exchange with me:

> The execution team is a nine-officer team and each one has certain things to do. When I train you, maybe you'd buckle a belt, and that's all you'd be expected to do. . . . When you're executin' a person, killing a person, I find the less you have on your mind, why the better you'll carry it out. So it's just very simple things. And so far, you know, it's all come together, we haven't had any problems.

Source: Robert Johnson, *Death Work* (Pacific Grove, Calif.: Brooks/Cole, 1990), pp. 70–76.

Table 7.2 PRISONERS UNDER SENTENCE OF DEATH, BY REGION AND STATE, YEAR END 1988 AND 1989

Region and state	Prisoners under sentence of death 12/31/88	Changes during 1989: Received under sentence of death	Changes during 1989: Removed from death row (excluding executions)[a]	Changes during 1989: Executed	Prisoners under sentence of death 12/31/89
U.S. total[b]	2,117	251	102	16	2,250
Federal	0	0	0	0	0
State	2,117	251	102	16	2,250
Northeast	124	17	9	0	132
Connecticut	1	1	0	0	2
New Hampshire	0	0	0	0	0
New Jersey	21	1	4	0	18
Pennsylvania	102	15	5	0	112
Midwest	337	26	17	1	345
Illinois	115	9	9	0	115
Indiana	51	1	4	0	48
Missouri	69	5	1	1	72
Nebraska	13	0	1	0	12
Ohio	89	11	2	0	98
South Dakota	0	0	0	0	0
South	1,246	145	68	13	1,310
Alabama	96	20	6	4	106
Arkansas	27	6	0	0	33
Delaware	7	0	0	0	7
Florida	287	37	33	2	289
Georgia	91	9	9	1	90
Kentucky	32	1	4	0	29
Louisiana	39	0	4	0	35
Maryland	14	2	0	0	16
Mississippi	47	3	5	1	44
North Carolina	79	9	0	0	88
Oklahoma	99	11	1	0	109
South Carolina	35	7	0	0	42
Tennessee	70	6	1	0	75
Texas	284	29	5	4	304
Virginia	39	5	0	1	43
West	410	63	8	2	463
Arizona	78	8	2	0	84
California	228	30	4	0	254
Colorado	3	0	0	0	3
Idaho	15	3	0	0	18
Montana	7	1	0	0	8
Nevada	45	10	1	2	52
New Mexico	2	0	1	0	1
Oregon	15	8	0	0	23

Table 7.2 (continued)

Region and state	Prisoners under sentence of death 12/31/88	Changes during 1989: Received under sentence of death	Changes during 1989: Removed from death row (excluding executions)[a]	Executed	Prisoners under sentence of death 12/31/89
Utah	8	3	0	0	11
Washington	7	0	0	0	7
Wyoming	2	0	0	0	2

Note: States not listed and the District of Columbia did not authorize the death penalty as of 12/31/88. The attorney general's office in Vermont has concluded that, although they have not been found unconstitutional, existing Vermont death penalty statutes do not conform to constitutional requirements; thus, the state has been removed from the listing of jurisdictions authorizing the death penalty. Some of the figures shown for year end 1988 are revised from those shown in *Capital Punishment 1988*, NCJ-118313. The revised figures include 18 inmates who either were reported late to the National Prisoner Statistics program or were not in the custody of state correctional authorities on 12/31/88 (four in Pennsylvania, two in Ohio, seven in Oklahoma, and one each in Missouri, Florida, Georgia, Tennessee, and Nevada) and exclude 25 inmates who were relieved of the death sentence on or before 12/31/88 (nine in Florida, four in Arizona, three in Illinois, and one each in Pennsylvania, North Carolina, South Carolina, Georgia, Tennessee, Alabama, Mississippi, Louisiana, and California).

[a]Includes five deaths due to natural causes (one each in New Jersey, Illinois, Georgia, Kentucky, and California) and one death due to suicide (Georgia).

[b]Excludes five males held under Armed Forces jurisdiction with a military death sentence for murder.

Source: Lawrence A. Greenfield, *Capital Punishment 1989* (Washington: Bureau of Justice Statistics, 1990), p. 6.

A PERSISTING DEBATE

The debate continues today among those who want to retain and those who wish to abolish the death penalty.

The Retentionist Argument

Defenders of the death penalty make several arguments supporting their position. First, they justify this punishment because of its deterrent value. They contend that crime is a rational process, and, therefore, it only stands to reason that the possibility of a death sentence will deter some of those who are contemplating murder.[12]

The most prolific defender of the death penalty in our time is Ernest van den Haag, a professor of social philosophy and jurisprudence whose views about crime and punishment are expounded in his *Punishing Criminals: Concerning a Very Old and Painful Question*,[13] in articles for law reviews and philosophical journals, and the debate he had with John P. Conrad.[14] Van den Haag's support for the death penalty is both retributivist and utilitarian. Like Stephen he is certain that common sense supports the deterrent effect of capital punishment.

> Our experience shows that the greater the threatened penalty, the more it deters. . . . [T]he threat of fifty lashes deters more than the threat of five. . . . [T]en years in prison deter more than one year in prison. . . . [T]he threat of life in prison deters more than any other term of imprisonment.

> The threat of death may deter even more. . . . [D]eath differs significantly, in kind, from any other penalty.[15]

Second, according to the **retentionist argument**, fairness dictates that "cold-blooded" killers pay for their crimes with their own lives. In an eloquent essay found in Box 7-2, the political scientist Walter Berns draws on humanity's anger against Nazi war criminals to justify capital punishment for retribution. Van den Haag also adopts a retributivist position when he says, "To refuse to punish any crime with death, then, is to avow that the negative weight of a crime can never exceed the positive value of the life of the person who committed it. I find that proposition implausible."[16]

Third, defenders of the death penalty charge that life imprisonment does not protect society, because prisoners who have committed murder are usually eligible for parole after 13 or 14 years. It is rare, they add, for a murderer to remain in prison for the remainder of his or her life. Thus, the person who has already victimized society once by taking a life will probably have an opportunity to do it again. Even if the murderer should remain in prison for life, these advocates say, he or she has the opportunity to hurt or even kill during incarceration.

Finally, proponents of the death penalty claim that it is too expensive to keep a murderer in prison for life. They estimate that at a cost of $10,000 to $20,000 a year, a 20-year-old who lives 60 years in prison would cost society more than $1 million.

The Abolitionist Argument

Contemporary opposition to capital punishment is based on **moral**, **constitutional**, and **pragmatic foundations.** Let us consider the arguments in that order.

The Moral Issue Moralists who reject the death penalty as a response to crime, even the crime of murder, hold that it is state-administered homicide.[17] In killing

Box 7-2 The Need for Social Revenge

I . . . reflect on the work of Simon Wiesenthal, who has devoted himself exclusively since 1945 to the task of hunting down the Nazis who survived the war and escaped into the world. . . . What did he hope to accomplish by finding them? . . . Punish them, of course. But why? To rehabilitate them? The very idea is absurd. To incapacitate them? But they present no present danger. To deter others from doing what they did? That is a hope too extravagant to be indulged. The answer—to me and, I suspect, everyone else who agrees that they should be punished—was clear: to pay them back. And how do you pay back SS Obersturmbannfuhrer Franz Stangl, SS Untersturmfuhrer Wilhelm Rosenbaum, SS Obersturmbannfuhrer Adolf Eichmann, or someday—who knows?—Reichsleiter Martin Bormann? As the world knows, Eichmann was executed, and I suspect that most of the decent, civilized world agrees that this was the only way he could be paid back.

Source: Walter Berns, *For Capital Punishment* (New York: Basic Books, 1979), P. 8.

the criminal the state engages in premeditated murder which the solemn proceedings of prosecution and conviction cannot disguise as anything else. They hold that if we believe that killing people is wrong, that lesson cannot be taught on the gallows or in a gas chamber. Following this line of reasoning, punishment of criminals must be limited to their restraint, never going so far as to harm or destroy their bodies.

Abolitionists recognize that it is impossible to "prove" it is wrong for the state to kill criminals. Charles Black, a professor of law at Yale University, makes the point that this judgment cannot be subjected to "proof":

> Those who, like me, oppose the penalty of death altogether, are simply making the judgement that it is too much, too cruel, too degrading to the offender and to society. We cannot prove this, but neither can the opponent of bone-breaking as a prelude to crucifixion prove his case. . . . Our part of the world, the western part, has by and large decided that torture is just too much, no matter what the offense. Four hundred years ago that decision had not been made. . . . The torture change is a shift of the moral emotions, of conscience—not of the intellect.
>
> Now if we look over the history of the world during the last century, we perceive in progress, I think, a similar world-wide shift with regard to the death penalty.[18]

The moralist's argument goes on to a consideration of the inevitable caprice in the administration of the death penalty. In a study of sentencing practice in American courts, Black argued that "mistake and arbitrariness are ineradicable in the administration of the death penalty."[19] The laws are irremediably vague in discriminating among the various degrees of homicide. Conviction of first-degree murder calls for proof that the killing was "premeditated," or committed "with malice aforethought." Where juries are allowed a part in the sentencing process, they may recommend the death penalty because of "special circumstances." In the states where jury participation is permitted, a separate sentencing hearing is required, in the course of which evidence about the defendant's background, criminal history, and other circumstances that had to be excluded from the trial as to guilt may be presented for consideration to justify the death sentence or to mitigate the sentence to life imprisonment. In charging the jurors, the court must instruct them regarding those elements of the evidence that may be considered in arriving at their recommendation. Where the jury departs from the instructions, the court may overrule it, or, on appeal, the higher court may find that the decision is inconsistent with the evidence.

Even with all these precautions, problems of definition remain. The meaning of premeditation is elusive. What is "malice"? Does "aforethought" call for one minute of "forethought" to arrive at an intention, or one hour, or several days? What is the evidence for the premeditation? The "special circumstances" may refer to exceptional brutality in the commission of the murder, but in the end the exceptional nature of the brutality is left to the jury to decide, opening latitude for prejudiced interpretation or caprice.

Abolitionists have always made the point that the majority of men and women executed have been black or Hispanic, in spite of all the precautions against prejudice that have been built into the judicial process. In all studies of this topic, black killers whose victims were white were much more likely to be sentenced to death than white killers of white victims. A review of the literature of racial discrimination in sentencing by the General Accounting Office turned up 28 statistical studies of the topic. Of these studies, 82 percent showed that the race of the victim determined the decision to sentence the convicted defendant to death. Those who murdered whites were more likely to be sentenced to death than those who murdered blacks.[20]

Van den Haag acknowledges that this disparity exists but rejects the argument that it is an objection to capital punishment:

> It is true that most of those currently under sentence of death are poor and a disproportionate number are black. But most murderers (indeed, most criminals) are poor and a disproportionate number are black. (So too are disproportionate number of murder victims.) One must expect therefore that most of our prison population, including those on death row, are poor and a disproportionate number black.[21]

Professor Black points to the enormous advantage that the death penalty places in the hands of the prosecution in negotiating justice. In the Ohio case of *State* v. *Lockett*, Black finds an example to demonstrate this point.[22] Sandra Lockett was a young black woman traveling with her boyfriend and another couple in the same car with the object of robbing a pawnbroker at gunpoint. One of the four, a man named Parker, got out of the car with the two others in the group to take care of the business they

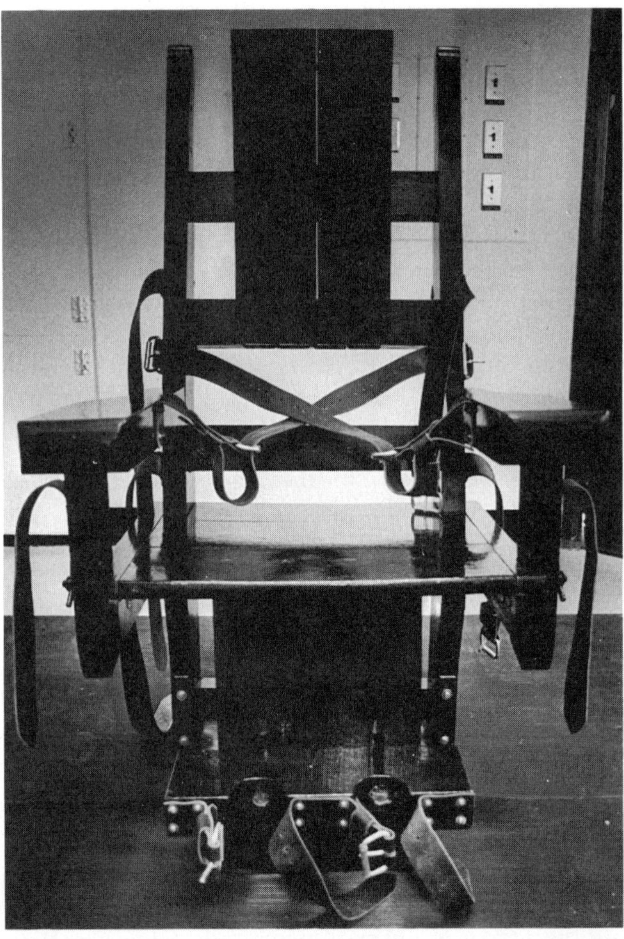

The chair. (*Source:* Tom Kelley.)

had in mind. Lockett stayed in the car because the pawnbroker knew her and would be able to identify her to the police. In a struggle with the victim, Parker's gun went off—accidentally, he claimed—and the pawnbroker was killed. All four were eventually arrested. In return for his testimony, Parker was able to negotiate a plea that limited his penalty to life imprisonment, even though he confessed to being the triggerman. Lockett was offered a bargain; she could plead guilty to voluntary manslaughter and aggravated robbery and thus escape trial for first-degree murder and the prospect of a death penalty. When she refused, the case went to trial and she was sentenced to death. Her appeal against the verdict and the sentence was rejected by the Ohio Supreme Court, but on appeal to the U.S. Supreme Court, the sentence was reversed on the grounds that the Ohio law did not require that the court consider mitigating factors in convictions leading to the death penalty.[23]

The Lockett case illustrates the risk that a defendant takes in plea bargaining, whether he or she is in fact innocent or guilty, if there is a serious prospect of a prosecutor's demand for the death penalty. Faced with this prospect, Parker saved his life by giving the state evidence. Lockett may have thought that she was guilty of nothing—she was in the car, she didn't shoot anybody, she didn't expect that the robbery would culminate in a shooting, she wasn't present when the shooting took place. She knew nothing about the provision in the law for "constructive guilt" in the case of murder in the commission of a felony. Of course her attorney should have explained the dangers to her, but whether he did or not, she stood her ground. She insisted on a trial. Against the advice of her attorney, but at the insistence of her mother, she refused to testify. She was found guilty of murder in the commission of a felony, and under Ohio law she could be—and was—sentenced to death. Her life was saved by the Supreme Court on a technicality.

Abolitionists argue that in the nature of policing and prosecution, mistakes are inevitable. The simplest kind of mistake occurs when the wrong person is arrested, prosecuted, and found guilty. Verified cases of mistaken identity in death penalty cases are very uncommon but do exist. The possibility is sufficient for the abolitionist to insist that this is reason enough to do away with capital punishment altogether. To this objection, van den Haag replied in a debate on capital punishment with John P. Conrad:

> Most human activities—construction, manufacturing, automobile and air traffic, sports, not to speak of wars and revolutions—cause the death of some innocent bystanders. Nevertheless, if the advantages sufficiently outweigh the disadvantages, human activities, including those of the penal system, with all its punishments, are morally justified.[24]

To which Conrad responded:

> The foolproof precaution against fatal errors in the administration of the death penalty is to legislate its abolition. It is unfortunate that few, if any, of the other accidents that may befall human beings are so completely preventable.[25]

Professor Black argues that the operations of criminal justice lead to more complex, not to say subtle, errors. We have mentioned previously the archaic language of the homicide statutes. It is left to a jury to decide whether the defendant committed a crime with "malice aforethought" and "with a malignant and abandoned heart," or whether guilt was mitigated by the defendant's being too inebriated to appreciate the nature of his or her acts and therefore is eligible for conviction of second-degree murder or nonnegligent manslaughter. Premeditation is not usually open to proof as where murderers announce their intention to credible witnesses that they will kill the victim. It is up to the jury to decide whether defendants' actions truly indicate premeditation. On appeal, the court may find in a split decision that the evidence was sufficient to support the verdict of the jury. If it was a 5-to-4 decision, as often is the case, the four who thought the evidence was insufficient believed the jury made a mistake. The margin for death in that case rests on one jurist's judgment. And who is to prove that the defendant's heart was "malignant and abandoned"?[26] Black argues that mistakes in the interpretation of the law, like mistakes in the identity of the defendant, cannot be corrected if the defendant has been put to death. Where the defendant has been represented by a less-than-competent attorney, mistakes are all too easily made. The abolition of the death penalty would assure that if a correction is needed it can be made while the defendant is still alive.

The Constitutional Issues Challenges to the legitimacy of capital punishment depend on the interpretation of two amendments to the Constitution of the United States, the Eighth and the Fourteenth. The Eighth Amendment specifies that:

> . . . excessive bail shall not be required, nor excessive fines imposed; nor cruel and unusual punishments inflicted.

The Fourteenth Amendment was adopted in 1868 as part of the reconstruction period after the Civil War. It provides that,

> . . . No State shall make or enforce any law which shall abridge the privileges or immunities of citizens of the United States; nor shall any State deprive any person of life, liberty, or property, without due process of law; nor deny to any person within its jurisdiction the equal protection of the laws.

From the ambiguous language of these two amendments to the Constitution abolitionist lawyers have built their case against the death penalty. The invocation of the Eighth Amendment is especially interesting. No one can doubt that for the framers of the Constitution capital punishment was a natural and perfectly legitimate punishment for a variety of crimes. The Fifth Amendment is clear: "No person shall be held to answer for a capital or otherwise infamous crime, unless on a presentment or indictment of a Grand Jury. . . ." Strict constructionists of the Constitution patiently explain that if the framers of the Eighth Amendment had meant to include the death penalty as cruel and unusual they would not have provided in the Fifth that those charged with a capital crime should be protected by a grand jury hearing and held to answer only if indicted.

To circumvent this inconvenient but undeniable historical fact, abolitionists seized on a theory of constitutional interpretation that horrifies retentionists. From the Supreme Court decision in *Trop* v. *Dulles*, a case in which excessive punishment, but not the death penalty, was the issue, the Warren Court held that "the Eighth Amendment must draw its meaning from the evolving standards of decency that mark the progress of a maturing society."[27]

In *Trop* the issue was whether the defendant, a deserter from the armed forces, should be denationalized as punishment for that offense. The court ruled that this was excessive, cruel and unusual, and contrary to the "evolving standards of decency." Abolitionists reasoned that this language could be applied to the death penalty. Whereas in the eighteenth century felons might be put to death for a wide variety of offenses, the evolution of the criminal law had modified its standards to exclude capital punishment for any crime other than murder and treason. Further, the penitentiary had yet to be invented when the Eighth Amendment was framed. Its availability in the twentieth century provides an alternative to the death penalty that could not have been foreseen by the framers.[28]

The Fourteenth Amendment was the principal foundation in the landmark decision of *Furman* v. *Georgia*. This was the case of a black man accused and convicted of murder and rape. In a 5-to-4 decision that elicited five differing opinions for the majority and four for the minority, the Supreme Court relied on the equal protection of the laws provision to overturn the sentence as well as the cruel and unusual punishment provision of the Eighth Amendment. In his opinion, Justice William O. Douglas wrote,

> The high service rendered by the "cruel and unusual" clause is to require legislatures to write penal laws that are even-handed, non-selective, and non-arbitrary, and to require judges to see to it that general laws are not applied sparsely, selectively, and spottily to unpopular groups.[29]

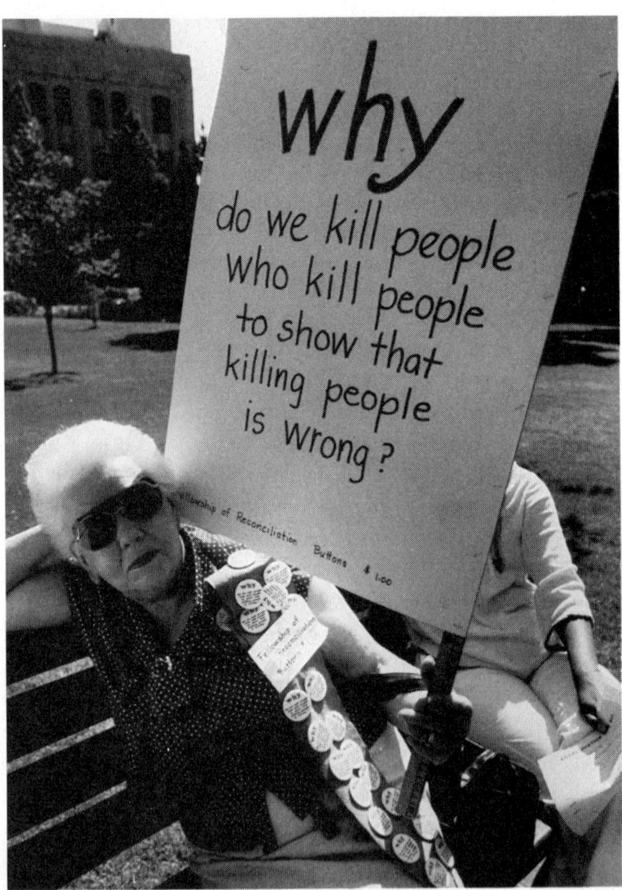

Anti–death penalty demonstrator. (*Source:* Robert V. Eckert Jr. / EKM-Nepenthe.)

Douglas went on to hold that the Georgia law violated the Fourteenth Amendment because, like those of the other states authorizing the death penalty, it provided trial courts with such discretionary freedom that it was imposed only on the poor, the unpopular, and the unstable:

> A law that stated that anyone making more than $50,000 would be exempt from the death penalty would plainly fall, as would a law that in terms said that blacks, those who never went beyond the fifth grade in school, those who made less than $3,000 a year, or those who were unpopular or unstable should be the only people executed. A law which in the overall view reaches that same result in practice has no more sanctity than a law which in terms provides the same.[30]

The decision and the nine differing opinions it comprised cannot be fully summarized here. We must take note of the essence of the four dissenting opinions as declared in Chief Justice Warren Burger's opinion:

> There are no obvious indications that capital punishment offends the conscience of society to such a degree that our traditional deference to legislative judgement must be abandoned. It is not a punishment such as burning at the stake that everyone would ineffably find to be repugnant to all civilized standards. Nor is it a punishment so roundly condemned that only a few aberrant legislatures have retained it on the statute books. Capital punishment is authorized by statute in 40 states, the District of Columbia, and in the federal courts for the commission of certain crimes. . . .
>
> . . . I cannot endorse the process of decision-making that has yielded today's result and the restraints that that result imposes on legislative action. I am not altogether displeased that legislative bodies have been given the opportunity, and indeed unavoidable responsibility, to make a thorough re-evaluation of the entire subject of capital punishment. . . .[31]

Four years later, and after intense national controversy, the Supreme Court arrived at a resolution of the ambiguities that cast the death penalty into a moratorium. Hundreds of prisoners occupying death-row cells had had their sentences commuted to life imprisonment. Legislatures across the land responded to the chief justice's invitation to reevaluate capital punishment's role in criminal justice.

The cast that ended the moratorium was *Gregg* v. *Georgia*, decided in 1976. By a 7-to-2 margin, the Court concluded that capital punishment was a justifiable expression of outrage at the commission of a heinous crime; that it was a deterrent to persons who might otherwise commit such a crime, and that it is not disproportionate to the gravity of the offense. The Georgia legislature had carefully drafted a statute ensuring that the sentencing judge would be furnished adequate information and guidance in deciding to impose this ultimate penalty. The Supreme Court found that "no longer can a jury wantonly and freakishly impose the death sentence; it is always circumscribed by legislative guidelines."[32]

After all this travail and deliberation, the constitutional questions were settled as follows.

Capital punishment is constitutional if the statutes clearly provide that in the sentencing process,

1. The court is informed about the defendant's background and criminal history.
2. Mitigating factors affecting his or her culpability are brought to the attention of the court.

3. There are standards to guide trial courts in making the sentencing decision.
4. Every death sentence will be reviewed by a state appellate court.[33]

Several important U.S. Supreme Court decisions concerning the death penalty were ruled upon in the 1980s (see Box 7.3). They related to such matters as the prediction of dangerousness, proportionality, juveniles, mental deficiency, and discrimination.

There the constitutionality of the death penalty stands. As we have seen, the latitude provided to the courts in sentencing murderers is seldom invoked. The sentence of death remains a constitutional option, but of the 38 states whose legislatures have authorized it, only 15 have made use of it since *Gregg*.

The Pragmatic Issues Leaving aside the moral and constitutional questions, all of which boil down to the question of right and wrong, we come to the difficulties of administering the death penalty under the conditions required by the Constitution and public opinion. Unlike any other punishment the state can impose, the full panoply of criminal justice procedures must be carried out. The case must come to trial. Almost always there will be a jury to convince one way or another. In pronouncing sentence the judge must clearly consider any factors that might mitigate guilt, as well as those "special circumstances" that justify the execution of the murderer. There must be a review of the case by an appellate court. Although in some cases the affirmation of judgment will not be further contested, most convicted defendants will proceed with appeals through the federal courts. Years may pass before all avenues of appeal are exhausted. In 1989 there were some men who had spent 14 years on condemned row. Advocates of the death penalty denounce these inordinate delays as the abuse of process. Abolitionists contend that although living so many years under the conditions of maximum custody constitutes cruel and unusual punishment, a man or woman facing death is justified in grasping at any legal procedure that will prolong life and possibly escape execution.

What causes these almost endless proceedings? Explanations are many, but all resolve into the deficiencies of the fallible human institutions comprised by the criminal justice system. The police may have obtained evidence using illegal methods. A confession may have been induced without cautioning the arrested person about the right to remain silent. A search may have been conducted without a proper warrant. There may have been a mistake in identifying the person responsible for the murder. Once the case is in the hands of a prosecutor, more mistakes may be made. The evidence against the defendant may not have been disclosed to the defense attorney in time to prepare for rebuttal. Inflammatory or misleading statements may be made in the presence of the jury. The selection of the jury may have failed to represent fairly all elements of the community in which the crime was committed. The trial judge is also human; in charging the jury he or she may have misconstrued the Constitution or the criminal laws. The judge may err in discussing the evidence against the defendant, or by minimizing the evidence in his or her favor. The application of the law defining first-degree murder to the facts in the case may have been incorrectly interpreted to the jury.

All these possible errors and many more can be challenged by competent and experienced defense counsel. What most homicide defendants get are public defenders or assigned counsel who at best are overworked. Too often they lack the

Box 7-3 Recent Supreme Court Decisions

We begin with the case of *Barefoot v. Estelle* (1983). Barefoot, a recidivist, had been found guilty in a Texas court of murder in the first degree. Texas law requires that capital punishment may be imposed only if in the opinion of the jury certain criteria are met. One such criterion is the probability that the defendant is a dangerous person who will probably commit more serious crimes if allowed to survive. In the opinion of two psychiatrists, neither of whom interviewed Barefoot, he presented such a danger. Barefoot's attorneys argues that psychiatrists are not competent to make such a prediction. In support of that contention they submitted a statement by the American Psychiatric Association that "the unreliability of predictions of dangerousness is by now an established fact within the psychiatric profession." The Association's best estimate was that two out of three predictions of long-term future violence made by psychiatrists are wrong.

Justice White, who delivered the opinion of the court majority, dismissed this point as "without merit." The decision as to dangerousness is up to the jury. "To accept the defendant's argument would call into question predictions of dangerousness that are constantly made." Justice Blackmun in a vigorous dissent held that the authority of a professional psychiatrist would inevitably carry great weight with a jury, especially when both the psychiatric experts felt themselves qualified to make predictions of dangerousness with a very high degree of accuracy.

In *Pulley v. Harris*, the question was whether California law was inconsistent with the constitutional requirements by not requiring that the court compare the facts of the case with the disposition of other similar cases in order to assure that the sentence was proportional to the seriousness of the crime. The court decided that the California law requiring the death penalty could be imposed if the court could find one or more of seven "special circumstances" obtained. These circumstances, as spelled out in the California statute, are (1) murder for profit; (2) murder perpetrated by an explosion; (3) murder of a police officer on active duty; (4) murder of a victim who was a witness to a crime; (5) murder committed in a robbery; (6) murder with torture; (7) murder by a person with one or more previous convictions of murder. In Harris' case, the murder was committed in the course of a robbery. The court was satisfied that the constitutional requirement of proportionality was met by the California statute and that Harris was eligible for execution.

In *Stanford v. Kentucky* (1989), the question had to do with the eligibility of a murderer for execution when the crime was committed while he was a minor. Stanford was 17 years and 4 months old when he was sentenced to death. Writing for a divided court, Justice Scalia ruled that inasmuch as the Common Law prescribed 14 as the minimum age for execution, the sentence of a 17-year-old did not violate the Eighth Amendment proscription of "cruel and unusual punishment. There was no settled consensus in the country about the minimum age for executions. Of the 37 states that provide for executions, 15 do not impose it on anyone under 16, while 12 do not impose it on persons under 17. The inference is that if there were a small minority of states that allowed the execution of minors the law might be opened to challenge, but here that was not the case.

In the related case of *Wilkins v. Missouri* (1989), the defendant, Wilkins, was 16 years and 6 months when he killed a woman clerk at a convenience store which he was robbing to make sure that he would not be identified. He was arrested, pled guilty, and declined counsel. He wanted to be executed, saying that he feared life imprisonment more than death. His case was taken up by civil liberties counsel on the score of his age and his apparent mental disturbance. Writing for a 5-to-4 majority, Justice Scalia rejected the argument that Wilkins' age disqualified him for execution. The question of his mental disturbance had been duly considered in court, and could not be raised on appeal.

In *Penry v. Lynch* (1989), the question related to mental deficiency. Penry had been convicted of rape and murder. On psychological examination he was found to have an IQ of 54, and a mental age of six. Justice O'Connor ruled that mental retardation was no bar to capital punishment.

The Georgia case of *McCleskey v. Kemp* (1987) has been through the federal courts several times. McCleskey is a black man who was convicted in 1978 of the murder of a white police officer in the course of an armed robbery. He contended that the imposition of the death penalty was cruel and unusual because black men killing white victims are sentenced to death with greater frequency than white men killing white victims. In support of this contention, he presented to the court a study by Professor David Baldus, showing that in Georgia 22 percent of black defendants with white victims received the death penalty as compared with only 8 percent of white defendants with white victims. Only 3 percent of white defendants charged with killing black victims were sentenced to death. The study further showed that prosecutors sought the death penalty in the cases of 70 percent of black defendants killing white victims, whereas capital punishment was sought for only 32 percent of white defendants killing white victims. It was argued that these figures showed that Georgia courts and prosecutors were discriminatory in their application of the laws. Justice Powell, writing for a 5-to-4 majority, rejected this argument. He held that the statistics did not prove that race entered into the decision of the court in this case. Further, following the defendant's line of reasoning, it could be claimed that any penalty could be challenged on the basis of unexplained discrepancies correlating to membership in minority groups or even to gender.

McCleskey returned to court for another attempt to overturn his sentence. In a decision announced on 15 April 1991, Justice Kennedy wrote for a 6-to-3 majority rejecting another contention and went on to pronounce a new rule on such appeals. Henceforth "a failure to press at the outset a claim of constitutional defect will be excused only if the inmate can show that something actually prevented raising that issue and can prove that the claimed defect made a difference in the outcome of the verdict or sentence."

This decision will have the effect of reducing the number of habeas corpus appeals to the federal courts on the basis of constitutional defect. The basis for appellate review at the highest level is the writ of habeas corpus. Proceedings on this writ, one of the most ancient in the Common Law, call on the custodian of any person detained, "to produce the body of the prisoner at a designated time and place, to do, to submit to, and receive whatever the court shall consider in that behalf." Prisoners on a death row argue in such a writ that their detention as condemned persons is based on some error in the administration of the law.

Source: *Barefoot v. Estelle*, 103 S. Ct. 3383 (1983); *Pulley v. Harris*, 104 S. Ct. 881 (1984); *Stanford v. Kentucky* 109 S. Ct. 2969 (1989); *Wilkins v. Missouri*, 109 S. Ct. 2969 (1989); *Penry v. Lynch*, 109 S. Ct. 2934 (1989), *McCleskey v. Kemp*, 107 S. Ct. 1756 (1987).

experience to make the best of a set of facts that usually includes the defendant's guilt of a homicide, but not necessarily of the first degree.

It is impossible to arrive at an estimate of the costs of capital punishment litigation. Some famous cases have incurred costs ranging in the millions of dollars. For abolitionists the cost of justice for a person facing the death penalty is irrelevant. Retentionists denounce the tortuous delays in administering capital punishment. Chief Justice William H. Rehnquist has called for congressional legislation restricting the right of appeal in death penalty cases to one round in the federal appellate courts with a six-month limit for prisoners to file their challenges.[34]

Much more important than the cost of litigation is the enormous amount of police and prosecutorial time that must be devoted to preparing a case for trial, trying it, and pursuing the appeal to a conclusion. Many prosecutors find that they must assign such litigation a low priority because of the pressing need to attend to other cases. In the metropolitan courts in which most capital cases are tried, a judicial gridlock has added to the delay caused by the rules assuring due process. One thing is certain: If prompt and speedy administration of justice is an essential element of deterrence, the present system of litigation results in the reverse of that requirement.

THE IMPACT OF THE DEATH PENALTY

Both abolitionists and retentionists have devoted ingenuity and rhetoric to establish answers to the question of deterrence that would favor their respective positions. Whether the death penalty should be given to those age 18 and under when the crime was committed is another issue that concerns both abolitionists and retentionists.

Deterrence and the Death Penalty

As we have previously noted, the ancient justification of revenge or retribution is not subject to proof. The **deterrence** of criminals, however, rests on a hypothesis that should be open to empirical test. There are many ways to frame the theory of deterrence. For the purpose of this chapter we will settle for the definition of the National Academy of Science:

> Deterrence is the inhibiting effect of sanctions on the criminal activity of people other than the sanctioned offender.[35]

From this definition it follows that criminal activity will be inhibited when sanctions are imposed. If so, the imposition of capital punishment, the most severe sanction of all, will inhibit the commission of crimes for which it is the penalty. At present, the only crime for which it is imposed is first-degree murder. We leave aside the unusual crime of treason, which remains on the statutes but for which no one has been sentenced to death for the past 30 years. If deterrence has an inhibiting effect on the commission of first-degree murder, that effect should be reflected in the homicide rates.

The first social scientist to engage in an empirical test of this hypothesis was the famous sociologist Thorsten Sellin. He reasoned that in the case of two or more states adjoining each other, one or more without the death penalty and others with it, homicide rates should be lower in the retentionist states if the deterrence hypothesis is valid.

As it happens, there are several such clusters of states. Sellin tabulated their experience with homicide over many years with the results shown in Table 7.3.[36]

Michigan abolished capital punishment in 1846 and has not revived it in the century and a half that has elapsed since. Ohio and Indiana have consistently executed murderers throughout their histories. Michigan and Ohio are about the same size in population and have about the same distribution among residents of very large cities, smaller towns, and rural districts. The distribution of the population among racial minorities is about the same in both states. They are, of course, contiguous. Abolitionists argue that if capital punishment were an effective deterrent of murder, the homicide rates in Ohio over the 54-year period under study would be significantly lower than in Michigan. They are not. The same holds true in Indiana.

Note that in the period from 1965 to 1969 the homicide rate in Michigan doubled and nearly doubled again between 1970 and 1974. The rates in Ohio and Indiana also rose, but more modestly. A hasty review might lead one to conclude that at last the benefits of capital punishment were taking effect. However, although Michigan had no death penalty, Ohio and Indiana, because of the moratorium on capital punishment, did not execute anyone. Capital punishment thus could not have had anything to do with increases cited. Reflection on the social and political history of the time suggests that there were other, much more potent influences contributing to the increase in homicide rates. Race riots in the large cities (especially Detroit), the turbulent conflict generated by the war in Vietnam, the growing traffic in narcotics, and a good deal of economic instability almost certainly had much more to do with more people being killed than operations of the criminal justice system.

Sellin made other comparisons among similar clusters of states: Minnesota and Wisconsin with Iowa, and Rhode Island and Maine with Massachusetts. In none of these comparisons was any evidence of the superior deterrence of capital punishment over life in prison found.

Retentionists dismiss Sellin's methodology as fatally flawed. They point out that other influences may affect the murder rate, even in states that may in many respects

Table 7.3 CRUDE HOMICIDE DEATH RATES, WITH NUMBERS OF EXECUTIONS, MICHIGAN, OHIO, AND INDIANA, 1920–1974 (MEAN ANNUAL RATES PER 100,000 POPULATION)

	Michigan	Ohio		Indiana	
	Rate	Rate	Number of executions	Rate	Number of executions
1920–1924	5.5	7.4	45	6.1	5
1925–1929	8.2	8.4	40	6.6	7
1930–1934	5.6	8.5	43	6.5	11
1935–1939	3.9	5.9	29	4.5	22
1940–1944	3.2	4.3	15	3.0	2
1945–1949	3.5	4.8	36	3.8	5
1950–1954	3.8	3.8	20	3.7	2
1955–1959	3.0	3.4	12	3.0	0
1960–1964	3.6	3.2	7	3.2	1
1965–1969	6.6	5.1	0	4.7	0
1970–1974	11.3	7.8	0	6.4	0

Source: National Office of Vital Statistics, *Vital Statistics of the United States*; William J. Bowers, *Executions in America* (Lexington, Mass.: D. C. Heath, 1974), Appendix A. Reprinted by permission of the publisher, from *Executions in America,* by William J. Bowers (Lexington, Mass.: Lexington Books, D. C. Heath & Co., copyright 1974, D. C. Heath & Company).

A California gas chamber. (*Source:* California Department of Corrections.)

be similar. Sellin did not control for the availability of handguns and lethal poisons, the rate of poverty and unemployment, the proportion of the population in the younger age groups, the amount of violence shown on television, the state of medical science, and the efficiency of the police.[37] Advocates of capital punishment argue that his disregarding these and other potentially influential variables invalidates Sellin's conclusions. They also point out that Sellin and others who have conducted similar studies are convinced that abolitionists and their bias to capital punishment may have distorted their research. They do not show how this might be the case.

Capital punishment gained more substantial support from the publication in 1975 of an article by the economist Isaac Ehrlich, showing that the deterrence effect of the death penalty was far from negligible or nonexistent.[38] Using the complex statistical methodology of regression analysis, he arrived at the conclusion that every execution deterred eight homicides. In doing so he included such variables as the arrest rate in murder cases, the conviction rate of murder suspects, the rate of labor force participation, the unemployment rate, the fraction of the population in the 14-to-20 age group, and per capita income. This analysis was applied to the data for executions and homicide rates for the entire United States for each year between 1932 and 1967. Note that there was a precipitous decline in the number of executions during that period.

In spite of the recondite statistical methods used, Ehrlich's article soon became famous. It was the first empirical study showing that capital punishment might be a very substantial deterrent. It was cited by the U.S. Solicitor General in a brief for the Supreme Court to show that capital punishment was an effective deterrent.[39]

Ehrlich's fellow economists as well as sociologists challenged him on many counts. Hardly any of their reviews supported his conclusions, but Ehrlich stoutly fired back at each salvo from his critics. Perhaps the most authoritative review is contained in the report of the Panel on Research on Deterrence of the National Academy of Sciences, which included several distinguished economists:

> In undertaking research on the deterrent effect of capital punishment . . . it should be recognized that the strong value content associated with decisions regarding capital punishment and the high risk associated with errors of commission make it likely that any policy use of scientific evidence . . . will require extremely severe standards of proof. The non-experimental research to which the study of the deterrent effects of capital punishment is necessarily limited almost certainly will be unable to meet these standards of proof. Thus, the panel considers that research on this topic is not likely to produce findings that will or should have much influence on policy-makers.[40]

Juveniles and the Death Penalty

According to Victor Streib, a professor of law at Cleveland State University, the United States has executed 281 juvenile offenders throughout its history. Thomas Graunger, a 16 year old (caught sodomizing a horse and a cow), was the first execution in 1642. Fourteen states have never executed juveniles, but Georgia leads all states with 41 juvenile executions, followed by North Carolina and Ohio, with 19 each.[41]

Of the 38 states that permit capital punishment, 27 allow it for those age 18 or under at the time the crime was committed (see Table 7.4). In Indiana, where Paula Cooper was condemned to die for a crime she committed when she was 15, executions were permitted for crimes committed from age 10. Partly because of the turmoil created by the sentencing of Paula Cooper to death, the Indiana legislature raised the minimum age for a death sentence to 16.

In 1982, in the case of Monty Lee Eddings, a 16 year old from Oklahoma who killed a police officer, the court ruled that "great weight" must be given to the youth's age.[42] Then, in late 1988, the court heard the case of *Thompson* v. *Oklahoma*.[43] Wayne Thompson was 15 when he was arrested along with his half brother, then 27, and two other men, also in their twenties, for the shooting and stabbing death of Charles Keene, Thompson's former brother-in-law. The court ruled by a 5-to-3 vote (Justice Kennedy abstained) that "the Eighth and Fourteenth Amendments prohibit the execution of a person who was under 16 years of age at the times of his or her offense."[44] The court finally upheld the constitutionality of the death penalty with juveniles in two 1989 cases, in which 16-year-old Heath A. Wilkins of Missouri and 17-year-old Kevin N. Stanford of Kentucky had been convicted of first-degree murder.[45] (See Box 7-3 for the background of these cases.)

Abolitionists are especially critical of what they consider the barbaric and uncivilized practice of sentencing a juvenile to the death penalty. They charge that the death penalty should never be applied to juveniles because age is a mitigating factor. In constraint, retentionists hold to the same reasons for sentencing a juvenile murderer to death as they would an adult who committed the same crime.

Table 7.4 MINIMUM AGE AUTHORIZED FOR CAPITAL PUNISHMENT, YEAR END 1989

Age less than 18	Age 18	None specified
Arkansas (15)	California	Alabama
Georgia (17)	Colorado	Arizona
Indiana (16)	Connecticut	Delaware
Kentucky (16)	Illinois	Florida
Louisiana (16)[a]	Maryland	Idaho
Mississippi (13)[b]	New Jersey	Nebraska[c]
Missouri (14)	New Mexico	Pennsylvania
Montana[d]	Ohio	South Carolina
Nevada (16)	Oregon	Washington
New Hampshire (17)	Tennessee	
North Carolina[a]	Federal system[f]	
Oklahoma (16)		
South Dakota[g]		
Texas (17)		
Utah (14)		
Virginia (15)		
Wyoming (16)		

Note: Ages at the time of the capital offense were indicated by the offices of the state attorneys general.

[a]Interpretation of attorney general's office based on La. R.S. 13:1571.1.

[b]Minimum age defined by statute is 13, but effective age is 16 based on an interpretation of U.S. Supreme Court decisions by the attorney general's office.

[c]Age can be a statutory mitigating factor.

[d]Youths as young as 12 may be tried as adults, but age less than 18 is a mitigating factor.

[e]Age required is 17 unless the murderer was incarcerated for murder when a subsequent murder occurred; then, the age may be 14.

[f]Age 18; less than 18 but not younger than 14 if waived from juvenile court.

[g]Age 10, but only after a transfer hearing to try a juvenile as an adult.

Source: Lawrence A. Greenfield, *Capital Punishment 1989* (Washington: Bureau of Justice Statistics, 1990), p. 5.

CONCLUSIONS

Capital punishment statutes remain in the codes. With 80 percent of the population of the United States in support, their disappearance will not occur soon. That this country is thus almost alone in the Western industrialized world does not trouble advocates of the death penalty. With a serious crisis on the sale and widespread use of narcotics facing policymakers, there is more than an inclination to enact laws that would extend capital punishment to drug dealing. The evidence that it will affect crime rates is tenuous. As Sellin noted,

> It is impossible to prove that there are no unicorns. All that we can prove is that we've found none so far. If the end result of a long argument . . . is nothing more than a statement that a particular theory can't be disproved, you are probably safe in putting it in the same class as unicorns.[46]

The debate over deterrence and its empirical support is furious. Since 1976 hundreds of men and women have accumulated on the nation's death rows, only a small fraction of whom have been executed. It is plausible to suppose that the end of capital punishment is in sight. That prospect is distant. So long as the rates of criminal violence appear to rise, so long as the public in our major cities lives in fear, capital punishment will seem to be a reasonable precaution to take against the men and women responsible for creating that fear. So long as our cities contain large numbers of people living in the conditions of an impoverished underclass, the fear of them will persist—and with good reason. Fear, however justifiable, is never a sound foundation for making public policy. The scattering of men and women killed by a few states may satisfy an angry public and aggrieved relatives of victims. The annals of criminal justice provide absolutely no reason to suppose that the number of homicides in the United States will be thereby diminished.

KEY TERMS

abolitionists

constitutional foundations

deterrence

moral foundations

pragmatic foundations

retentionist argument

DISCUSSION TOPICS

7.1 Summarize the early arguments on the death penalty.

7.2 What is the retentionist argument on the death penalty?

7.3 Define and discuss the moral, constitutional, and pragmatic issues of the abolitionist argument.

7.4 Summarize the debate on deterrence and the death penalty.

ANNOTATED REFERENCES

Bedau, Hugo Adam, ed. *The Death Penalty in America*, 3rd ed. New York: Oxford University Press, 1982. *Bedau is a convinced and consistent abolitionist, but this collection of articles scrupulously includes articles by such articulate retentionists as Walter Berns and Ernest van den Haag, as well as abolitionist articles by Anthony Amsterdam, Charles Black, and Hans Zeisel, among others.*

———, and Chester M. Pierce, eds. *Capital Punishment in the United States*. New York: AMS Press, 1975. *A collection of essays and articles on capital punishment, all of them written from the abolitionist perspective.*

Blumstein, Alfred, Jacqueline Cohen, and Daniel Nagin, eds. *Deterrence and Incapacitation: Estimating the Effects of Criminal Sanctions on Crime Rates*. Washington: National Academy of Sciences, 1978. *This important volume contains a review by Lawrence Klein, Brian Forst, and Victor Filatov on "The Deterrent Effect of Capital Punishment: An Assessment of the Estimates." Although this article discusses Thorsten Sellin's study of deterrence in abolitionist and retentionist states, most of its attention is devoted to the intricate Ehrlich statistical contention that capital punishment effectively deters homicide.*

Johnson, Robert. *Death Work: A Study of the Modern Execution Process.* Pacific Grove, Calif.: Brooks/Cole, 1989. *Johnson has compiled an account of the actual processes of execution in the United States, together with its effects on executioners, witnesses, and the men and women executed. He concludes with a powerfully written argument against the process.*

Sellin, Thorsten. *The Penalty of Death.* Beverly Hills, Calif.: Sage, 1980. *In this volume, the author reports on the validity of the utilitarian claim that capital punishment succeeds in deterring the crime of murder. His well-known study of the incidence of homicide in abolitionist and retentionist states will be found in Chapters 9 and 10, pp. 139–179.*

Van den Haag, Ernest, and John P. Conrad. *The Death Penalty: A Debate.* New York: Plenum, 1983. *An extended exchange of views between an uncompromising retentionist and an equally uncompromising abolitionist. Most of the significant policy and scholarly issues are examined vigorously.*

Zimring, Franklin E., and Gordon Hawkins. *Capital Punishment and the American Agenda.* Cambridge: Cambridge University Press, 1986. *The authors are candid: "This book is advocacy scholarship." They have examined the status of death penalty legislation and its actual implementation in a very few states, mostly southern. The fundamental question is whether capital punishment is "in harmony with a progressive vision of the American future."*

NOTES

1. Cesare Beccaria, *On Crimes and Punishments*, trans. Henry Paolucci (Indianapolis: Bobbs-Merrill, 1963), pp. 45–49. For a much older and more eloquent critique of the death penalty, see Thucydides, *The Peloponnesion War*, trans. R. Crawley (New York: Modern Library, 1934), pp. 167–170.
2. President Gorbachev of the Soviet Union declared his intention to revise the criminal codes as a phase of *perestroika*, the "restructuring" of society. There have been intimations that capital punishment may be abolished in the USSR, or at least drastically curtailed.
3. The shift in public opinion on the issue of abolition or retention has been dramatic. In 1965, the Roper poll reported that 47 percent of those surveyed were opposed to capital punishment, and 38 percent were in favor, 15 percent were unsure.
4. Dagobert D. Runes (ed.), *The Selected Writings of Benjamin Rush* (New York: The Philosophical Library, 1947).
5. Philip English Mackey (ed.), *Voices Against Death* (New York: Burt Franklin, 1976), pp. 14–33.
6. Sir James Fitzjames Stephen, "Capital Punishment," *Fraser's Magazine*, 1864. Quoted by Franklin E. Zimring and Gordon Hawkins, *Capital Punishment and the American Agenda* (Cambridge, England: Cambridge University Press, 1986), p. 159.
7. Sir James Fitzjames Stephen, *A General View of the Criminal Law of England* (London: Macmillan, 1963), p. 99.
8. In 1990, an anti-crime bill was passed in Congress that will extend the death penalty to 33 offenses, ranging from hostage taking to drug trafficking with profits exceeding $5,000,000.
9. In *Furman v. Georgia*, 408 U.S. 238 (1972).
10. In *Gregg v. Georgia*, 428 U.S. 153 (1976).
11. David C. Baldus, Charles A. Pulaski Jr., and George Woodworth, "Arbitrariness and

Discrimination in the Administration of the Death Penalty: A Challenge to State Supreme Courts," *Stetson Law Review* XV, 2: Spring 1986, pp. 146–149.

12. James Q. Wilson, *Thinking About Crime*, rev. ed. (New York: Basic Books, 1963).
13. Ernest van den Haag, *Punishing Criminals: Concerning a Very Old and Painful Question* (New York: Basic Books, 1975).
14. Ernest van den Haag and John P. Conrad, *The Death Penalty: A Debate* (New York: Plenum Press, 1983).
15. Ibid., p. 68.
16. Ernest van den Haag, "In Defense of the Death Penalty: A Practical and Moral Analysis." In Hugo Adam Bedau, ed., *The Death Penalty in America*, 3rd ed. (New York and Oxford: Oxford University Press, 1982), pp. 332–333.
17. It is important to keep in mind that the retentionist claims that his arguments are based on profoundly moral considerations. In this chapter we are impartially encapsulating the two opposing conditions.
18. Charles L. Black, *Capital Punishment: The Inevitability of Caprice and Mistake*, 2nd ed. (New York: Norton, 1978), pp. 161–162.
19. Ibid., p. 22
20. The United States General Accounting Office, Death Penalty Sentencing (Washington, D.C.: February 1990). However, the federal courts have rejected discrimination as grounds for reversal of the sentence of death. See *McClesky v. Kemp*, 753 E. 2d 877, (1989).
21. Van den Haag and Conrad, *The Death Penalty*, pp. 206–207.
22. *State v. Lockett*, 358 N.E. 2d 1062 (Ohio 1976).
23. *Lockett v. Ohio*, 438 U.S. 586, 98 S. Ct. 1891 (1978).
24. Van den Haag and Conrad, *The Death Penalty*, pp. 226–231.
25. Ibid.
26. Black, *Capital Punishment*, pp. 85–93.
27. *Trop v. Dulles*, 356 U.S. 86 (1957). In this case a military court martial convicted a soldier of desertion in time of war and sentenced him to be stripped of his nationality. The court held that this was cruel and unusual punishment.
28. For a spirited but learned denunciation of this interpretation of the Constitution, see Raoul Berger, *Death Penalties: The Supreme Court's Obstacle Course* (Cambridge, Mass.: Harvard University Press, 1982), pp. 116–122.
29. *Furman*.
30. Ibid.
31. Ibid.
32. *Gregg v. Georgia*.
33. Ibid.
34. For an extended discussion of delay from the retentionist point of view, see Berns, *For Capital Punishment*, pp. 112–127.
35. Alfred Blumstein, Jacqueline Cohen, and Daniel Nagin, editors for the National Research Council Panel on Research on Deterrent and Incapacitative Effects, *Deterrence and Incapacitation: Estimating the Effects of Criminal Sanctions on Crime Rates* (Washington: National Academy Press, 1978), p. 3.
36. Thorsten Sellin, *The Penalty of Death* (Beverly Hills, Calif.: Sage, 1980), p. 144.
37. See Berns, *For Capital Punishment*, for a full bill of particulars.
38. Isaac Ehrlich, "The Deterrent Effect of Capital Punishment: A Question of Life and Death," *American Economic Review* 65 (1975), p. 397. This article was followed by more elaborate studies focusing on capital punishment. For a full bibliography of Ehrlich's numerous articles defending his method of finding, and the articles of others supporting him and opposing him, see Deryck Beyleveid, "Ehrlich's Analysis of Deterrence," *British Journal of Criminology* 22, April 1982: 101–123.

39. *Fowler v. North Carolina*, 428 U.S. 904 (1976).
40. Blumstein et al., *Deterrence and Incapacitation*, p. 63.
41. Victor Streib, *The Death Penalty and Juveniles* (Bloomington, Indiana: Indiana University Press, 1988).
42. *Eddings v. Oklahoma*, 102 S. Ct. (1982).
43. *Thompson v. Oklahoma*, 102 S. Ct. (1988).
44. Ibid.
45. Decided on June 26, 1989, 57 LW 4973.
46. Sellin, *The Penalty of Death*, p. 178.

PART THREE

Community-based Corrections

Chapter 8

Community-based Corrections: An Overview

CHAPTER OUTLINE

Community-based corrections is made up of pretrial release and diversion, probation, residential and reentry programs, and parole. The most distinguishing feature of community-based programs is the frequency, duration, and quality of community relationships. The quality of community relationships, however, is even more important than the frequency and duration of community contacts. The chain gangs of an earlier era placed inmates in the community outside the prison walls, but they scarcely yielded the relationships that are needed for successful community-based programs.[1]

This chapter discusses the reasons for the rise and fall of the popularity of community-based programs from the late 1960s through the 1980s; examines the philosophical underpinnings of community-based corrections; considers state, local, and privately administered community programs; and forecasts the changing face of community-based corrections in the 1990s.

THE RISE AND FALL OF PUBLIC ACCEPTANCE

Community-based corrections had its origins in the nineteenth century and experienced a period of growth at the beginning of the twentieth century. In the mid-1970s, Richard McGee, director of the California Department of Corrections, encouraged his staff to see if the alarming growth of the prison population could be curbed by a strong parole program. Various experiments were conducted leading to confidence that credible programs of control and professional assistance could shorten prison terms and eventually keep many offenders out of prison. Not only would money be saved, but many relatively harmless men and women would be spared the destructive experience of confinement in overcrowded and underprogrammed prisons. Evaluation of these programs reached mixed results, and some succeeded better than others, but the overall findings were positive enough to gain acceptance by the state legislature and the law-enforcement community.

By 1961, enough experience with community corrections had accumulated for an ambitious experiment conducted by the California Youth Authority. Herman Stark, the agency's director, engaged the services of Marguerite Warren, a social psychologist, for the design and professional direction of the Community Treatment Project (CTP).[2] This experiment called for the random assignment of Youth Authority wards to control and experimental groups. The control group youths were committed to institutions and released on the standard basis after the customary reviews by the staff and a hearing by the Youth Authority. Wards assigned to the experimental group were released to the community immediately after commitment to the Youth Authority. After intensive psychological testing, they were assigned according to "maturity level" and "delinquent subtype" to specific treatment programs organized for their particular level and subtype. Evaluations were sufficiently positive to allow continuation for several years.

The moderate success of the community-based programs led McGee to propose to the legislature a **Probation Subsidy Statute**, through which counties would be subsidized by the state to organize 50-person probation caseloads for felony offenders who would ordinarily be committed to prison but who were placed on these special caseloads instead.[3]

The Probation Subsidy system worked well for several years. There was increasing criticism from the police and district attorneys, but the end came as the subsidies allowed by the law became insufficient to support the reduced caseloads. New legislation was enacted that provided for state subsidy of county correctional systems, to include jails as well as probation. The program of reduced caseloads came to an end with the new statute.

At the same time, crime was emerging as a major social problem. President Lyndon B. Johnson appointed the President's Commission on Law Enforcement and Administration of Justice to study the problem and make recommendations. Californians dominated the Task Force on Corrections; indeed, 8 of the 63 members were employees of the California Department of Corrections or Youth Authority, and 7 more were California academicians who had worked closely with the CTP and probation subsidy programs.

The recommendations of the Corrections Task Force captured the imagination and support of American citizens in the late 1960s and early 1970s. The spirit of the times was one of reform. The area of mental health had gone through a period of deinstitutionalization in the 1960s, in which greater numbers of mental patients were kept in the community rather than placed in large institutions. The turbulence brought on by the Vietnam War, urban riots and disturbances on college campuses, and the widespread questioning of traditional values by youth countercultures fostered a receptivity to new solutions. The bloody prison riots that erupted between 1971 and 1973 also helped support the conclusion that there must be a better way.

Federal funding, finally, provided the catalyst that linked correctional reform with social and political realities, thereby creating a huge array of community-based programs throughout the nation. For example, from the inception of the Law Enforcement Assistance Administration (LEAA) in 1967 to July 1975, $23,837,512 of the Safe Street Act federal monies was matched with $12,300,710 from state and local funds for grants devoted solely to residential aftercare programs for adults. Thus, guided by reintegrative philosophy, advocated by a number of blue-ribbon commissions, and supported by federal dollars, community-based programs sprouted in nearly every state.

Yet community-based corrections began to decline in popularity even more rapidly than it had gained public approval. In the mid-1970s, the mood of the country suddenly changed to a "get tough with criminals" approach as publications of official statistics and media coverage of street crime convinced the public that the crime problem had gotten out of hand. The "permissive" approach that kept offenders in the community became less and less acceptable. Supporters of the punishment model were quick to urge incarceration as a more fitting way of dealing with crime. This model would teach offenders that they had to pay for their crimes in prison rather than in their community, where they could come and go as they pleased. Institutional populations climbed to an all-time high.

By the late 1970s, it became apparent that the public was growing increasingly disillusioned with residential programs. Indeed, it was widely stated at the time that "community corrections is acceptable to the public until you give it an address." The unreceptivity of many communities made it extremely difficult for departments of corrections to establish new residential programs. In 1979, Perry M. Johnson, director of the Michigan Department of Corrections, commented on the difficulty his department experienced in establishing new halfway houses in the community:

> We have 70 halfway houses throughout the state; in fact, we've got a larger proportion of felons in the community than any other state: 1,600 of our 15,000 are in our halfway houses. Where we're established, we receive very little flak, but whenever we try to develop new centers we run into substantial resistance. Out of every ten attempts, we get one facility.[4]

The financial crunch affecting all levels of government, along with the demise of LEAA support of community programs, also made it difficult both to establish new programs and to sustain the ones already functioning in the community. In California, partly because of the inability of that state's legislature to deal with the demands for local tax relief, a citizens' tax revolt ("Proposition 13") led to a California constitutional amendment that rolled property tax rates back to the levels prevailing in 1975. The loss in probation subsidy, as well as the disappearance of one in four probation officer positions, were two consequences of this citizens' tax revolt.[5]

Moreover, in the late 1970s and 1980s, liberals who had supported community-based corrections with so much enthusiasm only a few years before now became increasingly critical. Stanley Cohen, one of the most articulate, has this to say about how community programs expand the net of the criminal justice system:

1. There is an increase in the total number of deviants getting into the system in the first place and many of these are new deviants who would not have been processed previously (wider nets).
2. There is an increase in the overall intensity of intervention, with old and new deviants being subject to levels of intervention (including traditional institutionalization) which they might not have previously received (denser nets).
3. New agencies and services are supplementing rather than replacing the original set of control mechanisms (different nets).[6]

Cohen explains that the popular strategies of **deinstitutionalization** and **diversion** were aimed at decreasing the size, scope, and intensity of the criminal justice system's interventions in offenders' lives. But instead of reducing the number of those sentenced to prison, Cohen and a host of others contend, "community control has supplemented rather than replaced traditional methods," resulting in an expansion of the overall system. Cohen also argues that the " 'wrong' populations are being swept into the new parts of the net." These populations are wrong because they are inappropriate placements and would not otherwise be incarcerated if the new programs did not exist. Finally, Cohen observes that proponents of community-based corrections promised that its forms of interventions "would be less intrusive, onerous, coercive, stigmatizing, artificial, and bureaucratic; more humane, just, fair, helpful, natural and informal." But he charges that the intensive observation and surveillance of intermediate sentencing models (intensive probation supervision, electronic monitoring, and house arrest), compulsory therapy of many community programs, and the stringent security conditions of residential settings simulate or mimic institutional life instead of providing a less intrusive or intense intervention for offenders.[7]

Yet, in spite of declining support given to community-based corrections in the 1970s, prison crowding had a dramatic effect on increasing the size of community-based corrections in the 1980s. Federal court orders in 36 states to relieve crowded prison conditions meant that the states had to do something. Although prison construction remained a possible long-term solution, more immediate relief was clearly needed. Community-based corrections, particularly probation and parole, suddenly gained the favor of judges and politicians, and the number of those on probation soon skyrocketed and of those on parole significantly increased.

Today, substantially more offenders are involved in community-based corrections than are confined in prisons. For example, on January 1, 1990, more than 4 million adults were under some form of correctional supervision. Nearly two-thirds

(62.2 percent) of these offenders were on probation, while an additional 11.3 percent were under parole supervision.[8]

PHILOSOPHICAL UNDERPINNINGS

The new challenge of corrections, according to the 1967 Corrections Task Force of the President's Commission on Law Enforcement and Administration of Justice, was to keep offenders in the community and to help reintegrate them into community living.[9] Community-based corrections responded to the widespread dissatisfaction with prison programs. The nominal quality of conventional probation was equally unsatisfactory to both criminal justice professionals and to the general public.

Anti-institutionalization

The President's Commission was perhaps the first national statement of the principle that there were far too many nonviolent property offenders serving too much time in prison, that they could be on probation or in some other community-based control. The Corrections Task Force stressed the need for alternatives to prison because too many of these long-term facilities were understaffed and deteriorating, had problems with crowding and violence, and were out of control.[10] The commission report also charged that prisons typically were remote from urban communities and that this inaccessibility made it extremely difficult to reintegrate inmates into community settings and to recruit correctional staff, especially professionals.[11]

In 1973, the National Advisory Commission on Criminal Justice Standards and Goals, a blue-ribbon commission that focused on developing standards for criminal justice, also explained why it was necessary to keep offenders out of long-term institutions:

> Prisons tend to dehumanize people. . . . Their weaknesses are made worse and their capacity for responsibility and self-government is eroded by regimentation. Add to these facts the physical and mental conditions resulting from overcrowding and from the various ways in which institutions ignore the rights of offenders, and the riots of the present time are hardly to be wondered at. Safety for society may be achieved for a limited time if offenders are kept out of circulation, but no real public protection is provided if confinement serves mainly to prepare men for more, and more skilled, criminality.[12]

Thus, both the President's Crime Commission and the National Advisory Commission established their case for community-based corrections by charging that correctional institutions were ineffective and inhumane. The National Advisory Commission report went so far as to recommend that "states should refrain from building any more state institutions for juveniles" and "should also refrain from building more state institutions for adults for the next ten years, except where total institution planning shows that the need is imperative."[13]

The anti-institutionalization emphasis is a minority position in American corrections today. In a 1990 interview, Janet A. Leban, director of the Pennsylvania Prison Society, forcefully challenged the practice of increasing the numbers of those incarcerated in long-term institutions (see Box 8-1).

Box 8-1 Interview with Janet A. Leban

Question: Where is Pennsylvania now in terms of corrections?

Answer: I see the picture in Pennsylvania as grim. We have a new commissioner who was just confirmed by the Senate last week. He is from the state of Washington, and I guess I was hopeful given that background. Washington is one of the better, more progressive states. I hoped that his early initiative would indicate that he was progressive and that he would make improvements. His first press release came out last Friday, and it's just more of the same. The focus was on building. There's going to be enough construction with money appropriated, if need be, for a total of over 15,000 new prison beds.

The budget for corrections increased by 11 percent over the last fiscal year. The price tag for just prison construction alone is going to be somewhere in the neighborhood of $250,000,000. Then, there's another $200,000,000 to counties to help them relieve their jail overcrowding. The education and environmental budgets have been cut, including cleaning up hazardous waste sites. We had a riot at Camp Hill at the end of October. This agency thought that would lead legislators, who in this state are very conservative, to come to grips with various problems. The only way they seem to be able to do that is construction.

Source: Interviewed in June 1990.

Reintegrative Philosophy

The President's Crime Commission and the National Advisory Commission also developed the basic assumptions of **reintegrative philosophy**, which can be defined as the priority given to returning offenders to the community as law-abiding citizens. It was reasoned that as nearly all offenders would eventually return to their communities, they should have help in dealing with the inherent problems sooner rather than later. All the resources of the community were to be mobilized to help offenders restore family ties, obtain employment and education, and find their place in society. Thus, meaningful community contacts are required in order for offenders to assume the normal roles of family member, employee, and citizen. Furthermore, proponents of reintegrative philosophy recommended community-based corrections for all but hard-core criminals. To those who had to be institutionalized they would offer a wide variety of reentry programs, permit inmates to be brought into the decision-making process so that they could choose their prison programs, and provide the necessary services so that offenders could restore family ties and obtain employment and education.[14]

Internalization is the process by which change takes place in the reintegration model. To achieve internalization, offenders must be presented with such options as employment, education, recreation, and any other activities needed to provide direct or indirect alternatives to criminal behavior. Proponents of this model reason that through a process of experimentation, offenders can learn how to meet their needs in law-abiding ways so that they will alter socially unacceptable values and behaviors.

However, reintegrative philosophy has encountered increased criticism in recent years. Critics charge that this high-sounding concept lacks meaning in the real world. These commendable sentiments, they explain, are extraordinarily unrealistic in a world in which narcotics, the underclass community, racism, and lack of opportunities define resocialization for adult offenders.

STATE, LOCAL, AND PRIVATELY ADMINISTERED COMMUNITY-BASED CORRECTIONS

Comprehensive state-sponsored, locally sponsored (usually by the courts), and privately administered programs are the three basic types of organizational structures in community-based corrections.

State-sponsored Community-based Corrections Programs

States administer community-based corrections in several ways. Forty-five states administer probation. State departments of corrections also are responsible for reentry programs, such as work release, home furloughs, and educational release. Moreover, parole supervision is administered by the state in every state that still conducts parole services. Finally, 15 states passed community corrections acts in the 1970s and 1980s.

Minnesota, Oregon, and Kansas indicated their support of community-based corrections by passing **community corrections acts** in the 1970s. California also passed a community corrections act in the late 1970s, but it is debatable whether this act, which replaces the Probation Subsidy Act, is a move toward or away from community-based programs. In the 1980s, Colorado, Connecticut, Indiana, Michigan, and Virginia were among those states that passed community corrections acts, but each state varies in how widely the corrections act has been implemented throughout the state.[15]

Minnesota The first step in the enactment of the broad and comprehensive Community Corrections Act in Minnesota was the formation in July 1972 of a study committee whose task it was to review and assess the correctional systems in the state.[16] This group, composed of legislators and their staffs, police, judges, representatives of state and county agencies, local elected officials, and staff from the department of corrections, drafted the Community Corrections Act. After extensive review and revision, the draft legislation was presented to the legislature in February 1973. The act became law during that session, with an appropriation of $1.5 million for the first phase of implementation in three pilot areas. The 1975 legislature appropriated more than $7 million to continue the program in the pilot areas and to expand it to include an additional 18 counties during the next two years. The 1977 legislature continued its support by providing $13.6 million to maintain the program in all the counties where it had been implemented and to extend it into nine additional counties. By 1980, at the peak of the Community Corrections Act's success, about 70 percent of Minnesota's counties were participating in the community corrections project.

Minnesota's Community Corrections Act has four major purposes: (1) reduction of commitments to state prisons; (2) encouragement of local units of government to maintain responsibility for offenders whose crimes are not serious (those who would receive a sentence of less than five years in a state facility); (3) promotion of community corrections planning at the local level; and (4) improved coordination among local components of the criminal justice system.

The establishment of a local community advisory board is basic to the implementation of the plan in each new area. This board, which represents the criminal justice system and other community groups, develops a local comprehensive plan that identifies correctional needs and defines the programs and services necessary to meet those needs. After the comprehensive plan has been completed, it is submitted to the county board (or joint power board in multicounty units) for final approval. The plan is then sent to the commissioner of corrections 30 days before the expected starting date. When the commissioner has approved the comprehensive plan, the county or multicounty unit becomes eligible for a state financial subsidy. (See Figure 8.1 for the organization of the community corrections act.)

In a 1990 interview, Jeff Martin, coordinator of the Community Corrections Act in Minnesota, gives an up-to-date report on this act:

> Our community corrections act has recently made some changes. We used to have a financial disincentive built in for short-term offenders, sentenced to less than five years. If they were sent to prison, the county had to pay a per diem for their care. We would pay for longer term offenders with five years or more. So, there was an incentive to keep clients at home. If they kept them there, the first time burglars and car thieves, they would be able to keep all of their subsidy money. They wouldn't have to pay the per diem to the state.
>
> In 1981 we passed a sentencing guidelines law in Minnesota that basically told the courts whom to sentence and for how long. We made a decision that it is unfair for one agency in the government to require payment for incarceration, while another agency tells the courts whom to send. We decided this financial disincentive, this charge-back idea, would be dropped. There is no charge for anyone sent by the local courts. This has gotten to be a windfall for the counties because they have gotten to keep all of their subsidy money, although we still have the financial disincentive for juveniles.[17]

Minnesota has used its Community Corrections Act to develop a large number of residential programs throughout the state, including what was the first restitution program in the United States for probationers, live-in probation centers, and therapeutic communities for both probationers and parolees.

The Probationed Offenders Rehabilitation Training (PORT) Center is one of the most noteworthy of these programs. The staff of this residential program includes an executive director, a group home director, 3 program assistants, an office supervisor, a secretary, and 12 live-in volunteer counselors who provide part-time services. The PORT advisory committee, a group of about 65 Rochester citizens, generates support in the areas of employment, social involvement, legislation and finance, prevention, and public awareness.

This residential center, which serves male adult offenders, has three purposes: residential placement for probationers, crisis intervention and placement, and post-trial sentencing alternatives. Problem-solving groups and individual counseling are used in an attempt to change the antisocial behavior of residents. Each resident is also expected to develop a contract for such specific objectives as social and financial restitution, employment, vocational education, and chemical dependency treatment.

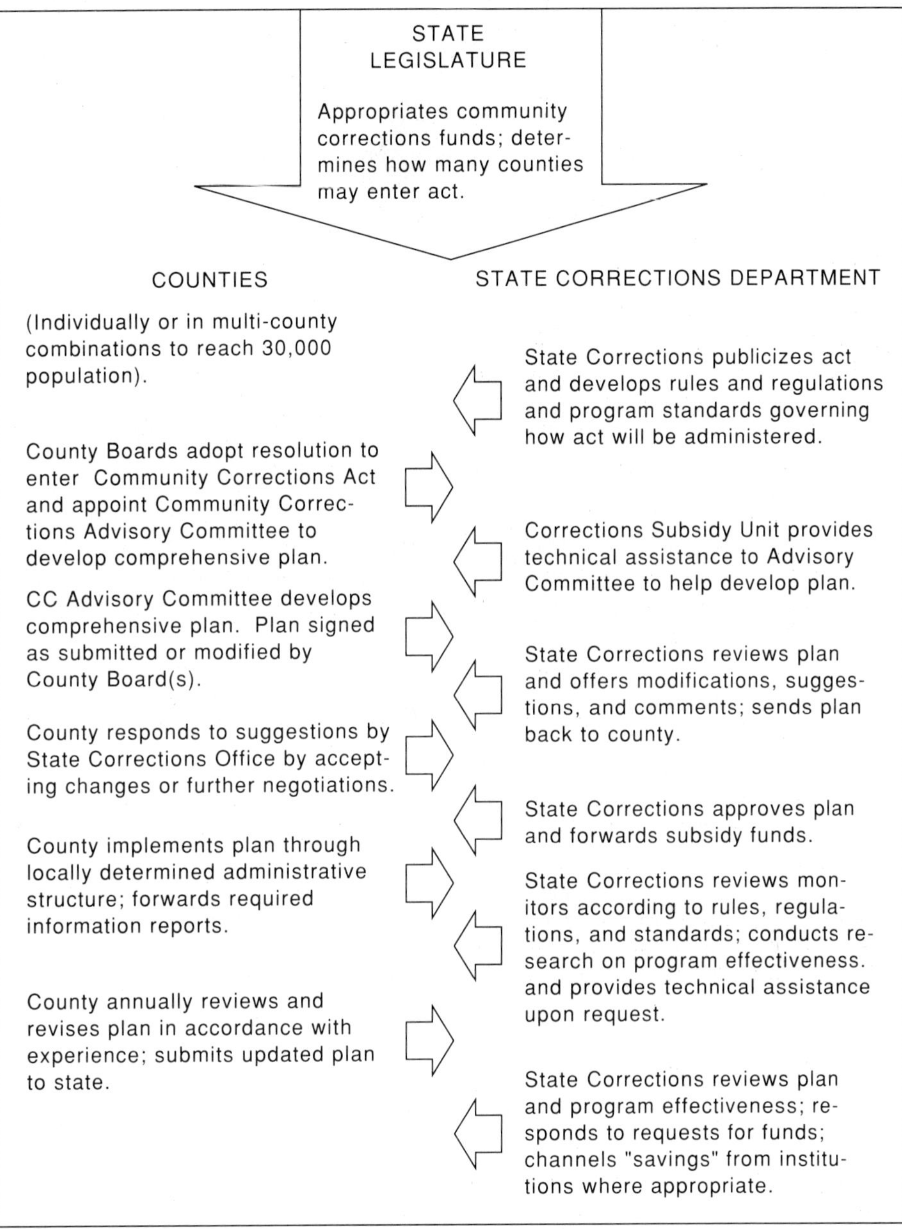

Figure 8.1 The Minnesota Corrections Act. (*Source*: E. Kim Nelson, Howard Ohmart, and Nora Harlow, *Promising Strategies in Probation and Parole* (Washington: Government Printing Office, 1978), p. 61.)

The PORT program has also established the Community Corrections Training Institute, designed to help train community-based corrections staff in other jurisdictions.[18]

However, not everyone is impressed by what has taken place in Minnesota. It is claimed that because this state does not have the urban crime problems that plague

PORT Halfway House, Rochester, Minnesota. (*Source*: PORT Halfway House.)

so many industrial states, there are limits to the application of the Minnesota model. Critics also have reservations about placing too much reliance on county corrections, since this area has traditionally been the least effective of the criminal justice system. Similarly, they argue that the end result of the Community Corrections Act will be a dramatic increase in the use of county jails, which increase will shortchange both the public and the criminal.[19]

Despite these reservations, Minnesota remains the pacesetter in community-based corrections. The Community Corrections Acts in Kansas and Oregon, especially, are modeled after the one in Minnesota. Representatives from many other states have visited Minnesota to see if the act is really effective and if the lessons learned there can be useful at home.

Kansas The 1978 Kansas Community Corrections Act (CCA) was influenced by both the 1965 California Probation Subsidy Program and the 1973 Minnesota Community Corrections Act. Yet, while the Kansas CCA adopted many of these principles, especially the encouragement of local delivery of correctional services, it is not a replica of these community corrections programs. Local counties in Kansas do not have a direct role in the administration of probation or parole services, nor in the improvement of local jail programs. Instead, community corrections in Kansas is narrowly focused on developing new programs not previously funded by either local or state agencies. Consequently, most community corrections programs can be described as intermediate sanctions, providing a sentencing alternative between probation and state incarceration.[20]

The Kansas CCA focuses on a "target population" of nonviolent offenders who have been convicted of Class D and E felony offenses and who have had no more than one prior felony conviction. By 1986, 8 of Kansas's 100 counties (including 4 with large populations) were participating in the CCA. In 7 of the 8 counties, intensive supervision was the primary component of the program. Three counties had adult work release/residential programs, and other components of the CCA included restitution and community service, employment and education services, substance-abuse programs, victim services, and social/psychological evaluations of offenders.[21]

In a 1984 study of the Kansas CCA, Peter Jones reported that "community corrections programs in the two largest participating counties did have a significant impact on prison admissions of program-eligible offenders." Equally significant, Jones added, "the programs appear to have drawn the majority of clients from a prison-bound population."[22] Thus, because the Kansas CCA has achieved a measure of success in targeting and diverting prison-bound offenders, this challenges the previously discussed net-widening criticism of community-based corrections.

Oregon Enacted in July 1977, Oregon's Community Corrections Act also provides a generous state subsidy to those counties choosing to participate. But for every Class C felon (convicted of a minor property offense) a participating county commits to a state correctional institution after January 1, 1979, the county is required to return a portion of its grant money in order to house and provide services for that offender during the first full year of incarceration.

The cornerstone of Oregon's community corrections act is the Central Referral Agency (CRA), which centralizes services at the point of entry into the system. This 24-hour service includes pretrial release, medical screening, referral to community facilities for substance abusers, and information and other support systems for clients. CRA, which is working particularly well in Multnomah County (Portland), has already reduced the number of individuals detained awaiting trial.

Michael C. Musheno et al., in evaluating the implementation of the Community Corrections Act in Colorado, Connecticut, and Oregon, found that the 263 respondents in Oregon, representing various segments of the criminal justice system, were mixed in their evaluation of the Community Corrections Act. About one-fourth (23.6 percent) indicated that the act had been very successful, about one-third (37.6 percent) viewed it as moderately successful, and the other 38.8 percent were either neutral (14.1 percent) or saw it as moderately unsuccessful (10.3 percent) or very unsuccessful (14.4 percent). Yet upper-level administrators (80 percent) were much more positive about the act's being implemented appropriately than those who worked directly with offenders (20 percent).[23]

Colorado Of the recently passed community corrections acts, Colorado's appears to be one of the most successful. The state Judicial Department contracts with those judicial districts that form advisory boards to identify and fund private agencies willing to provide correctional services within the community. The state delegates district court judges authority to sentence nonviolent offenders to community corrections rather than to state correctional institutions.[24]

Private agencies in most of the judicial districts are nonprofit, multiservice community agencies offering residential and nonresidential services for a variety of offenders. These private agencies are staffed by volunteers and paraprofessionals, including ex-offenders. Advisory boards play an active role in coordinating the corrections services of contracted agencies. These boards, made up of elected officials, administrators and line personnel of criminal justice agencies, and influential citizens, serve also as local advocates of community corrections.[25]

Musheno et al. found that 79 percent of the 296 respondents to their survey in Colorado felt that the Community Corrections Act had been very successful (24 percent) or moderately successful (55 percent). While 15 percent of the respondents were neutral, only 6 percent indicated that it was moderately unsuccessful (5 percent) or very unsuccessful (1 percent). Significantly, 59 percent of those interviewed also felt that the state's existing administration had been successful in its implementation of community-based corrections; only 15 percent disagreed, and the other 26 percent were neutral.[26]

Michigan The state of Michigan began to discuss a community corrections law in the early 1980s but did not pass an act until 1988. This act is presently generating considerable interest in community corrections circles across the nation. It is housed in the Office of Community Corrections, and Dennis Schrantz, who worked in community corrections in North Carolina, was brought in to be executive director. (See Figure 8.2 for a chart showing the comprehensive corrections planning process.)

The main purposes of this act are to

> Reduce crowding in state prisons and local jails by placing non-violent offenders in safe, highly structured community punishment programs which do not jeopardize public safety.
>
> Support and expand successful local programs and processes which can demonstrate a positive impact on the reduction of prison and jail admissions.
>
> Make offenders pay back victims through restitution and community service work.
>
> Develop additional middle-range sentencing options for the court in every jurisdiction throughout Michigan.
>
> Provide treatment and educational services to non-violent offenders aimed at reducing recidivism.
>
> Encourage greater involvement of local government officials and citizens in correctional programs.[27]

The Community Corrections Act in Michigan is different in several ways from other community corrections acts. First, rather than have the management and administration of the act under the department of corrections, there was created an independent agency. This autonomous agency is overseen by a state community corrections board appointed by the governor and confirmed by the senate. Second, the funding appears to be sufficient to do the comprehensive planning and implementation that is needed to reduce jail and prison crowding. The first-year funding was at $19 million, and second-year funding is at $26 million. Third, a major focus of this act is comprehensive planning and technical assistance; as part of this comprehensive planning, the Office of Community Corrections designed and implemented a data-driven decision-making instrument. In a 1990 interview, Dennis Schrantz notes, "What we're doing with this data-based approach is really unique. I suspect that it's going to give us the information we need to track in a statistical way whether or not these programs, policies, theories, and practices really have an impact."[28]

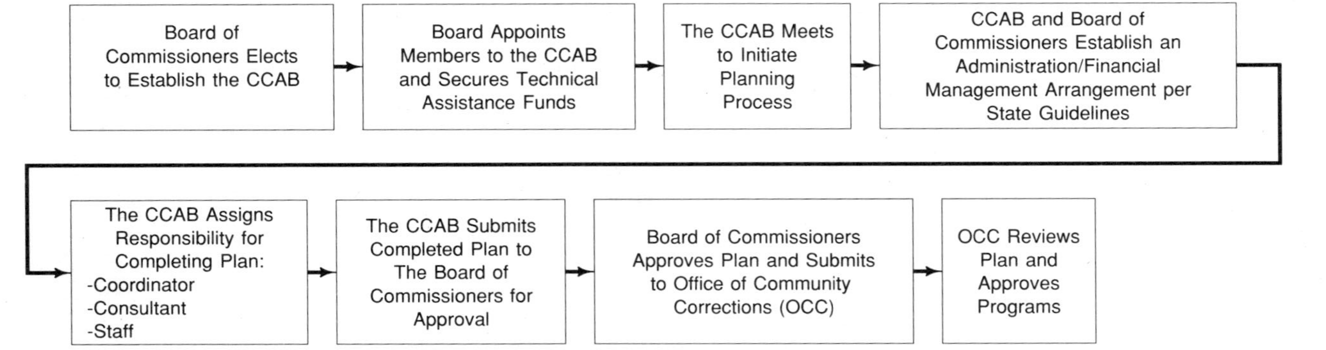

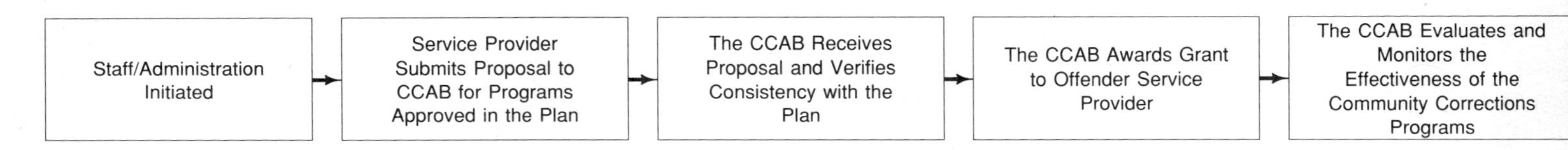

Definitions:

OCC = The State of Michigan Office of Community Corrections
CCAB = The Local Community Corrections Advisory Board

Figure 8.2 The Michigan Community Corrections process.

Locally Sponsored Community-based Corrections Programs

In five states probation is administered by the courts and funded by the county. Pretrial diversion programs are also frequently administered by the judiciary or the prosecutor's office. Some counties have established work release centers. A few counties have developed a continuum of services and a coordinated correctional effort, so that a comprehensive program that includes several subsystems of the correctional system is administered under local jurisdiction. Fragmentation is reduced and services are improved. Model comprehensive programs have been developed in Polk County, Iowa, and Montgomery County, Maryland.

The Des Moines Program The Des Moines Program which began in 1971, has four components that provide correctional services to defendants and convicted offenders at varying stages of the criminal justice process:

Pretrial release (ROR)

Supervised release

Probation/presentence investigation

Community corrections facility

The pretrial release stage is modeled on the Vera-Manhattan Bail Reform Project of New York City, and it stipulates release on the offender's own recognizance (ROR). Immediately after being processed, each booked defendant is interviewed and evaluated using objective criteria. If the defendant's scores indicate stable roots in the community, the staff recommends to the court that release on personal recognizance be granted.[29]

The supervised release program—which is the most innovative element—covers persons who do not qualify for ROR pretrial release. If defendants are willing to participate in a carefully structured program of supervision, counseling, and treatment and appear to be able to profit from such an experience, they are recommended for release to the custody of the supervised-release staff. If the court approves the release, the defendant is assigned a counselor and, following a battery of tests, assigned to a treatment plan. Job development assistance, marital and psychological counseling, and drug-abuse therapy are common areas of treatment.

Probation/presentence investigation is the third link in the chain of services provided to defendants and convicted offenders. Probation, a county responsibility in Polk County, is housed in the same building as the supervised-release staff, for the two programs complement each other. The intent of supervised release is to help defendants build a good "track record" that, if they are convicted, should assure assignment to probation; the probation effort is then directed to continuance of the treatment objectives of supervised release. Problem solving rather than surveillance is the main objective of the probation unit.

Up until the late 1980s, the community corrections facility, the fourth component, was a 50-bed, nonsecure, renovated barracks at Fort Des Moines, a partially deactivated army base at the edge of the Des Moines city limits. This facility, predominantly for males, was by statute a jail used to retain sentenced offenders for the entire duration of their sentences. Work release, referral to community agencies, counseling within the facility, and overnight or weekend furloughs were all offered at Fort Des Moines.

The Des Moines Program is being used as a model in other Iowa cities and has been replicated in Clark County (Vancouver), Washington; San Mateo County, California; Salt Lake County, Utah; St. Louis County (Duluth), Minnesota; and Orange County (Orlando), Florida.

Yet, in the late 1980s and early 1990s, it has become evident that community-based corrections in Iowa has lost much of its vision and dynamic flavor. Although the four components of the Des Moines Project remain in place throughout the judicial districts of Iowa, the 1980s represented a decade in which Iowa had to deal with a prison riot, inmate gangs, and prison crowding; as a result, the focus of correctional priorities was shifted from community to institutional corrections. In addition, questionable administration of community programs has created serious morale problems among probation officers and residential staff. For example, one judicial district during the 1980s suspended several top administrative staff members, had high turnover among probation officers and residential staff, and had a number of grievances filed by this staff. A probation officer in this district noted soon after her resignation, "I couldn't wait to get out of there. It's a lousy place to work."[30]

Privately Administrated Community-based Programs

Privately administered programs provide contract services to both probationers sentenced to residential facilities by the courts and to prison parolees. As Chapter 9 discusses, the Salvation Army Misdemeanant Program (SAMP) provides nearly all of the misdemeanant probation supervision in Florida,[31] and private firms are beginning to provide judges with presentence investigation reports.[32]

Residential Programs Residential programs depend upon a variety of funding sources, including federal, state, local, and private foundations. In addition to residential services for probationers and parolees, they sometimes offer programs to assist drug abusers, ex-offenders, and victims. Private agencies profit from being smaller operations and, thereby, escaping some of the bureaucratic red tape that affects state residential programs. The Magdala Foundation in St. Louis, the Talbert House in Cincinnati, and the Bureau of Rehabilitation of the National Capital Area in Washington, D.C., are especially respected for the high-quality services they offer to offenders. See Table 8.1 for the variety of services that Talbert House offers.

THE CHANGING FACE OF COMMUNITY-BASED CORRECTIONS

A new mission in community-based corrections, based upon expansion rather than retrenchment, is being shaped in the early 1990s. This new mission has a number of emerging themes. First, it is commonly agreed that intensive supervision is the means by which more offenders can be left in the community without endangering the protection of citizens. Second, electronic monitoring and house arrest are increasingly being used as a means by which the supervision of offenders can be

Table 8.1 TALBERT HOUSE PROGRAMS, CINCINNATI, OHIO

1. Alternatives (Residential)
Structured residential, chemical dependency treatment program for 13–17 year olds. Adolescent clients attend school on site. Referrals welcome.

2. Driver Intervention Program (DIP) (Residential)
72-hour residential program offering resources to local courts with a sentencing alternative for the disposition of DUI cases. State certified, court approved education and assessment program for first-time offenders.

3. Drug and Family Counseling (Nonresidential)
Structured outpatient program designed for treatment of drug and alcohol dependency. Provides services to adults and adolescents, their family members and friends.

4. Turning Point
Twenty-eight-day intensive, in-patient treatment program for individuals currently serving sentences in the Hamilton County Justice Center for multiple DUI convictions.

5. 281–CARE
A crisis intervention program which includes 24-hour telephone crisis counseling and short-term outpatient therapy. Community consultation and education services such as public speaking, specialized training (e.g., suicide intervention) and therapeutic support groups are also offered.

6. Victim Service Center
Aid to victims of crime, information/referral and counseling center. Primary goals include assisting victims in dealing with fear, anger, and frustration. Counseling and support groups.

7. Talbert House for Women (Residential)
Highly structured and individualized treatment program serving adult women offenders. Referrals from V.A. Hospital, Federal Prison System, State, County, and Municipal Courts.

8. McMillan House for Young Men (Young Male Residential)
Highly structured treatment facility for males 16–22 years old. Program emphasis on substance abuse and employment services. Referrals from Hamilton County Common Pleas Court, Direct Court Commitments, Department of Youth Services, Adult Parole Authority and Municipal Court.

9. Cornerstone (Male Residential)
Highly structured treatment program for adult male parolees, probationers and prereleases. Provides individual and group counseling on community adjustment problems like employment, chemical dependency, financial responsibility and residency. Referrals from State, Federal Bureau of Prisons, Common Pleas Court, Municipal Court.

10. Pathways (Female Residential)
Treatment program for women involved in criminal justice system. Specialized programming in substance abuse, parent effectiveness, career/personal development. Referrals from State or County and Municipal courts.

11. Beekman Work Release Center (Male Residential)
Highly structured work release program providing treatment services for releases having problems with substance abuse, employment and financial responsibility. Referrals from the Ohio Department of Correction and the Hamilton County Court System.

12. Forensic Services (Nonresidential)
The Forensic Services Program is designed to identify those with severe mental disabilities who are incarcerated in the Hamilton County Justice System. Staff serve as liaisons between the court and mental health systems.

13. Substance Abuse/Mental Illness Services
SA/MI services are designed to serve dually diagnosed individuals; those who suffer from substance abuse and a severe mental disability. SA/MI is composed of three separate programs: Case Management, Day Treatment, and Residential Support.

14. Case Management involves intensive outpatient service which provides outreach, advocacy and crisis intervention to severely mentally disabled, substance abusing adults. Emergency case management services are available 24 hours per day, seven days per week.

15. Day Treatment is a structured 6-month day program (9:00–3:00 M–F) for severely mentally disabled, substance abusing adults. This program offers prevocational and life skills, expressive and group therapy and aftercare support.

16. Residential Support is a structured residential program for severely mentally disabled, substance abusing adult women and men. Therapeutic support groups and on-site AA meetings are provided to all residents during evening and weekend hours; participation in Day Treatment is strongly encouraged on weekdays. Length of stay is three months.

Source: Talbert House brochure, revised 1990.

improved. Third, more attention is being paid to substance abusers, primarily because so many of these offenders have histories of substance abuse. Fourth, more adequate screening and classification systems are being developed regarding the level of probation supervision. Fifth, greater emphasis is being placed on community restitution programs and work orders as part of the victims' rights movement. In many court systems, restitution is an almost inevitable condition of probation status. Sixth, bureaucratic efficiency and accountability is being demanded of community-based programs. Finally, responsibility is being returned to the counties, while the courts simultaneously permit privately operated agencies to play a major role in administering community-based programs. In Box 8-2, Orville Pung, commissioner

Box 8-2 Interview with Commissioner Orville Pung

Question: Does the public still strongly support community-based corrections?

Answer: I think the public's awareness of community corrections is more along the lines of activities, such as electronic monitoring and house arrest. I think the public's interest in community corrections is more economical than it is philosophical. The public probably supports alternatives to prisons, not for broad notions of rehabilitation but because it might be perceived as being a little bit cheaper. I think the public today is looking for retribution and control, much more so than the broad notion of rehabilitation which was popular in the 1970s.

I think the public's understanding today of crime and corrections is influenced by drugs, fear, and the perception that it is under siege, the Willie Horton kind of notion. The people of Minnesota watch the same television shows, watch the same news broadcasts, and read the same magazines as they do anywhere else in the country. They may not perceive themselves as being under as much of a siege as you see everywhere else. Certainly, another thing that has had an impact on corrections in general are the much more organized victims groups, such as MADD [Mothers Against Drunk Driving] and programs for sexual assault or for battered women. I think we've felt an impact on the notion that individuals, as well as the state, are victims. I think the whole shift of more conservatism across the country also has impacted on corrections. Legislators that were probably perceived as liberals in the 1970s are saying things that would have been considered conservative then. As I said, I think what the public is looking for now is control.

Source: Interviewed in June 1990.

of the Minnesota Department of Corrections, suggests that control is a key component of the emerging mission of community-based corrections.

The major challenges in the implementation of this emerging mission is that community programs must deal with crowded caseloads, programs, and facilities without sacrificing delivery of services; must expand intermediate sanctions without sacrificing community safety; and must respond to the rising demand of victims' rights without sacrificing needed programs. The absence of an emphasis on diversion is a significant omission in this emerging mission.

Correctional Crowding and Community-based Corrections

Correctional crowding, a continuing theme of this text, is probably the most critical problem facing corrections today. The Bureau of Justice Statistics reported that between 1984 and 1990, the overall adult correctional population increased by 50 percent, from 2,475,100 to 4,053,946.[33] The correctional system clearly has been unable to meet the demand for incapacitation. The National Prison Project summarizes the court's reaction to this problem of crowding:

> The entire prison system was under court order (or consent decree) in 10 jurisdictions.
> At least one major institution was under court order (or consent decree) in 30 jurisdictions.
> The prison system was under court order and cited for contempt in six jurisdictions.
> Special masters, monitors, or mediators have been appointed to deal with the crowding problem in 20 jurisdictions.
> There is pending litigation in eight jurisdictions.[34]

The hope that community alternatives, such as probation and parole, can handle this overflow has been completely unrealistic. Probation and parole populations grew even faster (by 46.5 and 59 percent, respectively) than prison and jail populations (32.6 and 32.7 percent) between 1983 and 1989. Thus, a severe crowding problem has taken place in these agencies, at least in part because funding has not been increased for probation and parole. (See Table 8.2 for the causes of correctional crowding.) The intermediate sanctions of surveillance-oriented community-based programs have recently emerged "as a response to both the demand for alternatives to crowded institutions and the need for more control over offenders who are supervised in community settings."[35]

It can be argued that community-based corrections has exacerbated the problem of crowding by high rates of failure on probation and parole. About 15 percent of new probationers are committed to prison within one year because of technical violations, rearrest, or reconviction, and almost half of all parolees will return to prison within six years after initial release.[36] A response to this criticism is that community-based corrections must have a sanction that assures consequences in the event of noncompliance. If more people are placed in community corrections, the chances are that there will be more noncompliance than there was with nominal probation. There were not many people on probation in 1930, and they were haphazardly supervised. The increase to 19 percent in 1970 is a clear case of another time. The chances of failure increased in the 1980s when more felons were placed on probation. Also, the failure rate of probation, parole, and supervisory mandatory release from prison has been affected by the skyrocketing narcotics problem. Indeed, the situation is much worse in the 1990s than it was in the early 1980s.

nation. Diversion can be attempted either through the police and the courts or through agencies outside the formal justice system.

In the 1970s, **resolution of citizen disputes**, deferred prosecution, and Treatment Alternatives to Street Crime were the most widely used pretrial diversion programs for adults. Therapeutic communities were also called upon both at the pre- and posttrial stages to divert drug addicts from the criminal justice system.

In many states programs for the resolution of disputes have been established to prevent conflicts from escalating to a point where they must be adjudicated to court. Most of the 50 such programs that existed during the 1970s were based on mediation, whereby a third party recommended a solution to the conflict but did not have the authority to make a binding decision. These came under the jurisdiction of city governments, municipal courts, prosecuting attorneys' offices, bar associations, or grassroots citizens groups within the community.

Deferred prosecution programs deal with persons for whom conviction is likely, but they enable them to avoid the stigma of prosecution and a criminal record. The pilot deferred prosecution programs were the Flint (Michigan) Citizens Probation Authority, the Manhattan Court Employment Project, and the District of Columbia's Project Crossroads.

At their peak, 150 programs operated in 37 states, and 7 states (Arkansas, Colorado, Connecticut, Florida, Massachusetts, Tennessee, and Washington) had authorizing legislation. Deferred prosecution programs operate in one of two ways: An arrested offender is deemed eligible for the program on the basis of pre-established criteria, and the court is asked to defer formal charges because of willing participation in the formal diversion program; or formal charges are made before defendants are screened for their eligibility, but criminal proceedings are suspended for defendants accepted into the program, pending their successful completion of the deferred prosecution program.

The Special Action Office for Drug Abuse Prevention created **Treatment Alternatives to Street Crime (TASC)** in 1971 to identify and provide treatment for the greatest possible number of drug abusers entering the criminal justice system. More than 50 cities during the 1970s established TASC programs.

The three main stages of TASC were (1) a screening unit offered the program to drug abusers eligible under locally determined criteria, (2) an intake unit diagnosed each drug user referred and recommended the appropriate treatment program, and (3) a tracking unit monitored the progress of TASC clients and returned those who failed the locally determined success–failure criteria to the criminal justice system for appropriate action. TASC expanded its interventions to include services for prearrest and postarrest police diversion, pretrial intervention (conditional release), presentence referral, conditional probation, and conditional parole. Although initially only adult heroin addicts were accepted into TASC, all types of adult and juvenile drug abusers were eventually treated.

Therapeutic communities for drug offenders, such as Daytop Village and Phoenix House (New York), Delancey Street (California), and Gateway House (Illinois), were frequently called upon during the 1970s, both at the pre- and posttrial stages, to divert drug addicts from the criminal justice system (see Box 8-3).

While the most positive characteristic of diversion programs is that they minimize the penetration of offenders into the formal justice system, the past two decades have not been kind to these programs. The decline of federal funding was a major

Box 8-3 The Benefits of Diversion

I shot dope for as long as I did because I enjoy shooting dope. But that isn't the whole thing. There were a lot of things I felt bad about. I can't change it, but I can accept it. I appeared to enjoy being a dope fiend, a dope dealer, and having money. Basically, I can see now that I wasn't happy with that lifestyle. It didn't cause me anything but grief.

At the age of forty-two, after shooting dope since I was fourteen, I made a total commitment to myself. I've never made a commitment to myself before. The commitment started when a judge gave me a choice—either spend five years in the penitentiary or enter treatment. I signed myself into Gateway House and made up my mind not to do drugs again. The next time I get busted my sentence won't be for five years, and it won't be for eighteen, it will be for twenty. I've already been in the penitentiary twice; I made up my mind that I didn't want to go through life as a loser. I've peace of mind now. I don't have the material things I had before, but I'm free—free of a habit, free to do what I want within reason. When I lie down at night and get up in the morning, I don't have to worry about a fix. I may be broke, but I'm free.

Source: Interviewed in December 1980.

blow to the diversion movement, and many of these programs had to close their doors in the late 1970s when federal funding dried up. Then, in the 1980s, criticism mounted from both the left and the right. Conservatives wanted to "get tough" on criminals and refused to support diversion because they viewed it as a means of "mollycoddling" criminals. But from the traditionally supportive liberals came the empirical evidence that doing something (treatment or services) is not necessarily better than doing nothing. These researchers charged that the overlooked, negative consequences of diversion challenge the viability of this concept.[38] Some of these negative effects include widening the net of the formal system by increasing the number of offenders under the control of the system, increasing the size of the system (budget and staff), creating new legal entities, altering traditional programs, and ignoring clients' due process rights.[39] James Austin and Barry Krisberg went so far as to state:

> "Widening the net" describes the nightmare of the benevolent state gone haywire. This horror has already been vividly portrayed in Orwell's *1984*, Solzhenitsyn's *Cancer Ward*, Kesey's *One Flew Over the Cuckoo's Nest*, and Burgess's *Clockwork Orange*. Social scientists and criminologists have just caught up with the humanists.[40]

However, this criticism of diversion, both from the right and the left, ignores some complex issues.[41] For example, we need to consider how much social control is needed for criminal offenders and what forms this control should take. As to diversion without formal trial, Stanley Cohen and others are quite right; these processes do indeed allow for little or no due process. In a real sense, we need nets that are just wide enough to maintain social control of those people who require it if they are to abstain from crime.

In sum, diversion—one of the correctional panaceas of the late 1960s and 1970s—

has met hard times in the 1980s and 1990s. It is difficult to challenge the criticism that diversion sometimes needlessly widens the net of the criminal justice system. Yet the need to minimize penetration of offenders in the system was a viable concept, and many have profited from the intervention of diversion programs. A successful graduate of Gateway House, in this regard, noted, "Hey, I used heroin all my life until this program turned me around."[42] Significantly, as is discussed in the next chapter, traditional diversion agencies are being increasingly replaced by deferred sentencing and other means of informal probation that give participants an opportunity to expunge their criminal record by the successful completion of these sentencing options.

Increased Intermediate Sanctions

A new wave of **intermediate sanctions** has captured the attention of both liberal and conservative policymakers. These intermediate sanctions include such alternatives as intensive supervision, split sentencing, and house arrest (with and without an electronic monitoring component). To liberals, Intensive Probation Supervision (IPS) and the other intermediate sanctions represent a means for diverting offenders from prison and jail without their (the liberals) appearing "soft on crime." To conservatives, it provides a means to "get tough" with offenders in the community without adding to the high cost of incarceration. Indeed, it is this trying to be "all things to all people" that is one of the most salient characteristics of these intermediate sanctions.[43]

Intensive supervision of high-risk probationers has been used by jurisdictions since the late 1970s. Such programs reassure conservative policymakers by promising intensive surveillance of high-risk offenders, satisfy federal judges that official discretion is being properly used, and reduce the need to commit new funds for prison construction.[44]

As of June 1, 1988, 45 states had intensive supervision programs (ISP) or were in the process of developing them.[45] The vast majority of these programs (85 percent) are administered by departments of corrections or the circuit courts. Nationwide, more than 25,000 offenders, approximately 3 percent of all probationers, are participants in these projects.[46]

House arrest has a long history, but house confinement as a policy for use with adult offenders began to draw attention in 1983, with the publication of several scholarly papers on the topic, with the passage of the Correctional Reform Act, and with the use of an "electronic bracelet" to monitor compliance with home confinement of an offender in New Mexico. This electronic bracelet was inspired by a New Mexico district court judge's reading of a comic strip in which the character Spiderman was tracked by a transmitter affixed to his wrist. Approached by the judge, an engineer designed an electronic bracelet to emit a signal picked up by a receiver placed in a home telephone. The bracelet was so designed that if the offender moved more than 150 feet from the home telephone, the transmission signal would be broken, alerting the authorities that the offender had left his or her home.[47]

Following the trial use of the device in New Mexico, a research project funded by the National Institute of Corrections reported successful results with this "electronic monitoring."[48] Beginning in 1986, the federal government approved an experimental program for the Federal Prison System, the Probation Service of the U.S. Courts, and the Parole Commission that would permit a federal parolee's release dates to be advanced 60 days on the condition that "he remain in his place of residence during a specified period of time each night."[49] See Figure 8.3 for the key decision points where electronic monitoring (EM) programs are being used.

In sum, intermediate sanctions have generated considerable interest. There are those who question the ethics of using these intermediate sanctions.[50] Indeed, some believe that **electronic monitoring devices** conjure up fears of some Orwellian nightmare in which the state engages in total surveillance of its citizenry.[51] Yet there is wide support of intermediate sanctions, including home confinement and electronic monitoring devices. The various means of intermediate sanctions will be evaluated and further discussed in the next two chapters.

The Rise of the Victims' Rights Movement

Victims' rights is one of the most critical issues in corrections.[52] The public has become incensed that victimization occurs so frequently in American society; indeed, one in every four families in the United States has been victimized, involving financial loss, property damage, physical injury, or death of a loved one. The psychological traumas of victimization are often even more devastating.[53]

During the 1980s, a number of grassroots groups propelled the needs and rights of victims. The women's movement brought national attention to the victims of rape and spouse abuse and was influential in developing rape crisis centers and domestic violence shelters for women and children. Established in 1978, Parents of Murdered Children focuses on the needs of the next of kin of murder victims and provides peer counseling. Mothers Against Drunk Driving (MADD), founded in 1980, advocates stiffer punishment for intoxicated drivers. As a result of these grassroots movements,

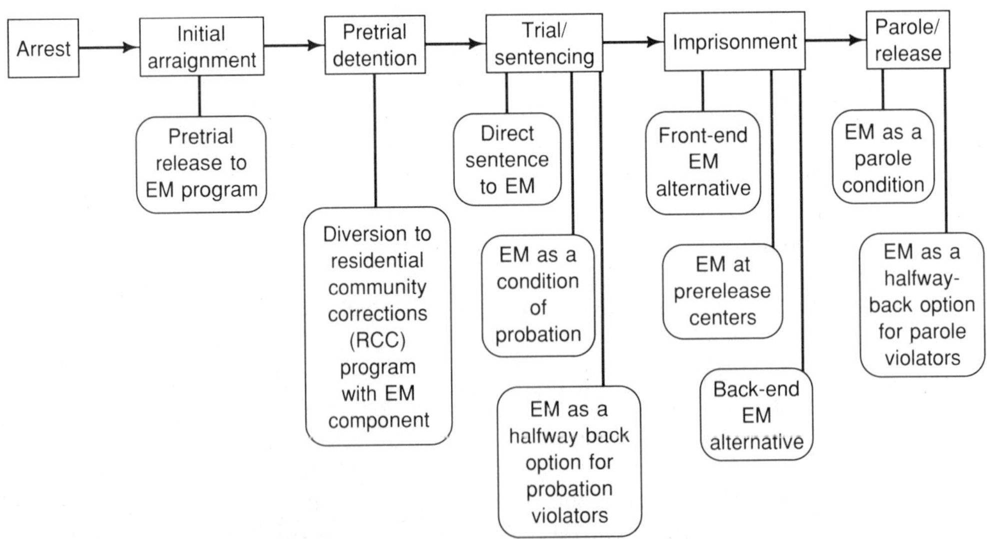

Figure 8.3 Key decision points where electronic monitoring (EM) programs are being used. (*Source*: James M. Byrne and Linda Kelly, *Restructuring Probation as an Intermediate Sanction: An Evaluation of the Massachusetts Intensive Probation Supervision Program* (Final Report to the National Institute of Justice, Research Program on the Punishment of and Control of Offenders, 1989), p. 19.)

as many as 4000 programs are presently helping crime victims cope with victimization and the complexities of the criminal justice process.[54]

The victims' rights movement has affected community-based corrections in several ways. First, corrections departments are increasingly mandated to provide programs for victims. Orville Pung, Minnesota's commissioner of corrections, notes that "we have a new mission and responsibility, which is to provide programs for victims, especially within the department of corrections. That's quite a substantial change from what was talked about in the 1970s."[55]

Second, financial restitution and community service projects are now commonly ordered by the court as a condition of probation and are becoming increasingly required at other points in the criminal justice process. In 1982, as part of a concern for both federal witnesses and victims, Congress passed the Victim and Witness Protection Act. This legislation pushed the use of restitution to the forefront of possible sanctions for criminal behavior. It also required that victim impact statements be included in all presentence investigation; that victims and witnesses be protected from intimidation, threat, or harassment; and that the victim's situation be considered in determining bail.[56]

Third, the fear of victimization has made it more difficult to establish halfway houses, work release centers, and diversionary projects in a community. Citizens are now more willing to mobilize against the establishment of such programs. Fourth, victims are increasingly becoming part of criminal justice decision making. In some jurisdictions, probation officers' presentence investigative reports (PSIs) may contain victim impact statements as well as the defendant's version of what took place. When inmates become eligible for parole, victims or relatives of victims are taking a more active role in influencing the parole board. Moreover, victims are sometimes given the opportunity to negotiate with offenders in terms of restitution settlements.

CONCLUSIONS

Community-based corrections is made up of pretrial release and diversion, probation, residential and reentry programs, and parole. The 1970s began with the policy of keeping all but violent offenders in the community; some students of corrections even projected that correctional institutions would soon be a relic of the past. But the late 1970s were not good years for community-based corrections. Indeed, residential programs and parole were subjected to a great deal of criticism, and reentry programs were dramatically reduced in jurisdiction after jurisdiction across the nation. Probation and pretrial diversion held their own, but they, too, were under attack. A few states, such as Minnesota, Oregon, Kansas, and Iowa, made the establishment of strong community-based programs one of their priorities, but sweeping offenders out of the way and into institutions was still the choice of most states.

The 1980s were a decade in which community-based corrections dealt with skyrocketing probation and parole caseloads; yet, this was a decade in which the retrenchment of the 1970s was replaced with expansion and new programs. The various means of intermediate sanctions were largely developed in the 1980s, especially intensive supervision programs, house arrest, and electronic monitoring devices.

Stanley Cohen has defined the history of social control as cycling between periods in which **exclusionary measures** predominate and those eras in which inclusionary methods are more widely used in dealing with crime. Cohen means by "exclusion" such measures as "banishment and expulsion, segregation and isolation, designation, signification and classification, stigmatization." In contrast, "inclusion" refers to measures that employ "integration, assimilation, accommodation, normalization, tolerance, absorption, engulfment, incorporation."[57]

Reformers in the early 1970s predicted that the Golden Age of Corrections was at hand, an age in which corrections would be community oriented and would use inclusionary measures. But the reality of community-based corrections in the 1990s is quite different from the 1970s rhetoric of the community-based movement. Today, the fact is that exclusionary measures are being increasingly used in community-based corrections, and the boundaries between institutions and community-based programs have become blurred.[58]

KEY TERMS

community corrections acts

correctional crowding

deferred prosecution

deinstitutionalization

diversion

electronic monitoring devices

exclusionary measures

house arrest

intensive supervision

intermediate sanctions

internalization

privately administered programs

Probation Subsidy Statute

reintegrative philosophy

resolution of citizen disputes

Treatment Alternatives to Street Crime (TASC)

victims' rights

DISCUSSION TOPICS

8.1 Community-based corrections keeps an offender in the community. Explain its changing popularity.

8.2 Several states legislate and fund extensive community correctional programs. Would you favor payments to counties that send fewer offenders to state prisons?

8.3 What community-based corrections options are available in your county?

8.4 Why is crowding likely to be a problem for community-based corrections?

8.5 Define what is meant by "intermediate sanctions." Why are these sanctions generating so much interest at the present time?

ANNOTATED REFERENCES

Ball, Richard A., C. Ronald Huff, and J. Robert Lilly. *House Arrest and Correctional Policy: Doing Time at Home.* Newbury Park, Calif.: Sage, 1988. *This book represents the most expansive examination of house arrest.*

Byrne, James M. "The Future of Intensive Probation Supervision and the New Intermediate Sanctions." *Crime and Delinquency* 36, January 1990: 6–41. *Byrne's article is helpful in that it provides a brief overview of intensive probation supervision.*

Cohen, Stanley. *Visions of Social Control.* Cambridge: Polity Press, 1985. *Cohen's analysis of social control is required reading for the student of corrections. It provides insights that are essential in understanding both community-based and institutional corrections.*

Hirsch, Andrew von. "The Ethics of Community-based Sanctions." *Crime and Delinquency* 36, January 1990: 62–173. *Von Hirsch, in examining the ethics of community-based sanctions, raises several ethical issues that are important considerations for the student of corrections.*

Jones, Peter R. "Community Corrections in Kansas: Extending Community-based Corrections or Widening the Net?" *Journal of Research in Crime and Delinquency* 27, February 1990: 79–101. *An evaluation of the Kansas Community Corrections Act that challenges the "net widening" criticism of community programs.*

Lewis, Dan A., and Cheryl Darling. "The Idea of Community in Correctional Reform: How Rhetoric and Reality Join." In *Are Prisons Any Better? Twenty Years of Correctional Reform*, edited by John W. Murphy and Jack E. Dison. Newbury Park, Calif.: Sage, 1990: 95–110. *Lewis and Darling do a very able job of comparing the rhetoric and reality of community-based corrections.*

McCarthy, Belinda, ed. *Intermediate Punishments: Intensive Supervision, Home Confinement and Electronic Monitoring.* Mousey, N.J.: Criminal Justice Press, 1987. *An excellent series of articles on intermediate punishments.*

Morris, Norval, and Michael Tonry. *Between Prison and Probation: Intermediate Punishments in a Rational Sentencing System.* Cary, N.C.: Oxford University Press, 1990. *Draws a distinction between alternative sanctions and intermediate punishments. Alternative sanctions, according to the authors, connote substitutes for punishment, whereas intermediate punishments constitute true punitive responses to crime.*

National Advisory Commission on Criminal Justice Standards and Goals. *Corrections.* Washington: Government Printing Office, 1973. *This report of this blue-ribbon commission provides the vision of community-based corrections in the 1970s.*

Niederberger, W. V., and W. F. Wagner. *Electronic Monitoring of Convicted Offenders: A Field Test.* Washington: National Institute of Justice, 1985. *This monograph provides a good overview of electronic monitoring.*

Petersilia, Joan. *Expanding Options for Criminal Sentencing.* Santa Monica, Calif.: Rand, 1987. *Petersilia discusses in some detail the intermediate sanctions presented in this chapter.*

NOTES

1. Robert B. Coates, "A Working Paper on Community-based Corrections: Concept, Historical Development, Impact, and Potential Dangers" (Paper presented at the Massachusetts Standards and Goals Conference, November 1974), pp. 3–4.
2. See Marguerite Warren, "The Community Treatment Project." In Norman Johnston, Leonard Savity, and Marvin E. Wolfgang, eds., *The Sociology of Crime and Punishment* (New York: Wiley, 1970), pp. 671–683.
3. For a full account and evaluation of the Probation Subsidy Program, see Edwin C. Lemert and Forrest Dill, *Offenders in the Community* (Lexington, Mass.: Lexington Books, 1978); Robert Lee Smith, *A Quiet Revolution* (Washington: Government Printing Office, 1971); and Floyd Feeney and Travis Hirschi, *Impact of Commitment Reduction on the Recidivism of Offenders* (Davis, Calif.: Center for the Administration of Justice, 1975).
4. Interviewed in January 1979.
5. Harry E. Allen, "The Organization and Effectiveness of Community Corrections." In Lawrence P. Travis, ed., *Probation, Parole, and Community Corrections: A Reader* (Prospect Heights, Ill.: Waveland Press, 1985), p. 194.
6. Stanley Cohen, *Visions of Social Control* (Cambridge: Polity Press, 1985), p. 44.
7. Ibid., pp. 43, 49, 69.
8. Bureau of Justice Statistics, *Probation and Parole 1989* (Washington: U.S. Department of Justice, 1990), p. 2.
9. The President's Commission on Law Enforcement and Administration of Justice, *Task Force Report: Corrections* (Washington: Government Printing Office, 1967), p. 7.
10. Ibid.
11. Ibid.
12. National Advisory Commission on Criminal Justice Standards and Goals, *Corrections* (Washington: Government Printing Office, 1973), p. 121.
13. National Advisory Commission on Criminal Justice Standards and Goals, *A National Strategy to Reduce Crime* (Washington: Government Printing Office, 1973), p. 187.
14. President's Crime Commission, *Task Force Report: Corrections*, p. 7.
15. Michael C. Musheno et al., "Community Corrections as an Organizational Innovation: What Works and Why," *Journal of Research in Crime and Delinquency* 26, May 1989: 139.
16. This statement on the Community Corrections Act in Minnesota is adapted from "A State Report, April 1978, The Community Corrections Act," pp. 1–4.
17. Interviewed in June 1990.
18. "Dodge-Fillmore-Olmstead: Community Corrections Systems" (Rochester, Minn.: Dodge-Fillmore-Olmstead Community Corrections System, n.d.), p. 3.
19. See Stephen Gettinger, "Community Corrections Begins to Pay Off," *Corrections Magazine* 5, June 1979; John Blackmore, *The Minnesota Community Corrections Act* (unpublished paper prepared for the National Institute of Corrections, 1982); and Gerald Straithman et al., *Minnesota Community Corrections Act Evaluation* (Minneapolis: Minnesota Department of Corrections Crime Control Planning Board, 1981).
20. Peter R. Jones, "Community Corrections in Kansas: Extending Community-based Corrections or Widening the Net?" *Journal of Research in Crime and Delinquency* 27, February 1990: 83.
21. Ibid., pp. 82–83.

22. Ibid., p. 96.
23. Musheno et al., "Community Corrections," pp. 151–152.
24. Ibid., p. 147.
25. Ibid.
26. Ibid., p. 152.
27. Mimeographed handout received from Dennis Schrantz in August 1990.
28. This information on the corrections act in Michigan was provided by Dennis Schrantz in a July 1990 interview.
29. David Boorkman et al., *An Exemplary Project: Community-based Corrections in Des Moines* (Washington: U.S. Department of Justice, 1976), pp. 1–4. For a recent evaluation of this project see David E. Duffee and Edmund F. McGarrell, *Community Corrections: A Community Field Approach* (Cincinnati: Anderson Publishing Co., 1990).
30. One of the authors had a number of probation officers and residential staff of this judicial district as students. This particular statement was made to him in 1987 by a probation officer who had worked in this agency for ten years.
31. See "The Salvation Army Conquers Florida," *Corrections Magazine*, February 1983: 40–41.
32. James S. Granelli, "Presentence Reports Go Private," *National Law Journal* 2, May 1983: 9.
33. Bureau of Justice Statistics, *Probation and Parole 1989*, p. 4.
34. Cited in James M. Byrne et al., "The Effectiveness of the New Intensive Supervision Programs." In Joan Petersilia, ed., *Research in Corrections* (Santa Monica, Calif.: Rand, 1989), p. 2.
35. Ibid.
36. See Table 8.2.
37. President's Commission on Law Enforcement and Administration of Justice, *Task Force Report on Juvenile Delinquency* (Washington: Government Printing Office, 1967), p. 2.
38. Charles E. Frazier, "Official Intervention, Diversion from the Juvenile Justice System, and Dynamics of Human Services Work: Effects of a Reform Goal Based on Labeling Theory," *Crime and Delinquency* 32, April 1986: 157–176; Thomas Blomberg, "Diversion and Accelerated Social Control," *The Journal of Criminal Law and Criminology* 68, 1977: 274–282; Andrew Rutherford and Robert McDermott, *National Evaluation Program Phase I Report: Juvenile Diversion* (Washington: Government Printing Office, 1976), pp. 2–3.
39. Cohen, *Social Control*, pp. 52–56.
40. James Austin and Barry Krisberg, "Wider, Stronger and Different Nets: The Dialectics of Criminal Justice Reform," *Journal of Research in Crime and Delinquency* 18, 1981: 165–196.
41. For an article that challenges some of the assumptions of "net widening," see Maeve McMahon, " 'Net-Widening': Vagaries in the Use of a Concept," *British Journal of Criminology* 30, Spring 1990: 121–149.
42. Interviewed in 1985.
43. James M. Byrne, "The Future of Intensive Probation Supervision and the New Intermediate Sanctions," *Crime and Delinquency* 36, January 1990: 6.
44. Neal Shover and Werner J. Einstadter, *Analyzing American Corrections* (Belmont, Calif.: Wadsworth, 1988), p. 137.
45. E. Herrick, "Intensive Probation Supervision," *Corrections Compendium* 12, 1988: 4–14.
46. Byrne et al., "New Intensive Supervision Programs," p. 11.
47. Richard A. Ball, C. Ronald Huff, and J. Robert Lilly, *House Arrest and Correctional Policy: Doing Time at Home* (Newbury Park, Calif.: Sage, 1988), pp. 35–36.
48. W. V. Niederberger and W. F. Wagner, *Electronic Monitoring of Convicted Offenders: A Field Test* (Washington: National Institute of Justice, 1985).

49. "Paroling, Recommitting, and Supervising Federal Prisoners," *Federal Register* 50, March 1986: 893.
50. See Andrew von Hirsch, "The Ethics of Community-Based Sanctions," *Crime and Delinquency* 36, January 1990.
51. Ball et al., *House Arrest and Correctional Policy*, p. 37.
52. See Paul Horner and Gilbert L. Ingram, "Victims and Witnesses: The Newest Constituency, the Newest Challenge" *Federal Prisons Journal*, Spring 1990: 23–27.
53. See Arthur J. Lurigio, Wesley G. Skogan, and Robert C. Davis, eds., *Victims of Crime: Problems, Policies, and Programs* (Newbury Park, Calif.: Sage, 1989).
54. Peter Finn and Beverly N.W. Lee, *Establishing and Expanding Victim-Assistance Programs* (Washington: National Institute of Justice, 1988).
55. Interviewed in June 1990.
56. Horner and Ingram, "Victims and Witnesses," p. 24.
57. Cohen, *Visions of Social Control*, p. 267.
58. Cohen, "The Punitive City: Notes on the Dispersal of Social Control," *Contemporary Crisis* 3, 1979: 339–363; D. F. Greenberg, "Problems in Community Corrections," *Issues in Criminology* 10, 1975: 1–33. *See also* Dan A. Lewis and Cheryl Darling, "The Idea of Community in Correctional Reform: How Rhetoric and Reality Join." In John W. Murphy and Jack E. Dison, *Are Prisons Any Better? Twenty Years of Correctional Reform* (Newbury Park, Calif.: Sage, 1990), p. 97.

Chapter
9

Probation

CHAPTER OUTLINE

Probation is a correctional service allowing an offender to remain in the community for the duration of a sentence under supervision by an officer of the court and requiring him or her to comply with such conditions as the court may impose. Keeping the adjudicated individual in the community is the real benefit of probation. The American Bar Association's *Standards Relating to Corrections* recommends that offenders be left in the community unless they are a danger to society, their needs cannot be met without confinement, or the seriousness of their crimes necessitates imprisonment.[1] The goal of probation is to promote law-abiding behavior by the offender. Because of criticism in the 1970s and 1980s that probation was "too soft" on crime, the means by which probation accomplishes this goal of promoting law-abiding behavior is more hard line than in the past. As this chapter documents, the current emphasis for probation is on risk control and reduction approaches, such as intensive supervision, house arrest, and electronic monitoring.

THE PRESENT LANDSCAPE OF PROBATION

The most recent statistics available indicate that 2,520,479 adult offenders were on probation status as of December 31, 1989. See Table 9.1 for the number of adults on probation on December 31, 1989. The probation population during 1989 showed a 5.6 percent gain over the previous year's count. The increase in the probation population occurred in every region, with the west reporting the highest gains (9.4 percent) and the northeast the lowest (1.2 percent). The states with the largest increases in probation populations were Rhode Island (24.5 percent), Oregon (16.7 percent), and Florida (16.3 percent).[2]

A real threat to probation services is governmental economy. In California, several counties have drastically reduced fiscal support; it seems that when budgets have to be rolled back, probation services are the first to be rolled. Even when times are good, probation has been hampered by modest resources. The dramatic increase in drug offenders also has put serious pressure on probation (see Box 9-1).

The conditions of probation vary from jurisdiction to jurisdiction and may also vary to meet the personal situation of particular offenders. The payment of fines, restitution to victims, community service assignments, random urine and alcohol testing, and regular employment are common requirements. These conditions satisfy the desire both to consider the needs of victims and to teach offenders responsible behavior. **Financial restitution** and **community service** are particularly widely used today. The use of restitution actually predates both incarceration and modern forms of community treatment; the current trend is toward a more purposeful and imaginative use of restitution. At times, the victim is even involved with the offender in the development of restitution agreements.[3]

Probation orders usually put offenders under supervision for a set period of time. Probationers must report to a probation officer as often as required. They must keep him or her informed of changes in their circumstances, especially as to contacts with the police, employment, address, marital status, and income or indebtedness.

Some jurisdictions allow the **deferred sentence.** This variation delays conviction on a guilty plea until the completion of a term of probation, at which time the offender withdraws the guilty plea. The court dismisses the charge, thereby clearing the offender's record of a conviction. One advantage of the deferred sentence is that it avoids the stigma of a conviction. This procedure is not the same as pretrial diversion, because the offender is supervised by a probation officer when the deferred sentence is imposed by a judge; in pretrial diversion the offender is diverted from the system.

Other jurisdictions suspend a prison sentence ordered after formal conviction, allowing the offender to serve the sentence in the community while on probation. The judge actually pronounces the sentence but then suspends it and places the offender on probation. Later in this chapter we will discuss shock probation. Here it is enough to say that it calls for the shock of a few weeks in prison for a first-time offender followed by a standard term of probation.

In addition to these legal variations, two other types of probation are used in the

Table 9.1 ADULTS ON PROBATION, 1988

Regions and jurisdictions	Probation population 1/1/89	1989 Entries	1989 Exists	Probation population 12/31/89	Percent change in probation population during 1989	Number on probation on 12/31/89 per 100,000 adult residents
U.S. total	2,386,427	1,567,156	1,433,104	2,520,479	5.6%	1,369
Federal	61,029	19,858	21,741	59,146	−3.1	32
State	2,325,398	1,547,298	1,411,363	2,461,333	5.8	1,337
Northeast	438,691	215,467	210,364	443,794	1.2%	1,147
Connecticut	46,086	27,839	31,083	42,842	−7.0	1,728
Maine	6,059	4,792	4,000	6,851	13.1	747
Massachusetts	92,353	47,026	50,850	88,529	−4.1	1,935
New Hampshire	2,948	2,552	2,509	2,991	1.5	361
New Jersey	57,903	31,891	23,041	66,753	15.3	1,131
New York	125,256	41,953	38,502	128,707	2.8	946
Pennsylvania	92,296	47,761	50,566	89,491	−3.0	973
Rhode Island	9,824	8,467	6,060	12,231	24.5	1,595
Vermont	5,966	3,186	3,753	5,399	−9.5	1,270
Midwest	510,253	395,440	362,928	542,765	6.4%	1,217
Illinois	90,736	58,023	54,815	93,944	3.5	1,083
Indiana	60,184	57,362	55,685	61,861	2.8	1,497
Iowa	13,099	12,180	11,557	13,722	4.8	644
Kansas	19,580	12,507	9,562	22,526	15.0	1,215
Michigan	115,132	92,400	86,096	121,436	5.5	1,778
Minnesota	56,901	48,079	46,332	58,648	3.1	1,819
Missouri	42,728	27,322	24,799	45,251	5.9	1,174
Nebraska	11,411	15,369	14,153	12,627	10.7	1,064
North Dakota	1,504	558	410	1,652	9.8	343
Ohio	70,088	53,111	44,976	78,223	11.6	967
South Dakota	2,585	4,277	4,146	2,716	5.1	523
Wisconsin	26,305	14,252	10,397	30,160	14.7	835
South	929,936	658,418	601,846	986,508	6.1%	1,565
Alabama	25,301	12,405	11,231	26,475	4.6	880
Arkansas	15,931	5,875	4,234	17,572	10.3	1,001
Delaware	9,576	3,959	3,834	9,701	1.3	1,925
District of Columbia	11,296	8,942	9,887	10,351	−8.4	2,226
Florida	166,475	241,462	214,442	192,495	16.3	1,964
Georgia	121,559	69,142	65,260	125,441	3.2	2,704
Kentucky	7,398	4,142	3,478	8,062	9.0	292
Louisiana	31,218	12,828	11,751	32,295	3.5	1,039
Maryland	78,619	50,145	44,308	84,456	7.4	2,390
Mississippi	6,854	3,142	2,663	7,333	7.0	396
North Carolina	67,164	37,972	32,811	72,325	7.7	1,467
Oklahoma	23,341	11,605	10,706	24,240	3.9	1,022
South Carolina	26,260	15,543	12,151	29,652	12.9	1,159

Table 9.1 (continued)

Regions and jurisdictions	Probation population 1/1/89	1989 Entries	1989 Exists	Probation population 12/31/89	Percent change in probation population during 1989	Number on probation on 12/31/89 per 100,000 adult residents
Tennessee	28,282	24,821	22,197	30,906	9.3	839
Texas	288,906	143,515	141,265	291,156	.8	2,419
Virginia	17,945	10,470	9,330	19,085	6.4	414
West Virginia	4,811	2,450	2,298	4,963	3.2	356
West	446,518	277,973	236,225	488,266	9.4%	1,290
Alaska	2,994	1,755	1,414	3,335	11.4	921
Arizona	25,446	11,490	9,286	27,650	8.7	1,074
California	265,580	163,575	144,137	285,018	7.3	1,335
Colorado	23,230	21,877	18,729	26,378	13.6	1,075
Hawaii	10,704	5,892	5,219	11,377	6.3	1,379
Idaho	3,587	1,976	1,538	4,025	12.2	567
Montana	3,275	1,528	1,344	3,459	5.6	588
Nevada	7,032	3,411	3,119	7,324	4.2	879
New Mexico	5,312	4,508	4,160	5,660	6.6	527
Oregon	27,320	12,018	7,460	31,878	16.7	1,502
Utah	5,595	3,615	3,686	5,524	−1.3	513
Washington	64,257	44,730	34,733	74,254	15.6	2,095
Wyoming	2,186	1,598	1,400	2,384	9.1	703

Note: Nine States estimated numbers in one or more categories. See detailed probation notes for further information.

Source: Bureau of Justice Statistics, *Probation and Parole 1989* (Washington: U.S. Department of Justice, 1990), p. 2.

United States. Some jurisdictions permit bench, or supervised, probation—especially with misdemeanants—under which probationers are not subject to probation supervision. The **split sentence** is also used by some jurisdictions: Offenders must spend a period of time in jail before being placed on probation in the community, or they are sentenced to so many weekends in jail while remaining in the community on probation status during the week.

Under **intensive probation**, a probationer is supervised far more strictly than under standard services. The skyrocketing increase in the numbers of defendants placed on probation across the nation is partly explained by the fact that courts now are sentencing to probation many more convicted felons than they have in the past. For example, in 1986, state courts across the nation sentenced to probation an estimated 306,000 convicted felons, representing 53 percent of those convicted of felony offenses.[4] Joan Petersilia and colleagues found that today more than one-third of California's probationers present a serious threat to public safety. During the fortieth-month follow-up period of this study, 65 percent were reconvicted, 18 percent were reconvicted of serious violent crimes, and 34 percent were reincarcerated. Even more significantly, 75 percent of the official charges filed against the subsample involved burglary/theft, robbery, and other violent crimes.[5]

Box 9-1 Glutted Probation System Puts Communities in Peril

Local and federal probation agencies, overwhelmed by the increase in drug-related crimes, are changing in ways that experts say are making communities less safe.

Probation departments have become seriously understaffed just as they are being relied on more heavily than at any point in their history; probation, rather than prison, is by far the most prevalent form of punishment.

Probation officers have become less and less involved in their traditional counseling and supervision roles, more akin to social work, and are more consumed with law enforcement, tracking down those who have violated the terms of their freedom.

In New York last year, almost 38 percent of the criminals who had been given probation were sent to prison for violating rules, mostly for new crimes. Five years ago, 20 percent of the probationers were sent to prison for violations.

1000 CRIMINALS TO AN OFFICER

In interviews, judges, prosecutors, probation officers, and probationers said the combination of these circumstances had become a serious community problem with high concentrations of drug offenders.

"There is not a probation department in the nation that is adequately staffed to handle the needs of the new high-risk offenders," said Cecil Steppe, chief probation officer for San Diego County. This year caseloads in his department are running as high as 700 probationers for each officer, up from last year's high of 400.

Most experienced supervisors say it is not unreasonable to ask an officer to keep track of 30 probationers, but they add that the system begins to become unsafe when the ratio nears 100 to 1. Yet in Los Angeles, which has the nation's biggest probation department, a single officer is expected to handle as many as 1000 criminals.

MORE FELONS, AND WORSE

"When people say that probation is the alternative to prison, right now they have got it backwards," said Mr. Steppe.

More than two-thirds of the nation's convicted criminals are now under the supervision of federal and local probation departments. With drug-linked crimes clogging the judicial system from courtrooms to prison cells, judges are increasingly handing out sentences of years on probation. When a prison sentence does precede probation, it is often for only a few weeks or months.

Probation systems are handling more felons and hard-core criminals than at any time in history. Although records showing the proportions of various categories of criminals were not kept until recent years, officials said that in the past, very few hard-core criminals were ever given probation. Today, sentences of probation are sometimes meted out even for brutal offenses like rape and child molestation.

Even as probation departments face increased demands, they are receiving fewer and fewer resources. Their budgets are declining in relation to other segments of the court system. In New York City in 1985, for example, the budget for the Department of Corrections was $302.5 million, and for the Probation Department $30.3 million.

Last year, the budget for corrections was $616.9 million, a 103 percent increase; the probation budget had risen just 49 percent, or $45.1 million. . . .

Many judges, prosecutors, and probation officials say that probation has become the weakest link in the judicial chain and that the public now perceives it as just another word for coddling criminals. Yet the only real alternative, they say, is to spend untold billions of dollars to expand prisons.

Source: Stephen Labaton, "Glutted Probation System Puts Communities in Peril," *New York Times*, 19 June, 1990, pp. A-1, A-10.

THE ADMINISTRATION OF PROBATION

State or county administrative structures, privately administered programs, probation subsidy, and rights of probationers are important considerations in the administration of probation.

State or County Administrative Structures

The administrative structure of probation is currently under debate. Should probation be administered by the judicial or the executive branch of government? Should probation be within a state or a local administrative structure? Should probation and parole be administered separately, or should they be combined?

There are arguments for both sides of these issues, but in about 25 percent of the states, probation is primarily a local responsibility, with the state accountable only for providing financial support, setting standards, and arranging training courses. This locally based approach accounts for about two-thirds of all probationers supervised in this nation. (See Figure 9.1 for the various probation administrative structures in the nation; see Table 9.1 for a breakdown of probationers by state.) The federal probation services are controlled by the district judges, but recruitment and training of personnel are administered by the Probation division of the Administrative Office of the United States Courts.

Those who favor judicial control of probation note that it is a service by which offenders are retained under the supervision of an officer of the court and subject to conditions imposed by the court. Revocation of probation and discharge from supervision are court functions. An important disadvantage to county or judicial district control of probation is the widely varying tax base from county to county. An affluent metropolitan county will be able to support a competent probation department, but poor or rural counties will have trouble scraping up funds to support minimal services. Assignment of probation to the executive branch on a statewide basis allows uniform standards of policy making, recruitment, training, and personnel management. Coordination with the state department of corrections and with the parole service is also facilitated. The most significant disadvantage is the development of a large probation bureaucracy with echelons of decision makers shuffling memoranda from out-basket to in-basket with little contact with the real world of the streets. Firm leadership with a grasp of sound management procedures can prevent this dismal prospect.

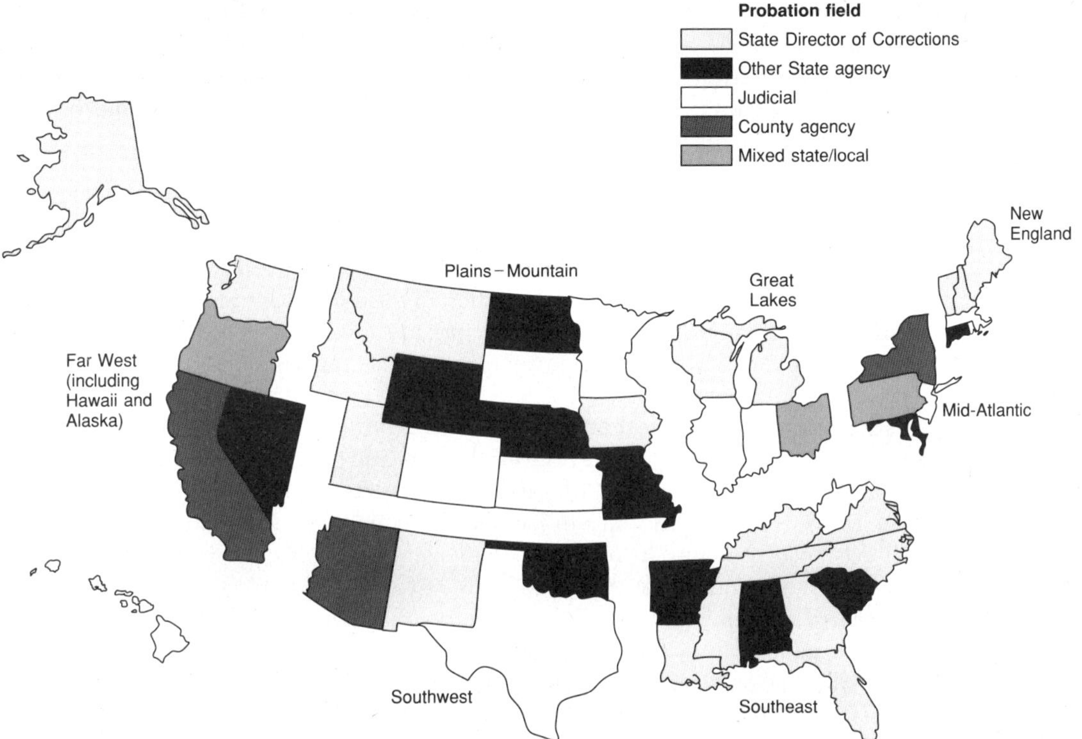

Figure 9.1 Probation structures, National Assessment Project. (*Source*: James M. Byrne and Linda Kelly, *Restructuring Probation as an Intermediate Sanction: An Evaluation of the Massachusetts Intensive Probation Supervision Program* (Final Report to the National Institute of Justice, Research Program on the Punishment and Control of Offenders, 1989), p. 61.)

The two most persuasive arguments for local administration of probation are, first, that citizens and agencies of the community more readily support programs that are open to their participation and that are responsive to local needs and problems and, second, that small operations are more flexible, adjust more quickly to change, and are less encumbered by bureaucratic rigidity.[6] Three arguments against local administration, however, have won the support of many policymakers: A state-administered probation system can set standards of service, thereby ensuring uniformity of procedures, policies, and services; a larger agency can make more effective use of funds and manpower; and greater efficiency in the disposition of resources is possible when all probation officers are state employees.[7]

Thirty states have executive branch agencies that provide both probation and parole services. Critics of the combined system argue that probationers, especially first-time offenders, should be kept separate from parolees and that probation is a service to judges and should be under their control. However, a combined system conserves scarce resources and has greater public acceptance. A combined system requires only one office, one set of directives, and one supervisory hierarchy. In both probation and parole, the same goals are sought and the same skills are required for supervision of offenders.[8]

In sum, the management of probation and parole can be organized in several different ways. On the whole, the statewide organization of combined services is the best assurance of accountability and economy, given firm leadership by an administrator who knows what has to be done and how to do it. Such administrators can also demonstrate strong leadership at a local level and deal with several obvious but not insurmountable disadvantages.

Privately Administered Programs

Probation, like other components of the criminal justice process, contracts services to private agencies. The private administration of misdemeanant probation supervision is currently taking place in Florida, and private investigative firms have begun to supply judges with presentence investigation (PSI) reports.

Misdemeanant Probation and the Private Sector In 1974, misdemeanant probation was left in limbo when the Florida legislature stripped the state Parole and Probation Commission of its authority to administer this form of probation supervision. The Salvation Army office in Jacksonville decided to take advantage of the void that existed by opening its own probation agency. It collected fines, counseled clients, and made social agency referrals.[9]

Armed with missionary zeal and military efficiency, the Salvation Army in Florida has expanded from this beginning in Jacksonville to the point that it has become essentially the only misdemeanant probation supervision arm of the Florida court system. The Salvation Army Misdemeanant Program (**SAMP**) presently employs 200 counselors in 37 counties, and they supervise 14,000 clients a month, or 90 percent of the state's probation caseload.

Two explanations can be given for this rapid and remarkable growth in Florida. First, the Salvation Army does its job very well. Hillsborough County District Attorney Douglas Roberts put it this way: "You think about the Salvation Army as the people who come and collect your old furniture, but, quite frankly, it's been nothing but pleasurable. They're always prepared, they write good case reports. They come across as fair and impartial people."[10]

Second, and probably more important, the Army has become excellent lobbyists for its new program. Through the tireless efforts of Jordan Rothbart, a civilian who founded the program, the Army was able to get its foot in the door of state government. Rothbart's political contacts eventually resulted in a 1978 law that allowed county officials to put misdemeanant probation in the hands of "any court-approved public or private entity." The legislation was formally entitled "The Salvation Army Act" and contained two references to the Army.

Probationers report monthly to the offices of the Army's correctional division. There they meet with counselors and pay fines and fees. Most of the SAMP counselors are civilians, and religious matters are kept out of the business of probation supervision. Interest in SAMP has developed in Alabama, New York, and California, and SAMP experiments are being conducted in Mississippi and Tennessee.

Private PSI The private investigative firms work in one of two ways to provide judges with **PSIs**. First, defendants enter contractual relationships with these firms to conduct comprehensive background checks on them so that judges can be provided with alternatives to incarceration sentencing options. In what is sometimes called "client-specific planning," the private agency becomes the defendant's advocate at the sentencing stage. A major criticism of this approach is that it represents an advantage to the middle- and upper-class offender who can afford to contract the private PSI.[11]

Second, instead of the state or county probation offices preparing the report, the court contracts with a private investigator to do the PSI. This neutral PSI, proponents claim, better ensures that the court will receive a fair and unbiased account upon which to base sentencing on the defendant. Critics, however, claim that private firms ought not to be involved in the quasi-judicial functions of making sentence recommendations. There is also the issue that the white-collar offender is more likely to receive this service than the street offender.[12]

Probation Subsidy

Several states offer rewards in the form of revenue support or labor to local probation systems that comply with state standards. By this means, states can attain greater uniformity of standards. A California innovation, the subsidy program was initiated because several studies suggested that many juvenile and adult offenders could remain safely in the community if they had good probation supervision. Thus, the **subsidy program** was expected to reduce prison populations and to delay further prison construction, an objective that was achieved for a few years. The studies also found that the expanded use of probation would demand state-supported financial incentives. (See Chapter 19 for an evaluation of the subsidy program in California.)

Until it was replaced in 1978 by another act, California's probation subsidy program provided state funds for participating counties (most of the 58 counties participated) if they committed fewer offenders to state institutions. The more cases that were diverted from the prison system, the larger the subsidy a county received. The level of subsidy was determined by comparing a county's actual commitment rate with an ideal normative commitment rate. If, according to this yardstick, a county committed only 100 persons within a period when it could reasonably be expected to commit 200, it had realized a 50 percent reduction. This reduction meant a savings to the state, and the county, in turn, received a portion of the money saved.

Participating counties also were required to improve probation services by employing additional probation officers, by reducing caseloads, and by demonstrating innovative approaches to probation. Some counties failed to provide adequate training for probation staff and did not match offenders' needs with available staff resources, thus causing the program critical embarrassment and contributing to the replacement of the subsidy act by a community corrections act.[13] But the fact of the matter was that the level of service required by the act could not be supported by the amount of the subsidy allowed.

The state of Washington also compensates counties for lower rates of commitment to state institutions. In New York state, a probation subsidy is given to local communities willing to conform to staffing patterns. These local units of government are reimbursed for up to 50 percent of their operating costs for probation services. Michigan assigns state-paid probation officers to work with local probation officers and makes direct payment to local units of government to defray part of the costs of probation services. In 1979, a probation subsidy law went into effect in Illinois. This law mandates officer training and minimum standards of operation, and, in turn, participating counties receive $400 a month for each probation officer.

Rights of Probationers

One of the major issues in the administration of probation concerns the **rights of probationers.** The most important cases litigated by the courts have been involved with disclosure of presentence reports and probation revocation.

The report of the presentence investigation (PSI) is a critical element of the sentencing process. Almost always prepared by a probation officer, it should contain a full review of the offender's social history, criminal history, financial condition, and any circumstances affecting his or her behavior that may be helpful in imposing sentence or planning correctional treatment. It should also include verified information of the financial, social, psychological, and medical impact of the offense upon the victim or victims.

In the preparation of a PSI a probation officer may gather information from persons who may wish to be anonymous. Their reasons—fear of retaliation by the offender or serious personal embarrassment—may be compelling. The question of disclosure of the PSI to defense counsel was first raised in *Williams* v. *New York* (1949).[14] In that case the U.S. Supreme Court rejected the defendant's contention that the sentencing procedure violated his due process rights. It was argued that "the sentence of death was based on information supplied by witnesses with whom the accused had been confronted and as to whom he had no opportunity for cross-examination or rebuttal." This argument failed because, in the view of the Supreme Court:

> We must recognize that most of the information now relied upon by judges to guide them in the intelligent imposition of sentences would be unavailable if information were restricted to that given in open court by witnesses subject to cross-examination. And the modern probation report draws on information concerning every aspect of a defendant's life. The types and extent of this information make totally impractical if not impossible open court testimony with cross-examination.[15]

In *Gardner* v. *Florida*, another capital punishment case, decided 28 years after *Williams*, the sentence of death was pronounced by the trial court after consideration of a PSI, some portions of which had been withheld from open court as confidential.[16] The jury had had no opportunity to review the PSI but had arrived at a recommendation that the court should impose a life sentence. After full consideration of the PSI, the trial judge chose to impose the death penalty. Justice John Paul Stevens, in delivering the opinion of the U.S. Supreme Court, held that circumstances had changed since *Williams*. If the PSI, including the confidential information, had been "the basis for a death sentence, the interest in reliability plainly outweighs the State's interest in preserving the availability of comparable information in other cases."[17] While both *Williams* and *Gardner* were cases in which the death sentence was at stake, there seems to be no reason why they should not apply to defendants facing prison sentences or other dispositions. There is a limit, however. In *Booth* v. *Maryland* (1987), still another death penalty case, the PSI included a Victim Impact Statement (VIS).[18] The adult son and daughter of elderly victims of a murder committed in the course of a burglary made eloquent comments on the brutality of the offense, the grief and sorrow they had experienced, the fears and depression that their parents' murder had caused, and on the fine qualities of their parents as citizens. In a 5-to-4 decision, the Supreme Court held that such information was likely to inflame the jury against the defendants and therefore could not be allowed.[19]

The U.S. Supreme Court has ruled on two important cases concerning probation revocation: *Mempa* v. *Rhay*[20] and *Gagnon* v. *Scarpelli*.[21] In *Mempa*, the court held that the Sixth Amendment's right to counsel applies to the sentencing hearing because it is a critical stage of criminal prosecution. The Court then extended this reasoning to apply to deferred sentencing and probation revocation hearings. Since Mempa did not have counsel at his revocation hearing, the Supreme Court reversed the decision of the lower courts and ordered his release from prison.

Gagnon v. *Scarpelli* involved an offender, Scarpelli, whose probation was revoked in Wisconsin without a hearing. Scarpelli had been sentenced to 15 years' imprisonment for armed robbery in Wisconsin, but his sentence was suspended and he was placed on probation for 7 years. He was given permission to reside in Illinois, where he was later arrested for burglary. His probation was then revoked without a hearing. This case was appealed on the grounds that probation revocation without a hearing and counsel violated Scarpelli's due process rights.

The Supreme Court held that the right to counsel should be decided on a case-by-case basis and that considerable discretion must be given the responsible agency in making the decision. The Court did indicate that counsel should be provided upon request when the probationer claims that he or she did not commit the violation and when the reasons for the violation are complex or otherwise difficult to present.

The revocation of probation is clearly a critical matter for the probationer, for it can send him or her to prison. Prior to these two Supreme Court decisions, considerable confusion existed over what procedural safeguards, if any, regulated probation. In *Gagnon*, the Court refused to find an absolute right to counsel in revocation hearings; however, it did find that in some cases counsel may be required. *Gagnon* has been heavily criticized, chiefly because the case-by-case approach for determining the right to counsel is arbitrary. It also has been argued that counsel should be appointed in all revocation cases because the effects of potential loss of liberty for the probationer outweigh any possible burden on the state in providing counsel.[22]

CHANGING GOALS OF PROBATION SERVICES

In the past two decades, three goals have been advocated for probation services: the rehabilitative goal of reintegration, the "just deserts" philosophy of the justice model, and an emphasis on public safety. The role of the probation officer changes significantly with each of these goals.

Reintegrative Philosophy

As previously discussed, the social context was one of reform in the late 1960s and early 1970s, and, supported by blue-ribbon commissions and funded by federal dollars, the reintegrative philosophy was widely accepted by probation officers across the nation. Elliot Studt makes clear the need for community involvement in the task of reintegration:

> It is too seldom recognized that reintegration is a two-way relationship requiring open doors and support from the community as well as responsible performance by the parolee [or the probationer]. No one can reintegrate in vacuo.[23]

Adopting the reintegrative philosophy required changes in probation and parole services, such as team approaches, pooled caseloads, service brokerage (arranging services through other agencies), referred services, and job placement development.[24] In the mid-1970s, as the rehabilitation model came under increasing attack, a number of probation administrators adopted the concept of the Community Resource Management Team (CRMT). Under this approach to probation services, officers are divided into teams, and each team takes responsibility for a caseload and makes decisions on what community resources are needed by clients. Team members are usually specialists in "needs subsystems," and the specialist links the probationer with whatever services in the community are necessary.[25]

The Justice Model

David Fogel's justice model argues that probation lacks direction, has low status, and is experiencing a decline in public confidence (see Chapters 5 and 6 for discussions of the justice model).[26] Fogel, P. McAnany, and D. Thompson have offered the following suggestions to provide direction for probation:

1. Probation is a penal sanction whose main characteristic is punitive.
2. Probation should be a sentence, not a substitute for a real sentence that is threatened after future violation—it should not be subject to reduction or addition.
3. Probation should be part of a single graduated range of penal sanctions and should be available as the sentence for all levels of crime, except the most serious felonies.
4. The gravity of the probation sentence should be determined by both the length of term and the quality and quantity of the conditions.
5. Conditions should be justified in terms of the seriousness of the offense, though other purposes may be served by such conditions, such as incapacitation.[27]

Fogel also wants to reduce the discretionary authority of probation officers and, therefore, recommends that the standard of proof for the revocation of probation be as strong as the original finding that resulted in the sentence of probation (i.e., beyond a reasonable doubt). Furthermore, the presentence investigation report should be regarded as a legal document, and defendants have the right to know the contents of this report. Fogel and other advocates of the justice model recommend increasing restitution programs because they believe it is only fair for offenders to pay for the social harm they have inflicted. Fogel emphasizes that probation should be as concerned with the victim of crime as it is with the offender.[28]

Risk Assessment and Increased Surveillance Models

In the late 1970s, probation came under criticism as a lenient measure that allowed offenders to escape their just punishment. R. L. Thomas explains why probation suffers from this "soft on criminals" image:

> Probation lacks the forceful imagery which other occupations in criminal justice can claim. Police catch criminals, prosecutors try to get them locked up, judges put them in prison, guards and wardens keep them there, [but] probation, in the public view, offers crime and the criminal a second chance.[29]

In an attempt to convince the public, as well as policymakers, that probation could be "tougher" on criminals, probation administrators began to emphasize a number of strategies that would better ensure public protection. (See Figure 9.2 for the risk control and risk reduction emphasis of probation in Massachusetts.) The most widely used of these strategies have been the combination of probation and incarceration, financial restitution and community service programs, classification systems, intensive probation, and electronic monitoring and house arrest.

Combination of Probation and Confinement A number of sentencing options require the probationer to serve a period of confinement. The "split sentence" combines incarceration with probation as a separate sentence. Intermittent confinement means weekend, night, or vacation confinement in jail during the time a person is on

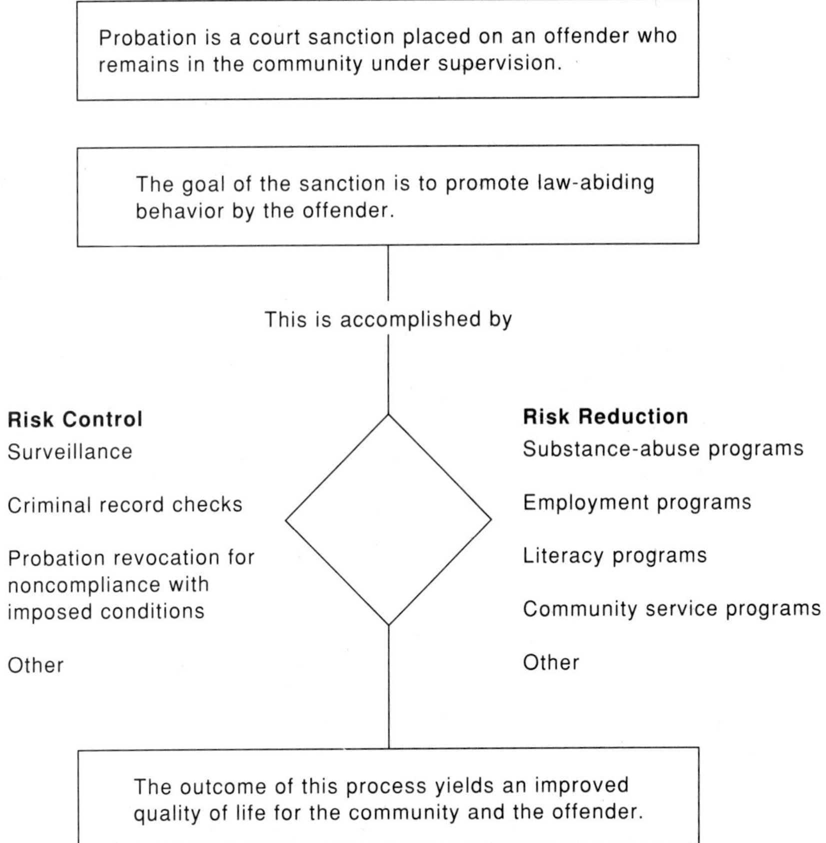

Figure 9.2 Probation structures, National Assessment Project. (*Source*: Randall Guynes, "Difficult clients, large caseloads plague probation, parole agencies," *Research in Action* (Washington: U.S. Department of Justice, 1988), p. 2.)

probation. The diagnostic study followed by probation, an option in a number of jurisdictions (California, Kansas, North Dakota, Pennsylvania, and the federal system), permits the judge to confine an offender for a limited period of time before sentencing him or her to probation.[30]

Shock probation has been a widely used option in which the judge sentences a defendant to prison and then releases this person to probation supervision after a period of time (frequently 90 days). In 1965, the Ohio General Assembly implemented what has become known as shock probation. Developed from the split sentence in the federal courts (in which the defendant receives a specific jail sentence to be served before being released on probation status in the community), shock probation in Ohio means that after a felon has served at least 30 but fewer than 60 days of the sentence, the offender, his or her attorney, or the sentencing judge can submit a motion to suspend the remainder of the sentence and to release him or her on probation. Within 60 days of the filing of the motion, the judge who heard the case must hold a hearing on the motion and is then permitted another 10 days in which to rule on the motion.[31] Until the court acts on the petition, the institutionalized inmate remains uncertain about how much more time he or she will spend in prison. Between 1985 and 1990, 12,003 offenders were committed to this program and released after completion of the shock: 1985, 1427; 1986, 1485; 1987, 1798; 1989, 2895; and 1990 (so far), 2602.[32]

Used also under various names and forms in Kentucky, North Carolina, Texas, Indiana, Idaho, and Maine, shock probation has generated considerable interest and debate. In the 1980s, however, shock incarceration has replaced shock probation in many states. The major difference between the earlier shock probation and shock incarceration programs relates to the required participation in drills and physical training in "boot camp" prison settings that are components of the recent shock incarceration programs.[33] Indeed, according to Doris L. MacKenzie, seventeen states now have shock incarceration programs, while three other states are developing such programs.[34]

Split sentencing is also a standard feature of many intensive supervision programs. For example, all offenders assigned to New Jersey's intensive supervision program must serve a minimum of 30 days of initial confinement. The intensive supervision programs of Arizona, Connecticut, Kentucky, Louisiana, Missouri, Ohio, Oregon, and Texas also include a period of confinement.[35]

The basic assumption of combining incarceration and community supervision has been aptly stated by Joan Petersilia:

> The rationale for such programs is that an offender who is "shocked" by a brief prison or jail experience will be deterred from returning to crime. The period of probation or parole may be part of the original sentence or may be granted to inmates who petition the court to suspend execution of sentence. The goal of shock incarceration is specific deterrence.[36]

Financial Restitution and Community Service Financial restitution and community service orders have become widely used conditions of probation in recent years. Interest in these programs, according to Joan Petersilia, "has recently increased due to growing interest in the rights of victims and the search for alternatives to incarceration."[37]

Financial restitution establishes a sum of money that the offender must pay either to the victim or to a public fund for victims of crime. A community service order requires that the offender perform a certain number of work hours at a private nonprofit or government agency. Two general patterns have emerged for structuring community service obligations: (1) to refer offenders to community agencies that handle the work placement and supervise completion of the community service obligation and (2) to assign a group of offenders to provide a community service. The number of hours of community services to be completed is generally determined by the court or sometimes by program staff.[38] Commonly assigned public service projects include clean-up work on the local streets or in city parks, volunteer service in hospitals or in nursing homes, and repair jobs in run-down housing.

Offenders who do not have the resources to make their restitution payments may be confined to a correctional facility at night while they are employed elsewhere during the day to earn money for such payments. About 30 states now operate restitution centers.[39] Residential restitution programs include the Restitution Shelters developed by Georgia's Department of Offender Rehabilitation, the Probation in Restitution Experiment of the Polk County (Des Moines) Iowa Court Services, the Mississippi Restitution Corrections Center, the Florida Restitution Centers, the Offender Restitution Program in Orleans Parish, Louisiana, and the Restitution Centers in Texas.

Joe Hudson and Burt Galaway, in an examination of 14 community service programs across the nation, developed a model of the structure and logic of the community service program activities, inputs, and outcomes. In this model, they also included the resources necessary to support the community service activities, the immediate results of the program activities, and the socially beneficial outcomes of the activities. (See Figure 9.3 for the schematic representation of this model.)

Since the mid-1960s, community service sentencing has been growing more popular. Initially, it was used to permit offenders, such as misdemeanants, traffic defendants, and minor property offenders, who could not pay their fines to work off their obligation by working without pay for the community. Usually add-ons to probation, rather than sentences unto themselves, community service sentences were considered a rehabilitative alternative to jail sentences.[40]

Today, community service has new advocates because it can relieve jail and prison crowding by diverting certain kinds of offenders. However, community service programs are difficult to design, implement, and manage. A program must appear punitive enough to satisfy the public that justice is being served. A sizable staff is also needed to keep track of convicted offenders' community service. Moreover, agencies willing to accept felons as volunteers, particularly those agencies having work compatible with offenders' skills, are not easily found.[41]

In the early 1980s, the Vera Institute of Justice designed a community service sentencing project in three New York City boroughs. The Vera project focused on persistent property offenders who were housed in jail and was quite clear in its objectives: "The community service sentence was to be first and foremost a punishment."[42] Vera decided to set up and operate its own program, with its staff supervising work assignments. All persons sentenced to community service in this project are required to perform 70 hours of unpaid labor, even though they have committed different crimes. About 85 percent of the offenders in the three Vera projects complete their community service obligations; most of those who fail are brought back to court and given a jail term.[43]

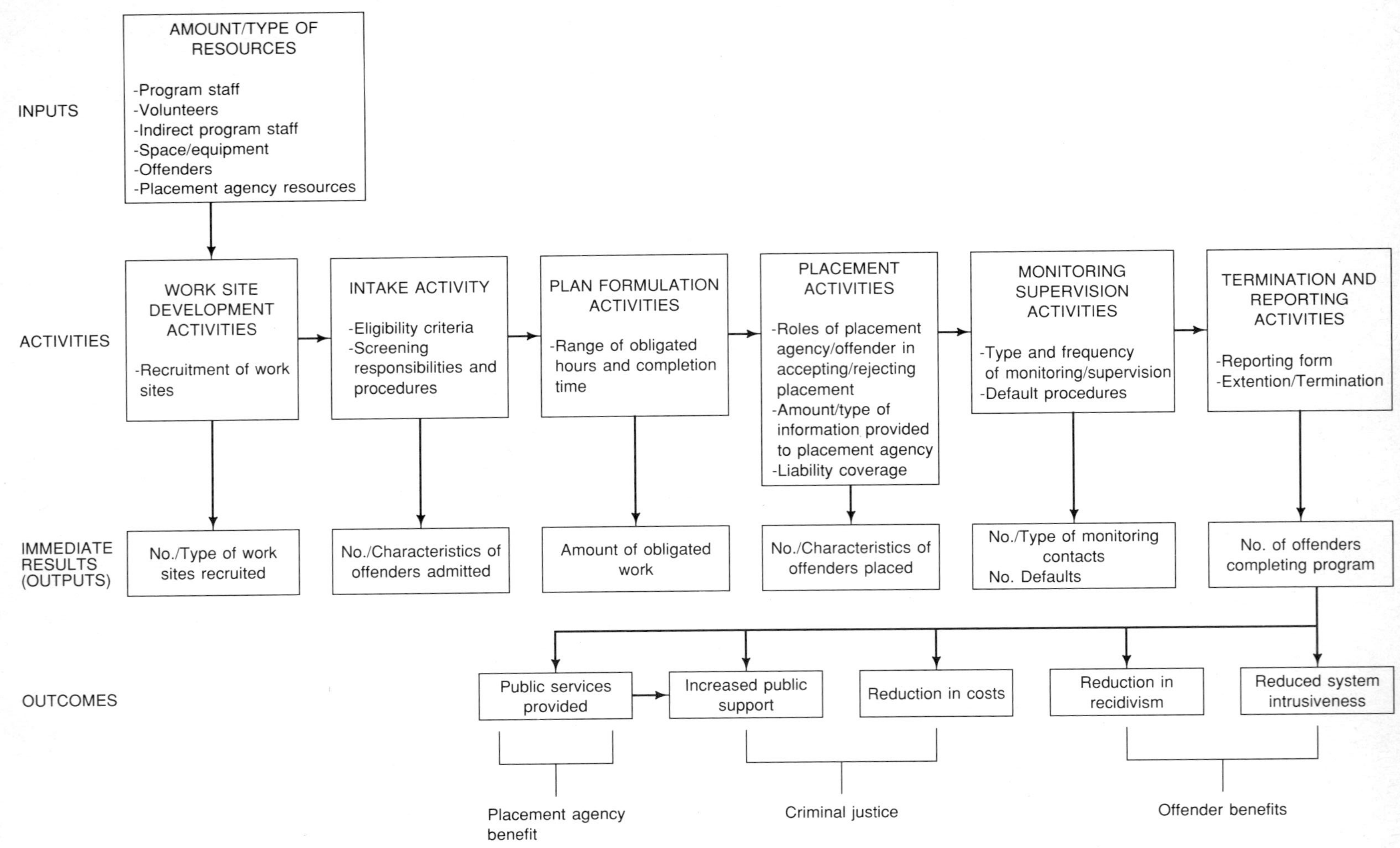

Figure 9.3 Federal probation. (*Source*: Joe Hudson and Burt Galaway, "Community Service: Toward Program Definition," *Federal Probation* (June 1990).)

Classification Considerations of public safety have led most probation departments to develop classification systems for placing offenders under intensive, medium, or minimum supervision. Most of these instruments are modeled after the Wisconsin system, or the NIC Model Probation Client Classification and Case Management System.[44]

On the basis of an objectively scored, structured interview, the **Wisconsin classification system** assigns clients to appropriate casework groups. The classification interview covers 40 items dealing with probationers' attitudes toward their offense, the offense history, family and interpersonal relationships, current problems, and future plans. One or two open-ended questions are asked in each general area, followed by more specific questions designed to elicit detailed information. There are also 12 objective background and offense-history items, 5 behavior ratings (based on interview behavior), and 7 items calling for the agents' impressions of the probationers' most and least important problem areas.[45]

Probationers are assigned to one of four case-management treatment strategies: a selective intervention group, a casework/control group, an environmental structure group, and a limit-setting group.[46] The most prominent characteristic of probationers in the selective intervention group is that they tend to have relatively stable and prosocial lifestyles. They are also usually employed and established in the community and have committed minor criminal offenses.

The most prominent characteristic of probationers in the casework/control group is a general instability as evidenced by problems in the home, inability to hold a job, and a lack of goal-directedness. Although these probationers require a great deal of an officer's time, direction, and support, it is believed that they are capable of substantial change if they can establish stability in their lives and can deal with their self-defeating behaviors.

Probationers in the environmental structure group tend to allow themselves to be led by others because they are deficient in social and vocational skills. These probationers require long-range, time-consuming support, guidance, and structure; but if they can find a challenging job, an adequate living situation, and noncriminal friends (very substantial "ifs"), they may be able to avoid further involvement in crime. Probationers placed in the limit-setting group usually have had a long-term involvement in crime. They need ground rules, maximum supervision, and a redirection of their intellectual and social skills.

Under the Wisconsin system a risk/needs assessment evaluation is made of each probationer at regular intervals. The risk scale was derived from empirical studies that showed certain factors, such as prior arrest record, age at first conviction, the nature of the offense for which the probationer was convicted, and employment patterns, to be good predictors of recidivism.

The needs assessment focuses on such indicators as emotional stability, financial management, family relationships, and health. The scores derived from the risk/needs assessment are used to classify probationers by required level of supervision, intensive, medium, or minimum. These levels, in turn, impose corresponding restrictions on liberty and requirements for contact between offenders and probation staff. Reassessment of cases takes place at regular intervals, and the level of supervision may be increased or reduced.[47]

In October 1977, this classification system was first implemented in two probation and parole units in Wisconsin. The system has since received further modification and has been used in additional units throughout the state. The Wisconsin system also is currently used in at least 100 jurisdictions throughout the United States and promises to make an impact on probation services in the future.

Intensive Supervision Intensive supervision, a new but already widely used program, seems especially useful with high-risk probationers. This type of program, initiated in Georgia, is based on the belief that increased contact and referral result in more positive adjustment—as evidenced, for example, by a higher employment rate and a lower rate of involvement in crime.[49] The typical pattern is for one or more probation officers to assume a small caseload made up of probationers who require intensive supervision. These probationers are contacted several times a week through unannounced home visits and other means.[50]

Proponents argue that these programs offer realistic prospects for a wide-ranging renovation of American penology.[51]

Intensive probation supervision is generally organized in six ways:

Supervision is *extensive*. Probation officers have multiple, weekly face-to-face contacts with offenders, as well as collateral contacts with employers and family members and frequent arrest checks.

Supervision is *focused*. Monitoring activities concentrate specific behavorial regulations governing curfews, drug use, travel, employment, and community service.

Supervision is *ubiquitous*. Offenders are frequently subjected to random drug tests and unannounced curfew checks.

Supervision is *graduated*. Offenders commonly proceed through IPS programs in a series of progressive phases—each of which represents a gradual tempering of the prescriptions and requirements of IPS—until they are committed to regular supervision as the final leg of their statutory time on probation.

Supervision is strictly *enforced*. Penalties for new arrests and noncompliance with program conditions are generally swift and severe.

Supervision is *coordinated*. IPS offenders are usually monitored by specially selected and trained officers who are part of a larger specialized, autonomous unit.[52]

The Georgia Intensive Probation Supervision (IPS) program is the strictest form of intensive probation in the United States. (See Chapter 19 for a more extensive evaluation of the Georgia program.) Thirteen teams across the state—each composed of a probation officer and a "surveillance officer"—watch over no more than 25 probationers at a time. They see their clients at least 5 times a week, sometimes more often. Probationers have a curfew that is checked on frequently.[53] A 1987 evaluation showed that offenders placed in IPS had lower rates of recidivism than comparison groups of offenders released from prison and supervised on regular probation, and that the majority who committed new crimes were involved in less serious forms of criminal behavior.[54] The positive evaluation of Georgia's project has encouraged 39 other states to develop their own intensive probation projects. Some large county probation offices—such as Lucas County, Ohio, and Multnomah County, Oregon—have also set up similar intensive programs.

Joan Petersilia has identified nine conditions for implementing successful IPS programs:

1. The project must address a pressing local problem.
2. The project must have clearly articulated goals that reflect the needs and desires of the community.

3. The project must have a receptive environment in both the "parent" organization and the larger system.
4. The organization must have a leader who is vitally committed to the objectives, values, and implementations of the project and who can devise practical strategies to motivate and effect change.
5. The project must have a director who shares the leader's ideas and values and uses them to guide the implementation process and operation of the project.
6. Practitioners must make the project their own, rather than being coerced into it. They must participate in its development and have incentives to maintain its integrity during the change process.
7. The project must have clear lines of authority and no ambiguity about "who is in charge."
8. The change and its implementation must not be complex or sweeping.
9. The organization must have secure administration, low staff turnover, and plentiful resources.[55]

A considerable amount of crime is committed by felons sentenced to probation. It is commonly agreed that IPS programs have a particularly important role to play with these more serious offenders. In 1986, the Bureau of Justice Assistance (BJA) funded an IPS demonstration project involving high-risk offenders. The intent of this project was to determine how participation in IPS programs affected offenders' subsequent behavior. The project took place in 14 sites in 9 states. The RAND Corporation was selected to evaluate the IPS project.[56]

Joan Petersilia and Susan Turner evaluated three counties in California (Contra Costa, Ventura, and Los Angeles) that participated in the project. They found that at the end of the one-year follow-up period, about one-fourth of the IPS offenders in each site had no new incidents (technical violations or new arrests); about 40 percent had technical violations only and about a third had new arrests. Furthermore, they found that there were no significant differences in the severity of the arrest offenses among experimental (IPS) and (non-IPS) offenders.[57] Evaluation of the IPS project at the other 11 sites also will reveal how effective this intermediate sentence is with high-risk offenders.

Electronic Monitoring and House Arrest House arrest is a sentence imposed by the court whereby offenders are ordered to remain confined in their own residences for the length of their sentence. They may be allowed to leave their homes for medical reasons, employment, and approved religious services. They may also be required to perform community service. Electronic monitoring equipment may or may not be used to monitor offenders' presence in a residence where they are required to remain.[58]

Through **electronic monitoring** devices, corrections staffs can verify that an offender is at home or in a community correctional center during specified hours.[59] According to a National Institute of Justice survey, officials in 33 states were using electronic monitoring devices to supervise nearly 2300 offenders in 1988; this number was about 3 times the number using electronic monitoring in 1987 (see Figure 9.4 for the location of these programs).[60] Electronic monitoring has been described in the *Wall Street Journal* as the "hottest new technology in crime control."[61] Georgette Bennett predicts in *Crimewarps* that electronic monitoring will be the "dominant means of probation and parole supervision within the next 20 years."[62] Box 9-2 explains how electronic monitoring equipment works.

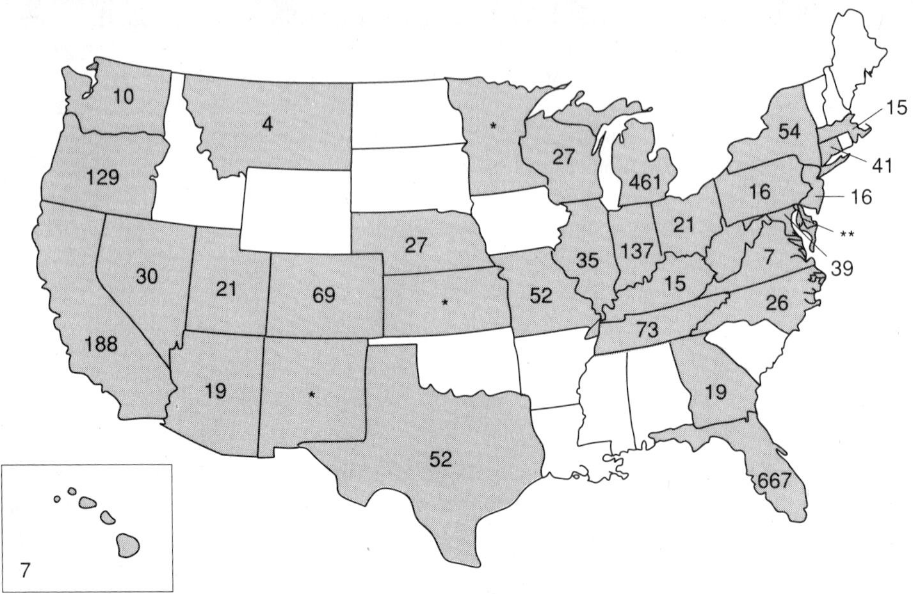

* Programs exist, but no offenders were being monitored on this date.
** No response.
Note: There are no programs in Alaska

Figure 9.4 Number of offenders being electronically monitored on February 14, 1988. (*Source*: Annesley K. Schmidt, "Electronic monitoring of offenders increases," *Research in Action* (Washington: U.S. Department of Justice, February 1989), p. 1.)

The level of monitoring varies widely among these states. For example, Florida's 667 and Michigan's 461 electronically monitored offenders accounted for 49.5 percent of the 2300 offenders monitored in 1988. The programs monitored primarily men, with women constituting only 12.7 percent of monitored offenders. Furthermore, 33.4 percent of the offenders monitored had been convicted of major traffic offenses, 18.2 percent of property offenses, 22 percent of multiple offenses and other crimes, and 13.5 percent of drug offenses. The remaining offenders being monitored had been convicted of a wide range of criminal violations.[63]

The application of high technology to the field of corrections raises a number of controversies that have yet to be resolved by research. On the positive side, to the limited extent that it can provide a genuine alternative to incarceration and its destructive consequences, electronic monitoring certainly is beneficial to both the offenders who escape the jails and to society, which can defer building more of them. Further, keeping the offender in the community reduces the task of resocialization that confronts those who wish to assist the released prisoner.

On the negative side, at least three perils could result in the wake of the proliferation of electronic monitoring. First, this new correctional "panacea" is a depersonalization of the relationship between the correctional agency and offenders. In the electronic model of control, there is no bureaucrat in sight to whom offenders might turn for help. There is no one who is interested in helping them. There is only the anklet or the bracelet and a telephone system that will keep them from bringing the system's representative to pounce on them if the invisible boundary is breached.

Box 9-2 How Electronic Monitoring Equipment Works

Electronic monitoring equipment receives information about monitored offenders and transmits the information over telephone lines to a computer at the monitoring agency. There are two basic types: continuously signaling devices that constantly monitor the presence of the offender at a particular location, and programmed contact devices that contact the offender periodically to verify his or her presence.

CONTINUOUSLY SIGNALING DEVICES

A continuously signaling device has three major parts: a transmitter, a receiver-dialer, and a central computer.

The transmitter, which is attached to the offender, sends out a continuous signal. The receiver-dialer, which is located in the offender's home and is attached to the telephone, detects the signals sent by the transmitter. It reports to the central computer when it stops receiving the signal and again when the signal begins.

A central computer at the monitoring agency accepts the signals from the receiver-dialer over the telephone lines, compares them with the offender's curfew schedule, and alerts correctional officials about any unauthorized absences. The computer also stores information about each offender's routine entries and exits so that a report can be prepared.

PROGRAMMED CONTACT DEVICES

These devices use a computer programmed to telephone the offender during the monitored hours, either randomly or at specified times. The computer prepares a report on the results of the call.

Most but not all programs attempt to verify that the offender is indeed the person responding to the computer's call. Programmed contact devices can do this in several ways. One is to use voice verification technology. Another is to require the offender to wear a wristwatch device programmed to provide a unique number that appears when a special button on the watch device is pressed into a touch-tone telephone in response to the computer's call.

A third system requires a black plastic module to be strapped to the offender's arm. When the computer calls, the module is inserted into a verifier box connected to the telephone. A fourth system uses visual verification at the telephone site.

Source: Annesley K. Schmidt, "Electronic Monitoring of Offenders Increases." In *Research in Action* (Washington: U.S. Department of Justice, 1989), p. 3.

Richard Ball and Robert Lilly, in examining **house arrests**, also concluded that the use of surveillance technology reduces the involvement of the community with the offender. They add that "the rapid development of electronic monitoring now suggests that the system . . . may be more interested in maintaining bureaucratic control . . . than involving the community in the monitoring of compliance."[64]

Second, the move toward technological supervision could undermine the status of probation as a profession. With electronic monitoring, there is the routine, straightforward clerical function of monitoring and responding to computer printouts. There are also reports of electronic monitoring programs changing, or de-skilling, the nature of probation officer training and redefining tasks typically carried out by probation officers. For example, new probation officer training in Florida—one of the first states to embark on an electronic monitoring program—stresses officer safety, self-defense, surveillance techniques, and search-and-seizure law.[65]

Third, the fact that electronic monitoring intrudes into the home by monitoring the activities of one of its inhabitants challenges the idea of "home" as a refuge, a sanctuary, and a bulwark. "What's next?" is a question that anyone concerned about civil liberties might ask. The sociologist Gary Marx has suggested that electronic monitoring has the potential for turning every home into a prison and every bedroom into a cell, and that we would do well to consider whether we want to take that risk.[66]

In sum, the real worry is that policy makers might once again become slaves to fashion, without sufficient planning and analysis of likely implications.[67] Depersonalization, the most serious criticism of electronic monitoring programs, can be largely prevented. Aware of the damage this system might do, a staff of probation officers can keep in touch, providing help and reassurance as needed throughout the experience. Yet the temptation of the bean counters will be to minimize the expensive staff and to maximize the cheaper electronics.

THE PROBATION OFFICER

The three basic functions of an adult probation officer are to manage a caseload, to supervise probationers, and to make reports to the courts.

Casework Management and Other Administrative Duties

The probation officer maintains a file on each probationer for whom he or she is responsible. This file consists of the court documents that establish the requirements of probation, chronological entries of contacts with the probationer and others whose relationships might be significant, items of correspondence, and periodic reports made to the courts or to officials of the agency. There will be a certain amount of paperwork, which in an enlightened agency will be kept to the barest minimum necessary, and some data submitted periodically to the statistical unit of the agency.

Commonly, probation departments divide probationers into several categories, based upon either their needs or the risk they present to the community. Some offenders are placed on minimum supervision status and are required only to mail in a report once a month or even less frequently. Others, classified as medium supervision cases, must visit their officers at least once a month. Still other offenders require maximum, or intensive, supervision and must be seen several times a month.

Supervision of Probationers

Traditionally, probation officers were expected to maintain a counseling relationship with probationers. But during the 1970s, the majority of probation officers began to see themselves as resource managers, or brokers, rather than as counselors. This role as community resource manager was based on the premise that "the probation officer will have primary responsibility for meshing a probationer's identified needs with a range of available services and for supervising the delivery of these services."[68] To fulfill this role effectively, the probation officer must assess the situation, be aware of available resources, contact the appropriate resources, assist a probationer in obtaining these services, and follow up on the case. If it is necessary to purchase community services, the task, then, is to monitor and evaluate them.

The probation officer is often called on to intervene in family crises as an agent for conflict resolution. His or her counseling role will also include assisting the probationer in getting and keeping employment. Many whose employment experience is meager or nonexistent will have much to learn—how to apply for a job and the habits of punctuality, dress, and diligence required in the world of work. In most situations, only the probation officer is available for these services.

As an officer of the court, the probation officer is responsible not only for assistance but also for surveillance. Depending on the policy of the agency and the community served, the emphases have shifted one way or the other since the 1940s. The conflict of roles bedevils officers who are interested in treatment. Offenders cannot easily trust personnel whose job requirements call for them to take action on apparent violations of the conditions of probation, whether such violations are real or not. In recent years, largely because of the failures of probation in crime-ridden neighborhoods, many probation officers have sloughed off their treatment roles in favor of surveillance and the collection of urine for drug testing.

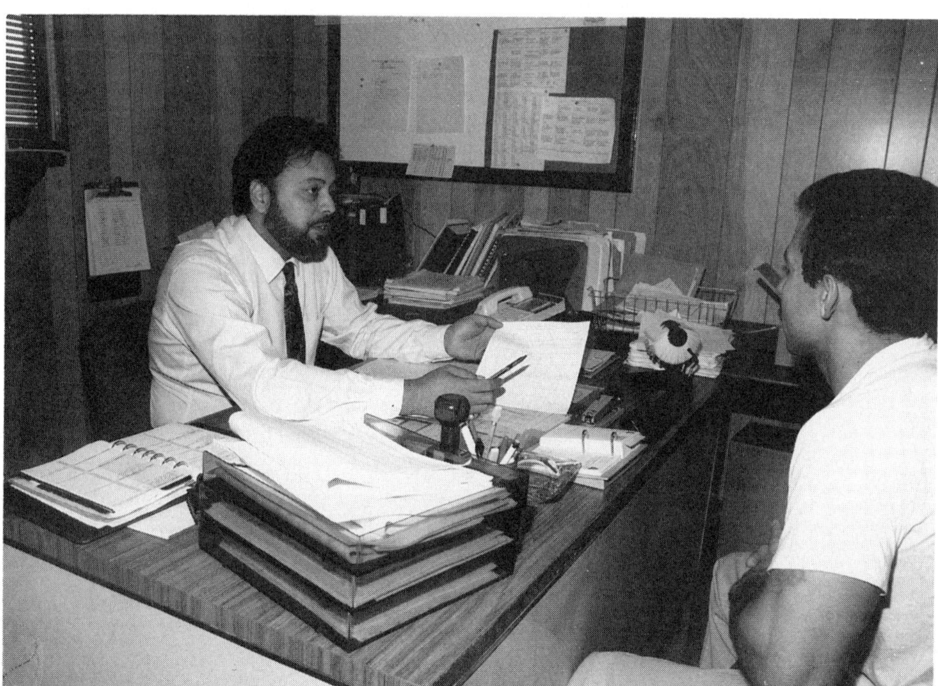

Probation counselor. (*Source*: Southern State Correctional Facility, New Jersey Department of Corrections.)

Reports to the Court

The third function of the probation officer is the preparation of investigative reports. The presentence investigation (PSI) is crucial to the sentencing decision of the court and in some jurisdictions may contain recommendations as to the sentence to be imposed. In most states, the PSI must be prepared whether or not the offender is eligible for probation. If he or she is sent to prison, the PSI will accompany the commitment document for the information of the prison authorities.

Subsequent to the PSI, the probationer's progress is recorded. Police contacts must be reported to the court, and where a serious violation of the conditions has taken place a full report must be presented to the court before the revocation hearing.

The PSI has five purposes:

1. The primary purpose is to assist the court in deciding the proper disposition of the offender. Except for the offenders convicted of crimes for which a prison sentence is mandatory, the options will range from a fine or suspended sentence to a prison term, including, of course, probation.
2. The presentence report also serves as a basis for probation supervision and treatment. It describes problem areas in the defendant's life, evaluates his or her capacity for using help, and notes the opportunities the community offers for meeting the defendant's needs.
3. The presentence report can also assist prison staff in classifying the defendant and providing programs for him or her. When prison staffs are overwhelmed with incoming inmates, these presentence reports can facilitate the classification process.
4. The presentence report provides parole authorities with pertinent information helpful in parole and release planning.
5. Ideally, the presentence report also serves as a source of information for research in corrections and criminal justice.[69]

The long form of a presentence report may take up to 20 hours to complete. Probation officers must first interview the defendant, preferably more than once, in order to verify information. Officers then review the defendant's arrest record, reports concerning the current offense, previous presentence reports, and any available psychiatric or psychological reports. Occasionally they must interview the arresting officer and the defendant's employer, and they often talk with the defendant's family. In a number of large departments, because of the increasing specialization of probation services, some officers' jobs consist only of preparing presentence reports. The importance of the PSI in those jurisdictions that require a recommendation is apparent in the fact that studies show a high correlation (95 percent) between the probation officer's recommendation and the judge's decision.[70]

Probation officers have the authority to file a notice of violation with the court when a probationer violates the conditions of probation or is arrested again. The prosecutor may decide to prosecute the new offense, especially if the penalty is greater than that of revocation and he or she has a solid case. If he or she does not decide to prosecute, the case is placed on the court calendar, and the probationer is directed to appear in court for a preliminary hearing. If a revocation hearing is scheduled following the preliminary hearing, the probation officer is charged before the hearing to present the judge a full violation-of-probation report documenting the charges and summarizing the probationer's degree of adjustment to supervision.

The Frustrations of the Job

Probation officers are faced with a number of pressures and role conflicts that interfere with the commitment they have to their jobs. The most frustrating of these pressures are feeling underpaid, overburdened, subject to stress from clients, and limited by bureaucratic constraints.

Probation officers continue to feel underpaid. The minimum annual starting salary for a probation officer in 1986 ranged from $9,592 in some counties in Pennsylvania to $25,466 in Massachusetts. Sixteen states paid a starting probation officer under $17,000 in 1986, and 30 states paid such an officer under $20,000. While 20 states paid a starting probation officer $20,000 or more that year, this increased salary base was still less than what parole and police officers were making in that jurisdiction.[71]

Indeed, because income is highly correlated with job prestige and status in American society, probation officers also experience low status. A black probation officer tells of his unique problem with status:

> I had the opportunity to go to a small town in Iowa for a revocation hearing of a white client. He had on a white T-shirt and a pair of blue jeans and beat-up tennis shoes. I had on the prettiest suit money could buy and a very sophisticated top hat and overcoat. The judge came into the courtroom and said, "Will the defendant please rise?" He asked for the defendant, so I did not move. But neither did the defendant next to me move. He banged the gavel and said, "Will the defendant please rise?" I saw him looking at me. I thought, he thinks I'm the client, but I'm not going to stoop so low as to explain to him that I'm not. He should be able to figure that I'm the PO by my briefcase and my suit. He beat the gavel once more and told the bailiff that if I didn't get up, I would be made to get up. Right then I knew how it felt for everybody else in the system.[72]

The large caseloads also make most probation officers feel overworked. In 1967, the President's Commission on Law Enforcement and Administration of Justice recommended that probation and parole caseloads should average about 35 offenders per officer. But the average caseload is usually several times that number. As stated in Box 9-1, caseloads for an officer are as high as 1000 in Los Angeles, 700 in San Diego, and several hundred in other urban areas.[73] The large caseloads, the number of presentence reports to be prepared, the never-ending paperwork, the time that must be spent in court, and the contacts that must be made in the community make the job seem overwhelming.

A major source of stress for probation officers is the pressure of working with individuals who are constantly involved in crisis and failure. One probation officer noted that "a PO never gets a client very far away from the crisis line."[74] The consequence of working with so many offenders who are "losers" makes it easy to generalize and to look upon all clients as "losers." It is easy for officers to become discouraged because they are confronted with so little success and so much failure. This situation leads to officers' withdrawal from clients and to job burnout. Probation officers also encounter stress because probationers are commonly resistant and sometimes hostile to them. Officers are occasionally threatened by probationers, and they stand the risk of physical assault, including rape.[75]

Finally, the increasing bureaucratic rigidity in probation services is a major source of frustration for probation officers. The overall pattern of probation in the late 1980s and early 1990s shows much defensiveness on the part of administrators and little tolerance for innovation in probation services. All too frequently, probation staff are informed that the first commandment of working in the office is not to embarrass the agency. This "play it safe" posture has led to a bureaucratic rigidity that has sometimes proved dysfunctional in delivering services to clients. In Box 9-3, the director of a public defender's office relates one such incident of how bureaucratic

Box 9-3 Imperfection in Probation

Ruth, an eighteen year old from Milwaukee, came to live with her father. When she arrived here, she found that her fifty-year-old father had a twenty-five-year-old girlfriend living with him. The father told Ruth she could stay with a friend of his. The first night there, this guy, about half drunk, tried to rape her. She somehow eluded that by getting him to have another drink and, at some point, he passed out. She stole one of his checks and rented an apartment forging his name. She cashed a $75 check; so she has a $75 crime.

She was given a deferred sentence, but she had no place to live. So they put her in the residential facility. She didn't want to go back to Milwaukee, and her mother didn't want her back. She had never been in trouble before. She had a friend in Las Vegas, so her probation officer agreed to let her transfer to Las Vegas. She got a job as a chambermaid at a strip hotel.

But a girl with the same name was arrested for prostitution out there. The Las Vegas probation department saw that in the paper and sent a copy of it to the probation department here. They went to a judge without anybody representing her with a recommendation to revoke probation. It was revoked, and the judge ordered that she be returned from Las Vegas. The sheriff and his wife flew to Las Vegas and brought her back. But she didn't lose her deferred sentence because we were able to prove it wasn't her. The judge did say that Las Vegas wasn't good for her and would not let her return.

She's now back at the facility, working two jobs. She brings home $172 every two weeks. The facility takes out all but $7 of that—not to apply toward the restitution but to pay them for letting her live there. On top of that, they've now presented her with a $2000 bill for the trip of the sheriff and his wife to Las Vegas to get her. Her original crime now has her owing about $3000. And the $172 she makes doesn't even apply toward it.

She was in here the other day and said, "I quit! Why should I try to improve?" She has a good point. The whole system is designed to build in failure. This happens far too frequently.

Source: Interviewed in December 1984.

rigidity resulted in the failure to deliver adequate services to a probationer. Most probation officers have their own war stories.

The Effective Officer

Newly hired probation officers usually begin their jobs with enthusiasm. They think of themselves as entering a helping profession and believe they have something to give to the clients under their care. There is a quality of being responsive to people, even people whom others might find rather repellent, that makes for superior performance. Very much involved in their work, they expend a great deal of physical and emotional energy during the day in providing direct services to probationers, and they may take their jobs home with them at night. A friend of one of the authors, since deceased, used to hold open house after hours and on his own time for any probationers who wanted to drop by and join in a "bull session." He had an extraordinarily low violation rate. But for most probation officers, before long the problems and frustrations of the job begin to weigh upon them. They wonder about how much good they are doing and question the whole philosophy of probation service. Effective officers, instead of succumbing to disillusionment, are able to work through these feelings and reach an even deeper dedication to their tasks.

The most effective probation officers have certain characteristics. They try to remain genuine in officer–client relationships; they will not play games. Effective officers are compassionate and respectful toward their clients; however, they are streetwise and will not be manipulated. The best probation officers have an uncanny ability to help others to achieve success. When a client fails, the officer can help him or her try again. Successful probation officers know themselves and keep their personal problems separate from their clients' problems. Most important, they are committed to their jobs, not just to a paycheck. Their motivation remains constant and strengthens them against burnout. Many remain as involved in their work as they were on their first day on the job.

Because of these characteristics, effective officers are respected by their clients. They can usually discipline offenders without alienating them. They develop a bank of successes to draw on when burnout threatens. Effective officers enjoy the respect of colleagues in the justice system and maintain good relationships within the office. Whether they are prompted or not (promotions are impossible in a one-person office), they are rewarded by an awareness of their reputations for fairness, genuineness, and commitment to their jobs. In short, their efforts do pay off, and they do make a difference in the lives of probationers.

CONCLUSIONS

Probation is not popular with hardline penologists. Their assumption that it is an indulgence to the convicted criminal that gives him or her further opportunities to rob and steal is not without foundation. Where probation is a nominal service carried out by underpaid, overworked, and untrained personnel, it is a sad mockery of a potentially essential service. A policy that provides for professional services carried out under professional conditions can keep the less menacing criminals safely in the community and will leave space in the prisons for the truly dangerous men and women from whom society must be protected. Much more of the taxpayers' money could be spent on probation without matching a fraction of the cost of prison building and maintenance.

KEY TERMS

community service

deferred sentence

electronic monitoring

financial restitution

house arrest

intensive probation

PSI

rights of probationers

SAMP

shock probation

split sentence

subsidy program

Wisconsin classification system

DISCUSSION TOPICS

9.1 You are about to appear before the court for sentencing. Naturally you and your attorney are worried, especially when you think of the interviews you have had with a probation officer who asked embarrassing questions. You'd like to know what's in her report before the judge decides what to do with you. Do you have a right to see it? Should you have such a right?

9.2 To your relief after your conviction of a felony, the judge has placed you on probation. You are new to the criminal justice system. What do you expect of your first contact with your probation officer? What kind of help will you need right now?

9.3 The probation officer seems like a nice young woman. She says that her job is to help you, and you know very well that you need a lot of help. How far should you trust her?

9.4 You have been transferred from the caseload of your original probation officer, who helped you a lot. The new P.O. is a young fellow who doesn't seem to know which way is up. He tells you that he wants to help, but when you need to see him, he's always too busy to take more than a minute. Other probationers say that that's good; he has a caseload of about 150, and you won't need to worry about him—you can do as you please. Are they right?

9.5 You are transferred again, this time to an intensive supervision caseload. The new probation officer says that she'll see you every day, and you must keep an 8:00 P.M. curfew. You have to pay $25 a month out of your meager earnings for this privilege, but it's explained to you that this is for your benefit. What is the benefit?

ANNOTATED REFERENCES

Ball, Richard, A., C. Ronald Huff, and J. Robert Lilly. *House Arrest and Correctional Policy: Doing Time at Home*. Newbury Park, Calif.: Sage, 1989. *An expansive treatment of house arrest in both juvenile and adult corrections.*

Byrne, James M., and Linda Kelly. *Restructuring Probation as an Intermediate Sanction: An Evaluation of the Massachusetts Intensive Probation Supervision Program*. Final Report to the National Institute of Justice, Research Program on the Punishment and Control of Offenders, 1989. *A highly recommended evaluation of the intensive probation supervision program in Massachusetts.*

Erwin, Billie, S. *Evaluation of Intensive Probation Supervision in Georgia*. Atlanta: Georgia Department of Corrections, 1987. *Erwin, the founder of Georgia's intensive probation supervision project, evaluates what is commonly considered the most demanding IPS project in the nation.*

Fogel, David. "The Emergence of Probation as a Profession in the Service of Public Safety: The Next 10 Years." In P. D. McAnany et al., eds., *Probation and Justice: Reconsideration of Mission*. Cambridge, Mass.: Oelgeschlager, Gunn, and Hain, 1984. *A recent application of the justice model to probation services.*

Hudson, Joe, and Burt Galaway. "Community Service: Toward Program Definition." *Federal Probation*, June 1990: 3–9 *A recent article by two of the pioneers in the field of community service orders.*

McCarthy, Belinda R., ed. *Intermediate Punishments: Intensive Supervision, Home Confinement, and Electronic Surveillance*. Monsey, N.Y.: Criminal Justice Press, 1987. *Highly recommended; contains a number of good papers on intermediate punishments.*

Petersilia, Joan. *Expanding Options for Criminal Sentencing*. Santa Monica, Calif.: Rand, 1987. *An excellent summary of intensive probation projects (IPS), house arrests, and electronic monitoring programs.*

Petersilia, John. *Probation and Felony Offenders*. Washington: U.S. Department of Justice, 1985. *A widely cited examination of felony probationers in California that shows the high rates of recidivism within this criminal population.*

NOTES

1. American Bar Association, *Standards Relating to Probation* (New York: American Bar Association, 1970).
2. Bureau of Justice Statistics, *Probation and Parole 1989* (Washington: U.S. Department of Justice, 1990), p. 1.
3. E. K. Nelson, Howard Ohmart, and Nora Harlow, "Promising Strategies for Probation and Parole." In Robert M. Carter, Daniel Glaser, and Leslie T. Wilkins, eds., *Probation, Parole, and Community Corrections: A Reader*, 3rd ed. (New York: Wiley, 1984), p. 410.
4. John M. Dawson, *Felons Sentenced to Probation in State Courts, 1986* (Washington: Bureau of Justice Statistics, 1990), p. 1.
5. Joan Petersilia, *Granting Felons Probation* (Santa Monica, Calif.: Rand Corp., 1985), p. 21.
6. The President's Commission on Law Enforcement and Administration of Justice, *Task Force Report: Corrections* (Washington: Government Printing Office, 1967), p. 35.
7. National Advisory Commission on Criminal Justice Standards and Goals, *Corrections* (Washington, D.C.: Government Printing Office, 1973), pp. 313–316.
8. Ibid.

9. The following discussion is adapted from "The Salvation Army Conquers Florida," *Corrections Magazine*, February 1983: 40–41.
10. Ibid.
11. Todd R. Clear and George F. Cole, *American Corrections*, 2nd ed. (Pacific Grove, Calif.: Brooks/Cole, 1990), p. 260.
12. Chester J. Kulis, "Profit in the Private Presentence Report," *Federal Probation* 47, December 1983: 12.
13. See Edwin M. Lemert and Forrest Dill, *Offenders in the Community* (Lexington, Mass.: Heath, 1978), for more information on the probation subsidy in California.
14. *Williams* v. *New York State*, 337 U.S. 241, 69 S. Ct. 1079 (1949).
15. Ibid.
16. *Gardner* v. *Florida*, 430 U.S. 349 (1977).
17. Ibid.
18. *Booth* v. *Maryland*, 482 U.S. 496 (1987).
19. Ibid.
20. *Mempa* v. *Rhay*, 339 U.S. 128 Cir. 3023 (1968).
21. *Gagnon* v. *Scarpelli*, 411 U.S. 778 (1973).
22. Sheldon Krantz, *Corrections and Prisoners' Rights* (St. Paul, Minn.: West, 1976), p. 314.
23. Elliot Studt, *Surveillance and Service in Parole* (Los Angeles: University of California Institute of Government and Public Affairs, 1972).
24. Harry E. Allen, "The Organization and Effectiveness of Community Corrections." In Carter, Glaser, and Wilkins, eds., *Probation, Parole, and Community Corrections*, p. 189.
25. Rob Wilson, "Probation/Parole Officers as 'Resource Brokers'," *Corrections Magazine* 5, June 1978: 48.
26. David Fogel, "Probation in Search of Advocate" (Paper presented at the 13th Annual John Jay Criminal Justice Institute, New York, 15 May 1981), pp. 2–6.
27. P. McAnany, D. Thompson, and D. Fogel, "Probation Mission: Practice in Search of Principle" (Paper presented at the National Forum on Criminal Justice, Cherry Hill, N.J., 1981).
28. For Fogel's thoughts on probation, see the interview in Clemens Bartollas, *Correctional Treatment: Theory and Practice* (Englewood Cliffs, N.J.: Prentice-Hall, 1985), pp. 45–46.
29. William P. Adams, Paul M. Chandler, and M. G. Neithercutt, "The San Francisco Project: A Critique," *Federal Probation* 35, 1971: 45–53.
30. Nicolette Prisi,"Combining Incarceration and Probation." In Carter, Glaser, and Wilkins, eds., *Probation, Parole, and Community Corrections*, pp. 68–70.
31. G. F. Vito, "Developments in Shock Probation: A Review of Research Findings and Policy Implications," *Federal Probation* 48, 1984: 22–27.
32. Figures supplied by the Ohio Department of Rehabilitation and Corrections.
33. Doris L. Mackenzie, et al., "Shock Incarceration: Rehabilitation or Retribution," *Journal of Offender Services and Rehabilitation* 14, 1989: 26.
34. Doris L. MacKenzie, "Boot Camp Programs Grow in Number and Scope," *NIJ Reports* 222, November–December 1990: 6.
35. James M. Byrne, Arthur J. Lurigio, and Christopher Baird, "The Effectiveness of the New Intensive Supervision Program." In *Research in Corrections* (Boulder, Colo.: National Institute of Corrections, 1989), p. 20.
36. Joan M. Petersilia, *Expanding Options for Criminal Sentencing* (Santa Monica, Calif.: Rand, 1987), p. 61.
37. Petersilia, *Criminal Sentencing*, Rand, p. 70.
38. Joe Hudson and Burt Galaway, "Community Service: Toward Program Definition," *Federal Probation*, June 1990: p. 6.
39. Ibid., p. 70.
40. Ibid., p. 73.

41. Ibid.
42. Douglas C. McDonald, *Punishment Without Walls* (New Brunswick, N.J.: Rutgers University Press, 1986).
43. Petersilia, *Criminal Sentencing*, pp. 73–74.
44. Todd R. Clear and Kenneth W. Gallagher, "Probation and Parole Supervision: A Review of Current Classification Practices," *Crime and Delinquency* 31, July 1985.
45. Department of Health and Social Services, *Project Report #7: Client-Management Classification Process* (Madison, Wis.: Bureau of Probation and Parole, August 1977), p. 2.
46. Ibid., pp. 3–5.
47. Joan Petersilia, *The Influence of Criminal Justice Research* (Santa Monica, Calif.: Rand, 1987), p. 72.
48. Ibid.
49. Billie S. Ervin, *Evaluation of Intensive Probation Supervision in Georgia* (Atlanta: Georgia Department of Offender Rehabilitation, Office of Evaluation, 1984).
50. Joan Petersilia, "Community Supervision: Trends and Critical Issues," *Crime and Delinquency* 31, 1985: 339–347; John P. Conrad, "The Penal Dilemma and Its Emerging Solution," *Crime and Delinquency* 31, 1985: pp. 411–422; Frank S. Pearson, "New Jersey's Intensive Supervision Program: A Progress Report," *Crime and Delinquency* 31, 1985: pp. 393–410.
51. Conrad, "The Penal Dilemma," p. 411.
52. D. Thomas, *Intensive Probation Supervision in Illinois* (Chicago: Center for Research in Law and Justice, 1985).
53. Stephen Gettinger, "Intensive Supervision: Can It Rehabilitate Probation?" *Corrections Magazine*, April 1983: 8.
54. Billie Erwin and Lawrence Bennett, "New Dimensions in Probation: Georgia's Experience with Intensive Probation Supervision (IPS)." In *Research in Brief* (Washington: National Institute of Justice, 1987).
55. Joan Petersilia, "Conditions for Implementing Successful Intensive Supervision Programs" (preliminary draft). (Santa Monica, Calif.: Rand, 1988), p. 8.
56. Joan Petersilia and Susan Turner, *Intensive Supervision for High-Risk Probationers* (Santa Monica, Calif.: The Rand Corp., 1990), p. vi.
57. Ibid., p. ix.
58. Petersilia, *Criminal Sentencing*, p. 32.
59. Daniel Ford and Annesley K. Schmidt, "Electronically Monitored Home Confinement." In *NIJ Reports* (Washington: National Institute of Justice, 1985), p. 2.
60. Annesley K. Schmidt, "Electronic Monitoring of Offenders Increases." In *Research in Action* (Washington: U.S. Department of Justice, 1989), p. 1.
61. Quoted in Ronald Corbett Jr., "Electronic Monitoring," *Corrections Today*, October 1989: 74.
62. Ibid.
63. Ibid., p. 2.
64. Richard A. Ball and J. Robert Lilly, "The Phenomenology of Privacy and the Power of the State: Home Incarceration with Electronic Monitoring." In J. E. Scott and Travis Hirschi, eds., *Issues in Criminology and Criminal Justice* (Beverly Hills, Calif.: Sage, 1987).
65. Corbett, "Electronic Monitoring," p. 79.
66. Gary T. Marx, "The Maximum Security Society" (Paper presented at the 38th International Criminology Congress, Montreal, Canada, 1987).
67. Corbett, "Electronic Monitoring," p. 80.
68. National Advisory Commission on Criminal Justice Standards and Goals, *Corrections*, p. 322.
69. Howard Abadinsky, *Probation and Parole: Theory and Practice* (Englewood Cliffs, N.J.: Prentice-Hall, 1977), pp. 92–93.

70. Eugene H. Czajkoski, "Exposing the Quasi-Judicial Role of the Probation Officer," *Federal Probation* 37, September 1973: 9–10. See also Curtis Campbell, Candace McCoy, and Chimezie A. B. Osigweh, Yg., "The Influence of Probation Recommendations on Sentencing Decisions and Their Predictive Accuracy," *Federal Probation*, December 1990: 13–20.
71. Contact Center, Inc., *Corrections Compendium* (Lincoln, Neb.: Contact Center, Inc., 1987), pp. 9–13.
72. Interviewed in December 1984.
73. Stephen Labaton, "Glutted Probation System Puts Communities in Peril." *New York Times*, 19 June 1990, p. A-1.
74. Interviewed in 1985.
75. For an examination of job burnout in probation, see J. T. Whitehead, "Job Burnout in Probation and Parole; It's Extent and Intervention Implications," *Criminal Justice and Behavior* 12, 1985: 91–110. Some evidence reveals that intensive supervision officers are more positive than other probation officers. See John T. Whitehead and Charles A. Lindquist, "Intensive Supervision: Officer Perspectives" In Belinda R. McCarthy, ed., *Intermediate Punishments: Intensive Supervision, Home Confinement and Electronic Surveillance* (Monsey, N.Y.: Criminal Justice Press, 1987), pp. 67–84.

Chapter

10

Parole and Reentry Programs

CHAPTER OUTLINE

Release from prison is effected in several ways: conditional or mandatory release, pardon, commutation of sentence, parole, or involvement in a reentry program. Offenders must be freed on conditional or mandatory release once they have served their sentence minus good time. In a state that grants 10 days of good time for each 30 earned, a prisoner serving a six-year sentence would be released in four years. Governors and the president of the United States have the power to grant pardons or executive clemency, an act of grace toward a convicted offender. Commutation of sentence reduces the time an inmate must serve. Inmates who assist the staff during a prison riot or who are terminally ill may have their sentences commuted. Inmates can also be granted parole, which for the past fifteen years has experienced serious challenges on several fronts.[1] As part of the parole process, inmates can participate in reentry programs, in the course of which they are gradually integrated into the community.

Parole can be defined as releasing offenders from a correctional institution, after they have served a portion of their sentence, under the continued custody of the state and under conditions that permit their reincarceration in the event of a violation. Parole stands on three legalities. First, the state extends to offenders a privilege by releasing them from prison before their full sentence is served. Second, the state enters a release contract with offenders in exchange for their promise to abide by certain conditions. Offenders who violate the law or the conditions of parole can be returned to prison to complete their sentence. Third, the state retains control over parolees until they are dismissed from parole.[2]

The administration of parole has five basic characteristics that are shared by all jurisdictions: (1) parole is a form of release from incarceration; (2) selection for parole release is discretionary; (3) authority to release rests with an administrative agency in the executive branch; (4) parole release involves the supervision of those released; and (5) release is conditional, and the parole authority retains the power to revoke liberty.[3]

On December 31, 1989, those on parole numbered 456,797, a record population.[4] (See Table 10.1 for the adults on parole on December 31, 1989.) The parole population grew 12.1 percent during 1989. Five states reported increases above 24 percent of their 1988 parole populations (Georgia, 54.2 percent; Oregon, 52.9 percent; Kansas, 37.1 percent; Oklahoma, 37 percent; and Michigan, 28.8 percent). Twelve states in 1989 reported a declining parole population; the average decline in these states was 8.7 percent. At the end of 1989, Texas maintained 91,294 on parole, the largest parole population of any reporting jurisdiction. California's total of 84,111 admissions to parole supervision during the year was the largest of any state.[5]

Parole is the prime concern of most prisoners. The thoughts and fantasies of those who remain locked up dwell on their appearance before the parole board. They anticipate what will please the board; they guess what will be asked and what should be said to the board. The exceptions to this rule are the well-known murderers and rapists, those who have major disciplinary problems, some recidivists, and those who are considered seriously disturbed. One of the most dubious practices of some parole boards is the annual hearing of an inmate with no action taken, and further consideration postponed for one or more years. A year spent in ambiguity is hard for anybody to take, especially in the conditions under which prisoners live.

For inmates, so much depends on being placed on parole. They are serving time, which is wasted time and sometimes very hard time. They long to be back on the streets. Some, of course, intend to continue their criminal careers but are determined not to be caught "this time." Some would like to stay out of trouble but know that they probably will be back; still, the action on the streets will be worth it—that first fix, that first sexual encounter, and the old friends. Others are determined to stay out of trouble. They are fed up with prison life. Someone is waiting outside for them, and they do not intend to waste any more of their lives within the walls.[6]

Table 10.1 ADULTS ON PAROLE, 1989

Regions and jurisdictions	Parole population, 1/1/89	1989 Entries	1989 Exits	Parole population, 12/31/89	Percent change in parole population during 1989	Number on parole on 12/31/89 per 100,000 adult residents
U.S. total	407,596	305,596	256,395	456,797	12.1%	248
Federal	20,451	10,910	9,949	21,412	4.7	12
State	387,145	294,686	246,446	435,365	12.5	236
Northeast	104,680	56,807	50,940	110,547	5.6%	286
Connecticut	371	101	150	322	−13.2	13
Massachusetts	4,333	5,124	4,769	4,688	8.2	102
New Hampshire	461	259	243	477	3.5	58
New Jersey	18,463	11,202	9,603	20,062	8.7	340
New York	33,962	18,841	16,118	36,685	8.0	270
Pennsylvania	46,466	20,802	19,566	47,702	2.7	519
Rhode Island	442	345	396	391	−11.5	51
Vermont	182	133	95	220	20.9	52
Midwest	51,062	40,437	35,578	55,921	9.5%	125
Illinois	14,369	12,096	11,915	14,550	1.3	168
Indiana	3,411	1,305	1,260	3,456	1.3	84
Iowa	1,945	1,392	1,437	1,900	−2.3	89
Kansas	3,497	3,137	1,841	4,793	37.1	259
Michigan	7,677	7,549	5,336	9,890	28.8	145
Minnesota	1,639	1,912	1,852	1,699	3.7	53
Missouri	7,207	4,228	3,797	7,638	6.0	198
Nebraska	447	679	636	490	9.6	41
North Dakota	134	198	193	139	3.7	29
Ohio	5,991	4,851	4,378	6,464	7.9	80
South Dakota	617	435	542	510	−17.3	98
Wisconsin	4,128	2,655	2,391	4,392	6.4	122
South	156,696	98,397	71,122	183,971	17.4%	292
Alabama	4,701	2,516	1,401	5,756	22.4	191
Arkansas	3,840	2,061	2,401	3,500	−8.9	199
Delaware	1,093	424	504	1,013	−7.3	201
District of Columbia	3,949	2,995	2,029	4,915	24.5	1,057
Florida	2,562	918	1,162	2,318	−9.5	24
Georgia	11,308	15,386	9,257	17,437	54.2	376
Kentucky	3,443	1,759	2,069	3,133	−9.0	114
Louisiana	7,387	5,493	3,703	9,177	24.2	295
Maryland	9,225	5,862	5,225	9,862	6.9	279
Mississippi	3,177	1,641	1,469	3,349	5.4	181
North Carolina	6,191	8,242	6,874	7,559	22.1	153
Oklahoma	1,455	1,195	657	1,993	37.0	84
South Carolina	3,626	1,039	1,035	3,630	.1	142
Tennessee	9,529	4,876	3,705	10,700	12.3	290
Texas	77,827	36,287	22,820	91,294	17.3	758
Virginia	6,576	7,184	6,368	7,392	12.4	160
West Virginia	807	519	383	943	16.9	68
West	74,707	99,045	88,806	84,946	13.7%	224
Alaska	489	555	511	533	9.0	147

Table 10.1 (continued)

Regions and jurisdictions	Parole population, 1/1/89	1989 Entries	1989 Exits	Parole population, 12/31/89	Percent change in parole population during 1989	Number on parole on 12/31/89 per 100,000 adult residents
Arizona	1,669	3,622	3,243	2,048	22.7	80
California	49,364	84,111	75,967	57,508	16.5	269
Colorado	1,743	1,571	1,515	1,799	3.2	73
Hawaii	1,108	625	446	1,287	16.2	156
Idaho	247	227	236	238	−3.6	34
Montana	671	370	289	752	12.1	128
Nevada	2,100	1,375	1,058	2,417	15.1	290
New Mexico	1,230	1,038	1,117	1,151	−6.4	107
Oregon	3,790	3,864	1,860	5,794	52.9	273
Utah	1,218	848	789	1,277	4.8	119
Washington	10,745	643	1,556	9,832	−8.5	277
Wyoming	333	196	219	310	−6.9	91

Note: Twelve states estimated numbers in one or more categories. Maine eliminated parole in 1976. See the detailed parole notes for further information.

Source: Bureau of Justice Statistics, *Probation and Parole 1989* (Washington: U.S. Department of Justice, 1990), p. 3.

This chapter considers parole practices today, including the parole board, intensive supervision and shock incarceration, and parole revocation. Postrelease life for the inmate, prerelease and community assistance programs, and working within a residential program are also discussed.

PAROLE PRACTICES TODAY

Parole, as previously suggested, has been challenged on a variety of fronts in the past 15 years. Although the movement to abolish parole may have peaked, significant limits have been placed on the discretion of paroling authorities in many states, particularly concerning the release and supervision of offenders. Guidelines, in this regard, have been developed to structure release decision making for inmates eligible for parole.

The degree of professionalization of the parole board itself, as well as the consistency of supervision practices both within and across jurisdictions, has been widely debated. Even more significantly, the parole board has been abolished in 11 states and the federal government. Moreover, parole has been called upon to be responsive to the competing concerns of the public, victims, and offenders. In addition, the proportion of inmates released by parole boards has declined for more than a decade, while the percent of mandatory releases from prison has dramatically increased. Despite these limitations placed on parole, the parolee population is now at a record number and represents the fastest growing of the four correctional components (parole, prisons, probation, and jails).[7]

Operation of the Parole Board

The **parole board** is administered either by an independent agency (autonomous model) or by a board that is part of a single large department that runs all state correctional programs (consolidated model). The parole board is an independent agency in all but five states; yet parole field services are administered by the department of corrections in two-thirds of the states (see Table 10.2).[8]

As Table 10.2 reveals, the majority of states have a full-time parole board. The membership of state parole boards varies from 3 to 17. New York has the largest parole board, with 19 members. Twenty-two jurisdictions have five members; 10 have three. In 19 states, the governor appoints the parole board; Wisconsin and Ohio are the only states that appoint members from a civil service list. Very few states require specific professional qualifications for board members.[9]

Parole decisions are made in a number of ways. Some jurisdictions have the entire board interview eligible inmates; in other jurisdictions, only part of the board interviews. A few jurisdictions use hearing examiners to interview inmates. Some states do not interview inmates at all; they make their decisions solely upon written reports. The percentage of prisoners released by parole boards varies from 90 percent in Kansas and New Hampshire to 20 percent in South Carolina, Wyoming, and Oklahoma.

Most states have recently taken measures to ensure due process at release hearings. For example, about half of the states now permit counsel to be present and witnesses to be called. Verbatim transcripts also are frequently kept of the hearings. Furthermore, inmates are typically provided with both a written and an oral explanation of the parole decision. However, inmates continue to be denied access to their files, which means they are unable to determine why their case was decided the way it was.

Parole eligibility is determined in several different ways across the nation. The common procedure is to make an inmate eligible for parole when he or she has served the minimum sentence minus good-time credits. But other states make an inmate eligible for parole at the parole board's discretion or at the completion of one-third or one-half of the maximum sentence.

The capricious and arbitrary manner in which parole boards, especially in the past, decided when an inmate was ready for release has drawn strong criticism from inmates, prison reformers, and practitioners in the criminal justice system. The riot at Attica in New York in 1971 and the subsequent report that identified parole as a source of inmate discontent have also contributed to the unfavorable scrutiny of parole boards. The unfairness of parole boards is legendary among inmates. Stories defying logic are told of how teetotalling inmates have been turned down for parole until they agree to join an Alcoholics Anonymous group in the prison. It often seems that those inmates who appear to be the poorest risks for community living are granted parole, while inmates with better chances are denied.

That the parole board reduces **disparity in sentencing** is one of the main arguments its supporters make for its retention. For example, offenders from various judicial districts may receive disparate sentences for committing the same crime: An armed robber in an urban area may receive a sentence that is half the length of that of an armed robber in a rural area. The parole board, according to its proponents, has the opportunity to "even" things out by granting both prisoners—assuming everything else is equal—parole after the same length of time.

A nationwide trend away from parole boards became apparent in 1977 when Maine, Indiana, California, and Arizona abolished parole and adopted determinate-sentencing systems. Illinois and New Mexico followed suit in 1978, and five other

Table 10.2 CHARACTERISTICS OF STATE AND FEDERAL PAROLING AUTHORITIES
By jurisdiction 1989

Jurisdiction	Name of agency	Administrator of parole field services	Independent agency	Number of board members	Full-time board
Alabama	Board of Pardons and Paroles	Board of Pardons and Paroles	Yes	3	Yes
Alaska	Board of Parole	Department of Corrections	Yes	5	No
Arizona	Board of Pardons and Paroles	Department of Corrections	Yes	7	Yes
Arkansas	Board of Parole and Community Rehabilitation	Department of Correction	Yes	7	No[a]
California[b]	Board of Prison Terms	Department of Corrections	Yes	9	Yes
Colorado	Board of Parole	Department of Corrections	Yes	7	Yes
Connecticut	Board of Parole	Department of Correction	Yes	11	No[c]
Delaware	Board of Parole	Department of Correction	Yes	5	No[c]
District of Columbia	Board of Parole	Board of Parole	Yes	4	Yes
Florida	Probation and Parole Commission	Department of Corrections	Yes	7	Yes
Georgia	Board of Pardons and Parole	Board of Pardons and Parole	Yes	5	Yes
Hawaii	Paroling Authority	Paroling Authority	Yes	3	No[c]
Idaho	Commission for Pardons and Parole	Department of Corrections	Yes	5	No
Illinois	Prisoner Review Board	Department of Corrections	Yes	13	Yes
Indiana	Parole Board	Department of Correction	Yes	5	Yes
Iowa	Board of Parole	Department of Corrections	Yes	5	No
Kansas	Parole Board	Department of Corrections	Yes	5	Yes
Kentucky	Parole Board	Corrections Cabinet	Yes	7	Yes
Louisiana	Board of Parole	Department of Corrections	Yes	5	Yes
Maine	Parole Board[d]	Department of Corrections	Yes	5	No
Maryland	Parole Commission	Department of Public Safety and Correctional Services	No	7	Yes
Massachusetts	Parole Board	Parole Board	Yes	7	Yes
Michigan	Parole Board	Department of Corrections	No	7	Yes
Minnesota	Department of Corrections, Office of Adult Release	Department of Corrections	No	4	No[c]
Mississippi	Parole Board	Department of Corrections	Yes	5	No
Missouri	Board of Probation and Parole	Department of Corrections	Yes	5	Yes
Montana	Board of Pardons	Department of Institutions, Corrections Division	Yes	3	No
Nebraska	Board of Parole	Department of Correctional Services	Yes	5	Yes
Nevada	Board of Parole Commissioners	Department of Parole and Probation	Yes	5	Yes
New Hampshire	Board of Parole	Department of Corrections	Yes	5	No
New Jersey	Parole Board	Bureau of Parole	Yes	9	Yes
New Mexico	Adult Parole Board	Corrections Department	Yes	4	Yes
New York	Board of Parole	Division of Parole	Yes	19	Yes
North Carolina	Parole Commission	Department of Corrections	Yes	5	Yes

Jurisdiction	Name of agency	Administrator of parole field services	Independent agency	Number of board members	Full-time board
North Dakota	Parole Board	Department of Corrections and Rehabilitation	Yes	3	No
Ohio	Department of Rehabilitation and Correction, Adult Parole Board	Department of Rehabilitation and Correction	No	9[e]	Yes
Oklahoma	Pardon and Parole Board	Department of Corrections	Yes	5	No
Oregon	Board of Parole	Department of Corrections	Yes	5	Yes
Pennsylvania[b]	Board of Probation and Parole and County Courts[f]	Board of Probation and Parole and County Courts	Yes	5	Yes
Rhode Island	Parole Board	Department of Corrections	Yes	6	No
South Carolina	Board of Probation, Parole and Pardon Services	Department of Probation, Parole and Pardon Services	Yes	7	No
South Dakota	Board of Pardons and Paroles	Board of Pardons and Paroles	Yes	3	No
Tennessee	Board of Paroles	Board of Paroles	Yes	7	Yes
Texas	Board of Pardons and Paroles	Board of Pardons and Paroles	No	18[g]	Yes
Utah	Board of Pardons	Department of Corrections	Yes	5	Yes
Vermont	Board of Parole	Department of Corrections	Yes	5	No
Virginia	Parole Board	Department of Corrections	Yes	5	Yes
Washington	Indeterminate Sentence Review Board	Department of Corrections	Yes	5	Yes
West Virginia	Board of Probation and Parole[h]	Department of Corrections	Yes	3	Yes
Wisconsin	Parole Board[i]	Division of Corrections	No	4	Yes
Wyoming	Board of Parole	Department of Probation and Parole	Yes	5	No
Federal[b]	Parole Commission	Administrative Office of the U.S. Courts	Yes	9	Yes

Note: The column "independent agency" refers to the status of the State paroling authority.

[a] Three full-time, four part-time.

[b] Accredited.

[c] The chairman serves full-time; members serve part-time.

[d] Parole Board hears pre-1976 cases of parole. Flat sentences with no parole under criminal code effective May 1, 1976.

[e] Nine hearing officers expand the functions of the Parole Board.

[f] The Board of Probation and Parole provides services when the sentence is over 2 years; the County Courts provide services when the sentence is 2 years or less.

[g] Plus a nine-member Parole Commission.

[h] Under state statute, parole is considered probation.

[i] The Secretary of the Department of Health and Social Services is the paroling authority. The Parole Board is part of the Secretary's executive staff and exists to advise and make recommendations to the Secretary on all matters pertaining to the parole of adults.

Source: American Correctional Association, *Probation and Parole Directory* (Laurel, Md.: American Correctional Association, 1989), p. 395; and American Correctional Association, *Vital Statistics in Corrections* (Laurel, Md.: American Correctional Association, 1991), p. 38.

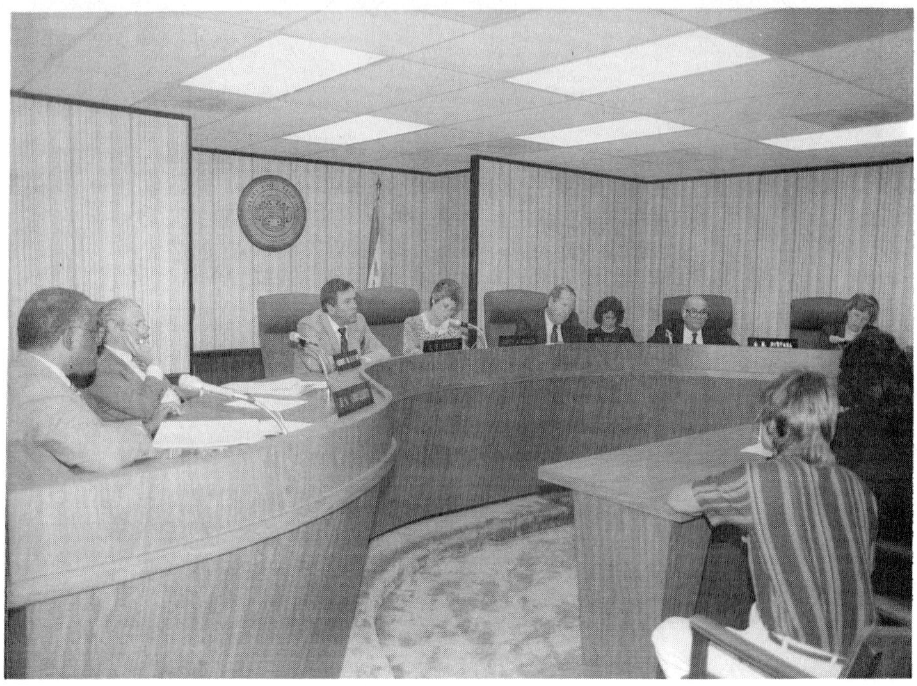

Florida Parole Commission. (*Source*: Florida Department of Corrections.)

states have since adopted determinate-sentencing laws. But parole boards began to fight back by adopting parole guidelines that set, early in prisoners' terms, the exact time they would serve.

The American Correctional Association's Task Force on Parole conducted a national survey on the status of parole from 1986 to 1988 and found that 23 states use some form of guidelines, while 28 states do not. A matrix approach is used in some states, while other guidelines list the aggravating and mitigating factors that determine the decision to release. Furthermore, 19 states that use guidelines also have incorporated some form of risk assessment into the system.[10]

The new federal guidelines are based on the abolition of parole for prisoners received after 1989. (See also the discussion in Chapter 6 of federal parole guidelines.) The U.S. Parole Commission now has jurisdiction only over prisoners received before 1989, which will keep the commission in business for a good many years to come. The U.S. Parole Commission does not have jurisdiction over federal probation. The Federal Probation Service presently administers both probation and parole.

The Parole Officer

Parole officers have much in common with probation officers. They share duties that are investigatory and regulatory. They face similar role conflicts and frustrations: They both handle excessive caseloads, lack community resources, and are inadequately trained for their jobs.

The vast majority of states require a bachelor's degree as an entry requirement for parole officers. Some states requiring a bachelor's degree also specify that the degree should be in a related field, such as sociology, psychology, social work, or administration of justice. In those states that do not require a bachelor's degree (Idaho, Indiana, Iowa, Kansas, Maine, Massachusetts, Minnesota, Nevada, and Wisconsin), several years of experience is generally substituted as an entry requirement.[11]

The number of parole officers in a state varies from 3,600 in Florida, 750 in New York, 700 in California, 577 in Michigan, and 572 in Maryland to 17 in South Dakota, 14 in Hawaii, and 10 in Nebraska. The administrative office of the U.S. Court employs 2,376 probation officers who also cover a parole caseload. The minimum annual starting salary, as of February 1987, ranges from $31,644 in California, $25,460 in Alaska, and $22,500 in Colorado to $13,620 in Louisiana and $12,768 in West Virginia. Thirty states and the administrative office of the U.S. Courts pay between $15,000 and $19,000 as the minimum starting salary of a parole officer (10 states, $15,000-plus; 6 states, $16,000-plus; 9 states, $17,000-plus, and 5 states and the U.S. Courts, $18,000-plus).[12]

In David Stanley's sample of parole officers in Colorado, Wisconsin, Georgia, California, the District of Columbia, and the federal prison system it was consistently found that parole officers' only on-the-job training was a week or two of observing before they were assigned their own caseloads. He also found that the caseloads of parole officers averaged 100 or more.[13]

In many states and the federal government, the same officer provides both probation and parole services. In separated departments, state-administered parole services usually pay their officers somewhat better than do county-funded probation services. Parole officers usually place a higher priority on surveillance than do probation officers. Because parole officers are often better paid than probation officers, they tend to be older and more experienced in the criminal justice system.

Even though parole officers may no longer visit bars to catch violators, the **"watchdog" role** remains firmly rooted in the minds of parolees. They know that the officer can have them returned to prison; indeed, many parolees have been personally escorted back to prison by their parole officers. In some jurisdictions, parole officers have the power of arrest. Accordingly, hostility and distrust often exist in the relationship between officer and parolee. Officers, in turn, know that some parolees are dangerous and require little provocation for assault.

In a few states, parole officers are now required to carry firearms. But not all parole officers wish to carry firearms. For example, an experienced and excellent parole officer once remarked to one of the authors that his effectiveness would be ended if he ever actually fired a pistol at a parolee. So he refused to consider arming himself.

The surveillance role of the parole officer has also increased because of the wide implementation of intensive supervision programs, including electronic monitoring of parolees, and because so many parolees have histories of drug addiction. The epidemic of drug addiction, especially, has had a horrible impact on the practice of parole supervision and has resulted in parole officers' spending much of their time collecting urine.

Yet parole officers are in a position to help parolees significantly if they understand that service remains the most important part of their job. In this regard, there are parole officers who have managed to become effective treatment agents. To put it in the words of one of the themes of this book, good parole agents can make a difference.

Alfred Anderson, an ex-offender, relates the effect his parole officer had upon him:

> I had what I feel everyone should have. I had a coach and that was my parole agent. He and his supervisor gave me a lot of basic confidence. They believed in me, and I can't say enough about them. He used to say that it was in me to succeed, but he made it a lot more comfortable.[14]

The organizational constraints appear to be as strong in parole as they are in probation departments. Both Richard McCleary, in an examination of a large district parole office in Illinois, and Robert C. Prus and John R. Stratton, in their study of parole agents in a midwestern state, found that bureaucratic, or organizational, constraints were extremely influential on officers' supervision of parolees.[15]

The decisions of parole officers, according to research conducted by Paul Takagi and James Robison, are affected in part by their perceptions of their supervisors' likely response. In considering whether to revoke parole, Takagi and Robison found, a powerful influence

> appeared to be at the district supervisor level, where there is a high degree of correspondence between district supervisors and their subordinates on the case-recommendation task. This finding suggests that the selective enforcement of some [parole] rules is as much a characteristic of the officials as selective adherence to rules is a characteristic of the [parolee].[16]

Parole officers' decisions are also affected by the organizational goal of avoiding public criticism, or "heat." In a period in which the "get tough" approach prevails, parole executives are extremely sensitive about decision making that could be interpreted as "coddling" the criminal. This organizational goal of avoiding public criticism tends to be focused much more toward maintaining the equilibrium, or stability, of the agency than toward taking a chance on parolees, or "giving them a break."

Intensive Parole Supervision

The movement toward more intensive means of supervising parolees actually had its origins with shock parole in the 1970s and early release statutes in the 1980s. Shock parole was more extensively developed in Ohio than in any other state, no doubt because of the state's experiment with shock probation. The Ohio shock parole statute allowed shock parole for many prisoners after six months in prison. In the 1980s, because of overcrowded prisons and pressure from federal courts, a number of states began to develop **early release programs**—sometimes called emergency parole—for inmates. The public's backlash against early release of inmates has been one of the factors causing pressure on departments of corrections to intensify parole supervision.

Two major trends have emerged in the past fifteen years to reduce the risk of parolees committing more crimes. First, formal classification systems have been developed for community supervision, and second, risk instruments have been widely adopted to assess more accurately the parolee's likelihood of renewed criminal behavior. Both of these trends received a major stimulus from the Model Probation/

Parole Classification and Case Management Project sponsored by the National Institute of Corrections.[17]

The survey results of the American Correctional Association's Task Force on Parole found that nearly all of the 45 parole field agencies used case classification to determine the level of supervision. Of these agencies, 43 indicated they used a risk instrument and 37 a needs instrument as part of the classification process.[18] (See Table 10.3 for the parole risk assessment instrument that was developed in Tennessee.)

Intensive parole, like probation, is sometimes combined with such strategies as home incarceration or electronic monitoring.[19] For example, Oklahoma prison ad-

Table 10.3 PAROLE RISK ASSESSMENT INSTRUMENT

Risk factor	Category	Score	
Number of previous paroles on this sentence	None	0	____
	One or more	5	
Maximum sentence length at time of release	5 years or less	0	____
	6–9 years	2	
	10 years or more	5	
Age at first juvenile adjudication	No juvenile record	0	____
	13 or younger	1	
	14 or over	3	
Number of previous felony incarcerations	None	0	____
	1 or more	4	
Instant offense was burglary, forgery, or fraud	No	0	____
	Yes	3	
Living arrangement with spouse or parents	Yes	0	____
	No	3	
Age at incarceration on current offense	32 or older	0	____
	22–31	1	
	21 or younger	3	
Employment status at first parole contact	Employed	0	____
	Unemployed	2	
Parole officer assessment of attitude	Positive	0	____
	Generally positive	2	
	Generally negative	5	
	Negative	7	
Parole officer assessment of risk	Minimum	0	____
	Medium	1	
	Maximum	2	
		Total Score:	____

Score Ranges: 0–10 minimum, 11–17 medium, 18–24 maximum, 25 + intensive supervision.

Source: Tennessee Department of Corrections, 1986.

ministrators use "house arrest" as an early release program, and at least 15 parole agencies use electronic monitoring in order to justify early release (see Box 10-1).[20] Furthermore, intensive supervision programs have been used as "halfway-back" alternatives for offenders who violate the technical conditions of parole or are rearrested for minor offenses.

Shock incarceration programs began in 1983 in Georgia and Oklahoma, and, as discussed more extensively in Chapter 12, have spread throughout the nation.[21] As an alternative to a standard prison sentence, offenders in shock incarceration spend a short period of time in a "boot camp" atmosphere. In some programs, following their 90 to 180 days in the rigorous "boot camp" setting, they are placed under intensive parole supervision.[22]

Doris Layton MacKenzie and James W. Shaw, in evaluating the Louisiana Department of Corrections' shock incarceration program, concluded that those who participated in this program "have more positive attitudes in regard to their experience in prison, toward society in general, and toward their ability to make positive change."[23] They reason that "if more prosocial attitudes are associated with more positive adjustment in the community, it would appear that the shock offenders are leaving prison with a much better chance of being successful on parole."[24]

However, Shaw and MacKenzie found that the effectiveness of shock incarceration differed for substance abusers and problem drinkers. After one year of parole supervision, problem drinkers who were involved in shock incarceration adjusted better on parole than inmates paroled from regular imprisonment.[25] In contrast, shock incarceration with substance abusers appeared to be unrelated to performance during one year of community supervision.[26]

Parole Revocation

In the 1972 *Morrissey* v. *Brewer* decision, the U.S. Supreme Court first ruled on **parole revocation procedures.** Morrissey was a check writer who had been paroled from the Iowa State Penitentiary. Seven months after his release, his parole was revoked for a technical violation, and he was returned to prison. At about the same time, a second petitioner, Booher, was returned to prison on a technical parole violation. Both men petitioned for habeas corpus on the grounds that they had been denied due process of the law and returned to prison without opportunities to defend themselves at an open hearing. The two cases were consolidated for appeal and eventually reached the U.S. Supreme Court. In his opinion, Chief Justice Warren Burger laid down the essential elements of due process for parole revocation. The first requirement was a hearing before an "uninvolved" hearing officer, who might be another parole officer or perhaps an "independent decision maker," who would determine whether there was reasonable cause to believe that a parole violation had taken place. If so, the parolee might be returned to prison, subject to a full revocation hearing before the parole board. Due process in such a proceeding was outlined as follows:

> Our task is limited to deciding the minimum requirement of due process. They include: (a) written notice of the claimed violation of parole; (b) disclosure to the parolee of evidence against him; (c) opportunity to be heard in person and to present witnesses and documentary evidence; (d) the right to confront and cross-examine adverse witnesses (unless the hearing officer specifically finds good cause for not allowing confrontation);

Box 10-1 Community Control Project

On March 3, 1986, the United States Parole Commission implemented the experimental "Curfew Parole Program" to provide a substitute for Community Treatment Center residence for the 60-day period preceding the otherwise scheduled parole release date. A joint effort of the U.S. Bureau of Prisons, the U.S. Probation System, and the U.S. Parole Commission, this program is designed for prisoners who would otherwise qualify for Community Treatment Center residence but who do not require the support services provided by the Community Treatment Center because they have acceptable release plans. Under this program, qualified and approved inmates have their release date advanced for up to 60 days on the condition that they remain at their place of residence between the hours of 9:00 P.M. and 6:00 A.M. each night, unless they are given permission in advance by their supervising U.S. Probation Officer.

The Parole Commission implemented this program as a cost reduction procedure through which the Bureau of Prisons might reduce the number and expense of inmates confined in Community Treatment Centers. In establishing this program, the Parole Commission intended that the Probation Service provide high activity supervision of the parolee during the Special Curfew parole period, including at least weekly contact with the parolee as well as monitoring compliance with this special condition by random, periodic telephone contacts.

This program has been a success in reducing the cost of Community Treatment Center placements; the Bureau of Prisons reports a savings of over three million dollars since 1986. But because a number of Chief Probation officers expressed concern concerning the ability of the probation officer to enforce adequately a curfew through random telephone contact, the decision was made to experiment with electronic monitors as a means of enforcing a curfew in the Central District of California and the Southern District of Florida. Renamed the Community Control Project, the decision was made that the probation system would select the electronic monitoring equipment and the cost would be reimbursed by the Bureau.

The selected proposal was from Guardian, Inc., using equipment manufactured by BI, Inc. The first parolee entered the program on January 19, 1988, and the study will continue for thirty months. When entering the program, participants are required to be at home at all times, except for work and approved absences for treatment programs, religious services, and medical appointments.

Exit interviews were conducted with 45 participants who completed the program and agreed to be interviewed. Approximately half of the interviewees thought electronic monitoring was more punitive than being in a halfway house. But those living with their spouses generally preferred home confinement to residing in a halfway house, while those living alone or with individuals other than a spouse preferred halfway house placement. Most of those interviewed stated that the most stressful part of the program was the time restriction; for example, some participants stated that it was sometimes difficult getting home from work on time when traffic was heavy. Others complained about having personal telephone calls interrupted by the computer; the size of the equipment was larger than most anticipated but eventually they became accustomed to it.

Source: James L. Beck and Jody Klein-Saffran, "Community Control Project." Report 44 of the U.S. Parole Commission Research Unit, September 1989.

> (e) a "neutral and detached" hearing body such as a traditional parole board, members of which need not be judicial officers or lawyers; and (f) a written statement by the fact finders as to the evidence relied on and reasons for revoking parole.[27]

The importance of this decision to the administration of parole cannot be exaggerated. Before *Morrissey*, parole boards and parole officers were free to administer very summary justice to parolees for technical violations of parole of little significance, the justification being that parole was only an extension of confinement. Parolees were prisoners serving part of their sentences outside the prison. Like any other convicts, they were subject to a change in program at the discretion of the system's officials. Due process of the law was irrelevant at this stage; prisoners had had at the time of conviction all the due process to which they were entitled. By imposing strict requirements before the paroling authorities could inflict the "grievous loss" of freedom, the Supreme Court drastically revised the whole concept of parole.

Several other issues have been ruled upon since *Morrissey*. It has been held that parolees have no legal right to bail pending a revocation hearing.[28] The courts have also held that all that is needed to satisfy the parole board at the revocation hearing is a demonstration that the parolee has failed to meet the conditions of parole.[29] In other words, the standard of proof does not need to be beyond a reasonable doubt.

The actual revocation procedures begin when the parole officer requests a warrant based on an alleged violation of parole. An issued warrant can be enforced by a parole officer, a warrant officer, or a police officer. Once parolees are in custody, they are given a list of the charges against them. The next step in this process, which tends to vary from state to state, gives prisoners an opportunity to challenge at a preliminary hearing the allegation of violation and to confront adverse witnesses, including parole officers. The hearing officer is usually a senior officer, whose chief task is to determine whether or not there are reasonable grounds for believing that parolees have violated one or more of the conditions of parole—that is, if there is "probable cause." If probable cause exists, parolees will be held in custody for a revocation hearing; if probable cause is not found, parolees will be returned to supervision.

A more comprehensive revocation hearing is held to determine if the violation of parole is serious enough to justify returning parolees to prison. If parole is not revoked, parolees are returned to supervision. Jurisdictions vary greatly in determining how much time revoked parolees should spend in prison; they also vary in their decisions on whether parolees should receive credit for the time they spend under parole supervision.[30]

RELEASE FROM PRISON

More than 80 percent of those released from prison receive supervision in the community. Inmates enter parole supervision either by a discretionary parole board decision or by being given a mandatory release. In indeterminate-sentencing systems, the parole board releases inmates to conditional supervision in the community based on statutory or administrative determination of eligibility. Inmates usually must serve some fraction of the minimum or maximum before becoming eligible for parole. But in determinate-sentencing systems, prisoners are conditionally released from prison when they have served their original sentence minus time off for good behavior; this type of release is referred to as **supervisory mandatory release.**[31]

In contrast, **unconditional prison releases** are those in which the offender's obligation to serve a sentence has been satisfied. For example, "expiration of term" refers to a release from prison after a sentence has been fully served or after earned credits have been reduced. When this happens, no further conditional supervision in the community is required.[32]

The percent of supervised mandatory releases increased more than fivefold during the past 11 years: from about 6 percent of all releases in 1977 to more than 30 percent in 1989 (see Table 10.4). Not surprisingly, the number of prisoners released by a parole board decision declined from almost 72 percent of all releases in 1977 to about 39 percent in 1989. During this period of time, the number of unconditional releases remained basically the same.[33]

Felons go through four stages before and subsequent to release from prison: (1) prerelease stress, (2) the early days at home, (3) the frustrations of "making it," and (4) the decision of whether or not to return to crime.

The Prerelease Stress

The problems found by newly released men and women have been recognized almost since the invention of the prison. For example, as early as 1817, a commission of the Massachusetts legislature recommended the construction of a halfway house to ease the difficulties of readjustment.[34]

Table 10.4 STATE PRISON RELEASES, BY METHOD, 1977–1989

		Percent of prison releases							
			Conditional releases				Unconditional releases		
Year	Total releases from prison	All	Discretionary parole	Supervised mandatory release	Probation	Other*	Expiration of sentence	Commutation	Other
1977	115,213	100%	71.3%	5.9%	3.6%	1.0%	16.1%	1.1%	.4%
1978	119,796	100	70.4	5.8	3.3	2.3	17.0	.7	.5
1979	128,954	100	60.2	16.9	3.3	2.4	16.3	.4	.6
1980	136,968	100	57.4	19.5	3.6	3.2	14.9	.5	.8
1981	142,489	100	54.6	21.4	3.7	3.1	13.9	2.4	1.0
1982	157,144	100	51.9	24.4	4.8	3.6	14.4	.3	.6
1983	191,237	100%	48.1%	26.9%	5.2%	2.5%	16.1%	.5%	.6%
1984	191,499	100	46.0	28.7	4.9	2.7	16.3	.5	.9
1985	203,895	100	43.2	30.8	4.5	3.0	16.9	.4	1.2
1986	230,672	100	43.2	31.1	4.5	4.6	14.8	.3	1.4
1987	270,506	100	40.6	31.2	4.4	5.7	16.2	1.0	.9
1988	301,378	100	40.3	30.6	4.1	6.0	16.8	1.0	1.2
1989	364,434	100%	39.1%	30.5%	4.4%	8.9%	16.0%	.2%	.9%

Note: The data are from the National Prisoner Statistics reporting program. The total releases from State prison are those for which the method of release was reported. Deaths, unspecified releases, transfers, and escapes were not included. Altogether, 385,479 persons were released or removed from State prisons in 1989.

* Other conditional releases include prisoners discharged under special procedures that included early release because of crowding, supervised work furloughs, release to home detention, release to community residence, release to special programs with required supervision, supervised reprieves, and emergency releases. Nearly 87% of the 32,281 "other conditional releases" in 1989 occurred in four states: Arizona, Connecticut, Florida, and Georgia.

Source: Bureau of Justice Statistics, *Probation and Parole 1989* (Washington: U.S. Department of Justice, 1990), p. 4.

The stress and problems found during the reintegration period actually begin as prisoners' release dates near. The "short time" syndrome, also described as "getting short," "shortitis," and **"gate fever"** is quite real. B. N. Cormier et al. describe this syndrome as including irritability, anxiety, restlessness, and a variety of psychophysiological symptoms.[35]

Marc Renzema, in examining the stress of inmates before and after release, found that the most stressful period for respondents was the period before release from prison. He contends that both the effects of the prison environment itself and the effects of stresses produced by anticipation of release contribute to "gate fever." It seems, Renzema reasons, "that knowing of upcoming problems without having the means to cope with them actively may be worse than the time when one is totally immersed in coping activities."[36] But beyond the stress, most prisoners intend to stay out of trouble following their release. Daniel Glaser's extensive study of the impact of imprisonment and postrelease supervision, in this regard, observes, "It seems that over 90 percent of the men released from prison initially seek legitimate employment and try to achieve self-sufficiency without engaging in crime."[37]

John Irwin said of 41 felons whom he interviewed shortly before release from prison:

> Most of them express the belief that making it is up to the individual, and now that they had decided to try to make it their chances were very good. Most of those who come back, they believed, don't want to make it. Only four of the sample expressed doubts about their chances of making it.[38]

The Early Days at Home

The return to the streets after years of confinement is usually a shocking event. One of the reasons for the popularity of reentry programs is that both correctional officials and prisoners generally agree that the gradual re-integration of offenders into society is preferable to an abrupt return to community living.

Some prisoners experience an unexpected jolt when released suddenly and without preparation. They often feel disoriented and confused by the transition from controlled living to life in free society. *An Eye for an Eye*, a book written by former prisoners, puts it this way:

> Upon arriving in the city [following release from prison] the pedestrians scared me almost as much as the traffic. They seemed to flow along the street in a controlled hysteria, determined, set upon goal and destination, and when one of them approached, I didn't know whether to jump to one side, freeze, or keep right on walking toward the inevitable collision. You didn't have all this confusion in prison. There everyone walked in neat, orderly lines in a sort of half-shuffle. The noise of the traffic, the horns, the whistles, the music coming from somewhere, coupled with the clatter of high heels and the chatter of voices welled up, a cacophonous crescendo. Hey! I'm free![39]

The euphoria of release often gives way to a letdown. This is particularly true of those who return after several years away. Friends have moved away or perhaps have changed. Families also are not the same as when the offender was sent to prison. The attempt to restore new ties may be a threatening experience and may make the ex-offender feel like a stranger or an outsider. Moreover, the slow pace of prison life is replaced by hundreds of people shoving and crowding on streets and in shopping malls. Returned felons soon discover that the way to acceptance in prison does not work in the community. Trust in prison is problematic in a world where everyone is for himself or herself. Outside, not to trust is to isolate oneself.

In contrast to this general reaction of confusion and disorientation, Renzema's study found that the experience of reentry after exposure to furloughs or work release was "a time of coping, a time of relaxation. The new releases were not disoriented, anxious, depressed, or immediately overwhelmed by tasks of coping."[40] He argues that reentry programs have helped these parolees deal with the critical first few days: "Over half of my respondents had been, at some time during their imprisonments, on furloughs, on work-release, or on both: These people may be presumed to have been less isolated from the community than most parolees who have been studied in the past."[41]

The Frustration of "Making It"

The major frustration of "making it" is usually related to employment. Ex-offenders must deal with barriers to employment—some legal, some social—that stand as a wall between them and job opportunities. Examinations of statutory barriers have found that as many as 300 occupations require licenses specifically excluding persons with felony convictions. Although legal restrictions on the hiring of ex-offenders appear to be loosening, the options for most offenders still are severely limited. In most states, occupational restrictions are still enforced against a felon's being licensed to be a nurse, barber or beautician, real estate salesperson, cashier, or worker in a place where alcoholic beverages are sold.

In addition to the statutory barriers, ex-offenders are often disqualified by limited work experience, inadequate training, inability to accept supervision, and unrealistic expectations of income and promotion. The knack for dealing with the public or with fellow workers has seldom been cultivated in prison life, leaving the ex-offender at a disadvantage in any job calling for interaction with strangers.

REENTRY PROGRAMS

A number of reentry programs have been developed to assist offenders in making the transition from the institution to the community. These programs include prerelease instruction, work release, educational release, home furloughs, and halfway house placements.

Prerelease Programs

A number of institutions conduct formal **prerelease programs** for inmates, who are excused from work in prison industries or from academic or vocational programs in order to attend prerelease classes. Some prisons transfer inmates ready for prerelease programs to facilities outside the main prison compound. At Ohio's Lebanon Correctional Institution, the prerelease program is housed in a facility a short distance from the main prison. There is a somewhat similar arrangement at Colorado's Canon City complex, where a separately administered prerelease unit housing 80 prisoners has been in operation since 1983. In other correctional systems, inmates ready to be released are transferred to prerelease guidance centers in the community; there they receive the benefit of work release, home furloughs, and formalized prerelease instruction.

California provides a 3-week, full-time training program for inmates who are within 15 to 45 days of release. As part of this training, inmates are exposed to the attitudes and skills needed to get and keep a job, to establish sound money managements, to improve communication skills, and to seek and receive community and parole resources. After inmates' needs are evaluated, they are given a list of five objectives to be achieved within 30 days of being paroled and the names and addresses of five public or private agencies that can be called upon for assistance. Inmates also participate in a mock job interview and acquire a California driver's license.

The South Carolina Prerelease Employment Training Program, a 30-day course mandated by the South Carolina Probation, Parole and Pardon Board, is also representative of these programs. It provides information and instruction on on-the-job safety practices; loyalty to the employer; the importance of being on time; the development of needed skills for business and industry; job opportunities and employment aids; the purpose and function of the law; motor vehicle driver training; insurance; legal problems and contracts; basic financial management; the importance of establishing and maintaining credit; personal health practices and proper diet; buying a car; Social Security and Medicare benefits; perspectives on family responsibilities; community agency assistance; human relations; and the dangers of alcohol, drugs, and cigarettes.[42]

Overall, high expectations for a brief prerelease program appear to be unrealistic. The best justification for their continuation is that some inmates do find prerelease programs helpful.

Work Release Programs

A national survey indicates that the generally agreed-upon objectives of **work release** are to (1) ease the transition from prison to community life; (2) place offenders in jobs they can retain following release; (3) give inmates a means of financial support; (4) help them support their families; (5) enable correctional officials to determine their readiness for parole; and (6) preserve family and community ties.[43]

Work release programs are conducted in community-based facilities, jails, and prisons. In a jail- or prison-based work release program, inmates leave the facility in the morning, usually with lunch and enough money for transportation, and return at the end of the work day. Some inmates are provided transportation to and from work; others depend on public transportation. Commonly, it is the minimum security facilities that sponsor work release programs. Community work release programs are usually held in halfway house facilities called work release centers, prerelease guidance centers, or community treatment centers.

There are several reasons for placing prisoners involved in work release in community settings. Inmates who return to prison after a day's work in the free community are set apart, with damaging consequences for prison morale; they are resented by those prisoners who have had to remain in the institution. Prisoners involved in work release programs, who must pay for room and board, object to having to continue to live in a 6′ × 9′ cell. Furthermore, work release inmates are pressured by other inmates to smuggle contraband in and out of the institution, which threatens security.[44]

South Carolina has three work release programs. Under one program, male prisoners live in seven work release centers in the community, and female prisoners reside in a center in the South Carolina Department of Corrections' Broad River Road complex. Under a second program, inmate construction workers are housed in a special dormitory in Broad River. Inmates may qualify for this program earlier than for work release because there is tighter supervision on the way to and from the job. A third program, Extended Work Release, allows nonviolent offenders who have proved themselves able, through work release, to live in the free community.[45]

All but a few states have laws permitting work release programs, but states vary on the commitment they have made to work release. For example, California, Texas, New York, and Illinois are examples of large departments of corrections that involve only 1 or 2 percent of the state's prison population in work release. The diminishing popularity of work release in the late 1970s and 1980s can be traced to at least three causes: the unwillingness of citizens to have work release centers in their communities, high rates of unemployment, and the occasional major crime committed by work release participants.

The tight job market of the late 1970s and early 1980s affected work release, because when free citizens are having difficulty finding jobs, it becomes even harder for prisoners to obtain them. Furthermore, the commission of only one or two serious

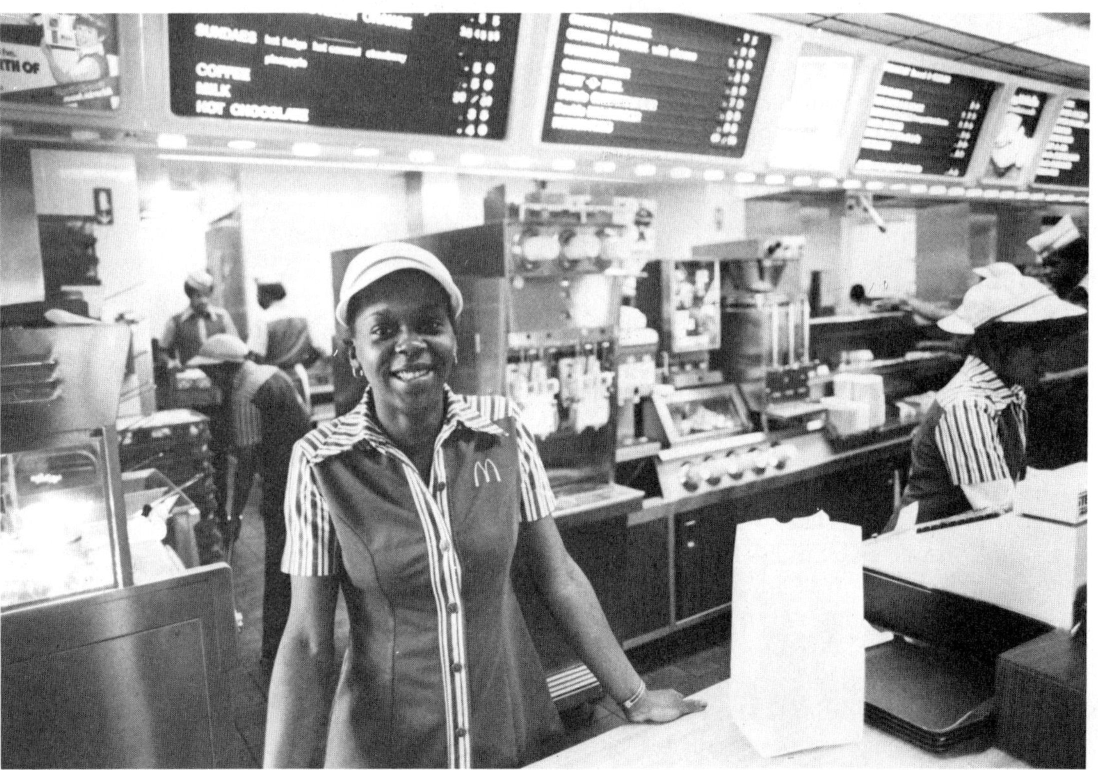

Work-release under the Golden Arches. (Copyright © 1980 Tony O'Brien. Corrections Magazine.)

crimes can just about destroy a work release program; the next session of the legislature is likely to see the introduction of bills to end work release. To attempt to protect work release programs from increased attack, many departments of corrections have tightened up the eligibility criteria for work release, thereby reducing the number of offenders on work release.

State, federal, and local governments all profit from work release programs. Enrolled inmates pay for their room and board, pay state and federal taxes on their income, and require less public aid for their families. Prisoners also profit from these programs, for they are able to spend the work day in the community interacting with free citizens; they make far more money than they could earn in prison industry; they learn skills and disciplines in the world of work; and they see themselves as productive members of society.

However, work release can also have damaging consequences for both inmates and society. Stuart Adams concludes that work release

> may in fact operate to reduce the compression that a prisoner is reported to experience in the institution . . . [but] it introduces him to stresses of its own. It places him under temptation to violate curfew hours, thus opening him to charges of absconding. It keeps him under daily surveillance by the center administrators when he had been anticipating freedom from the correctional regime. And by reducing some of the "pains of imprisonment," the work release center may [actually encourage] the commission of new crimes.[46]

An inmate who was feeling the tension of work release exclaimed, "Man, get me off this work program. I'm going to blow it. The pressure is starting to get to me."[47]

The national picture indicates that work release has not lived up to its potential. Particularly disappointing is the fact that large industrial states, such as California and New York, place so little emphasis on work release programs. Yet other states' work release programs remain a vital part of their correctional mission.

Educational Release Programs

Under **educational release,** inmates, instead of going to work, attend school in the community. Forty states, the District of Columbia, and the federal prison system have had study release programs.

New York's Ossining State Correctional Facility has one of the largest study release programs in the United States; up to 60 inmates from this facility have attended a community college in the Bronx. Inmates from Trenton, Rahway, and Leesburg state prisons in New Jersey have studied at Mercer Community College. Inmates from the Terminal Island, California, federal facility for women have been enrolled in 11 different colleges and trade schools. Several California inmates live on the campuses of the University of California and, like other college students, attend classes and return in the evening to facilities provided by the state.

There are several reasons why educational release occurs less frequently than work release: (1) Many inmates cannot qualify for college-level work because they are not high school graduates or do not have the GED (equivalency) certificate; (2) community colleges and universities often offer courses within the prison for those who are interested and qualified; (3) video college and correspondence courses are

South Carolina prisoner on work-release program studying at University of South Carolina. (*Source*: South Carolina Department of Corrections.)

frequently made available to interested inmates; (4) corrections institutions are often isolated from college or university campuses; and (5) work release simply has a longer history and more public acceptance than educational release.

Instructors who have taught inmates in the community are generally quite positive about inmate performance in the classroom. Inmates themselves usually look upon educational release as a worthwhile program.

Home Furlough Programs

Also called home visits, temporary leaves, and temporary community releases, **home furlough** programs began in the late 1960s. In 1987, more than 53,000 inmates in federal and state prisons were allowed to leave custody on more than 200,000 separate occasions. Furloughs are usually 48 to 72 hours in length and given on weekends. Half or more of all such visits are awarded to residents of work release centers or halfway houses.

To qualify for a home furlough, an inmate usually must have minimum security status and a clean disciplinary record and be near the end of confinement. Spotlighted by the press, home furloughs have probably been hit harder by the "get tough on criminals" attitude than any other community-based program. California, for example, which granted 14,000 furloughs in the early 1970s, grants only a few today. Several serious incidents, including the fatal shooting of a Los Angeles police officer by an offender on furlough, hastened the withdrawal of the furlough program there.[48] More recently, Willie Horton, a prisoner who had been furloughed, became a pivotal issue during the 1988 presidential campaign (see Box 10-2).

Halfway Houses

Typically "way stations" for parolees, halfway-out houses have many characteristics in common with halfway-in houses, which are generally used for probationers. Indeed, probationers and parolees are sometimes placed in the same center. One of the best-known **halfway houses** in the United States is Dismas House in St. Louis, Missouri. Founded in 1959 by Father Charles Dismas Clark, Dismas House represents the resurgence of correctional halfway houses. As of May 1991, Dismas House had provided services to 7,700 ex-offenders. Both individual and group counseling are offered to residents, especially in such areas as alcohol and drug abuse, family life, and employment. Dismas House's capacity is 90 residents, and both the Bureau of Prisons and the state department of corrections have contracted for space for parolees.[49] Dismas, whom early church history defined as "the good thief," has been used as the name of halfway houses in other cities. Of the 400 or so halfway houses presently in operation, which are found in nearly all states, about 50 percent focus on offenders newly released from prison.

The federal Bureau of Prisons operates 11 halfway houses, called Community Treatment Centers (CTC), in Atlanta, Dallas, Chicago, Detroit, Houston, Kansas City, Long Beach, Los Angeles, New York, Oakland, and Phoenix. CTC programs provide extensive prerelease services to federal inmates serving the last 60 to 120 days of their sentences. These centers also accept, for evaluation and diagnosis, offenders committed by the federal courts. Most residents are free to leave the centers in the evenings and on weekends, and they are encouraged to spend time with their families if they are in the community.

A study of Blackburn House, a private, nonprofit halfway house in San Antonio, Texas, conceptualizes four phases that residents pass through during their 90- to 120-day stays. Residents have just been released from prison and go through a period of detachment during their first stage. They enter the second stage when they become involved in community life by looking for a job or by going home on weekends. The third stage occurs when they come to terms with both the challenges and the problems of community life. The final stage takes two or three weeks before release when residents get "prerelease jitters." In addition to the anxiety and anticipation of release, residents often have behavioral problems during this final stage.[50] These four stages are somewhat typical for the inmate who is paroled to a halfway house.

Robert Martinson and Judith Wilks's report "Knowledge in Criminal Planning" found that the mean recidivism rate for "partial physical custody following imprisonment" was 24.82 percent. Only inmates who "max out" (are not paroled but must finish their sentence minus good time) have a higher recidivism rate—27.39 percent.[51] The high recidivism rate of parolees placed in halfway-out houses is not surprising when it is remembered that these individuals either were not considered good risks in the first place or had no place to go. Halfway-out houses are forced to work with the most marginal of the criminal population.

Box 10-2 **Bush's Most Valuable Player**

William Horton. Black. Murderer. Rapist. Most valuable player in George Bush's no-holds-barred bid for the White House.

Of all the tactics used by Bush's strategists to brand Michael Dukakis a goofy liberal out of touch with mainstream values, none worked better than the relentless pounding of Horton's horrible tale. By the end of the campaign, scarcely a voter had not been exposed to the lurid details of the rapacious spree Horton committed while on weekend furlough from the Massachusetts prison to which he had been sentenced to life without parole for a brutal 1974 homicide.

Like most attack ploys, there was a grain of truth to be exploited: The prison-furlough policy used by Massachusetts went beyond the boundaries of common sense. Unlike other states and the federal government, which usually employ furloughs to gradually acclimate prisoners near the end of their sentences to living outside the walls, Massachusetts granted weekend leaves to convicts whom judges had condemned to remain behind bars until they died. Horton is precisely the sort of criminal that people have in mind when they say someone should lock him up and throw away the key.

It was one of Dukakis' rivals for the Democratic nomination, Tennessee Senator Al Gore, who first unearthed the furlough policy as a campaign issue. The fact that it was inaugurated by Dukakis' Republican predecessor is irrelevant. As Governor, Dukakis stubbornly resisted attempts to rescind furloughs for first-degree murderers until a drive to ban such leaves through a state referendum gathered steam. By then, the presidential-primary season was under way.

If the Republican assault on Dukakis' furlough policy had stopped with making these valid points, Democrats and blacks would have no just cause for complaint. But the Republican attack did not stop there. Instead, Bush's handlers tapped into the rich lode of white fear and resentment of blacks that the G.O.P. staked out more than 20 years ago, when the party of Lincoln recast itself as the embodiment of the white backlash. . . .

The fear of crime is, to be sure, deeply implanted among Americans of all races. No group is more victimized by street thugs than the law-abiding citizens of the ghetto. Doubtless the G.O.P. would have exploited Dukakis' furlough policy if Horton were white. Yet the glee with which Bush's campaign team leaped upon the Horton affair belies its denials that it intended to tweak white prejudices. In Horton, Bush's staff found a potent symbolic twofer: a means by which to appeal to the legitimate issue of crime while simultaneously stirring racial fears.

How else to explain Bush campaign manager Lee Atwater's remark to Republican activists gathered in Atlanta last July? Observing that Jesse Jackson, then pressing his demand to be selected as Dukakis' vice-presidential running mate, had visited Dukakis' home on July 4, Atwater suggested that "maybe he will put this Willie Horton on the ticket after all is said and done." Or the relish with which Bush press secretary Mark Goodin posted a mug shot of Horton on the wall above his desk. Or the ardor with which Bush's media guru Roger Ailes declared, "The only question is whether we depict Willie Horton with a knife in his hand or without it." In the end, the Bush campaign refrained from using Horton's likeness in its campaign spots, leaving an independent political-action committee to saturate the airwaves with the rapist's glaring visage while a few state Republican parties stuffed mailboxes with flyers banging home the same message. . . .

Source: Jack E. White, "Bush's Most Valuable Player," *Time*, 14 November 1988, pp. 20–21.

Community-based Assistance Programs

Various programs, especially those designed to find jobs for ex-offenders, have been established in recent years to help ease the transition from prison to community. They are located throughout the United States. Some are associated with parole departments; others are adjuncts of a state employment service. Many other groups are committed to helping ex-offenders. These buffering agencies often make the difference between a parolee's success and return to prison.

The Fortune Society in New York City has gained considerable publicity for helping ex-offenders adjust to community living. The society serves the largest group of ex-offenders in the country; it has 38,000 names on its mailing list and receives more than 20,000 financial contributions. Between 4,000 and 5,000 persons come for help each year, and about 1,500 actually receive some form of concrete assistance.[52] The credo of the Fortune Society, shown in Figure 10.1, expresses the philosophy of the buffering agency. In a 1990 interview, JoAnne Page, executive director of the Fortune Society, explains further:

> Most of the people we see come from abusive families. They're used to seeing two roles, the victim and the victimizer. Most of the people we see don't have anything to lose. They are caught in that same cycle of violence and vengeance. We're trying to provide an alternative to criminal involvement and, at the same time, to educate the public. To "go straight" means that you've to take a whole life history and turn it around. It is incredibly difficult to do this. People with substance abuse histories who go back to the same neighborhoods have a real problem. People need jobs; they need a social life. Our job is to help people feel there is hope for the future.[53]

In Ohio, the Cincinnati Comprehensive One-Stop Offender Aid Program (COSOAP) has been quite successful in helping parolees deal with community life; COSOAP offers social, vocational, and psychological services, all in one location. In Illinois, the John Howard Association helps ex-offenders with college tuition, vocational training, and needed tools for employment. Some programs are run under religious auspices. The Salvation Army has a long history of helping inmates; others, such as the Women Help Women Organization in Minnesota, are known outside their immediate communities. In Box 10-3, Louise Wolfgramm, executive director of AMICUS in Minneapolis, Minnesota, talks about the importance of **friendship** to inmates.

WORKING WITHIN A RESIDENTIAL PROGRAM

Probation and parole officers, staff of pretrial release and diversion programs, staff of residential programs, and volunteers operate community-based corrections. The staff patterns of residential programs for probation and parole have much in common and therefore will be considered together.

I THINK, THEREFORE, I AM . . .

As a thinking person, I believe that I am worthy of being loved and accepted. I believe that my ability to accept myself is a part of my real freedom. It is vital that I develop a foundation of belief about myself—for freedom and love and respect are not an "end result" but, rather, a process which changes, refines, and grows. My ability to offer love and respect and my acceptance of freedom is a reflection of my view of myself.

SUGGESTED STEPS

Facing the truth about ourselves, we decided to change.

Realizing that there is a power from which we can gain strength, we decided to use that power.

Evaluating ourselves by taking an honest self-appraisal, we examined both our strengths and weaknesses.

Admitting to God (as we understand him), to ourselves, and to another human being the exact nature of our weaknesses.

Endeavoring to help ourselves overcome our weaknesses, we enlisted the aid of that power to help us concentrate on our strengths.

Deciding that our freedom is worth more than our resentments, we are using that power to help free us from those resentments.

Made a list of all persons we had harmed and become willing to make amends to them all.

Made direct amends to such people wherever possible, except when to do so would injure them or others.

Observing that daily progress is necessary, we set an attainable goal toward which we can work each day.

Continued to take personal inventory, and when we were wrong promptly admitted it.

Maintaining our own freedom, we pledge ourselves to help.

Figure 10.1 A wall poster at the Fortune Society.

The line staff member of state, local, and private residential programs does not have an easy job.[54] Low pay, long hours, hectic work schedules, and lack of appreciation from clients are among the reasons for the high staff turnover and for staff "burnout." In privately administered residential programs, line staff members are frequently more poorly paid than they would be in state residential programs.

Line staff in residential programs actually face problems comparable to those of line staff in correctional institutions. They are, after all, running a 24-hour-a-day, 7-days-a-week operation. They also are charged with providing services to residents.

Box 10-3 Friendship: The Best Penology of All

AMICUS grew out of one person's need for affirmation. This person was not unusual. He needed to know that he was not alone in the world; he needed to talk with someone he could trust; he needed a relationship in which he could be himself and be respected. This person needed a friend. AMICUS was incorporated in 1967, two years after the AMICUS founder's release from Stillwater prison. Since then 2,500 citizens of the Minneapolis/St. Paul metropolitan area have identified with a prisoner's need for a friend and have been paired with an inmate asking for an AMICUS volunteer. Why do inmates need an agency to find them a friend, and why do busy people make time to build a relationship with a lawbreaker? Why does the community support this activity?

Inmates who really want to change have realized two things: One, that the responsibility for success or failure is on their shoulders; and two, that nobody is really happy without a friend who cares whether or not they succeed or fail. The friend that they seek is not only one who is going to cheer them on, but one who is going to be honest with them when they see unrealistic expectations or self-destructive behavior. To an inmate, a friend is one who wants the best for him or her and who brings no agenda to the relationship. Most inmates who request an AMICUS volunteer can imagine such a friendship but have never in their lives experienced one. Those who are capable of this imagination already have the crucial ingredient for success: hope.

People who volunteer for a friendship with an inmate already have much in common with the inmates they seek to befriend. They have imagination and hope. These are people motivated to help someone because they can imagine circumstances in which they themselves could have broken the law and ended up in prison, and they can imagine the need for a friend at such a time. Usually these people fall into two groups, those who say, "My life has brought me close to the edge—I know what it must be like to feel estranged, isolated, afraid" and those who say, "By grace, my life has been blessed with the security of knowing that I am loved—I would like to share what I have been given." Both groups know that there are no guarantees that their investment in a friendship with an inmate will keep that person out of trouble. They volunteer because they haven't given up hope that people, inmates included, at their core want to live in peace with themselves and their neighbors.

What is needed in addition to well-intentioned volunteers and willing inmates to build a program like AMICUS? Essential to this program's success have been procedures for careful screening, orientation, matching, and ongoing support for the volunteers and inmates involved.

The hope upon which AMICUS was built continues to be fulfilled. While there are certainly cases where inmates who have participated in AMICUS have returned to a life of crime, there is solid evidence that many AMICUS participants have changed their lifestyles and have become contributing members of the community.

Why does the community support this organization? Well, it doesn't really. People do. People who reason and know that most people who go to prison return again to their community. They know that people who have the affirmation of a good friend are less likely to put the community at risk than those who return feeling alone, frightened, and unwelcome. Those who contribute financially to a program like AMICUS may or may not be willing to make a personal investment in an inmate, but they are glad that there are others who will—for the good of the community.

Source: This statement on friendship was supplied by Louise Wolfgramm, executive director of AMICUS, Minneapolis, Minnesota.

Furthermore, like institutional staff, they face problems with the physical facility, as when the heating unit breaks down or when the pipes freeze. Residential and institutional line staffs both work with the losers of the system. The "cream of the crop" tends to remain on regular probation or receive parole, while those placed in residential programs often have few resources and no employment history.

Yet residential staff do not have the physical control over offenders that institutional staff have over their inmates. This leads to problems because residents usually have the freedom to leave the halfway house for part of the day and to be exposed to the temptations of the community. In probation referrals, the family and friends of residents are still in the immediate area, and they are often the source of the offenders' problems.

Unlike prison line staff, who work in an environment in which life is fairly predictable, residential staff must function daily on a very irregular routine. In smaller facilities they usually are alone after 5 to 6 o'clock in the evening, and even in larger ones, there are usually not more than two staff members on the premises after 6 o'clock.

Neither do counselors have easy jobs. The limited size of residential programs builds an intensity into the job that is usually not found in a prison job; nor do probation or parole officers face the intensity of working with the same small caseload on a daily basis. Moreover, residential counselors hear complaints from clients so frequently that it is sometimes difficult to recognize a legitimate complaint. The most important skill that counselors or caseworkers possess is the ability to listen to and communicate with residents.

Top-level staff, directors and assistant directors, are responsible for administrative duties, supervision of staff, and decision making concerning residents.[55] Administrative duties include preparing monthly, quarterly, and annual reports on program performance. Monthly billing reports must be submitted to various funding agencies; these reports are frequently sent to the executive offices for agency-wide billing by the business manager. Other duties include liaison work with other criminal justice and mental-health agencies and speaking engagements outside the facility. Budget planning and review are also important, although the final approval usually comes from an executive director.

Staff supervision can sometimes be a very frustrating task and may cause more problems for the director than any other area. The director often must learn to adjust job descriptions to staff needs and abilities, which may mean that he or she must delegate some of his or her own responsibilities. The maintenance of the house is assigned to staff and residents, but it is a big job to ensure that everything is clean, safe, and in good repair.

Decision making concerning disciplinary action toward residents is the third major responsibility of top-level staff. These decisions will often affect a resident's freedom. For example, a bad disciplinary report to a probation officer may result in the revocation of probation and the imposition of a prison sentence.

However, directors and assistant directors usually like their jobs. They complain about the frustrations, the long hours, the dubious capability of line staff, and the way the job interferes with their lives. Still, there are many satisfactions in this work: The possibility for personal growth is unlimited; considerable professional freedom is possible, as the job permits a casual lifestyle; and morale is enhanced because the director and assistant director can assume "ownership" of the program.

CONCLUSIONS

This chapter has considered the recent developments of parole. Parole boards have few friends; guidelines for parole boards have many supporters. Some parole officers want guns; others want to be treatment agents. Some citizens want to improve parole by wiring parolees with electronic monitors; others are determined to provide parolees with every possible constitutional safeguard. Some jurisdictions do not provide community resources for parolees, leaving them to sink or swim on their own; other jurisdictions provide extensive resources. Some students of parole predict that it is in a final decline; others claim that the drive to abolish parole has stalled and may prove to be a "flash in the pan." In other words, the debates on parole are endless.

Reentry programs, consisting of prerelease, work release, educational release, home furloughs, halfway houses, and community-based assistance for ex-offenders, have been established recently throughout the United States. In some ways, these reentry programs have been a disappointment, for only a few years ago they were looked to as the vehicle for significant correctional reform.

The public has been less than enthusiastic about the placement of these programs in their communities. Yet inmates look forward to the programs because they provide an escape from fortresslike prisons. Instead of worrying about being raped at night when they fall asleep or stabbed during the day, inmates are able to do "easy" time and, if they are involved in work release, perhaps even save a little money in the process. The families of inmates also look forward to these programs. They are able to occasionally spend time with a son or a daughter, a husband or a wife, or a mother or a father. If the inmate is on work release, the family may also receive some financial assistance.

KEY TERMS

disparity in sentencing

early release programs

educational release

friendship

"gate fever"

halfway house

home furloughs

parole board

parole revocation procedures

prerelease programs

supervisory mandatory release

unconditional prison releases

"watchdog" role

work release

DISCUSSION TOPICS

10.1 "Parole boards are arbitrary and discriminatory, and they ought to be abolished," says John Q. Liberal. "Yes, but so is the whole criminal justice system," says Sally Middle. "At least the boards are trying to remedy inequities." What are likely to be the reasons behind each opinion?

10.2 Watchdog or counselor—which is the modern parole officer more likely to be?

10.3 What is the purpose of reentry programs?

10.4 In many prerelease programs, inmates hear lectures about the etiquette of life in the real world. Imagine yourself in such a prerelease session. What would you want to hear? Be honest.

10.5 Inmates on work release combine working at a job with serving the last months of their prison sentences. What is your evaluation of these programs?

10.6 Study release programs let inmates out part of the day to go to school in the community. Should convicts get a free education?

10.7 Do the occasional relapses (or even the violent crimes) of prisoners on home furlough (48 to 72 unsupervised hours) convince you that such programs do more harm than good?

10.8 How strong is your state's commitment to reentry programs? Which programs do you feel have the most value?

ANNOTATED REFERENCES

Beck, James L., and Jody Klein-Saffran. "Community Control Project," Report 44. Washington: U.S. Parole Commission Research Unit, September 1989. *A description of the recently implemented "Curfew Parole Program" of the United States Parole Commission.*

Citizen's Inquiry on Parole and Criminal Justice, Inc. *Prison Without Walls: Report on New York Parole.* New York: Praeger, 1978. *An examination of the failure of parole in New York state.*

Irwin, John. *The Felon.* Englewood Cliffs, N.J.: Prentice-Hall, 1970. *A revealing account of how prisoners feel about parole and the problems they encounter when they are released from prison.*

McCleary, Richard. *Dangerous Men: The Sociology of Parole.* Beverly Hills, Calif.: Sage, 1978. *A case study of parole in Washington, D.C.*

Renzema, Marc. "The Stress Comes Later." In Robert Johnson and Hans Toch, eds., *The Pains of Imprisonment.* Beverly Hills, Calif.: Sage, 1982. *A portrayal of why reintegration into the community is so stressful for ex-offenders.*

Shane-DuBow, S., A. P. Brown, and E. Olsen. *Sentencing Reform in the United States.* Washington: U.S. Department of Justice; National Institute of Justice, 1985. *A good overview of the changing sentencing structure in this nation and how that has affected parole supervision.*

Smith, William R., Edward E. Rhine, and Ronald W. Jackson. "Parole Practices in the United States." *Correction Today,* October 1989: 24–28. *An up-to-date examination of parole practices in this nation.*

NOTES

1. William R. Smith, Edward E. Rhine, and Ronald W. Jackson, "Parole Practices in the United States." *Corrections Today,* October 1989: 22.
2. James L. Galvin et al., *Parole in the United States: 1976 and 1977* (Washington: Government Printing Office, 1978), p. 13.
3. Ibid.
4. Bureau of Justice Statistics, *Probation and Parole 1989* (Washington: U.S. Department of Justice, 1990), p. 1.
5. Ibid., p. 1.
6. Thomas Meisenhelder, "An Exploratory Study of Exiting from Criminal Careers." *Criminology,* November 1977: 318–334.
7. Smith, et al., "Parole Practices in the United States," pp. 24–25.
8. American Correctional Association, *1988 Directory of Juvenile and Adult Correctional Departments, Institutions, Agencies and Paroling Authorities* (College Park, Md.: American Correctional Association, 1988), pp. xiv, xv, 2–45.
9. Ibid.
10. Smith, et al., "Parole Practices in the United States," p. 24.
11. Contact Center, Inc., *Corrections Compendium* (Lincoln, Neb: Contact Center, Inc., December 1987), pp. 10–14.
12. Ibid.
13. David T. Stanley, *Prisoners Among Us: The Problem of Parole* (Washington, D.C.: Brookings, 1976), p. 93.
14. Interviewed in February 1977.
15. Richard McCleary, *Dangerous Men* (Beverly Hills, Calif.: Sage, 1978), and Robert C. Prus and John Stratton, "Parole Revocation Decisionmaking: Private Typings and Official Designations." *Federal Probation* 40, 1976: 48–53.
16. Paul Takagi and James O. Robison, "The Parole Violator and Organizational Reject." *Journal of Research in Crime and Delinquency* 5, 1969: 78–86.
17. Smith, et al., "Parole Practices in the United States," p. 25.
18. Ibid.
19. Daniel Ford and Annesley K. Schmidt, "Electronically Monitored Home Confinement." In *NIJ Reports* (Washington, D.C.: National Institute of Justice, 1985), pp. 2–6.
20. James Austin, "Political Realities in Solving the Prison Crowding Problem" (Presentation at the Annual Meeting of the American Society of Criminology, Chicago, Illinois, November 1988).
21. Dale Parent, *Shock Incarceration: An Overview of Existing Programs* (Washington: National Institute of Justice, 1989), p. 10.
22. For an extensive examination of the shock incarceration program in New York state, see *The Second Annual Report to the Legislature: Shock Incarceration in New York State: The Corrections Experience* (New York: Division of Program Planning, Research and Evaluation, 1990).
23. Doris Layton MacKenzie and James W. Shaw, "Inmate Adjustment and Change During Shock Incarceration: The Impact of Correctional Boot Camp Programs." *Justice Quarterly* 7, March 1990: 146.
24. Ibid.
25. James W. Shaw and Doris Layton MacKenzie, "Shock Incarceration and Its Impact on the Lives of Problem Drinkers" (unpublished paper, 1991), p. 1.
26. James W. Shaw and Doris L. MacKenzie, "Boot Camp: An Initial Assessment of the Program and Parole Performance of Drug-Involved Offenders" (unpublished paper, 1991), p. 1.
27. *Morrissey* v. *Brewer,* 408 U.S. 1971, 92S. (1972).

28. *In re Whitney*, 421 F.2d 337, 1st Cir. 1970.
29. *United States* v. *Strada*, 503 F.2d 1081, 8th Cir. 1974.
30. Howard Abadinsky, *Probation and Parole: Theory and Practice* (Englewood Cliffs, N.J.: Prentice-Hall, 1977), pp. 189–190.
31. Bureau of Justice Statistics, *Probation and Parole 1989*, p. 2.
32. Ibid.
33. Ibid.
34. Elmer H. Johnson, *Crime, Correction, and Society* (Homewood, Ill.: Dorsey, 1968), p. 331.
35. B. N. Cormier, M. Kennedy, and M. Sendbuehler, "Cell Breakage and Gate Fever." *British Journal of Criminology* 7, 1967.
36. Marc Renzema, "The Stress Comes Later." In Robert Johnson and Hans Toch, eds., *The Pains of Imprisonment* (Beverly Hills, Calif.: Sage, 1982), p. 152.
37. Daniel Glaser, *Effectiveness of a Prison and Parole System* (Indianapolis, Ind.: Bobbs-Merrill, 1969) p. 30.
38. J. Irwin, *The Felon* (Englewood Cliffs, N.J.: Prentice-Hall, 1970), p. 112.
39. H. Griswold et al., *An Eye for An Eye* (New York: Pocket Books, 1971), p. 235.
40. Renzema, "The Stress Comes Later," p. 159.
41. Ibid., p. 159.
42. "Community Programs" (brochure published by the South Carolina Department of Corrections, n.d.), p. 4.
43. "Graduated Release." In Benjamin Frank, ed., *Contemporary Corrections* (Reston, Va.: Reston, 1973), pp. 232–234.
44. The rural location of many prisons also makes it necessary to maintain work release centers in urban areas where there are work opportunities for inmates.
45. *The Intercom* 8 (Columbia, S.C.: South Carolina Department of Corrections, Summer 1978), pp. 1–2.
46. Stuart Adams, "Evaluation of Work Release." In Emilio Viano, ed., *Criminal Justice Research* (Lexington, Mass.: Heath, 1975), p. 210.
47. Statement made to the author, while he was conducting a prerelease program in a North Carolina prison (1975).
48. *Corrections Magazine* 1, July–August 1975: 3–4.
49. Interviewed in May 1991.
50. Paul F. Cromwell, Jr., "Release from Prison: Transition and Re-Assimilation." In Paul F. Cromwell, Jr., ed., *Corrections in the Community: Alternatives to Imprisonment* (St. Paul, Minn.: West, 1974), pp. 492–499.
51. The Center for Knowledge in Criminal Justice Planning, 38 East 85th Street, New York, New York.
52. Information provided by JoAnne Page, executive director of the Fortune Society, September 20, 1990.
53. Interviewed in September 1990.
54. Stanley Swart, a former director of the Young Men's Fellowship of Lake County, Illinois, provided these materials on line staff in residential settings.
55. Materials on top-level staff provided by Neil F. Tilow, who is director of Talbert House for Men, Cincinnati, Ohio.

PART

FOUR

Local, State, and Federal Institutions

Chapter 11

Local Institutions

CHAPTER OUTLINE

Jails, lockups, workhouses, and houses of corrections are the main types of local institutions. Jails have the authority to detain individuals for periods of 48 hours or longer; they also hold convicted inmates sentenced to short terms (generally 1 year or less). Jails are usually administered by the county sheriff but are sometimes managed on a regional basis or, in a few cases, by the state government. Lockups, sometimes called temporary holding facilities or police lockups, are generally found in city police stations or precinct houses, and they hold persons for periods of less than 48 hours. The primary function of workhouses and houses of corrections—which are operated by cities and counties and are sometimes known by other titles, such as county prisons—is to hold convicted inmates sentenced to short terms.

This chapter focuses upon the jail because this pivotal institution touches the lives of more people than does any other correctional institution. Thousands of people stream in and out of jails all year, but most people in jail stay there for short periods of time, to be replaced by more people of the same kind. A key difference between the jail and state and federal institutions is that jails handle unconvicted individuals, many of whom are first-time offenders. In addition to being an intake center for the entire criminal justice system, the jail also serves as a place of first or last resort for individuals who more properly belong in public health, welfare, or social service agencies.

Among researchers, jails are no longer the neglected institutions they once were.[1] John Irwin has skillfully analyzed the jail's role in the community,[2] and John Gibbs has examined inmate adjustment in jail.[3] Several recent studies have been done on judicial intervention,[4] inmate subcultures,[5] jail suicides,[6] and jail management.[7] Moreover, many useful studies have been done on the causes of, and solutions to, jail crowding.[8]

Beginning with the history of the jail, this chapter also considers "doing time" in jail, jail structure and problems, pretrial release programs, and proposals for reform.

HISTORY OF THE JAIL

The jail had its origin in medieval England. County correctional institutions spread throughout England in 1166, when Henry II ordered that the sheriff in each county shire establish a jail.[9] Although initially conceived as places for detaining suspected offenders until they could be tried, jails gradually came to serve the dual purpose of detention and punishment. The English jail became an expression of the dominant authority of the county, which maintained control over the jails because the state had not developed its own institutions. Lack of adequate transportation to other county towns also made it necessary to hold suspected offenders within the counties until they could be tried.

An estimated 200 jails existed in England throughout the sixteenth, seventeenth, and eighteenth centuries. They were operated by several different authorities: The sheriff operated the county jail; corporation officers ran the town jails; and church and political leaders maintained private jails. The keeper of the jail ordinarily did not draw a salary, but a system of fees made it a very profitable job. Indeed, some sheriffs charged a fee to prisoners about to be released before they could actually leave; this was the practice that first interested John Howard in the jail. Although the fee system varied from jail to jail, inmates usually paid for every service they received. Rates varied by the class of the inmates; upper-class prisoners paid more for their beds, mattresses, bedclothes, and so forth. A prisoner who had enough money could live with his wife and family in a private suite outside the jail.[10]

The concept of the English jail was brought to the colonies soon after the settlers arrived from Europe. The jail was used to detain those awaiting trial and those awaiting punishment. The stocks and pillory, and sometimes the whipping post, were usually located nearby. Instead of cells, the early colonial jails consisted of small rooms that housed up to 30 prisoners each. An example of these early colonial facilities is the one at Williamsburg, Virginia, which was built by Henry Clay in 1703 and 1704 (see Figure 11.1). Prisoners in each county were placed under the jurisdiction of the sheriff, who fed and lodged them. The fee system was also used in the colonies.

Virginia established the first colonial jail, but it was the Pennsylvania jails that became the model for other states. The penal law and codes of Massachusetts in

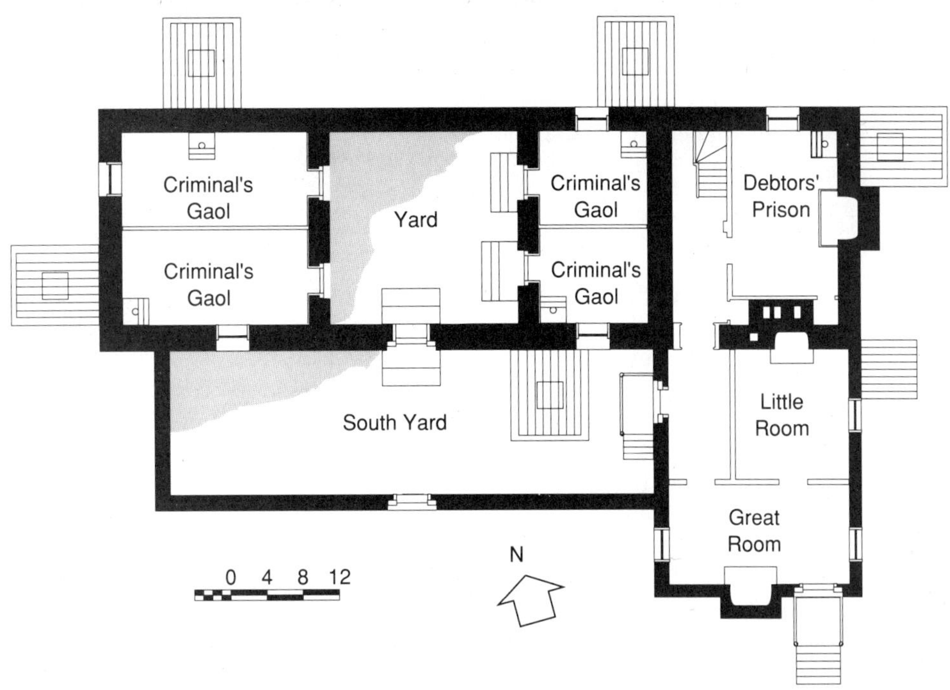

Figure 11.1 The Gaol Plan of the reconstructed building. (*Source*: Marcus Whiffen, *The Public Buildings of Williamsburg*, The Colonial Williamsburg Foundation, Williamsburg, Virginia, 1958. Courtesy, the Colonial Williamsburg Foundation.)

1699, New Jersey in 1754, South Carolina in 1770, and Maryland in 1811 also established jail systems.[11] The Walnut Street Jail in Philadelphia, as Chapter 3 pointed out, gave birth to the modern penitentiary when a separate wing was constructed in 1790 for the purpose of reforming convicted offenders.

At the beginning of the nineteenth century, children, debtors, slaves, the mentally ill, and the physically ill all were housed in jails, but as the century progressed, children and the mentally ill were more often sent to other institutions. Jails began to house both pretrial and posttrial prisoners; some jails also held felons as well as misdemeanants.[12]

Public outrage and official condemnation have characterized the history of the jail in the United States. In 1831, a Protestant clergyman in an eastern state wrote, "In regards to our county prisons nothing has been done in the way of reform."[13] In 1911, the penologist E. C. Wines warned the National Conference on Charities and Corrections that the only hope was "overthrow of the county jail system."[14] In the early 1930s, the Wickersham Report referred to jails as "dirty, unhealthy, unsanitary, and ill-fitted to produce either a stabilizing or beneficial effect on inmates."[15] A speaker informed the 1934 Attorney General's Conference on Crime that jail conditions were "so medieval, and barbarous, and so contrary to the ordinary tenets of democracy and social justice that [he was] shocked beyond experience."[16] Jails continued to draw criticism throughout the next three decades, culminating in the report of the Corrections Task Force of the National Advisory Commission on Criminal Justice Standards and Goals in 1973: "Outmoded and archaic, lacking the most basic comfort, totally inadequate for any program encouraging socialization, jails perpetuate a destructive rather than reintegrative process."[17] The Task Force on Prisoner Rehabilitation also described the jail as "the most glaringly inadequate institution on the American correctional scene."[18] Thus, nobody seems to like the jail; it has no constituency and few supporters.

WHO GOES TO JAIL?

Nationally, local jails held 395,553 inmates on June 30, 1989, 15 percent more than a year earlier. The overall occupancy rate was 116 percent of rated capacity. Significantly, one in every 469 adult residents of this nation was in jail on June 30, 1989. During the fiscal year ending June 30, 1989, there were 19 million jail admissions and releases. Unconvicted inmates (those on trial or awaiting arraignment or trial) made up 52 percent of the adults in jail.[19]

The 1988 Jail Survey revealed that jails were filled with youthful male offenders between the ages of 18 and 30. About 43 percent of all inmates in local jails were white (non-Hispanic), 41 percent were black (non-Hispanic), 15 percent were Hispanics of any race, and 1 percent were other races. There were about 10 times more males than females in jails.[20]

The jail has always confined a diverse population. For example, jails:

- Receive individuals pending arraignment and hold them awaiting trial, conviction, and sentencing
- Readmit probation, parole, and bail-bond violators and absconders
- Temporarily detain juveniles pending transfer to juvenile authorities
- Hold mentally ill persons pending their movement to appropriate health facilities
- Hold individuals for the military, for protective custody, for contempt, and for the courts as witnesses
- Release convicted inmates to the community upon completion of sentence
- Transfer inmates to State, Federal or other local authorities
- Relinquish custody of temporary detainees to juvenile and medical authorities[21]

Mandatory arrests for drunken driving, known across the nation as DWI (driving while intoxicated), DUI (driving under the influence), and OMVI (operating motor vehicle while intoxicated), are contributing to the diverse population of the jail. More than 30 states since 1981 have enacted legislation directed at drunken driving control, most frequently by prescribing such sanctions as mandatory confinement.[22]

Jails more than anything else are **dumping grounds for the poor** and catch-alls for uneducated, unemployed, homeless, and impoverished offenders. John Irwin, in spending more than a year of observation of the San Francisco jail and shorter periods in observation at several other jails, concluded that jails were primarily occupied by persons deemed disreputable or offensive to the larger society. He refers to these disorderly and disorganized persons as "**rabble**" and contends that the jail was invented and continues to be operated in order to manage society's rabble. Even with the felony prisoners in the San Francisco jails, Irwin found that offensiveness of acts was a more important factor than crime severity in leading to their arrests.[23]

Steven Spitzer's more radical interpretation suggests that the local jail is society's catch basin for the two types of deviant produced in monopoly capitalist society, "social junk" and "social dynamite." The former type, which, according to Spitzer, is "a costly yet relatively harmless burden to society," includes the mentally ill and chronic alcoholics. The latter is made up of criminal offenders who represent a potential threat to property relations and social order and, therefore, are the objects of more intense legal controls. Spitzer, like Irwin, concludes that the basic role of the jail is to manage disreputable and potentially disruptive persons.[24]

PAINS OF JAIL CONFINEMENT

Pretrial confinement, as Box 11-1 vividly shows, is disruptive, debilitating, and even traumatic because the jail prisoner is faced with four interrelated problems: "Withstanding entry shock, maintaining outside ties, securing stability or even safety, and finding activities to occupy otherwise empty time."[25]

Even those who engage in persistent criminal behavior and are not strangers to the jail environment often describe jail entry as a disruptive and disorganizing experience. But if the rapid transition from street to jail is unsettling for the jail veteran, it can be a cataclysmic experience for the novice. It can result in serious psychological disturbance and even self-injury.[26] In this regard, suicide is more prevalent in jails than in prisons. In 1988, there were 284 suicides in local jails, which was the leading cause of death among jail inmates.[27]

Jail prisoners find themselves in two worlds. They are neither serving time nor on the streets. The jolt of the street–jail transition presses prisoners to establish links with those in the community, usually family members. Thus, the support from family and friends on the outside is seen as important to maintaining their bearings during the street–jail transition. These significant others are looked to for tangible assistance in the form of money and emotional support, which can give a person a sense of hope in an uncontrollable situation.[28]

The detained prisoner also lives in an uncertain world. The jail experience shatters one's sense of predictability and order, an ingredient necessary for psychological health and effective coping. The uncertainties of jail include length of confinement; disposition of case; chances of obtaining pretrial release; competence of counsel, usually a public defender; and the intentions of prosecutors, judges, and juries.[29]

Moreover, the jail experience is typically one of marginality. In a study of three New Jersey jails, James Garofalo and Richard D. Clark found that an inmate subculture—the adherence of inmates to a set of norms that reflected opposition to institutional rules and staff—existed among a few experienced inmates. These prisoners were already familiar with the norms when they entered the jail and readapted to them upon determining that they would not be gaining their freedom in the near future. However, most inmates, especially first-timers, did not adhere to these subcultural norms and felt even more alienated because of them.[30]

Finally, inactivity and the resulting boredom is a problem faced by the jail prisoner. Boredom aggravates the tension created by enforced inactivity. The failure to reduce tension and anxiety can become an added frustration producing a new cycle

Box 11-1 "You're in Jail"

A van backs into what appears to be an ordinary municipal garage. You are ordered off the van, and a door leading into a narrow corridor swings open. The force of the noise from within seems enough to open the door. It's not like the roar of the fans at a football game or the din of machines, people, and tools in a factory. Individual sounds—bells, voices, doors—are more recognizable and seem more personal. Yet it doesn't seem real. It's like a radio station tuning in and out.

You step into the corridor. On one side, there are a half dozen holding cells. Some hold men who are on their way out; others hold men who are on their way in. Each cell holds between five and ten men. Some of these men just sit and stare into space. Others are more active, almost hyperactive. They climb up on the cell bars and shout bitter denunciations. They make exaggerated lewd gestures to intimidate newcomers, and they make comments to humiliate those they consider vulnerable and contemptible.

On the other side, there is a long office that runs the length of the corridor. The office stands about five feet above the corridor floor, and it is separated from the corridor by thick glass. Behind the quiet of the glass, one hears the bustle and hum of the control room. It is similar to a taxi dispatch station or an air traffic control tower. The major concern is the smooth and safe flow of human traffic. In this office, guards process the papers that represent the prisoners with whom their fellow officers are dealing directly in the flesh and in full view.

Someone barks your name. With all the pandemonium, however, you're not sure it was your name you heard. Your name is barked again. This time there is no question; a guard stationed at a small stand grabs your right wrist and hand, and presses your thumb on an ink pad. You're in jail!

You're in jail. Here the pains of imprisonment begin. This is the first step after you have been arrested and charged. Here you can look out on streets where you walked only a few hours ago, and wonder, as every jail inmate wonders, "What's happening with my case?" Here you will stay while your future is being decided by judges, prosecutors, defense attorneys, jury members, and others.

Source: John J. Gibbs, "The First Cut Is the Deepest: Psychological Breakdown and Survival in the Detention Setting." In *The Pains of Imprisonment*, edited by Robert Johnson and Hans Toch (Beverly Hills, Calif.: Sage, 1982), pp. 97–98. Reprinted by permission of Sage Publications, Inc.

of anxiety and tension. When people have nothing to take their minds off the present, this can escalate to crisis proportion and can result in psychological breakdowns[31]:

> It bothers me every day. I feel very guilty, and it's something that I can't get out of my mind, that I can't run away from. . . . And I try to tell myself, "The money's gone, you've done it, it's over. So just forget it." But I can't forget it. Every time I think of it, my woman comes back in my mind, the kids come back in my mind. The fact that there were so many things that I needed with the money, that I needed to do with the money, so many constructive things that I needed to do, material things that I needed to do. I just threw it away.[32]

JAIL STRUCTURE

The administration of the jail, its physical characteristics, and inmate programs are three important aspects of jail structure.

Administration of the Jail

The most frequent means of jail administration is to give county sheriffs operational responsibility for the jail. Indeed, that is how more than 3,000 counties in the United States are run.[33] A major problem with this kind of jail administration is that sheriffs are politically accountable to the county's voters, which make jails one of the most political institutions in adult corrections. Accordingly, jails tend to face both political conservatism and fiscal constraint.[34]

There are at least four alternatives to local control: state-run jails, cooperative (regional) arrangements, state subsidy programs, and private services. Six states—Alaska, Connecticut, Delaware, Hawaii, Rhode Island, and Vermont—currently have full operational responsibility for jails. Although state-run jails offer greater operational efficiency than locally operated jails, political opposition by the counties is one of the chief reasons why this approach is not likely to be selected by more states.[35]

A widely used alternative to local or state control is regional or multicounty arrangements. This arrangement typically occurs when a jurisdiction with an adequate jail is willing to contract with neighboring cities and counties to house prisoners on a per diem basis. It also occurs when a group of local governments decides that no existing facility is adequate and makes the decision to build a new regional jail or "detention center." Furthermore, local governments may decide to specialize and house different populations, such as juveniles, females, pretrial detainees, or convicted felons awaiting transportation to state prisons. Yet transportation problems, multijurisdiction funding problems, and turf disputes limit or prohibit the even wider use of cooperative arrangements among local governments.[36]

State subsidies provide a third way to reach beyond locally operated jails, with their politics and financial constraints. Almost 60 percent of the states provide technical assistance to local governments with jail problems, and about 50 percent provide jail personnel training. In addition, some subsidy programs assist jails in complying with state standards and in making capital improvements ordered by courts.[37]

Furthermore, jails, like other components of correctional services, utilize private services to some degree in the areas of medical and mental health care, food service, jail work programs, community-based inmate programs, facility financing, architectural services, and facility construction. The private sector is even being used in a few jails for total facility management.[38] Norman R. Cox, Jr., and William E. Osterhoff suggest that a public–private partnership offers more advantages to local governments than private agencies running jails. They picture this public–private partnership in the following way:

> The public–private partnership concept can be visualized as a continuum with exclusively public sector responsibilities at one end and exclusively private sector involvement at the other. Other responsibilities would fall along the continuum depending on their respective public and private involvement. At the end of the continuum where private sector involvement is more acceptable are jail services and programs, including

> medical and mental health care, food service, and alcohol and drug treatment programs. At the end of the continuum where public control is more acceptable are jail management, operation, and facility ownership. Toward the center of the continuum are community-based correctional facilities and programs, jail industries, and selected special-purpose facilities and programs that can be operated jointly by the public and private sectors.[39]

Yet, whatever means is used to administer the jail, personnel management remains an important concern. Jail training is either poor or nonexistent for the corrections officer. Salaries are typically low and sometimes incredibly low. Officers can suffer severe motivational problems, especially when sheriffs' deputies are used as jail personnel in place of career-line corrections officers. In Box 11-2, a corrections officer in a Florida jail reveals some of the problems facing the line officer.

Physical Characteristics

Most jails are small. Approximately 67 percent of all jails in 1988 held an average daily population of fewer than 50 inmates (see Table 11.1). The midwest had the highest percentage of small jails (80 percent), and the northeast the lowest (30 percent). But large jails held a growing percentage of this nation's inmates during the 1980s. Approximately, 63 percent of all jail prisoners in 1988 were in facilities for 250 or more, including 28 percent in jails with capacities for 1000 or more.[40]

Jails range from ancient, dilapidated dungeons to modern, attractive facilities. But in many the cagelike atmosphere and barbarous facilities of the nineteenth-century jail still exist. Inflexible cells face inflexible dayrooms. Prisoners spend most of the day in large cages or bullpens. Alcoholics, drug abusers, psychotics, and others with serious medical and behavioral problems are placed in isolation cells, or "drunk tanks," generally unfurnished cubes of steel and concrete, many of which contain only an eastern-style floor toilet. Health problems are created by the shortage of such items as towels, soap, toothbrushes, clean bedding, and toilet paper. As the late Hans Mattick said, "If cleanliness is next to godliness, most jails lie securely in the province of hell."[41]

The crowding characteristic of the nation's jails has led to the use of existing structures or old buildings as makeshift jails, a convenient and economical way to continue the rate of detention and incarceration. Some counties have converted old school buildings into minimum security detention centers. An abandoned gas station in Denton, Texas, was converted into a makeshift jail. The Bibby Venture, a floating barge moored at the New York City's waterfront, is designed to ease crowding at Rikers Island. The success of this barge, which held 355 inmates as of May 1989, is leading to plans to purchase another jail barge, the Bibby Resolution, which will hold approximately 800 inmates.[42]

The Boulder County Correctional Center (Colorado), the Fairfax County Adult Detention Center (Virginia), and the Metropolitan Correctional Centers (New York, Chicago, San Diego, Tucson, and Miami) of the Bureau of Prisons are newer facilities that are several cuts above the average American jail.

Opened in 1976 after nearly five years of planning and preparation, the Boulder Center emerged as the result of extensive citizen involvement. Community citizens and county officials made a joint decision to support a more humane, carefully planned facility. The correctional center is part of the $8 million Boulder County

Box 11-2 Interview with Richard A. Clark

As a correctional officer, when I enter the jail every night, I never know what kind of problems I am going to be faced with. Entering the jail is like entering a different world. It is very difficult to explain to other people what it is like working in a jail environment.

To understand what types of inmates we have in our jail population, you have to think of the jail population as a microcosm of our troubled society. To be an effective line officer, you must be able to deal with inmates who are from different ethnic and economic class backgrounds than what you are. This can appear to be an impossible task at times.

Most Americans have grown up with a value system where we are taught the difference between right and wrong, but people in jail seem to have a different set of ethics. In a jail or prison environment, inmates have to play by a different set of rules in order to survive. In other words, inmates have to become "jail wise."

As a line officer, you also have to become "jail wise" if you want to keep your sanity and live to receive your pension some day. As a line officer, you can learn a lot by observing how inmates handle different jail situations they are confronted with each day.

Today's inmates are more violent and are quicker to exhibit aggressive behavior toward officers and support staff. Our American society has become more violent and it is obvious inmates don't leave their violent behavior back home.

To make it in a modern correctional environment, a correctional officer must have good insight into human behavior. A good officer must also keep his or her sense of humor in such a negative environment as a jail. The average officer and staff member must be able to deal with inmates who have very serious emotional problems.

If you say "no" to a request from the average person because it will get you into trouble with your boss, that is usually the end of the story. However, if you say "no" to some inmates, they may become very upset with you.

As a line officer, you will find inmates who want to confront the officers and the jail administration with all kinds of demands. Some complain to you about the jail food being bad or the room temperature being uncomfortable or that an officer on a different shift likes to "pick on" the inmates.

I have seen some inmates who will play one correctional officer against another to help divide the shift. This can happen a lot when there is a personality conflict between different officers. This kind of situation can become very serious if it gets out of hand in a jail environment. I call this one the "mind game" that a lot of inmates use in jails.

Most inmates see the average floor officer as their only link to the jail administration. A lot of the jail administrators do not have the time or do not want to talk to the inmates. As a rule, inmates as well as floor officers must go through the chain of command to solve problems.

From my own personal experience, most of the serious problems are handled by the floor officer or a sergeant. As a jail officer, if you are assigned to a certain area for a long period of time, you soon learn to sense problems in your work area. After a while, I have been able to tell when there is a growing race conflict or when a gang fight is about to take place.

Source: Richard A. Clark, a correctional officer in a Florida jail, was interviewed in January 1991.

Table 11.1 NUMBER OF LOCAL JAILS AND SIZE OF FACILITY, BY REGION, 1983 AND 1988

Region and year	Number of jails	Average daily population	Percent of jails in categories of daily population: Fewer than 50	50–249	250–499	500–999	1000 or more
U.S. total							
1983	3,337	68.2	74.0%	20.2%	3.5%	1.6%	.6%
1988	3,316	101.3	66.9	24.1	4.8	2.7	1.5
Northeast							
1983	223	168.2	42.6	39.0	11.2	4.5	2.7
1988	223	255.0	30.0	40.4	13.9	11.2	4.5
Midwest							
1983	972	42.5	84.3	12.8	1.6	1.0	.1
1988	964	51.6	80.4	16.3	2.1	.8	.4
South							
1983	1,606	57.2	75.2	20.7	2.6	1.2	.4
1988	1,599	87.2	66.9	25.8	4.4	1.9	1.1
West							
1983	536	105.9	65.1	24.4	6.5	2.8	1.1
1988	530	169.6	58.1	26.2	7.0	4.9	3.8

Source: Bureau of Justice Statistics, *Population Density in Local Jails, 1988* (Washington: Department of Justice, 1990), p. 3.

Criminal Justice Center, which houses the courtrooms, state probation offices, the Boulder city police department, and the county sheriff offices.[43]

Jail residents are housed in single rooms arranged in clusters of ten. Windows face an interior courtyard on one side and dayrooms on the other. Male prisoners live in eight of the units, which are arranged around the courtyard in four modules; each unit has a different level of security. There is also a 14-man dormitory for inmates on a work release program and a 10-room unit for women, who share dayrooms with male prisoners. A well-stocked library, a full-size gymnasium, a game room, and a small dining area are available for the use of the prisoners. The design gives the overall impression of a small residential school. The highly trained, casually dressed staff contributes to this impression by their informal relationships with inmates.

The Fairfax County Adult Detention Center, which can accommodate 240 male and female prisoners, has shatter- and bulletproof glass rather than bars. Each modern cell has a stainless steel commode, a bed, and a small writing table. The hooks in the cells are designed to give way under more than 5 pounds of pressure in order to prevent suicides. Two deputies in a central control room use 12 cameras to monitor the problem areas of the jail. Medium security prisoners can open and shut the doors to their cells and go back and forth to an adjoining dayroom. Cameras monitor the dayrooms of the maximum security sections. Prisoners' menus are planned by the state board of corrections, and the meals are prepared by civilian employees. The jail also has an outdoor recreation yard, an indoor gymnasium, classes in which prisoners can prepare for the GED (General Equivalency Diploma) test, groups led by Alcoholics Anonymous, art classes, and a work release program for prisoners during the last 120 days of their sentences.[44]

Boulder County Correctional Center. (*Source*: Federal Prison System.)

The Metropolitan Correctional Center (MCC) in Chicago is a 26-floor triangular structure that was completed in June 1975. The MCC is designed to accommodate 400 inmates in 10 separate living units. The security system is largely electronic, with doors, elevators, TV monitors, alarms, intercoms, and telephones centrally controlled with the assistance of a computer. Most units consist of two floors, with a split-level design. The outside rows of 44 individual inmate rooms are divided into four 11-room modules, each with its own lounge area. Midway between the two floors is a multipurpose area with kitchenette, dining room, recreation and exercise areas, and visitors' lounge. The individual rooms provide both privacy and security for the inmate.[45]

In startling contrast to the grim picture of the remaining nineteenth-century jails and most of the makeshift jails, the **New Generation jail** is a concept that attempts to use the physical plant to manage the jail population. By late 1988, direct supervision jails were either in operation or planned in 41 jurisdictions, including the Boulder County Correctional Center and the 5 MCCs (see Figure 11.2 on page 299 for a list of direct supervision jails).[46] This new management concept offers a possibility of reducing costs of jail construction as well as providing an innovative management method known as direct supervision.[47]

Local governments have earmarked approximately $3 billion for jail facilities presently being designed or under construction. Additional increases in the jail population are estimated at 21,000 each year—the equivalent of one new 400-bed jail every week. The rising costs of jail construction are resulting in increased interest in the New Generation jail, because it is less reliant upon expensive construction, such as high-security hardware and advanced technology. For example:

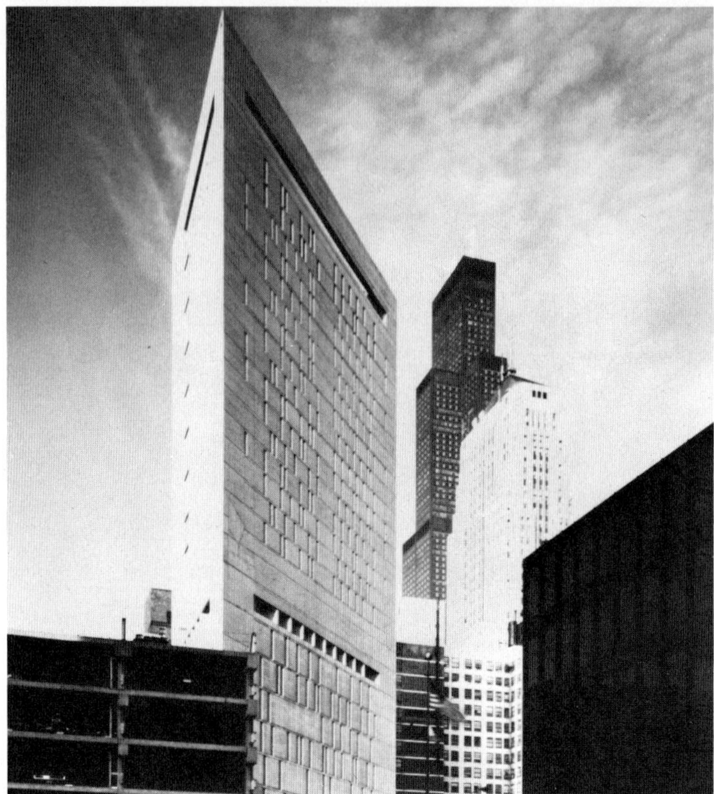

Metropolitan Correctional Center, Chicago, Illinois. (*Source*: Federal Prison System.)

- Commercial-grade plumbing fixtures can replace vandal-proof stainless steel fixtures in general population living areas.
- The cost of secure control stations on each living unit can be eliminated.
- The cost of walls and glazing to divide 48-cell living units into smaller 12- or 16-cell subunits, as is the custom in "remote surveillance" detention facilities, can be eliminated.
- Furniture for use by inmates in general population living areas can be of normal commercial quality rather than the more expensive vandal-proof line.
- Cell doors, frames, and hardware in the general population living areas can be commercial or institutional types rather than heavy steel doors and sliding gates.[48]

Direct supervision is probably the most dominant feature of the New Generation jail. A direct supervision jail is different from the intermittent surveillance and remote surveillance jails because the officer is stationed inside the housing unit (see Figure 11.3). Direct supervision permits direct interaction between staff and inmates to prevent negative behavior. It groups prisoners into living units of about 50 cells that can be managed by one officer. Thus, rather than the traditional procedure of separating staff from inmates by security barriers, the new approach places officers in direct contact with inmates at all times.[49]

*Santa Clara County, San Jose, California
Larimer County, Fort Collins, Colorado
Metro-Dade County Stockade, Miami, Florida
Contra Costa County, Martinez, California
Prince Georges County, Upper Marlboro, Maryland
Manhattan House of Detention, New York, New York
Clark County, Las Vegas, Nevada
Alexandria City Jail, Alexandria, Virginia
Multnomah County, Portland, Oregon
*Horry County, Conway, South Carolina
*Charleston County, Charleston, South Carolina
Boulder County, Boulder, Colorado
Bucks County, Doylestown, Pennsylvania
Erie County Correctional Facility, Alden, New York
Erie County Jail, Buffalo, New York
*Hillsborough County, Tampa, Florida
*Genesee County, Flint, Michigan
Middlesex County, New Brunswick, New Jersey
Licking County, Newark, Ohio
*Sonoma County, Santa Rosa, California
Pima County, Tucson, Arizona
Washoe County, Reno, Nevada
Bexar County, San Antonio, Texas
Spokane County, Spokane, Washington
Shawnee County, Topeka, Kansas
*Marin County, San Rafael, California
*Los Angeles County, Los Angeles, California
*San Joaquin County, Stockton, California
*Tarrant County, Fort Worth, Texas
*Milwaukee County, Milwaukee, Wisconsin
*Lake County, Waukeegan, Illinois
*Will County, Joliet, Illinois

Metropolitan Correctional Centers (Federal Bureau of Prisons)
1) New York City, New York
2) Chicago, Illinois
3) San Diego, California
*4) Los Angeles, California
5) Tucson, Arizona
6) Miami, Florida

* Planned or under construction

Figure 11.2 Direct Supervision Jails. (*Source*: W. Raymond Nelson. *Cost Savings in New Generation Jails: The Direct Supervision Approach* (Washington: U.S. Department of Justice, 1988), p. 8.)

Another feature of the New Generation design is that prisoners have greater freedom to interact with other prisoners and, unlike the traditional jail, which separates guard and prisoners, the New Generation jail places them in the same room with guards. Furthermore, the New Generation jail provides prisoners with more personal space than the other two types of jail designs, for they may stay in their own cells if they so desire.[50]

The advantages of this new design include programming for specialized offender groups, the ability to shut a pod down when populations are low, and placing correctional officers in closer contact with prisoners. Disadvantages include the difficulty of "selling" the jail to a public that tends to see it as a means of "coddling" prisoners, the possibility of the jail's becoming outmoded between the time it is planned and completed, and the fact that overcrowding makes this design hard to implement.[51]

Several studies support the efficacy of direct supervision jails. For example, Linda L. Zupan and Ben A. Menke found that correctional officers in New Generation jails were more satisfied with their jobs, were more positive about the organizational climate, and experienced more job enrichment than did officers in traditional jails.[52] Zupan and Stohr-Gillmore also found that inmates in direct supervision facilities were significantly more positive in their evaluation of the jail climate, the physical environment, and officers than were inmates in traditional jails. In addition,

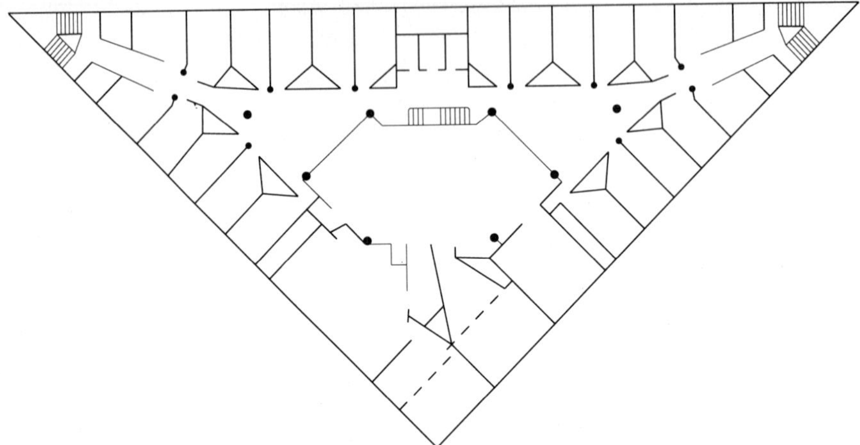

Figure 11.3 Direct supervision. (*Source*: W. Raymond Nelson, *Cost Savings in New Generation Jails: The Direct Supervision Approach* (Washington: U.S. Department of Justice, 1988), p. 3.)

inmates in direct supervision jails experienced less psychological and physical stress than those in traditional settings.[53]

Jail Programs

John Knoll, former education director of the Bexar County Detention Center in San Antonio, Texas, expresses the positive attitude of some jail administrators: "You're cut off emotionally in prison. Jails have a better chance to make an impact upon prisoners."[54] The President's Commission on Law Enforcement and Administration of Justice reached the same conclusion:

> The deeper the offender has to be plunged into the correctional process and the longer he has to be held under punitive (though humane) restraints, the more difficult is the road back to the point of social restoration. It is logical, then, to conclude that the correctional process ought to concentrate its greatest efforts at those points in the criminal justice continuum where the largest numbers of offenders are involved and the hope of avoiding social segregation is the greatest.[55]

However, most small jails and many large ones offer little programming. It is difficult for small jails to develop a variety of programs because they lack space, staff, and fiscal resources. Large jails have more programs, but the overcrowded conditions make it difficult to offer adequate programming for each inmate.[56] In a humorous note, Box 11-3 talks about jail programming.

A 1988 jail survey found that 1,787 jails had work release programs involving 19,700 inmates, or about 6 percent of the jail population (see Table 11-2). Approximately 68 percent of the jails in the Midwest maintained work release programs, compared to 62 percent in the Northeast, 55 percent in the Northwest, 44 percent in the West, and 44 percent in the South. A total of 2,405 facilities operated weekend sentence programs involving 4 percent of the jail population. About 78 percent of the jails in the Midwest maintained weekend sentencing programs, compared to 73

Box 11-3 LA County Jail—The No Frills Business School

Prison, as Richard Nixon has observed, has proved to be fertile ground for writers and social observers in this century. Idealists and visionaries like Mahatama Gandhi and Martin Luther King Jr., and lunatics like Adolf Hitler, spawned powerful books and articles about their movements from behind bars. Now, from that center of the new and the relevant, Los Angeles, come some poignant thoughts about management and organization in modern corporations, also germinated in jail.

The source of this data is a man I will call Donald. He was a student of mine some years ago at a glittering university overlooking the ocean in Malibu. Donald was an intelligent and articulate guy, but he was also an incorrigible (I thought) wise guy, troublemaker, and arguer.

I had heard, off and on, that the same traits had dogged him when he had gone to work for a very major corporation here in Los Angeles. Promotion had been slow, and he had been in constant jeopardy of being dismissed—always because of his bad attitude.

When he pulled up behind me at a gas station in Malibu a few days ago in a gleaming sports car, looking like a vastly more confident, far smoother, far easier to talk to—far, far better dressed—guy than I had known, I was surprised. He looked, as one might say, like a successful version of his old self.

He said that he had, in fact, been doing incomparably better at his work, had been promoted, was told what an asset he was, and was on the fast track to plutocracy. Over veggie burgers at an outdoor restaurant, he told what had happened.

It all began, he said, when he had been sentenced to 60 days in LA County Jail for drunken driving while on probation. It was, he said, a kind of education he had never expected, but had badly needed.

From the first moment that he had been handcuffed to a hardened convict and attached by leg irons to five others—all of whom were terrifying—Donald had realized that he had better learn the rules of prison life fast, or he was going to wind up either dead or with some truly horrible stories to tell for the rest of his life. "There are rules of how to get by," he said, "and if you follow them, you do."

Rule One, he said, ". . . is that no matter what kind of crap is being dished out by the cops and the guards, you absolutely have to put up with it. You can't say one word back or you get hit so hard you can't believe it, and you can't do a thing about it. That's rule one: Be humble and don't talk back to those who have power over you.

"Rule Two is that you can't take any crap at all, not any, from anyone on your level. You can't let yourself be pushed around at all, not even a little bit, by the other prisoners. If they ask you for a cigarette, you tell them to go —— themselves. If they ask you for money, you tell them you'd rather kill them than give them a cent. You can be friendly, but don't ever back down from anything, and even if the guy is 10 times your size, you let him know you'll put up a fight and he'll at least have some scars on him. Respect is everything in jail, and if you don't have the guts to fight, take it until you do (while I was in jail, I told people I was there for whacking my old lady, just so they wouldn't think I was another drunk driving wimp).

"Third, beware of anyone who seems to be doing you a favor that's too good to be true. The first night I was there, a little guy offered me his bed—and there weren't anywhere near enough beds to go around—for five bucks. I paid him, and 10 minutes later, this huge Chinese guy comes by and says it's his bed and he's going to kill me. We swore at each other for a while, so I at least looked tough, and then I went and got my money back from the little guy. Guys who (make offers) too good to be true are nothing but trouble, at least in jail.

"Fourth, stay out of other people's fights. You don't need to speak up for someone who's being hassled unless you're part of his group. The guy who started teaching me about this told me at first I should just go off into a corner and not talk to anyone. He was totally right—totally. And it saved me a lot of trouble.

"Fifth, hook up with a larger group who can protect you. Don't ever be alone in jail. In LA County (jail) there were mostly blacks and Hispanics, and since I'm not black and I speak Spanish, I got with the Mexicans. That way I wasn't just one lone guy who they could kill in the shower for laughs.

"Sixth, have a goal, and pay attention to it. My goal was to get out of there alive, in one piece, in good health, and without any horror stories to tell my friends. I did it, but it meant giving up being a wise ass; no more arguing for the fun of it, no more disrupting everybody else just to be the center of attention. Just staying alive. That was my goal.

"The point is that when I got out, one month early for good behavior, and went back to work—they thought I was in Germany on vacation—I just reflexively started to do the same things I had done in County.

"They worked even better there. Being humble to my bosses, not taking any guff at all from the people on my same level, not getting into other people's fights, making myself part of a group that could protect me, staying away from people who offered me unreal favors, paying attention to my goal (which was to get promoted), not showing off—all that works incredibly well in a large white-collar organization.

"Prison is the most unforgiving, rigorous large competitive organization. It's the essence of human relationships in groups without any of the politeness or the etiquette. It's what business should teach you about what competing is really like—boot camp, in a way, for other more compromising situations. It sure worked for me," Donald said.

"Anyway, now that you know," he added, "don't feel you have to try it."

(Thanks, I won't.)

Source: Benjamin J. Stein, "LA County Jail—The No-Frills Business School" (*The Wall Street Journal,* 13 August 1990), p. 3.

percent in the South, 67 percent in the Northeast, and 64 percent in the West. In addition, 503 facilities sponsored community service programs or other activities to provide other options for offenders than staying overnight in jail. Approximately 19 percent of all jails in the West sponsored such alternative programs, compared to 17 percent in the South, 12 percent in the Northeast, and 10 percent in the Midwest.[57]

Some jails have exemplary health care delivery systems; others have virtually no health care systems. Yet even the most exemplary systems are unable to manage inmates thought to be infected with the human immunodeficiency virus (HIV), the causative agent of acquired immunodeficiency syndrome (AIDS). James E. Lawrence and Van Zwisohn suggest that a comprehensive jail system for management of HIV disease in jail would have the following elements:

1. Early detection and diagnosis
2. Medical management

Table 11.2 PROGRAMS FOR JAIL INMATES, 1988

Region	Total number of jails	Number of jails with: Work release programs	Weekend sentence programs	Alternatives to jail incarceration*
U.S. total	3,316	1,787	2,405	503
Northeast	223	138	148	27
Midwest	964	654	749	97
South	1,599	702	1,169	277
West	530	293	339	102

* Includes jail-sponsored community service and other activities in which participants do not stay overnight but would be incarcerated in the jail if the program did not exist.

Source: Bureau of Justice Statistics, *Census of Local Jails, 1988* (Washington: U.S. Department of Justice, 1991), p. xii.

3. Inmate classification
4. Transmission risk reduction
5. Education and training
6. Resource allocation[58]

Substance dependency is a serious problem with offenders today, and the lack of sufficient programming for substance abusers is a severe criticism of the jail. Alcoholic prisoners also exist in great numbers, and the early identification of both the chemically and alcohol-dependent detainee can help the institution deal more adequately with withdrawal symptoms, physical illness, and emotional distress. In addition, early identification can prevent self-injury and help relieve the depression resulting from drug and alcohol withdrawal.

Mentally ill prisoners also pose special problems for the jail. For example, studies in California have found that 5 percent to 8 percent of jail populations are psychotic.[59] Untrained staff and insufficient intervention make the mentally ill high risks for jail confinement. Ideally, the mentally ill prisoner ought to be transferred to a psychiatric facility, but these facilities are often reluctant to accept troublesome prisoners with criminal histories.[60]

PROBLEMS OF THE JAIL

The specific problems of the jail are overcrowding, court orders and inmate suits, fiscal constraints and the costs of running the jail, and violence.

Crowding

Jails, like other correctional institutions in the United States, have not escaped the skyrocketing influx of prisoners; indeed, the jail population increased from 223,551 in 1983 to 343,569 in 1988. To accommodate this 54 percent growth, local jails added 5.3 million square feet of housing (a 44 percent increase). In addition to a greater increase of inmates than new housing, there were 177 fewer local jails in operation in 1988 than there had been in 1983. The end result is that the average daily population of a local jail increased from 68.5 in 1983 to 101 in 1988.[61] Another indication of **jail crowding** is that in 1988 the local jail population was at 101 percent of the total rated capacity, up from 85 percent of capacity in 1983.[62]

Standards on spatial density established by the American Correctional Association suggest that each prisoner have 60 square feet of floor space and spend 10 hours or less per day in a confinement unit or cell. Local jails during the 1983 and 1988 surveys reported confining their inmates 13.5 hours per day in housing units. When considered by state, jails varied significantly in both spatial density and social density. North Dakota jails reported the largest amount of space per inmate, while New Jersey jails reported the least space per inmate (see Table 11.3 for the average square feet of floor space per inmate in local jails, by region and state, 1988). Nine states, six of them in the south, had less than the 50.9 percent average square feet per inmate reported by this nation's jails. Four western states, four midwestern states, and one northeastern state had local jails with an average of at least 65 square feet per inmate.[63]

Table 11.3 AVERAGE SQUARE FEET OF FLOOR SPACE PER INMATE IN LOCAL JAILS, BY REGION AND STATE, 1988

Average square feet per inmate	Northeast (54.2)	Midwest (58.4)	South (48.3)	West (48.8)
80–89		North Dakota (88.8)		
70–79		Iowa (75.6)		Montana (76.7) Wyoming (76.1) Nevada (70.5)
60–69	Maine (65.5)	Kansas (67.7) Minnesota (66.8) South Dakota (63.7) Wisconsin (63.6) Missouri (63.5) Nebraska (62.0)	Arkansas (63.6) West Virginia (61.8)	Idaho (69.9) Washington (63.9) Colorado (62.7) Oregon (61.0) New Mexico (60.8)
50–59	New York (59.2) Pennsylvania (58.7) New Hampshire (57.9)	Ohio (56.5) Michigan (56.3) Illinois (53.2) Indiana (52.2)	Dist. of Columbia (57.2) Oklahoma (57.2) Kentucky (56.9) Alabama (54.3) Florida (54.3) Maryland (52.4) Mississippi (52.3) North Carolina (50.9)	Arizona (57.8) Utah (51.4)
40–49	Massachusetts (49.0)		South Carolina (49.6) Texas (44.0) Georgia (43.9) Louisiana (43.1) Tennessee (42.3) Virginia (40.4)	California (43.0)
30–39	New Jersey (39.6)			

Source: Bureau of Justice Statistics, *Population Density in Local Jails, 1988* (Washington: U.S. Department of Justice, 1990), p. 5.

A contributing factor to jail crowding is that 42,000 inmates, or one in every eight inmates, were being held for other correctional authorities. About 26,500, or 8 percent of all prisoners in 1988 compared with 7,700, or 3 percent, in 1983—were being held because of crowding in other institutions.[64] In this regard, the Clark Foundation reported in 1982 that a frustrated county sheriff in Arkansas attempted to get rid of the state inmates confined in his jail by chaining them to the state prison fence. However, state officials confronted the sheriff with shotguns and a court order to return the inmates to the county jail.[65]

What makes jail crowding such a serious problem is that jails have even fewer alternatives for dealing with overcrowded facilities than do state and federal institutions. States and the Federal Bureau of Prisons can transfer inmates from one facility to another. They can relieve some of the overcrowding by makeshift jails. Parole boards in some overcrowded states release prisoners early. Such options are not usually available to jail administrators, who are dependent on bail reform acts, speedy trials, and the benevolence of judges to alleviate overcrowded jail conditions.

Overcrowding is particularly acute in large urban jails; few in number, they hold more than 50 percent of the U.S. jail population. In the 1970s and the 1980s, the Tombs in New York City, the Cook County Jail in Chicago, the old District of Columbia jail, and the jails in Atlanta, Dallas, and Houston suffered from scandalously overcrowded conditions.

One of the problems resulting from overcrowded conditions is inmate idleness. A few jails run work farms, and the city workhouses usually have labor gangs. But the few existent jail programs, makeshift work, and maintenance tasks simply are not adequate. A long-accepted adage is that busy inmates create fewer problems than idle inmates; the endless empty hours in dayrooms accompanied by the usual restricted movement within the jail result in restless prisoners.

Civil Suits and Court Orders

Civil and class-action suits have become a real concern for most jail administrators. In the 1988 Jail Survey, a total of 404 jails, or 12 percent of all facilities, were under state or federal court order or consent decree to limit the number of inmates. At the same time, 412 jails were under state or federal court order or consent decree for specific conditions of confinement, such as inmate classification, library services, medical facilities or services, food service, and the totality of conditions. More than 75 percent of the jails that courts had cited for specific conditions were also under court order to limit the number of inmates (see Table 11.4).

A landmark case involving jail overcrowding was *Bell* v. *Wolfish*, which attacked the double-bunking policies of the Metropolitan Correctional Center (MCC) in New York City. A dramatic rise in pretrial detainees caused the Bureau of Prisons to double-bunk sentenced and unsentenced inmates in single-occupancy accommodations. The *Bell* class-action suit alleged violations of other constitutional rights, such as undue length of confinements, improper searches, and inadequate employment, recreational, and educational opportunities. The U.S. Supreme Court rejected all allegations as not violating inmates' constitutional rights. Significantly, double-bunking was not deemed unconstitutional, particularly because nearly all pretrial detainees were released within 60 days.[66]

Sheriffs and wardens are concerned because the courts can hold them, as they

Table 11.4 JAILS UNDER COURT ORDER OR CONSENT DECREE FOR SPECIFIC CONDITIONS OF CONFINEMENT ON JUNE 30, 1988, BY REASON AND WHETHER ORDERED TO LIMIT THE NUMBER OF INMATES HELD

Whether under court order and reason	Total	Ordered to limit population	Not ordered to limit population
Total number of jails	3,316	404	2,912
Not under court order or consent decree for specific conditions	2,904	84	2,820
Under court order or consent decree for:	412*	320*	92*
Crowded living units	306	278	28
Recreation facilities	190	147	43
Medical facilities or services	161	128	33
Staffing patterns	137	102	35
Visiting practice or policies	132	103	29
Library services	137	111	26
Inmate classification	123	102	21
Food service (quantity or quality)	122	97	25
Disciplinary procedures or policies	111	85	26
Grievance procedures or policies	106	83	23
Totality of conditions	92	74	18
Fire hazards	90	69	21
Other reasons	242	183	59

* Detail adds to more than total number of jails under court order for specific conditions because some jails were under judicial mandate for more than one reason.

Source: Bureau of Justice Statistics, *Census of Local Jails 1988* (Washington: U.S. Department of Justice, 1990), p. 2.

have held other jail administrators, personally liable for damages. Civil damages and legal fees in excess of $1 million have been awarded by the courts. Sheriffs can also lose their jobs and expend what seems to be an endless amount of time dealing with lawsuits.

Fiscal Constraints and the Costs of the Jail

The fiscal constraints so common in state correctional systems are even more acute in county corrections. County or city commissioners are not known for their generosity, and shoestring budgeting affects every aspect of jail life. Jailers usually receive low salaries; the food service cuts every possible corner; and money is seldom available for recreational equipment or leisure-time activities. There is little public pressure to spend money on jails because the jail lacks a political constituency. To express this in another way, there are no votes in jail.[67] Commissioners understandably favor such politically attractive institutions as hospitals and schools.

However, in spite of this history of fiscal austerity, local jail expenditures throughout the nation totaled slightly more than $4.5 billion during the year ending June 30, 1988 (see Table 11.5). This total (not adjusted for inflation) was 67 percent higher than in 1983. Salaries and wages, employer contributions to employee benefits, food, supplies, contractual services, and other operating costs accounted for 78

Table 11.5 JAIL EXPENDITURES, BY REGION AND STATE, FOR THE ANNUAL PERIOD ENDING JUNE 30, 1988

Region and state	Annual expenditures: Total	Operating	Capital	Capital expenditures as a percentage of total expenditures	Operating expenditures per inmate*
U.S. total	$4,555,649,319	$3,574,940,241	$980,709,078	22%	$10,639
Northeast	$1,347,000,062	$1,007,214,597	$339,785,465	25%	$17,710
Maine	16,333,648	9,415,438	6,918,210	42	14,463
Massachusetts	88,575,784	75,564,427	13,011,357	15	13,962
New Hampshire	16,054,306	11,852,048	4,202,258	26	15,098
New Jersey	137,619,407	127,876,387	9,743,020	7	11,648
New York	872,290,218	578,439,309	293,850,909	34	22,698
Pennsylvania	216,126,699	204,066,988	12,059,711	6	15,046
Midwest	$ 704,049,758	$ 549,300,832	$154,748,926	22%	$11,036
Illinois	106,562,460	100,470,540	6,091,920	6	10,628
Indiana	60,321,691	34,514,000	25,807,691	43	6,820
Iowa	29,213,939	16,777,584	12,436,355	43	15,798
Kansas	23,775,112	19,092,297	4,682,815	20	10,243
Michigan	128,310,624	116,604,955	11,705,669	9	12,347
Minnesota	62,401,146	44,349,375	18,051,771	29	14,778
Missouri	41,159,938	39,010,370	2,149,568	5	9,081
Nebraska	15,593,883	14,183,515	1,410,368	9	12,778
North Dakota	7,118,989	4,787,689	2,331,300	33	17,099
Ohio	140,205,813	104,198,710	36,007,103	26	11,498
South Dakota	5,061,433	4,422,593	638,840	13	8,604
Wisconsin	84,324,730	50,889,204	33,435,526	40	11,001
South	$1,453,370,251	$1,174,081,570	$279,288,681	19%	$ 8,418
Alabama	47,379,649	33,834,840	13,544,809	29	6,905
Arkansas	25,683,951	17,311,209	8,372,742	33	8,837
District of Columbia	14,113,253	13,562,805	550,448	4	8,745
Florida	360,767,037	316,730,177	44,036,860	12	11,718
Georgia	144,876,348	97,237,101	47,639,247	33	6,013
Kentucky	46,478,850	37,898,822	8,580,028	18	8,045
Louisiana	84,484,712	65,241,755	19,242,957	23	5,882
Maryland	97,842,235	88,030,850	9,811,385	10	12,059
Mississippi	21,147,521	17,341,645	3,805,876	18	5,341
North Carolina	51,756,230	41,955,997	9,800,233	19	7,556
Oklahoma	21,238,729	19,426,587	1,812,142	9	7,150
South Carolina	24,076,359	23,340,302	736,057	3	6,629
Tennessee	106,466,694	71,706,962	34,759,732	33	7,112
Texas	280,381,295	215,108,299	65,272,996	23	7,386
Virginia	114,466,881	103,560,888	10,905,993	10	11,367
West Virginia	12,210,507	11,793,331	417,176	3	8,388
West	$1,051,299,248	$ 844,343,242	$206,886,006	20%	$ 9,392
Alaska	4,257,439	1,227,409	3,030,030	71	43,836
Arizona	48,233,240	48,085,953	147,287	—	8,279
California	659,717,625	523,497,555	136,220,070	21	8,262
Colorado	97,214,038	71,862,700	25,351,338	26	15,998
Idaho	7,322,921	6,831,030	491,891	7	8,331
Montana	7,696,447	7,427,830	268,617	3	12,463

Table 11.5 (continued)

Region and state	Annual expenditures: Total	Operating	Capital	Capital expenditures as a percentage of total expenditures	Operating expenditures per inmate*
Nevada	37,043,814	35,134,916	1,908,898	5	16,087
New Mexico	25,473,791	25,120,756	353,035	1	11,657
Oregon	65,366,001	38,906,446	26,459,555	40	13,861
Utah	14,148,762	13,907,857	240,905	2	10,272
Washington	65,667,372	64,901,258	766,114	1	11,178
Wyoming	19,087,798	7,439,532	11,648,266	61	15,276

* Operating expenditures per inmate were determined by dividing the amount spent on salaries, wages, supplies, utilities, transportation, contractual services, and other current items paid for during the fiscal year by the average daily inmate population.

—Less than 0.5%.

Source: Bureau of Justice Statistics, *Census of Local Jails 1988* (Washington: U.S. Department of Justice, 1990), p. 2.

percent of all expenditures. Construction costs, major repairs, improvements, equipment, land purchases, and other capital outlays accounted for the remaining 22 percent.

A major issue facing county government is how to finance the increased costs of the jail. Court orders concerning crowded conditions and inadequate services mandate that increased monies be placed in jail operations. Local bond issues for jail construction generally meet resistance from a tax-weary public. But even with the construction of a new and larger jail, the new jail is usually crowded and in danger of another court order by the time it receives its first inmates.

Violence

Violence, especially in large facilities, is a way of life in the jail. Overcrowding and idleness among heterogeneous populations provide an ideal setting for a lawless society in which the strong take advantage of the weak. Physical assaults, including sexual rapes, are more frequent, but mass disturbances sometimes erupt among jail populations.

The accounts of physical assaults in jail are legion. In one such account, Clifford Spears had been reassigned to a cell in one of the tanks in the Los Angeles jail reserved for inmates who were labeled assault risks. The Crips, a street gang from Los Angeles, controlled this row of 26 cells. They had decided the day before to extort $5 a week from any non-Crips assigned to the row. Spears, 24, had only a month left on a 6-month sentence for petty theft and battery. A physically large person, he just wanted to be left alone. That is what he told a Crips gang member who approached him within minutes of his arrival on the tier. "Sodbuster," the gang member yelled, invoking a term used for nonmembers; then, he struck Spears in the face with his fist. Spears was killed in the beating that lasted for ten to twenty minutes and was undetected by the deputy stationed in the glass walkway running along the row.[68]

Sexual assaults in jail have been documented from time to time, with women, children, and first-offending males being the most likely victims. In the 1970s, southern rural jails gained a reputation as places where women were sexually abused by their jailers. The trial of Joan Little, who fatally stabbed jailer Clarence Alligood in the Beaufort County Jail in North Carolina, spotlighted this accusation. In her 1976 study of women in southern jails, Patsy Sims claimed that there are a thousand Joan Littles all over the south, in small county jails:

> In my interviews with more than 50 women serving time in southern jails or work-release programs, inmate after inmate repeated virtually the same stories of what happened to them, or to the woman in the next cell: the oral sex through bars; the constant intrusion of the trusties who slither in and out of the women's cells as unrestricted as the rats and roaches; the threats of "you do, or else"; the promises of "Girl, you got 30 days; we'll knock off 10 if you take care of my friend here."[69]

No recent study has documented the sexual victimization of women in jail, but there appear to be two reasons why it is unlikely that women today are being sexually exploited with the frequency that they were purported to be in the past. First, the fear of lawsuits felt by all jail staff makes predatory behavior toward female prisoners extremely risky. Second, the increased number of female drug violators is creating a population of female prisoners who tend to be more aggressive than previous female prisoners. Male jailers are more reluctant to "mess" with this increasingly aggressive jail population.

Nor have urban jails been kind to juveniles; many have been sexually and physically abused by adult prisoners. Pat Barker, an official of the Oklahoma Crime Commission, recalls his own jail experience:

> I've seen people raped, especially young kids. . . . These young boys would come in, and if they were fresh and young, the guys who run the tank and lived in the first cell, they would take these young guys if they wanted to. They would take the kid, forcibly hold him, and someone would rape him right in the rear.[70]

The sexual victimization of children, however, has dramatically decreased. The biggest reason is that fewer children are placed in jail, and those who are jailed are likely to be separated from adult prisoners.

Males, especially first-time offenders, continue to fear sexual victimization in jail. Although recent research suggests that adult male prisoners are now less likely to be raped, that prospect does remain a serious problem for some male prisoners.[71] John P. DeCecco and James R. Randolph, in a study of sexual assaults in the San Francisco jails, developed a profile of the victim and the assailant. Victims were more likely to be middle class, white, somewhat effeminate, and lacking previous jail experience. Assailants were more likely to have had previous jail experience; to be aggressively macho; to be lower class; to be black rather than Asian, Hispanic, or white; and to prefer heterosexual rather than bisexual or homosexual relations.[72]

Finally, mass disturbances, or jail riots, occasionally take place. When they do occur, the jail typically is a large, old, crowded facility with a history of violence. A good example is the Rikers Island jails in New York which saw a riot in 1990 (see Box 11-4).

PRETRIAL RELEASE PROGRAMS

Defendants who are accepted into **pretrial release** programs are spared weeks or months of notoriously poor living conditions in jails or pretrial detention centers.

Box 11-4 Prisoners Riot in N.Y.! 47 Injured

About 800 prisoners at the city's Rikers Island jails, angered by a two-day blockade of the lockup by protesting guards, rioted last night. Officials said the melee left at least 12 guards and 35 inmates injured.

The disturbance started shortly before 6:30 P.M., just before a settlement was announced in the guards' job dispute. Guards using tear gas quelled the disturbance by 9:45 P.M. and captured an inmate who had escaped briefly, jail spokeswoman Ruby Ryles said.

A captain for the Correction Department, who spoke on the condition of anonymity, told the Associated Press that the inmates had clubs and knives.

"We had to gas them," he said. "They came at us with homemade knives. They had broken up the bed frames. They were just fed up and they knew there weren't too many of us, and that we were tired."

Officials said the riot apparently resulted from prisoners' frustration over the job dispute. The guards blocked the bridge leading to Rikers Island, which is in the East River between Queens and the Bronx, so no one could enter or leave.

The protest had kept hundreds of prisoners from making court appearances and thousands of workers from going home, halted visits and food deliveries, and forced jails to handle 400 extra prisoners.

The guards, protesting the robbery and beating of a guard last week by three prisoners, were demanding measures to protect themselves from inmates.

Last night's uprising left broken pipes and windows at the jail's Otis Bantum center, where inmates barricaded themselves in 14 dormitories, Ryles said.

There were varying reports of injuries. Ryles said 35 prisoners and 12 officers were injured. Robert Leonard of the Emergency Medical Service said 20 injured guards were taken to hospitals and 26 other guards were treated on the island.

Yesterday's settlement, agreed to by Correction Commissioner Allyn Sielaff and Phil Seelig, leader of the Correction Captains Association, ended the guard's blockade.

Joseph Dike, spokesman for the Correction Captains Association, said all the union's demands had been met, but refused to give details.

Source: *Chronicle Wire Services*, 15 August, 1990. © *San Francisco Chronicle*. Reprinted by permission.

They also have the advantages of continuing their jobs, of being free to collect evidence in the community, of benefiting from the financial and emotional support of their families, and of coming into court as free citizens rather than being brought in handcuffed and in custody. Defendants accepted for pretrial release programs are also free to continue criminal activities, often with the objective of paying the expenses of trial. There is some evidence that sentencing judges are usually more reluctant to imprison defendants who stand before them as free men and women, holding a job and supporting a family, than to imprison defendants who are already in jail. (See Table 11.6 for the offense history of those released on bail.)

Field citation and station house citation are the two most widely used prebooking release programs.[73] An arresting police officer has the option of releasing on the spot

Table 11.6 FELONY DEFENDANTS RELEASED BEFORE OR DETAINED UNTIL CASE DISPOSITION, BY TYPE OF RELEASE AND THE MOST SERIOUS ARREST CHARGE, 1988

	Felony defendants in the 75 largest counties												
		Percent of defendants released before case disposition									Percent of defendants detained until case disposition		
			Financial release					Nonfinancial release					
Most serious arrest charge	Number of de-fendants	Total released	Total	Surety bond	Full cash bond	Deposit bond	Other	Total	Recogni-zance* cita-ton release	Un-secured bond	Total de-tained	Held on bail	Held without bail
All offenses	44,719	66%	31%	16%	8%	6%	1%	35%	29%	6%	34%	31%	4%
Violent offenses	9,435	59%	32%	13%	10%	8%	2%	27%	24%	3%	41%	34%	6%
Murder	580	39	32	14	10	7	1	7	6	1	61	35	26
Rape	755	55	32	12	10	9	2	22	17	5	45	41	5
Robbery	3,601	52	29	8	12	7	1	23	21	2	48	42	7
Assault	3,495	69	35	17	7	9	2	34	31	3	31	27	4
Other	1,004	66	30	15	10	4	1	36	28	8	34	30	4
Property offenses	16,114	62%	25%	13%	5%	6%	1%	37%	30%	7%	38%	34%	4%
Burglary	5,107	53	22	10	5	7	—	31	24	7	47	43	4
Theft	6,355	64	25	13	6	5	1	39	33	6	36	33	4
Other	4,653	70	29	17	5	5	2	41	32	8	30	27	3
Drug offenses	15,520	72%	36%	10%	10%	6%	1%	36%	30%	7%	28%	26%	2%
Sale/trafficking	6,109	69	37	20	13	3	1	32	28	4	31	29	2
Other	9,411	75	35	19	8	8	—	39	31	9	25	24	1
Public-order offenses	3,650	70%	31%	17%	9%	4%	1%	39%	34%	5%	30%	24%	5%
Driving-related	852	86	39	27	9	2	2	47	44	3	14	13	1
Other	2,798	66	29	14	9	4	1	37	32	5	34	28	7

Note: Data on detention-release outcome were available for 95% of all cases. Detail may not add to total because of rounding.

* Released on own recognizance.

—Less than 0.5%.

Source: Bureau of Justice Statistics Bulletin, *Pretrial Release of Felony Defendants, 1988* (Rockville, Md., U.S. Department of Justice, 1991), p. 2.

in field citation any person being charged with a misdemeanor who does not demand to be taken before a magistrate. The date of the initial hearing usually must be set within five days following the arrest. Station house citation, the other type of prebooking release, takes place after a police officer has transported a person arrested on a misdemeanor to a police station, where the information provided by the arrested person is verified. Station house release permits a police officer to make a decision on the basis of valid information and avoids prearraignment custody or detention for the defendant.

The California Citation Release law allows both means of prebooking release. The statute, which applies only to misdemeanant offenses, allows officers some freedom in assessing a suspect's eligibility. If an officer decides not to write a citation, the suspect is taken to a detention facility and booked. However, the statute requires the police department to conduct a background investigation of any misdemeanant who is not given a citation release. If the investigation is favorable, the suspect must be given a station house release.

Several options exist for postbooking release. The most widely used types are **Release on Own Recognizance (ROR)**, unsecured bail, percentage bail, and supervised release. In ROR, defendants are put on their own honor to report when scheduled. Arrestees are first interviewed by an ROR staff member, who gathers and verifies data about each defendant. If a defendant scores the required number of verified points, as determined by established criteria, he or she is recommended for ROR. (See Figure 11.4 for the pretrial release criteria used in the judicial districts of Iowa.) The defendant is released, after signing a promise to keep all appearances, provided that the presiding judge of the criminal court agrees with the recommendation and the district attorney decides not to contest it in court.

Unsecured bail allows release without a deposit or bail arranged through a bondsman. It differs from ROR in that the defendant is obligated to pay an established fee upon default, but, because the full bond amount is rarely collected, the program is basically the same as ROR. In percentage bail, the defendant deposits a portion of the bail amount, usually 10 percent, with the court clerk. In Illinois, where percentage bail is the most common form of pretrial release, only the defendant is permitted to execute the bond; thus, no professional bail bondsman, surety, or fidelity company can pay the bail. In Kentucky and Oregon defendants who have failed to receive ROR or conditional release have a right to be released under percentage bail, provided they can afford the deposit. The defendant is released from custody once the specified percent is paid, and when the defendant appears in court, 90 percent of the original 10 percent is refunded.

Supervised-release programs require more frequent contact with a pretrial officer, including phone calls and office interviews. Although the main purpose of supervision is to enforce the conditions imposed, the defendants are also helped with housing, finances, health problems, employment, and alcohol- or drug-related problems. Percentage bond, cash bail, or unsecured bail may also be part of supervised release; in high-risk cases, intensive supervision may be used, requiring several contacts a week with a pretrial release officer.

Home detention with electronic monitoring is also beginning to be used with pretrial defendants to relieve jail crowding. For example, such a program was established in Marion County, Indiana, in 1988. Defendants were screened for pretrial release on home detention only after they had been denied other forms of pretrial

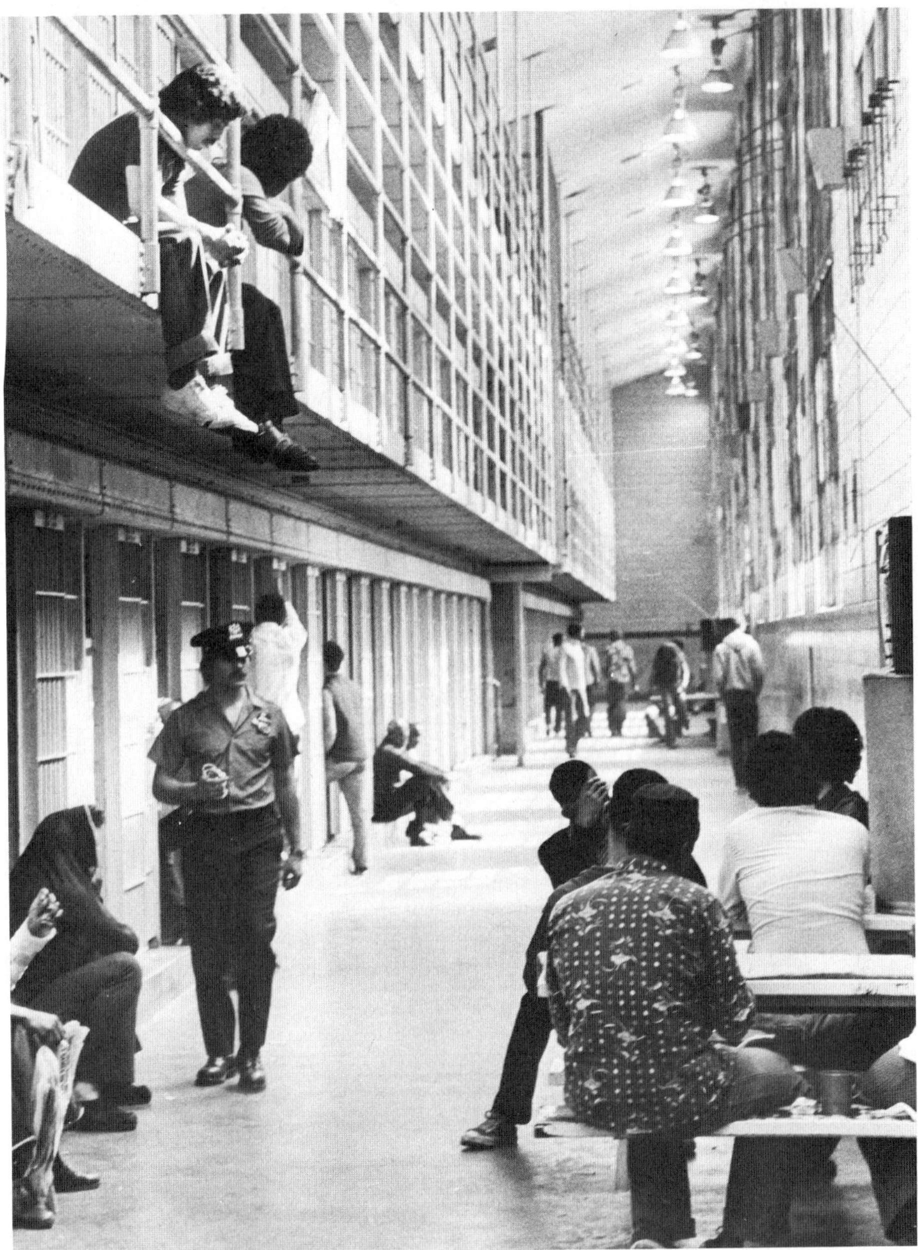

The House of Detention for Men on Rikers Island, New York City. With nearly 8,000 inmates, it is the largest correctional complex in the United States. (*Source*: Edward Hausner/NYT Pictures.)

Interviewed by________
Date____________

Interview	Verified	Residence
3	3	Present residence 1 year or more or owns dwelling.
2	2	Present residence 6 months or more or present and prior 1 year.
1	1	Present residence 3 months or more or present and prior 6 months.
0	0	Present residence 3 months or less.
		Family Ties
3	3	Lives with family (spouse or dependents).
2	2	Lives with relatives or lives w/non-family individual 1 year or more.
1	1	Lives with non-family individual.
1	1	Lives alone and has sufficient support and/or family contact in the area.
0	0	Lives alone.
		Time in Area
2	2	Five years or more continuous, recent.
		Employment / Support
4	4	Present local job 1 year or more.
3	3	Present local job 6 months or present and prior 1 year.
2	2	Social Services or Social Security income or full-time student for 6 months.
1	1	Unemployment Compensations, family support.
1	1	New student status, new job, part-time job.
0	0	Unemployed, not sufficient support.
		Alcohol/Drug Abuse
−1	−1	Present involvement.
−2	−2	Present involvement and history of abuse.
		Criminal Record
2	2	No convictions.
1	1	One simple/serious misdemeanor conviction within last 5 years.
0	0	One felony/aggravated misdemeanor or 2 simple/serious within last 5 years.
−1	−1	Two or more felony convictions or 3 or more simple/serious convictions.
−1	−1	Six months or more jail term or 3 or more jail sentences.
−2	−2	Served prison term.
		Current Offense Charge
−3	−3	Forcible felony/mandatory sentences.
−2	−2	Present on probation or parole.
−1	−1	Other criminal charges pending of aggravated misdemeanor or felony nature.
		Miscellaneous (more than one may apply)
−2	−2	Previous Pre-Trial/Probation/Parole violations.
−2	−2	Failure to appear or contempt of court charges.
−3	−3	Flight to avoid prosecution or AWOL.
		Health/Psychiatric (indicate if applicable)
______	______	____________________

Comments: ____________________

Figure 11.4 Pretrial services release criteria. (*Source*: First Judicial District, State of Iowa.)

release. Clients who were accepted into this program were fitted with a coded wristlet matching a base unit attached to their home telephone. Successes in the program whose cases had not reached disposition by the courts after 90 days typically were recommended for release on recognizance.[74]

However, a backlash among the public in terms of crimes committed by pretrial releases is reducing the popularity of pretrial release. This backlash is giving rise to a **preventive detention movement** in more and more jurisdictions across the nation. The objective of preventive detention is to retain in jail defendants who are deemed dangerous or are likely to commit crimes while awaiting trial.

The origins of this movement can be traced to a 1970 law that was passed in the District of Columbia permitting pretrial preventive detention.[75] This law cited defendant dangerousness as one criterion to be used in determining release conditions or in denying pretrial release. The Comprehensive Crime Control Act of 1984 (Bail Reform Act) also authorizes the holding of allegedly dangerous federal defendants without bail if the judge finds that no conditions of release would ensure their appearance at trial and at the same time ensure community safety.[76] The concern for public safety became so strong that by the mid-1980s well over half of the states had enacted laws reflecting the notion of preventive detention:

- Colorado, the District of Columbia, Florida, Georgia, Michigan, Nebraska, and Wisconsin excluded certain crimes from automatic bail eligibility.
- Alaska, Arizona, California, Delaware, the District of Columbia, Florida, Hawaii, Minnesota, South Carolina, South Dakota, Vermont, Virginia, and Wisconsin defined the purpose of bail to ensure appearance and safety.
- Colorado, District of Columbia, Florida, Georgia, Hawaii, Indiana, Michigan, New Mexico, Texas, Utah, and Wisconsin limited the right to bail for those previously convicted.[77]

The U.S. Supreme Court decided in favor of juvenile preventive detention in *Schall* v. *Martin* (1984),[78] and in *U.S.* v. *Salerno* (1987)[79] the Court upheld the Bail Reform Act of 1984. Yet three recent studies challenge the feasibility of preventive detention. Patrick G. Jackson, in examining pretrial detention in California jails, found that most pretrial inmates are arrested for relatively minor offenses and do not have extensive criminal histories.[80] The General Accounting Office[81] and the Bureau of Justice Statistics,[82] in evaluating the new federal pretrial detention law, concluded that this new law has resulted in (1) an increased number of detained defendants; (2) longer periods of pretrial confinement; and (3) more serious problems with jail crowding. These changes have not led to a decrease in pretrial crime.[83]

CONCLUSIONS

The typical jail is racked with many problems—overcrowding, victimization, inadequate programs, and archaic physical facilities. There is little question that the American jail is ill-equipped and ill-prepared to do its job. Or to express this in another way, the American jail remains in a state of crisis. Indeed, being jailed for the first time is a bewildering experience. Although the ideal of "innocent until proven guilty" is part of our criminal justice system, the steps involved in processing a person into jail represent a series of attacks on self-respect. After a person is placed in a cell with other prisoners, he or she may have even more humiliating experiences. First offenders often learn much in jail that has nothing to do with rehabilitation. If staff are brusque, impersonal, and uncaring, then the jail experience can create even deeper feelings of inferiority, fear, and degradation.[84]

The reform of the jail has been proposed in every generation since its inception. Local politics, or local control, seem to be one of the most serious impediments to reform. In recent years, six proposals for jail reform have been recommended. First, minimum standards for the construction and operation of jails have been developed by the Federal Prison System and the American Correctional Association. Second, seven states in recent years have enacted legislation that transfers control of local jails to state government, and many more states have established procedures for state inspection of local jails. Third, increased development of regional jails serving multiple cities or counties has been proposed. Fourth, development of diversified facilities for the jails's heterogeneous population has been suggested. Fifth, the New Generation jail and its direct supervision is becoming increasingly popular across the nation. Finally, as part of the privatization movement in corrections, some support has been given to contracting with private corporations to operate jails.

Whether these proposals or others have any effect on improving the jail will be seen in the 1990s. Until then, the jail remains one of the most inadequate institutions in American society.

KEY TERMS

direct supervision

dumping grounds for the poor

jail crowding

new generation jail

pretrial release programs

preventive detention movement

"rabble"

release on own recognizance (ROR)

DISCUSSION TOPICS

11.1 Why are jails the central institutions in criminal justice systems?

11.2 Jails have been called "brutal, filthy cesspools." Are there exceptions?

11.3 Is there such a thing as a good jail? Imagine yourself inside a good one and describe it.

11.4 Prison sentences are usually long, jail terms short. What kinds of programs can work in a jail?

ANNOTATED REFERENCES

Advisory Commission on Intergovernmental Relations. *Jails: Intergovernmental Dimensions of a Local Problem.* Washington: Advisory Commission, 1984. *Provides a good policy analysis of the local jail.*

Bolduc, A. "Jail Crowding." *Annals of the American Academy of Political and Social Science* 478, 1985: 47–57. *Examines the causes of and proposes remedies for jail crowding.*

Garofalo, James, and Richard D. Clark. "The Inmate Subculture in Jails." *Criminal Justice and Behavior* 12, December 1985: 415–434. *Examines the existence of an inmate subculture in three New Jersey jails.*

Gibbs, John H. "The First Cut Is the Deepest: Psychological Breakdown and Survival in the Detention Setting." In Robert Johnson and Hans Toch, eds., *The Pains of Imprisonment.* Beverly Hills, Calif.: Sage, 1982, pp. 97–114. *Provides useful analyses of inmate adjustment in jail.*

Goldfarb, Ronald. *Jails: The Ultimate Ghetto of the Criminal Justice System.* Garden City, N.Y.: Doubleday, 1976. *Discusses the shortcomings of the jail and its negative impact on offenders placed within.*

Irwin, John. *The Jail: Managing the Underclass in American Society.* Berkeley: University of California Press, 1985. *The underclass, or "rabble," thesis proposed in this book merits serious consideration by society's policymakers.*

Thompson, Joel A., and G. Larry Mays. *American Jails: Public Policy Issues.* Chicago: Nelson-Hall Publishers, 1991. *An excellent and up-to-date examination of the jail.*

NOTES

1. John Klofas, "Measuring Jail Use: A Comparative Analysis of Local Corrections." *Journal of Research in Crime and Delinquency* 27, August 1990: 296.
2. John Irwin, *The Jail: Managing the Underclass in American Society* (Berkeley: University of California Press, 1985).
3. John Gibbs, "The First Cut Is the Deepest: Psychological Breakdown and Survival in the Detention Setting." In Richard Johnson and Hans Toch, eds., *The Pains of Imprisonment* (Beverly Hills, Calif.: Sage, 1982), pp. 97–114.
4. N. E. Schafer, "Jails and Judicial Review: Special Problems for Local Facilities." In David Kalinich and John Klofas, eds., *Sneaking Inmates Down the Alley: Problems and Prospects in Jail Management* (Springfield, Ill.: Charles C Thomas, 1986); A. Champagne, "The Theory of Limited Judicial Impact: Reforming the Dallas Jail as a Case Study." In S. Nagel, E. Fairchild, and A. Champagne, eds., *The Politics of Criminal Justice* (Springfield, Ill.: Charles C Thomas, 1983).
5. J. Garofalo and R. Clark, "The Inmate Subculture in Jail" (*Criminal Justice and Behavior* 12, 1985), pp. 15–34.
6. L. M. Hayes, "And Darkness Closes In . . . a National Study of Jail Suicides." *Criminal Justice and Behavior* 4, 1983: 461–484; L. T. Winfree, "Toward Understanding State-Level Jail Mortality: Correlates of Death by Suicide and Natural Causes, 1977 and 1982." *Justice Quarterly* 4, 1987: 51–72.
7. Mark Pogrebin, "Scarce Resources and Jail Management." *International Journal of Offender Therapy and Comparative Criminology* 26, 1982: 263–274.
8. See A. Bolduc, "Jail Crowding." *Annals of the American Academy of Political and Social Science* 478, 1985: 47–57.
9. For a more extensive history of the jail, see J. M. Moynahan and Earle K. Stewart, "The Origin of the American Jail." *Federal Probation* 42, December 1978: 41–50.
10. Henry Burns, Jr., *Corrections: Organization and Administration* (St. Paul, Minn.: West, 1975), pp. 147–148.
11. Ibid., p. 154.
12. Moynahan and Stewart, "Origin of the American Jail," p. 45.
13. Orlando F. Lewis, *The Development of American Prisons and Prison Customs, 1776–*

1845. Reprint Series in Criminology, Law Enforcement and Social Problems, no. 1 (Montclair, N.J.: Patterson Smith, 1967), p. 278.

14. Ibid., p. 269.
15. National Commission on Law Observance and Enforcement, Report of the Advisory Committee on Penal Institutions, Probation and Parole, *Report on Penal Institutions, Probation and Parole* (Washington: Government Printing Office, 1931), p. 272.
16. Joseph C. Hutcheson, "The Local Jail," *Proceedings of the Attorney General's Conference on Crime, December 10–13, 1934* (Washington: n.d.), p. 233.
17. National Advisory Commission on Criminal Justice Standards and Goals, *Corrections* (Washington: Government Printing Office, 1973), p. 4.
18. The President's Commission on Law Enforcement and Administration of Justice, *Task Force Report: Prisoner Rehabilitation* (Washington: Government Printing Office, 1967).
19. Bureau of Justice Statistics, *Jail Inmates 1989* (Washington: U.S. Department of Justice, 1990), p. 1.
20. Bureau of Justice Statistics, *Census of Local Jails, 1988* (Washington: U.S. Department of Justice, 1991), p. VIII.
21. Ibid., p. IV.
22. The National Institute of Justice, *Jailing Drunk Drivers: Impact on the Criminal Justice System* (Washington: U.S. Department of Justice, 1984).
23. Irwin, *The Jail*, pp. 26–38.
24. Steven Spitzer, "Toward a Marxian Theory of Deviance." *Social Problems* 22, 1975: 645.
25. Gibbs, "The First Cut Is the Deepest," p. 99.
26. Ibid., p. 100.
27. Bureau of Justice Statistics, *Census of Local Jails, 1988*, p. viii.
28. Gibbs, "The First Cut Is the Deepest," p. 100.
29. Ibid.
30. Garofalo and Clark, "The Inmate Subculture in Jails," pp. 415–434.
31. Gibbs, pp. 101, 103.
32. Ibid., p. 103.
33. G. Larry Mays and Francis P. Bernat, "Jail Reform Litigation: The Issue of Rights and Remedies," *American Journal of Criminal Justice* 12, 1988: 254–273.
34. G. Larry Mays and Joel A. Thompson, "The Political and Organizational Context of American Jails." In Joel A. Thompson and G. Larry Mays, eds., *American Jails: Public Policy Issues* (Chicago: Nelson-Hall Publishers, 1991), p. 11.
35. Ibid., p. 12.
36. Advisory Commission on Intergovernmental Relations, *Jails: Intergovernmental Dimensions of a Local Problem* (Washington: Advisory Commission, 1984).
37. Ibid., p. 170.
38. Norman R. Cox, Jr., and William E. Osterhoff, "Managing the Crisis in Local Corrections: A Public-Private Partnership Approach." In *American Jails*, p. 228.
39. Ibid., p. 236.
40. Bureau of Justice Statistics, *Census of Local Jails, 1988*, p. 6.
41. National Advisory Commission on Criminal Justice Standards and Goals, *Corrections*, p. 276.
42. Michael Welch, "The Expansion of Jail Capacity: Makeshift Jails and Public Policy." In *American Jails*, p. 150.
43. John Blackmore, "Prison Architecture: Are 'Advanced Practices' Dead?" *Corrections Magazine* 4, September 1978: 48–49.
44. The Washington Crime News Services, *Jail Administration Digest* (February 1978), pp. 5–6.
45. Federal Prison System, "Metropolitan Correctional Center," n.d., pp. 1–2.
46. W. R. Nelson, "The Origins of the Popular Direct Supervision Concept: A Personal

Account." In Ken Kerle, ed., *Proceedings of the 3rd Annual Symposium on Direct Supervision Jails* (Boulder, Colo.: National Institute of Corrections Jail Center, 1988).
47. W. Raymond Nelson, *Cost Savings in New Generation Jails: The Direct Supervision Approach* (Washington: National Institute of Justice, 1988), p. 1.
48. Ibid., pp. 4–5.
49. Ibid., p. 2.
50. Todd R. Clear and George F. Cole, *American Corrections*, 2nd ed. (Pacific Grove, Calif.: Brooks/Cole, 1990), p. 226.
51. Ibid., pp. 226–227.
52. Linda L. Zupan and Ben A. Menke, "Implementing Organizational Change: From Traditional to New Generation Jail Operations." *Policy Studies Review* 7, 1988: 615–625.
53. L. L. Zupan and M. Stohr-Gillmore, "Doing Time in the New Generation Jail: Inmate Perceptions of Gains and Losses." *Policy Studies Review* 7, 1988: 626–640.
54. Interviewed in December 1978.
55. The President's Commission on Law Enforcement and the Administration of Justice, *Corrections* (Washington: Government Printing Office, 1967).
56. Hans Mattick, "The Contemporary Jails of the United States." In Daniel Glaser, ed., *Handbook of Criminology* (New York: Rand McNally, 1974), p. 785.
57. Bureau of Justice Statistics, *Census of Local Jails, 1988*, p. xii.
58. James E. Lawrence and Van Zwisohn, "AIDS in Jail." In *American Jails*, pp. 119–120.
59. H. L. Lamb and R. W. Grant, "The Mentally Ill in an Urban County Jail." *Archives of General Psychiatry* 39, 1982: 17–22.
60. For discussion of mental health services in jail, see David Kalinich, Paul Embert, and Jeffrey Senesa, "Mental Health Services for Jail Inmates: Imprecise Standards, Traditional Philosophies, and the Need for Change." In *American Jails*, pp. 79–99.
61. Christopher A. Innes, *Population Density in Local Jails, 1988* (Washington: Bureau of Justice Statistics; U.S. Department of Justice, 1990), p. 1.
62. Bureau of Justice Statistics, *Census of Local Jails, 1988*, p. 1.
63. Innes, *Population Density in Local Jails*, p. 5.
64. Bureau of Justice Statistics, *Census of Local Jails, 1988*, p. 7.
65. Clark Foundation, *Overcrowded Time: Why Our Prisons Are So Overcrowded and What Can Be Done* (New York: Edna McConnell Clark Foundation, 1982).
66. *Bell* v. *Wolfish*, 441 U.S. 520 (1979).
67. Charles Perrow, *Complex Organizations: A Critical Essay*, 3rd ed. (New York: Random House, 1986).
68. Ted Rohrlich, "Jail Inmate Dies While Rules Hold Guard 'Prisoner.' " *Los Angeles Times*, 30 April, 1983, part 2, pp. 1, 8.
69. Patsy Sims, "Women in Southern Jails." In Laura Crites, ed., *The Female Offender* (Lexington, Mass.: Heath, 1976), pp. 137–147.
70. Ben Bagdikian, "A Human Wasteland in the Name of Justice." *Washington Post*, 30 January 1972, p. A-16.
71. For this viewpoint that sexual exploitation has decreased in jail; see Irwin, *The Jail*, p. 64.
72. John P. DeCecco and James R. Randolph, "Report on the Study and Prevention of Sexual Assault in Men's Jails" (mimeographed, January 15, 1979), p. 9.
73. The materials on pretrial release programs are adapted from John J. Galvin et al., *Alternatives to Pretrial Detention* (Washington: Government Printing Office, 1977), pp. 23–30.
74. Michael G. Maxfield and Terry L. Baumer, "Home Detention with Electronic Monitoring: Comparing Pretrial and Postconviction Programs." *Crime and Delinquency* 36, October 1990: 522–528.
75. D. C. Code, Sections 23–1321 et seq.
76. Comprehensive Crime Control Act of 1984 (H.R. 5963; S. 1763).

77. Bureau of Justice Statistics, *Report to the Nation on Crime and Justice* (Washington: U.S. Department of Justice, 1988), p. 77.
78. *Schall* v. *Martin*, 1–4 D/ Vy 24–3 (1984).
79. *U.S.* v. *Salerno*, 107 S. Ct. 2095 (1987).
80. Patrick G. Jackson, "The Uses of Jail Confinement in Three Counties." *Policy Studies Review* 7, 1988: 592–606.
81. U.S. General Accounting Office, *Criminal Bail: How Bail Reform Is Working in Selected District Courts*. Subcommittee on Courts, Civil Liberties, and the Administration of Justice, Committee on the Judiciary, U.S. House of Representatives.
82. Bureau of Justice Statistics, *Pretrial Release and Detention: The Bail Reform Act of 1984* (Washington: U.S. Government Printing Office, 1988).
83. Patrick G. Jackson, "Competing Ideologies of Jail Confinement." In *American Jails*.
84. Frances O. Jansen and Ruth Johns, *Management and Supervision of Small Jails* (Springfield, Ill.: Charles C Thomas, 1978), p. xi.

Chapter 12

State and Federal Institutions

CHAPTER OUTLINE

Prisons have few friends. They have been described as dark, dingy, deteriorating, and depressive dungeons where the senses are deprived and the human spirit is destroyed by endless monotony and regimentation. Because this description is often all too accurate, dissatisfaction with prisons is widespread. Small cages, stone walls, and multitiered cellblocks make them seem oppressive and unfit for human habitation. They are also too frequently the scene of brutality, violence, and racial unrest. Furthermore, although these institutions purport to cure offenders of crime, their record in that area has not been encouraging.[1] Few would share the vision of the Reverend James Finley, chaplain at Ohio Penitentiary in 1851:

> Could we all be put on prison-fare for the space of two or three generations, the world would ultimately be the better for it. Indeed, should society change places with prisoners . . . taking to itself the regularity, temperance, and sobriety of a good prison, the goals of peace, light, and Christianity would be furthered . . . taking this world and the next together . . . the prisoner has the advantage.[2]

But of the nearly 1,100 correctional institutions in the United States, about one-fourth fit this description of an ancient, maximum security fortress. Beginning with a discussion of crowding in American prisons, this chapter examines the different types of correctional institutions, considers the variety of services that prisons offer, and evaluates prison industries and private prisons.

PRISON OVERCROWDING

When asked about his most serious problem, Orville Pung, commissioner of corrections in Minnesota, responded: "I would say that my comment would be like what you would hear anywhere in the country, and that would be overcrowding. The centerpiece of that would be the new kinds of prisoners coming into the system, primarily sex offenders and drug abusers."[3] In Box 12-1, Director Michael Quinlan adds his views on the consequences of crowding in the Bureau of Prisons. Morris Thigpen, commissioner of corrections in Alabama, further states:

> I think the most obvious problem we have is the rapid population growth that we're encountering right now. I would say that the second problem would be the budget shortfalls here in Alabama; the department of corrections is already consuming about 17 percent of the general fund budget. There's just no way that sort of growth can continue year after year.[4]

The Bureau of Justice Statistics reports that the number of prisoners under the jurisdiction of federal and state correctional authorities at year end 1989 reached a record 710,054. The states and the District of Columbia added 73,223 prisoners during the year, and the federal system added 9,243. The total increase of 82,466 inmates set a new record as it exceeded the 1982 record increase by more than 38,000. Equally significant, the total growth in the prison population since 1980 was 380,233, an increase of approximately 115 percent.[5] (See Table 12.1 for the percent change in sentenced prison population by region and state.)

Since 1980, the number of women imprisoned in this nation has nearly tripled. Women inmates numbered 40,556 at year end 1989, increasing at a faster rate during the year (24.4 percent) than males (12.5 percent).[6] Increases in the number of incarcerated women have surpassed male rates each year since 1981, and an unprecedented number of expensive prison spaces are presently being built for women.[7]

Empirical research indicates that prison crowding has an adverse effect on both institutional management and maintenance and on employee satisfaction and stress.

Box 12-1 Interview with Director J. Michael Quinlan

Question: Where is the Bureau of Prisons now in terms of construction and population? What directions or projections do you have for the future?

Answer: We have grown dramatically. The Bureau's population is currently 57,000 offenders. That is up from 24,000 in the last ten years. Right now, a total of 35,000 prison beds that have been funded by Congress are in construction. The problem is that we are operating severely crowded institutions in which there are about 70 percent more offenders than we have rated beds. The facilities are designed to hold about 33,000 prisoners, and, as I said, we have 57,000. That is 170 percent of capacity.

One of the major new initiatives that the Bureau has undertaken is the building of institutions in complexes. Although our traditional way had been to put one institution at each location, we will now be putting four institutions at one location. We are going to be building eight complexes in the next three years. These complexes will have a minimum or low security, a medium security, and a high security prison all at the same location. This will enable us to have a number of economies of scale. Staff will be able to move up the ladder without actually being transferred, which should improve morale.

Question: Now let's talk about the problems and challenges you see.

Answer: The biggest challenge is going to be continuing to get the support of the Congress and the administration in relieving the crowding crunch. That has been very successful in the past, but it needs to be emphasized continually. Our population is expected to grow to 100,000 by 1995, and from there we expect it to grow even higher. We can't lose sight of that problem. The second most important issue that I deal with and am concerned about is that as we grow from an agency of 17,000 employees to what we expect to be about 38,000, how do we maintain the same quality of staff? How do we maintain the same atmosphere, the same attitude of a "family type" agency? This is going to demand a great deal of attention and dedication on the part of our staff.

We have managed our programs, institutions, and inmates very effectively despite the crowding crunch that we've been suffering from for the past five years. I think the main reason we've been successful with classification is our ability to separate out the worst offenders at facilities like Marion. In addition, separating the gang leaders has very effectively disarmed gangs within the Federal Bureau of Prisons. We have new intelligence systems and networks that help us identify and provide early warnings of potential problems in institutions.

All of these things are in place and are working very well, so we want to continue them and improve upon them. But the main issues and the problems that we face are in the area of getting the resources to continue expansion, to relieve overcrowding, and to have a quality staff.

Source: Interviewed in June 1990.

Table 12.1 PERCENT CHANGE IN SENTENCED PRISON POPULATION FROM 1980 TO 1989, BY REGION AND STATE

	Percent increase									
Region	0–49 percent		50%–79 percent		80%–99 percent		100%–149 percent		150 percent or more	
Northeast					Vermont	80.4	Rhode Island	140.1	New Hampshire	257.7
							New York	136.7	New Jersey	249.4
							Massachusetts	130.7	Pennsylvania	162.0
							Connecticut	129.4		
							Maine	113.4		
Midwest	Iowa	44.6	Wisconsin	70.2	Indiana	94.6	Missouri	143.1	Ohio	162.0
			Nebraska	65.5			Illinois	130.4		
			Minnesota	55.1			Kansas	125.4		
							North Dakota	118.4		
							Michigan	109.9		
							South Dakota	109.7		
South	Texas	36.5	Georgia	64.6	S. Carolina	90.4	Dist. of Col.	149.0		
	W. Virginia	22.2	Tennessee	50.4	Maryland	98.9	Oklahoma	138.2		
	N. Carolina	15.5			Florida	97.7	Kentucky	131.0		
					Louisiana	94.1	Arkansas	116.6		
					Virginia	89.6	Delaware	115.0		
							Alabama	113.2		
							Mississippi	103.0		
West			Washington	57.5	Wyoming	92.1	New Mexico	138.6	California	262.5
					Montana	84.6	Idaho	126.4	Alaska	234.2
					Colorado	80.5	Oregon	112.6	Nevada	192.9
									Arizona	191.9
									Hawaii	157.4
									Utah	153.8
Regional totals			South	74.8			Midwest	111.2	West	202.8
									Northeast	155.3
U.S. summary							States	114.0		
							Federal	128.8		
							Total	115.0		

Note: Sentenced prisoners are those with sentences of more than 1 year.

Source: Bureau of Justice Statistics, *Prisoners in 1989* (Washington: U.S. Department of Justice, 1990), p. 3.

Prison crowding also promotes rule infractions by inmates, transmission of diseases, mental-health problems, and collective and interpersonal violence.[8] Moreover, prison crowding has resulted in lawsuits in many states; for example, in 1987, 36 states and the District of Columbia were under court order or involved in litigation concerning conditions of confinement in their prison systems.[9] There is little disagreement concerning the reality of crowded prisons, but sharp disagreement exists over what should be done about it.

ARCHITECTURAL DESIGNS FOR TODAY'S PRISONS

A variety of architectural designs are used in today's prisons. The early prisons, such as the Pennsylvania model, incorporated a structural design with a specific function. The architecture of these structures supposedly served the purpose of the moral reformation, or penitence, model; that is, the created space was intended to facilitate contemplation, industry, and isolation. Beginning with Jeremy Bentham's Panopticon model in the nineteenth century (see Chapter 3), institutional security or control, rather than reformation, was the basic function that architectural designs were supposed to fulfill.

The radial design, the telephone-pole design, the courtyard style, and the campus style have been the four most widely used architectural designs in American prisons. (See Figure 12.1 for these designs.) The Eastern Penitentiary, the first **radial design** and prototype of many to follow, had a control center at the hub, and the "spokes" went outward from this central core. This radial design is used in the Federal Penitentiary at Leavenworth (Kansas) and state penitentiaries at Rahway and Trenton (New Jersey). In his examination of prison architectural design, William G. Nagel found that the radial design has been used in few new prisons.[10]

The **telephone-pole design** is characterized by a long central corridor serving as the means for prisoners to go from one part of the prison to another. Jutting out from the corridor are cross-arms, containing housing, school, shops, and recreation areas. This design, the most widely used for maximum security prisons in the United States, is used at the Federal Penitentiary in Marion, Illinois, and state correctional institutions at Graterford, Pennsylvania; Somers, Connecticut; and Jackson, Georgia. One of the advantages of this design is that it is possible to house prisoners by classification levels. A major disadvantage of the telephone-pole design is that it creates a corridor that can be barricaded by militant convicts. In the event of a riot or a hostage-taking situation, it is easy for the convicts to take control and difficult for guards to take it back.

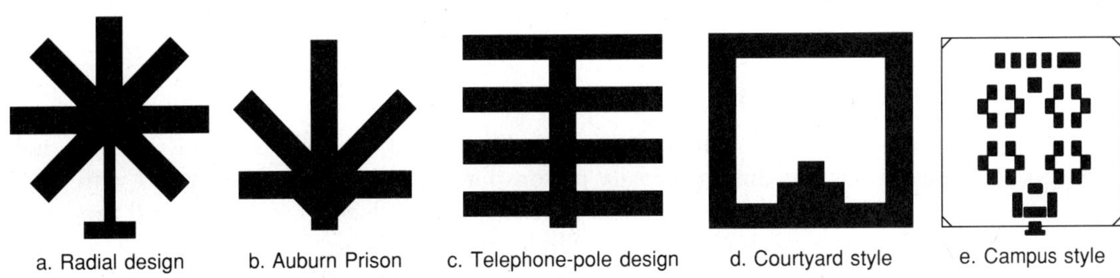

Figure 12.1 Prison designs used in the United States.

The **courtyard-style design,** which is more likely to be found in newer prisons, has a corridor surrounding the courtyard. The housing units, as well as educational, vocational, recreational, prison industry, and dining areas, also face the courtyard. The Women's Treatment Center at Purdy in Washington state has become the showplace among women's prisons. It is built around multilevel and beautifully landscaped courtyards, and the attractive buildings provided security without fences, until a number of escapes in the mid-1970s caused a greater emphasis on security, resulting in the construction of eight-foot fences. Small housing units with pleasant living rooms imply that the women will behave like human beings and, therefore, should be treated as such. The education, recreation, and training areas are ample and roomy. A short distance from the other buildings are attractive apartments, each containing a living room, kitchen, dining space, two bedrooms, and a bath; these apartments are occupied by women approaching release who work or attend school in a nearby city. Significantly, these apartments are normally off limits to staff except by invitation.[11]

The **campus design,** contained in minimum security and a few maximum security prisons, has become an architectural design used to depict openness and freedom of movement. Smaller housing units are scattered among the other educational, vocational, recreational, and dining units of the prison. Women's prisons frequently use the campus design, with living units in cottages scattered around the institutional grounds. Minimum security men's prisons at Vienna in Illinois and Leesburg in New Jersey are built around an open courtyard with a campuslike plan. The campuslike design is especially found in showplace institutions that allow more generous visiting policies, have more frequent furloughs, offer better services and programs, and provide a safer environment for both staff and inmates.

TYPES OF CORRECTIONAL INSTITUTIONS

Men's prisons are designated as maximum, medium, and minimum security facilities. Women's prisons usually incorporate all levels of security in the same facility. Co-correctional, or coeducational, institutions and boot camps are other forms of adult institutions.

There are presently 64 federal and 521 state prisons in the United States. The average prison in this nation is medium security, has fewer than 500 inmates, has been built since 1925, and houses male prisoners (see Table 12.2). But what these figures do not tell is the serious problem with crowding in today's prisons, the violence that plagues prison life, the increasing minority status of prisoner populations, and the deteriorating conditions of many prison facilities.[12]

Maximum Security Prisons for Men

Designated by such names as reformatories, correctional centers, penitentiaries, and state prisons, **maximum security prisons** for men have been bombarded with criticism, much of it deserved. Ancient, large, rurally located fortresses still predominate. Like the pyramids, they were built to stand forever: Thick stone walls, massive gates, tall gun towers, and steel doors bear testimony to their permanence. Their age and the years of shoddy maintenance have resulted in dilapidated conditions, but the

Table 12.2 CHARACTERISTICS OF STATE PRISONS

Characteristics	Percentage of prisons	Percentage of inmates
Total	100	100
Region		
Northeast	15	17
Midwest	20	20
South	48	44
West	17	19
Size		
Fewer than 500 inmates	65	22
500–1,000	20	27
More than 1,000	15	51
Custody level		
Maximum security	25	44
Medium security	39	44
Minimum security	35	12
Sex of inmates housed		
All male	88	91
All female	7	3
Co-ed	5	5
Age of facility		
Over 100 years	5	12
50–99 years	16	23
25–49 years	22	18
15–24 years	14	13
5–14 years	23	20
5 years or less	20	15

Note: Totals may not add up to 100 percent because of rounding.

Source: U.S. Department of Justice, Bureau of Justice Statistics, *Report to the Nation on Crime and Justice* (Washington: Government Printing Office, 1988), p. 107.

crowding of prisons, the need for maximum security facilities, and the costliness of building new fortresslike prisons make it unlikely that many of these institutions will be replaced in the near future.

The deficiencies of the old fortresses from the standpoint of economy in management and safety of personnel and prisoners also mandate that they be replaced as soon as possible. For example, if manned 24 hours a day, each tower will cost about $100,000 a year to maintain. Most of these nineteenth-century prisons were built without any thought to economy: The builders seemed to think that the more gun towers were installed, the better.

Most maximum security prisons are large physical plants, housing 44 percent of all state prisoners. The State Prison of Southern Michigan at Jackson has held as many as 6,500 prisoners; San Quentin State Prison in California, Stateville Correctional Center in Illinois, and the Ohio Penitentiary in Columbus have each held more than 4,000 inmates in the recent past. The Florida State Prison in Raiford and the Missouri Penitentiary in Jefferson City have each housed more than 3,000

The Bastille by the Bay, San Quentin Correctional Center. (*Source*: State of California, Department of Corrections.)

prisoners. The prison at Jackson is so big that more than 57 acres are enclosed within its walls.

Reformatories As previously noted, **reformatories** were created by prison reformers in the late nineteenth century. They presently are used to imprison 18- to 30-year-old male offenders. Some reformatories, such as the Ohio State Reformatory in Mansfield and the Kansas State Reformatory, have kept the old name, while others, such as the Pontiac Correctional Center in Illinois, use new titles. Euphemisms, however, do not change old realities.

Both the Ohio State Reformatory and the Pontiac Correctional Center are notorious. The Ohio State Reformatory, which receives young offenders from Cleveland and other northern Ohio urban centers, has long needed demolition. When one of the co-authors last visited Mansfield, the stench of decaying foodstuffs from the kitchen was overpowering; one hopes that the kitchen has been sanitized since then. The cells at Mansfield are the smallest this co-author has ever seen, and still inmates were double celled. Mansfield also has long had a reputation for violence.[13] An ex-offender who is now working in community-based corrections put it this way: "Mansfield is pandemonium. The conditions there and the overcrowding are awful. I felt I was in an overcrowded zoo."[14] Loud, clanging steel doors and dark cellblocks make Mansfield a forbidding place even to the visitor.

Pontiac is also a difficult institution in which to do time, especially for the white inmate, for this 80 percent black facility has for some time been controlled internally by Chicago gangs. Wardens have tried different strategies to make the institution manageable; in the early 1970s, Warden John Petrilli attempted to bring the prison under control by dividing it into functional units and by making gang leaders responsible for the behavior of their members.[15] One of the co-authors visited Pontiac a few days before the gang takeover. He has never seen such a complacent staff. They *knew* that they had the gangs where they wanted them. In fact, they said, all the hysteria about gangs was just that—hysteria.

Pontiac wardens in the mid- and late 1970s adopted other strategies to keep the lid on this facility, but in July 1978, three officers were killed and three others seriously wounded in an inmate takeover. As a result, the institution was on lockup for several months, and it took a court order to end it. In the 1980s, no more successful than their predecessors, a series of wardens attempted to regain control of the institution from inmate gangs.

State Penitentiaries The nation is slowly emerging from its reliance on costly old fortresses for the control of maximum custody convicts. The history of these dreadful places is studded with needless tragedies. The most famous of these prisons was Alcatraz, situated on an island in San Francisco Bay, facing the Golden Gate Bridge. It was escape-proof; escapes were tried, but no one ever succeeded. Like all such facilities, it was dangerous. In 1946 there was a riot in which the convicts managed to take over the prison briefly. It was reclaimed a day or so later, at the cost of much bloodshed and several fatalities. It housed about 250 prisoners, and the cost of maintenance was so prohibitive that it was decommissioned and converted into a tourist attraction in the 1960s.

Not far from Alcatraz is the California State Prison at San Quentin. For years it was the main maximum custody prison in California. It was famous for the benign

Interior of West Cellhouse, Illinois State Penitentiary, Pontiac, Illinois. (Illinois Department of Corrections)

regime of Warden Clinton Duffy. Long after his departure, it became the focus for radical intervention. A militant faction of blacks was encouraged by far-left lawyers and intellectuals to rebel against the prison administration. The argument of the rebels was that blacks and Hispanics were political prisoners, not criminals in any sense that a progressive society should recognize. Both guards and prisoners were killed in the successive insurrections of the 1970s. The movement that supported this ideology lost its momentum after a horrifying incident in which a judge was abducted at gunpoint in his courtroom while hearing the trial of accused perpetrators of the murders that climaxed in the San Quentin rebellion. While being taken in a truck to an unknown destination, he was shot and killed. Since that time, San Quentin has been relatively quiet, although far from free of violence.

Many other prisons have been the scenes of disasters. Outrageously incompetent management led to the infamous riot of 1971 at the Attica Correctional Facility in New York in which 43 guards and prisoners lost their lives. In 1980, there was a riot at the Penitentiary of New Mexico at Santa Fe in which 33 prisoners were killed and 12 officers were held hostage and subjected to abuse and severe treatment. The immediate cost of the riot to the state was $4.5 million for travel and out-of-state housing for the prisoners; this was followed by the expenditure of $35 million for reconstruction of the penitentiary and increased salaries for staff. An investigation of the causes of the riot concluded that the prison had been understaffed by poorly paid and untrained personnel for years. One observer commented before the event that a riot was inevitable, given the incompetence that prevailed in the prison.[16]

But the Pelican Bay State Prison located near Crescent City, California, and the Oak Park Heights Correctional Facility in Stillwater, Minnesota, do not deserve association with these dungeonlike facilities. The Pelican Bay State Prison includes a 200-bed minimum security complex; two 512-bed maximum security (Level IV), general population facilities; and a 1,056-bed security housing unit (SHU). A Prison Industry Authority manufacturing facility and an advanced $11.6 million tertiary wastewater treatment plan are other elements of the project. The Pelican Bay project utilized the fast-track method of construction. There were nine separate construction packages, ranging in cost from $2.2 million to $50.2 million. Inmate occupancy of the prison began in December 1989.[17] (See Figure 12.2 for other prisons in California that are new and under construction.)

The design of the Oak Park Heights Facility incorporated advanced architectural concepts and technology into its security, correctional living environment, and energy conservation construction. Completed in the early 1980s, this three-story facility has some walls below ground level, with living space looking out on a sunken central courtyard. This design gives an impression of openness while ensuring a secure institution. The design saves energy, as it is below ground and has a heat-reclaiming unit. Another key concept of this innovative facility is that freedom of movement will decrease as an inmate approaches the institution's outer boundaries. This restricted movement at the security perimeters makes it possible to minimize the degree of guard tower surveillance necessary and thereby reduce costs.[18]

The facility is located on a 160-acre site that includes a 60-acre secured area within its fenced perimeter. The land occupied by the 330,000-square-foot building and the area it encircles is slightly more than 8 acres. The institution's housing units are staggered along the building's exposed wall, which encircles both the main yard and smaller, separate athletic courts adjacent to each unit. In 1987 an addition was

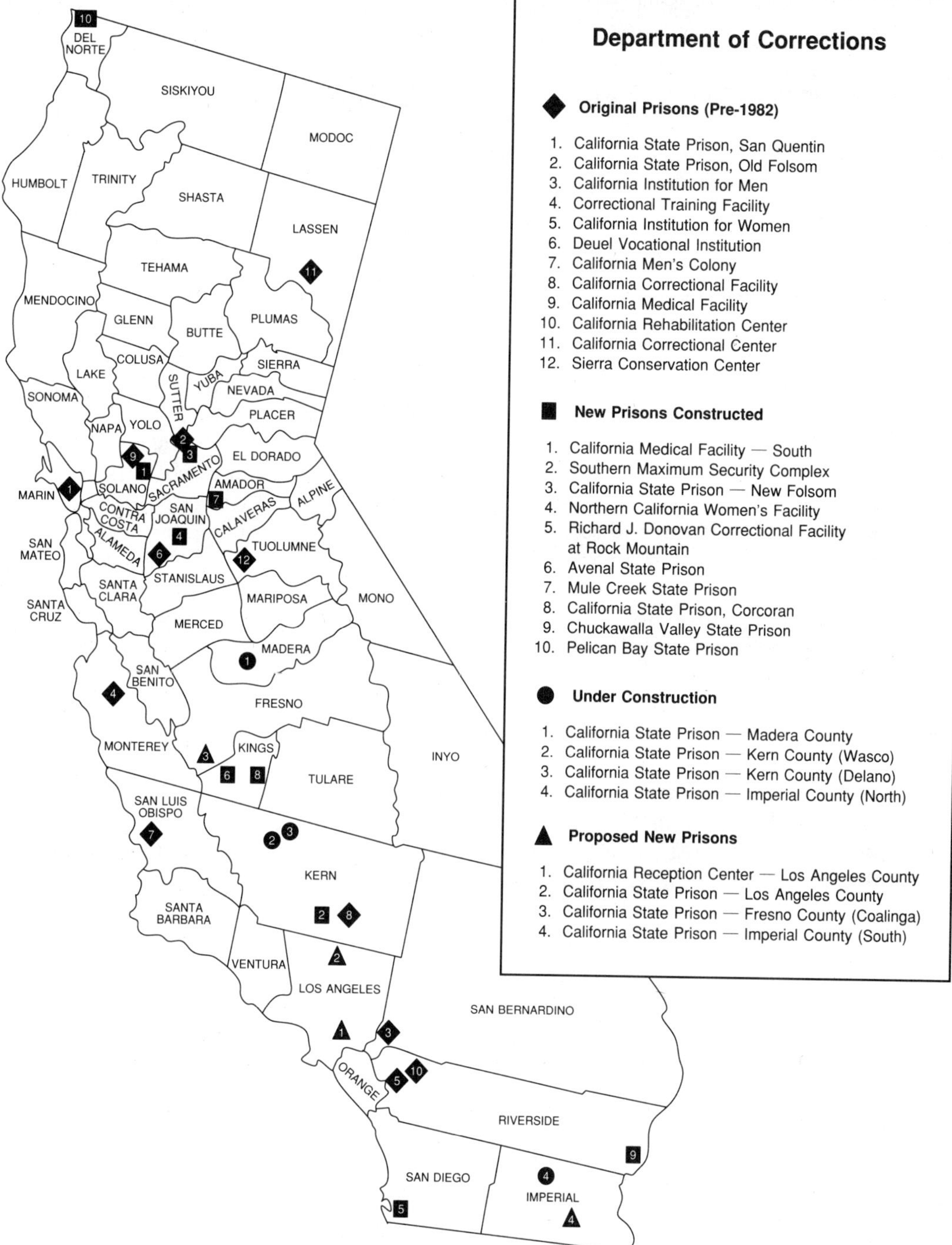

Figure 12.2 California state prisons. (*Source*: Brochure of the Pelican Bay State Prison, June 14, 1990.)

completed, adding 25,000 square feet, which included industry and commissary warehouses, vehicle storage, and an indoor firearms range. This addition increased the total square footage of the facility to 355,000. The 400-bed earth-sheltered facility consists of eight attached complexes with housing on the lower two levels and industry/program space above. Arranged in a U-shape built into a hillside, the complexes are connected by two traffic corridors on separate levels: one corridor primarily for staff traffic, the other corridor for routine inmate and staff traffic.[19]

Medium and Minimum Security Prisons

There are some major distinctions between maximum and medium security prisons. The assumption underlying maximum security design is that the physical characteristics of the prison will be such that complete control of any and all prisoners can be realized at any time. Whether so many prisoners require this degree of control is irrelevant; this is the governing principle of maximum security. In **medium security prisons,** the emphasis is, or should be, on controlled access to programs. Prisoners assigned to medium custody are under a lot of control and can be locked down in emergencies, but it is expected that they will be in industrial or educational activities. Many maximum security prisons—perhaps most of them—are in reality medium custody facilities with units provided for housing those who cannot be allowed any freedom of movement. In effect, we are moving away from the old dungeon thinking, providing for the programmed prison that allows for a good deal of freedom of movement within a technologically secured perimeter. Oak Park Heights is an excellent example of this kind of planning. In this regard, sensors on the fences at Oak Park Heights warn the central control room of any approach to the fence so that officers can be dispatched to apprehend anybody thinking of escape.

Medium security prisons typically have single or double fencing, guarded towers or closed-circuit television monitoring, sally port entrances, and control of inmate movement within the institution by zonal security systems. **Minimum security prisons,** in contrast, frequently have far more relaxed perimeter security, sometimes without fences or any means of external security.

Medium and minimum security prisons for men that have abandoned the old fortress-type structure include Leesburg in New Jersey, Allenwood (a federal institution) in Pennsylvania, Fox Lake in Wisconsin, Jean in Nevada, and Vienna in Illinois. They all demonstrate that a more humane philosophy of imprisonment is possible. Openness sets these facilities apart from other prisons. Jean resembles a condominium, and Vienna and Leesburg are built around an open courtyard with a campuslike plan.

The Vienna Correctional Center in Illinois is probably the most innovative correctional facility in the country. No riots and few escapes have occurred in its nearly 20-year history. Even more surprisingly, Vienna offers a variety of exciting community-based and institutional programs. Inmates provide around-the-clock emergency paramedical care to surrounding counties, teach cardiopulmonary resuscitation to local citizens, act as umpires at Little League games on a baseball field they built and maintain, and assist firefighters in nearby communities with labor and a fire truck. Southern Illinois University and Shawnee Community College have offered vocational and educational courses at the prison; these are also open to citizens of nearby communities. Local high schools, too, have started to use the prison recreational and vocational equipment. Most important, the residents are quite involved in both institution- and community-based programs.

Prisons for Women

The first prison for women in the United States was not opened until 1863, but by the 1960s there were 29 separate institutions for women. South Carolina, Florida, and Michigan are among the states that have recently constructed new **women's prisons.** (See Table 12.3 for the number of state and federal correctional institutions for women.) By the 1990s, the number of women sentenced to prison had increased in most states, with the result that women's prisons began to be crowded.[20]

Ruth M. Glick and Virginia V. Neto, in the summary report of the National Study of Women's Correctional Programs, described four different architectural designs among the 16 women's prisons that were included in the survey: the complex, the campus, the single building, and the cottage. The complex design of several buildings clustered around a central administration building is used at Goree Unit (Texas), Bedford Hills (New York), the Minnesota Correctional Institution for Women, and the Nebraska State Center for Women. The single-building design, in which one major building houses all functions of the prison, is found at the Georgia Rehabilitation Center for Women and the Colorado Women's Correctional Center. The campus design is used at the Purdy Treatment Center for Women (Washington), the California Institution for Women, the Florida Correctional Institution, the North Carolina Correctional Center for Women, and the Massachusetts Correctional Institution (Framingham). The Detroit House of Corrections uses the cottage design, which consists of self-sufficient living units.[21]

Some states also house women on the grounds of prisons for men, just off the main area of the institution, or in county institutions where the states have contracted for space. Fifteen states place women only in open institutions, while six states do confine women in maximum security facilities.[22] The female prisoner, thus, may be housed in a variety of settings, but instead of being sent to the most appropriate institution, she goes to whatever the state has available.

Glick and Neto evaluated their national sample in terms of physical adequacy (actual physical dimensions and state of repair), normalization (the quality of the living/working environment in which staff and residents interact with each other), and the degree of autonomy (the amount of freedom inmates have within the institution). Purdy in Washington and Vienna in Illinois—both coeducational at the time of the study—are the only two institutions that were ranked as excellent or very high in all three categories. Women's prisons in Texas, Indiana, and Georgia were ranked low in two of the three categories, and those in Michigan and North Carolina were ranked low in all three categories.[23]

Women's prisons are generally smaller, more attractive physically, and more homelike than men's prisons. Some have fewer recreational programs and facilities than do men's prisons, while other women's prisons are almost overprogrammed. For example, the California Institution for Women had so many programs that some women complained that they did not have time to do their time. The real difficulty in programming women's prisons is the traditional assumption that a paroled woman is limited to factory work in textiles, cosmetology, and typing. Women's institutions

Table 12.3 STATE AND FEDERAL CORRECTIONAL INSTITUTIONS FOR WOMAN, 1873–1975

State	Title at opening	Date of opening
Indiana	Woman's Prison	1873
Massachusetts	Reformatory Prison for Women	1877
New York	House of Refuge for Women, Hudson	1887
New York	House of Refuge for Women, Albion	1893
New York	Reformatory Prison for Women, Bedford Hills	1902
New Jersey	State Reformatory for Women	1913
Maine	Reformatory for Women	1916
Ohio	Reformatory for Women	1916
Kansas	State Industrial Farm for Women	1917
Michigan	State Training School for Women	1917
Connecticut	State Farm for Women	1918
Iowa	Women's Reformatory	1918
Arkansas	State Farm for Women	1920
California	Industrial Farm for Women	1920
Minnesota	State Reformatory for Women	1920
Nebraska	State Reformatory for Women	1920
Pennsylvania	State Industrial Home for Women	1920
Wisconsin	Industrial Home for Women	1921
United States	Industrial Institution for Women (now Federal Reformatory for Women)	1927
Delaware	Correctional Institution for Women	1929
Connecticut	Correctional Institution for Women	1930
Illinois	State Reformatory for Women	1930
Virginia	State Industrial Farm for Women	1932
North Carolina	Correctional Center for Women	1934
California	California Institution for Women	1936
Kentucky	Correctional Institution for Women	1938
South Carolina	Harbison Correctional Institution for Women	1938
Maryland	Correctional Institution for Women	1940
Alabama	Julia Tutwiler Prison for Women	1942
West Virginia	State Prison for Women	1948
Puerto Rico	Industrial School for Women	1954
Georgia	Rehabilitation Center for Women	1957
Missouri	State Correctional Center for Women	1960
Louisiana	Correctional Institute for Women	1961
Ohio	Women's Correctional Institution	1963
Nevada	Women's Correctional Center	1964
Oregon	Women's Correctional Center	1965
Tennessee	Prison for Women	1966
Colorado	Women's Correctional Institute	1968
Washington	Purdy Treatment Center for Women	1970
Oklahoma	Women's Treatment Facility	1973
South Carolina	Women's Correctional Center	1973

Source: Estelle B. Freedman, *Their Sisters' Keepers: Women's Prison Reform in America, 1830–1930,* (Ann Arbor: University of Michigan Press, 1981), p. 302. Reprinted by permission.

that are attached to or are satellites of men's institutions typically are more security oriented than those that are not. Moreover, the staff–inmate ratio of women's prisons is normally higher than in men's prisons, and the staff is more sexually mixed than in men's prisons. Finally, inmates in treatment-oriented institutions tend to be less negative toward staff than those in custody-oriented institutions.

Co-correctional or Coeducational Institutions

The first **coeducational institutions,** known among corrections practitioners as co-correctional, opened in 1971. There are presently nine coed adult correctional institutions: Chittenden Community Correctional Center (Vermont); Correctional Institution for Women (New Jersey); Deberry Correctional Institution (Tennessee); Federal Correctional Institution at Lexington (Kentucky); Federal Correctional Institution at Pleasanton (California); Maine Correctional Center; Muncy State Correctional Institution (Pennsylvania); North Idaho Correctional Institution; and Renz Correctional Center (Missouri).[24] (See Table 12.4 for institutions that were formerly co-correctional but are no longer.)

Correctional officials have not publicized this innovation because of the perceived low tolerance by the public for heterosexual contact among prisoners behind the walls. These institutions have emerged as a pragmatic way of housing the increasing numbers of women being sent to prison.

John Smykla, who has done extensive research on coed prisons, summarizes the generally agreed-upon advantages of the coed facility: (1) It creates a more normal environment and reduces some of the pain of imprisonment; (2) predatory homosexuality is reduced, assaultive behavior is lessened, and inmate interest is diverted; and (3) the adjustment problems that inmates experience upon return to the community are reduced.[25] A study of the coeducational institutions at Fort Worth (Texas)

Table 12.4 COEDUCATIONAL CORRECTIONAL INSTITUTIONS

Institution	Location	Implementation date
*FYC–Morgantown	Morgantown, West Virginia	July 1971
**FCI–Fort Worth	Forth Worth, Texas	November 1971
Muncy State Correctional Institution	Muncy, Pennsylvania	December 1971
Massachusetts Correctional Institution	Framingham, Massachusetts	March 1973
FCI–Lexington	Lexington, Kentucky	February 1974
*Dwight Correctional Center	Dwight, Illinois	May 1974
*Vienna Correctional Center	Vienna, Illinois	May 1974
**FCI–Pleasanton	Pleasanton, California	July 1974
Correctional Institution for Women	Clinton, New Jersey	August 1974
*Claymont Institution for Women	Claymont, Delaware	October 1974
*Metropolitan Training Center	Circle Pines, Minnesota	March 1975
*FCI–Terminal Island	Terminal Island, California	March 1975
**Taycheedah Correctional Institution	Taycheedah, Wisconsin	July 1975
*Connecticut Correctional Institution	Niantic, Connecticut	September 1975
Renz Correctional Center	Cedar City, Missouri	September 1975
Chittendon Community Correctional Center	South Burlington, Vermont	January 1976
Maine Correctional Center	South Windham, Maine	April 1976
North Idaho Correctional Institution	Cottonwood, Idaho	May 1976
**Memphis Correctional Center	Memphis, Tennessee	April 1977
**Westville Correctional Center	Westville, Indiana	August 1977

* Phased out prior to 1978.

** Phased out after 1978.

Source: John Smykla, "The Impact of Co-correctionals." In S. E. Zimmerman and H. D. Miller, eds., *Corrections at the Crossroads* (Beverly Hills, Calif.: Sage, 1981), p. 112. Reprinted by permission of Sage Publications, Inc.

and Morgantown (West Virginia) found that personal hygiene seemed to be better, inmates learned or relearned appropriate behavior in the presence of the opposite sex, both sexes seemed to develop healthy relationships, and inmates' self-esteem appeared to improve.[26] One satisfied warden put it this way: "It's a place safe for inmates who couldn't survive in other institutions."[27]

Sexual activity and increased costs seem to be the greatest disadvantages of the coed prison. Surveillance to prevent sexual activity takes a great deal of correctional officers' time, but unwanted pregnancies create embarrassment for the department, and they obviously are not well received by spouses on the outside. Increased cost enters the picture because most coed facilities require larger staffs than do unisexual institutions.

Boot Camps

In several states, correctional **boot camps**, styled after the military model for basic training, are being used as an alternative to prison in order to deal with the problem of prison crowding and public demands for severe treatment.[28] Participants are primarily young, nonviolent, and first-time male offenders. In Dale Parent's survey of existing boot camp programs, he found the typical pattern to be the use of strict discipline, physical training, drill and ceremony, military bearing and courtesy, physical labor, and summary punishment for minor violations of rules.[29]

By the end of 1989, boot camps—also known as shock incarceration—were operating in one county (Orleans Parish, Louisiana) and in 17 states. Eighteen other states were either planning or considering such programs (see Figure 12.3). Moreover, in the summer of 1989, the boot camp model was put forth by the House Crime Subcommittee chairman as a national strategy for treating drug abusers.[30]

William Raspberry wrote of the Louisiana boot camp that "the idea [is] to turn a score of lawbreakers into disciplined, authority-respecting men."[31] He quoted the warden: "[W]e're giving an inmate a chance to get out of prison in 90 days instead of seven years. But you're making him work for it. . . . We keep them busy from the time they wake up until they fall asleep with chores that include such sillinesses as cleaning latrines with a toothbrush."[32] Douglas Martin, in a similar vein, wrote about the New York program:

> Days are 16 hours long, and two-mile runs and calisthenics on cold asphalt are daily staples. Work is chopping down trees or worse. The discipline recalls Parris Island [the Marine base]. . . . Those who err may be given what is genteely termed "a learning experience," something like carrying large logs around with them everywhere they go or, perhaps, wearing baby bottles around their necks.[33]

Doris Layton MacKenzie, a highly respected researcher on boot camps, draws the following conclusions:

> There is some evidence that the boot camp experience may be more positive than incarceration in traditional prison.

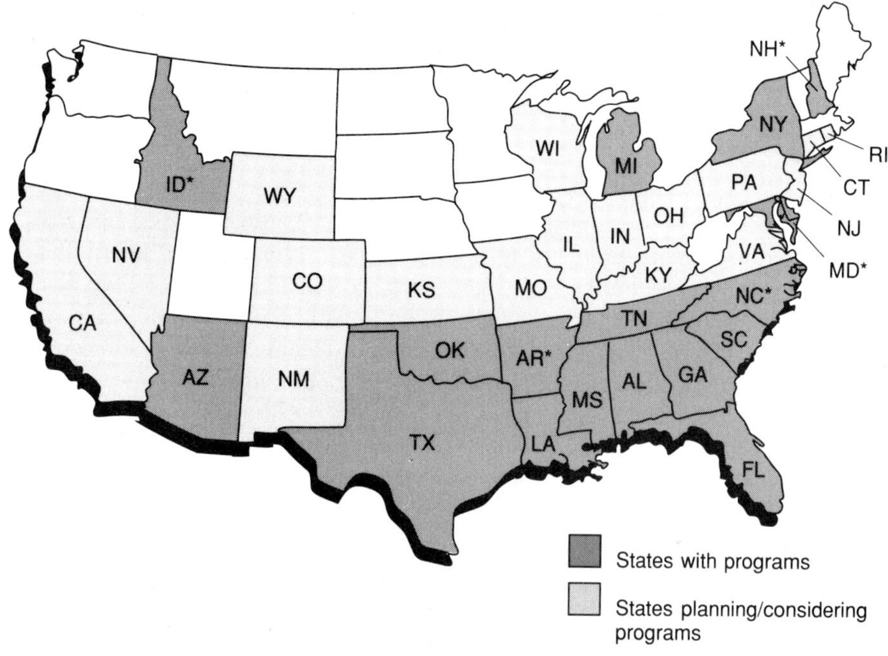

Figure 12.3 Shock Incarceration Programs in the United States, July 1990. (*Source*: Doris L. MacKenzie, " 'Book Camp' Programs Grown in Number and Scope," *National Institute of Justice/Research in Action* 222, November–December, 1990, p. 7.)

There is no evidence that those who complete boot camp programs are angrier or negatively affected by the programs.

Those who complete shock programs report having a difficult but constructive experience. Similar offenders who serve their sentences in a traditional prison do not view their experience as constructive.

Boot camp recidivism rates are approximately the same as those of comparison groups who serve a longer period of time in a traditional prison or who serve time on probation.

Success may be contingent on the emphasis on rehabilitation—giving offenders the training, treatment, and education needed to support new behavior—during incarceration and on aftercare during community supervision.[34]

Yet there are a number of disturbing issues raised about this new approach to correcting offenders. First, the journalistic accounts of boot camp celebrate a popular image of a dehumanizing experience marked by hard and often meaningless physical labor. The inmate is portrayed as deficient and requires something akin to being clubbed over the head to become "a man." This imagery is particularly troubling when it is remembered that the inmates are disproportionately minorities and members of the underclass. Second, why would an approach developed to prepare people to go into war be considered to have such potential in deterring or rehabilitating offenders? Third, why is the emphasis on unquestioned obedience to authority and aggression consistent with prosocial behavior?[35]

TREATMENT PROGRAMS

Treatment technologies, self-help programs, and service programs are the three expressions of treatment that take place within correctional institutions.

Treatment Modalities

The rehabilitation model brought therapy into the program. Supporters wanted to turn the prison into a hospital and to treat the "disease" of criminality. Even with the present debunking of treatment, prison administrators are aware that increasing numbers of inmates have mental-health problems and need appropriate therapy programs. Transactional analysis (TA), reality therapy, behavior modification, drug and alcohol counseling, and skill development are the most widely used **treatment modalities.**

Transactional Analysis (TA) Based on interpreting and evaluating relationships among people, **transactional analysis** (TA) has generated interest because offenders, like their counterparts outside, can see its immediate value. TA uses catchy language to promise people who feel "not OK" that several easy steps can make them feel "OK."

The TA leader and the inmate usually first do a "script analysis" in which they estimate the effect that negative "tapes" have on the offender's present behavior. The TA leader's role is to teach offenders to change their negative, or self-defeating, tapes and to assure them that it is possible to become winners and to attain their life goals. If the offender decides to negotiate a treatment contract with both short- and long-range goals, treatment begins.

Once offenders become part of a TA group, they are taught that they act according to three roles in dealing with others: the "child," "parent," and "adult" roles. The goal is to help each offender use the adult ego state more frequently and to turn off the "not OK" feelings buried in the childhood tape.[36] Offenders undergoing TA also learn that four life positions describe the judgments they make about themselves and others: "I'm OK—You're OK," "I'm not OK—You're OK," "I'm not OK—You're not OK," and "I'm OK—You're not OK."[37] Furthermore, offenders learn that people play games to protect themselves from knowing themselves and, therefore, from growing up.

TA has several advantages for adult offenders, for it is easy to learn, offers hope, and provides a future job possibility for inmates who become highly skilled in its use. Administrators also profit because TA serves to reduce disciplinary problems in units where it is used. TA works less well for those offenders who are not motivated to examine their own problems, who are evading personal change, and who have serious behavior problems. Adults with borderline intelligence, with sociopathic tendencies, and with immature personalities also tend not to profit from this modality. But overall, TA remains one of the most promising of the treatment modalities used in prison.

Reality Therapy William Glasser and G. L. Harrington, two Los Angeles psychiatrists, developed reality therapy, which assumes that all persons have basic needs and act irresponsibly when they are unable to fulfill those needs. The basic human needs are relatedness and respect; they are satisfied by actions that are realistic, responsible, and right—the three R's of **reality therapy.**[38] Three steps are involved in reality therapy. The inmate is expected to form an honest and real relationship with the therapist. The therapist must then demonstrate that the inmate is accepted but his or her irresponsible behavior is not. Finally, the therapist teaches the inmate better ways to fulfill his or her needs within the current situation.

Although there is no empirical evidence to demonstrate the effectiveness of reality therapy in prison, it has been well received in some adult institutions, such as Rentz in Missouri, because its emphasis on behavior makes sense to those inmates and staff who are turned off by insight therapy. Staff members also like the authority and power this treatment modality gives them. However, critics have charged that reality therapy is an oversimplification of human behavior, that it is not always wise to ignore the past, and that it can lead to paternalistic and authoritarian attitudes on the part of the therapist.

Behavior Modification Behavior modification, which is basically a learning theory applied to problems of behavior, assumes that behaviors that are rewarded positively, immediately, and systematically will increase. But if certain behaviors are not reinforced, their frequency will decrease. **Behavior modification,** sometimes called behavior therapy or contingency management, uses a variety of techniques to reinforce positive and extinguish negative behaviors. Systematic desensitization, extinction of undesirable responses, and counterconditioning are the basic tools of behavior modification. Positive reinforcers are attention, praise, money, food, and privileges; negative reinforcers include threats, confinement, punishment, and ridicule.

Because of the controversy raised by what critics refer to as the bizarre methods of people changing, behavior modification is formally on the decline in adult corrections. But behavior modification is still informally practiced in a great many correctional institutions. Commonly, inmates receive additional privileges as they become more accepting of institutional rules and procedures and as they give evidence of more positive attitudes. The North Carolina Youthful Offender Center in Morganton uses this principle. Offenders begin their orientation period in the spartan existence of the fourteenth floor and progress to the relative luxury of the fifth floor. Each successive lower floor, representing advances and tractability, offers more amenities, privileges, and better living arrangements. By the time offenders reach the fifth floor, they are ready for release and have keys to their rooms, comfortable furniture, attractive china on which to eat, and a wide range of options for recreation, visiting, eating, canteen use, and dress.[39]

Do these programs at Morganton and other institutions work? Does changing the external environment actually change the behavior of offenders? Certainly not as much as critics who fear a scenario like that in the film *A Clockwork Orange* might think, but it is human nature to exhibit outward compliance to seek rewards and amenities. Yet little evidence exists that outward compliance in terms of positive behavior will eventually stabilize the attitudinal change. The prison, as documented throughout this book, is about the least satisfactory setting in which to use a behavior modification program, for inmates have considerable control over the environment, little consistency exists among staff, and few staff are committed to this modality.

On balance then, it is probably just as well that corrections is moving away from behavior modification programs.

Drug and Alcohol Counseling Groups devoted to the special problems of inmates have increased significantly in the past decade. In 1979, for example, an estimated 4.4 percent of inmates in the 50 state correctional systems were in drug treatment. By 1987, 11.1 percent of inmates were enrolled in treatment programs. In spite of this 150 percent increase, however, the number of drug-using inmates far exceeds the enrollment level. Indeed, 62 percent of inmates reported using illicit drugs regularly before incarceration, and 35 percent used major drugs. Over half of prisoners also were regularly involved in using drugs before their last arrest but were not enrolled in drug-abuse programs.[40]

The Cornerstone Program (Oregon), the Lantana Program (Florida), the Simon Fraser University Program (British Columbia), and the Stay'n Out Program (New York) are four promising programs that have reported relatively low rates of recidivism among program participants. Box 12-2 lists the noteworthy characteristics and features that these four programs share:

The **therapeutic community,** focusing on the total environment and using all the experience of that environment as the basic tools for therapeutic intervention, has sometimes had marked success with drug abusers in prison. Evolving from the work of Maxwell Jones, this approach attempts to give persons within the therapeutic unit greater authority in the operation of their living units.[41]

The most widely hailed therapeutic community (TC) in adult institutions was developed by Dr. Martin Groder at the federal penitentiary at Marion, Illinois; this program has been copied in correctional facilities at Terminal Island, California; Oxford, Wisconsin; Stillwater, Minnesota; and the Fort Grant Training Center, Arizona. Other therapeutic communities have been established at Niantic in Connecticut, Patuxent in Maryland, St. Cloud in Minnesota, and the prison systems of California and New York.

Groder, influenced by transactional analysis as well as by Synanon in California, managed to convince institutional administrators to sanction an inmate group of about 25 volunteers who would evolve their own treatment programs. Inmates initially lived in a separate unit in the prison hospital, attended lectures on TA, and participated in Synanon-type confrontation groups. The basic rules, prohibiting physical violence or threats of violence, gambling, drugs, or homosexual behavior, were rigidly enforced, and violation resulted in automatic expulsion from the group.[42]

In sum, in view of the ever-increasing drug abuse found among prison inmates, it is imperative that drug treatment programs be dramatically increased. The replications of the characteristics and features of the four programs cited here would do much to ensure the effectiveness of other drug treatment programs. But self-contained therapeutic communities are difficult to establish in institutional settings. Prison authorities are reluctant to delegate responsibility and authority to TCs and to modify traditional rules to accommodate an atypical prison social system.[43]

Skill Development Programs **Skill development** programs are presently enjoying considerable popularity in adult correctional institutions. These programs are concerned with developing communication, daily living and survival, educational advancement, and career skills. (See Figure 12.4 for the communication skills module that is used in Tennessee prisons.) Anger management, relaxation exercises,

Box 12-2 Characteristics and Features Shared by Noteworthy Programs

1. [The programs] have special sources of funds, earmarked for their use and administered separately from other correctional services.
2. The programs exist as guests of established host institutions; thus they can focus on program activities rather than such institutional matters as housing and food preparation.
3. The programs use a comprehensive approach and wide range of activities that are commonly found in freestanding residential programs rather than in traditional prison drug programs.
4. The program providers are more likely to come from professions other than corrections, although they are sensitive to security regulations and willing to work within them.
5. Program participants typically were involved heavily in drug use and committed many serious crimes before incarceration.
6. In carrying out program activities, these participants learn a range of practical life skills.
7. Program staff members maintain contact with participants after release and provide follow-up support.

[The features shared by these programs include:]

1. Clear statements of the program rules and the consequences of breaking them.
2. Obvious concern by program staff about the welfare of participants.
3. Participant regard for staff members as persons worth imitating.
4. Utilization of community resources.

Source: Marcia R. Chaiken, *Prison Programs for Drug-Involved Offenders* (Washington: U.S. Department of Justice, 1989), p. 2.

assertiveness training, decision making, and problem solving are also particular skills that are taught in these programs.

The increasing popularity of these programs stems from the fact that both corrections officials and inmates are aware that the lack of these skills spells disaster in adjusting to community living. For example, the inability to manage anger is why many inmates end up in prison, the inability to make constructive decisions is why many inmates perpetuate a revolving door between prison and community life, and the inability to trust and relate outside the prison walls continues the stigma of marginality.

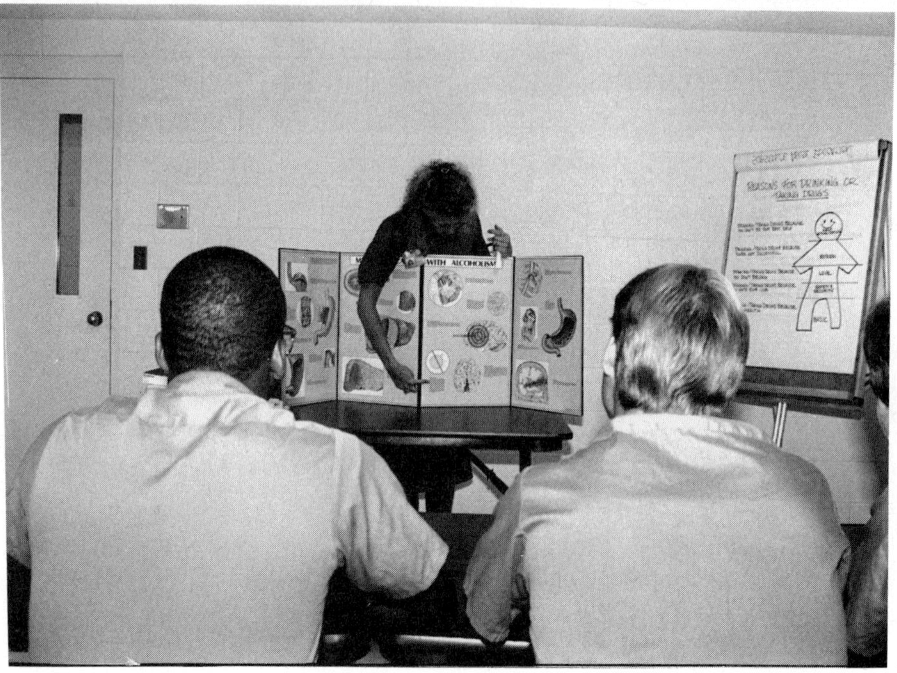

Substance abuse class. (*Source*: Florida State Department of Corrections.)

Self-help Programs

Departments of corrections frequently encourage inmates to establish **self-help groups**. These groups are operated primarily by the inmates themselves and often express ethnic and cultural goals. The groups meet in the evenings or on weekends. They usually are required to have a staff member sponsor and to establish bylaws and procedures for governing themselves. Among the self-help groups that meet in the California Department of Corrections institutions are these:

Seventh Step
Organization to Help Every Race
Hillel
People Builders
Alcoholics Anonymous
No Other Reason Than Help
Winners (Placement)
20 Psych Counseling
Gamblers Anonymous
Inner Wisdom Study
Black Culture
Humanist
Toastmasters
Narcotics Anonymous
Community Awareness
Wives and Husbands in Prison
Mexican-American Culture
Transactional Workshop
Asian Culture
American Indian

Other self-help groups offered in prisons are Jaycees, Life, Dale Carnegie, Checks Anonymous, Native American Spiritual and Cultural Awareness Group, Yoga, Transcendental Mediation (TM), T'ai Chi, Insight Incorporated, positive mental attitude (P.M.A.), assertiveness training, anger management, moral development, and Emotional Maturity Instruction.

Communication Skills

PARTICIPANTS: 15–20

TARGET POPULATION: Graduates of Self-Awareness Module

OBJECTIVE: To improve the participant's knowledge of what constitutes good communication skills, also, to have the participant exhibit appropriate communication skills.

GOAL: To provide participants with the information regarding good communication skills. To allow them to practice these skills with other group members and to use these skills with other individuals. (Staff and inmate)

1. *SESSION I* – Introduction to Communication Skills:
   - Verbal
   - Non-verbal
2. *SESSION II* – Matching Behaviors:
   - Voice Characteristics
   - Body Language
3. *SESSION III* – Non-verbal Listening Behavior:
   - "SOLER Model"
   - Roadblocks to Communication
4. *SESSION IV* – Self Expression, Model I:
   - Thoughts, Feelings and Behaviors
   - Genuineness and Respect
5. *SESSION V* – Self Expression, Model II:
   - Explanation or Clarification
   - Desire or Preference
6. *SESSION VI* – Active Listening Skills, Model I
   - Content and Feeling
7. *SESSION VII* – Active Listening Skills, Model II
   - Encouraging Responses
   - Open Questions
8. *SESSION VIII* – Review and Summarization
   - The Use of Fantasy and Imagery

Figure 12.4 Communication skills. (*Source*: Tennessee Department of Corrections.)

A national service organization, Jaycees is probably the largest self-help group, having 16,000 inmate members in 420 chapters in state and federal prisons. Sponsored by Jaycee chapters in the community, Jaycee groups in prison raise money for charities, refurbish visiting rooms, donate toys to children's hospitals, sponsor entertainment and sport events for prisoners, and operate radio stations.

Lifers, an organization made up of those sentenced to life imprisonment, is a popular organization and usually has a waiting list. Yoga and TM are both rapidly gaining recognition in correctional institutions; both have been established in more than 20 prisons. Teaching motivation for inmates—through such programs as Zzoom, P.M.A., and Guide for Better Living—is important in many institutions. The growing interest in self-help groups reflects a concern for consciousness raising as well as a desire to impress the parole board.

Service Projects

Inmates seem increasingly eager to become involved in projects involving service. These projects may have both self-help and service aspects or may focus on a needed institutional or community service. Some **service projects** are ongoing, while others arise because of a disaster or emergency in the community. Service projects include providing child care for prison visitors, fighting forest fires and floods, adopting war orphans, doing peer counseling, recording books for the blind, donating blood, participating as paramedics or in other lifesaving roles, and acting as umpires for Little League baseball games in the community.

PROGRAMS AND SERVICES

Correctional institutions are expected to provide a variety of services—among them food services, medical and dental care, visiting facilities, and libraries, as well as commissary services, mail delivery, and recreational services. Because of the questionable quality of these services in many institutions across the United States, the National Prison Project, the Osborne Association, and the John Howard Association have been most active in pressing for reform. Until the federal courts jettisoned the hands-off policy in the 1960s, the recommendations of these groups were usually ignored by correctional policymakers—except when riots and major disturbances brought the need for change to their urgent attention.

Food Services

The quality of food services varies from one correctional system to another and even from one correctional facility to another. But food services have improved dramatically from the days when inmates formerly sat at long rows of tables, all faced in the same direction to avoid personal interaction, and ate in enforced silence. They were fed on a few cents a day, sometimes going without such things as fresh fruit for months. In view of the general conditions, it is not surprising that the dining hall has been the setting for many prison disturbances.[44]

Today, in more and more prisons, inmates sit at four-person tables, menus have greater variety, and meal planning takes into consideration all cultural groups. For example, Muslims may receive a pork-free diet, the dietary laws of Jewish prisoners are respected, and vegetarians are served well-balanced meals. Diabetics and ulcer patients also receive special foods.

But, regardless of how appealing the food might be, inmates are still commonly marched in and out of the dining hall, given only a few minutes to eat, and often not permitted to smoke after the meal. In short, most prisoners continue to find institutional meals an unsatisfying experience.

Medical Services

Inmates have leveled many complaints against institutional medical care: They charge that it is inadequate, improper, and available only during the day; that requested treatment is often denied; that special diets are not provided; that medical treatment and drugs are often forced on them and that inmates are used in medical experimentation; and that prisoners are forced to work when they are physically unable to do so. Unquestionably, many of these charges have been true in the past.

Lawsuits in Alabama, *Pugh* v. *Locke*, and *Newman* v. *Alabama*, were concerned with the gross inadequacy of medical services.[45] One of the highest priorities of the prisoners at Attica was improvement of the medical services, which were managed by one physician whose interest in treatment of prisoners seems to have been minimal. The trend toward contracting out medical services appears to be an avenue toward major improvements. With very few exceptions, prison physicians have been drawn from the least successful practitioners of their profession or have been foreigners with an inadequate command of English. Fortunately, the organizations with which departments of corrections have contracted have been able to recruit men and women of reasonable competence.

Acquired immune deficiency syndrome (**AIDS**) has rapidly become one of the most difficult and complex public health issues facing the United States. The rapid increase in cases in recent years, as well as the continued uncertainty as to the future course of the disease's spread, led President Ronald Reagan to term AIDS "the nation's number one health priority."

Corrections officials believe that dealing with the problem of AIDS poses particularly difficult problems because inmate populations may include high proportions of individuals in AIDS risk groups, particularly intravenous drug users.[46] The National Institute of Justice's 1989 survey found that as of October 1989 correctional agencies had a total of 5,411 prisoners with AIDS; this was an increase of 72 percent over the previous year.[47]

Shortly after President Reagan's comment, the Bureau of Prisons began screening all incoming inmates and releases, becoming the sixth prison system to adapt some type of mandatory screening program. Nine other jurisdictions had instituted similar programs by October 1989, and in eight other jurisdictions all inmates in high-risk groups (including pregnant women) were subject to mandatory screening. Thus, some form of mandatory screening for HIV infection is found in nearly half of the states and the Bureau of Prisons, and about 60 percent of the remaining state systems report receiving some degree of political pressure to implement it.[48]

Whether inmates should be required to undergo testing for exposure to the HIV virus is only one of the difficult questions posed by the threat of AIDS in prison. How should HIV positive inmates be treated? Should they be hospitalized, segregated, or paroled? Should officers be notified that an inmate tests positive? How about notifying past or prospective sexual partners? Does educating inmates about "safer sex" and needle hygiene imply that the state condones such behavior in prison? Or does this education obligate prison officials to provide the means for prisoners to practice "safer sex" and good needle hygiene while imprisoned?[49]

Visiting

The quality of the visiting experience has improved greatly in recent years. Visiting arrangements tend to fall into the following categories: (1) closed visit; (2) limited-contact visit; (3) informal-contact visit; (4) freedom of the grounds; and (5) conjugal or family visit.

Closed visits do not allow any physical contact between prisoner and visitor, who are separated by a partition extending from floor to ceiling. The limited-contact visit substitutes a long table with a center partition that extends from the floor to a few inches above the surface of the table. The informal-contact visit usually takes place in a visiting room furnished with chairs, small tables, and, often, food-vending machines. Some institutions also extend the informality of their visiting arrangements to include picnic and play areas. Freedom of the grounds is permitted in some forestry camps, satellites, prerelease guidance centers, and minimum security prisons.

Finally, several states permit **conjugal visitation** for inmates who have earned the privilege. It is a hotly debated issue. Mississippi instituted a program of conjugal visitation at the turn of the century at the Parchman prison, but it was not until 1963 that the Department of Corrections formalized this practice.[50] South Carolina had a similar practice of permitting inmates to spend a certain period of time alone with their families that was in existence even prior to the informal system in Mississippi. In 1968, the California State Prison at Tehachapi initiated family visitation, and this program has been used throughout the California prison system.[51]

More recently, Alabama, Alaska, Connecticut, Minnesota, New York, and Washington state have initiated family visitation programs; this euphemism has replaced the term "conjugal visit," in part because the focus now provides for children and other relatives to be included. These programs have been expanded in most of the participating states to include female inmates. The federal Bureau of Prisons, however, does not have family visitation programs. A special task force appointed by the director of the Bureau evaluated several state programs in 1980 and advised against such a policy.[52]

Conjugal, or family, visitation usually means that prisoners enjoy 24 or 48 hours of privacy with their families. A trailer is frequently used for the visit, with the wife or family member bringing food to prepare, and a correctional officer checking on the inmate once a day or so. Some of the benefits of family visitation programs are that they keep the families together, permit the inclusion of children, permit extended visits by family members with unmarried inmates, relieve the tension of the prison environment, and maintain emotional closeness and mutual understanding with inmates' families. The most serious criticisms of conjugal, or family, visitation programs are that they pamper inmates by permitting sexual intercourse and that they present a security problem. Inmate families, for example, can bring drugs or perhaps even weapons into the institution.

In general, institutions have become more liberal about the frequency and length of visits and the amount of contact permitted. The drug appetites of prisoners and the tendency of visitors to bring narcotics into the prison make it uncomfortable for administrators to expand further the visiting rights, but it is still likely that other states will develop variations of family visitation in the near future.

Prisoners in California, South Carolina, New York, and Mississippi may earn family visits in private quarters without guards. (*Source*: State of California, Department of Corrections.)

The Inmate Commissary

The prison commissary, sometimes called the canteen or store, makes it possible for prisoners to buy a number of needed articles. Prison commissaries usually stock tobacco products, candy, instant coffee, prepared foods, hair tonics, shaving supplies, dental hygiene items and toilet articles, and writing supplies. Some commissaries also sell clothing, radios, television sets, canned meats, and watches. Institutions vary in how much they permit inmates to spend per week or month in the commissary, but they generally permit prisoners to visit the commissary more frequently and to spend more time there than they had in the past.

The profits from the commissary, which may reach a quarter of a million dollars or more per year in a large facility, are often used to purchase recreational equipment, movies, special entertainment, and newspapers and magazines. Nonetheless, the commissary is often one of the first places hit when a riot breaks out because inmates view it as one more example of exploitation by the establishment.

The Library

In recent years prison libraries have been expanded and made available to all inmates. In most prison libraries, inmates are now permitted to obtain from the state library books that are not available in the prison. In contrast to the days when law books were kept in the warden's office or in other inaccessible places, well-equipped law libraries generally are available for inmate use.

PRISON INDUSTRIES

Prison labor began as enforced labor, inflicted as punishment. Forcing inmates to break up rocks or to move coal from one pile to another was intended to break their spirits. Later, it was decided to use inmate labor to help pay the costs of imprisonment, and some prison systems at the end of the nineteenth century found themselves making considerable revenue from prison industries. However, labor union resistance resulted in the passage of state and federal laws early in the twentieth century that prohibited inmate-made goods from competing in the free market.

Prisoners have several responses to prison labor. In some correctional systems, they are required to work at some job, and these prisoners typically feel negative about such work, especially when they receive no or little compensation for what they do. Indeed, some prisoners will go to nearly any extreme to get out of such required labor:

> To show you how devious I was, just how I thought, they had a thing that if you had a tooth pulled you got a three day lay-in. It was cold when I was on the coal pile, and I had fairly good teeth. Every Wednesday I went to have one tooth pulled so I could lay-in Wednesday, Thursday, Friday, Saturday, and Sunday. At the end of six months, I had them all out. I gave them all up. But you only had to do six months on the coal pile, so I got my plates and was done with the job.[53]

More typically, inmates choose to become involved in a prison industry because it enables them to make much-needed income. Nevertheless, the hourly wage for most state inmates is still pitifully low. Federal Prison Industries (FPI) has consistently made a profit through the sale of goods to federal agencies; the FPI also pays prisoners reasonably well, at least as compared with the pay they get in most state systems. Inmates are also quick to point out that their work experiences in a prison industry are generally worthless following their release from prison. Making license plates, upholstering and refinishing furniture, processing meat, making soap, and producing metal products usually are not marketable skills in the community.

The **Free Venture model,** a federally funded program that began in Connecticut and has spread to six other states, attempted to achieve productive labor with private-sector efficiency, wages, and relevance. The goal of the Free Venture model is a realistic work environment with a full work day, inmate wages based on work output, and training for job skills that can be transferred to work in the community.[54] But in only two states, Minnesota and Washington, did private firms come within the prison and set up industry programs.

The Prison Industries Enhancement program (**PIE**) has followed up on the Free Venture model by requiring the actual involvement of private business in prison industries, either inside the prison or in plants nearby. Gordon Hawkins describes one of these projects:

> The best known of the PIE operations is Zephyr Products, Inc., in Leavenworth, Kansas. The plant, built by the city and leased to the company, makes sophisticated

for missiles, radios, television sets, and self-propelled combines. It employs thirty-five inmates and pays them the prevailing wage plus bonuses and stock options every three months they are on the job. In the first year of operation, Zephyr lost money, but now it is running at a profit. Inmate productivity matches that of private industry.[55]

The 1980s were the era of the revival of prison industries. This trend has emerged as a result of renewed interest in prison industries on the part of the public, the pioneering involvement of private corporations, and the driving force of former Chief Justice Warren E. Burger.[56] Since 1980, more than half the states have adopted legislation providing for private-sector involvement in prison industries.[57] The Justice Assistance act of 1984 also has liberalized restrictions on interstate markets.

Former Chief Justice Berger, long an advocate of prison industries, formulated the "factories with fences" concept and began promoting it with great energy. One of Burger's widely quoted sayings is, "To put people behind walls and bars and do little or nothing to change them is to win a battle but lose a war. It is wrong. It is expensive. It is stupid."[58] In February 1984, the chief justice and the Brookings Institution convened a national conference on prison industries at the Johnson Foundation Wingspread Center in Racine, Wisconsin. This conference gave rise to a much larger meeting at George Washington University in Washington, D.C., in June 1984. At this assembly, individuals representing many views on prison industry outlined their perspectives before a national audience. Chief Justice Burger argued for the establishment of a national panel to consider approaches to revolutionize and improve prison industries in the United States. In the fall of 1984, the National Task Force on Prison Industries was formed. This task force and its committees, under the guidance of Burger and the Brookings Institution, convened at the Wingspread Center in February 1985.[59] The task force developed a number of primary and secondary principles for policymakers to consider:

Principles

1. Prison industries should provide meaningful and relevant work opportunities for inmates.
2. Prison industries should operate in a businesslike manner.
3. Prison industries should reduce inmate idleness.
4. The private sector should be involved in prison industries.
5. Practices and regulations that impede the progress of prison industries should be rescinded, changed, or otherwise streamlined.

Secondary Principles

1. Inmates should not be exploited.
2. Wage and benefit structures must be dramatically improved.
3. Chargebacks are encouraged, particularly for institutional cost defrayment and victim compensation.
4. Standards of professional conduct should be incorporated more thoroughly into industry practices.
5. Industries should not operate in isolation from internal (prison) and external environments.[60]

The task force, in offering these recommendations, was aware that they are neither formulas nor panaceas. Committee members were also aware that prison industries are not the cure-all for all the correctional ills that plague this nation. But they contend that prison industries can significantly improve the quality of life in a correctional system, with benefits for staff, offenders, victims, and taxpayers alike.[61]

PRIVATE PRISONS

The private sector's involvement in corrections, as previously discussed, is not new. Prison labor was used by private industry in several ways during the late nineteenth century. Under the contract labor system, prisoners's labor was used to manufacture goods for private contractors who furnished tools and materials and supervised the work in prison. The piece-price system involved contractors' furnishing raw materials, with prisoners being paid for the completed goods on a per-piece basis. The lease system involved the leasing of prisoners to work in farming, construction, mining, and plantations, with contractors having complete control over prisoners.[62]

Current involvement of private enterprise in correctional institutions now includes three areas: (1) participation in prison work programs; (2) financing of prison or jail construction; and (3) managing and operating prisons.[63]

In early 1985, 26 projects involved private business in various arrangements with prison industries. Moreover, Merrill Lynch is arranging the financing and construction of correctional facilities, and, in the most comprehensive involvement of private enterprise in corrections, a number of private corporations already manage and operate a correctional facility under a lease arrangement with the federal, state, or local government. Indeed, the Corrections Corporation of American (CCA) even proposes to take over the Tennessee correctional system and run it as a private corporation.[64]

Yet increasing the involvement of private enterprise in corrections raises a number of important legal, financial, and moral questions that have not been adequately addressed. For the state to abdicate its power of punishment to the lowest corporate bidder will seal off prisons more completely from constitutional and popular controls. It will also sever any connection between justice and punishment, transforming the terms of the debate over the social objectives of incarceration from retribution, deterrence, and rehabilitation to productivity and profit. In a 1988 letter to the *Philadelphia Inquirer*, Norman Nusser, who has served 17 years of a 20- to 40-year prison term, wrote:

> Corrections is already too much of a business and needs to become less so. Too many people already are making a living from our misery. It is now subsidized sadism. Is our society to put sadism on a profit-making basis? . . .
>
> Look in the financial section of your daily newspaper to see how many points Prison Industries went up today. If there has been a prison riot and $50 million worth of machinery and plant are destroyed, the stockholders will be out in droves.[65]

CONCLUSIONS

One of the co-authors asked two inmates working outside a southern prison where the front gate of the penitentiary was. One responded, "It is around the other side of that fence, but we don't call it the penitentiary anymore. It's now the correctional center." To which this co-author replied, "Is it any different now?" "No, it's still the penitentiary."

The names may change, but maximum security institutions in most states continue to be violent, inhumane, ineffective, and costly. Even employees refer to them as garbage dumps, cesspools, and "the pits." An employee at Stateville in Illinois said, "You've got to be out of your mind to work here."[66]

Correctional administrators are willing to admit that much of this criticism has been justified. The recent desire to establish standards suggests that practitioners are at last beginning to deal with the immense problems of operating correctional institutions. Newer institutions are usually several steps ahead of the old fortresses in which offenders are confined. They are smaller, usually have better services and programs, are more liveable in decor and design, and are safer for inmates and staff. However, correctional institutions today still have many problems, a subject that will receive more extensive examination in the next four chapters.

KEY TERMS

AIDS
behavior modification
boot camps
campus design
coeducational institutions
conjugal visitation
courtyard-style design
Free Venture model
maximum security prisons
medium security prisons
minimum security prisons
PIE
radial design
reality therapy
reformatories
self-help groups
service projects
skill development
telephone-pole design
therapeutic community
transactional analysis

treatment modalities

women's prisons

DISCUSSION TOPICS

12.1 Are all prisons like the "Big House" in movies of the 1930s? Explain your position using examples from your reading.

12.2 If you have not visited a prison, make arrangements to do so. Compare what you see with what you have read.

12.3 You wake up one morning to find yourself in prison. Based on your reading of this chapter, what sort of prison do you hope it will be?

12.4 What pressures are behind recent changes in such areas of prison life as food services, medical care, libraries, commissaries, and visiting privileges? What has been the effect of these pressures?

12.5 What are conjugal, or family, visits? Why are they such a hotly debated issue?

ANNOTATED REFERENCES

Burstein, Jules. *Conjugal Visits in Prison: Psychological and Social Consequences.* Lexington, Mass.: Heath, 1977. *An examination of the conjugal visitation program adopted by the California Department of Corrections.*

Carroll, Leo. *AIDS and Human Rights in the Prison: A Comment on the Ethics of Screening and Segregation.* Paper presented at the Annual Meeting of the American Society of Criminology, Reno, Nevada, November 1989. *An insightful paper on the procedures and ethical issues involved in handling cases of AIDS in today's prisons.*

Logan, Charles. "Proprietary Prisons." In Lynne Goodstein and Doris J. MacKenzie, eds., *The American Prison: Issues in Research and Policy.* New York: Plenum, 1989. *This article presents a positive—perhaps too positive—discussion of privatization.*

Mullen, Joan. *Corrections and the Private Sector.* Washington: U.S. Department of Justice, 1985. *A good discussion of the emerging private involvement in the prison business.*

Nagel, William G. *The New Red Barn: A Critical Look at the Modern American Prison.* New York: Walker, 1973. *A dated but fascinating examination of the architectural designs, programs, and problems of prisons in the United States.*

Sherman, Michael, and Gordon Hawkins. *Imprisonment in America: Choosing the Future.* Chicago: University of Chicago Press, 1981. *An insightful book generally, but particularly helpful when it comes to what to do about prison crowding.*

NOTES

1. Norval Morris, *The Future of Imprisonment* (Chicago: University of Chicago Press, 1974), p. ix.
2. William G. Nagel, "An American Archipelago: The United States Bureau of Prisons" (Hacksensack, N.J.: National Council on Crime and Delinquency, 1974), p. 1.
3. Interviewed in June 1990.
4. Interviewed in July 1990.

5. Bureau of Justice Statistics, *Prisoners in 1989* (Washington, D.C.: U.S. Department of Justice, 1990), p. 1.
6. Ibid., p. 4.
7. Russ Immarigeon and Meda Chesney-Lind, "Women's Prisons: Overcrowded and Overused." (Paper presented at the Annual Meeting of the American Society of Criminology in Baltimore, Maryland, November 1990), p. 3.
8. Paul B. Paulus, et al., "The Effects of Crowding in Prisons and Jails." In *Reactions to Crime: The Public, the Police, Courts and Prisons*, eds. David Farrington and John Gunn (New York: J. Wiley, 1986).
9. Joan Petersilia, *The Influence of Criminal Justice Research* (Santa Monica, Calif.: Rand Corporation, 1987).
10. William G. Nagel, *The New Red Barn: A Critical Look at the Modern American Prison* (New York: Walker, 1973), p. 36.
11. Joan Potter, "In Prison, Women Are Different." *Corrections Magazine* 4, December 1978: 14–24.
12. See Scott Christianson, "Our Black Prisons." In Kenneth C. Haas and Geoffrey P. Alpert, eds., *The Dilemmas of Punishment: Readings in Contemporary Punishment* (Prospect Heights, Ill.: Waveland Press, Inc., 1986), pp. 64–76.
13. One of the authors has interviewed a number of ex-offenders who have served time at Mansfield; they have consistently emphasized its violent environment.
14. Interviewed in March 1979.
15. See the interview with John Petrilli in Clemens Bartollas and Stuart J. Miller, *Correctional Administration: Theory and Practice* (New York: McGraw-Hill, 1978), pp. 99–109.
16. For a full account of the riot and its antecedents, see Jeff Bingaman, *Report of the Attorney General on the February 2 and 3, 1980, Riot at the Penitentiary of New Mexico* (Santa Fe: Office of the State Attorney General, 1980).
17. Taken from a brochure made for the dedication of this prison on June 14, 1990, p. 2.
18. Minnesota Department of Corrections, "A New High Security Facility for Minnesota" (St. Paul, Minn.: Department of Corrections, n.d.), p. 2.
19. Material adapted from a brochure, "Minnesota Correctional Facility—Oak Park Heights," Department of Corrections, n.d.
20. Bureau of Justice Statistics, *Prisoners in 1989*, p. 4.
21. Ruth M. Glick and Virginia V. Neto, *National Study of Women's Correctional Programs* (Washington: Government Printing Office, LEAA, 1977), p. 20.
22. U.S. Department of Justice, *Survey of Inmates of States Correctional Institutions* (Washington: Government Printing Office, March 1976), p. 1.
23. Glick and Neto, *National Study of Women's Correctional Programs*, p. 34.
24. This information was obtained from the *American Correctional Association Directory* (Rockville, Md.: American Correctional Association, 1989).
25. John Ortiz Smykla, "Co-ed Prisons: A State of the Art" (Paper presented at the Annual Meeting of the Academy of Criminal Justice, New Orleans, La., March 1978), pp. 4–6.
26. B. Rubeck, "The Sexually Integrated Prison—A Legal and Policy Evaluation." *American Journal of Criminal Law* 3, 1975: 313–327.
27. Smykla, "Co-ed Prisons."
28. For up-to-date discussions of boot camps, see Doris L. MacKenzie, " 'Boot Camp' Programs Grow in Number and Scope." *National Institute of Justice/Research in Action* 222, November-December 1990: 6–8; Doris L. MacKenzie, "Boot Camp Prisons: Components, Evaluations, and Empirical Issues." *Federal Probation*, September 1990: 44–52; Doris L. MacKenzie, Larry A. Gould, Lisa M. Riechers, and James W. Shaw, "Shock Incarceration: Rehabilitation or Retribution?" *Journal of Rehabilitation* 14, 1989: 25–40; Doris L. MacKenzie and James W. Shaw, "Inmate Adjustment and Change During Shock Incarceration: The Impact of Correctional Boot Camp Programs." *Justice Quarterly* 7,

1990: 126–150; James W. Shaw and Doris L. MacKenzie, "Boot Camps: An Initial Assessment of the Program and Parole Performance of Drug-Involved Offenders" (Paper presented at the Annual Meeting of the Society of Criminology in Baltimore, Maryland, November 1990).

29. Dale Parent, "Shock Incarceration Programs" (Paper presented at the American Correctional Association Winter Conference, Phoenix, Arizona, 1988).
30. Doris Layton MacKenzie, " 'Boot Camp' Programs Grow in Number and Scope."
31. Gannett News Service, "Boot Camp Prisons." *Lansing State Journal* 135, 19 June 1989: 11.
32. Ibid.
33. Douglas Martin, "New York Tests a Boot Camp for Inmates" (*New York Times*, 4 March 1988), p. 15.
34. Doris Layton MacKenzie, " 'Boot Camp' Programs Grow in Number and Scope," p. 7.
35. M. Morash and L. Rucker, "Boot Camps as a Correctional Reform." *Crime and Delinquency* 36, 1990: 206.
36. Eric Berne, *What Do You Say After You Say Hello?* (New York: Grove Press, 1972).
37. Thomas A. Harris, *I'm OK—You're OK* (New York: Harper & Row, 1965).
38. William Glasser, *Reality Therapy* (New York: Harper & Row, 1965).
39. Nagel, *The New Red Barn*, p. 14.
40. Christopher A. Innes, *Profile of State Prison Inmates, 1986* (Washington: Bureau of Justice Statistics, 1988).
41. Maxwell Jones, *Social Psychiatry in Prison* (Baltimore, Md.: Penguin, 1968).
42. Martin Groder, "An Angry Resignation." *Corrections Magazine* 1, July/August 1975: 33.
43. Maxwell Jones, "Desirable Features of a Therapeutic Community in a Prison." In Hans Toch, ed., *Therapeutic Communities in Corrections* (New York: Praeger, 1980), p. 37.
44. Henry Burns, *Corrections: Organization and Administration* (St. Paul, Minn.: West, 1975), p. 399.
45. *Pugh* v. *Locke*, 406 F. Supp. 318 (MD Ala. 1976); *Newman* v. *Alabama*, 559 F.2d. 283 (5th Cir. 1977).
46. Leo Carroll, "AIDS and Human Rights in the Prison: A Comment on the Ethics of Screening and Segregation" (Paper presented at the Annual Meeting of the American Society of Criminology, Reno, Nevada, November 1989), p. 3.
47. Barbara A. Belbot and Rolando V. del Carmen, "Aids in Prison: Legal Issues." *Crime and Delinquency* 37, January 1991: 135.
48. Theodore M. Hammett, *AIDS in Correctional Facilities: Issues and Options*, 3rd ed. (Washington: National Institute of Justice, 1989).
49. Carroll, "AIDS and Human Rights in the Prison."
50. Columbus B. Hopper, *Sex in Prison: The Mississippi Experiment with Conjugal Visiting* (Baton Rouge: Louisiana State University Press, 1969).
51. Jules Burstein, *Conjugal Visits in Prison: Psychological and Social Consequences* (Lexington, Mass.: Heath, 1977), pp. 79–80.
52. Ann Goetting, "Conjugal Association in Prison: Issues and Perspectives." *Crime and Delinquency* 28, 1982: 52–71.
53. Interviewed in December 1980.
54. Connecticut Department of Corrections, *Free Venture Model in Corrections* (Hartford: Department of Corrections, n.d.).
55. Gordon Hawkins, "Prison Labor and Prison Industries." In Michael Tonry and Norval Morris, eds., *Crime and Justice*, vol. 5 (Chicago: University of Chicago Press, 1983), pp. 107–108.
56. Gail S. Funke, ed., *National Conference on Prison Industries: Discussion and Recommendations* (Washington: National Center for Innovation in Corrections, 1986).

57. Gordon Hawkins and Geoffrey P. Alpert, *American Prison Systems: Punishment and Justice* (Englewood Cliffs, N.J.: Prentice-Hall, 1989), p. 223.
58. Quoted in Funke, ed., *National Conference on Prison Industries.*
59. Ibid., pp. 17–18.
60. Ibid.
61. Ibid.
62. Joan Mullen, *Corrections and the Private Sector* (Washington: U.S. Department of Justice, National Institute of Justice, 1985).
63. G. E. Sexton, F. C. Farrow, and B. Auerback, "The Private Sector in Private Industries." In *Research in Brief* (Washington: U.S. Department of Justice, National Institute of Justice, 1985).
64. Neal Shover and Werner J. Einstadter, *Analyzing American Corrections* (Belmont, Calif.: Wadsworth, 1988), p. 141.
65. Craig Becker and Amy Du Stanley, "Incarceration, Inc.: The Downside of Private Prison" (*The Nation*, 15 June 1985), pp. 728–730.
66. Comment made to one of the authors in 1978.

PART FIVE

Institutional Administration

Chapter

13

Institutional Management

CHAPTER OUTLINE

CHANGING ROLES OF INSTITUTIONAL WARDENS
- *The Autocratic Warden*
- *Rise of Statewide Bureaucracy*
- *Views of Contemporary Correctional Administrators*

MANAGEMENT STYLES OF CONTEMPORARY WARDENS
- *Wardens of the 1970s*
- *Wardens of the 1980s*
- *Wardens of the 1990s*

SCOPE OF ADMINISTRATION
- *Establishment of Policy*
- *Planning*
- *Institutional Monitoring*
- *Staff Supervision*
- *Personnel Direction*
- *Fiscal Management*
- *Professional and Personal Integrity*

HUMANIZING CORRECTIONAL INSTITUTIONS
- *The Lawful Prison*
- *The Safe Prison*
- *The Industrious Prison*
- *The Hopeful Prison*

CONCLUSIONS

Prison administration is not an easy job. The job of a warden, as well as those of other prison workers, is thankless and demands enormous physical and emotional stamina on the part of those engaged in it. A warden in North Carolina puts it this way: "There is no question that the prison has taken its toll on me. I had ulcers at twenty-eight, heart problems at thirty-nine, and have hypertension now."[1] A warden in Illinois noted, "It is a hard struggle, and you just have to be prepared for it. Any decision you make takes a toll on you. If you make a mistake, you may not have a job tomorrow. If you make a mistake, the [prison] population won't let you forget it."[2]

Yet it cannot be denied that some wardens thrive on their jobs. They are innovative, resourceful, fair, and resilient; indeed, they may remain for 10 or 15 years at the same facility. They see correctional administration as interesting and challenging and speak with pride when they discuss their careers. They not only understand management theory, but they are also effective managers within their institutions.[3] Finally, they do their best to anticipate problems rather than be constantly involved in crisis-centered decision making. As Box 13-1 indicates, one such person is W. H. Dallman, warden of the Lebanon Correctional Institution in Ohio.

Box 13-1 Interview with W. H. Dallman

A lot of wardens forget what they're hired for, and that is to manage problems. Some wardens somehow expect that everything is supposed to be problem free and that if you follow a set of rules and policies, then the prison is going to run fine. They perceive all the lawsuits, all the overcrowding, all the other problems we face as some kind of plot against them to upset their apple cart. Actually, we wouldn't need anybody to do these jobs if it weren't for the fact that we constantly manage problems that keep changing.

For example, I get sued a lot. I get sued four and five times a week. I have hundreds of lawsuits pending against me. Fortunately, I don't lose many of them, but it takes an awful lot of my time. I try not to get too upset about all of this, even though that's easier said than done. We can get frustrated, aggravated, and tied up in emotional knots in this job. We can get so upset that we will end up with ulcers and have heart attacks.

But the reason for the lawsuits is because we have a good and strong country, a Constitution that was written to protect all of us. We all need to remember that this is our responsibility—to protect the rights of those who frequently stomp on the rights of others. Another way of looking at this is that our forefathers had strong beliefs about freedom, and didn't want government interference. They didn't want the government telling them how to run their lives. But we're in the business of taking peoples' liberties away from them. There are certain places where you can lose your freedom, and prison is one of them.

To make it in this business, the warden has to be in charge. I run this prison. We expect the prisoners to adjust to the prison and not the other way around. But at the same time we need to be fair and firm and honor the due process rights of inmates. I am probably the oldest warden in the world; I have been warden for over eighteen years. I have seen a lot of changes take place during this time, but I am still at it, excited about what I'm doing, and looking forward to what tomorrow brings.

Source: Interviewed in September 1990.

This chapter examines the types of administrators in this nation's prisons and places a special emphasis on the characteristics and decision-making styles of innovative wardens in the 1990s. Of the various metaphors available to understand the prison, this chapter also contends that the **rational, or learning, metaphor** provides a promising new approach to correctional administration.

CHANGING ROLES OF INSTITUTIONAL WARDENS

The autocratic and the bureaucratic warden have been the two basic types found in correctional institutions in the United States.

The Autocratic Warden

From the birth of the penitentiary in the 1820s until the years following World War II, the institutional warden was sovereign; as long as he kept in favor with the governor's office, his word was unquestioned law. Believing that no one else could run their organizations, these autocratic wardens took total responsibility for planning, staffing, and controlling. They refused to accept either staff or inmate resistance; indeed, the prisoners, like slaves, were denied nearly every human right beyond survival. Wardens mixed terror, incentives, and favoritism in order to keep their subjects "fearful but not desperate, hopeful but always uncertain." Guards who were subject to the absolute power of the wardens were dependent on their favor for job security and promotion.[4]

To protect his authority, the **autocratic warden** divided the prison community. The formation of groups of either prisoners or guards was never permitted. The warden's intelligence system assured that neither guard nor prisoner could trust anyone. The paramilitary model of management, with its military terminology, downward flow of communication, rigid rules and regimentation, and impersonal relationships, further protected the warden's absolute power and helped maintain an orderly, neat, and secure institution. Bloody uprisings did take place, but they were dealt with harshly. Ringleaders especially felt the heavy hand of unregulated authority.

Joseph Ragen, warden of Stateville and Joliet Penitentiaries in Illinois from 1936 to 1961, is the best-known autocratic warden. Ragen, sometimes called "Mr. Prison," ran the two penitentiaries by exercising personal control over every detail of prison life. He permitted no one to challenge him and had such control that there were no riots and escapes from within the walls during his 25 years as warden; only two guards and three inmates were killed during this time. Ragen demanded absolute loyalty; he kept outsiders out, and, within the walls, he maintained absolute power. Ragen made a policy of recruiting guards from southern Illinois, which in his time was a chronically depressed area. These men were just about totally dependent on him for their livelihoods. If they incurred his wrath, it was a catastrophe for them.[5]

Rise of Statewide Bureaucracy

Prison absolutism withstood many attacks: the opening of prisons to official inspection, the introduction of professionals, the adoption of the Principles of the National Prison Association in 1870, and the commitment to the rehabilitation ideal. But its collapse finally occurred following World War II, when governors and legislators demanded the creation of management systems that would assure their control of prisons through chains of accountability. As with every other department of government, this led to the **bureaucratization of corrections,** which involved the development of a statewide correctional system made up of both institutional and community facilities and programs. Set up in the bureaucratic tradition, corrections systems worked toward greater efficiency, clear accountability, higher standards, more flexible programming, and better allocation of resources. Thus, the absolute authority of the autocratic warden was replaced by specific, limited, and delegated power. The czars who had ruled as they pleased became field officers whose performance and recommendations were reviewed in the central office; the sovereigns, in effect, became accountable bureaucrats.[6]

Following World War II, corrections discovered, as did other departments of state government, that no organization, private or public, could survive without bureaucratization. However, bureaucratization has been a dubious blessing. The volume of paper generated in any professional bureaucracy far exceeds that of the simpler generations of management. All that paper must be read, initialed, and shuffled off to other desks or to accessible files. Many wardens spend far too much time in their offices, coping with memoranda and urgently required reports. Some of them are too busy to inspect their cellblocks from one end of the week to the next.

Bureaucratization also led to the development of civil service. The comfortable blanket of civil service has protected correctional employees—from almost the top down to the bottom—from political interference. In principle, the lowliest guards must qualify for their uniforms by examination, and their progress up the ranks depends on their performance on the examinations they will be required to take. This aspect is well and good, but civil service has also protected the incompetent, the time server, and the downright brutal from easy removal or, in many cases, from removal at all. This problem is not limited to corrections, but exists in all government services. While much thought has been given to possible solutions, no satisfactory ones have been found.

The head of the corrections department, whether titled director, commissioner, secretary, or administrator, runs the department from the state capital. His or her responsibility is to make certain that there are no cracks, no categories or decisions that are not governed by regulations. The problem, however, is to assure that the bureaucrats understand their roles as implementers but not formulators of policy. As an appointee of the governor, he or she is also responsible for supervising wardens of state institutions as well as public relations, political contacts with the legislature, fiscal management, policy implementation, and long-range planning. Chase Riveland, secretary of corrections in the state of Washington, discusses the importance of establishing good relationships with the legislature and the governor:

> Well, the encouraging part is that we are not in the shape that most states are. Although our prison population is climbing like everyone else's, we've been able to fashion the type of relationship with the legislature and the governor that they have supported, putting the necessary resources into meeting our needs. Our probation and parole populations are also doubling. But at least we feel we have the resources on schedule to take care of our needs, in contrast to having to fight the alligators after the fact.[7]

Directors may supervise wardens directly, or they may turn that responsibility over to a subordinate, who then reports back to the director. But personnel other than the director also have ongoing contact with institutions. Other headquarters staff involved in the inspection of institutions include the deputy director for operations, the deputy director for programs, the business manager and the budget analysts, the supervisor of classification, the personnel officer, and the staff attorney.

A number of other changes have also limited the warden's power: Professional duties are carried out by middle managers and treatment staff; civil service rules set limits for hiring and firing; professional associations hold the warden responsible for meeting their requirements; unions and employee associations impose rules about working conditions and promotions by seniority for their members; and courts insist upon inmate due process rights.

Not surprisingly, the changes in the role of the correctional administrator attracted a new type of employee. In a 1968–1969 national survey of top and middle managers in both correctional institutions and community-based corrections, the Joint Commission on Correctional Manpower and Training found that administrators had reached their present positions through a slow upward progression. Of top administrators, 75 percent were over 45 years of age, as were 55 percent of middle managers. Women made up less than 20 percent of the sample. Furthermore, the education of administrators usually was not related to their work; the most conspicuous shortcoming in their training was their lack of formal education in management.[8]

Today, top managers are more professional and more knowledgeable about managerial concepts. They are usually college graduates and may even have advanced degrees; some have studied correctional administration. Although the percentage of women in top management has not significantly changed, several women have been

Complex of administrative offices and institutions of the South Carolina Department of Corrections, Columbia, South Carolina. (*Source:* Carolina Department of Corrections.)

directors of state systems (Ward Murphy in Maine, Ali Klein in New Jersey, Elayn Hunt in Louisiana, and Ruth L. Rushen in California), and many are wardens or superintendents of state institutions. Today's correctional administrators appear to be younger than were the managers in the 1968–1969 national sample. Associate wardens are now often appointed when they are in their early thirties and become wardens or superintendents before they are forty.

Views of Contemporary Correctional Administrators

A 1983 survey of 44 state commissioners of corrections and 106 wardens once again highlighted prison crowding and staff shortages as the biggest problems of the correctional system. With regard to staff shortages, respondents noted needs in several areas: mental health, security, counseling, medical, and clerical assistance. Several recruitment and retention problems listed included problems in locating qualified professional staff, obtaining qualified minority applicants, overcoming the poor image of correctional work, combatting staff "burnout," and improving career incentives.[9]

When asked to identify specific program needs, respondents focused on jobs, education, and special inmate needs. The order of priority varied between the commissioners and wardens, but the overall results were the same (see Figure 13.1). Programs for protective custody and other segregation of prisoners were needed more acutely in the correctional systems that were operating in the middle range of crowding (between 96 percent and 120 percent of capacity). A possible explanation is that most crowded facilities have already been forced to take corrective action while less crowded systems have not yet encountered serious problems. Moreover, the need for industrial programs emerged strongly in systems under court order. The systems were experiencing an acute need of combatting inmate idleness with programs, reflecting recent court decisions that attributed findings of unconstitutionality to inmate idleness.[10]

Staff training was clearly a primary personnel need, as indicated by the high percentage of commissioners and wardens expressing such a need. The order of priorities, not surprisingly, varied somewhat between the two groups, but the predominant areas were management training, handling special problem inmates, and report writing (as seen in Table 13.1). The handling of special problem prisoners was a greater problem for systems under court order for conditions of confinement.[11]

Table 13.1 TRAINING NEEDS OF CORRECTIONAL ADMINISTRATORS

Training need	Percent of commissioners	Percent of wardens
Management training	75	64
Handling special problem inmates	70	72
Report writing	68	63
Liability issues	66	52
Interpersonal relations	57	65
Handling prisoners with AIDS	53	26
Stress management	52	62
Security	50	46

Source: National Institute of Justice, *Wardens and State Corrections Commissioners Offer Their Views in National Assessments* (Washington: U.S. Department of Justice, 1988), p. 7.

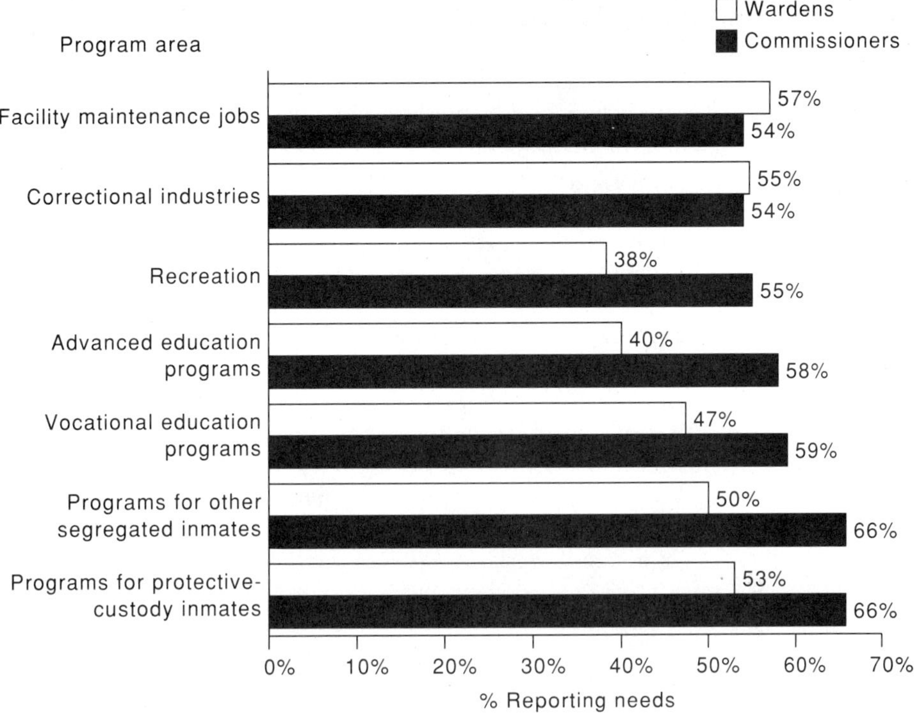

Figure 13.1 Most critical program needs. (*Source*: National Institute of Justice, *Wardens and State Corrections Commissioners Offer Their Views in National Assessment* (Washington: U.S. Department of Justice, 1988), p. 4.)

In sum, the findings of this nationwide survey reflected a correctional system already extended beyond the limits of its capacity. Correctional administrators were clearly in need of additional space, programs, and services to keep pace with an increasing population. In addition, they required more training and programs for dealing with specialized offender needs.[12]

MANAGEMENT STYLES OF CONTEMPORARY WARDENS

Wardens' management styles of the 1970s differ greatly from those of the 1980s and those emerging in the 1990s. The major of bureaucratic wardens of the 1970s used **participatory management** schemes with staff and sometimes with inmates; many wardens of the 1980s chose either the control, consensual, or responsibility models to manage their institutions. In contrast, the emerging wardens of the 1990s increasingly view themselves as professionals and team players dealing with institutional problems in innovative ways.

Wardens of the 1970s

Correctional administrators in the 1970s found themselves thrust into the center of a shifting and volatile field of forces. They had to not only relate to the staff and inmates of their institutions but also interact successfully with the director, the legislature, the press, labor unions, employee organizations, law-enforcement agencies, the courts, and the various special-interest groups in the community. They knew that their negotiations within this web of relationships had to protect and maintain the institution; yet, at the same time it was necessary to generate needed internal development and change.

Participatory management philosophy, adapted largely from the private sector, and the **shared-powers model** were the two styles of management developed to meet the challenges of managing a correctional institution.

Participatory Management Philosophy Those correctional administrators holding to this managerial philosophy tended to view themselves as generalists rather than as specialists. The generalist is charged with the responsibility of conceptualizing the whole organization and of developing a systemwide plan to manage it. Conceptualization involves the ability to see the whole and to rise above the organizational parts. Obviously, to be a generalist in as complex a physical, economic, and social system as a correctional facility is no easy task. It requires great dedication and endless hours of work, knowledge of all areas of institutional functioning, and the security that comes when one is comfortable with oneself and knows where one is going. This philosophy of administration requires participatory management and input from all levels of staff. The effective generalist does not try to carry the total weight or responsibility of a correctional institution on his or her shoulders, knowing that it is necessary to bring others into the decision-making process.

Correctional administrators at the time turned to the private sector for participatory management models. This approach to correctional management became known as the **corporate management model.** In this approach, great emphasis is placed upon modern management techniques and meaningful tables of organization. This model also develops lines of authority and accountability; too, feedback and quantitative evaluations are widely used.

But it did not take long for these correctional administrators to discover that the new management theory did not solve the problems in American prisons. By the 1980s, most of these correctional administrators had come to realize that in spite of this private-sector management theory, most prisons had more violence, worse living conditions, and fewer programming opportunities than those under the autocrat of old.

Shared-powers Model In the 1970s, many correctional administrators throughout the nation turned to a shared-powers model to manage prisons. Inspired by a rehabilitative ideal, wardens attempted to enhance the "respect," "dignity," and "status" of both staff and inmates by granting them some power in the governance of the prison. Still bureaucrats, they wished to bring inmates, as well as staff and central office, into institutional decision making.

This push for the democratization of the prison created a power vacuum to which prisoners, as well as guards, responded quickly by attempting to advance their respective interests. Specific groups grounded in some ideology and the advocacy group were the two main forms of inmate association developed in the prison. The Black Muslims represented the most notable of the ideological groups. Advocacy groups attempted to advance all inmate rights—locally, statewide, and even nationally. For example, inmate councils and inmate grievance systems were developed, and prisoner unions were talked about in several American prisons.[13]

As a result of the introduction of inmate councils, prisoners were assured greater representation and participation in institutional committees, such as superintendents' staff meetings and adjustment and classification committee hearings. Thus, prisoners managed to gain some power and authority, often at the expense of the custodial staff. The development of inmate grievance systems probably represented the greatest gains for prisoners. In some institutions, this grievance system actually did represent shared powers for inmates. The prisoner union, however, never shared any power and was never an even moderately successful venture, even in California, where it started.

The inmates' gain in power antagonized the custodial staff, who, along with the warden, were losing power and authority. To regain what they had lost, guards began to organize into unions so that they could present demands as a united force. But beyond the traditional "bread and butter" issues, guard unions became concerned about issues related to personal safety and security behind the walls. The increased authority of correctional officers' unions is seen in the fact that they now control work assignments and many other job security decisions.

In sum, the shared-powers model resulted in inmates seeking to become politicized and "recitizenized." The guards, as well as the warden, paid the price in loss of power. This correctional model also hastened the erosion of authority and power of corrections staff and contributed significantly to the widening alienation between guards and institutional administrators.[14]

Wardens of the 1980s

In the 1980s, nearly all correctional systems abandoned the shared-powers model, but a few states, particularly California and Illinois, came close to sliding into an **inmate control model.** In these states, inmate gangs wielded such power within the walls that they attempted, sometimes successfully, to dictate prison policy.[15]

John J. DiIulio Jr., in examining prison management during the 1980s, identified three main approaches: the **Texas control model,** the **California consensus model,** and the **Michigan responsibility model.**[16] The differences in these approaches, according to DiIulio, are rooted in differences of correctional philosophy. He adds that the importance of prison management is that it determines the quality of prison life—the order, the amenities, and the available services. Indeed, he claims that the prison disorders of the 1980s were the "simple tales of failed prison management."[17] Bert Useem and Peter Kimball's recent study of prison riots supports this viewpoint:

> If one accepts our thesis that the cause of prison riots is the disorganization of the state, then it follows that maintaining a strong, coherent prison administration is the crucial ingredient in avoiding disturbances. New Mexico and the other prison systems under study "blew," not because they chose the wrong style of management, but because their efforts were so thoroughly disorganized and incoherent. In short, good administration is the key. This may be an obvious point, but if so it has been missed by other students of prison riots.[18]

DiIulio is most supportive of the control model in Texas that has been dismantled by the *Ruiz* v. *Estelle* court decision.[19] He recognized the internal and external defects of this control model. Internally, the "building tenders" (B.T.) system gave the inmates too much power; externally, under Director Estelle, the control model lost political support and badly handled the long-term *Ruiz* v. *Estelle* court decision. Yet DiIulio strongly supports the order that the control model achieved, especially during the ten years (1962–1972) George Beto was director of the department. Objectively, according to DiIulio, there was less overt violence under the control model, and infractions were less frequent and less severe. This meant that prisoners were less at risk in Texas prisons than in other prisons across the nations. Subjectively, life within the prison system of the control model during its heyday was calm, stable, and predictable.[20]

DiIulio is far more critical of the other two approaches to correctional management. He believes that the Michigan responsibility model maximizes inmates' responsibility for their own actions. Prisons, according to this model, are to be run by imposing minimum constraints on inmates, an approach that supposedly fosters prison community. DiIulio charges that the major internal defect of this model is the alienation and lack of support from correctional officers.[21]

The California consensus model, concludes DiIulio, is even more of a disaster. This model "is a crazy-quilt pattern of correctional principles and practices."[22] He claims that the management of California prisons eventually evolved into the question of how to manage prison gangs. He charges that former directors Raymond Procunier, the father of the consensual model, and J. J. Enomoto, his successor, consulted and negotiated with the gangs. Thus, because of California's preoccupation with gang organization and violence and the enduring instability that brings to the institution, DiIulio believes that California has "given the store away" to the inmates.[23]

An Illinois warden in the early 1980s admitted that gang leaders placed great pressure on prison administrators to deal or negotiate with them. He added that although this usually is a serious mistake, it is also a serious mistake not to communicate with gang members. He explained why:

> We don't deal with them [gangs], but we listen to what they have to say. I tell them what I expect, and find out what they expect. Recently, a gang leader came to me and said, "You served bad meat over the weekend." We investigated and found that we had thrown out 120 pounds of bad meat the previous weekend. I called several of the gang leaders in and told them about it. This prevented a major incident. Gangs can get us over a barrel. We only have them over a barrel with the use of force during a disturbance. We don't want to see any of our people get hurt, and we don't want to see any of their people get hurt.[24]

In sum, with some variations, DiIulio wants a return of the departed Texas control model. He seems to buy into Warden Ragen's adage that either the inmates or the staff is in control, and he believes that a paramilitary operation and unflagging discipline will recapture the prison from inmates. He adds in another place that "to punish rule violators proportionately" is the key to prison discipline and control.[25]

Wardens of the 1990s

Present-day wardens appear to be divided into those who are disillusioned and overwhelmed and those who are innovative and in control of their facilities. Disillusioned wardens tend to feel that they have lost their reform ideology, because they no longer have the rehabilitation ideal, human relations model, participatory management philosophy, or shared-powers model to provide the hope that the present state of imprisonment can be changed. Faced with overwhelming problems, especially in maximum security prisons, this group would agree with the pessimistic Illinois warden who said, "The pressure is heavy duty, and I feel numb when I leave the institution at night. I don't think any warden can make it three years in this institution."[26]

Another group of wardens is attempting to develop a new approach to correctional administration. These wardens are different in a number of ways from the first group.[27] First, they believe that they can have an impact and that they do not need to be limited by what others have done. Or to express this in another way, they believe there is a way to run a prison so that both inmates and staff can have hope and can have mutual confidence in and respect for each other.

Second, these wardens have a hands-on approach; they spend a good deal of time walking the cellblocks, visiting inmates in their cells, touring the yard, and talking with staff at their assignments. They believe that to reduce the frequency, scope, and seriousness of institutional problems, the top administrator must set the climate by interacting directly with inmates and all levels of staff on a regular basis. This system provides information needed to avoid or defuse pending problems.

Third, a major goal of these wardens is to build a team of supportive staff. In Box 13-2, Warden Frank Wood discusses how important this supportive team is to the management of the prison. Note that Wood wants senior staff who supplement his skills as well as those who are willing to stand up to him.

Box 13-2 Interview with Frank Wood

Question: What type of ideal staff should a warden have? What type of people are you looking for?

Answer: Each of us has our own strengths and limitations, and what I look for to fill the positions that answer directly to the warden are those people who can fill in the gaps where I have limitations. I also look for people who have the following characteristics:

- Who challenge me to be my very best
- Who in their own right are confident and quite capable of running the institution as well as or better than I
- Who have knowledge, skills, experience, and personal characteristics that I don't exhibit as well as they do
- Who have differing perspectives and viewpoints than myself and can articulate those opposing views in a nonadversarial way, but yet are consistent with the ultimate philosophy and goals that I consider to be crucial to the pursuit of excellence in managing and operating an enlightened institution
- Who I believe will not only enhance my confidence and decision making but also will bring to the entire administrative team a higher level of review deliberation

and consideration to ensure that we, as a team, have explored all of the possibilities and options in making tough, very complex decisions

- Who are not easily provoked and have the capacity to be restrained even under extreme provocation
- Who demonstrate and have a track record of demonstrating maturity, good judgment, insight, and wisdom. There usually is not a relationship between wisdom and intelligence. Many people are very bright, intelligent, and knowledgeable, but rarely is true wisdom reflected in their work or personal lives. In fact, in my experience I find wisdom in very unexpected places. Wisdom appears to flow from our spiritual side. I look for people who recognize their place in Creation, have a high priority on investing in their spiritual lives, and are searching for insight, truth, and wisdom through a strong faith
- Who for the most part agree with my philosophy and can communicate that they believe in it with the same sincerity and intensity that I do. This is essential because they are the linkage with subordinate staff
- Who are honest and have integrity so that they will take stands on issues after thoughtful analysis and deliberation and not be wetting their finger and holding it up to find which way the wind is blowing on a given day
- Who are tactful and are able to articulate things well so that they can be understood by staff at all levels and the inmate clientele
- Who have perseverance and tenacity and are in the profession for the long haul
- Who have the courage to tell the emperor that he's naked and do that appropriately, privately, and not to elevate themselves at the expense of others
- Who are not easily intimidated
- Who have the capacity to understand and relate to inmates
- Who don't have biases about particular people or the crimes they commit or other personal biases
- Who are not arrogant, pompous, know-it-all, offensive, condescending, caustic, abrasive, and self-righteous
- Who have the intellectual depth to know that rarely will we find simplistic solutions to society's and mankind's very complex problems.

In summary, I look for the best and the brightest. I look for people who don't just talk golden rule but those who practice it, people who are loyal, and people who will be responsible to both the real and the imagined concerns of inmates and staff. I look for staff who have commitment and are dedicated and able to convince other people that our profession is important and noble and that we can make a difference.

Source: Interviewed in June 1990.

Fourth, this new breed of correctional administrator in the 1990s is quick to use the technological advantages that have recently become available to corrections. Today, innovations within the prison combined with external supervision are enabling federal and some state corrections officials to shape a new prison environment based on accountability, functional integration, risk assessment, and institutional differentiation. Management information systems (MIS) have led to systemwide changes. For example, inmates are tracked more effectively throughout the system, personnel have been upgraded, and population needs can be projected. Smaller and newer prisons, better classification systems, and unit management have helped to defuse institutional violence.[28]

Fifth, there is a real commitment among these correctional administrators to administer institutions in a rational way. One of the ways this can be done is to reduce uncertainty among inmates and staff. J. D. Thompson's excellent book *Organization in Action* suggests that organizations are expected to produce results, and, therefore, their actions must be reasonable or rational. Accordingly, managers must act rationally in a way that will produce the desired results.[29] But the problem that organizations face when attempting to act reasonably is uncertainty. As Frank Wood says in the interview quoted in Chapter 1, "We operate on the philosophy that there should be no surprises. I don't want to be surprised; my supervisors don't want to be surprised; staff and inmates don't want to be surprised."[30]

Sixth, these innovative wardens are receptive to the improved means of supervising correctional institutions that have been developed. They welcome legislative task forces that examine everything from free time (recreation) on death row to T.I.E.—Training, Industry, and Education vocational programs. They also are re-

High-security facility. Minnesota Department of Corrections, Stillwater, Minnesota. (*Source:* Public Information Office, Department of Corrections, St. Paul, Minnesota.)

ceptive to inmate grievance procedures and ombudsmen. Unlike their predecessors, they do not resist court supervision of prisons, including American Civil Liberties Union attorneys, defense counsel, representatives of the attorney general, and attorneys litigating for prisoners.

Seventh, these correctional administrators attempt to model the behaviors that they want to elicit from inmates and staff. They believe that a crucial component of this human relations approach is their willingness to demonstrate to others what involvement in and understanding of others entails. They also affirm that before they can expect this response from staff, they must demonstrate to others their job commitment, trustworthiness, loyalty, and high moral integrity. Also, as part of this modeling they attempt to show staff how to interact effectively with inmates without losing their respect and without being compromised, manipulated, or "taken for a ride."

Finally, they usually enthusiastically endorse the accreditation process of the American Correctional Association. An institution or a community-based program is accredited when it meets the minimum standards proposed by the American Correctional Association (now the standards of the Commission on Accreditation for Corrections). The accreditation process has been so widely supported because wardens feel that the standards were created by understanding fellow correctional administrators, that the standards of ensuring accreditation provided an attainable goal, and that the accreditation process made them seem more professional.

In sum, the development of correctional administration with these individuals can be understood as the attempt to become "rational," which means to become receptive to information and knowledge, or learning, as the means of effecting organizational change. The purpose of rational action is to know the end to be achieved and the proper means to reach this goal.[31] These correctional administrators pursue the learning, or brain, metaphor, rather than traditional prison metaphors. (See Box 13-3.)

Box 13-3 Metaphors for Prison Organizations

Correctional institutions have undergone more change over the past 20 years than they had in the previous 160 years. This change has been widely documented in a rich literature that has explored many incidents of change as well as the reactions of correctional administrators. Thomas Murton describes the scandal-reform-scandal cycle of prison change in Arkansas; John Irwin focuses on racial consciousness and the politics of power within California prisons; Leo Carroll describes changing race and social relations in Rhode Island; James Jacobs examines the relationship between outside society and the administration of Stateville Penitentiary; John Dilulio, Steve Martin and Sheldon Ekland-Olson, and Ben Crouch and James Marquart describe the impact of court decisions and administrative reaction on the management of penal institutions.

In this literature, it appears that four metaphors for prisons as organizations play a dominant role in the thinking of both the staff and administrators involved and those who analyze prison organizations.

PRISONS AS MACHINES

The metaphor of the mechanistic perspective dominates the analysis in speaking of the "paramilitary" nature of correctional staff. According to Gareth Morgan, the order and efficiency that should characterize prison management are achieved "through the creation of a fixed division of tasks, hierarchical supervision, and detailed rules and regulations."

As Dilulio and Jacobs describe the institutions they studied, it is clear that these paramilitary systems functioned more effectively during the period prior to the early 1960s, the era of the "Big House" prison. However, when the politics of race entered prisons and the "hands-off" doctrine of the courts vanished, then prison organizations perceiving themselves in ways described by the mechanistic metaphor experienced greater difficulties in coping with their changing environment.

PRISONS AS CULTURES

The metaphor of thinking about prisons as cultures can be traced back to Donald Clemmer's *The Prison Community* and is found in nearly all sociological studies of the prison produced since. Clemmer states that "the prison, like other social groups, has a culture."

A cultural approach, according to Morgan, focuses attention on the ways members of an organization create, share, and transmit the meanings for various aspects of organizational life. Today, the major shortcoming in applying this metaphor is that generational change among both staff and inmates has resulted in new and competing cultural meanings being imported into the prison. In other words, this metaphor is no longer as useful as it once was because "the good old days" of a unified staff and inmate culture have long passed from the prison scene.

PRISONS AS ORGANISMS

Jacobs's *Stateville* has most extensively described the relationship between prisons and their environment and the transformation of prisons as machines to prisons as organisms.

> The realization of mass society as expressed by such trends as the growth of prisoners' rights and the intrusion of judicial norms into the prison has provided the impetus toward the transformation of institutional authority and administration. When the prison as an autonomous institution was located at society's periphery and beyond the reach of the courts and other core institutional systems, there was no need for the system of internal authority to become rationalized. It was only when outside interest groups began making demands on the prison and holding administrators accountable for their decisions that traditional authoritarian systems of the institutional authority became untenable.

Jacobs's analysis actually results in an "open system" perspective. Morgan states that "the idea of openness emphasizes the key relationships between the environment and the internal functioning of the system." Unquestionably, while the environmental influences on prisons are more pervasive and acknowledged today than ever before, this metaphor is limited in understanding the change process and the internal functioning of the prison.

PRISON AS POLITICS

The political metaphor is another that has been applied to the study and practice of understanding the prison organization. This perspective, according to Morgan, focuses on "interest, conflict and power." Different constituencies within (and external to) the prison organization has interests in how prisons organize themselves. The ability of a particular constituency to achieve its goals will be determined by its ability to exercise power. This perspective also recognizes a variety of sources of power, such as formal authority, control over scarce resources, organizational structure, decision-making processes, knowledge and information, organizational boundaries, and control of technology.

In sum, these four metaphors may be inadequate in themselves to explain the prison as an organization, but each continues to influence the operation of the prison. The prison, especially the maximum security one, remains a paramilitary organization and is likely to retain much of this structure as long as security remains the dominant concern of institutional administrators. The unified prison culture of the past has been replaced by a number of competing groups, or subcultures, that shape the attitudes and outlooks of members. The day that the prison could keep outsiders out is long gone; indeed, one of the most widely examined research findings in recent years is that prisoners are affected as much by importation from outside the prison as by the deprivations of confinement. Finally, the political metaphor will always be found on all levels of prison management and inmate life, because power, authority, and conflict are likely to continue explaining the dynamics of prison life.

The problem is that the machine, culture, and political metaphors, especially, foster conservative and often reactionary agendas in the prison. The fact is that the repressiveness and rigidity of the prison are not likely to change until another metaphor begins to influence prison operations. Morgan proposes that this new metaphor, which incorporates the need to change, is the brain metaphor. The perspective of the brain metaphor is on learning. As Morgan describes it:

> the whole process of learning hinges on an ability to remain open to changes occurring in the environment, and on an ability to challenge operating assumptions in a most fundamental way.

Source: This box is adapted from Lucien X. Lombardo, "Metaphors for Prison Organizations and Correctional Officer Adaptation to Change." Paper presented at the Annual Meeting of the American Society of Criminology, Reno, Nevada (November 1989). Lombardo bases his brain, or learning, metaphor on Gareth Morgan, *Images of Organization* (Beverly Hills, Calif.: Sage, 1986).

This new breed of correctional administrator, then, tries to provide leadership for a culture of learning to take place within prison organizations. This will be accomplished to a much larger extent when (1) administrators across the nation believe that they can make a difference; (2) more wardens adopt a hands-on approach; (3) they develop a team of supportive staff, while at the same time recognizing the importance of different viewpoints on their team; (4) they seek out technological advances and improve means of supervising correctional institutions to improve the safety and security of staff and inmates; (5) they avoid imposing limited structures of goals and objectives and allow direction to emerge from ongoing organizational processes;

(6) they value openness and reduce uncertainty in a complex and changing environment; (7) they develop organizational structures that encourage the above processes, and (8) they are willing to model the humane behaviors they want to elicit from staff and inmates.

SCOPE OF ADMINISTRATION

The warden, or superintendent, is ultimately responsible for everything that takes place within a correctional institution. The warden delegates the responsibility for custodial services and for program services to associate wardens. In large correctional institutions, an associate warden for management services and an associate warden for industrial and agricultural services is charged with the responsibility for those areas. The associate wardens, in turn, rely on middle managers and line staff to operate the various departments that make up their sphere of responsibility (see Figure 13.2).

Institutional administration encompasses establishment of policy, planning, institutional monitoring, staff supervision, personnel direction, and fiscal management.[32]

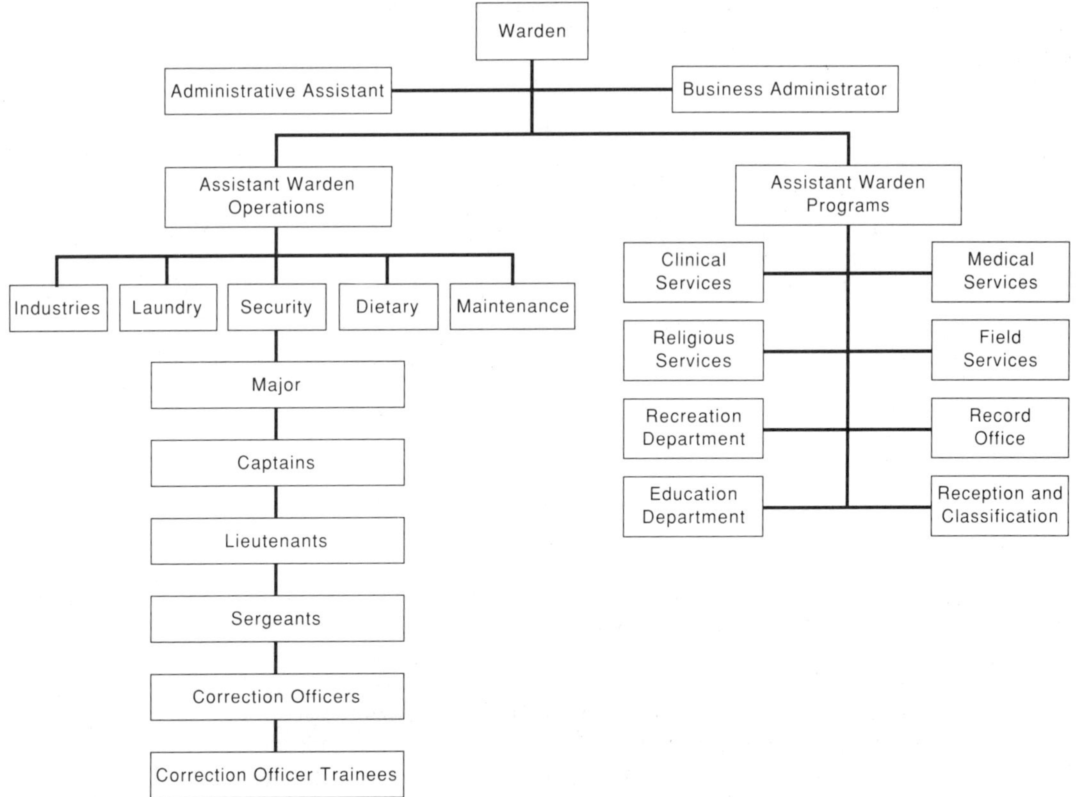

Figure 13.2 Institutional table of organization. (*Source*: Illinois' Menard Correctional Center.)

Establishment of Policy

Wardens determine policy for their particular institutions, although major policy changes must be cleared with the central office. One of the problems of determining policy stems from the number of groups that must be satisfied: the public, the inmates, the various levels of institutional staff, and the director of corrections. As policy makers, most wardens continue to see themselves as generalists who must develop the ability to see the whole and to function above the organizational parts. Or to express this in another way, this conceptual skill requires that the warden see the organization as a whole and recognize how the various functions and groups of the organization interrelate and depend upon one another.

Planning

The warden is expected to develop goals for the future and methods of achieving them. Some top administrators continue to find modern management principles to be helpful tools in the goal-setting process. If no long-range plan exists, most wardens know they will become involved in crisis-centered management, in which they face the same problems day after day. Staff burnout and inappropriate reactions to organizational problems are the consequences of crisis-centered management.

Civil lawsuits by inmates is another area in which planning is needed. Autocratic wardens used to stroll through the prison yard, priding themselves on their ability to relate to convicts. As inmates stood at attention, the warden would make friendly inquiries about how they were doing. Contemporary institutional administrators are faced with much more complex relations with inmates, because administrators who are sued by several prisoners each week must spend much of their time responding to charges, preparing affidavits, and testifying in court. This time-consuming process is not only frustrating and draining on administrative resources but also intimidating. Administrators may end up paying exorbitant attorney's fees or sustaining extensive damages, possibly losing everything they own. Court decisions that impose new procedures, standards, and personnel requirements on a state system can also be expensive, time consuming, and full of problems for administrators. To deal more effectively with civil suits, the wise administrator uses planning to eliminate any inhumane conditions exposed by these court actions, documents all decision making relating to inmates, develops expertise in correctional law, and swiftly complies with the orders of the court.

Institutional Monitoring

The effective institutional supervisor must have adequate information about what is taking place within the facility and must provide for special inmate needs. To keep informed, wardens must find ways to maintain good communication with prisoners. The day when a warden can act as an isolated autocrat is gone. Smart wardens now spend time in the yard relating with inmates. They insist that the assistant wardens also spend time working to maintain open relationships with inmates. Wardens can also improve rapport with inmates by "running a call line," extending an open invitation to inmates who wish to see them.

Yet maintaining effective communication with inmates is more difficult than in the past because of inmate gangs in many prisons. Gangs want prison administrators to recognize their existence and, if they can persuade them to do so, to negotiate with gang leaders. As administrators who supported the shared-powers model discovered in the 1970s and 1980s, any type of negotiation with prison gangs usually ends up in greater gang control of the prison and in increased levels of violence.

Another important aspect of institutional monitoring is providing for special inmate needs. In Box 13-4, J. Michael Quinlan, director of the Federal Bureau of Prisons, suggests that classification of inmates is one means of identifying and providing for special inmate needs. Prisoners with special needs vary from youthful prisoners, mentally ill and mentally retarded prisoners, to sexually deviant and long-term prisoners.

The surge of drug-trafficking gangs across the nation in the late 1980s and early 1990s has resulted in higher rates of adult institutionalization for juveniles involved in these gangs. Survival is no easy matter for most juveniles sentenced to prison, and they frequently are victimized in every possible way.

Mentally retarded prisoners, like emotionally retarded prisoners, constitute a small but nevertheless significant proportion of inmates housed within correctional institutions in this nation. Statistics are sparse for the number of mentally ill and mentally retarded inmates, but figures available for New York prisons report that 3 percent of the inmate population is mentally retarded.[33]

Both mentally retarded and mentally ill prisoners clearly have difficulty adjusting to the prison environment. Like many youthful prisoners, these inmates require self-protection and demand a great deal of staff time and attention. Without staff's watching out for them and giving them special attention, they become victims and rule-violators, and perhaps even self-destructive.

The number of prisoners who have committed incest appears to be increasing dramatically across the nation. As Commissioner Orville Pung of the Minnesota Department of Corrections notes in the following interview, sentencing guidelines and mandatory-sentencing acts that call for a prison sentence for sexual assaults explain why most of these offenders are being sentenced to prison.

> When I took over in 1982, 7 percent of our inmates were sex offenders; this has gone up to almost 20 percent. Many of these sex offenders aren't rapists; they're in for incest, which creates a whole new set of problems, because many of them are older inmates.
>
> I don't know if many intrafamilia sex offenders in the past were even charged, to be honest with you. There was a certain lack of concern about intrafamilia sex offenses, and this kind of thing was hush-hush. I think when a priest was involved with an altar boy or when a teacher was involved with a student, the thing was handled administratively. The laws were not geared up, nor was the aggressiveness of the victimization notion prevalent. I don't think the system had a way of handling victims or a way of having them come forth. Prosecutors weren't prosecuting these offenders, and when they did, people tended to see these people as mentally ill or they just said, "Incest, that's none of our business." Once it was moved into the area of sexual assault, it took on a whole new meaning. The sentencing guidelines call for a certain reaction to sexual assault, which is a presumptive prison sentence.[34]

Offenders who have been incarcerated for incest find imprisonment very difficult. They receive no respect from their peers and, indeed, are on the bottom of the

Box 13-4 Interview with J. Michael Quinlan

Question: I've always been impressed with the Bureau's approach to staff development. Can you give us some insight into its workings?

Answer: One of the real strengths of the Bureau of Prisons is the fact that it's a career agency. It is the only agency in the government, at least to my knowledge, that is still headed by a career administrator, and all the positions within the agency are filled with people who have worked their way up to management ranks.

We have a fundamental belief that we have talent and can train and groom people for the top jobs in the agency. The training continues throughout the individual's career. We start out with three weeks at the Federal Law Enforcement Training Center in Georgia. This provides the fundamental precepts for correctional work in the Bureau, but then that's augmented by institutional training as well as specialty training in our management training center. We feel that that is one of the mainstays of the Bureau's ability to manage effectively and efficiently in having the training programs and then offering people, not only good job experiences, but also the opportunity to compete for higher responsibilities and promotions.

In moving people to positions of greater responsibility, they get the opportunity to see other programs in action. They work with all types of people, which prevents stagnation because of working with one type of institution, one type of management. Through this, they grow into much more effective managers. They are more creative and more willing to start new initiatives because they learn along the way that there are other programs that are successful at other institutions. They are able to function at the highest levels at which we need them to function.

The major topic of discussion for the 1990s is: How do we most effectively categorize offenders? We are looking at how to stratify the program resources that we offer. We do not want them offered at every one of our institutions, of which we now have 64. This number will soon increase to around 100. The question becomes: How can we offer, at certain institutions, a very effective program and only offer it to those prisoners who are in most need of it and are the most deserving? We're doing that now with drug treatment. We have identified eight institutions in which intensive or comprehensive drug treatment programs are being offered. Eligible and interested prisoners from other institutions are being transferred to those programs. This type of stratification can be expanded in the future to include education programs, vocational training programs, and work programs. Prisoners who have come back many times and are virtually career criminals would not be put in institutions where they would use up valuable program space. These prisoners would be put in institutions where they can work. Obviously, we would make sure they have literacy programs available, but we wouldn't offer them valuable vocational and educational programs.

Source: Interviewed in June 1990.

inmate social hierarchy. Unless they are protected from other inmates, they are likely to be assaulted and perhaps even killed.

Finally, the "greying" of the prison is one of the features of contemporary prisons. Determinate and mandatory sentences have contributed to increasing the length of time inmates are spending in prison. Life without the benefit of parole (LWOP) sentencing options are also contributing to increasing the numbers of long-term prisoners. Twenty-three states report having a life-without-parole sentence. In 1988, more than 41,000 were serving a life sentence, and there were 7,072 inmates sentenced to life without parole, a 24 percent increase from 1984.[35]

As the number of LWOP inmates continue to increase, it is likely the mounting frustration of these inmates will contribute to mass disturbances and killings within prison walls.[36] D. L. Peck and R. Jones's examination of LWOP inmates led them to conclude that the potential for violence is high as their life sentence seems to give them a license to kill.[37]

Staff Supervision

The warden is expected to develop training programs for new staff and to make changes in job assignments when necessary. In Box 13-4, Director Quinlan discusses how staff training is related to making the Bureau of Prisons a career agency.

The leadership pattern the warden chooses to follow also affects the way subordinates do their jobs. Most institutional administrators continue to believe that staff morale and job involvement are enhanced when all levels of personnel participate in decision making, but the degree of personnel involvement is a decision that the top manager must make. This shared decision making can take many forms. One top administrator may sell an already formulated decision to the group; another may present a tentative decision subject to change; still another will describe the problem, take suggestions for its resolution, and make the final decision independently. Other administrators define the limits but allow the group to make the decision.[38]

Organizational restructuring through **unit management,** or the creation of functional units, is probably the most widely used basic method of sharing decision making with staff. The concept of a functional unit includes housing together a relatively small number of offenders throughout the length of their institutional stay; working in a close, intense relationship with a multidisciplinary, permanently assigned team of staff members whose offices are located in the unit; providing these personnel with decision-making authority for all within-institution aspects of programming and disciplinary actions; and assigning offenders to a particular living unit contingent upon a need for the specific type of treatment program offered. Dividing the prison into smaller units establishes both authority and communication links within each unit. It also places nearest the top of the organizational hierarchy those units with the most direct contact with inmates.[39] The rationale behind this organizational structure is that the close contact between unit managers and top-level administration will better assure maximum services to inmates.

Nearly all the correctional institutions of the federal Bureau of Prisons use unit management; so do several institutions in Kansas, Michigan, Indiana, and other states. Illinois' Vienna Correctional Center has used a similar concept, called zone management, and Illinois' Stateville Correctional Center has instituted unit management to break up inmate gang control of the institution.

Personnel Direction

The warden is involved in routine hiring and suspension decisions, employee relations and grievances, and negotiations with union officials. Although the warden makes the final personnel decision, the personnel manager is directly involved with the personnel process. He or she initially interviews any applicants, guides them through the civil service process, and then arranges further interviews with appropriate institutional staff. Other staff are often permitted to interview candidates for openings in their departments and may have some say about who is appointed. Supervisors are also expected to evaluate annually all individuals who report to them.

Fiscal Management

"A good warden," as one administrator put it, "always has a handle on the budget."[40] Fiscal management should be a year-long process. There should be periodic (perhaps monthly) staff meetings to keep abreast of developments and the status of the budget. The warden should maintain his or her own file on changes that will be needed and others that will be recommended for the next year's budget. Where emergencies have required unexpected expenditures, there must be immediate planning for the necessary budgetary adjustments. All of this calls for close collaboration with the deputy director for administrative services in the central office. The warden's staff should prepare and justify the institutional budget to the commissioner or director well in advance of the submission of the department budget to the department of finance. A warden who cannot or will not go through this year-long exercise is likely to get a budget that neither the warden nor subordinates are going to like. The lower-level staff people should by all means know how the budget affects their jobs. The guard in the cellblock should not be left to speculate about these matters; the training program should keep him or her thoroughly informed.

But, even if lower-level staff are not involved in the formal process of fiscal management, they usually must learn to do without, as money, staff, and equipment never seem to be adequate. Clinical supervisors must help counselors deal with their large caseloads. The chief engineer must repair rather than replace old plumbing. Because of the policies of scarcity that exist in correctional institutions, the mark of a good supervisor is the ability to get things done even when resources are in short supply. He or she sometimes must beg, borrow, or use other strategies to obtain what is necessary to run the department.

Professional and Personal Integrity

Wardens daily make decisions that have important moral, ethical, and legal implications. When their jobs are on the line, wardens sometimes resort to solutions that involve questionable tactics. A warden may make a promise without any intent of keeping it, or may resort to directing subordinates to solve a problem, and then ignore the means by which the staff accomplishes the directive. Even the most enlightened wardens may lose control in the heat of an inmate disturbance or the murder of a staff member and unprofessionally retaliate against inmates. One such warden had scantily dressed troublemakers loaded into an unheated bus on a cold winter night and transferred to an institution six hours away. Not surprisingly, some of the inmates suffered severe frostbite.

Top-level administrative staff who must deal directly with the problems of the prison often do more soul searching than any other institutional employee. From time to time, he or she must deal with such considerations as: "Is the organization's influence on me so subtle that I'm not aware of it?" "How extreme will the compromises I make here have to be before I am forced to sit down and take stock of myself?" "Even if I faced up to my compromises, would I be able to do anything about them?" "Am I so conditioned to seeing things the accepted way that I've lost my objectivity?" The answers to these questions will affect the employee's level of job satisfaction and ability to function satisfactorily in the institution.[41]

HUMANIZING CORRECTIONAL INSTITUTIONS

Nearly all institutional administrators face these general problems in varying degrees; yet each institution has unique problems of its own. The warden of a coeducational institution must watch for sexual contact between male and female inmates; the warden of a maximum security institution is likely to have more problems with staff turnover. Community relations are a vital concern in minimum security prisons that have active work release and furlough problems, and the possibility of institutional violence is a problem of which any maximum security warden must always be aware.

In attempting to improve the quality of institutional life for inmates, a worthwhile goal is to create humane institutions that simulate as much as possible the conditions of the real world. The simulation of the real world can be accomplished only when prisons are lawful, safe, industrious, and hopeful.[42]

The Lawful Prison

The purpose of the lawful prison is to prevent proscribed actions and conduct and to provide inmates with all the rights granted by case law. Violators within the prison must be punished appropriately under conditions in which due process procedures prevail. If the administration tolerates unlawful conduct by staff or prisoners—such as the free flow of drugs, thriving gambling rackets, and prostitution rings—nothing else that it attempts will succeed.[43]

The Safe Prison

Both prisoners and staff must be assured of their safety in prison. Although physical attacks on staff and inmates do take place in minimum security institutions, medium and maximum security prisons are the most likely settings for physical and sexual victimization, stabbings, and homicides. Guards across the nation express a common complaint—that they have neither the control nor the respect they used to have. Nor do inmates feel any safer. The new breed of inmates brings with it the criminal expertise of street gang sophistication, the mechanics of narcotics distribution, and an inclination to commit mayhem at a level hitherto unknown in American prisons.

To ensure inmate and staff safety, changes are needed in the design and administration of prisons. Small prisons holding no more than 400 inmates should be built. The physical design of the prison and its operations must ensure that adequately trained guards are in close contact with inmates in living quarters and at work assignments. Guards can best serve the interests of order and safety when they are competent in human relations so that information can flow freely between prisoners and guards without fear that it will be misused, without expectation of special favor, and under conditions of respect and responsibility.

The Industrious Prison

Idleness is one of the real problems of prison life today. Because of overcrowded prisons, what work there is to be done is spread so thin that it is no longer work. The yards and cellblocks are full of inmates trying to copy with their ennui. Some inmates engage in physical activities, such as lifting weights, but too many inmates scheme during idle hours about drug drop-offs, prostitutions rings, and "hitting" (stabbing) inmates in competing gangs.

As a step toward easing the idleness, inmates need to be provided with more work and to have the work they do valued. Inmates must be paid for their work. Workers in prison are denied the value of their labor when they are paid at the low rates allowed in most correctional systems; although paying inmates the rates prevailing in the free market may be unrealistic, higher pay will produce benefits more than commensurate with the increased cost. Finally, work that is more marketable must be found. The useless and menial work characteristic of most prison industries is inappropriate because it fails to equip inmates for employment in the free community.[44]

Fortunately, the 1980s saw the revival of prison industries. This trend has emerged as a result of the pioneering involvement of a few private corporations and the driving force of former Chief Justice Warren E. Burger. Burger formulated the "factories with fences" concept and promoted it with great energy.[45] As prisons in the 1990s are filled with more prisoners who are serving longer sentences, it is important that the prison industries revival of the 1980s be continued and expanded in the 1990s.

The Hopeful Prison

Finally, prisons should provide renewed hope. The loss of hope is one of the consequences of a criminal career. To provide renewed hope, prisons should offer inmates such programs as remedial elementary education, vocational training, individual and group therapy, and self-help techniques. No penalty should be levied against an inmate for failure to participate in a program, but there most be some incentive to engage in treatment. In the hopeful prison, inmates must feel that they have say in their own lives. There is strong evidence that the freedom to make some decisions is needed to build a sense of responsibility. Finally, in the hopeful prison, prisoners must feel that they have acceptance in the outside community. Without such contact, the only reality for the inmate is the cellblocks, the yard, and the prison industrial plant.[46]

CONCLUSIONS

We have outlined wardens' administrative role as it has evolved during the past two or three decades. From princely autocrats, lords of all that they surveyed in the prisons of the nineteenth century and most of the twentieth, they have become field managers for the department of corrections in which they are employed.

The princes of the old days were accountable to no one, unless a headline-making scandal or a radical political change upset their regimes. Warden–field managers are civil service bureaucrats, directly accountable to their superiors, directors or commissioners in the state capital. Their autocratic predecessors could ignore the outside world. They could exclude both the public and the press from their institutions. The new wardens cannot fend off many intruders. Journalists, lawyers, union representatives, professional associations, prison societies, and a host of other outsiders—people who would not have been given the time of day by the old autocrats—must be accommodated.

The problems differ in nature and in magnitude. Today's problems of violence and contraband far exceed in danger and prevalence the nineteenth-century state of affairs. Exacerbating these conditions is the unprecedented overcrowding of the contemporary prison. Also, the turnover of top administrators is high. Many are appointed without sufficient experience; others lack the stamina for a 24-hour-a-day job and the imagination to prepare for contingencies. Nevertheless, a substantial number of wardens have developed the knack of penal administration to a high degree. Their success indicates that this extraordinarily difficult job can be carried on for many years. Their secret is intelligence and continuous examination of experience.

KEY TERMS

autocratic warden

bureaucratization of corrections

California consensus model

corporate management model

inmate control model

Michigan responsibility model

participatory management

rational, or learning, metaphor

shared-powers model

Texas control model

unit management

DISCUSSION TOPICS

13.1 What were the advantages of the autocratic regime of prison management? To the staff? To the prisoners? To the political establishment?

13.2 Should prison wardens be selected by civil service procedures? Discuss the advantages of recruitment by civil service as contrasted with selection by the director from his or her knowledge of available candidates nationwide.

13.3. You have just been assigned to the warden's office in a maximum security prison. In your initial conference with the associate warden custody you are told that his most critical problem is violence between members of rival prison gangs. What questions will you ask him to inform yourself of the extent of the problem and the measures he has taken to control it?

13.4 To what extent should the warden involve him- or herself with the institutional budget? Why could this problem not be left with the central office staff?

ANNOTATED REFERENCES

DiIulio, John. *Governing Prisons: A Comparative Study of Correctional Management.* New York: Free Press, 1987. *A controversial book because of the author's support for the Texas control model.*

England, David. "Development in Prison Administration." In John W. Murphy and Jock E. Dison, eds., *Are Prisons Any Better? Twenty Years of Correctional Reform.* Newbury Park, Calif.: Sage, 1990, pp. 61–75. *A highly recommended article on the need for rationality in correctional administration.*

Fox, James G. *Organizational and Racial Conflict in Maximum-Security Prisons.* Lexington, Mass.: Lexington Books, 1982. *This study of five state maximum security prisons assesses the relationship between management policies and the dynamics of prisoner communities.*

Martin, Steve, and Sheldon Ekland-Olson. *Texas Prisons.* Austin: Texas Monthly Press, 1987. *Examines the correctional administration of the Texas Department of Corrections during the* Ruiz *v.* Estelle *case.*

Morgan, Gareth. *Images of Organization.* Beverly Hills, Calif.: Sage, 1986. *Develops the brain, or learning, metaphor discussed in this chapter.*

Stastny, Charles, and Gabrielle Trynauer. *Who Rules the Joint? The Changing Political Culture of Maximum-Security Prisons in America.* Lexington, Mass.: Lexington Books, 1982. *An interesting account of the failed experiment in inmate self-government at Washington's Walla Walla Penitentiary.*

Useem, Bert, and Peter Kimball. *States of Siege: U.S. Prison Riots, 1971–1986.* New York: Oxford University Press, 1989. *Argues that faulty prison management is usually related to inmate disturbances.*

NOTES

1. Interviewed in October 1978.
2. Interviewed in February 1983.
3. More and more wardens are pursuing graduate training in management theory. We know

of two such wardens who received a year off to study management at the Harvard Business School.
4. The following section on the changing role of correctional administrators is largely adapted from John Conrad and Simon Dinitz, "Position Paper for the Seminar on the Isolated Prisoner" (Paper presented at the Academy for Contemporary Problems, National Institute of Corrections, Columbus, Ohio, December 8–9, 1977), pp. 4–11.
5. James B. Jacobs, *Stateville* (Chicago: University of Chicago Press, 1977).
6. Conrad and Dinitz, "Position Paper for the Seminar on the Isolated Prisoner," pp. 4–11.
7. Interviewed in June 1990.
8. Elmer K. Nelson Jr. and Catherine H. Lovell, *Developing Correctional Administration*, Research Report of the Joint Commission on Correctional Manpower and Training (Washington: Government Printing Office, 1969).
9. Robert C. Grieser, *Wardens and State Corrections Commissioners Offer Their Views in National Assessment* (Washington: U.S. Department of Justice, 1988), p. 1.
10. Ibid., p. 4.
11. Ibid., p. 7.
12. Ibid., p. 8.
13. Israel L. Barak-Glantz, "Toward a Conceptual Schema of Prison Management Styles" *The Prison Journal*, August–Winter, 1981: 49.
14. Ibid., p. 50.
15. Ibid., p. 51.
16. John DiIulio, *Governing Prisons: A Comparative Study of Correctional Management* (New York: Free Press, 1987), p. 5.
17. Ibid., p. 30.
18. Bert Useem and Peter Kimball, *States of Siege: U.S. Prison Riots, 1971–1986* (New York: Oxford University Press, 1989), p. 227.
19. For the history of this court decision, see Steve Martin and Sheldon-Ekland Olson, *Texas Prisons* (Austin: Texas Monthly Press, 1987).
20. DiIulio, *Governing Prisons*, pp. 50–53.
21. Ibid., pp. 118–123.
22. Ibid., p. 128.
23. Ibid., pp. 128–134.
24. Interviewed in January 1983.
25. DiIulio, *Governing Prisons*, p. 144.
26. Interviewed in July 1985.
27. The assistance of Frank Wood, warden of Oak Park Heights in Minnesota, was invaluable in shaping this section.
28. For a discussion of these new classification systems, see Joan Petersilia, *The Influence of Criminal Justice Research* (Santa Monica, Calif.: Rand, 1987), pp. 60–61.
29. J. D. Thompson, *Organization in Action* (New York: McGraw-Hill, 1967).
30. Interviewed in June 1990.
31. David England, "Developments in Prison Administration." In John W. Murphy and Jack E. Dison, eds., *Are Prisons Any Better? Twenty Years of Correctional Reform* (Newbury Park, Calif.: Sage, 1990), p. 62.
32. Richard Gramley, a former Illinois warden, defined these basic responsibilities of the correctional administrator and helped shape this discussion.
33. G. Denkowski and E. Denkowski, "The Mentally Retarded Offender in the State Prison System." *Criminal Justice and Behavior* 12, 1985: 55–70.
34. Interviewed in June 1990.
35. E. Herrick, "Number of Lifers in U.S. Jump 9 Percent in Four Years." *Corrections Compendium* 13, April 1988: 9–11.
36. Dennis L. Peck and John O. Smykla, "Legal Mandates and Changes in Prisons." In John

W. Murphy and Jack E. Dison, eds. *Are Prisons Any Better? Twenty Years of Correctional Reforms.* Newbury Park, Calif.: Sage, 1990 p. 27.

37. D. L. Peck and R. Jones, "Life Without Parole: A License to Kill: An Unanticipated Cost Factor." *Corrective and Social Psychiatry and Journal of Behavior Technology Methods and Therapy* 31, 1985: pp. 116–125.
38. Robert Tannenbaum and Warren Schmidt, "How to Choose a Leadership Pattern" *Harvard Business Review* 51, May–June 1973: 164.
39. See Ron Ziegler et al., "Innovative Programming in a Penitentiary Setting: Report from a Functional Unit" *Federal Probation* 40, June 1976: 44–49, for a description of the Alcohol Treatment Unit at the U.S. Penitentiary at Leavenworth, Kansas; and W. Alan Smith and C. E. Fenton, "Unit Management in a Penitentiary: A Practice Experience" *Federal Probation* 40, September 1978: 40–46, for a description of the steps involved in developing a unit management system at the U.S. Penitentiary at Lewisburg, Pennsylvania.
40. Interviewed in July 1985.
41. Samuel A. Culbert, *The Organization Trap and How to Get Out of It* (New York: Basic Books, 1974), p. 4.
42. This section on policy is adapted from John P. Conrad and Simon Dinitz, "The State's Strongest Medicine." In John P. Conrad, ed., *Justice and Consequences* (Lexington, Mass.: Lexington Books; Heath, 1981), pp. 51–70; and Simon Dinitz, "Are Safe and Humane Prisons Possible?" *Australia and New Zealand Journal of Criminology* 14, March 1981: 11–16.
43. Dinitz, "Are Safe and Humane Prisons Possible?" p. 11.
44. Ibid., p. 13.
45. See Gail S. Funke, ed., *National Conference on Prison Industries: Discussion and Recommendations* (Washington: National Center for Innovation in Corrections, 1986).
46. To add another dimension of hope, John P. Conrad says that the prison should be a school of citizenship; see John P. Conrad, "Where There's Hope There's Life." In David Fogel and Joe Hudson, eds., *Justice as Fairness* (Cincinnati: Anderson, 1981), pp. 16–19.

Chapter

14

Institutional Security

CHAPTER OUTLINE

A warden's first priority is to maintain a secure, escape-proof institution. Secure **custody** and control of inmates are prescribed by law and custom and expected by the public. To assure control, most of the maximum security prison budget is allocated to custodial staff and equipment. A warden who is negligent in these matters will not be warden for long. A director of corrections who experiences a spate of riots or escapes will soon find him- or herself in the governor's office signing a letter of resignation.

Most escapes are from minimum security prisons where trust replaces walls.[1] Prisoners in such a setting may and often do walk away. Their absence counts in the statistics of escape. In a hostile legislative audit, a large number of "walkaways" counts against the department as much as the occasional escape from high security. This is not unreasonable. Escapes from minimum custody are failures of the classification process. Too many failures of this kind seriously impair public confidence in the competence of the administration.

The methods that inmates have used to escape from maximum security institutions are legion: placing dummies in their bunks and scaling the wall; using a smuggled gun to take hostages and to demand release; commandeering a prison garbage truck and ramming the gate; hiding in the garbage or in a container taken out of the prison. In another escape, inmates used smuggled guns to blast their way out of a prison bowling alley. Eleven inmates escaped from the New Mexico State Penitentiary by cutting their way through a window, using knotted sheets to climb, first down to the ground, then over the roof of the penitentiary's central corridor, crossing the lighted yard in full view of the tower, and cutting their way through the chain-link fence. Other escapes illustrate the impact of modern technology. Helicopters were used in escape attempts both at the State Prison of Southern Michigan and at the Federal Penitentiary at Marion, Illinois. Four other inmates at Marion opened electrically controlled gates with a computer they had made.[2]

The attempt to prevent escapes is simple compared with the attempt to prevent lethal violence. Keeping the peace within the walls is the most difficult task facing custodial staffs. A small band of guards must maintain control over a large number of unruly and insubordinate prisoners, men and women who do not want to be confined and have never acquired habits of self-control. The tension inherent in such a situation has always existed in prisons, but in these times it has become far more dangerous. The organization of ethnic gangs into cohesive forces has come to rival the official control.[3]

BREAKDOWN OF ORDER

The primacy of imprisonment as the dominant form of punishment, replacing guillotine and pillory, whipping and hanging, is achieved through the use of observation and surveillance to achieve security and control. Michael Foucault discussed Jeremy Bentham's panoptical design as "a dream building in which surveillance of dependent and docile bodies is achieved in its ideal form."[4]

The autocratic warden without question achieved this orderly environment more than contemporary correctional administrators. Convicts were told on their first day, both by staff and other inmates, that they could do "easy time" or "hard time." The staff assured prisoners that if they disturbed the order within the walls, they would lose the good time accumulated in many cases over many years. James Jacobs's *Stateville* aptly describes how Joe Ragen ran Stateville Penitentiary:

> Ragen mentioned "that if you stress the small things, you will never have to worry about the big ones." Then, under his fully elaborated system of administration the inmates were subjected to intense supervision under innumerable rules blanketing every aspect of prison life.[5]

The **inmate code** had a special role in the system that developed, for it was functional to both administrators and prisoners.[6] In the eyes of prison staff, the code promoted order in that it encouraged just doing one's time rather than creating problems. Prisoners knew that disorder within the walls could mean that the informal arrangements between leaders and staff would be set aside, and they would lose privileges it had sometimes taken years to obtain.

In the orderly days of the past, inmate trusties, especially in the south, were widely used to control other inmates because they were able to do many of the tasks usually performed by custodial staff. Arkansas, Mississippi, and Louisiana even permitted such inmates to carry firearms. Until the *Ruiz* v. *Estelle* decision ruled that the **"building tenders"** system in the Texas Department of Corrections was unconstitutional, inmate "building tenders" (B.T.s) were given authority by prison administrators to discipline erring inmates who disturbed the social order.[7] Building tenders were aware that they would be held responsible for inmate disorders and that they might be sent back to stoop labor in the fields for their inability to bring a conflict under control. They ruled the cellblock by terrorizing ordinary inmates. An inmate found stealing another's property was likely to receive a slap across the face, a punch in the stomach, or both. The erring inmate who continued to steal was summarily beaten and, with the staff's approval, moved to another cellblock. But the B.T.s were much more effective in controlling inmates' behavior in the cellblock by preventing incidents. They secured and relayed information on such matters as work strikes, loan sharking, stealing of state property, the distilling of liquor, homosexual acts, revenge plans, and escapes.[8]

Today, many prisons are out-of-control dumping grounds for lower-class "losers." Riots, disturbances, and disorders, as well as ever-present abuses and indignities, are simply the overt manifestations of anomie within the walls. Staff members seem powerless to prevent the periodic "blowouts" and violent eruptions. Robert Johnson suggests that the prison is a "pain limiting" institution as well as a "pain delivering" institution.[9] But the disorder of the contemporary prison unquestionably delivers far more pain than can be justified in a free and democratic society.

Inmate gangs in 32 states, drug appetites of most prisoners, inmates doing longer periods of time in determinate-sentencing states, the more limited involvement of the courts with prisoners' rights, and, most serious of all, overcrowded prisons do not make it easy to recapture order within the walls. Correctional officers for the past decade have been quick to tell outsiders that the inmates are running the prison; today, in many prisons, that is more true than ever before.

One example of inmate power within the walls is the highly developed **contraband market.** David B. Kalinich, in examining the contraband market at the State Prison of Southern Michigan (SPSM), found that the flow of contraband through the prison was extensive. "Contraband" can be defined as "any unauthorized substance or material" possessed by inmates—for example, weapons, drugs, alcoholic beverages, prohibited appliances, and clothing. Gambling, institutional privileges, special food and canteen services, and prostitution can also be acquired through the contraband market. Contraband has always been found in American prisons, but the drug appetites and addictions of today's inmates have encouraged the expansion of this market. Kalinich found that the most visible and widely used drug was marijuana, with large amounts of heroin, some cocaine, and an assortment of amphetamines and tranquilizers also being available.[10]

A perhaps even more telling example of the internal disorder within prison walls is the increased use of **protective custody** (PC) today.[11] Although no nationwide or recent statistics on protective custody are available, California in 1980 reported that

4 percent and Illinois that 17 percent of their populations, respectively, were housed in protective custody. In that same year, institutions reporting protective custody populations included the Massachusetts Correctional Institution at Walpole with 12 percent and the Washington State Penitentiary at Walla Walla with 9 percent of their populations. Walla Walla's superintendent, James Spaulding, noted at the time: "I believe it has gotten to the point where the count for protective custody depends on the space you have available."[12]

The PC unit is typically in the same cellhouse in which the administrative segregation unit is located, and inmates in the PC unit, like those in the administrative segregation unit, are locked up 23 or 24 hours a day. In addition to the frightened newcomer and prison snitch, PC volunteers in the late 1980s increasingly included experienced prisoners, the traditional experts in prison survival. A large part of the dramatic increase in protective custody has to do with gang members' willingness to murder at the command of gang leaders. The prudent inmate locks up in many prison settings rather than deals with the population on a day-to-day basis.

INSTITUTIONAL SECURITY

To maintain secure institutions, departments of corrections usually divide prison structures into levels of security. Strong **perimeter security** is essential in maintaining custody. **Internal security** is achieved through the security of the living area, the control of the yard, and the control of inmate movement. A strong perimeter security guards society against escaping inmates; a high level of internal security attempts to prevent the violent and lawless prison.

Levels of Security

Levels of security are generally described as maximum, medium, and minimum. In its Master Plan, the Iowa Department of Corrections defines the typical characteristics of each level (see Table 14.1).

Perimeter Security

The buffer zone and the fence are the two aspects of perimeter security common to every maximum and most medium security institutions. Many correctional institutions are built out in the country on acres of relatively undeveloped land to enable guards to observe any person approaching or leaving the prison. In many institutions, especially those in the west, guards stop all traffic and ask the drivers the purpose of the visit. They will usually check the trunk before permitting visitors to drive into the main prison compound. The driver may also be told where to park. A variation on this procedure is used in a federal maximum security facility in the midwest, where all visitors are directed to an intercom. A disembodied voice asks for names and the purpose of the visit. Upon receiving clearance, the driver is directed to a parking space.

High, thick masonry walls, fortified with gun turrets, surround most older prisons. Because of the prohibitive cost of masonry walls, many maximum and medium

Table 14.1 LEVELS OF SECURITY
Levels of security are generally described as maximum, medium, and minimum. In its Master Plan, the Iowa Department of Corrections defines the typical characteristics of each level:

Maximum security	Characteristics
High Perimeter Security	Walled institution Guarded towers Limited access to institution sally port
High Internal Security	Officer-controlled cell-locking system Extensive observation by correctional officers Frequent shakedowns of inmate areas Strict control of access to non–housing areas Limitations on personal possessions
Medium Security	**Characteristics**
Moderate Perimeter Security	Single or double fencing Guarded towers or closed-circuit television monitoring Sally port entrances
Moderate Internal Security Cells	Individually locked Control of inmate movement within the institution by zonal security system
Minimum Security	**Characteristics**
Perimeter Security	Fences, or absence of barriers
Internal Security	Individually locked rooms Inmate movement restrictions based on scheduling and security officer observation

Source: Iowa Department of Corrections, *Architectural and Programmatic Analysis of Institutional Corrections*, Vol. 2 (Des Moines, Iowa: Department of Corrections, n.d.), p. 40.

security prisons are surrounded by heavy-gauge cyclone fences. These fences, topped with aprons or concertinas of barbed wire, are usually double, with an open space between the two. Razor wire is now more popular than barbed wire. Some institutions have sensitive electronic sensors near the fences; they sound an alarm at a touch. The Texas and Alabama departments of corrections use Perigrad—an electronic sensory device—in a number of their institutions. Other correctional facilities are installing microwave systems that sound an alarm when an approaching body interrupts the wave between stations. All these methods of perimeter security are intended to slow an escaping inmate or to alert the officer in the nearest tower.

Pedestrian and vehicular **sally ports** usually have double electrically operated doors that cannot be opened simultaneously. This permits the officer to stop anyone between the doors before entering or leaving the institution. Maximum security institutions sometimes have two or more of these sets of double doors separating outsiders from the prison interior. In some prisons, visitors must pass through a metal detector. The U.S. Bureau of Prisons and other state correctional systems now ask visitors to sign a statement that they are not bringing contraband into the institution. In nearly all correctional institutions, visitors are searched before they enter the prison. Generally, a visitor signs in and is taken to an adjoining room to be frisked by a guard of the same sex.

The Marion (federal) Correction Center, Marion, Illinois, was built in the 1960s to replace the "Rock" (Alcatraz). (*Source:* Federal Prison System.)

Internal Security

The control room, design of living quarters, control of the yard, and control of inmate movement are the main determinants of internal security.

Control Room The hub of institutional security is the **control room.** Counts are received in this room, and closed-circuit television cameras that monitor areas of the institution are often located in the control room. When institutional problems or escapes occur, the control room takes charge of the situation until the warden arrives.

Design of Living Quarters Inside cells, outside cells or rooms, segregation cells, squad rooms, open wards or dormitories, and cubicles are the basic living accommodations in adult correctional facilities. Inside cells have no outside walls or windows. They generally have built-in sanitary facilities and a grillwork cell front that ensure maximum surveillance and minimum privacy. As might be expected, this type of cell is popular with custodial staff. Outside cells or rooms have exterior walls and windows and are therefore less secure. Outside cells frequently have a solid door with an observation panel; they may or may not have self-contained sanitary facilities. Segregation cells, special facilities built to contain inmates undergoing discipline, are designed to be the most secure facilities in an institution. Squad rooms usually are small wards or large cells holding four to eight beds.

Open dormitories predominate in correctional institutions for males, especially in the south. Yet dormitory housing should never be used for prisoners with maximum or close-custody rating. Although they are less expensive to construct, both inmates and staff dislike them, for they make it nearly impossible to protect inmates from one another. Texas meets this problem by placing officers in an elevated observation room to supervise prisoners in dormitories; entrance to this room can be made only through a secure outside door. Many institutions, such as Kilby Correctional Facility in Alabama, Sommers in Connecticut, Lake Butler in Florida, and Bordentown in New Jersey, use both cells and open wards.

Cubicles, which use partial walls built around an inmate's living space, are also

Tiered housing unit. (*Source:* California Department of Corrections.)

used in some facilities.[13] These partitions within a dormitory space are intended to allow some privacy to minimum or medium custody prisoners, thereby making the dormitory assignment more acceptable.

Massive five-, six-, and seven-tier cellhouses are no longer built; construction costs are prohibitive for facilities higher than two or three floors of open galleries. Jackson in Georgia, Sommers in Connecticut, Leesburg in New Jersey, Moverly in Missouri, Ionia in Michigan, and Canon City in Colorado are newer two- and three-tiered cellhouses. Newer institutions with single-floor living units include Fox Lake and Lincoln in Wisconsin, Purdy in Washington, and Kennedy in West Virginia.[14]

Control of the Yard Traditionally, the yard is the scene of much of a prison's drug traffic and much of the violence of institutional life. Guards equipped with firearms in towers and officers who roam the yard are the primary security forces. The latter, however, should never carry firearms but may be armed with batons. Inmates are not permitted in the yard when there is low visibility, as during fog or storms. The senior custodial staff know that the inmates of some cellblocks are more unmanageable in the yard than others. If an incident does occur in the yard, security staff members immediately try to break it up before it becomes uncontrollable. If a situation appears to be getting out of hand, the officer in the nearest tower will usually fire a warning shot.

Control of Inmate Movement Security problems arise any time line movement takes place to and from the cellblock. If meals are served in a central dining hall, inmates of each cellhouse must arrive promptly at an assigned time. Inmates generally have 20 or 25 minutes to eat before they must move out of the dining hall to permit another cellblock group to take their places. In a time when racial and gang conflicts abound in so many institutions, fights can quickly erupt in the dining hall. The California Department of Corrections has built separate dining halls for each cellblock in certain of its institutions in an attempt to avoid the confusion that takes place when an entire institution must be fed in a single dining facility.

Visiting presents a security problem in institutions that permit inmates and

Inmates and yard time. (*Source:* Pennsylvania Department of Corrections.)

visitors to sit together around tables. When inmates always were separated from families and friends by a glass partition, there was no way visitors could pass contraband. Presently, it is increasingly difficult to prevent the smuggling of contraband. Institutions try to control this situation by permitting only those on an approved list to visit an inmate, but because it is so easy to enter a name on a list, often there is little control over who comes into the prison. Drugs are frequently passed along in a deflated balloon that inmates can either swallow or conceal on their bodies. To prevent this, some prisons require skin searches of visitors who are on a suspected drug trafficker's visiting list. Inmates are usually stripped and searched after they leave the visiting area, but swallowing the evidence makes it impossible to detect.

Pass tickets that allow inmates to move from one part of the institution to another present another security problem. In a large institution, 200 tickets may be issued during a day. In a well-run prison, it is not difficult to know where a particular person should be at any given time. A pass ticket or ducat should be issued for a specific place at specific times, and the control room should have lists of prisoners who have the ticket or ducat by time and place. This kind of bookkeeping differentiates competent administration from administration so sloppy that it should not be thought of as administration.

METHODS OF CONTROL

Methods of control include rules and regulations; counts, searches, and shakedowns; tool, key, and weapon control; enforcement of disciplinary procedures, including administrative segregation; and use of technology.

Rules and Regulations

Everyone is subject to rules and regulations, whether as a citizen or as a prisoner. The rules of prison are more restrictive, partly because they are seldom carefully thought out and partly because they are restraining individuals who do not wish to be there. The basic objective of **rules and regulations** is to provide formal guidelines for custodial officers in the institution. The President's Crime Commission described how many of the restrictive rules came into existence:

> Under conditions of mass treatment and great concern for custody there is a tendency to accumulate numerous restrictions on inmate behavior. Each disturbance inspires an attempt to prevent its recurrence by establishing a new rule. Once established, rules have great success at survival. Rarely is there any systematic review that looks at elimination of unnecessary restrictions.[15]

Prohibited acts listed in inmate handbooks, as the President's Crime Commission Report surmised, are numerous and reflect the experience of a particular institution. But within a particular facility, the enforcement of the rules varies from shift to shift and from officer to officer. Some officers are called "super cops" because they try to enforce all the rules; other officers tend to let a great deal slide. In Box 14-1, Jean Harris, former headmistress now serving a sentence following her conviction on murder charges, describes the inane and countless rules, the ever-changing regula-

Box 14-1 Rules in Women's Prisons

A lieutenant pulled me aside tonight as I was on my way to medication and said in a very serious tone, "Mrs. Harris, we're having a good deal of trouble with several of your packages."

I said, "Why? What's the matter?"

He said, "Some of them have no address on the outside so they have to be returned to the sender without opening them."

"How do you do that?"

"Return them to the sender without opening them? Just stamp 'return to sender'! I'm just telling you, you better tell your friends to be sure to put an address on the outside, because, by law, we cannot open them if they don't have an address."

"But how will the mail know where to return them to if there isn't any address on the outside?"

"That's what I'm saying, Mrs. Harris. They just return it to the people who sent it."

"But if there isn't any address on it how do they know where to send it? You have to open the package to see if there's a name and address inside."

"I've just told you, Mrs. Harris, the law says you can't open a package that doesn't have an address on the outside."

Finally, I said, "OK, just do whatever you have to do with it." God alone knows what was in the packages, or who sent them, or where they finally ended up.

The lieutenant must be a cousin of the C.O. who refuses to let me alphabetize the many names of my visiting list to make it easier for the C.O.s at the gate to find the names when the people come to visit me.

"Mrs. Harris," he said, in the sort of tone one uses with a not very bright child after you've explained something simple to them at least five times, "it ain't gonna do no good to put 'em in alphabetical order. Those people don't visit you in alphabetical order."

Source: Jean Harris, *Stranger in Two Worlds* (New York: Kensington, 1986), pp. 452–454.

tions, and the staff's abuse of authority that are characteristic of both many women's and men's prisons.

The following rules are consistently present in inmate handbooks or rulebooks:

1. No fighting, threatening, or extorting from another person
2. No sex with other prisoners
3. No disrespect or insolence toward a staff member
4. No leaving a cell, a place of assignment, or other appointed place without permission
5. No use of alcohol
6. No stealing
7. No gambling
8. No disobeying an order from an institutional employee

9. No giving of false information to an employee or trying to bribe an employee
10. No forging or altering a pass
11. No smoking in unauthorized areas
12. No failure to report to work or failure to perform work as instructed by a supervisor

Counts, Searches, and Shakedowns

Counts are one of the important functions of custody. In maximum security institutions, counts take place as frequently as every two hours; in minimum security they may be made only at mealtime and at bed check. All counts are called in to the control room by telephone, followed by the count slips. If the count is not cleared the second time around, the missing prisoner or prisoners must be identified, and procedures set in motion to look for hide-outs or escapees.

Shakedowns are conducted to identify contraband, the possession of which is against the rules of the institution and which sometimes can aid in an escape. The most common shakedown is the "frisk" search, which is used when inmates enter or leave the institution or when custodial staff suspect that inmates are hiding contraband on their persons. When it is suspected that inmates have concealed drugs, weapons, or other contraband on their bodies, a strip search may be conducted. The strip search has sometimes been used to degrade inmates; it should be confined to cases of suspected violation.

Cell searches are vitally important to prevent the use of weapons. Regular shakedowns are desirable, but they should be supplanted by unannounced and unscheduled searches of entire living units. The result of such a policy is that weapons will not be found in anybody's cell, a most desirable outcome. However, cell searches are not as easy as they used to be because inmates now are permitted to have many more personal possessions. Correctional officers do not have time to search all the cells in the cellhouse and, therefore, tend to rely on tips from inmates.

Such searches can be abused by officers who accidentally or intentionally harm or destroy inmates' personal belongings. Officers may take out their anger at particular inmates in this manner. Whether accidental or intentional, an incident of this nature humiliates and infuriates an inmate. To calm an inmate whose picture of a sweetheart, a wife, or a mother has been torn is no easy matter.

Tool, Key, and Weapon Control

Tool control is of major importance because stolen tools can be used for making weapons and for assistance in escape. Tool control requires an effective check system in the shop and a pilfer-proof system of storage. Welding torches, which can cut steel, must be stored overnight in the arsenal. Machine shop tools can be stored in the shop. Tools such as screwdrivers and pliers can also be kept in the shop tool crib.

Tools are often stored on shadow boards on which their outlines have been painted. The work supervisor can then tell immediately at the end of the day which tools are missing. If a tool is missing, the work supervisor calls for help, and inmates are not permitted to leave the shop until the missing tool is located.

Key control is also important for security. Key rings are stored in the control

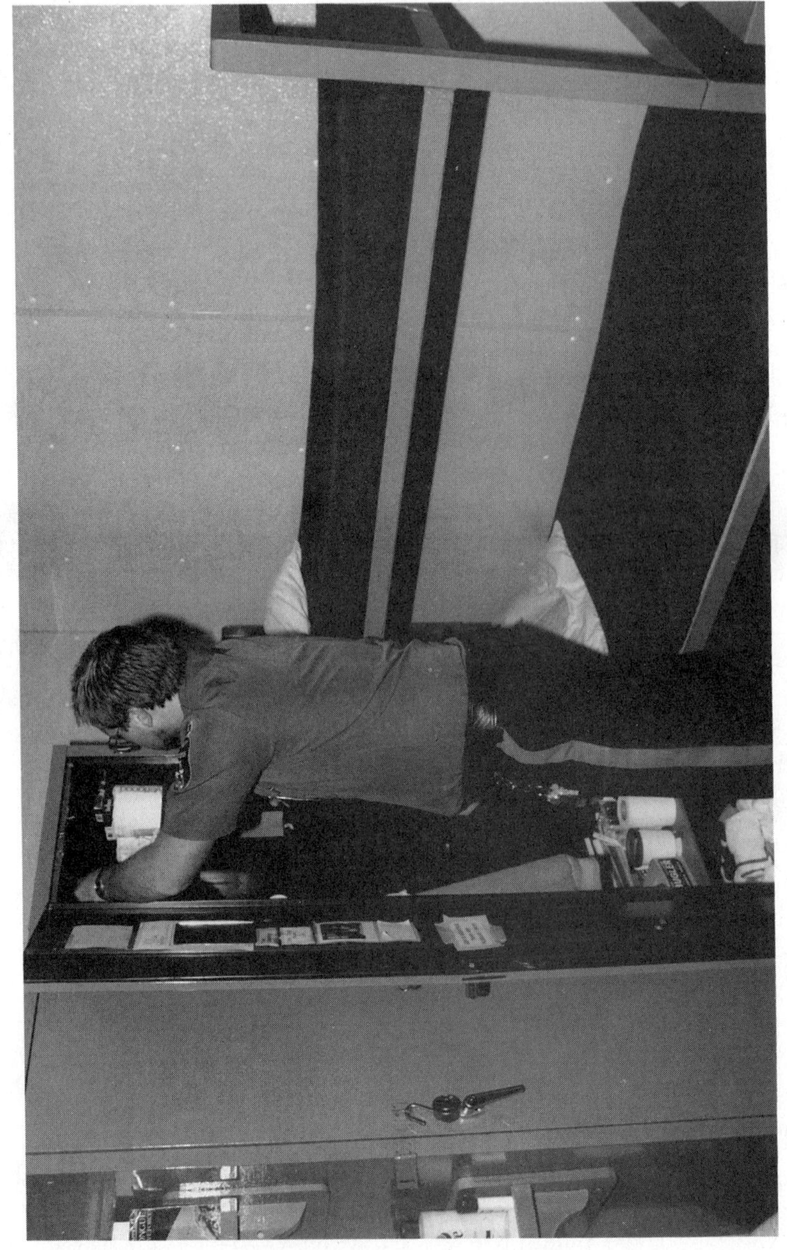

Locker inspection. (*Source:* Southern State Correctional Facility, New Jersey Department of Corrections.)

room and are checked out to officers coming on duty and checked in when they finish their shifts. Keys should always be concealed from inmates, who may study a key and then duplicate it. Loss of keys is, of course, a serious matter. The only solution is to change the locks and to issue new keys in the affected areas.

Weapon control is imperative, especially of those used in inside towers. In those institutions in which officers have firearms in an inside tower, in the dining room, or in the cellhouse, the shells are locked in the arsenal after all the inmates have left these areas. This prevents inmates from capturing firearms and shells simultaneously.

One of the most important problems of security is that of determining when to use firearms against inmates. Institutions vary in delegating the authority to decide when to fire on an inmate inside the walls, although an escaping felon must be controlled by the tower officer. If the inmate does not stop on command, a warning shot is fired. If this does not work, the officer is instructed to bring the inmate down.

Disciplinary Procedures

Three models of the **disciplinary committee** have been used in corrections in the United States. The oldest type consisted of a group of custodial officers who met and decided upon the inmate's punishment. The disciplinary committee in this outdated model was a summary court serving all the functions of police officer, prosecutor, judge, and jury. More recently, a disciplinary committee composed of custody and treatment personnel appointed by a warden has come into use. Frequently made up of three members, one of whom is a noncustodial employee, this committee attempts to be impartial. Ordinarily, no one who has personal knowledge of the case is permitted to sit on the committee. Since *Wolff* vs. *McDonnell* (1974) and several related state decisions, inmates have been given increased due process rights at these hearings.[16] The newest model, the Minnesota model, is composed solely of a hearing officer, who conducts disciplinary meetings. The hearing officer is answerable only to the commissioner of corrections and is a member of the commissioner's staff. In reviewing the decisions of the hearing officer, the commissioner of corrections can reduce the punishment to be administered but cannot increase it.

The first step in the disciplinary process occurs when a correctional officer gives an inmate a ticket. In many correctional systems, tickets are labeled either major or minor. A minor ticket is dealt with by a program team, chaired by a lieutenant; a major ticket is referred to the disciplinary committee. Serious infractions include such offenses as assaulting an officer or other inmate; participating in a riot; becoming involved in arson, escape, or theft; disobeying orders; possessing a weapon or drugs; and entering an unauthorized area. Minor infractions include such offenses as failing to maintain good hygiene, playing a radio too loud, and smoking in a no-smoking area.

If a disciplinary committee finds an inmate guilty, several types of disciplinary action can be taken. First, an inmate can be reprimanded and warned not to commit the infraction again. Second, a prisoner can lose yard, movie, phone, or commissary privileges for a certain period of time. Third, an inmate can be placed in segregation (also called administrative detention, segregation, isolation, disciplinary segregation, and punitive segregation). The disciplinary committee usually sets the number of days an inmate will spend in segregation, but some correctional systems provide for scheduled meetings with inmates in segregation, keeping them there until their attitude and behavior improve. Fourth, the committee can recommend a transfer, usually to a more secure institution. Fifth, the committee can recommend that some of the inmate's good time be withheld or revoked. Finally, the committee can recommend to the parole board that an inmate's parole date be set back. Segregation is examined in detail here because of the controversy it is creating in corrections.

Segregation There are two types of segregation: isolation and administrative segregation. Isolation is punishment; the prisoner is sent for a specific number of days, in most states not to exceed 30. Administrative segregation is just what the term implies. The prisoner is to be removed from the main population because his or her behavior is dangerous to others. The removal may be for an indefinite period of time, subject to case review, or for some specific period. The distinction is important in principle, but life in segregation is about the same either way.

California inmates sometimes call the **segregation unit** "the shoe"; this is the pronunciation of the acronym SHU, for Security Housing Unit. Alabama's prisoners refer to it as "the doghouse." More commonly, it is known as "'the hole." Whatever it is called, segregation has changed significantly in recent years. Gone are the days when inmates would be restricted to a diet of bread and water and shut in a dark, damp cell until the warden felt like letting them out. Segregated inmates today have many of the privileges of prisoners in the general population. Legally, they must receive the same food served to the general population, must be granted showers and exercise periods, must be permitted to correspond with persons outside the prison, and must be permitted television sets and radios in their cells. But officers frequently complain that by prohibiting "tough time," the courts have taken away their means of controlling inmates. One midwestern officer put it this way: "The inmates don't have to work. All they do is sit around and watch television during the day and raise hell at night."[17]

Inmates, in turn, complain that they do not receive proper medical attention during segregation. They also complain that their food is often cold or dirty, which is not surprising when it is remembered that their food trays may be slid underneath the door. Furthermore, inmates complain that it is inhumane to be locked up for most of the day and that they shout and yell obscenities simply to release tension. Finally, they maintain that their rights are abused in a miscarriage of justice in disciplinary meetings.

Several studies have been done on the impact of solitary confinement upon prisoners. One study found a "restlessness, yelling, banging and assaultiveness" in some inmates and in others "a kind of repressed, dissociated, withdrawn hypnoid state."[18] P. Suedfield and C. Roy reported two cases of reactive psychosis, which eventually resulted in a hallucinatory and incoherent state.[19] Stuart Grassian, in a psychiatric examination of 14 inmates restricted to periods of increased solitary confinement, found substantial psychopathological effects with all inmates. The psychiatric symptoms included hyperresponsivity to external stimuli, hallucinations, massive free-floating anxiety, paranoia, lack of impulsive control, shortness of breath and panic, disorientation, and aggressive fantasies of revenge, torture, and mutilation of the guards.[20]

Inmate isolation policies and practices have been implicated in prison riots and disturbances at the Indiana State Prison, the Penitentiary of New Mexico at Santa

Fe, the Idaho State Prison, and three Michigan prisons.[21] This prison within the prison is one in which inmates do not want to do time and in which officers do not want to work.

Israel L. Barak-Glantz, in a study of segregation at Walla Walla State Penitentiary in Washington state, identified four types of inmates who experienced solitary confinement at Walla Walla. The "incidental/accidental" type (nearly half of the solitary confinees) got into trouble only once, and even then it was likely to have been only accidentally. The "early starter" type was made up of inmates who had initial problems, but their records of violations began to diminish as they became assimilated. The misconduct of the "late bloomer" type took place at a later phase of the institutional stay, primarily because of traumatic stimuli [such as a parole board "flop" (rejection), distressing correspondence from the outside, intimidation from another inmate, or even the fear of being released]. The "chronics" were those individuals engaging in predatory behaviors involving injury, drugs, and other contraband, which behavior eventually resulted in their administrative removal from the prison yard, usually for exceedingly long periods of time. This group, constituting about 20 percent of the solitary confinees, accounted for most of the disciplinary committee action.[22]

The new Segregation Unit at the U.S. Penitentiary, Leavenworth, Kansas—which received inmates in March 1989—is considered a prototype for future segregation units around the nation. Staff involvement was increased by their participation in the design of the unit from the "think tank" stages through actual construction. To enhance the security of inmates and staff, the decision was made to build single-person cells, to place a shower in each room, to include phone jacks outside the cells, and to include a wall down the center hall of each cellrange. Inmates are taken out of their cells regularly to use the recreation yards; each wing has its own indoor and outdoor locked recreation yards that will hold four to five people. In addition, inmates are restrained any time they are outside of their cells. (See Figure 14.1 for the floor plan of the segregation unit.)[23]

Technology

Modern prisons have come to rely on **technology** to assist in the operation and security of the institution. Staff persons taken from the guard towers and other assignments have now been placed in control rooms watching dozens of TV monitors, opening electric doors, and operating intercoms. A control room that might have taken one officer to operate a couple decades ago now requires three.[24]

Today, there is starting to unfold a fourth generation of correctional facilities whose design is intended to make correctional institutions more humane without sacrificing security. More sophisticated electronic aids, such as closed-circuit television, personal staff alarm systems, and dual-technology perimeter security systems, will be used. Electronic technology will enhance the security of facilities, yet allow more contact and communication between staff and inmate populations. Perimeter security may even assume the form of laser fields that will replace more conventional methods of fencing used in the 1980s. Finally, as time goes on, new technology in locking systems and the control of these systems using various biometric systems, such as fingerprint or retinal eye identification, will be used more exclusively.[25]

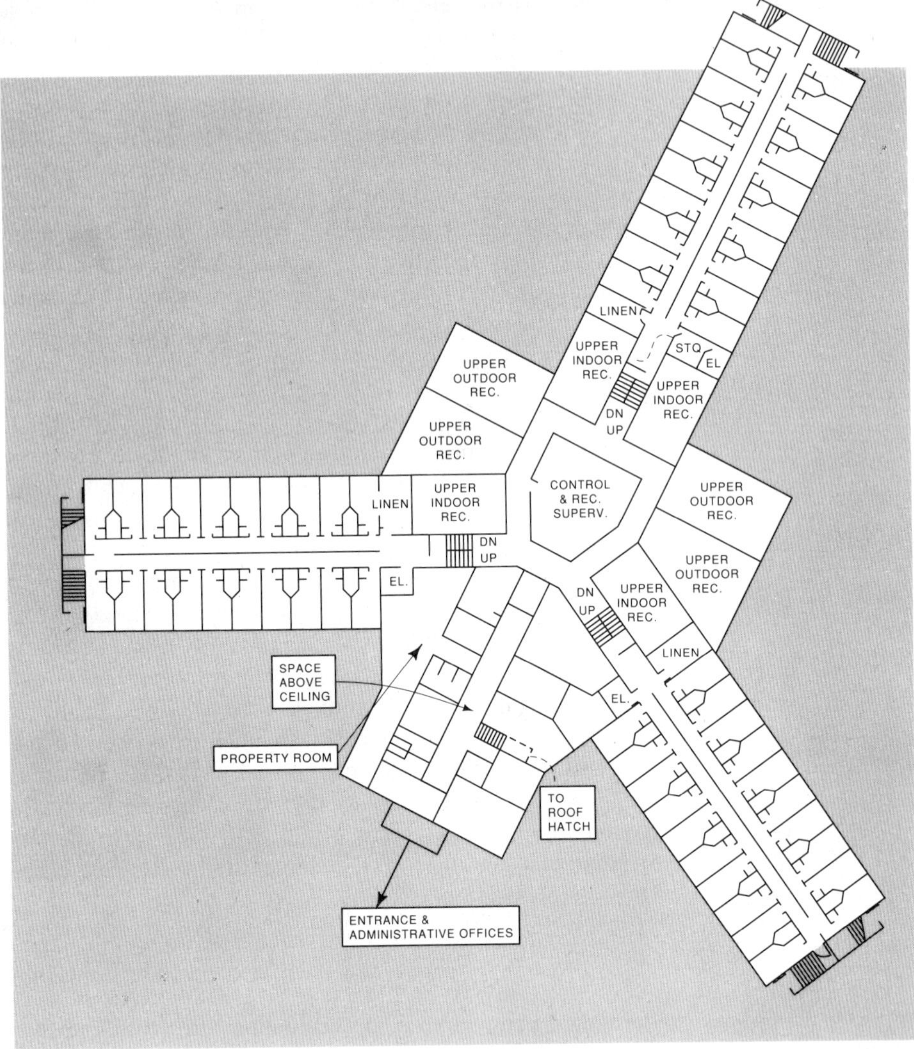

Figure 14.1 Floor plan of the segregation unit at the U.S. Penitentiary, Leavenworth, Kansas. (*Source*: Connie Gardner, " 'State of the Art' Segregation: Enhancing Security Planning Through Staff Involvement," *Federal Prisons Journal* [Spring 1990], p. 31.)

The Minnesota Correctional Facility–Oak Park Heights (opened 1982) and the California Pelican Bay State Prison (opened 1989) are two of the most technologically advanced and secure prisons in the nation. At Pelican Bay, a state-of-the-art electronic surveillance system monitors the Security Housing Unit (SHU). At Oak Park Heights, a sophisticated, computerized building status system monitors security. Routine events, such as the opening and closing of doors, are monitored by the computer. Any deviation must be cleared with security staff to avoid triggering alarms. The system also monitors perimeter security and fire safety and controls the heating and ventilation systems. Other security elements at Oak Park Heights include a closed-circuit television monitoring system and an electronic alarm network on the roof of the facility and on the perimeter's double security fence. Institutional electrical systems are backed up with an independent emergency generator that is automatically started during power outages. The 60-acre secure circular perimeter of the site is also patrolled by officers who monitor the institution perimeter systems. The patrol officers are armed and maintain two-way radio communication with a central control station by way of the vehicle mobile unit and a handheld two-way radio unit.

L. Travis, E. Latessa, and B. Oldenrich recently evaluated 105 correctional facilities and 12 large jails built within the past 10 years. The key findings of this study reveal:

> The majority of states reporting new prison construction indicate that some form of electronic perimeter security system will be installed.
>
> About half the institutions surveyed reported having some type of electronic intrusion system.
>
> About 80 percent of facilities surveyed use some type of electronic pneumatic locking system.
>
> About 90 percent of the institutions in our survey reported using some sort of internal security equipment (metal detectors, magnetic scanners, x-ray or fluoroscope machines, etc.).
>
> Half of the institutions surveyed reported using some type of internal surveillance equipment (closed circuit television, listening devices, etc.). The higher the security level of the institution, the more likely it is that internal surveillance equipment will be used.
>
> Only a small percentage of the institutions surveyed reported using new technologies such as nonlethal weaponry or infrared scopes.[26]

In summarizing this survey's findings, Latessa and Oldenrich conclude that while the impact of new technology has usually been positive, it has not produced major changes in staff size, staff composition, or the operation of the institution. Technology, the authors add, can help well-run and well-managed prisons operate more efficiently, but it will not solve the problems of poorly run facilities. They add that before sophisticated technology will improve institutional life, planning and evaluation must be upgraded.[27]

THE CUSTODIANS

Historically, the **paramilitary model** has been used for security in most institutions. Custodial staff wear uniforms and badges; are assigned such titles as sergeant, lieutenant, captain, and major; use such designations as company, mess hall, drill, inspection, and gig list; and maintain a sharp division between lower- and higher-ranking officers. The procedures and organizational structures that control inmates are also militaristic in form. For many years, prisoners marched to the dining hall and to their various assignments. They removed their hats in the presence of a captain and stood at attention when the warden approached.

Although it has been stripped of the autocratic warden and some of the regimentation, the paramilitary model is still alive and flourishing. Associate warden custody (often called the deputy of custody or the assistant for custody) is ultimately responsible for knowing the whereabouts of all inmates at all times. Guard captains, few in number, are usually assigned to full-time administrative responsibilities or to shift commands. They often chair assignment and disciplinary committees. Guard lieutenants are known as troubleshooters and roam the institution dealing with volatile incidents. "The lieutenant's job," said one, "is to be right there with his men. If a problem arises, the lieutenant goes in first."[28] The lieutenants take troublesome inmates out of their cells and walk them to segregation. Guard sergeants, like army sergeants, manage particular units, such as cellhouses or the hospital, and supervise several other guards.

The correctional officer is responsible for enforcing the security measures devised by supervisors. Officers open and close steel-barred doors allowing entrance and exit; take inmate counts several times a day; distribute medicine, mail, and laundry; oversee maintenance activities; supervise feeding, either in the cellhouse or in a central dining facility to which they transport prisoners; and supervise the daily showers of the inmates. They are also assigned to the yard, the canteen, the visiting area, and prison industries. They may be given the responsibility of taking an inmate home on an emergency leave or of supervising inmates on a trip to the community. Some correctional officers also are assigned to the tower and gate, keeping prisoners under constant surveillance. Officers at the gate check all outsiders who enter the prison, frequently frisking and stamping them.[29]

The Changing Role of the Correctional Officer

Higher salaries, improved standards, greater training, and unionization are signs that the role of the correctional officer is undergoing change. Guards, now called correctional officers in most states, are beginning to make a living wage. More than 75 percent of the states pay overtime to officers who work more than 40 hours a week; and with overtime pay, some officers make as much as $20,000 to $25,000 a year. More than half the states now require a high school diploma or a GED certificate as

Control room. (*Source:* Southern State Correctional Facility, New Jersey Department of Corrections.)

their minimum employment requirement. Many states have academy training programs for pre-service and in-service officers, which appear to be effective in assuring that officers bring basic skills to their jobs. The U.S. Bureau of Prisons requires three years of college for correctional officers. All the correctional officers at the coeducational Lexington Correctional Center have M.A. degrees and wear blazers.

The growth of unions among correctional officers has encouraged them to seek greater rights, more recognition, and higher pay. By 1981 correctional officers in 29 of 52 jurisdictions (state, federal, and District of Columbia) were unionized.[30] The unions that represent correctional officers include AFSCME (American Federation of State, County, and Municipal Employees, AFL-CIO), SEIU (Service Employees International Union), the International Brotherhood of Teamsters, and local state employee associations. Officers in Connecticut, New Jersey, New York state, and Ohio have struck to protest low wages or poor working conditions. When correctional officers walk out, administrators, other personnel, the state police, and sometimes even the National Guard are forced to run the institution until the strike is settled.

The Female Correctional Officer

Affirmative-action measures have resulted in more minority officers, with the result that the percentage of racial minorities among officers is now equal in many states to that of the minority population of the state. But it was not until the enactment of equal employment legislation—specifically Title VII, which prohibited sex discrimination in hiring by state and local governments—that doors began to open for women in men's prisons.

Women working as correctional officers in men's prisons have received three criticisms: First, women are not fit for the job; for example, they are not strong enough, are too easily corrupted by inmates, or are poor backup for other officers in trouble. Second, women are a disruptive influence; that is, inmates will not follow their orders or will fight for their attention. Third, the presence of women violates inmate privacy, especially when women are working in shower areas or conducting strip searches of inmates.[31]

Dothard v. *Rawlinson* (1977) and *Gunther* v. *Iowa State Men's Reformatory* (1979) have been the most important U.S. Supreme Court cases examining whether women are qualified to work in men's prisons.[32] The former was an Alabama lawsuit filed by Diane Rawlinson, a recent college graduate in correctional psychology who was denied a job as a correctional officer because she was five pounds below the minimum weight requirement. Her class-action suit challenged the state's height and weight requirement; the suit also charged that a department of corrections' regulation preventing female officers from "continual close proximity" to prisoners in maximum security prisons for men (known as the no-contact rule) was discriminatory. The Supreme Court, in a 5-to-4 decision, overturned a lower court decision that had invalidated the no-contact rule. The Court was unwilling to let women work in maximum security prisons for men in Alabama because of the danger of sexual attack and because the extra vulnerability of women to attack would weaken security and endanger other prison employees.[33]

However, in *Gunther* v. *Iowa,* the Court dismissed security issues as a reason for limiting women's employment as guards in that state. The *Gunther* decision defined that job requirements to strip search male inmates or witness them in showers constituted an attempt to prevent women from working as correctional officers.[34]

These and other cases demonstrate that the courts have generally established procedures that both guarantee women the right to employment and protect inmate privacy as much as possible. Departments of corrections can achieve this by administrative policies preventing women from doing some types of searches, such as strip searches. The installation of modesty half-screens, fogged windows that permit figures to be seen, or privacy doors on toilet stalls offer another solution to privacy issues. Security does not have to be sacrificed, and these modifications can be made to the physical environment at little cost.

Several studies have compared male and female correctional officers.[35] They have generally found that men and women do not differ on the quality of job performance. This still does not mean that they are equal in all tasks. While men may be able to handle physical assault better than women, women may more effectively defuse an incident before violence erupts.[36] Leo L. Meyer, a former warden in the Illinois correctional system, describes the role of women officers in a male medium security institution:

> We probably have more female officers than any other correctional center because of the transfers from mental health. Two are lieutenants, and one of them just passed the NRA [National Rifle Association] test for instructor in firearms. I think she is the first woman in history to do this. A female who wants to be a warden has a real good opportunity. I say one thing about females, they're dependable and they seem to try harder. In terms of qualifying for their firearms test: Their scores are better than some men, and many have never shot a gun before.[37]

A female correctional officer in a men's prison usually finds that the stress of working in a violent environment is coupled with conflict with male co-workers. But even assuming that problems with male co-workers can be resolved, the role confusion or uncertainty of the job may cause her to seek out or be assigned low-contact positions.[38] This, in turn, results in dead-end work assignments or limited promotional possibilities.[39]

Problems of the Correctional Officer

In most state systems, correctional officers have at least as many problems as the guards of yesterday. Theirs can be a dangerous, dead-end, low-status job with confusing role expectations. Hans Toch aptly describes how guards are imprisoned in their roles:

> Prison guards are truly imprisoned: They are not physically confined but are locked into movie caricatures, into pejorative prophecies (sometimes self-fulfilling), into anachronistic supervision patterns, into unfair civil service definitions, into undeserved hostilities and prejudgments of their actions. Officers are imprisoned by our ignorance of who they are and what they do, which is the price they pay for working behind walls.[40]

Attitudes and behaviors are so rigidly built into the prison structure that only a certain kind of working personality survives. A study at Stateville supports the opinion that the behavior of correctional officers is a product of organizational roles and is independent of such variables as education, age, race, and political orientation. This study compared black and white correctional officers. Although the black officers were typically younger, better educated, and more liberal than white officers, they manifested no consistent difference in their attitudes toward jobs, correctional goals, other staff, and inmates.[41]

The skills acquired through guarding are usually transferable only to even lower-paying private security jobs. A few officers are promoted through the ranks, but these opportunities frequently disappear early in an officer's career. Furthermore, professional training is increasingly required of prison managers, which training reduces the possibility of top administrative openings for officers.

The conflict of goals and expectations creates a new problem for officers. In the days of autocratic wardens, guards knew what was expected of them, including the avoidance of undue familiarity with inmates. Prisons were custodial in nature. Today, requirements for shakedowns and counts seem to change with each new supervisor, and policies on relations with prisoners are often open to interpretation. The lack of predictability of officers' behavior, as well as the inconsistent rule-enforcement structure, has contributed to the creation of stress with inmates.[42]

Alienation is a common problem among correctional officers. Lucien X. Lombardo found in New York state and James Jacobs and Harold G. Retsky found in Illinois that many guards are pushed into prison work by circumstances, such as the unavailability of other jobs, which makes it difficult for them to accept their problem-laden circumstances.[43]

In addition to the problems of low status, role confusion, and inmate defiance, correctional officers also must deal with the reality that they sometimes are treated no better than inmates. For example, they are subjected occasionally to strip searches, although many union chapters have been strong enough to resist this kind of control. Strip searches are necessitated by the fact that one route for contraband drugs into the prison is the guard whom prisoners have identified as a willing conduit, but guards view these searches as unjust because they have committed no crimes. Correctional officers also share the same environment and many of the deprivations as inmates, and, as a result, officers often see themselves as doing time.

Increased inmate defiance makes prisons, especially maximum security ones, dangerous and stressful places in which to work. Security staff across the nation express a common complaint—that they have neither the control nor the respect they used to have. Correctional officers know that life is cheap in the contemporary prison, and they feel that they are at the mercy of the inmates. It is no wonder that high blood pressure and heart disease, psychological problems, and alcoholism are some of the common effects of working in this violent atmosphere.[44]

The Response to Such Problems

New correctional officers are socialized by the old-timers concerning acceptable behavior on the job. Experienced officers know that all will be punished severely for violation of security. A mistake that leads to an escape may cost them several weeks "on the streets" (suspension) or may even result in termination. The erosion of security also makes it more likely not only that inmates will initiate a disturbance, but that the disturbance will mushroom into a full-scale riot. Moreover, experienced officers know that inmates cannot be given too much leeway or they will end up controlling the institution and abusing staff. These officers try to teach newly certified correctional officers the midpoint between rigidly enforcing all the rules and allowing the inmates to gain control. Finally, experienced officers know that the best hope for security is fair treatment of inmates. Simply put, the inmate who is treated fairly and with respect is much less likely to become a security problem than the prisoner who feels humiliated and abused by staff.[45]

However, some correctional officers respond in violence to their alienating roles. These officers go around looking for trouble in order to prove who is in control. H. Toch and J. Klofas, in an examination of correctional officers in the northeast, found that about a quarter of the guard force could be classified in this way.[46] The officers believe that acting tough, dominating the weak, threatening violence, and putting inmates in their place will show the captives who is in control.[47] James Marquart found that the escalating aggressive strategies used by this group moved from "verbal assaults," to physically abusive "tune-ups," to overt violent "ass-whippings" and "severe beatings."[48]

Moreover, there are always a few officers who become involved in corrupt and illegal behavior that jeopardizes security. They may agree to bring contraband into the institution because they have been set up by inmates. This often occurs when a correctional officer agrees to do something against the rules in order to be well liked. For example, one correctional officer agreed to mail a birthday card to an inmate's daughter on his way home from work. Although this was against policy, it meant that the card would reach the child on her birthday. Subsequently, the inmate demanded that the officer comply with other requests, using the threat that the first violation would be reported to the captain. Sam P. Garrison, former warden of Central Prison, Raleigh, tells how another correctional officer was set up:

> In talking with an officer over the space of a year, an inmate can learn a great deal about him. The last officer bringing drugs into the institution was married and had a family. The whole thing was set up by inmates finding out that he went to a certain bar one night a week. All of a sudden this officer found himself in a motel room with a prisoner's girlfriend. Then two days later she said, "There'll be a package mailed to you that you'll take into the prison." When he resisted, she said, "Well, do you want your wife to know that you slept with me night before last?" The prisoners had him in the jaws of a vice.[49]

Some officers carry contraband for profit. Those inmates who have a large drug appetite are usually able to make cash and street contacts and need only someone to bring drugs into the prison. According to an ex-offender who has spent time in several federal institutions, inmates watch and talk with each new officer and soon figure out who can be corrupted.[50] An example is the correctional officer in a midwestern state who was caught in a strip search with two large bags of marijuana taped across his chest. This particular individual apparently had been bringing drugs into the prison for some time and had been able to buy a Cadillac and expensive clothes with his additional tax-free income.[51]

Job Enrichment

Perhaps the best hope for bringing order within prison disorder is to use such incentives as career development programs to reinforce and encourage the number of officers who want to provide human services to inmates. A number of studies appear to indicate that at least some officers enjoy providing such services.[52] N. C.

Jursik adds that many officers see correctional work as a worthwhile endeavor.[53] Robert Johnson even more strongly emphasizes this point:

> It is by helping prisoners—by promoting secure and responsive prison regimes—that some officers rise above the limitation of their formal custodial role. They use their authority to help inmates cope with prison life; they provide human services rather than custodial repression. They do the best they can with the resources at their disposal to make the prison a better place in which to live and work.[54]

Female officers seem more likely than males to take a human relations view of the correctional officer's job. The "softening" effect that some women officers have in men's prisons seems to make these institutions more livable and less violent.[55] Yet, as with any generalization, glaring expectations exist, especially in women's prisons, to women officers' bringing a "softening" effect. Indeed, some women officers feel obliged to be more "macho" than their male colleagues.

Daniel Glaser's examination of the prison more than two decades ago found that officers who are fair and friendly and who relate to inmates as human beings are liked and obeyed.[56] Stan Stojkovic's more recent examination of the prison found that officers themselves agree that "consistency, fairness, and flexibility in the enforcement of rules were what made a good officer," and that "effective officers are able to develop a sense of respect with inmates by being fair and consistent."[57]

John Hepburn's study similarly concluded that "the level of institutional authority appears to be greatest among those guards who also have a less punitive and less custodial orientation, who maintain a lower degree of social distance from inmates, and who express a higher level of job satisfaction."[58] Thus, this human relations approach leads not only to improved personal relationships with inmates but also to a greater degree of correctional authority.

The **human relations approach** can help calm the prison by officers' providing needed goods and services to inmates, by their acting as referral agents or advocates, and by their helping inmates with institutional adjustment problems.[59] The importance of delivering services is aptly expressed by Michael J. Mahoney, executive director of the John Howard Association:

> An interesting measure of the inhumanity of prison life appears in what prisoners are asking for today. If you examine prison riots, such as Attica, New Mexico, and the 1979 takeover of death row at Stateville, you will find that what prisoners are bargaining for are basic human rights. For example, they aren't asking for a 747 to leave the country or a million dollars to go to Africa. They aren't asking to make prisons into a Holiday Inn. But they are asking for safety, adequate food, showers, access to the law library, sufficient recreation, and more time out of their cells. Particularly in maximum security prisons those are the commodities people desire the most. Until we can guarantee prisoners these basic human rights, then we are wasting our time talking about rehabilitating them.[60]

CONCLUSIONS

A popular adage in corrections is that security should be as strong as the strongest inmate. One of the problems with control is that it tends to lead to more control, and the end result is a more repressive and alienating environment. Another problem is that tight security has different effects on inmate populations. To inmates primarily concerned about safety and structure, tight security offers protection from assault, but to other inmates, tight security means a loss of freedom and the reduced ability to control one's life.[61] Correctional administrators receive strong pressure to ensure that the headline "Killers Escape from Prison" never appears. Staff who do not commit themselves to maintaining a secure institution will not be around for long.

Although prisons, for the most part, have been effective in keeping offenders confined, most correctional systems face sizeable problems in providing safe institutions and in preventing inmates from creating their own violent and lawless society. Joe Ragen, former warden of Illinois Stateville Correctional Center, used to say, "You either run the prison or the inmates run the prisons." In U.S. prisons, prisoners do run the prison, with dire consequences to both staff and inmates. One of the most hopeful steps correctional administrators can take is expanding the role of the correctional officer to include human service, or "people work," with prisoners.

KEY TERMS

"building tenders"

cell searches

contraband market

control room

counts

custody

disciplinary committee

human relations approach

inmate code

internal security

key control

paramilitary model

perimeter security

protective custody (PC)

rules and regulations

sally ports

segregation unit

shakedowns

technology

tool control

weapon control

DISCUSSION TOPICS

14.1 Draw a mental picture of a prison. What security features have you included? What have you forgotten?

14.2 Why is disorder within the walls a more serious problem today than escapes?

14.3 What should be the minimum qualifications for employment as a correctional officer?

14.4 Prisoners in administrative segregation are restricted until their behavior warrants return to the institutional population. How can a prisoner's behavior change for the better be verified?

14.5 Some observers say that prisoners applying for protective custody (PC) do so in order to enjoy "easy time." If you had the decision to make, how would you make sure that a prisoner applying for PC really needed protection?

ANNOTATED REFERENCES

Atlas, Randall I., and Roger G. Dunham, "Changes in Prison Facilities as a Function of Correctional Philosophy." In John W. Murphy and Jack E. Dison, eds., *Are Prisons Any Better? Twenty Years of Correctional Reforms.* Newbury Park, Calif.: Sage, 1990, pp. 23–42. *A discussion of architectural design and new technological innovations and how they are affecting correctional institutions.*

Johnson, Robert. *Hard Time: Understanding and Reforming the Prison.* Belmont, Calif.: Wadsworth, 1987. *An excellent examination of the deprivations of confinement as well as a valuable section on the human services role of the correctional officer.*

Kalinich, David B., *Power, Stability, and Contraband: The Inmate Economy.* Prospect Heights, Ill.: Waveland Press, 1986. *The most up-to-date study of the contraband market in a male prison.*

Kauffman, Lesley. *Prison Officers and their World.* Cambridge, Mass.: Harvard University Press, 1988. *One of the best recent studies of the correctional officer's role.*

Lombardo, Lucien X. *Guards Imprisoned*, 2nd ed. Cincinnati: Anderson, 1989. *Lombardo's study of the Auburn Prison in New York state is one of the most perceptive examinations of the correctional officer.*

Marquart, James W., and Julian B. Roebuck. "Prison Guards and 'Snitches.' " *British Journal of Criminology* 25, 1985: 217–233. *Examines the activities and control function of the "building tenders" (B.T.s) in Texas before the* Ruiz *v.* Estelle *decision.*

Martin, Steve, and Sheldon Ekland-Olson. *Texas Prisons: The Walls Came Tumbling Down.* Austin: Texas Monthly Press, 1987. *This fascinating examination of the* Ruiz *v.* Estelle *decision in Texas raises many questions about the relationship between due process rights and a secure institution.*

Zimmer, Lynne E. *Women Guarding Men.* Chicago: University of Chicago Press, 1986. *Shows clearly the problems of women working as correctional officers in men's prisons.*

NOTES

1. Contact Center, Inc., *Corrections Compendium* (Lincoln, Neb.: Contact Service Center, Inc., March 1988), pp. 10–14.
2. The escapes from the Penitentiary of New Mexico took place in December 1979. See Bert Useem and Peter Kimball, *States of Siege: U.S. Prison Riots, 1971–1986* (New York:

Oxford University Press, 1989), p. 99. Dale O. Remling was picked up from the yard of the State Prison of Southern Michigan at Jackson on June 6, 1975, by a helicopter.

3. George M. Camp and Camille Graham Camp, *Prison Gangs: Their Extent, Nature and Impact on Prisons* (Washington: U.S. Government Printing Office, 1985).
4. Michael Foucault, *Discipline and Punish: The Birth of the Prison,* trans. Alan Sheridan (New York: Pantheon, 1977).
5. James B. Jacobs, *Stateville: The Penitentiary in Mass Society* (Chicago: University of Chicago Press, 1977), p. 77.
6. Gresham Sykes, *The Society of Captives* (Princeton, N.J.: Princeton University Press, 1958), Gresham M. Sykes and Sheldon M. Messinger, "The Inmate Society System." In Richard A. Cloward et al., eds., *Theoretical Studies in the Social Organization of the Prison* (New York: Social Science Research Council, 1960).
7. *Ruiz* v. *Estelle,* 503 F. Supp. 1265 (S.D. Tex. 1980); 679 F. 2d 1115 (5th Cir. 1980); *cert. denied,* 103 S.Ct. 452 (1983); *Modified on reh'q,* 688 F.2d 266 (5th Cir. 1982); *cert. denied,* 103 S.Ct. 1438 (1983). The best authority on the building tenders of the Texas Department of Corrections is Steve J. Martin and Sheldon Ekland-Olson, *Texas Prisons: The Walls Came Tumbling Down* (Austin: Texas Monthly Press, 1987). See also John J. DiIulio Jr., *Governing Prisons* (New York: Free Press, 1987), pp. 111–113.
8. James W. Marquart and Julian B. Roebuck, "Prison Guards and Snitches: Social Control in a Maximum Security Institution." In Kenneth C. Haas and Geoffrey P. Alpert, eds., *The Dilemmas of Punishment* (Prospect Heights, Ill.: Waveland Press, 1986), pp. 158–176; J. W. Marquart and B. M. Crouch, "Coopting the Kept: Using Inmates for Social Control in a Southern Prison." *Justice Quarterly* 1, December 1984: 502.
9. Robert Johnson, *Hard Time: Understanding and Reforming the Prison* (Belmont, Calif.: Wadsworth, 1987), p. 129.
10. David B. Kalinich, *Power, Stability, and Contraband: The Inmate Economy* (Prospect Heights, Ill.: Waveland Press, 1986), p. 42
11. David C. Anderson, "I Can't Go Back Out There." *Corrections Magazine,* August 1980: p. 9.
12. Ibid.
13. William G. Nagel, *The New Red Barn: A Critical Look at the Modern Prison* (New York: Walker, 1973), pp. 70–73.
14. Ibid., pp. 74–75.
15. The President's Commission on Law Enforcement and the Administration of Justice, *Task Force Report: Corrections* (Washington: Government Printing Office, 1967), p. 67.
16. *Wolff* v. *McDonnell,* 94 S.Ct. 2963 (1974).
17. Interviewed in 1985.
18. M. Meltzer, "Solitary Confinement." In *Group for the Advancement of Psychiatry Symposium Number 3: Factors Used to Increase the Susceptibility of Individuals to Forceful Indocrimination, Observations and Experiments* (New York, 1956).
19. P. Suedfield and C. Roy, "Using Social Isolation to Change the Behavior of Disruptive Inmates." *International Journal of Offender Theraptive and Comparative Criminology* 19, 1975. 90–99.
20. Stuart Grassian, "Psychopathological Effects of Solitary Confinement." *American Journal of Psychiatry* 140, November 1983: 1450–1454.
21. Israel L. Barak-Glantz, "A Decade of Disciplinary, Administrative, and Protective Control of Inmates in the Washington State Penitentiary." *Journal of Criminal Justice* 10, 1982. 481.
22. For these four types, see Israel L. Barak-Glantz, "Patterns of Prisoner Misconduct: Toward a Behavioral Test of Prisonization" *Sociological Focus* 16, April 1983: 141–143.
23. Connie Gardner, " 'State of the Art' Segregation: Enhancing Security Planning Through Staff Involvement." *Federal Prison Journal,* Spring 1990: 28–33.

24. Randall L. Atlas and Roger G. Dunham, "Changes in Prison Facilities as a Function of Correctional Philosophy." In John W. Murphy and Jack E. Dison, eds., *Are Prisons Any Better? Twenty Years of Correctional Reform* (Newbury Park, Calif.: Sage, 1990), p. 55.
25. Ibid., pp. 56–57.
26. Lawrence F. Travis, III, Edward J. Latessa, Jr., and Robert W. Oldendick, "The Utilization of Technology in Correctional Institutions." *Federal Probation*, September 1989: pp. 36–39.
27. E. Latessa and B. Oldendich, *Impact of Technology on Adult Correctional Institutions* (Washington: National Institution of Justice, 1988).
28. Interviewed in August 1983.
29. James B. Jacobs and Harold G. Retsky, "Prison Guard" *Urban Life* 4, April 1975: 5–29.
30. David Duffee, "Careers in Criminal Justice: Corrections." In Sanford H. Kadish, ed., *Encyclopedia of Crime and Justice* (New York: Free Press, 1983), p. 1232.
31. Richard Hawkins and Geoffrey P. Alpert, *American Prison Systems: Punishment and Justice* (Englewood Cliffs, N.J.: Prentice-Hall, 1989), p. 359.
32. *Dothard* v. *Rawlinson*, 433 U.S. 321 (1977); *Gunther* v. *Iowa State Men's Reformatory*, 612 F2d 1079 (8th Circ. 1979).
33. *Dothard* v. *Rawlinson*.
34. *Gunther* v. *Iowa State Men's Reformatory*.
35. Geoffrey P. Alpert, "The Needs of the Judiciary and Misapplications of Social Research: The Case of Female Guards in Men's Prisons." *Criminology* 22, 1984: 441–455; Cheryl Bowser Peterson, "Doing Time with the Boys: An Analysis of Women Correctional Officers in All-Male Facilities." In B. R. Price and N. J. Sokoloff, eds., *The Criminal Justice System and Women* (New York: Clark Boardman, 1982); and Sandra Nicolai, "The Upward Mobility of Women in Corrections." In R. Ross, ed., *Prison Guard/Correctional Officer* (Toronto: Butterworths, 1981).
36. Peterson, "Doing Time with the Boys," pp. 444–445.
37. Interviewed in July 1978.
38. Lynne E. Zimmer, *Women Guarding Men* (Chicago: University of Chicago Press, 1986).
39. Nancy C. Jurik, "An Officer and a Lady: Organizational Barriers to Women Working as Correctional Officers in Men's Prisons." *Social Problems* 32, 1985: 375–388.
40. Hans Toch's foreword in Lucien X. Lombardo, *Guards Imprisoned* (New York: Elsevier, 1981), p. xiv.
41. James B. Jacobs and Lawrence S. Kraft, "Integrating the Keepers: A Comparison of Black and White Prison Guards in Illinois." *Social Problems* 25, February 1976.
42. Lucien X. Lombardo, "Alleviating Inmate Stress: Contributions from Correctional Officers." In Robert Johnson and Hans Toch, eds., *The Pains of Imprisonment* (Beverly Hills, Calif.: Sage, 1982), p. 293.
43. Lombardo, *Guards Imprisoned*, p. 21; and Jacobs and Retsky, "Prison Guard," p. 6.
44. F. E. Cheek and M.D.S. Miller, "The Experience of Stress for Correction Officers: A Double-Bind Theory of Correctional Stress." *Journal of Criminal Justice* 11, 1983: 105–120.
45. B. M. Crouch and J. W. Marquart, "On Becoming a Prison Guard." In B. M. Crouch, ed., *The Keepers: Prison Guards and Contemporary Corrections* (Springfield, Ill.: Charles C Thomas, 1980), p. 91, and Lombardo, *Guards Imprisoned*, p. 63.
46. H. Toch and J. Klofas, "Alienation and Desire for Job Enrichment Among Corrections Officers." *Federal Probation* 46, 1982: 35–44.
47. Johnson, *Hard Time*.
48. J. W. Marquart, "Prison Guards and the Use of Physical Coercion as a Mechanism of Prisoner Control" (Paper presented at the Annual Meeting of the American Sociological Association, August 1984).
49. Interviewed in October 1978.

50. Interviewed in July 1981.
51. This incident was reported to one of the co-authors during a 1985 interview.
52. Charles A. Lindquist and John T. Whitehead, "Guards Released from Prison: A Natural Experiment in Job Enlargement." *Journal of Criminal Justice* 14, 1986: 283–294.
53. N. C. Jurik, "Individual and Organizational Determinants of Correctional Officer Attitudes Toward Inmates." *Criminology* 23, 1985: 523–539.
54. Johnson, *Hard Time*, pp. 137–138.
55. P. J. Kissel and P. L. Katsampes, "The Impact of Women Corrections Officers on the Functioning of Institutions Housing Male Inmates." *Journal of Offender Counseling, Services and Rehabilitation* 4, 1980): pp. 213–231; and B. A. Owen, "Race and Gender Relations Among Prison Workers" *Crime and Delinquency* 31, 1985: 147–159.
56. Daniel Glaser, *The Effectiveness of a Prison and Parole System* (Indianapolis: Bobbs-Merrill, 1969).
57. Stan Stojkovic, "An Examination of Compliance Structures in a Prison Organization: A Study of the Types of Correctional Power" (Paper presented at the Annual Meeting of American Criminal Justice Sciences, March 1984).
58. John R. Hepburn, "The Erosion of Authority and the Perceived Legitimacy of Inmate Social Protest: A Study of Prison Guards" *Journal of Criminal Justice* 12, 1984: 579–590.
59. Lombardo, "Alleviating Inmate Stress," p. 287.
60. Interviewed in March 1980.
61. Lucien X. Lombardo, "Stress, Change, and Collective Violence in Prison." In *The Pains of Imprisonment*, p. 80.

Chapter 15

Institutional Violence

CHAPTER OUTLINE

A serious and perplexing problem, institutional violence manifests itself in a variety of forms—riots and major disturbances, victimization of one inmate by another, staff brutality toward inmates and inmate assaults on staff, and self-inflicted mutilation by prisoners. Whatever form it takes, institutional violence is a severe indictment of the current policy of imprisonment. John Irwin sums up his view of the contemporary prison as "not chaos, but a dangerous and tentative order."[1] The 300 prison riots since 1970 have established both the dangers and the tentative character of contemporary prisons.[2]

The 1971 prison uprising at Attica, in which 43 persons died, is considered one of the bloodiest one-day encounters between Americans since the Civil War.[3] Six people also died—3 inmates and 3 correctional officers—in the disturbance following the 1971 George Jackson shooting at San Quentin. During 1977 and 1978, 9 inmates were murdered by other inmates at the Atlanta Penitentiary of the federal prison system. In 1978, 3 guards were killed and 3 more were seriously injured at the Illinois Pontiac Correctional Center, and 2 inmates and a guard were killed at Georgia State Prison at Reidsville. In early 1980, during a 36-hour rampage of burning and convict infighting, inmates seized the New Mexico State Penitentiary at Santa Fe, brutally killing 36 inmates and injuring 57 inmates and 9 prison employees.[4] The violence continued in the 1980s with the Kingston and Archambault riots in Canada (the latter taking the lives of 3 guards and wounding 5 others), as well as the killing of 3 prisoners in the torching of the Idaho prison and the uprisings in Holmsburg in Pennsylvania, Sing Sing in New York State, and the Iowa State Penitentiary.

The ongoing "lockdown" at the Federal Penitentiary at Marion, Illinois, attests to the difficulty of reestablishing control in a prison that has been through a period of violent disruptions.[5] The murders, riots, and general disruption at this facility from February 1980 to October 1983 led administrators to institute a total lockdown of the institution. Inmates are kept isolated in their cells and when they are moved to a different cell, they frequently resist and fight with correctional officers. In a situation that both sides define as "combat" and "war," it has become normal behavior for inmates to resist any of the staff's attempts at control. Since the 1983 lockdown, Marion has experienced numerous killings and assaults of both correctional officers and inmates. This underlying conflict between staff and inmates at Marion is seething immediately below the surface and is kept at bay only through very expensive physical containments.[6]

In the prisons of this nation, young, passive, or weak inmates are repeatedly victimized by those who are stronger and more aggressive. Robbery, extortion, theft, assault, and rape are everyday occurrences among prison populations. This volatile environment creates a pressure chamber in which there is constant fear that the lid may come off at any time, and administrators know that they stand to lose their jobs if it does. Counselors and treatment staff know that a major disturbance will probably cause cancellation of treatment programs until control can be restored to the institution, which may take months. Correctional guards and other line staff know that they may be taken hostage and possibly killed. Inmates, in turn, know that such a disturbance will give the predators an even greater chance to victimize the weak.

Following an examination of the causes of institutional violence, this chapter considers the expressions of such violence and the measures that may possibly reduce it.

CAUSES OF INSTITUTIONAL VIOLENCE

The violent characteristics of inmates; social factors including inmate gangs, racial unrest, and the increased use of drugs; and the institutional, or structural, factors of prisons are the main causes of violence within the walls.

Violent Characteristics of Inmates

Four personal factors seem to be directly related to violent behavior in prison: youth, lower-class attitudes, the fear of humiliation, and a personal history of violent behavior.[7] Prisons are filled with men and women between 18 and 30, an age span that tends toward violence. Furthermore, the young seem to be less receptive to institutional control because they usually have faced few responsibilities before imprisonment, usually have spent less time in prison and therefore are less prepared to submit to discipline, and seldom have become firmly established in an occupation.

Most offenders are lower-class males who carry with them subcultural values and attitudes that quickly erupt into violence. These inmates often regard superior strength as a criterion of maleness, and this **machismo complex** makes them retaliate quickly for any episode they consider to be an attack on their manhood. In fact, those who fail to resort to physical combat are contemptible in their eyes. They prefer privately administered "justice," taking punishment into their own hands. They have also learned that survival on the streets and in prison dictate the intimidation of others, the exploitation of the weak, and the protection of self.

The fear of humiliation is an important underlying impetus for creating an image as a "bad ass," someone whom others dare not confront. As inmates vie for such violent reputations, confrontational incidents between inmates increase, especially among younger inmates. "Winners" in this violent competition for the "victimizer," "bad ass" roles gain power in the inmate social structure. But the losers in the struggle become labeled with the humiliated, "victim" role.[8]

In Mark Colvin's study of the Penitentiary of New Mexico, inmates reported that they placed a premium on gaining a violent reputation. "The young ones, I don't know, I guess they're trying to think they are cool. They walk around pushing everybody around. They're just trying to get them a name, a reputation," said an inmate. "They want to be recognized as being real tough," added another inmate. Said a third inmate, "This new generation is very aggressive. . . . They're all out to build a reputation here quick. As quick as possible. . . . They don't care if they leave or not."[9]

Today, prison populations are composed of more violent offenders than in the past. "Big House" prisons were filled primarily with property offenders, but beginning in the 1960s and continuing through the 1970s and 1980s, increased numbers of violent offenders were sentenced to prison. The law-and-order emphasis of the late 1970s and 1980s has also resulted in new criminal codes that provide severe penalties for violent offenses. Thus, individuals who have a history of violence are likely to be sent to prison for extended periods of time.

Social Factors

The major social factors that contribute to prison violence are continuing racial unrest, the presence of organized gangs within the walls, and the widespread drug appetites of the inmate population. The traditional prison was predominantly white, and the black inmates, who seldom made up more than 10 percent of the population, were usually docile. Now, the percentage of blacks in the prison population may be as high as 40 to 80 percent. In western states, Chicano prisoners may constitute as much as 30 percent or more of the population. Both Chicano and black inmates are now much more aggressive. Blacks resentful of white privileges in society use imprisonment as an opportunity to express a domination over whites that is denied them in the free community.[10]

Whites sometimes fight back by forming gangs and cliques; but because they are less streetwise and ready for the test of prison, more often they permit themselves to be physically and sexually assaulted by blacks. This **victimization of whites** has received considerable documentation. Leo Carroll, Anthony M. Scacco, Daniel Lockwood, and Hans Toch describe this pattern of victimization in prisons in the northeast; and the Dangerous Offender Project of the Academy of Contemporary Problems in Columbus, Ohio, provides a national perspective on white victimization.[11] In Florida, a white inmate filed a suit seeking reestablishment of racially segregated prisons. Louis Wainwright, former top correctional administrator in Florida, commented on this suit and the racial disorder that preceded it: "It is an extremely hazardous situation. White prisoners are begging to be locked in cells because of the increasing aggressive activities by blacks."[12] In Rhode Island, the following statement by a black inmate vividly portrays his rage:

> To the general way of thinking it's 'cause they're confined and they got hard rocks. But that ain't it at all. It's a way for the black man to get back at the white man. It's one way he can assert his manhood. Anything white, even a defenseless punk, is part of what the black man hates. It's part of what he's had to fight all his life just to survive, just to have a hole to sleep in and some garbage to eat. . . . It's a new ego thing. He can show he's a man by making a white guy into a girl.[13]

James Jacobs claims that the most important factor contributing to violence at Stateville was the presence of four Chicago street gangs—the Blackstone Rangers (who later renamed themselves the Black P Stone Nation and now are the El Rukns), the Devil's Disciples, the Conservative Vice Lords, and the Latin Kings.[14] A 1985 national study of prison gangs found gangs in 32 states and the Federal Bureau of Prisons. The most gangs were reported by Pennsylvania (15) and Illinois (14); the largest number of gang members was found in Illinois (5300), Pennsylvania (2400), and California (2050). Gang members made up 3 percent of all inmates in state and federal prisons.[15]

Prison gangs vary from loosely organized to highly organized and structured groups. The gangs that are imported from the streets in California and Illinois are particularly highly organized. For example, the Conservative Vice Lords, a Chicago-based street gang, has 21 divisions. This gang, as well as the other Chicago "supergangs," has a well-established leadership structure and clearly defined social norms. Violations of these social norms bring punishment ranging from a beating to death.

In California, the Mexican Mafia (chiefly from East Los Angeles) vies for power with the Nuestra Familia (consisting of rural Chicanos). Chicanos join gangs when it is necessary to fight the whites and the blacks. Blacks in California are organized into the Black Guerilla Family, the Black Muslims, the Black Panthers, and other groups; the Neo-Nazis and the Aryan Brotherhood are white gangs that have organized to provide protection against abuse and sexual molestation. In Illinois the El Rukns, the Black Gangster Disciples, and the Conservative Vice Lords are struggling for control and supremacy at the three maximum security institutions (Stateville, Menard, and Pontiac). The Latin Kings, a Spanish gang, and the Young Nobles, a white gang, attempt to protect themselves from the superior organization and greater numbers of the black gangs.

Mafia gangs are spreading throughout eastern prisons; the gangs from Illinois are also beginning to appear in Michigan, Wisconsin, and Iowa; and members of the California gangs are found in other states. Prison gangs spread from one state to another in several ways. Gang members may be sometimes transferred to a federal or another state correctional institution, and there they spread the teachings of the mother gang. Gang members may move to another state and, when imprisoned for criminal activities, start a gang organization in the new correctional facility. Or gang members may be traveling through a state and be imprisoned in that state because of a crime they commit. Finally, some street gang leaders send gang members to other states specifically to establish a gang organization. One chief of a Chicago street gang reported, "We want a national organization of the Unknown Vice Lords, and so we have sent our people to Wisconsin, Minnesota, and Michigan. It won't be long before we are coast to coast."[16]

Prison gangs usually specialize in economic victimization. They typically force all independent operators out of business and either divide among themselves the spoils of drugs, gambling rackets, and prostitution rings or fight to the death to determine who will establish a monopoly within the prison.[17] High levels of violence may occur when gangs are in conflict with each other. Interracial conflict also disrupts institutional life when such conflict is made a deliberate policy of large gangs organized along racial and ethnic dimensions.

The Bureau of Justice Statistics, in examining the use of drugs by prisoners, found that 42.6 percent had taken drugs on a daily basis in the month before the current offense, 35.3 percent were under the influence of drugs at the time of their offense, and 62.3 percent had used drugs on a regular basis.[18]

Mark Colvin has documented the relationship between drugs and violent behavior at the New Mexico state prison. Drug consumption at this prison dramatically increased from about 1971 to 1976, as did the number of inmate groups involved in trafficking. Staff's toleration, and in some cases collusion, with drug trafficking became an important feature of social control during these years. Inmates were willing to "keep the lid" on the prison because they did not want drug connections jeopardized or "heat" brought upon traffickers. But when a new administration took office in 1975, curtailment of drug use within the penitentiary became one of its major goals. Increased drug searches took place, and possible conduits for drugs were clamped down. The removal of incentives in drug trafficking disrupted inmate sources of nonviolent power, and a power vacuum developed, triggering a struggle for power among the inmates. As nonviolent power diminished, power became increasingly based on violence. Violence begets violence, and, according to Colvin, "a reputation for violence became a necessary requisite for survival—and especially for protection from sexual assault."[19]

Structural and Institutional Factors

Prison violence also results from double and triple celling of inmates; indefensible space; the frustration of living in a setting characterized by filth, lack of privacy, and enforced idleness from lack of jobs; the easy availability of violent weapons; a general high level of tension because of the deprivations of prison life; the influx of state-raised inmates; and a crisis of authority within the walls.

Overcrowding contributes to the victimization of weak prisoners. When two or three inmates are placed in a cell, the weakest is clearly vulnerable to the demands of the strongest. Or, to put it another way, in a cell housing three, it is usually two against one. The great amount of **indefensible space** in most prison compounds makes it difficult for staff to protect the weak from predatory peers. The weak have few places to go for protection in the conventional prison.

Violence also arises from the lack of private space. Violence-prone people particularly need space; instead, in prison they are placed in 6′ x 9′ cells that they must share with at least one other person. This increases tension and reduces the options in conflict resolution. The easy availability of weapons, usually made by the inmates themselves, provides a lethal means of striking out at others.

Scarcity of valued commodities (cigarettes, money, clothing, alcohol, and drugs), idleness, powerlessness, sexual frustration, and institutional routines all contribute to unrest and violence.[20] Understandably, the deprivations of imprisonment trigger acts of aggression and result in a frustrated and alienated inmate population. In turn, this environment generates a lack of trust. Indeed, inmates in the prison social system can do themselves a great deal of harm by becoming involved in the affairs of other residents; therefore, the prudent inmate will not see or hear if a peer is being harassed or exploited.

State-raised convicts have more opportunities for violence in prison these days with the power vacuum among inmates and the crisis of authority with staff. Jack Abbott, who in many ways is a prototype of the state-raised convict, has this to say about this population:

> He who is state-raised—reared by the state from an early age after he is taken from what the state calls a "broken home"—learns over and over all the days of his life that people

Overcrowding at San Quentin: Lack of privacy builds tension. (*Source:* Granger.)

in society can do anything to him and not be punished by the law. Do anything to him with the full force of the state behind them.[21]

As Abbott suggests here and elsewhere, state-raised convicts are bitter and prone to violence. They are at war with themselves as well as with the world around them, and they view violence as the only means they have of being taken seriously. State-raised convicts tend to find sexual gratification in the violation of other men. With their veneer of cool and hard manliness, they have a façade of adult maturity. They usually are chronically defensive, assuming a tough and menacing pose because they are angry and frightened. Moreover, state-raised convicts generally use poor judgment, react with rash and impulsive emotions, exhibit profound self-centeredness, and are consumed by a festering rage that touches nearly everything and everyone in their world.[22]

In short, the prison is a violent environment because the characteristics of inmates combine with abnormal social factors and institutional, physical, and structural imperfections to generate aggression and violence. The claim can be made, of course, that the prison is not as violent as some of the neighborhoods from which prisoners come, but this is difficult to substantiate. It does appear that institutional violence is tapering off as administrators recapture some of the control they once had. For example, the period from 1985 to 1990 was less violent than the decade before. Yet most prison staff, as well as inmates, continue to see violence as one of the most troubling problems of prison life.

EXPRESSIONS OF PRISON VIOLENCE

Institutional violence is expressed through **riots** and major disturbances, inmate aggression toward other inmates, inmate and staff conflict, and self-inflicted inmate injuries.

Riots and Major Disturbances

The 300 riots since 1970 can be divided into violent and nonviolent uprisings. Nonviolent **inmate disturbances** include hunger strikes, sit-down strikes, work stoppages, voluntary lockdowns (staying in one's cell even when the cellblock is open), excessive numbers of inmates reporting for sick call, and the filing of grievances by nearly everyone in a cellblock or even in the entire institution. Violent inmate disturbances include crowding around a correctional officer and intimidating him or her so that a disciplinary ticket is not written; assaulting officers; sabotaging the electrical, plumbing, or heating systems; burning or destroying institutional property; and taking control, with or without hostages, of a cellblock, a yard, or an entire prison.

The violent uprisings, best characterized by those at Attica and Santa Fe, include the taking of staff hostages and sometimes the killing of fellow inmates and staff. (See Box 15-1 for the background of the Santa Fe riot.) The most frequent pattern of nonviolent riots is widespread arson and vandalism.

The 1980s were also a decade in which widespread arson and vandalism took place during numerous inmate uprisings in men's prisons. In 1981, five such riots

Box 15-1 The New Mexico Prison Riot

The watershed riot at the New Mexico State Prison in Santa Fe began shortly after midnight on Saturday, February 2, 1980. As things go in maximum security prisons these days, it had been a quiet week—no killings, no stabbings, and only the usual amount of physical mayhem and personal indignities. Nothing, in short, to warn of the savagery which would eventually cost 33 lives, inflict many injuries, some critical, and produce hundreds of beaten, raped and psychologically scarred prisoners.

The weekend had begun peacefully, despite rumors of impending trouble, for the 1136 prisoners in this facility designed to hold no more than 800 men. A few of the inmates were taking their leisure; most were asleep. In the dormitory end of the complex and in Dormitory E-2 specifically, some of the men were watching the late movie on TV; two boisterous prisoners, feeling no pain, were lying in their bunks drinking prison-made raisinjack. The noise attracted Captain Roybal, a tough and seasoned veteran in the system. One of only 22 officers on duty that night either on the towers or inside the prison perimeter, the captain tried to confiscate the prison-made raisinjack. In the process, he was jumped by the intoxicated prisoners and by unknown others in the dormitory, taken hostage and relieved of his keys—all the keys needed to gain entry to the corridor leading to the control room. Two other officers who came to his assistance were also taken hostage. All three were beaten and raped into unconsciousness.

Within moments of the taking of the Captain and his two colleagues in Dormitory E-2, the corridor and the cellblocks belonged to the prisoners. Down the corridor they stormed in a wave that must have been as terrifying to the guards as the breaching of an ancient fortress—a Bastille—to its undermanned defenders. Curiously, the impregnable control room was readily breached; the shatterproof glass, shattered; the control room operative fled, of all places, into the solitary confinement wing. The buttons were pushed, the electronically controlled gates opened. The remaining interior guards were soon captives; the tower guards powerless to report the riot since all phone lines were cut. The infirmary was invaded and looted of all mood-altering drugs.

The carnage began. Old inmate scores were settled; real or imagined slights redressed; the very thin layer of moral development peeled right down to the atavistic core. Unlike other riots in recent years, there was no carnival atmosphere, no leadership, no lists of grievances, no organization, nothing. Only unspeakable brutality. In all these respects, New Mexico represents a turning point in U.S. prison history.

Dazed, stuporous, and revengeful, the prison intractables, the violent few, were soon in possession of the warden's secret list of informers, weaklings, debtors, and vulnerables. In almost less time than it takes to tell, the 50 to 150 hard-core and violent men reached the sturdy protective cellblock. In uncontrollable frenzy, using blowtorches, and an assortment of prison-fashioned and smuggled weapons, 12 snitches were burned, decapitated, castrated, and eviscerated. One unfortunate had a metal rod jammed in one ear and out the other. Another was burned systematically from his legs up. Such was the brutality that many in the protective custody unit were beyond physical identification.

Source: Simon Dinitz, "Are Safe and Humane Prisons Possible?" *Australia & New Zealand Journal of Criminology* 14, March 1981, pp. 3–4.

Sit-down strike in a Southern prison.

rupted at three Michigan prisons (State Prison, Southern Michigan; Michigan Reformatory; and Marquette) over a five-day period. Three similar riots took place in 1986 at the West Virginia Penitentiary, South Carolina's Kirkland Correctional Institution, and Iowa State Penitentiary. Considerable damage also took place in 1987 riots at two federal penitentiaries, in which Cuban detainees demanded not to be transported to a "non-imperialist" country.[23]

Women, traditionally passive and docile during imprisonment, were also influenced by the political and social events of the late 1960s and early 1970s and began to match men in mob violence. During the 1972 and 1973 riots at five institutions for females—Federal Reformatory for Women in Alderson, West Virginia; Muncy in upstate Pennsylvania; Ohio Reformatory for Women; Philadelphia House of Corrections; and Niantic Women's Prison in Connecticut—hunger strikes were staged, institutional property was destroyed, hostages were taken, staff members were injured, and escapes occurred. Women in these and other institutions gave vent to their frustrations and began to demand more rights. However, women's prisons have had relatively few inmate disturbances since the mid-1970s.

Riots may be expressive, or spontaneous, or instrumental, or planned with some goal in mind.[24] The planning required for an instrumental riot generally requires inmate solidarity. When prison riots break out today, they tend to be more like the New Mexico riot than the inmate revolt at Attica. In Attica, inmates had a high degree of organization, solidarity, and political consciousness, while the New Mexico riot is notable for inmates' fragmentation, lack of effective leadership, and disorganization. Indeed, the 1980 New Mexico riot showed the extent to which relations between prisoners had become fragmented during the 1970s and 1980s; political apathy and infighting had replaced the politicization and solidarity of the earlier years.[25]

Five stages usually take place in the loss, then reestablishment, of state control. First, during the pre-riot stage, inmates and the forces of the state develop the resources that will determine the course of the riot event. Second, inmates initiate action in which they cross the line into open rebellion, and the state responds. Third,

The clean-up at the Penitentiary of New Mexico. (*Source:* Norman Bergsma/Sygma.)

assuming that the disturbance is not crushed immediately, a stage of expansion occurs, during which the inmates most often attempt to take control of the prison. Fourth, a stage of siege then usually follows, during which the inmates control some territory in the prison, the state assembles its forces and concentrates its options for recapture, and bargaining may go on among the state, inmates, and other parties. The final stage is termination or recapture.[26]

There have been four prison riot epidemics in this century.[27] The first took place at the time of World War I and led to the introduction of "moral regeneration" activities, such as the start of library education, the introduction of counseling services, a reduced emphasis on regimentation and the lock-step, and minor improvements in health care and sanitary conditions.

The second wave, coinciding with the onset of the Great Depression, peaked in 1929–1930. The medical model contributed to these revolts in that the introduction of classification and diagnosis, psychiatric treatment, psychological testing and counseling, and indeterminancy in sentencing undermined the institutional power arrangements. Ironically, the subsequent rioting led to the acceptance of these programs as well as other reforms.

The third wave took place in the early 1950s, the time of the Korean War, and continued for over a decade. The Utah State Prison and the Michigan State Prison at Jackson blew up in the early 1950s. In both instances, hostages were taken as a matter of course; hostage taking began the policy of trading guards for concessions. Between 1950 and 1966, as the repressive principles of autocratic management gave way to reform philosophy and participative management, more than 100 riots and major disturbances took place.

The fourth wave of prison riots took place during the late 1960s and early 1970s and continues to the present. These were the most riotous years since the Civil War, and the turmoil in the streets quickly moved into the prisons. The street slogan

"Burn, baby, burn" soon entered prison lingo, and the politicalization of inmates spread from California throughout the nation. Several serious riots occurred at the San Quentin and Folsom prisons in California and at the Holmesburg Prison in Philadelphia during the late 1960s, but it was the 1971 shooting of George Jackson at San Quentin that became the rallying point for inmates throughout the country. On September 9, less than a month after Jackson's death, a riot at the Attica Correctional Center catapulted this prison in northwestern New York state from anonymity to infamy. Following the Attica riot, protests, strikes, and riots in epidemic numbers occurred in state prisons, federal institutions, and county jails during the 1970s and 1980s.

In sum, collective violence has always been endemic in prisons in this nation, but since 1951, there have been, on the average, more than ten prison riots a year. These riots have occurred in all areas of the country, have usually not involved the taking of guards as hostages or the loss of life, and have nearly always featured widespread arson and vandalism. The targets of destruction consistently have been the schools, shops, and infirmaries. Riots recently have tended to be more spontaneous outbursts rather than planned rebellions by inmates. Apparently, the main reason that the violent, fragmented, and tense prison setting remains intact is that inmates ultimately prefer order to disorder. As one gang leader stated, "We're in control around here. If we wanted to, we could take the prison apart, but we choose not to. We've too much to lose."[28]

Inmate Against Inmate

The prison environment combines a number of factors that contribute to what can be called a controlled war among inmates. These factors include (1) inadequate supervision by staff members, (2) architectural designs that promote rather than inhibit victimization, (3) the easy availability of deadly weapons, (4) the housing of violent-prone inmates in close proximity to relatively defenseless victims, (5) a high level of tension produced by close quarters and crosscutting conflicts among both individuals and groups of inmates, and (6) feedback systems through which inmates feel the need to take revenge for real or imagined slights or past victimizations.[29]

Violence among inmates has reached a new high. A misspoken word, a slight bump of another inmate, an unpaid gambling debt, a racial slur, or an invasion of the "turf" of another can bring a violent attack. The expected arrival of a visitor who never appears, news about problems being experienced by a spouse or child, cancellation of a scheduled and looked-forward-to bit of entertainment, an unanticipated cell search, or even an unusually hot and humid day also can produce explosive consequences.[30]

Emotional harassment; physical assaults, including rapes and stabbings; and homicides are part of prison life, especially in large maximum security prisons. One inmate expressed the feelings of many inmates when he said, "Man, it's a jungle in here, and only the strong survive."[31] Another inmate speaks of the violence of prison life:

> At San Quentin there is a terribly hostile atmosphere. You have to adapt yourself. Everyone puts up a front that they are strong. If you are weak, people know that you won't fight back and you will be used. You will be forced into homosexual relations and be forced to buy dope. When you first arrive you are tested. We call that "getting your

> face." The first month I was here I had to physically defend myself. I didn't want to fight—I wanted to just do my number, but I had to fight in order to show that I couldn't be pushed around, and once I had shown that, I was left pretty much alone. There is a really strong protection racket here; if you let yourself be pushed around and don't defend yourself, you can get forced to pay for your own protection.[32]

In 1964, John P. Conrad identified 146 fights in California prisons that were sufficiently serious to require disciplinary action. That was a rate of 0.62 fights per 100 prisoners in a prison system that had about 25,000 inmates. In 1980, the most recent year for which figures are available, there were 775 fights and assaults, involving 339 weapons, in a population of about the same size as that in 1964. That works out to a rate of 3.31 fights per 100 prisoners, more than 5 times the rate in 1964. Five incidents in 1964 resulted in fatalities, but in 1980, 14 were killed, including one staff member.[33]

Sylvester Sawyer, John H. Reed, and David O. Nelson, in a study of homicides in prisons housing 200 or more male inmates, found that 113 of the 128 homicides were inmate against inmate. These researchers found that there appeared to be two distinguishable types of prison homicides: single-assailant homicide and multiple-assailant homicide. The first seemed to be more spontaneous, more often victim-precipitated, and related to homosexuality; the second appeared to be premeditated homicide. Single-assailant instances appeared to stem from personal involvements, while multiple-assailant occurrences seemed to have more to do with maintenance of the inmate social order.[34]

The divisions among inmates contributes to the unpredictable nature of prison violence. While some prison violence is gang and clique related, other incidents can be found in personal pathology, drug-induced hallucinations, or the danger of an accidental meeting. Most inmate violence appears to be of a situated nature, almost a chance occurrence—that is, being in the wrong place at the wrong time.[35] The national study done by Sawyer et al. found that the most frequent type of homicide (25 percent) had no apparent motive.[36] Research in California also found that the largest category of inmate-on-inmate assault (35 percent) fell into the category of "accidental, real or imagined insults combined with hypersensitivity."[37]

Understandably, inmates make every effort to protect themselves. Weaponry has replaced fists as the primary means of self-protection in male institutions. A variety of objects can be weapons: chisels, screwdrivers, sharpened shanks of spoons, broomsticks, baseball bats, clubs, chunks of concrete, stiff wire, heavy-gauge metal, metal from beds, boilerplate metal, and zip guns. Smuggled weapons also appear. Barrelfuls of knives and other weapons have been collected by security staff during shakedowns in some institutions.

Sexual Victimization

Sex occurs in men's prisons in three contexts: (1) consensual sex involving affection and sexual release, (2) coercive sexual behavior that combines force and domination; and (3) sex for hire, where sexual release is purchased at various levels of domination.[38]

The violence and brutality of inmates toward other inmates is probably expressed more often in **sexual victimization** than in stabbings or slayings. Most first arrivals in prison—especially white males who have committed minor crimes—are "on trial." If they have the willingness and capacity to fight, they will usually pass the examination. If not, then prison time will indeed be "hard time":

> Any new person, they hollered obscenities at them and all sorts of names, and throwing things down from the galley and everything. They told me to walk down the middle of this line like I was on exhibition, and everybody started to throw things and everything, and I was shaking in my boots. . . . They were screaming things like, "That is for me" and "This one won't take long—he will be easy." And, "Look at his eyes" and "her eyes" or whatever, and making all kinds of remarks.[39]

Daniel Lockwood found that in the correctional settings he studied in New York state, violent sexual incidents among men in prison fell into two groups. In the first group, aggressors use violence to coerce their targets. The causes of this violence can be traced to subcultural values upholding the right to use force to gain sexual privileges. In the second category, targets react violently to propositions they view as threatening. In other words, victims, or targets, have a tendency to answer sexual propositions with counterthreats.[40] Hans Toch adds that some prisoners use violence against those who make sexual approaches to them in order to get the predators to leave them alone.[41] Lockwood concluded that since violent incidents in prison appear to be divided about equally between these two categories, programs to reduce prison sexual violence should be aimed at both targets and aggressors.[42]

Prisoners who escape physical assault and sexual victimization are able to accomplish this feat because they follow these rules:

1. Never show weakness to anybody.
2. Never take anything from another inmate, unless you are certain you can pay it back.
3. Never go into another inmate's cell, unless you know the inmate well.
4. Never get into a threatening position, unless you have some lethal means to protect yourself.[43]

A study by Peter L. Nacci, William G. Saylor, and Thomas R. Kane documenting sexual victimization in the Federal Bureau of Prisons found that about 10 percent of inmates had had to defend themselves against a sexual attack at some time during their incarceration in state or federal institutions. Nacci et al. also found that about 12 percent of their sample had participated at least once in a sex act in other institutions. Sexual participation does not seem to alter sexual orientation significantly; however, these researchers did find a tendency for any existing attraction to males to increase during incarceration.[44]

Colvin's study of the Penitentiary of New Mexico led him to conclude that rapes and assaults in the late 1970s sharply increased in this correctional facility. The instability of the environment forced inmates into marking themselves as powerful and dominant by humiliating others. Newly arriving prisoners, especially, had their "character" tested. The weak lost everything, including their manhood and perhaps their lives.[45]

However, John Irwin, a widely published corrections writer who was an inmate himself for a period of time, believes that the reports of sexual assaults are exaggerated. He admits that during the 1960s the naïve white youth was too often the victim of the more streetwise black, but he feels that this period has passed and that white inmates now know the game and are able to avoid the interpersonal interaction that leads to rape.[46] Dan A. Fuller and Thomas Orsagh studied the prison system in North Carolina and also concluded that the occurrence of rape is exaggerated. They claim that a male in prison in this southeastern state is no more likely to be raped than is a female in the free community.[47]

Regardless of whether sexual assaults are seen as epidemic or as relatively infrequent, few would deny that sexual victimization has many unfortunate effects. It curbs victims' freedom to act; indeed, many victims feel that their only viable alternative is to check into protective custody. Sexual victimization also leads to feelings of helplessness and depression, fear of AIDS, damaged self-esteem, possible self-destructive acts such as self-mutilation or suicide, lowered social status, psychosomatic illnesses, sometimes increased difficulty in adjusting to life after release, and possibly even increased risk of recidivism.[48]

Inmates Versus Staff

Correctional officers are very aware of the dangers present in their jobs, for they daily experience the hostility of inmates. The axiom "If the inmates want you, they can get you" reminds officers that their lives can be snatched away at any time. In addition to the physical danger, officers also experience other types of abuse from inmates. As a warden noted, "Who wants a bucket of urine in his face? Who wants human excrement thrown upon him? Who wants to be the recipient of continual sneers and profanity?"[49]

A senior member of the headquarters staff of the California Department of Corrections describes the present status of prisoner–guard relations:

> Social contacts between officers and inmates are getting more distant. When I was on the line, I would get assignments like supervision of a dormitory on the third watch [4:00 P.M. to midnight] and sometimes I got pretty scared. I'd be alone, and my chief protection was that I knew guys and they knew me and we had a sort of rapport. I was always talking with them. But now, on account of the violence, we've had to introduce a sort of buddy system, and I won't say we could have avoided it. The officers do their patrolling in pairs. They rap with each other and hardly ever talk with the inmates. They don't need to. In the days when an officer was alone on a cellblock or in a dorm, he wouldn't have anyone to talk to except the inmates he was working with. I'm convinced that kind of interaction was helpful and important, but we're losing it. We don't know what's going on, and we don't have an opportunity or occasion to build rapport.[50]

Officers in maximum security prisons now generally prefer total lockup; they feel safer when inmates are in their cells 24 hours a day. Tower positions, though they represent a dead-end job, are beginning to become desirable because they exclude contact with inmates. Thus, correctional officers, like inmates, serve time. The values they bring into the institution are reshaped by the necessities of institutional control and by nagging anxieties about their personal safety.

One correctional officer expresses the conflict between inmates and officers this way: "They tell us that if we would treat them like men, they would act like men. But we tell them that if they would act like men we would treat them that way." He went on to say, "Physical abuse follows verbal abuse, and we are getting a lot of verbal abuse."[51]

Self-inflicted Violence

During imprisonment, many men and women lose hope and feel alienated from their families and other inmates. Of those who feel isolated, some break, direct their hostilities and frustrations toward themselves, and try to take their own lives. An ex-offender who was talking about a prison suicide put it this way: "He couldn't handle it; prison was too much for him."[52]

In 1988 109 suicides were recorded in this nation's prisons (99 in state facilities and 10 in federal institutions).[53] Cases clearly are missing from these official suicide counts because they were counted as something else. For example, some prison homicides are suicides, because inmates let themselves be murdered by violent inmates. Inmates have also been known to charge the fence, knowing that guards will shoot them down. Furthermore, prisoners on death row who have lost their will to live may call off their appeals, letting the state fulfill the suicidal act.[54]

The fact is that there are several times as many attempted suicides as there are actual suicides. It is difficult, however, to estimate accurately the genuine self-destructive acts, and differentiate them from those in which inmates are seeking attention or wishing to receive protection. What is common among inmates who engage in self-destructive acts is a sense of desperation or hopelessness.

Three types seem to be likely candidates for **self-inflicted injuries** in correctional institutions. First are the inmates who do not have a criminal history and are embarrassed at having brought disgrace upon themselves and their families. These persons generally inflict injury upon themselves soon after admission to the prison. Second are the inmates who have been confined in the prison for months or years and who have developed a feeling of hopelessness and futility about the future. Third are antisocial persons who exhibit suicidal behavior in order to manipulate others; they tend to choose methods that will ensure their survival.[55]

An inmate who attempted suicide discusses why some prisoners focus their rage on themselves rather than on others:

> There are many reasons why I feel a man in prison would take his own life. In prison he is away from loved ones and the ones he cares about. Prison restrains him from any communications where he can see, could touch or reach out and feel a loved one or dear friend. . . . You have to be mentally strong to survive in prison no matter how short the term is.[56]

Prison suicide is most common among young, unmarried white males.[57] Suicide generally occurs early in confinement, and hanging is the usual method. Inmates also use razor blades to commit suicide. If razor blades are not available, fragments of metal, glass, wire, or even eating utensils can be transformed into lethal instruments. Swallowing objects or toxic substances, such as mercury from a thermometer, is sometimes tried.

REDUCING PRISON VIOLENCE

Institutional violence, which does vary in seriousness and expression from state to state, may possibly be reduced by these methods: making the prison more humane; developing quality correctional leadership; developing better-trained staff; screening more adequately the violent and vulnerable; making prison space defensible; and denying recognition to inmate gangs.

More Humane Institutions

Small facilities and humane institutions can do much to reduce institutional violence. The fact is that large maximum security prisons are the most likely to have frequent and violent inmate disturbances. Full employment of inmates is a strong deterrent to violence, but inmates are most likely to be idle in large institutions. Large prisons also have difficulty providing the necessary services to inmates, and this lack of services generates considerable animosity among the kept. Finally, in larger institutions it is more difficult to control the possession of weapons and drug trafficking than in smaller ones. Co-correctional, or coeducational, facilities show that smaller institutions providing a more humane environment will usually have reduced rates of inmate disturbances, physical and sexual assaults, and self-destructive behaviors.

Effective Correctional Administration

A breakdown in administrative control and operation is usually found in the riot-prone prison. Typical elements of this breakdown include scandals, escapes, inconsistent rules for inmates and guards, fragmentation, instability within the system, conflict between administration and guards, and the disruption of everyday routines for eating, work, and recreation. Thus, poorly managed prisons, lacking stability and uniformity, perpetuate the feelings among inmates that they must do something about the inadequate conditions of confinement.[58]

The progressive wardens of the 1990s, as suggested in Chapter 13, are good managers who bring stability and uniformity to their institutions. Staff members feel safer and better about working within the walls. As a result of higher staff morale, there is less turnover, sick leave, and tardiness, thus contributing to more institutional stability. These wardens are also more on top of what goes on in the institution, and they are less likely to let an incident get out of control or to overreact to an institutional problem. Moreover, they contribute to the reduction of prison violence by communicating to inmates that they are doing everything possible to make conditions more humane and by providing inmates with effective channels for expressing their needs and frustrations.

Line Staff and Defusing Violence

The erosion of the security system is unquestionably one of the quicker ways to promote institutional violence. For example, at Attica, steel gates broke and there were no radios; at New Mexico, guards left the doors open and the supposedly unbreakable glass quickly shattered.[59] Equally as true, correctional systems are beginning to discover that one of the most effective ways to defuse violence is by having well-trained line staff. California sends correctional staff to conflict-resolution training as a means of more effectively handling tension within the walls. Training staff in conflict-resolution techniques is likely to promote the idea that correctional officers work jointly with inmates to resolve differences or grievances, whether they take place between officers and inmates or between inmates themselves.[60] Most states are aware that the recruitment of staff members from minority groups is another helpful factor in controlling prison violence; a higher percentage of minority staff clearly eliminates many of the problems created by a core of white guards controlling predominantly black inmates. Finally, as discussed in Chapter 14, expanding the role of the correctional officer to include human service work is likely to contribute, perhaps significantly, to reducing institutional tensions and violence.[61] What is clearly needed are line staff who will more fully understand the needs of correctional clients, who will work with them effectively, and who will help them achieve full citizenship.

Correctional Ombudsmen

Ombudsmen who demonstrate integrity in their dealings with inmates and staff can often resolve some of the tension-producing prison problems that lead to violence. Ombudsmen also serve as a channel of information from inmates to administrators, which channel can be used to focus resources on conditions and situations appearing to be most conducive to victimization.[62]

Adequate Screening

Violence can also be reduced by more adequate **screening of the vulnerable** from the aggressive. Special programs and isolation cells can be provided for emotionally disturbed, disabled, or defenseless inmates. Another strategy is to remove the weak from the presence of the strong through a classification process that would prevent violent and nonviolent prisoners from being housed together. Some states protect such inmates as informants, delinquent debtors, or homosexual targets by assigning them to institutions restricted to those who cannot survive in other correctional facilities. It is hoped that the new prisons being constructed throughout the United States will more adequately provide for such needs.

Defensible Prison Space

Violence can be reduced by making prison space defensible because victimization rates tend to be high in those areas of prisons that are not open to the view of staff members. For example, a covered walkway can have the roof removed so that tower guards can have an open view of what takes place there. A cul-de-sac in the hallway that precludes staff observation can be walled off or can be monitored with a remote television camera.[63] Some of the new prisons have been designed to minimize the extent of indefensible space. Leesburg in New Jersey is a newer secure prison that is designed to hold about 500 adult male felons. All living units are constructed around landscaped open courts, with each of the four sides containing outside rooms built in two tiers. The self-contained rooms have secure, solid prison doors, which, like the walls, are painted in pleasant colors. The inside walls are glass from ceiling to floor, giving the impression of no walls at all.[64]

Gang Control Measures

The lockup, punitive segregation, sharing power, and institutional transfers are the four most widely used methods of dealing with gang control, and all four methods have their shortcomings. Wardens and superintendents can always resort to the lockup or lockdown to keep the lid on gang violence. But although keeping gang members in their cells 24 hours a day may enable staff to regain control of the institution initially, ultimately gang members must be released from their cells, and the repressed tension may create even greater problems. Gang leaders have been frequently handled by being isolated for long periods in punitive segregation. Yet federal courts are increasingly unwilling to tolerate placing inmates in segregation for long periods. Also, even in segregation, gang leaders often are able to continue ruling their followers. As previously discussed, a number of institutions have found that the process of sharing power with gangs has usually ended up in disaster. Institutional transfers, of course, permit prison administrators to send troublemaking inmates, including gang members, to other institutions, but this merely spreads the problem from one prison to another. Indeed, one reason why gangs have spread throughout the nation is this policy of institutional transfers for troublemaking inmates.

The best strategy for controlling gangs at the present time appears to be for the entire department of corrections to adopt a policy of denying recognition of these inmate groups. Frank Wood cogently presents this position:

> The first thing you have to do with gangs once they come into the prison is for the entire department of corrections to follow the same policy. We are not going to give recognition to gangs, or leaders of gangs, or give them a special status, or a special form in which to interact with the administration or staff.
>
> If we do so, what we've done is set up a system where we've communicated to inmates that to make anything happen, they've got to go through these self-appointed thugs. They have emerged as leaders largely because of their physical abilities and their capacity to treat life with such abandon that they're prepared to kill over a pack of cigarettes. It's important that you don't give up your future to any group or organized group of inmates, because their agenda is going to be quite different from the one that would be good for the future of the institution.[65]

Wood's nonrecognition strategy is much easier to accomplish in Minnesota, which is at the onset of inmate gang prisons. It is clearly much more difficult to accomplish in Illinois, California, and other states where gangs have an entrenched power base and have a sizable membership within the population. Yet, as gangs increase in number in the 1990s because of the recent nationwide expansion of drug-trafficking groups on the streets, this ultimately appears to be the best strategy of avoiding gang takeover of prisons.

Many other factors leading to violence are beyond the control of prison officials: Among them are the size of megaprisons and the crowding of facilities; the injustice in the criminal justice system, such as shortsighted sentencing and parole practices; the enforced idleness of too many inmates; inadequate financial support from the state legislature; public indifference; and the increasing number of violent and aggressive criminals, including gang members from the streets, being sentenced to prison. Furthermore, prison officials cannot alter the belief of prisoners that the only way they can gain the public's attention and overcome public apathy is through a prison riot.

CONCLUSIONS

Within the contemporary prison, the worst of society's rejects create a world in which the reality of violence can take place at any time. The violent characteristics of inmates, the abnormal social environment, and the institutional physical and structural imperfections all combine to produce violent surroundings. Overcrowding, the drug appetites of prisoners, and racial and gang skirmishes seem to be the most important factors that create an incendiary situation. If inmates can be tough enough, they will turn themselves into the worst kind of predators, forcing themselves on the weak and enjoying the spoils of their predation. The background of prisoners suggests that there will always be some violence, predation, and corruption, but violence, predation, and corruption need not have the upper hand. The fact remains that creating a lawful prison—in which compliance with the law and reasonable regulations prevail—will be no easy task.

Nevertheless, every inmate is entitled to protection from physical and sexual assault. Rapes do not occur in the warden's office or on the front lawn; they take place in back rooms, in crowded cells, and in other indefensible areas of the institution. Prisons must be made more humane, and the inmates themselves must come to the aid of victims and assume responsibility for creating a safer prison. Staff members also deserve every available protection. To guard 50 or 100 hostile prisoners is a frightening task, and to have to guard them without every precaution's being taken for protection of staff is inexcusable.

KEY TERMS

indefensible space

inmate disturbances

machismo complex

prison gangs

prison suicide

riots

screening of the vulnerable

self-inflicted injuries

sexual victimization

state-raised convicts

victimization of whites

DISCUSSION TOPICS

15.1 Gangs are the most powerful social units in some prisons. How do gangs escalate violence in the cellhouse?

15.2 Crowding, filth, deprivation, and enforced idleness—what effect do these conditions of prison life have on prison behavior.

15.3 Violence isn't only other-directed. What prisoners are most likely to be their own victims? Why?

15.4 Can prisoner violence be reduced? How? Will any one method do it?

ANNOTATED REFERENCES

Attica: The Official Report of the New York State Special Commission on Attica. New York: Praeger, 1972. *This official report on the Attica riot is required reading for the serious student of corrections.*

Carroll, Leo. *Hacks, Blacks, and Cons.* Lexington, Mass.: Heath, 1974. *Portrays the growing racial conflict between blacks and whites in a prison in the northeast.*

Colvin, Mark. *From Accommodation to Riot: The Penitentiary of New Mexico in Crisis.* Albany: State University of New York Press, 1991. *An excellent study of the 1980 riot at the Penitentiary of New Mexico.*

Fleisher, Mark S. *Warehousing Violence.* Newbury Park, Calif.: Sage, 1989. *Examines the methods of social control used to maintain order at Lompoc, a federal institution in California.*

Irwin, John. *Prisons in Turmoil.* Boston: Little, Brown, 1980. *A lively account of the social factors behind the violence found in today's prisons.*

Remick, Peter, as told to James B. Shuman. *In Constant Fear.* New York: Reader's Digest Press, 1975. *Remick's account of life at Walpole Prison in Massachusetts is one of the most important books written by an inmate in the past two decades.*

Useem, Bert, and Peter A. Kimball. *States of Siege: U.S. Prison Riots, 1971–1986.* New York: Oxford University Press, 1989. *A first-rate study of the Attica, New Mexico, Michigan, Joliet, and West Virginia penitentiaries riots.*

NOTES

1. John Irwin, *Prisons in Turmoil* (Boston: Little, Brown, 1980), p. 212.
2. Bert Useem and Peter A. Kimball, *States of Siege: U.S. Prison Riots, 1971–1986* (New York: Oxford University Press, 1989), p. 3.
3. *Attica: The Official Report of the New York State Special Commission on Attica* (New York: Praeger, 1972), p. xi.
4. For more information on the New Mexico State Prison riot, see Mark Colvin, "The 1980 New Mexico Prison Riot." *Social Problems* 29, June 1982: 449–463.
5. J. Michael Olivero and James B. Roberts, "Marion Federal Penitentiary and the 22-Month Lockdown: The Crisis Continues." *Crime and Social Justice*, 27–28, 1987: 234–255; "A New Home for Noriega? The Federal Prison in Marion, Ill., the Nation's Most Secure Pen, Holds Hard Men Doing Hard Time." *Newsweek*, 1 January 1990: 66–69.
6. Mark Colvin, *From Accommodation to Riot: The Penitentiary of New Mexico in Crisis* (Albany: State University of New York, 1991), pp. 374–375.
7. Albert K. Cohen, "Prison Violence: A Sociological Perspective." In Albert K. Cohen, George F. Cole, and Robert C. Bailey, eds., *Prison Violence* (Lexington, Mass.: Heath, 1976), pp. 10–14.
8. Colvin, *From Accommodation to Riot*, pp. 305–306.
9. Ibid., p. 306.
10. John P. Conrad, "The Survival of the Fearful." In John Conrad and Simon Dinitz, eds., *Fear of Each Other* (Lexington, Mass.: Heath, 1977), pp. 122–124.
11. Leo Carroll, *Hacks, Blacks, and Cons* (Lexington, Mass.: Heath, 1974), pp. 181–187; Anthony M. Scacco Jr., *Rape in Prison* (Springfield, Ill.: Charles C Thomas, 1975), pp. 47–65; Clemens Bartollas, Stuart J. Miller, and Simon Dinitz, *Juvenile Victimization: The Institutional Paradox* (New York: Halsted Press, A Sage Publication, 1976), pp. 53–67; Conrad, "Survival of the Fearful," pp. 123–124.

12. "Wainwright Says Black Prison Majority Feared." *Orlando Sentinel Star*, May 1973: 2.
13. Carroll, *Hacks, Blacks, and Cons*, pp. 184–185.
14. James B. Jacobs, *Stateville: The Penitentiary in Mass Society* (Chicago: University of Chicago Press, 1977), p. 146.
15. George M. Camp and Camille Graham Camp, *Prison Gangs: Their Extent, Nature and Impact on Prisons* (Washington: Government Printing Office, 1985), p. vii.
16. Interviewed in March 1984.
17. Jacobs, *Stateville;* Lee Bowker, *Prison Victimization* (New York: Elsevier, 1980).
18. Katherine M. Jamieson and Timothy J. Flanagan, *Sourcebook: Criminal Justice 1988* (Washington: U.S. Department of Justice, 1989), p. 662.
19. Colvin, "The 1980 New Mexico Prison Riot," pp. 454–455.
20. See Gresham Sykes, *Society of Captives* (Princeton, N.J.: Princeton University Press, 1959), for the classic statement on the deprivations of imprisonment.
21. J. H. Abbott, *In the Belly of the Beast* (New York: Vintage, 1981), p. 12.
22. Robert Johnson, *Hard Time: Understanding and Reforming the Prison* (Belmont, Calif.: Wadsworth, 1987), pp. 87–88.
23. Useem and Kimball, *States of Seige.*
24. Richard Hawkins and Geoffrey P. Alpert, *American Prison Systems: Punishment and Justice* (Englewood Cliffs, N.J.: Prentice-Hall, 1989), p. 254.
25. Colvin, "The New Mexico Prison Riot," p. 448.
26. Useem and Kimball, *States of Siege,* p. 5.
27. Simon Dinitz and George Beto, "In Fear of Each Other." *Sociological Focus* 16, August 1983: 158–159.
28. Interviewed in May 1981.
29. Colvin, "The New Mexico Prison Riot," p. 448.
30. Charles W. Thomas, *Corrections in America* (Newbury Park, Calif.: Sage, 1987), p. 126.
31. Interviewed in April 1981.
32. Erik Olin Wright, *The Politics of Punishment* (New York: Harper, Colophon Books, 1973), p. 150.
33. John P. Conrad, "What Do the Undeserving Deserve?" In Robert Johnson and Hans Toch, eds., *The Pains of Imprisonment* (Beverly Hills, Calif.: Sage, 1982), p. 319.
34. Sylvester Sawyer, John R. Reed, and David O. Nelson, *Prison Homicide* (New York: Spectrum, 1977), p. 80.
35. Hawkins and Alpert, *American Prison Systems,* p. 268.
36. Sawyer et. al., *Prison Homicide.*
37. John J. Gibbs, "Violence in Prison." In R. R. Robert and V. J. Webb, eds., *Critical Issues in Corrections* (St. Paul: West, 1981), pp. 121–122.
38. Hawkins and Alpert, *American Prison Systems,* p. 275.
39. Hans Toch, *Living in Prison: The Ecology of Survival* (New York: Free Press, 1977), pp. 147–148.
40. Daniel Lockwood, "Reducing Prison Sexual Violence." In *The Pains of Imprisonment,* p. 257.
41. Hans Toch, "Institutional Violence Code, Tentative Code of the Classification of Inmate Assaults on Other Inmates." Report prepared for the California Department of Corrections Research Division, September 1965.
42. Lockwood, "Reducing Prison Sexual Violence," p. 257.
43. These survival lessons were described by several ex-offenders.
44. Information provided in personal correspondence with Peter L. Nacci; also Peter L. Nacci, William G. Saylor, and Thomas R. Kane, *The Federal Study of Sexual Aggression in Federal Prisons* (Washington: The Federal Prison System, 1979).
45. Colvin, *From Accommodation to Riot,* p. 303.
46. Discussion in *Prison Violence,* p. 53.

47. Dan A. Fuller and Thomas Orsagh, "Violence and Victimization within a State Prison System" (Paper presented at the Annual Meeting of the American Society of Criminology, Tucson, Arizona, November 1976).
48. Lee H. Bowker, "Victimizers and Victims in American Correctional Institutions." In Robert Johnson and Hans Toch, eds., *The Pains of Imprisonment* (Beverly Hills, Calif.: Sage, 1982), p. 64.
49. Interviewed in August 1985.
50. Conrad, "The Survival of the Fearful," p. 127.
51. Interviewed in April 1983.
52. Interviewed in February 1986.
53. Bureau of Justice Statistics, *Correctional Populations in the United States, 1988* (Washington: U.S. Department of Justice, 1991), p. 77.
54. Hawkins and Alpert, *American Prison Systems,* p. 294.
55. Bruce L. Danto, "The Suicidal Inmate." In *Jail House Blues* (Orchard Lake, Mich.: Epic Publications, 1973), pp. 20–21.
56. Dave, "Voice from Solitary." In *Jail House Blues,* p. 169.
57. Hawkins and Alpert, *American Prison Systems,* pp. 295–296.
58. Useem and Kimball, *States of Siege,* pp. 218–219.
59. Ibid., p. 220.
60. Ronald I. Weiner, "Management Strategies to Reduce Stress in Prison: Humanizing Correctional Environments." In *The Pains of Imprisonment,* p. 303.
61. Lucien X. Lombardo, "Alleviating Inmate Stress: Contributions from Correctional Officers." In *The Pains of Imprisonment,* p. 287.
62. Lee H. Bowker, "Victimizers and Victims in American Correctional Institutions." In *The Pains of Imprisonment,* p. 72.
63. Ibid.
64. William G. Nagel, *The New Red Barn: A Critical Look at the Modern American Prison* (New York: Walker, 1973), p. 110.
65. Interviewed in August 1990.

Chapter
16

The Rights of Wrongdoers

CHAPTER OUTLINE

THE INDIVIDUAL RIGHTS OF PRISONERS
- *First Amendment Rights*
- *Fourth Amendment Rights*
- *Fourteenth Amendment Rights*
- *Eighth Amendment Rights*

THE CONDITIONS OF CONFINEMENT
IMPACT OF THE PRISONERS' RIGHTS MOVEMENT
CONCLUSIONS

Any discussion of **rights** must begin with a definition of the term. We open with our own formulation: A right is a claim by an individual or group of individuals that another individual, a corporation, or the state has a duty to fulfill.

That definition is only the beginning of a complexity into which we will not venture far. Philosophers and jurists have written volumes about the source of rights. Legal positivists claim that the only rights anyone possesses are those that are conferred by law. Many other philosophers disagree, asserting that we all possess "natural" rights—from which legal rights are derived—as necessary to our survival in the human community. In this view a law that is inconsistent with natural rights cannot and should not survive. Examples would be the race laws of National Socialist Germany before World War II, or the apartheid laws of South Africa.

Whether natural rights exist independent of statutory law, as for example the right to life, is an important issue for moral philosophers and for ordinary people, too, but not for an understanding of criminal justice. The rights of persons accused or convicted in criminal offenses are defined in the statutes and interpreted in case law. The laws of every civilized state recognize the natural right to life—subject, of course, to the requirements of military service and the right of the state to impose the death penalty for certain law violators.

Jeremy Bentham, about whom we had much to say in Chapter 3, thought that the very idea of natural rights was nonsense and that the idea of inalienable rights—the right to life, liberty, and the pursuit of happiness claimed in our Declaration of Independence—was "nonsense on stilts." He has had much company. Positivist legal philosophers hold that the only rights are those conferred by the laws of the state.

We will not be further detained by this debate. Except for the right to life—that is, the right to survive one's prison sentence—convicted felons do not have rights other than those conferred on them by law. In America, those rights are derived by the courts from the Constitution of the United States, from the state constitutions, and from the laws that Congress and the state legislatures enact.

Until well into the twentieth century, those laws assumed that the convicted felon was "civilly dead." There were centuries of precedent. The philosopher Immanuel Kant (1724–1804), a liberal moralist in most respects, thought that an incarcerated robber or thief enjoyed no rights: "He has nothing and can also acquire nothing, but he still wants to live, and this is not possible unless others provide him with nourishment." Kant added that "the state will not support him gratis," and, therefore, he must do whatever kind of work the state may wish to use him for, "and so he becomes a slave, either for a certain period of time or indefinitely, as the case may be."[1]

American courts had little to say on this subject in the nineteenth century. The 1871 Virginia case of *Ruffin* v. *Commonwealth* expressed the prevailing view that a prisoner was a slave with no rights other than those his keeper might choose to allow him:

> During his term of service in the penitentiary, he is in a state of penal servitude to the State. He has, as a consequence of his crime, not only forfeited his liberty, but all his personal rights except those which the law in its humanity accords to him. He is for the time being the slave of the State. He is civiliter mortuus; and his estate, if he has any, is administered like that of a dead man.[2]

Under this rule, convicted felons while on probation, or in prison, or on parole could not sign contracts, could not marry, could not vote or hold public office, or enjoy any of the ordinary privileges of a citizen, except as a single such right might be restored by the court or other legal authority, as, for example, to sign a specific contract. As slaves, the only rights they had were those that the state might allow them, either through statutes or under the regulations of the prison system. The courts would not intervene to protect prisoners from major abuses, or to prevent the authorities from interfering with prisoners' access to the courts. This general principle was referred to as the **"hands off" doctrine.** So far as the courts or anyone else bothered to justify the "doctrine," the thinking was that a prison was at best very difficult to manage, and the warden's tasks would be made only more difficult by the intrusion of the courts.

Change in legal doctrine is slow. In 1944, the Sixth Circuit Court of Appeals made the first significant modification of the principle of *Ruffin*. In *Coffin* v. *Reichard*, a case in which physical abuse of a prisoner was the issue, the court announced a new doctrine: "[C]onviction and incarceration deprive [the prisoner] only of such liberties as the law has ordained he shall suffer for his transgression." "A prisoner," according to the Court, "retains the rights of an ordinary citizen except those expressly or by necessary implications taken from him by the law."[3]

No longer is the prisoner a slave. Under this ruling he or she is, theoretically, a citizen whose liberty has been restricted. The change is obvious enough, but the practical difference it makes is less than clear. Commenting on this substantial step forward in legal doctrine, Sheldon Krantz, a leading commentator on the law of corrections, questions how much this shift in prisoners' rights actually changes things, because "incarceration brings about necessary withdrawal or limitation of many privileges and rights, a retraction justified by the considerations underlying our penal system."[4]

Thus, the issue has become what privileges and rights can necessarily be withdrawn or limited and under what circumstances. In other words, when must constitutional rights give way to the various governmental problems and needs relating to custody, security, rehabilitation, discipline, punishment, or resource limitations?[5]

We shall see that at the present time both federal and state courts have grappled with the conflict between the due process rights guaranteed by the Constitution and institutional necessities. The caution with which the courts approached the establishment of prisoners' rights is clearly expressed in *Siegel* v. *Ragen.*[6] In this case the Seventh Circuit Court of Appeals considered a class-action suit brought on behalf of prisoners in the Illinois state penitentiaries alleging gross abuses by the director of the Illinois system and his subordinates. The case was brought under the Civil Rights Act, which states that,

> Every person who, under color of any statute, ordinance, regulation, custom, or usage, or any State or Territory, subjects, or causes to be subjected, the citizen of the United States or other person within the jurisdiction thereof to the deprivation of any rights, privileges, or immunities secured by the Constitution and laws, shall be liable to the party injured in an action at law, suit in equity, or other proper proceeding for redress.[7]

The court found that prisoners are entitled to invoke the provisions of this statute. However, it was willing to proceed under that Act only insofar as it applied to serious physical abuse by the prison authorities. The reasoning was that the Fourteenth Amendment required due process of law for the actions of any state. The Eighth Amendment, forbidding cruel and unusual punishment, did not apply to actions on the part of any state. (As we shall see, later decisions by the Supreme Court ruled that the Eighth Amendment does indeed apply to all states.) The court then went on to say: "This court is prepared to protect State prisoners from death or serious bodily harm in the hands of prison authorities, but it is not prepared to establish itself as a 'co-administrator' of State prisons along with duly appointed State officials."

The general principles established by the federal courts up to the present time are summarized in the American Bar Association's Standards Relating to the Legal Status of Prisoners:

> *Standard 23–1.1*
> Prisoners retain the rights of free citizens except:
> [a] As specifically provided to the contrary in these standards; or
> [b] When restrictions are necessary to assure their orderly confinement; or
> [c] When restrictions are necessary to provide reasonable protection for the rights and physical safety of all members of the prison system and the general public.[8]

There these matters stand. The standards are grounded on four principles laid down by the Supreme Court: (1) Prisoners do not forfeit all their constitutional protections; (2) prisoners do not "possess the full range of freedoms of an unincarcerated individual"[9]; (3) institutional security, order, and discipline may take precedence over the individual exercise of constitutional rights; and (4) prison administrators "should be accorded wide-ranging deference in the adoption and execution of policies and practices that in their judgement are needed to preserve internal order and discipline and to maintain institutional security."[10]

The standards and principles that have emerged after decades of litigation in the courts have left plenty of room for further lawsuits on the rights of prisoners. These lawsuits fall under two general headings: the conditions of confinement, applicable to all prisoners or to a class of prisoners, and the rights individual prisoners may possess under the general provisions of the Constitution and its Amendments. In Box 16-1, Vincent Nathan, a former law professor who has served as special master of several state correctional systems, documents the need for judicial intervention.

Prisoners have used several means of legal challenges to remedy prison conditions and practices. These include (1) state habeas corpus, which is a hearing on the conditions of confinement initiated by an inmate; (2) federal habeas corpus, which is available only after exhausting state remedies; (3) state tort suits, which are civil actions against a correctional employee for "negligence, gross, or wanton negligence, or intentional wrong"; (4) Section 1983 of the federal Civil Rights Act of 1871, which may involve both injunctive relief and monetary damages; and (5) the Civil Rights of Institutionalized Persons Act of 1980, which entitles the federal government to bring civil suits for equitable relief, but not damages, against employees of any state correctional institution.[11]

THE INDIVIDUAL RIGHTS OF PRISONERS

As we have seen, the civilly dead prisoner was a slave without rights, except for those rights accorded by the "law in its kindness" or specifically restored to him or her by duly constituted authority. The "kindness of the law" has been extended not only to the conditions of confinement but also to a number of individual rights enjoyed by all citizens. In this section, we shall review the status of the more important prisoners' claims that the state must honor.

Prisoners have sued to establish rights in four areas: (1) the right to physical security and the minimum conditions necessary to sustain life, (2) the right to receive their constitutionally guaranteed safeguards, (3) the right to challenge the legality of their convictions through the courts, and (4) the right to receive the benefit of reasonable standards and procedural protections.

First Amendment Rights

> Congress shall make no law respecting an establishment of religion, or prohibiting the free exercise thereof; or abridging the freedom of speech or of the press, or the right of the people peaceably to assemble, and to petition the government for a redress of grievance.
>
> The First Amendment to the Constitution

Box 16-1 Interview with Vincent Nathan

Question: What are the problems in turning prisons around? What's wrong, and what ought to be done about it?

Answer: That is a question that could be answered on several levels. I think that most of those who work in the field today would say that the crowding of institutions is simply creating unmanageable problems and indeed threatening a fair amount of the progress that has been made over the past 15 to 20 years. There is no question about the difficulties involved in maintaining constitutional conditions which are magnified enormously by populations of 170 to 180 percent of the designed capacity.

More than that, however, is something that I think you hear a little less about. The correctional systems that are building at such a rate to maintain a reasonable degree of control over crowding are becoming such enormous bureaucracies that the demands on the day-to-day administration are becoming simply overwhelming. This occurs in systems like those in Florida, Texas, and California. All of the problems which have led to judicial intervention in prison management are being magnified by these megasystems that are challenging even the best administrators.

Furthermore, although this is probably not a fair statement, corrections reflects the apathy of management skill and creativity. That isn't to say there aren't a number of very firm managers. However, corrections managers are not paid Wall Street salaries, and you have to accept that you are often going to be dealing with average management skill.

Going to a different kind of response, the real problem in correctional reform is analogous to other kinds of institutional inertia. It is very difficult to change the status quo in an institutional setting. It is important that people understand that corrections is nothing more than an example of that. For example, I've taught for 18 years at two universities. If someone had come in and turned one of them on its head, changing virtually every policy and procedure relating to recruitment of staff, treatment of students, academic standards, and all things that make up a university, that person would encounter two major problems. First, is overt hostility from a number of interests. Second, and even worse, is the enormous amount of body weight that would stand in the way of change. We've seen it when we've tried to change our mental-health institutions.

Prisons are an even better example of inertia. When you go into the state that has been found to be unconstitutional, you find a blend of problems. You find some people who are outright resistant to change, who believe the old ways are the best ways and should be followed. These people actively oppose what the court has suggested to do. People must be persuaded all the way down to the front line of the institutions, that things have to be done differently. You're really talking about the implementations of written policies, practices, procedures, and norms that aren't familiar to people. They've got to understand what they are aiming for and they have got to buy into it. Ultimately you've got to expect the people who are responsible for the prisons to buy into the change. There is an element of spoon feeding in the process, but ultimately the people have got to learn to and want to maintain a system that is in keeping with a new status quo.

Source: Interviewed in August 1990.

The rights of prisoners under the First Amendment have been widely ruled upon, especially as they pertain to religion, speech, the press, and assembly.

Religion A number of cases in the 1960s held that the Black Muslim faith was an established religion and that therefore its disciples were entitled to the same rights as those of more conventional faiths. Federal courts ordered prison officials to allow Black Muslim ministers to conduct services and to permit Muslim prisoners the use of the Koran and other religious materials. The court has also been willing to apply the freedom of religion clause to other religious groups, such as the Buddhists.[12] However, the Fifth Circuit Court of Appeals, in ruling upon the "Church of the New Song" movement, decided that it was inappropriate to give First Amendment protection to "so called religions which tend to mock established institutions and are obviously shams and absurdities and whose members are patently void of religious sincerity."[13] Harry Theriault originated the Church of New Song (so named because it fit the acronym CONS) while serving time in a federal prison. This "religion" also included dietary requirements of porterhouse steaks and sherry for its members.

In general, the federal courts have consistently held that the religious rights granted to one religious group must be accorded to all such groups within a correctional institution. Religious freedoms have also been looked upon as preferred freedoms, and, therefore, the burden of proof is on institutional administrators when they wish to limit religious practices.[14] However, the courts have not usually required prison administrators to give religious groups special diets, nor are they willing to allow the free exercise of religion to jeopardize the security and safety of the institution.

Censorship of Personal Correspondence No area of correctional law has attracted as much litigation as prisoner correspondence. This may be because personal correspondence involves a person in the free community who is also protected by the First Amendment.

Administrators feel that there is strong reason to place stringent limitations on inmate correspondence. Censorship of incoming mail is necessary, prison officials reason, to detect contraband—including instruments of escape, pornographic materials, and narcotics or drugs. According to administrators, censorship of outgoing correspondence is necessary to protect the public from insulting, obscene, and threatening letters; to avoid defaming the prison; and to detect escape or riot plans.

In an important 1974 case, *Procunier* v. *Martinez*, the U.S. Supreme Court ruled on a California case concerning the constitutionality of censoring prisoners' incoming and outgoing personal mail.[15] But the Supreme Court surprisingly avoided the question of the extent to which inmates retain First Amendment rights, basing its decision on the First Amendment rights of the citizens with whom an inmate corresponds: "Censorship of prison mail works a consequential restriction on the First and Fourteenth Amendment rights of those who are not prisoners." The Court then defined the criteria for determining when the regulation of inmate correspondence constitutes a violation of First Amendment liberties:

> Prison officials may not censor inmate correspondence simply to eliminate unflattering or unwelcome opinions or factually inaccurate statements. Rather, they must show that a regulation authorizing mail censorship furthers one or more of the substantial govern-

> mental interests of security, order, and rehabilitation. Second, the limitation of First Amendment freedoms must be no greater than is necessary or essential to the protection of the particular governmental interest involved.[16]

This was a disappointing decision for those who wanted greater procedural restrictions on inmate correspondence, for the Supreme Court placed a relatively light burden of proof on prison censors. An even more discouraging decision was *Pell* v. *Procunier*, in which California inmates challenged prison rules that prohibited them from conducting interviews with the press. The Supreme Court ruled that prisoners do not have an automatic right to meet the press because the legitimate state interest in security, order, and rehabilitation has to be considered.[17] The *Pell* decision solidified the balance test established in *Martinez*, but it also gave corrections officials the major role in determining when the interests of security, order, and rehabilitation were involved.

Freedom of Speech Most court decisions have rejected the argument that prisoners should be able to express their views freely. The courts have been dubious about giving prisoners the right to speak where such speech may create an insurrection. In one case, the court upheld the punishment of a prisoner who circulated materials calling for a collective protest against the administration.[18]

Censorship of Publications and Manuscripts The extent to which prison officials can censor the publications prisoners receive and can restrict the freedom of prisoners to publish articles and books while in prison has been the subject of much litigation. Although the courts have cautiously advised a broadening of these rights, they have reserved discretionary responsibility to prison administrators. The need for lawsuits is seen in Box 16-2.

The U.S. Supreme Court. (© Johnson, Gamma Liaison.)

Box 16-2 The Right to Write

The United States Penitentiary at Lompoc is a maximum security prison, holding many men who are serving long terms. Among them was one Dannie Martin, a middle-aged bank robber, serving a 33-year term, who discovered a talent for narrative in a creative writing class. In 1986 he submitted an article about AIDS in prison to the *San Francisco Chronicle*. It was accepted and published with a byline. There followed a series of 30 articles that the *Chronicle* published and for which it paid fees to Martin's lawyer.

The articles were mostly about prison life: "what's it like in there?—how do the days go by?" The contributions to the *Chronicle*'s "Sunday Punch" section were widely read and continued until June 1988, when an article appeared to which the editor gave the title "The Gulag Mentality: Some wardens know how to make hell burn a little hotter." Newspaper practice is to leave the headlines to the writer; this title was the *Chronicle*'s idea.

This article caught the attention of the Lompoc staff. Martin had recounted the actions of a new warden, Richard Rison, who had begun his tenure by closing down the exercise yard in the mornings, thereby denying night workers the opportunity to exercise. This decision provoked a good deal of annoyance, and one prisoner remarked to Martin that the warden was trying to provoke a riot. Then, without warning the guards descended on the TV room and confiscated the old-timers' chairs:

> For as long as most of us can remember, we've had our own chairs in the TV rooms as well as in our cells. There's little enough in here for a man to call his own, and over the years these chairs have been modified and customized to an amazing degree—legs bent to suit the occupant, arm rests glued on, pads knitted for comfort. The final personal touch is always the printing of the name on the back . . . Shorty Blue, Big Red, Monster Mack and Mukilteo Slim. Names that run from somber identification of the occupants to bizarre sobriquets. But whatever the name on the back or the condition of the chairs, those chairs were ours.

These prized possessions were replaced by metal folding chairs, which certainly were not as comfortable nor capable of personalization. A memorandum was posted to the effect that defacing a chair in any way would be an offense subject to disciplinary action. No advance notice of the change, no explanations.

All that was written up with the concluding sentences,

> We wait and watch for the next move. Many of us older convicts feel that if the lids stay on until our next "landlord" arrives it will be a small miracle.

When Warden Rison read the article, he ordered Martin into segregation. His writing materials were taken from him, and it was explained to him that he was segregated for his protection because other prisoners might attack him. Why? Because they might think that the article would bring about a lockdown. Martin was instructed not to write any more articles.

On 16 July 1979, seven years before Martin began writing his articles, the Bureau of Prisons issued Rule 540.62b, which reads as follows:

> An inmate currently confined in an institution may not be employed or act as a reporter or publish under a by-line.

However, it was explicit that an inmate might write a letter to the editor of a newspaper, signing his name, or he might even write a book. The problem for the Bureau was that prisoners could not be allowed to conduct a business—as for example selling stocks and bonds, or a medical practice—and writing articles for pay constituted a business by the Bureau's definition. Further, that Martin was writing with a byline would make him a "big wheel" around the prison. That would give him prestige among his fellow prisoners, and that would be undesirable.

There had been no explanation as to how it came about that Martin's articles were published for two years without interference from the warden or other officials of the Bureau of Prisons.

Martin was released from segregation after two days. Later he wrote an article about his experience. It sounded like a session in "the Hole" rather than the relatively benign conditions of protective segregation. A week later he was transferred to the Federal Correctional Institution at Phoenix, Arizona.

He sued the Bureau of Prisons on the ground that his First Amendment right to free speech had been infringed. The suit was joined by the *San Francisco Chronicle.* A federal court issued a preliminary injunction, ruling that "there's been substantial showing that the acts against Mr. Martin were indeed retaliation." Martin's articles continued to be published until June 1990, when the court, after an extended hearing, dissolved the preliminary injunction and entered judgment for the Bureau of Prisons.

In his opinion, Judge Charles Legge ruled that "the penological interest of prison security was invoked by Martin writing and *The Chronicle* publishing the 'Gulag' article. The fact that there was a genuine concern for security was established by a preponderance of evidence."

Martin continues to write for the *Chronicle,* but anonymously. As of mid-1990, the case is on appeal.

Right to Assemble Prisoners are also restricted in their right to assemble. The emergence of prisoner unions in ten states in the early 1970s brought about litigation on this subject.[19] *Goodwin* v. *Oswald* brought a decision upholding the right to prisoners to form unions.[20] The Court stated that nowhere in state or federal law is the formation of prison unions outlawed or prohibited. However, in *Jones* v. *North Carolina Prisoner Union,* the Supreme Court overruled a favorable decision and held that a state regulation prohibiting prisoners from soliciting others to join a union and barring union meetings did not violate the First Amendment.[21]

The *Jones* decision represented another setback for prisoners' rights. On the one hand, the Supreme Court extended the position in *Pell,* in which prison officials were looked to as the party that would decide when institutional security and order were threatened. On the other hand, the *Jones* decision extended the power of prison officials to limit First Amendment rights if they believed the potential existed for disruption of order.[22]

Fourth Amendment Rights

> The right of the people to be secure in their persons, houses, papers, and effects, against unreasonable searches and seizures, shall not be violated, and no warrants shall issue but upon probable cause, supported by oath or affirmation, and particularly describing the place to be searched, and the persons or things to be seized.
>
> The Fourth Amendment to the Constitution

The courts have consistently held that the protection the Fourth Amendment affords against unreasonable searches and seizures does not extend to prison. For example, the *Moore* v. *People* decision concluded that searches conducted by prison officials "are not unreasonable as long as they are not for the purpose of harassing or humiliating the inmate in a cruel or unusual manner."[23]

The privacy issue has arisen concerning cell searches. The *Bell* v. *Wolfish* (1979) decision made it clear that the Supreme Court felt that unannounced cell searches, or "shakedowns," were necessary for security and order.[24] The 1984 *Hudson* v. *Palmer* decision shattered even further any hope that Fourth Amendment rights could apply to cell searches. The Court ruled that "the Fourth Amendment has no applicability to a prison cell."[25]

Strip searches have also been allowed by the courts, which generally have permitted prison officials to conduct pat searches and body cavity examinations in the name of institutional order and security.[26]

Fourteenth Amendment Rights

> All persons born or naturalized in the United States, and subject to the jurisdiction thereof, are citizens of the United States and of the State wherein they reside. No State shall make or enforce any law which shall abridge the privileges or immunities of citizens of the United States; nor shall any State deprive any person of life, liberty, or property, without due process of law; nor deny to any person within its jurisdiction the equal protection of the laws.
>
> The Fourteenth Amendment to the Constitution (Section 1)

Due Process Rights in Disciplinary Hearings The 1974 *Wolff* v. *McDonnell* decision has been heralded as a landmark because of its impact on correctional administration and prisoners' rights.[27] McDonnell, a prisoner, had filed a class-action suit against the state of Nebraska, claiming that its disciplinary procedures—especially those pertaining to the loss of good time (time subtracted from an inmate's sentence for good behavior)—were unconstitutional. He petitioned the court to restore the good time he had lost and to assess damages against correctional officials. The Supreme Court ruled that the state of Nebraska had properly enacted laws pertaining to the granting and revoking of good time. Nonetheless, the procedure used to revoke good time was found to be a violation of the due process rights granted in the Fourteenth Amendment. In reviewing these disciplinary procedures, the Court held that the procedure was not part of a criminal prosecution and that a prisoner does not have full rights of a defendant on trial. Nevertheless, the Court specified certain minimum requirements for disciplinary proceedings:

1. The inmate must receive advanced written notice of the alleged rules infraction;
2. The prisoner must be allowed sufficient time to prepare a defense against the charges;
3. The prisoner must be allowed to present documentary evidence on his or her behalf and therefore may call witnesses, as long as the security of the institution is not jeopardized;
4. The prisoner is permitted to seek counsel from another inmate or a staff member when the circumstances of the disciplinary infraction are complex or the prisoner is illiterate;
5. The prisoner is to be provided with a written statement of the findings of the committee, the evidence relied upon, and the rationale for the action. A written record of the proceedings must also be maintained.[28]

The Court left it to the discretion of correctional administrators whether or not a witness could be confronted and cross-examined by the prisoner. The Court further ruled that a prisoner's incoming mail from his or her attorney can be opened in the presence of the inmate to check for contraband, but it cannot be read by institutional staff.[29]

This case was significant because it tended to standardize certain rights and freedoms within correctional facilities. Although inmates received some procedural safeguards to protect them against the notorious abuses of disciplinary meetings, they did not receive all the due process rights of a criminal trial. Nor did the Court question the right of correctional officials to revoke the good time of inmates.

Legal Assistance to Inmates Until well past the time when the hands-off doctrine was cast into obsolescence, correctional authorities were obsessed by their belief that prisoners should not trouble the courts with their complaints. Particularly discouraged were "writ-writers" who prepared complaints for themselves and other prisoners. In many states, the preparation of writs was a disciplinary offense, calling for a session of punitive isolation.[30] Access to the courts was vigorously prevented. In 1941 the Supreme Court took notice of the obstacles to writs of habeas corpus in *Ex Parte Hull.*[31]

In this case, Hull had filed for a writ of habeas corpus only to have the papers he filed returned to him by the officials without submission to the court. When ordered by the Supreme Court to show cause why Hull's petition for a writ should not be granted, the warden replied that he had issued a regulation that all such petitions had to be referred to the legal investigator for the parole board. The regulation went on to say that "documents submitted to [the investigator], if in his opinion are properly drawn, will be directed to the court designated or will be referred back to the inmate." Justice Frank Murphy's opinion pronounced this regulation invalid; "the state and its officers may not abridge or impair petitioner's right to . . . apply for writ of habeas corpus."

The principle is clear and has consistently been upheld. However, as one commentator has pointed out, "The problem . . .—as with any 'right' possessed by prisoners—is not with the principle but with the implementation."[32] After all, it is one thing to allow a prisoner to petition the court, but quite another to equip him or her to submit such a petition in a form that will allow the court to proceed. The solution should be to create a modest law library in which prisoners could assemble the information and authorities they might need to make an intelligible case.

The Supreme Court took notice of this problem in *Bounds* v. *Smith.*[33] In a 5-to-4 decision, the Court ruled that the state of North Carolina had a duty to provide adequate law libraries in each of its correctional facilities. Although the state's proposal for a standard library is rather generous in its content, including the standard legal references, the Supreme Court Reports, and the North Carolina reports as well as the federal and state statutes, other states have gone far beyond North Carolina in the provision of law libraries, some of them so extensive as to be the envy of practicing attorneys.

In the 1969 *Johnson* v. *Avery* decision, the Supreme Court ruled that institutional officials may not prohibit inmates from assisting one another with legal work unless the institution provides reasonable legal assistance to inmates.[34] This decision denied the constitutionality of a Tennessee prison regulation that provided: "No inmate will advise, assist or otherwise contract to aid another, either with or without a fee, to prepare Writs or other legal matters. . . . Inmates are forbidden to set themselves up as practitioners for the purpose of promoting a business of writing Writs." The Court denied the jailhouse lawyer the right to receive legal assistance from a fellow inmate. The Court also stated that the activities of the jailhouse lawyer could be restricted as to time and place and that jailhouse lawyers could be prohibited from receiving fees for their services.[35]

Some prisons have avoided the use of jailhouse lawyers by establishing their own legal assistance programs. Although they vary from prison to prison, these programs generally use lawyers or law students to represent inmates in postconviction proceedings. The Correctional Institution at Graterford in Pennsylvania developed a paraprofessional law clinic to provide legal assistance to inmates. Experienced writers, with some help from legal organizations, study transcripts, undertake legal research, and write legal briefs.[36]

Eighth Amendment Rights

> Excessive bail shall not be required, nor excessive fines imposed, nor cruel and unusual punishments inflicted.
>
> The Eighth Amendment to the Constitution

The three principal tests of conformance with the Eighth Amendment deal with these questions: Does the punishment shock the conscience of a civilized society? Is the punishment unnecessarily cruel? Does the punishment go beyond legitimate penal aims? Considerable case law has been concerned with violation of the Eighth Amendment in terms of solitary confinement, physical abuse, deadly force, the death penalty, access to medical treatment and services, and segregation.

Solitary Confinement Generally, the courts have supported the segregation of troublesome prisoners. They have ruled that segregation is necessary to protect the inmate, other prisoners, and the staff, and to prevent escapes. Although several courts have ordered the release of inmates from harsh solitary confinement, most courts have been unwilling to interfere unless the conditions are clearly "shocking," "barbarous," "disgusting," or "debasing." One decision held that subhuman conditions that constituted cruel and unusual punishment existed when prisoners were denuded, exposed to the winter cold, and deprived of such basic elements of hygiene as soap and toilet paper.[37]

Physical Abuse Not until the mid-1960s did a court decide that the disciplinary measure of whipping a prisoner with a leather strap constituted **cruel and unusual punishment.**[38] The courts have generally been unwilling to impose liability on prison officials for failing to protect prisoners from physical abuse and sexual assault by other inmates. The courts have usually agreed that prisoners deserve some protection against predatory inmates, but they have rarely provided for it in individual cases.

Deadly Force The courts have ruled that the use of deadly force is permissible to prevent the commission of a felony or the infliction of severe bodily harm.[39] These rulings permit the use of deadly force to prevent an inmate from escaping if a state has classified escape as a felony. Nevertheless, the courts have ruled that to avoid civil and/or criminal liability, deadly force must be used only as a last resort—after all other reasonable means have failed.

Medical Treatment and Services A convict serving time in an American correctional facility will be understandably concerned about his or her access to medical care. One of the principal grievances underlying the destructive and lethal 1971 riot at the Attica State Penitentiary in New York was the inmates' belief that medical care was inadequate and indifferently administered by physicians whose competence was in question. The Official Report of the New York State Special Commission on Attica noted that medical staff conducted the daily sick call from behind a wire mesh screen. That was hardly a setting to inspire a confident doctor–patient relationship. The report went on to conclude that "the purpose of medical care at Attica was limited to providing relief from pain or acute anguish, correcting pathological processes that may have developed before or while the inmates were serving their terms, and preventing the transmittal of sickness among the prison population."[40] Chronic disabilities, whether correctable or not, were not assessed or treated. "Part of this . . . was due to lack of personnel and time, but much reflected a lack of commitment to attempt restorative efforts." Prompted by this report, the state took, without court intervention, remedial action in the improvement of medical care.

Elsewhere, intervention by the courts has been called for, but their remedies have been cautious. In Texas, the Department of Corrections was brought into court on a complaint by a prisoner that the medical staff had failed to treat him competently for an injury received when a bale of cotton fell on him while he was unloading a truck.[41] Many treatments had been administered, but the patient's condition had only gotten worse. Both the medical and the custodial staffs decided that the plaintiff was malingering. The case found its way to the Supreme Court, which ruled that the state could not be held liable for medical malpractice, a misfortune that could befall anyone, prisoner or free individual. The Supreme Court would not decide against the state because its physicians' treatment was ineffective, but it made it clear that "deliberate indifference to serious medical needs" constituted "unnecessary and wanton infliction of pain" within the meaning of cruel and unusual punishment.

This is the state of doctrine on medical care at the present time. It must be recognized that medical practice in a correctional setting will never attract the stars of modern medicine, although many have made themselves available as consultants. For the most part, physicians employed in prisons are young and inexperienced, or old and weary, or foreign born and trained, often with poor command of the English language. Under the circumstances, professional and public vigilance is warranted to ensure that the care of sick felons, many of whom arrive in prison with badly abused bodies, does not descend to a level of callous indifference.

Right to Treatment and to Refuse Treatment For ordinary citizens the right not to submit to medical treatment is settled. It is a right that is open to some question in prisons and mental hospitals where inmates live under conditions of coercion. In a ground-breaking tract, the American Friends Service Committee vigorously argued that prisoners were unfairly retained in confinement when they refused rehabilitative services.[42] The system on which the committee reported was the California Department of Corrections, but the practices in California were certainly in effect in many other states. Prisoners who failed to engage in group counseling or group therapy would be denied parole because they had refused rehabilitative benefits. If a therapist's report to the parole board indicated an unsatisfactory response to therapy, that was sufficient reason to postpone parole. Refusal to attend school or to engage in vocational training would be good cause to defer release.

Brought out into the open by *The Struggle for Justice*, the value of coerced rehabilitation became a target for prison reformers. Obviously, without the indeterminate sentence no prisoner could be coerced into rehabilitation. It was only a matter of time before legislation to abolish both the indeterminate sentence and the parole boards was adopted in California and in many other states.

The right to be treated comes up in individual cases. The courts have been firm in their insistence on informed consent. In *Knecht* v. *Gillman*, the Eighth Circuit Court of Appeals ruled that although prisoners might give their consent to a procedure, they should be allowed to later withdraw that consent.[43] In this case, the plaintiff was an inmate of the Iowa Security Medical Facility, where he was subjected to an especially nasty kind of aversive therapy. When any inmate in his living group might see another in violation of institutional rules—for example, not getting up from bed, swearing, lying, or even talking when silence was in order—he was injected with apomorphine by a nurse. The effect of this drug was to induce vomiting that would last 15 minutes to an hour. The plaintiff claimed that this was cruel and unusual punishment within the meaning of the Eighth Amendment. Expert evidence was submitted showing that the effectiveness of this treatment in extinguishing undesirable conduct was unproven. The rules prescribed for the Iowa Security Medical Facility for the administration of psychopharmacological treatments carefully circumscribe their use:

1. A written consent must be obtained from the inmate specifying the nature of the treatment, a written description of the purpose, risks and effects of treatment, and advising the inmate of his right to terminate treatment at any time. This consent must include a certification by a physician that the patient has read and understands all of the terms of the consent and that . . .

[he] is mentally competent to understand fully all of the provisions thereof. . . .

2. The consent may be revoked at anytime after it is given and if an inmate orally expresses an intention to revoke it to any member of the staff, a revocation form shall be provided for his signature at once.
3. Each apomorphine injection shall be individually authorized by a doctor and be administered by a doctor or a nurse. It shall be authorized in each instance only upon information based on the personal observation of a member of the professional staff. . . .

Information is the essence of informed consent. Where a prisoner is incompetent, the courts have been solicitous, going so far as to rule that a mentally disturbed prisoner cannot be considered capable of giving informed consent to an experimental psychosurgical procedure.[44]

Racial Segregation Until well into the 1960s, racial segregation in prisons, both northern and southern, was general. Cellblocks were either black or white, and so were mess-hall lines. The good jobs went to deserving white prisoners; black prisoners had to be specially deserving to be assigned as runners, clerks, or other desirable positions. That began to change in a few states in the 1950s, but wardens and custodial staffs are naturally conservative. Apprehensions of riots and other violence if the traditional segregation was disturbed inspired stubborn resistance to change. The right to equal opportunity for minority prisoners had to be adjudicated. The first court to hear arguments on this matter was presided over by a judge whose primary concern was the ascendency of the Constitution.

The Alabama case of *Washington* v. *Lee* was the first judicial intervention on the desegregation of prisons.[45] Judge Frank Johnson, who later was to preside over *Pugh* v. *Locke*, held that "this court can conceive of no consideration of prison security or discipline which will sustain the constitutionality of state statutes that on their face require complete and permanent segregation of the races in all Alabama penal facilities." The state was therefore ordered to provide for the total desegregation of all the prisons within one year. This was done. There were no riots and no other unpleasant consequences. Throughout the nation, desegregation of the prisons has been achieved with remarkably little difficulty, even though the anxieties of many wardens had seemed to be self-fulfilling prophecies.

THE CONDITIONS OF CONFINEMENT

The "hands off" doctrine allowed correctional systems to abide by the standards, or lack of them, that state governments would tolerate. In some states progressive commissioners managed prisons with reasonably humane policies. The best that could be said for most states was that without professional administration, without trained personnel, and without public interest in correctional policy and practice, conditions in the prisons did not descend to the levels of brutality and outright corruption that were to be found in the worst of them.

A breakthrough came in 1970 with the class-action case of *Holt* v. *Sarver*.[46] The plaintiffs in this case were prisoners in the Cummins Farm Unit and the Tucker Intermediate Reformatory of the Arkansas Penitentiary System. Their complaint was that their "forced, uncompensated labor" violated the Thirteenth Amendment to the Constitution, and that the conditions and practices within the system were such that their confinement was cruel and unusual punishment within the meaning of the Eighth Amendment. They also contended that racial segregation in these facilities violated the Fourteenth Amendment.

Responding to these complaints, the state of Arkansas admitted that it was not operating a good or modern prison system. In announcing its decision, the court noted that "with Commendable candor [the state had conceded] that many of the conditions existing at the Penitentiary were bad." The state's attorneys pointed out that officials were doing the best they could with limited funds and personnel.

As described in the court's opinion, the conditions in both units of the Arkansas system were in serious need of remedy, to put the best face possible on a dreadful state of penal anarchy. The Cummins Unit, with about 1000 prisoners, held all black convicts and the "more hardened white convicts." There were 35 free employees, of whom 8 were guards. The operation of the unit devolved upon trusty prisoners. They were armed, were responsible for the maintenance of security, had access to all prison records, and operated the gates to the unit. They were free to leave the prison for shopping tours and other purposes, and free to bring back liquor and other items usually considered contraband for sale, at handsome profits, to nontrusty prisoners. The court remarked that "in a very real sense trusty guards have the power of life and death over other inmates. . . . It is within the power of a trusty guard to murder another inmate with impunity, and the danger that such will be done is always clear and present."

There were eight barracks at Cummins, each one an overcrowded dormitory housing more than 100 men, far more than the number considered a maximum for medium custody prisoners under the observation of experienced correctional officers.[47] At night, supervision was left to convict "floorwalkers" who were expected to report disturbances to the two free guards on night duty. This control was ineffective in preventing violence. Sleeping prisoners were often stabbed by their enemies. Floorwalkers could not and did not interfere with homosexual acts whether by force or by consent. Drugs and alcohol were freely available and in use by anyone who could afford the exorbitant prices exacted by the trusties.

Prisoners assigned to solitary confinement for disciplinary offenses were jammed into windowless 8′ × 10′ cells with no facilities other than a water tap and a toilet that could be flushed only from outside the cell. Four men would usually occupy a cell, but as many as 11 were sometimes so accommodated. At night filthy mattresses were spread on the floor. The diet consisted of "gruel," a mixture of meat, potatoes, margarine, and syrup mashed together and baked. The caloric value was less than 1000 a day.[48]

Finally, the court turned to the complete absence of any programs that might be considered rehabilitative. Unwilling to hold that the absence of such programs in an otherwise unexceptional prison would be unconstitutional, the court found that such absence "may have constitutional significance where in the absence of such a program conditions and practices exist which actually militate against reform and rehabilitation."

Granted that the conditions in the Cummins Unit were shocking, what justification did the federal court have to intervene in the administration of a state prison system? The hands-off doctrine assumed that no matter what abuses might occur, they were none of the business of a federal court. In *Holt* v. *Sarver*, the court made obvious recourse to the Eighth Amendment, which prohibits cruel and unusual punishment. The term is vague, and the court attempted a fuller definition:

> The term cannot be defined with specificity. It is flexible and tends to broaden as society tends to pay more regard to human decency and dignity and becomes, or likes to think it becomes, more humane. Generally speaking, a punishment that amounts to torture, or that is grossly excessive in proportion to the offense for which it is imposed, or that is inherently unfair, or that is unnecessarily degrading, or that is shocking or disgusting to people of reasonable sensitivity is a "cruel and unusual" punishment. And a punishment that is not inherently cruel and unusual may become so by reason of the manner in which it is inflicted.

This attempt to sharpen the meaning of the Eighth Amendment necessarily relies on subjective terms—as does "cruel and unusual"—but it was accepted. The final determination was that "confinement in a given institution may amount to cruel and unusual punishment prohibited by the Constitution where the confinement is characterized by conditions so bad as to be shocking to the conscience of reasonably civilized people. . . ."

Based on this definition, the court specified that measures had to be taken to remedy the trusty system and the barracks conditions, to provide for inmate safety, and to clean up the filthy isolation cells. It ordered the state to submit a report and plan to show what would be done to accomplish these ends and when it would be done. The first report was unsatisfactory; so was the second. By 1973, at a third hearing, the court decided that enough improvement had been accomplished to allow the termination of supervision. That decision was appealed by the plaintiffs, and the court of appeals reversed the district court. A fourth hearing revealed that conditions were much worse. At the time of the trial, the barracks had been crowded with 1000 inmates, but they now confined 1500 without any expansion of the facilities. Continued supervision by the court eventually resulted in the elimination of the conditions on which the original complaint had been based. New and modern facilities were built, and personnel were recruited and trained to manage the system in a manner consistent with modern correctional standards.

It will be noted that in *Holt* compliance was achieved on the basis of periodic reports to the court. The court declined to take steps to provide for independent monitoring of the state's correction of the conditions specified in the decree. The Arkansas governor and legislature were motivated to make sweeping changes in the prison conditions that the state had deemed disgraceful. A "compliance coordinator" was appointed by the state by agreement between parties to the suit. This was a potential precedent, successful in achieving its ends, that no state with a similar problem has followed.

Holt v. *Sarver* made an enormous difference in correctional law. Following that decision, similar litigation was introduced in many other states. Under the direction of Alvin Bronstein, a seasoned civil rights lawyer, the National Prison Project was organized to identify serious prison abuses. The Project has engaged in numerous lawsuits designed to obtain relief from substandard conditions of confinement. Sometimes negotiations with the state authorities were sufficient to correct the procedures or deal with the personnel at fault. In many situations it was necessary to initiate a lawsuit seeking injunctive relief.

When a court enjoins a defendant from performing certain actions, it takes control of some or all of that defendant's freedom of action. This is the case in bankruptcy proceedings, where the assets of an insolvent debtor are impounded so that they can be distributed fairly among his or her creditors. The court will usually appoint a master or a receiver to control the process and make a final report to the court when all the creditors have been satisfied in accordance with the court's decree. This process has been adapted for the administration of injunctive relief in most of the proceedings to enjoin state departments of corrections from failing to take measures to meet the court's requirements for change.

Correctional systems in states facing requirements to make substantial changes to achieve court ordered reform are subjected to "**special masters**" whose task is to develop a plan for the implementation of the changes ordered by the court. When it is approved, the special master then is charged with supervision of the plan's implementation, reporting progress periodically to the court. A receiver occupies a more powerful position, becoming the manager of the department or agency that is under court order and deciding how the changes are to be made.

The common law and legislative history of the use of masters in equity proceedings has been authoritatively reviewed by Vincent Nathan, himself a special master for several courts issuing prison reform decrees.[49] Nathan emphasized that the appointment of a master calls for a decree that limits his or her powers to specific matters that require remedies. The master need not be a lawyer, and in fact some masters have been appointed whose experience and training have been entirely in correctional administration. Those who are appointed must expect that their role will be resented, and that their intrusion into institutional management, their contacts with prisoners, and their inspection of the files will probably be met with sullen compliance at best. In Box 16-3, Vincent Nathan discusses his work as a master.

The case of *Pugh* v. *Locke*, brought in the federal district court for Alabama before Judge Frank Johnson as a class-action suit complaining of the conditions of confinement in Alabama prisons, demonstrates the difficulties confronting the courts when the state resists the decrees requiring remedies.[50] It also illustrates the procedures that a determined judge can adopt to enforce his orders. In *Pugh*, the court found that the state of Alabama had not met constitutional standards for the administration of its prison. To provide for relief from these deficiencies, the court enjoined the governor and other officers of the state government from failing to implement its statement of the "Minimum Constitutional Standards of the Alabama Prison System" contained in its decrees. These standards comprised 11 categories of requirements, ranging from the overcrowding of facilities to the installation of a modern system of prisoner classification. Each category was laid out in a great deal of specificity for which officials would be held accountable. Deadlines for compliance were established in the decree, to all of which the state consented. In passing, Judge Johnson rejected the plaintiffs' claim to entitlement to rehabilitative services. He recognized, however, that where the conditions of confinement denied prisoners the opportunity to rehabilitate themselves a claim was made that entitled them to relief. He added that a penal system must not be "operated in such a manner that it impeded an inmate's ability . . . simply to avoid physical, mental or social deterioration."

The decree met with furious response from Governor George C. Wallace, who

Box 16-3 Interview with Vincent Nathan

Question: Would you briefly talk about your work as a special master and about some of your impressions of what you've done in various states?

Answer: Well, let me start with a descriptive response to give you some sense about what I have done. I've worked as a court monitor or a special master for a number of courts, beginning in about 1974: Cases that have involved single institutions, and relatively narrow issues, either prisons or jails, all the way to systemwide cases that have involved the entire correctional system of the state. I guess the two largest cases in which I've been involved have been the *Ruiz* case, which related to the entire Texas Department of Corrections, and the case I'm working on involving the Puerto Rico correctional system, which deals with some 30 institutions scattered about the island.

My job as a special master, or court monitor—these are interchangeable terms—is first to act more or less as the eyes and the ears of the court. The judge is largely tied to the bench, and my job is to monitor, to observe, to find facts, and to issue reports that will keep the parties, and particularly the court, abreast of what progress is being made toward implementation of a remedial order. I have come into these cases after the court entered a remedial order or at least after a finding of unconstitutionality has been made. So, in general, there is a set of obligations that have been imposed on the system by the time I'm appointed.

The other major role that a court monitor or special master plays is the role of mediator, or helping the parties craft effective remedial plans. This typically involves taking the somewhat broader obligations that are set forth in the court's remedial degree and converting those into operationally, practical, and effective means of accomplishing those objectives. There are other roles, but those are the two primary ones: the monitoring and reporting on one hand and the mediation on the other.

Source: Interviewed in July 1990.

proclaimed that "thugs and judges" had taken charge of Alabama's prisons. Although there was strong public support for prison reform, Wallace denied the court's right to intervene and heaped scorn on those who sympathized with prisoners' living in conditions virtually identical to those that had prevailed in Arkansas before *Holt* v. *Sarver*. His opposition softened over the years, but many influential politicians found it expedient to advocate measures that amounted to maximum resistance.

The court recognized that compliance would be difficult to achieve. A Human Rights Committee comprising 39 prominent citizens was appointed to monitor the implementation of the order. It was Judge Johnson's expectation that the committee would mobilize public support for what he knew would be a difficult and expensive process. Dr. George Beto, formerly the director of the Texas Department of Corrections, was engaged as a consultant to the committee, responsible for inspection of the prisons and recommendations as to steps that should be taken to meet the requirements of the consent decree.

From the first, the Human Rights Committee found itself playing a role that neither its members nor the court had intended. Instead of assisting the Department to bring about change by undertaking a public relations role in support of prison reform, the committee was forced into an adversarial position. Under the influence of the Board of Corrections, which felt itself aggrieved by the outcome of this litigation, Commissioner Judson C. Locke Jr. was at best a reluctant reformer, consistently at odds with the committee. Dr. Beto's function was divided between negotiating with the legislature, the Board, and the commissioner and informing the committee about the department's lack of progress in achieving compliance.

The state appealed *Pugh* v. *Locke*. On review by the Circuit Court of Appeals, the orders were upheld with the exception that the committee was dissolved because supervision should have been placed in the hands of a monitor rather than a large and unwieldy committee. The court held that such a committee, largely composed of persons with no experience in the administration of prisons, placed an unfair burden on the state's administrators as defendants. The task of reviewing the adequacy of plans to implement the decree would be better assigned to a special master who would be qualified to make findings of fact.[51]

In 1979 Fob James replaced Wallace as governor. Convinced that it was his constitutional duty to comply with the orders of the court, James decided that it was unlikely that he could achieve compliance without direct control of the department, hitherto reserved to the independent Board of Corrections. He petitioned for appointment as the receiver for the Department of Corrections, setting forth eight objectives that he would pursue if appointed. His petition was granted by Judge Johnson, after a scathing review of the state's inaction during the three years since his order in *Pugh*.[52] The governor then abolished the independent Board of Corrections, which was the appointing authority for the Commissioner of Corrections and to which the commissioner was solely accountable. He dismissed the refractory Commissioner Locke, which he could not have done with the Board in control of the department. A new and professional administrator from outside Alabama was appointed as commissioner.

The entire department was reorganized. Funding of new prisons relieved some of the overcrowding, but never all. Although each prison was kept at its rated capacity, as mandated by the order, hundreds of felons waited in the county jails pending the availability of accommodation in the penitentiaries. Most of the other requirements laid down in the court's orders of 1976 were met by the end of Governor James's term of office.

In 1982 Governor Wallace was reelected. Returned to office, he was determined to remove the problems of corrections from the political agenda. There remained the one problem of the large number of state prisoners retained in the county jails under conditions that were in most places worse than those that had prevailed in the prisons before the adjudication of *Pugh*. Judge Robert Varner, who had replaced Judge Johnson upon the latter's appointment to the Circuit Court of Appeals, refused to relinquish jurisdiction for so long as this state of affairs continued. In place of the receivership from which Governor James had withdrawn, he appointed a special Implementation Committee to supervise the final stages of compliance.

This committee consisted of four persons: two lawyers representing both sides of the litigation and two penological experts recommended by the two attorneys. From 1983 to the end of 1988, the committee observed, prodded, made recommendations, and reported periodically to the court. It was finally dissolved in late 1988 when measures taken by the Parole Board to reduce the population of the prisons brought about a balance between the number of prisoners and the number of beds. *Pugh* v. *Locke* was dismissed "with prejudice"—that is, the case could not be reactivated in court.

The history of Alabama prison reform illustrates in dreary relief the dilemma that confronts a court when it enjoins a state to take specific actions to reform its prison system. Usually the intervention of the court is resented by the government and by the penal establishment. Funds required to make the mandated changes are scarce and may not be appropriated by the legislature, which will usually rank prison reform low on its scale of priorities. Advocates of a hard line with criminal offenders are indifferent to the humanitarian concerns of reformers and will see no reason to spend large sums of tax dollars on "undeserving" convicts. Conditions are only grudgingly improved or not at all. The court is then faced with a limited number of unattractive options for the enforcement of its orders. It may undertake a wholesale release of prisoners to reduce the population. It may hold officials in contempt and impose fines for their noncompliance—an action that was taken by the court at one point in the *Pugh* litigation. Some courts have entertained the possibility of committing one or more officials to jail for criminal contempt, but so far this option has not been put into effect. The court may even elect to close a prison down entirely, another option that no court has yet adopted.

Rather few commissioners of corrections have accepted court orders in the spirit that one commissioner in another state adopted. Said he: "I welcomed the order because it compelled me to do things that I had always wanted to do but which I'd never been able to sell to the legislature. It gave me leverage to get things done."[53] For the most part, commissioners and their staffs have seen themselves as embattled protectors of the status quo, resentful of what they saw as attacks on their competence and personal integrity. In the Texas case of *Ruiz* v. *Estelle*, the entire Department of Corrections was placed under court orders to make sweeping changes.[54] A battle between the department and the special master appointed by the court was protracted by the officials' angry denial of any deficiencies that might call for remedial action. On appeal the orders of the court have been consistently upheld.[55]

The administrative problems brought about by the presence of a special master or other officer of the court monitoring compliance are by no means trivial. Unless the orders are amicably accepted, the special master or other monitoring officers inevitably become alternative administrators, with powers that compromise the authority of the commissioner or warden. (See Box 16-4).

IMPACT OF THE PRISONERS' RIGHTS MOVEMENT

In 1991 there were 37 state correctional departments that were operating under court order. The improvements that have resulted are undeniable and would not have been achieved without judicial intervention. Whether the courts will continue to intervene where class-action cases are brought to remedy conditions of confinement remains to be seen.

Some believe that since the mid-1970s, a **"restrained-hands" doctrine** seems to guide judicial intervention in corrections. During the spring of 1976, this more restrained approach was expressed in four U.S. Supreme Court decisions: *Baxter* v. *Palmigiano*,[56] *Enomoto* v. *Clutchette*,[57] *Meachum* v. *Haymes*,[58] and then most clearly in *Meachum* v. *Fano*:

Box 16-4 Interview with Vincent Nathan

Question: Would you talk about the advantage that special masters offer to the process of reform?

Answer: These lawsuits, as you know, are highly charged affairs. They are very political, and the litigation phase tends to end on a very sour note. The lawyers and the parties have both been fighting each other for years. You begin, obviously, with groups who are not particularly fond of each other. Inmates don't love their keepers, and in many cases keepers don't love their inmates. A neutral agent coming in at that point can often build a bridge between the parties and make possible constructive negotiations and resolutions. I don't want to overstate that because the monitor of the suit is closely identified with the judge and generally has some pretty strong feelings there. At the end of the litigation stage, when the judge finds liability because of the opposition toward the remedial decree, there is a fair amount of resentment between the defendants and the judge.

Keep in mind that I come into these cases only when the defendants lose. I'm not involved in those in which they prevail. Nonetheless, the first thing I attempt to do is to establish my own identity. I want the parties to know that I have not been a part of the disagreements that preceded my appointment. They ought to try to separate me in their minds from other actions by the lawyer and the judge. I make it very clear that my job is not to be responsive to the prisoners. They are not my clients. The person to whom I am accountable is the judge, and his concern is for me to pursue obedience to his orders.

A master or monitor can also help by establishing some priorities, thus making it possible to craft an overall compliance plan which assumes first things have to be done first, that certain conditions have to be met before you can move forward in other areas. This is particularly true in a correctional agency faced with a myriad of mandated reforms. Puerto Rico is a good example. The prisons in Puerto Rico, when I was appointed in 1986, were literally so crowded that inmates were assigned to individual window ledges and individual steps on stairways. I guess that the square foot per inmate was about the size of the inmate's body. It seemed pretty hopeless to think about implementing some of the reforms that were required by court order: Medical care, mental-health care, adequate security, inmate activity, and programming could hardly be worked on under the conditions of crowding. I could not understand how the role was to be accomplished as long as the population density remained at that level. We spent roughly the first year or two of that case tackling the population problem. My responsibility is to suggest a process that will not leave the corrections administration feeling that it has to fight the war on all fronts simultaneously. Rather, I need to help things flow in some type of orderly fashion.

A monitor or master also provides a source of factual information that is probably superior to that obtained from any other source. It is very difficult, and in fact unfair, to expect plaintiffs' counsel, if they serve as monitors, to adopt a neutral position. They are by definition not neutrals. They are representing a group of prisoners who are not likely to ever acknowledge that things are okay in a prison. An unconstitutional prison is a very bad thing, but so is a constitutional prison from the point of view of the people who are living there. It's not to be expected that the plaintiffs will look at a situation and treat it with complete objectivity any more than it's fair to expect the defendants to critique their own efforts in an entirely objective fashion. It is human nature to be partial toward your own side and therefore virtually impossible to render an entirely objective opinion. The finding of facts is a significant advantage that should be expected to flow through a mastering or monitoring position.

Source: Interviewed in July 1990.

> Given a valid condition, the criminal defendant has been constitutionally deprived of his liberty to the extent that the state may confine him and subject him to the rules of its prison system so long as the conditions of confinement do not otherwise violate the Constitution.[59]

The retreat of judicial intervention appeared to continue as the U.S. Supreme Court ruled 8 to 1 in 1981 that "double celling" in the maximum security Ohio prison at Lucasville does not violate "constitutional standards of decency" under the Eighth Amendment. In overturning the lower court's decision, the Court ruled that "cruel and unusual punishment" does not necessarily forbid more than one person in a cell but is more involved with the "totality of circumstances" in prison. The tone of this decision was particularly discouraging to those who had looked to the courts for relief in concerns related to the Eighth Amendment.[60]

Other cases that reflected more of a "restrained-hands" doctrine phase were the *Bell* v. *Wolfish* and *Hudson* v. *Palmer* decisions. As previously suggested, the 1979 *Bell* v. *Wolfish* decision ruled that unannounced cell searches were necessary for security and order,[61] and the Court ruled in the 1984 *Hudson* v. *Palmer* decision that the protection against unreasonable searches afforded by the Fourth Amendment "has no applicability to a prison cell."[62]

The good news is that the bad conditions of the worst prisons in the 1970s have been corrected. Prisoners have made the greatest gains in the right to send and receive letters, but they also have made strides regarding their right to communicate with lawyers and the courts. Furthermore, the courts have permitted the right of religious freedom as long as it does not jeopardize institutional security. Courts have additionally been willing to rule on the totality of conditions in a prison setting when prisoners appeared to be undergoing severe dehumanization and deterioration in their mental and physical well-being. It can be argued that many of these improvement are probably irreversible and that the states can be trusted to maintain constitutionally acceptable prisons.

The bad news is that in an era when prison costs are mounting along with the numbers of offenders convicted and committed, overcrowding and its associated evils are reappearing and will be difficult to correct. Prisoners may retain basic human rights, but they are not entitled to the same degree of constitutional protections that they enjoyed before conviction. The conditions of confinement can never satisfy prisoners. Convicts and their plight attract little public sympathy, and, therefore, action to correct intolerable conditions is usually delayed until a crisis occurs. At that point, remedies must be drastic and therefore costly, far more so than would be the case if foresighted planning, development, and fiscal support were available to implement changes as soon as they were needed.

All litigation initiated on behalf of a prisoner or prisoners to obtain the exercise of rights calls for the intervention of a judge, usually a federal judge. If relief must be granted, the court assumes a burden that may remain on the docket for months, and sometimes, as we have seen in *Holt* v. *Sarver* and *Pugh* v. *Locke,* for many years. A judge may appoint a special master or even a receiver to manage the implementation of the decree. No matter how competent the master and the supporting monitors, the judge must be continuously informed about the progress of compliance.

The difficulty of the judicial tasks that we have explored in this chapter has been nicely summed up by Judge Irving Kaufman in his article, "Prison: The Judge's Dilemma":

> [T]he relationship between the courts and the jailors, and the relationship between jailors and prisoners, are ones in which there is an attempt to coerce virtue as defined by the coercer. Even if we were of one mind about the function of prisons, it is hard to imagine a more inefficient system of administration than the coercion of unwilling people over whom one has authority.[63]

Coercion is an essential and irremovable element of corrections. Enlightened administrators should need a minimum of judicial coercion, if any at all. Resistance to a court order may occasionally be seen as politically advantageous, and sometimes an appeal is reasonable and necessary. But when all avenues toward modification of a decree have been exhausted, the task of the responsible administrator is to collaborate with the court on achieving speedy compliance.

As we have pointed out, the recalcitrance of state officials will often be expressed in active and determined fashion. Where timely compliance is not achieved, the judge faces difficult options, most of which will have a punitive effect without achieving the end sought by the decree. A judge can do many things, but compelling a legislature to make necessary modifications of the penal laws or to increase appropriations for the prisons exceed judicial powers. Fining officials for contempt, closing a prison as unconstitutionally unfit for habitation, or dismissing an incompetent administrator are available but disruptive options. They may capture gubernatorial or legislative attention, but at the cost of reluctant and hostile compliance. Willing collaboration should be the objective in these matters.

CONCLUSIONS

Despite the difficulties confronting the courts in rectifying conditions of confinement that have been unacceptable in a decent society and in expanding the rights of prisoners, much has been accomplished in the past three decades. Courageous judges and public officials have changed the nature and quality of corrections beyond the reasonable expectations of reformers earlier in the century. Much remains to be done, but the lesson of this chapter emphasizes the solid constitutional support for decency in corrections. That support has been provided by judges. Nevertheless, their decrees will be futile unless capable administrators are on hand to carry out their implementation.

With a full understanding of the importance of as full a panoply of constitutional rights as is practicable in the correctional context, future litigation of the kind we have described may call for much less judicial attention. The slave of the state could rarely struggle back to full humanity. The prisoner whose rights have been abridged only to the extent of the limits imposed by confinement may return to full citizenship. And that should be the ultimate objective of the administration of justice.

KEY TERMS

cruel and unusual punishment

"hands off" doctrine

"restrained-hands" doctrine

rights

"special masters"

DISCUSSION TOPICS

16.1 What did it mean that the convicted felon was "civilly dead"?

16.2 What are the general principles on prisoners' rights established by the federal courts up to the present time?

16.3 Summarize the most important cases establishing the "hands off" doctrine.

16.4 Why is the right to due process of the laws so difficult to disentangle from institutional priorities?

16.5 Why has the implementation of prisoners' rights been so difficult for the courts?

ANNOTATED REFERENCES

Jacobs, James B. "The Prisoners' Rights Movement and Its Impacts, 1960–1980." In Norval Morris and Michael Tonry, *Crime and Justice: An Annual Review*. Chicago: University of Chicago Press, 1980. *Jacobs, whose writings on the prisoners' rights movement have always been highly respected, provides in this article a perspective on the accomplishments of this movement.*

Krantz, Sheldon. *The Law of Corrections and Prisoners' Rights*, 3rd ed. St. Paul, Minn.: West, 1986. *A good summary of recent correctional laws.*

Martin, Steve J., and Sheldon Ekland-Olson. *Texas Prisons: The Walls Came Tumbling Down*. Austin: Texas Monthly Press, 1987. *The authors of this fascinating study of the* Ruiz *decision in Texas take the readers through the lengthy legal process of this court case.*

Palmer, John W. *Constitutional Rights of Prisoners*, 2nd ed. Cincinnati: Anderson, 1977. *An excellent review of correctional law.*

NOTES

1. Immanual Kant, *The Metaphysical Elements of Justice*, trans. John Ladd (Indianapolis: Bobbs-Merrill, 1965), p. 102.
2. *Ruffin* v. *Commonwealth*, 62 Va., 790, at 796.

3. *Coffin* v. *Reichard,* 143 Fed. 2nd 443, at 445. (1944). Note that this decision was applicable only within the Sixth Circuit. The hands-off doctrine survived elsewhere long past 1944.
4. Sheldon Krantz, *The Law of Correction and Prisoners' Rights,* 3rd ed. (St. Paul, Minn.: West, 1986), p. 292. For a comprehensive account of case law on corrections, this volume is invaluable and unrivaled.
5. *Price* v. *Johnston,* 334 U.S. 266. (1948).
6. *Siegel* v. *Ragen,* 88F. Supp. 996. (1948).
7. U.S.C.A., S43.
8. American Bar Association, 1980. Quoted in full in Krantz, *The Law of Corrections and Prisoners' Rights,* pp. 308–310.
9. *Bell* v. *Wolfish,* 441 U.S. 520.
10. Ibid.
11. Richard Hawkins and Geoffrey P. Alpert, *American Prison Systems: Punishment and Justice* (Englewood Cliffs, N.J.: Prentice-Hall, 1989), p. 368.
12. *Cruz* v. *Beto,* 405 U.S. 319 (1972).
13. *Theriault* v. *Silber,* 391 F. Supp. 578 (W. D. Texas, 1975).
14. John W. Palmer, *Constitutional Rights of Prisoners,* 2nd ed. (Cincinnati: Anderson, 1977), p. 85.
15. *Procunier* v. *Martinez,* 416 U.S. 396 (1974).
16. Ibid.
17. *Pell* v. *Procunier* 417 U.S. 817 (1974).
18. *Roberts* v. *Papersack,* 256 F. Supp. 415 (D.Md. 1966).
19. Ronald Huff, "Unionization Behind the Walls" *Criminology* 12, August 1974: 184–185.
20. 462 F2d, 1245–46 (ed Cir. 1972).
21. *Jones* v. *North Carolina Prisoners' Union,* 433 U.S. (1977).
22. C. Ronald Huff, "The Discovery of Prisoners' Rights: A Sociological Analysis." In G. P. Alpert, ed., *Legal Rights of Prisoners* (Beverly Hills, Calif.: Sage, 1980), pp. 60–61.
23. *Moore* v. *People,* 171 Colorado 338, 467 P.2d (1970).
24. *Bell* v. *Wolfish* 441 U.S. 520 (1979).
25. *Hudson* v. *Palmer* 82 L Ed 2d 393 (1984).
26. See *Wolfish.*
27. *Wolff* v. *McDonnell,* 418 U.S. 538 (1974).
28. Prisoner Law Reporter, "Prison Discipline Must Include Notice," hearing, Commission on Correctional Facilities and Services of the American Bar Association, vol. 3 (July 1975), pp. 51–53.
29. Clemens Bartollas and Stuart J. Miller, *Correctional Administration: Theory and Practice* (New York: McGraw-Hill, 1978), pp. 14–15.
30. For examples of the measures taken to stamp out such activities, see Steve J. Martin and Sheldon Ekland-Olson, *Texas Prisons: The Walls Came Tumbling Down* (Austin: Texas Monthly Press, 1987), pp. 32–45, 50–58.
31. *Ex Parte Hull,* 312 U.S. 546. Rehearing denied, 312 U.S. 716., (1941).
32. Fred Cohen, *The Legal Challenge to Correction* (Washington: Joint Commission on Correctional Manpower and Training, 1969), p. 69.
33. *Bounds* v. *Smith,* 430 U.S. 817 (1977).
34. *Johnson* v. *Avery,* 393 U.S. 483 (1969).
35. Palmer, *Constitutional Rights of Prisoners,* p. 92.
36. David Rudovsky, Alvin J. Bronstein, and Edward I. Koren, *The Rights of Prisoners: The Basic ACLU Guide to a Prisoner's Rights* (New York: Avon, 1977), pp. 51–52.
37. 387 F.2d 519 (2d Cir. 1967).
38. *Jackson* v. *Bishop,* 404 F2d 571 (8th Cir. 1968).
39. *Beard* v. *Stephens,* 372 F2d 685 (5th Cir. 1967).

40. *Attica: The Official Report of the New York State Special Commission on Attica* (New York: Praeger, 1972), pp. 60–62.
41. *Estelle* v. *Gamble,* 429 U.S. 97 (1976).
42. The American Friends Service Committee, *The Struggle for Justice* (New York: Hill & Wang, 1971).
43. *Knecht* v. *Gillman,* 488 F.2d 1136 (8th Cir. 1973).
44. See *Kaimowitz* v. *Department of Mental Health for the State of Michigan* (Civ. Action No. 73–19434–AW) (Cir. Ct. for Wayne County, Mich. 1973). Reproduced in Krantz, *The Law of Corrections and Prisoners' Rights,* note 4, pp. 445–457. In this case, the court ruled that the three elements of informed consent are "competency, knowledge, and voluntariness."
45. *Washington* v. *Lee,* 263 F. Supp. 27 (M.D. Alabama 1966). Affirmed, *Lee* v. *Washington,* 390 U.S. 333 (1968).
46. *Holt* v. *Sarver,* 309 F. Supp. 362 (E.D. Ark. 1970), affirmed, 442 F. 2d 304 (8th Circuit, 1971).
47. At that time prisoners were not classified in Arkansas. One of the benefits of modern classification systems is the identification of violence-prone prisoners, who should not be housed in dormitory conditions, even when the dormitory is competently supervised.
48. *Hutto* v. *Finney.* 437 U.S. 678 (1978). The Supreme Court's ruling in this case explicitly affirmed the applicability of the Eighth Amendment's prohibition of cruel and unusual punishment to state correctional systems and the jurisdiction of the federal courts in enforcing that constitutional provision.
49. "The Use of Masters in Institutional Reform Litigation." *The University of Toledo Law Review,* Vol. 10, No. 2, Winter 1979: 419–464.
50. *Pugh* v. *Locke,* 406 F. Supp. 318 (M.D. Ala. 1976). This case was introduced as *James* v. *Wallace,* 382 F. Supp. 1177 (M.D. Ala. 1974). James was consolidated with Pugh for reasons explained in John P. Conrad, "From Barbarism Toward Decency: Alabama's Long Road to Prison Reform," *Journal of Research in Crime and Delinquency,* Vol. 26, No. 4, November 1989: 307–328. A longer account of this litigation, which lasted for 15 years, will be found in Larry W. Yackle, *Reform and Regret: The Story of Federal Judicial Involvement in the Alabama Prison System* (New York: Oxford University Press, 1989).
51. *Newman* v. *Alabama,* 559 F. Supp. 283, 1977.
52. For Johnson's order and Governor James's petition, see *Newman* v. *Alabama,* 466 F. Supp. 628 (M.D. Ala. 1979).
53. Comment made to one of the authors.
54. This case has been adjudicated in several courts. The most relevant citations are 503 F. Supp. 1265 (1980) and 460 U.S. 1042 (1983).
55. The long and elaborate history of this legislation has been thoroughly narrated in Steve J. Martin and Sheldon Ekland-Olson, *Texas Prisons,* pp. 92–234. These authors are severely critical of the Texas authorities and supportive of the court's intervention. For a differing view, much more sympathetic to the Department of Corrections, see John J. DiIulio, *Governing Prisons* (New York: Free Press, 1987), pp. 53–60, 104–117, 195–234.
56. *Baxter* v. *Palmigiano,* 96 S. Ct. 1551 (1976).
57. *Enomoto* v. *Clutchette,* 96 S. Ct. 1551 (1976).
58. *Meachum* v. *Haymes,* 96 S. Ct. 2543 (1976).
59. *Meachum* v. *Fano,* 427 U.S. 216 (1976).
60. *Rhodes* v. *Chapmen,* 29 *Criminal Law Review* 3061 (1981).
61. *Bell* v. *Wolfish,* 441 U.S. 520 (1979).
62. *Hudson* v. *Palmer,* 82 L Ed 2d 393 (1984).
63. Irving Kaufman, "Prison: The Judge's Dilemma." *Fordham Law Review* 41, 1973: 495.

PART SIX

The Female Prisoner and the Male Prisoner

Chapter 17

The Female Prisoner

CHAPTER OUTLINE

The woman in prison has sometimes been called the "forgotten offender." There are several reasons for the lack of interest in the female prisoner. First, few women are incarcerated: Of approximately 771,000 state and federal prisoners, only about 40,000 are women.[1] Second, women's prisons are smaller than most prisons for males, and there are fewer of them.[2] Third, reform groups have ignored the plight of the confined woman because female prisoners have called so little attention to themselves. Treated as disgraced stepchildren, incarcerated women have traditionally responded with appropriate contrition. Up until recently, they have been content to do laundry, mend institutional clothes, and scrub prison floors. Finally, female offenders have not been involved in organized crime, in crimes that involved high property losses, or in crimes that have endangered large groups.[3] Yet female prisoners have increasingly been involved in drug-related offenses.

The literature on women's prisons began almost 30 years after research began to be conducted on men's prisons. Apart from E. Lekkerkerker's examination of women's prisons in 1931,[4] Rose Giallombardo and D. Ward and G. Kassebaum pioneered the present-day works describing women's prisons.[5] Alice Propper later published a study exploring homosexuality within women's correctional institutions,[6] and E. Heffernan and A. Mitchell followed in the 1970s with examinations of the subcultures within women's prisons.[7] More recently, E. Freedman and N. Rafter have published books on the history of women's prisons.[8] Finally, J. M. Pollock-Byrne's 1990 study of women's prisons shows that aspects of the prisoner subculture other than homosexuality must be explored to understand the female prisoner's adaptation to confinement.[9]

As Chapter 18 depicts in greater detail, researchers such as Donald Clemmer have found that prisoners become part of an antisocial culture within the walls that encourages them to become more committed to criminality, or to become "prisonized." Clemmer adds that the more imprisonment deepens inmates' criminality, the more difficult it is for them to reenter free society.[10] The studies on female prisoners are beginning to examine the negative effects of imprisonment upon them. Phyllis Jo Baunach has suggested that "the lack of autonomy, powerlessness, and the loss of identity create for incarcerated women an exaggerated dependency upon those in authority," and reactions to this environment may result in despondency, frustrations, heightened tensions, anxiety, and apathy.[11] Conversations with female prisoners also leave little doubt about the negative effect of institutionalization upon them. For example, in Box 17-1, a woman in Iowa expresses her reaction to imprisonment.

PROFILE OF FEMALE PRISONERS

Various studies have shown that the incarcerated woman has much in common with her male counterpart. She tends to be poor, young, and a member of a racial or

Box 17-1 The Deprivation of Imprisonment

[Being in] the penitentiary is the most humiliating thing I have ever experienced. For instance, if a matron wants you to strip down to bare skin, you must do so or face disciplinary action for disobeying a direct order. If you are sick and would like to rest for the day, you must get the nurse's permission. If they can't come up with a conclusion about your ailment immediately and you decide to rest anyway, then you will be locked up in your room the entire day. They say that I'm a mature adult, yet they tell me my every move and treat me as a child.

I don't feel that the penitentiary is the right place to learn and grow. I know more about crime now than when I came here. Being here makes you more of a criminal. That is why people may spend years incarcerated and are not reformed.

Source: Interviewed in October 1985.

ethnic minority. More than 50 percent have received welfare at some point during their lives, and two-thirds are under 30 years old. They have been arrested at a young age, and nearly one-third have spent time in juvenile institutions. Early in the century, women were frequently incarcerated for public-order crimes, such as prostitution, but the majority of female prisoners today are likely to be minor property offenders, often drug related. They rarely develop techniques in the way a professional criminal would, and their criminal histories reflect this lack of commitment to a criminal way of life. Or to express this in another way, more female than male prisoners subscribe to society's value system.[12] The percentage of women incarcerated for violent crimes (10 to 11 percent) has not changed much for the past 20 years.[13] White female prisoners are better educated, followed by black and Hispanic women. Fewer than one-fifth were living with a spouse, but nearly three-quarters had children. At the time of their arrest, more than 50 percent of the women had children living at home.[14]

Institutionalized females as a group have had somewhat different experiences with the criminal justice system from those of male offenders. However, the "chivalry" that was typically displayed toward women in the past appears to be decreasing. This is particularly true at the arrest stage: "If it's equality these women want, we'll see that they get it," one officer said.[15] But if "chivalry" is less evident at the arrest stage, Rita Simon found from her study that it is still very much alive in the other stages of the correctional process. Not only are women less likely to remain in custody during the pretrial period than are men, but they are also less likely to be convicted when they come to trial. If they are convicted, they are likely to receive lighter sentences than would a man convicted of the same crime. Only in parole decisions does gender appear to make little difference.[16]

Simon found that the greatest discrepancy between the treatment of males and females occurs in sentencing. For several reasons, judges seem less inclined to send a woman to prison. First, women usually pose a lesser threat to the community because their crimes are less violent than those of male offenders. Second, the violent crimes that women do commit are usually tied to their sex roles—their victims are generally family members or lovers. Few of these violent crimes are premeditated, and most are the outcome of frustration and abuse, motives that judges and society find easier to excuse. Third, the secondary role played by many women in the crimes in which they are involved makes it easier for judges to be lenient. Fourth, a judge cannot avoid considering who will take care of a woman's family if she is sent to prison. A superintendent of the California Institution for Women explained:

> If a man goes to prison, the wife stays home and he usually has the family to return to and the household there when he gets out. But women generally don't have the family support from the outside. Very few men are going to sit around and take care of the children and be there when she gets back. So, to send a woman to prison means you are virtually going to disrupt the family.[17]

D. Steffensmeir found that preferential treatment for women consistently showed up at each stage of the criminal justice process, although it was of a small magnitude. This widely respected research concludes that chivalry contributes to this differential treatment but that more important factors appear to be the perceived unlikelihood of future criminality on the part of female offenders and the absence of perceived danger. These factors, as well as the offender's naïveté, create a situation in which women are more likely to be given probation than imprisonment. Steffensmeir speculates that determinate sentencing and increased bureaucratization and professionalism will reduce this differential in sentencing.[18]

W. Wilbanks reported that women in the California court system experienced some leniency, but not consistently. Interestingly, they received even harsher treatment than males in some crime categories. Consistent with other findings, Wilbanks's study revealed that the greatest differential between the treatment of male and female offenders occurs at sentencing. A possible explanation for this differential, according to this researcher, is whether or not the woman offender has other social controls.[19] C. Kruttschnitt, in expanding on Wilbanks's finding about the relationship between social controls and sentencing, determined that a woman is more likely to receive probation if she is dependent on a male as daughter or wife. This finding suggests that consciously or unconsciously the court system permits informal social control systems to operate if they are present. Thus, if a female offender is under the control of another authority figure, she is likely to be left to that person's informal control, but if she is free from informal social controls, then this increases the chances that the state will step in to take control.[20]

Furthermore, in a study comparing institutionalized males and females, P. C. Kratcoski and K. Scheuerman found that male prisoners were more likely than female prisoners to have had contacts with the criminal justice system from early adolescence, to view the police as unnecessarily hard and harassing, to not have been released on bail, and to have entered guilty pleas without going to trial. But females received swifter dispositions of their cases than the males. When asked about their impressions of the criminal justice system and their feelings about justice in America, the vast majority of both males and females felt that their sentences were too harsh and expressed dissatisfaction with their lawyers' services. Most also felt that the poor cannot get a fair trial in the United States.[21]

Drugs and Alcohol Use

The 1990 drug use forecasting research of the National Institute of Justice reveals that among female arrestees the range of drug use was 44 percent in San Antonio to 88 percent in Cleveland. Cocaine was the most prevalent drug used among female arrestees in all but two cities of the sample. Multiple drug use was highest among females in Portland (36 percent) and San Diego (34 percent).[22] See Figure 17.1 for further breakdown of drug use by female arrestees.

A number of studies report that female prisoners frequently have histories of drug and alcohol use. The Department of Justice found that female inmates were five times more likely to abuse alcohol than women in the general population.[23] S. L. Weitzel and W. R. Blount found that 63 percent of the population of females in Florida's prisons reported sufficient use of drugs and alcohol to be classified as abusers (only 11 percent reported use of no substances).[24] In a 1986 survey of inmates in state correctional facilities, the Department of Justice found that women were more likely to have used "hard drugs" (cocaine, heroin, PCP, LSD, and methadone) on a daily basis than men.[25] A 1987 survey of state inmates reported a dramatic rise in the number of substance abusers in women's prisons; some states reported a threefold increase in the number of women admitted to their prisons for alcohol- or drug-related offenses.[26] Finally, in a review of studies of women who had committed homicide, I. J. Silverman, M. Vega, and T. Danner concluded that from

City	Percent Positive Any Drug*	Range of Percent Positive: Low	Date	High	Date	Percent Positive*: 2+ Drugs	Cocaine	Marijuana	Amphetamines	Opiates	PCP
Females											
Cleveland	88	Data Not Available				29	80	14	0	4	0
Wash., D.C.	85	70	2/89	88	6/89	33	78	12	**	20	6
Philadelphia	81	77	1/89	90	7/89	28	64	14	0	16	0
Ft. Lauderdale	79	56	12/89	79	3/90	22	60	28	0	1	0
Kansas City	76	68	10/89	83	8/89	23	66	22	5	1	0
Portland	76	57	11/89	82	8/88	36	43	34	20	19	0
Los Angeles	73	72	7/88	80	7/89	30	59	12	0	16	**
New York	71	71	1/90	83	2/88	31	67	6	0	24	4
Dallas	71	42	9/89	71	3/90	29	57	25	0	15	0
San Diego	70	70	1/90	87	12/87	34	34	16	38	18	4
St. Louis	69	45	11/88	75	4/89	16	54	15	0	7	0
Phoenix	69	54	7/88	78	3/89	31	38	25	8	16	**
Houston	66	48	10/89	66	1/90	30	56	13	5	11	0
Birmingham	66	43	11/89	77	4/89	33	40	11	0	6	0
New Orleans	65	46	11/87	65	1/90	26	57	16	0	14	0
San Jose	64	59	12/89	64	2/90	24	31	10	5	20	22
Denver	62	Data Not Available				15	46	15	4	3	0
Indianapolis	56	42	9/89	56	2/90	18	18	35	0	10	0
San Antonio	44	43	12/89	55	9/89	20	18	11	4	17	0

* Positive urinalysis, January through March 1990. Drugs tested for include cocaine, opiates, PCP, marijuana, amphetamines, methadone, methaqualone, benzodiazepines, barbituates, and propoxyphene.
** Less than 1 percent.

Figure 17.1 Drug use by female arrestees. (*Source*: National Institute of Justice. *Drug Use Forecasting Program.* (Washington: Department of Justice, 1990), p. 3.)

one-fourth to two-thirds of these offenders were substance abusers, with alcohol predominating.[27]

William R. Blount, Terry Danner, and Manuel Vega, in using a 90 percent sample of the women incarcerated in Florida prisons, found that these women were not a homogenous group. A greater proportion of casual/recreational users were non-white (70 to 30 percent), while the "problem user" and non-user were more evenly divided at 55 percent non-white and 45 percent white. A greater proportion of non-users had been or were married and had completed more grades of schooling than did the other two groups. Moreover, the extent of substance abuse was directly related to age at first arrest as an adult, age at incarceration, broken parental home, criminality in the family origin, child abuse, and crimes other than homicide. Non-users were more likely to be convicted of homicide, but casual recreational users were the most violent.[28]

Frequency of Offending

Criminologists generally agree that females commit fewer criminal offenses than do males. However, it is unclear whether arrested women behave in ways that pose a serious threat to society or whether their behavior conforms to patterns of less serious offending.

In their second cohort study, Wolfgang and colleagues found that of 14,000 female juveniles in this study, the prevalence of arrest was 14 percent before age 18. As to the level of delinquency, Wolfgang found that among the 1972 females ever arrested 60 percent were one-time offenders, 33 percent were nonchronic recidivists, and 7 percent were chronic recidivists (five or more arrests).[29] Moreover, the California Department of Justice Adult Criminal Justice Statistical System identified a cohort of 17,842 females whose first adult arrest occurred in 1973 and were followed for 15 years. Female offenders in the cohort were classified into one of three groups: (1) chronic offenders (five or more arrests), (2) moderately recidivistic (two to four arrests), and (3) those arrested only once as an adult. Ray Lewis reported that 58.6 percent of the cohort were one-time offenders, 30.4 percent were recidivists, and 11.1 percent were chronic offenders. Chronic offenders had been arrested an average of 10 times and averaged 14 charges over the 15-year follow-up period. Furthermore, chronic offenders contributed to 47.9 percent of all charges in all offense categories. For example, chronic offenders committed 45.5 percent of all violent offenses and 55 percent of all drug-related offenses.[30]

When female chronic offenders were compared with male chronic offenders in the same study, their patterns were observed to be very similar. Both female and male chronic offenders commit about the same proportion of felonies versus misdemeanors. Moreover, it is interesting that the 1,974 female chronic offenders in the study had been charged with more offenses (28,034) than had been the 19,873 one-time-only male offenders (26,601). Finally, as women become more involved in crime, these data suggest, they increase the likelihood that they will become involved in prostitution, felony property offenses, and felony drug-type offenses. Indeed, assault and robbery, once thought to be dominated by male offenders, constituted 11.3 percent of all felony offenses among female chronic offenders.[31]

The Violence of Offending

The amount of violence committed by female offenders is attracting a great deal of attention. Many assume that women are committing more violent and aggressive crimes than they have in the past.

In the mid-1970s, several factors converged to convince the public that women were definitely involved in more violent crimes. The activities of the Symbionese Liberation Army brought Patty Hearst, Emily Harris, and other female offenders into the public eye. Television carried films of armed women pulling a bank robbery, tough-looking women engaging in guerilla warfare. Sara Jane Moore and Lynette "Squeaky" Fromme were each charged with attempted assassinations of President Gerald Ford. No longer arrested merely for shoplifting or passing bad checks, women now were making the FBI's most-wanted list. Finally, Freda Adler's *Sisters in Crime* appeared, seemingly in answer to the public's bewilderment over what to make of the new female criminal. In her book, Adler offered a plausible answer: A violent, aggressive female criminal was now committing crimes traditionally committed only by male criminals. Professor Adler's appearance on a number of television programs gave her views nationwide publicity. She states:

> Women are no longer behaving like subhuman primates with only one option. Medical, educational, economic, political, and technological advances have freed women from unwanted pregnancies, provided them with male occupational skills, and equalized

> their strength with weapons. Is it any wonder that, once women were armed with male opportunities, they should strive for status, criminal as well as civil, through established male hierarchical channels?[32]

However, there is little evidence that women in the 1970s were more violent than they had been in the past or that they have become more violent in the 1980s or 1990s. In a study of crime among women in Washington, D.C., Rita Simon found that in 1974 and 1975, 82 percent of the women arrested for violent crimes had attacked someone they knew. Slightly more women than men used weapons when they committed violent acts: 79 percent of women arrested for crimes against persons versus 78 percent of the men in 1974 and 84 percent of the women versus 78 percent of the men in 1975. In 1974, 16.7 percent of those arrested for violent crimes in Washington, D.C., were women, compared with 14.1 percent nationally; in 1975, 15.4 percent were women as opposed to 14 percent nationally.[33] Thus, the typical violent female offender, as she is revealed in this study, arms herself against a known person, her husband, her lover, or a pimp. She differs only slightly from the stereotype of an enraged woman stabbing her husband with a carving knife. Such women, Simon argues, are less desperate and more rational in their violence than ever before.

A 1986 survey of inmates in state correctional facilities reveals similar violent behaviors of women in state prisons. Women in state prison for a violent crime reported that they had victimized adults and men. White women were more likely than black women to report having victimized someone of their own race (92 percent) and someone with whom they had had a close relationship (40.4 percent). Among white women in prison for a violent offense, 28.6 percent reported that they had killed a relative or intimate; among black women, 24.7 percent.[34]

Thus, researchers generally challenge the popular assumption that women are becoming more violent in their crimes. They say, in effect: Women may be hungrier, more greedy, or more unhappy, but, as a group, they do not appear to be any more violent than they were in the past.

Sexual Victimization

The fact that the majority of female prisoners have been sexual victims is becoming common knowledge. Meda Chesney-Lind states that it has long been understood that a major reason for girls' presence in juvenile courts is the fact that their parents insist on their arrest. But what researchers, as well as those who work with female status offenders, are discovering today is that a substantial number are the victims of both physical and sexual abuse.[35]

Chesney-Lind proposes that a feminist perspective on the causes of female delinquency include the following propositions: First, girls frequently are the victims of violence and sexual abuse (estimates are that three-quarters of sexual-abuse victims are girls), but, unlike boys, girls' victimization and their response to it are shaped by their status as young women. Second, their victimizers (usually fathers) can invoke official agencies of social control to keep daughters at home and vulnerable. Third, as girls run away from abusive homes characterized by sexual abuse and parental neglect, they are forced into the life of an escaped convict. Unable to enroll in school or take a job to support themselves because they fear detection, female runaways are forced to engage in panhandling, petty theft, and occasional prostitution to survive.

Finally, it is no accident that girls on the run from abusive homes, or on the streets because of impoverished homes, become involved in criminal activities that exploit their sexuality. Because American society has defined as desirable physically "perfect" young women, girls on the streets, who have little else of value to trade, are encouraged to use this resource. Not surprisingly, the criminal subculture also views them from this perspective.[36] In Box 17-2, Meda Chesney-Lind expands on this notion of the feminist theory of delinquency.

Their victimized role is likely to continue as they become adults. They may become victims of males and eventually are incarcerated for striking out at their victimizers. They may become prostitutes, simply because they feel that they have no better options. Viewed as criminals under state statutes, prostitutes are continually harassed by the law and threatened with fines and jail terms. Throughout history, prostitutes have been seen as feebleminded, sexually and economically deprived, and morally corrupt. But the real victim of this "victimless" crime is often the prostitute herself, who is permitted to keep only a small part of what she earns.

CONDITIONS OF CONFINEMENT

Women's prisons, unlike men's, tend to resemble college campuses rather than fortress penitentiaries. There are no gun towers, armed guards, or stone walls. With a few exceptions, there are no fences strung on top with concertina wire. The visitor's eye in many states is struck by the neatly pruned hedges, well-kept flower gardens, attractive brick buildings, and wide paved walkways. These institutions are frequently in rural, pastoral settings that suggest tranquility and "easy time" for the inmate.[37] Women's prisons may be more attractive in appearance than men's prisons, but this peaceful appearance is deceptive.[38]

The **assault on personal identity** is frequently more intensive in women's prisons than in men's. First, women are faced with status-stripping losses, such as the prohibition against wearing rings and other articles of jewelry. Cosmetics use is often forbidden or severely restricted. Personal-hygiene items also may be limited or dispensed to prisoners in embarrassing ways. Personal clothing is generally not permitted, and prison-issue clothes typically are drab and well worn.[39]

Second, restrictions on the type of clothing and how it should be worn are coupled with innumerable other rules that make female prisoners feel like children. "You have to eat everything on your plate," one inmate noted. "You can't even decide for yourself what you want to eat."[40] Often referred to as "girls" by the staff, prisoners are looked upon as immature and unable to make decisions. A female prisoner in Bedford Hills (New York) tells how this can carry over to the thinking pattern of an inmate:

> I find myself sometimes, if I'm writing a letter, I'll say, "the girls here . . . ." The officers make you feel as if you're definitely not equal. They look down to you, so you begin to look at yourself as a child.[41]

Third, another assault on personal identity is the fact that imprisoned mothers are burdened with the knowledge that their own behavior has caused the separation from children. This separation can generate feelings of emptiness, helplessness, anger and bitterness, guilt, and fear of loss of or rejection by the children.[42] In a

Box 17-2 Meda Chesney-Lind on the Need for a Feminist Theory of Delinquency

The question now is whether the theories of "delinquent behavior" can be used to understand female crime, delinquency, and victimization. Will the "add women and stir" approach be sufficient to rescue traditional delinquency theories? My research convinces me that it will not work. Gender stratification or the patriarchal context within which both male and female delinquency is lodged has been totally neglected by conventional delinquency theory. This omission means that a total rethinking of delinquency as a social problem is necessary.

The exclusion of girls from delinquency theory might lead one to conclude that girls are almost never delinquent and that they have far fewer problems than boys. Some might even suspect that the juvenile justice system treats the few girls who find their way into it more gently than it does the boys. Both of these assumptions are wrong.

Current work on female delinquency is uncovering the special pains that girls growing up in a male-dominated society face. The price one pays for being born female is upped when it is combined with poverty and minority status, but it is always colored by gender. Consequently, sexual abuse is a major theme in girls' lives, and many girls on the run are running away from abusive and violent homes. They run to streets that are themselves sexist, and they are often forced to survive as women—to sell themselves as commodities. All of this is shaped by their gender as well as by their class and their color.

You might ask: How about the system's response to girls' delinquency? First, there has been almost no concern about girls' victimization. Instead, large numbers of girls are brought into juvenile courts across America for noncriminal status offenses—running away from home, curfew, truancy, and so forth. Traditionally, no one in the juvenile justice system asked these girls why they were in conflict with their parents; no one looked for reasons why girls might run away from home. They simply tried to force them to return home or sentenced them to training schools. The juvenile justice system, then, has neglected girls' victimization, and it has acted to enforce parental authority over girls, even when the parents were abusive. Clearly, the patterns described here require an explanation that places girls' delinquent behavior in the context of their lives as girls in a male-dominated society—a feminist model of delinquency, if you will.

Source: Interviewed in 1988. Meda Chesney-Lind is a professor of sociology at the University of Hawaii at Manoa.

study of the effects of separation from their children on 138 inmate mothers incarcerated in Washington state and Kentucky, Phyllis Baunach also found that for female drug users, incarceration represented the first extended time period they were not using drugs and had an opportunity to evaluate the effects of their behavior upon their children.[43]

Fourth, women in prison are typically treated according to sexual stereotypes in terms of recreational and vocational programs. This failure to prepare the majority of women for meaningful employment following release is one of the serious indictments of this nation's policy of confinement.

Finally, women prisoners may be subjected to sexist medical evaluations and prescription routines. For example, women usually receive more psychotropic drugs than men.[44] One study found in 1984 that incarcerated women received from 2 to 10 times higher rates of psychotropic drugs than incarcerated men.[45]

Moreover, while female prisoners do not usually face the violence or deal with gangs that male prisoners do, crowding is increasingly becoming a problem. Female inmates increased at a faster rate during 1989 (24.4 percent) than males (12.5 percent). The female prison population has grown more rapidly than the male population each year since 1981. This higher growth rate for women over this period has raised the percentage of women in American prisons from 4.2 percent in 1981 to 5.7 percent in 1989. In 1989, 21 states, the District of Columbia, and the Federal Bureau of Prisons had more than 500 female inmates (see Table 17.1). Twenty of these

Table 17.1 WOMEN UNDER THE JURISDICTION OF STATE OR FEDERAL INSTITUTIONS, YEAR END 1989

Jurisdiction	Number of female inmates	Percent of all inmates	Percent change in female inmate population, 1987–88
U.S. total	40,556	5.7%	24.4%
Federal	4,435	7.5	36.8
State	36,121	5.5	23.1
States with at least 500 women inmates:			
California	6,000	6.9%	22.6%
Florida	2,551	6.4	26.9
New York	2,465	4.8	40.1
Texas	2,044	5.0	24.0
Ohio	1,995	6.5	26.5
Michigan	1,586	5.0	19.0
Georgia	1,110	5.3	19.5
Illinois	1,019	4.1	13.3
Pennsylvania	944	4.4	23.1
South Carolina	929	5.9	16.3
Oklahoma	900	7.9	23.1
New Jersey	886	4.6	25.9
Alabama	845	6.1	12.4
North Carolina	845	4.8	7.9
Virginia	794	4.8	35.0
Arizona	780	5.9	9.2
Louisiana	742	4.3	10.9
Maryland	728	4.4	41.1
Missouri	717	5.2	13.8
Connecticut	647	7.0	17.6
Indiana	624	6.7	24.3
District of Columbia	574	6.2	54.3

Source: Bureau of Justice Statistics Bulletin, Prisoners in 1989 (Washington: U.S. Department of Justice, 1990), p. 4.

jurisdictions had increases of at least 10 percent from 1988 to 1989, led by the District of Columbia's increase of 54.3 percent.[46]

Russ Immarigeon and Meda Chesney-Lind argue that "the current level of women's imprisonment is disproportionate to the absolute need for such confinement" because "women commit far fewer serious or violent offenses than men." Indeed, they add "that the proportion of women imprisoned for violent crimes has actually declined in the past decade" and that female offenders overwhelmingly commit crimes that pose little threat to public safety.[47] Instead of building more prison cells, Immarigeon and Chesney-Lind propose that alternatives to incarceration should be more widely used with women offenders. In Box 17-3, George Beto, former director of the Texas Department of Corrections, also recommends a reduction of women's prisons because he feels they are overused.

Immarigeon and Chesney-Lind suggest a number of community-based programs that are better suited to meet women offenders' diverse needs and, thereby are more effective in enabling women to lead law-abiding lives in the community:

1. The Program for Female Offenders. The nation's oldest multiservice center working with women offenders. Started in Pittsburgh in 1974, it has now expanded to three other Pennsylvania communities, Allentown, Harrisburg, and Philadelphia.
2. Community Services for Women. Operated by Social Justice for Women in Boston, Massachusetts. Prepares alternative sentencing plans for women convicted of misdemeanor and felony offenses.
3. The Neil J. Houston House. Also operated by Social Justice for Women and is a residential treatment program for pregnant women.

Box 17-3 Interview with George Beto, Ph.D.

Question: Why do we have so many women locked up today?

Answer: I think it is because of drugs. But women involved in the drug operations are not the big-time operators, usually they are just users. I'm not so sure you are making any gains by locking up all the users. For that matter, I believe we should get rid of women's prisons. I know some women need to be locked up, but I think states could provide for them by having a small—and I mean a very small—facility on state hospital grounds for them. We should certainly reduce the number of women we have locked up. I believe one day it will be commonly agreed that the concept of women's prisons is untenable.

I don't think releasing a lot of the women presently locked up is going to endanger society. Many imprisoned women have been abused, and they often commit violent crimes, even murder, against those who abuse them. A friend of mine put it this way, "They generally kill men who need to be killed." Parole boards are worried about when a violent parolee is released. But I have never heard of a woman parolee who embarrassed the parole board. One final thought is that the parole board shouldn't apply the same standards to locked-up women that they do to men prisoners.

Source: Interviewed in September 1990. Dr. Beto has served on the parole board in Illinois and for 10 years was the director of the Texas Department of Corrections. He is presently a professor at Sam Houston State University.

4. The Elizabeth Fry Center. Located near the Golden Gate Park in San Francisco and is one of five residential centers in the state for low-risk women prisoners who have children under six years of age.
5. Our New Beginnings. Initially conceived by seven women prisoners in Oregon's Women's Correctional Center in 1980 and today provides a broad array of transitional services to female offenders.
6. Summit House. An alternative to prison program in Greensboro, North Carolina, for prisoners who are pregnant or have children under seven years of age.
7. The Helen B. Ratcliff House. A transitional program in Seattle, Washington, for female felons released on work release from the state prison system.
8. The Women at Risk Program. Developed by a citizen's reform group in Asheville, North Carolina, and is a treatment program for victims of physical or sexual abuse who have been charged with or convicted of criminal charges.
9. Genesis II for Women. A day treatment program in Minneapolis, Minnesota, that provides assistance in a number of ways for women in conflict with the law.[48]

THE INMATE SUBCULTURE

A discussion of the female prisoner, as previously suggested, tends to examine only her kinship and homosexual relations with other prisoners; yet, to understand her means of coping with prison life, it is also necessary to explore the inmate code, leadership roles, and the social organization that develops during imprisonment.

Inmate Code

The **inmate code** in men's prisons in the 1940s and 1950s has been described in several studies (see Chapter 18). Although there is little current research on the inmate code in women's prisons, anecdotal evidence shows that women prisoners have weak commitment at best to an inmate code.[49] Yet, Esther Heffernan, in a study of a women's prison near Washington, D.C., found that inmates have an inmate code, which she stated in the maxim: "Mind Your Own Business."[50] More recently, Joycelyn Pollock-Byrne compared men's and women's prisons on three tenets of the inmate code: "do your own time," "keep away from staff," and "avoid snitching," and found some evidence of the inmate code in women's prisons.[51]

Pollock suggests that "do your own time" is followed more in men's than women's prisons because more women are involved in dyads or **kinship systems.** These relationships are filled with emotional involvement and concerns, and, therefore, female prisoners do not have subcultural proscriptions against involving themselves in other women's problems. Women also do not have subcultural proscriptions that men do regarding interaction with correctional officers. Male prisoners generally want to avoid interaction with officers because they are afraid of being labeled snitches. Women, in contrast, traditionally have had more casual and social interaction with staff. Although there is evidence that more female prisoners are becoming aggressive toward staff and defiant of their authority, the average female prisoner is still far more receptive to interaction with staff than are male prisoners.

Finally, the rule against "ratting" is observed much more frequently in men's prisons because the sanctions enforced against "rats" are more severe in men's than in women's prisons. Or to express this in another way, "taking a person out" (killing or assaulting another inmate) for ratting is a rather common experience in men's prisons but rarely takes place in women's prisons.[52]

Social Organization

The social organization of women's prisons is different in several ways from that of men's prisons. First, in most men's prisons today, the social organization is shaped primarily by inmate gangs. These gangs control drugs, as well as other types of contraband; and prisoners who do not join gangs risk victimization. However, gangs have not invaded women's prisons, and there is no evidence that one group of women prisoners binds together to control other prisoners.

Second, women's prisons do not have the racial conflict characteristic of men's prisons. (Indeed, racial violence has become one of the most salient factors related to the high rates of violence in men's correctional institutions.) In contrast, racial integration, rather than racial conflict, is more typical of women's correctional institutions. For example, one study found that although black prisoners felt that job placement and other staff treatment was racially discriminatory, there was a high degree of informal racial integration among inmates. In this study, 55 percent of white women had close ties with one or more black women, and 75 percent of black women had one or more close ties with white women.[53]

Third, the power and control of inmate leaders is different in men's and women's prisons. In men's prisons, leaders are usually connected with gangs. Prisoner leadership in men's correctional institutions is typically fragmented because inmate gangs are competing with one another for contraband and rackets, especially narcotics. In men's prisons, leadership tends to be based on domination and aggression; that is, gang leaders hold their place through fear rather than respect. Domination and aggression are also highly valued in women's prisons, but women inmate leaders usually develop within the kinship, or **pseudofamily,** system.[54] Giallombardo found from her study of the federal prison in Alderson, West Virginia, that the male or father figure was a leader for that family and gained status in the eyes of those outside the family by virtue of "his" position.[55] This implies, of course, that women value in a leader qualities paralleling those present in the traditional male role in society. Heffernan adds that masculine qualities in a woman are valued and that female prisoners tend to respond to such a person as they might to a male.[56] Pollock-Byrne illustrates this by an experience she had in a women's prison. An inmate who held three of the formal leader slots—head of the inmate grievance committee, representative to the administration for her unit, and president of an inmate club—was a transsexual who had completed several of the operations necessary for making her a male. With facial hair and a deep voice, this individual literally was the only male in a female prison and held most of the leadership roles.[57]

Other studies have found that female leaders in prison tend to be young, black, high interacters, and homosexually active.[58] Female leaders also tend to be narcotic offenders with prior felony records and previous prison incarcerations. Imogene Moyer defines leaders as those who stand up to others, get what they want, and are known for their ability to fight.[59] Heffernan, in discussing types of female leaders, described the "real woman." The "real woman" was one who told the truth regardless of consequences, was loyal, and never did anything spiteful.[60] However, female prisoners appear to have more difficulty than men in organizing and cooperating with a leader.

> Men are more organized than females. With the leaders they'll stand there and they'll face whatever's necessary. But with the females, they'll start something, I won't call them leaders, instigators really, and then fade into the background and then leave their followers to continue on.[61]

Finally, homosexuality in men's prisons is often the result of violent assaults or coercion. Experienced "cons" offer protection to inexperienced prisoners (punks) for sexual favors and commissary items. But the social organization of women's prisons is ultimately based on pseudofamilies and homosexual liaisons. The expressions of attachment that take place are almost always consensual. The majority of females (femmes) compete for the favors of those who have assumed the male role (butches). One officer explains the consensual basis of sex in women's prisons:

> The homosexuality that is done in the male facilities is usually masked, and there is a percentage of rapes, but I think a lot more of it is permissive, it is sold and so forth. In the female facilities it's not sold, it's not rape, it's just an agreement between two people that they're going to participate and there is a lot of participation. In this facility of 420 people or 430, I would say that maybe 50 percent of the population tends to deal in homosexual acts.[62]

Pseudofamilies In the Federal Reformatory for Women at Alderson, Rose Giallombardo discovered that the major difference between male and female prisons is that the women's inmate society establishes a substitute world in which women can identify or construct family patterns similar to those in the free world, whereas male prisoners design a social system to combat the social and physical deprivations of imprisonment. Family life—with "mothers and fathers," "grandparents," and "aunts and uncles"—was at the very center of inmate life at Alderson. Giallombardo also notes that membership in kinship groups took place more frequently than participation in homosexual activity and occurred earlier than sexual involvements. Providing a sense of belonging and identification, she adds, enabled inmates involved in "family affairs" to do easy time.[63]

In most women's prisons, pseudofamilies, or the kinship system, are at the heart of an inmate's life. The mother–daughter relationship is typically the most common, and some mothers have many daughters within the institution. She listens to their problems and gives advice. Still, commitment to this kinship system differs among women prisoners. Although some female prisoners take it very seriously, others regard it as a joke or a game. Women, for example, who are close to release or who have maintained close ties with their natural families tend to have little interest in pseudofamilies. In contrast, the real candidates for the kinship system are women isolated from communal ties, those who come from abusive backgrounds, and still early in their imprisonment. They are likely to look upon the prison world as their only world and may try to create the type of family they wish they had had on the outside.[64]

James Fox, in his examination of Bedford Hills in New York, found that the number of inmates involved in the kinship system fell significantly during the 1970s because of the new interest among inmates in prisoners' rights litigation, the in-

Federal Prison for Women, Alderson, West Virginia. (*Source*: Federal Prison System, Media Services Center, Washington.)

creased number of prison programs with their reduction of inmate idleness, and the new channels of communication with the outside world that outside volunteers introduced to inmates. In 1973, according to Fox, 52 percent of the Bedford Hills female prisoners held membership in a kinship unit and 45 percent had formed a close relationship with another prisoner; however, by 1978, prisoners holding membership in the kinship system had fallen to 27 percent, and only 25 percent were involved in a personal relationship with another woman.[65]

Homosexuality In studies made at the Federal Reformatory for Women at Alderson, West Virginia, at Frontera Correctional Institution in California, and at the District of Columbia Women's Reformatory in Occoquan, Virginia, researchers found that much of the inmate life is woven around lesbian relationships.[66] David A. Ward and Gene G. Kassebaum found that in the Frontera Correctional Institution, the prison love affairs appeared unstable, short lived, and explosive, and they involved strict role differentiation between the butch and the femme. The butch, who plays the dominant, or male, role, is expected to pursue the femme and to always be strong, in control, and independent.[67]

However, most research and inmate accounts suggest that only a small group of women involved in homosexuality in prison are committed to it as a lifestyle. These women typically had adopted a homosexual style before incarceration, but most women involved in lesbian relationships in prison revert back to a heterosexual lifestyle upon release. In this regard, it would appear that much of what is described as homosexuality does not even include a sexual relationship. Instead, the women involved in these relationships receive the affection and attention they need with a sexual connotation. Several studies have reported, for example, that most female prisoners are engaged in holding hands and kissing rather than actual consummation of lesbian affairs.[68]

One study found that black women were more likely to be active in prison homosexuality than white women. Nelson concluded that the black woman's socialization is to be aggressive and strong, and this predisposes her to take up the "butch" role. She also found that black women were more likely to have had homosexual relationships before prison.[69] It does seem to hold true that black women dominate the subcultures of women's prisons, emerging as the inmate leaders, and constitute the most active proponents of prison homosexuality. Similar to black men in prison, they usually have had more experiences in institutional environments, coming from foster homes, detention and training schools, and other state facilities. This background, as well as their other experiences, provide them with better coping skills for prison life.

COPING WITH PRISON LIFE

The female prisoner adjusts to prison life in the same ways that the male prisoner does; the aggressive, legalistic, withdrawal, and positive reactions to prison life are also found among women. But there are differences. Fewer women prisoners display aggressive, collective, and legalistic reactions, and a greater percentage consent willingly to homosexuality. Women also seem to exhibit fewer withdrawal reactions to prison life, for they ordinarily do not feel the need to be placed in protective custody. Nor do they commit suicide as frequently as do male prisoners. But equally few female and male prisoners show a positive reaction to prison life.

Aggressive Reaction

The traditional passivity of female prisoners began to disappear in the 1970s. Kathryn Burkhart learned from her nationwide interviews in the early 1970s what administrators of women's prisons were also discovering—that confined women were developing more behavioral problems and were becoming increasingly more difficult to manage.[70] Louisa D. Brown, warden of the Women's Correctional Center in Columbia, South Carolina, observed: "The needs of a woman are different. Women tend to be more emotional. You have to be very cautious about everything you do because their emotions are more on the surface."[71]

Charles A. Lindquist, in a study of the violators of prison discipline at the Florida Correctional Institution for Women and at the minimum security institution for men in Florida, discovered a similar pattern of disciplinary offenses. The majority of the disciplinary offenses were committed by a few women who had been incarcerated for less than a year. Verbal disrespect, movement into an unauthorized area, disobeying of institutional orders, possession of contraband, and fighting were the most frequent disciplinary offenses. But women tended to be treated more leniently than men who had committed these same disciplinary offenses.[72] The Bureau of Justice Statistics more recently examined prison rule violations among male and female prisoners in state correctional institutions. They found that more men than women were involved in prison rule violations and violated these rules more frequently (see Tables 17.2 and 17.3).

Women in prison. (*Source:* David E. Kennedy/TexaStock.)

Much less violence is reported in women's prisons than in men's prisons. One major reason for this is that women are usually less likely to manufacture or carry weapons than are men, because women's prisons generally do not have metal shops or other industries that provide materials for weapons. Even when women carry weapons, these weapons tend to be less lethal than weapons found in men's prisons. Accordingly, during an altercation, women generally pick up nearby objects, such as chairs, brooms, or irons, or they fight without weapons. The result is that female prisoners typically do not suffer serious injuries from this violence.[73]

Yet female prisoners are capable of committing violent acts behind bars. In South Carolina, correctional officers were attacked on two different occasions; during one of these attacks, two inmates tried to castrate a male correctional officer. In Illinois, a female officer was seriously injured when she was hit on the head by two female inmates during a 1977 escape. In Missouri, a superintendent was stabbed and seriously wounded by angry female prisoners.[74]

Withdrawal into Self

Given the increased numbers of women involved in drug violations and other crimes that have to do with drug use, the use of drugs represents for many a viable way to handle the pains of imprisonment. The "good news" for female prisoners with drug addictions or appetites is that psychotropic drugs are more likely to be used with

Table 17.2 STATE PRISON INMATES CHARGED WITH VIOLATING PRISON RULES DURING THEIR CURRENT SENTENCES

Characteristic	Percent of inmates charged with violating prison rules during current sentence	Percent of charged inmates found guilty
All inmates	52.7	94.0
Sex		
Male	52.9	94.0
Female	47.0	93.2
Race/ethnicity		
White (non-Hispanic)	51.2	93.8
Black (non-Hispanic)	56.8	94.3
Hispanic[a]	46.9	93.1
Other race[b]	57.0	94.9
Age		
17 or younger	44.3	—
18–24	60.2	95.0
25–34	55.1	94.3
35–44	46.0	92.6
45 or older	29.2	89.5
Marital status		
Married	41.2	91.9
Widowed	42.8	92.5
Divorced/separated	48.1	92.7
Never married	59.8	95.0
Education		
Less than 12 years	55.6	94.4
12 years or more	47.9	93.1
Military service		
Served in Vietnam	47.5	92.2
Served elsewhere	48.4	93.5
Never served	53.8	94.2
Immediate family members served time		
Yes	58.2	94.5
No	49.3	93.6

Note: Up to 2% missing data are excluded from the categories of race/ethnicity, age, marital status, education, military service, and immediate family members who served time.

—Too few cases to obtain a statistically reliable estimate.

[a]Any race.

[b]American Indians, Alaska Natives, Asians, and Pacific Islanders.

Source: Bureau of Justice Statistics, *Prison Rule Violators* (Washington: U.S. Department of Justice, 1989), p. 2.

women than men to control their institutional behaviors.[75] A correctional officer comments on the tendency of prison officials to use prescription drugs to control women prisoners:

> I don't see as much drunkenness, for example, among women in prison. . . . An awful lot of people will tell you that psychotropic drugs are used more and they're used probably legally perhaps because the medical staff are more prone to give out Valium, probably the same way, you know, if you went into everybody's pocketbook on this floor you'd find a lot of Valium. Doctors seem to give it to the women and it's a drug that's very easily abused.[76]

Table 17.3 NUMBER OF TIMES STATE PRISON INMATES WERE FOUND GUILTY OF VIOLATING PRISON RULES DURING THEIR CURRENT SENTENCES

		Percent of inmates, by number of times found guilty of violating prison rules during current sentence				
Characteristic	Total	0	1	2–5	6–10	11 or more
All inmates	100	50.6	15.2	20.3	6.3	7.6
Sex						
Male	100	50.3	15.3	20.4	6.3	7.7
Female	100	56.4	13.2	18.3	5.5	6.6
Race/ethnicity						
White (non-Hispanic)	100	53.1	14.8	19.2	6.4	6.5
Black (non-Hispanic)	100	48.1	15.2	21.0	6.8	8.9
Hispanic[a]	100	57.5	14.7	17.6	4.2	6.0
Other[b]	100	47.7	16.0	24.9	4.3	7.1
Age						
17 or younger	100	63.4	12.6	18.6	5.4	0
18–24	100	42.4	15.6	22.9	9.0	10.1
25–34	100	48.1	15.5	21.7	6.4	8.3
35–44	100	57.2	15.9	18.0	4.2	4.7
45 or older	100	74.6	11.0	9.5	1.6	3.3

Note: Categories excluding 2% missing data.

[a] Any race.

[b] American Indians, Alaska Natives, Asians, and Pacific Islanders.

Source: Bureau of Justice Statistics, *Prison Rule Violators* (Washington D.C. U.S. Department of Justice, 1989), p. 3.

The "bad news" is that female prisoners have less variety and quantity of contraband, including drugs, than male prisoners. Plausible explanations for why women have fewer street drugs are that they lack the outside community contacts, have fewer financial resources, and do not have the organization within the walls to develop widespread narcotics trafficking rackets.[77]

Legalistic Reaction

Female prisoners in the 1980s were no longer content merely to form homosexual alliances and to complain among themselves about the conflicts and emotional hurts resulting from fractured relationships. Instead, they began to see themselves more as aggrieved citizens of the state. Less afraid to express their grievances toward the institution, women began to file more federal suits and to use these suits to strike out at staff.

Nevertheless, A. Aylward and J. Thomas's comparison of women's and men's prison revealed that women were still much less likely to bring suits than men. In examining the summary decisions of all federal civil rights complaints filed in the Illinois Northern Division under 42 U.S.C. section 1983 between August 1977 and December 1983, they found that female inmates constituted 13 percent of the population but represented only 6 percent of the cases brought to the courts.[78] K. Gabel, in surveying several women's prisons to determine why women initiate less litigation than men, found that female prisoners cited jail credit or good time and child-custody issues as reasons why they did not use the court process to have their needs met.[79]

Gabel also concluded that female prisoners more likely to use the legal process were better educated, had some history of employment in the community, and were serving long sentences.[80] Fox predicted that more legal action would be forthcoming from female prisoners as younger and more aggressive females are imprisoned.[81] Both Gabel and Fox also found that such institutional variables as legal resources, outside legal volunteers, and communication among prisoners influenced the rate of litigation.

Positive Response

Most inmates, men as well as women, want to do their time and get out of prison. They have little interest in vocational, educational, or therapeutic programs. They frequently have even less respect for staff who run these programs. Also, as previously suggested, women's prisons have fewer vocational programs than do men's prisons, and what programs are available fail to address adequately women's needs when they return to the community.

There are two encouraging signs for those women who want to profit from their

Auto-mechanics class at Bedford Hills in New York. (© 1980, Tony O'Brien, *Corrections Magazine*.)

imprisonment. First, because of recent litigation, vocational programs in women's prisons are beginning to increase in number and to improve in the ability to meet the needs of women following their release. Second, there is some evidence that female prisoners are using the group process more frequently to have their needs met (see Box 17-4).

THE COSTS OF MOTHERHOOD

One of the most serious problems faced by female prisoners is separation from children: Two out of every three female prisoners have one or more children under 18 years of age.[82] Inmate mothers, not surprisingly, are particularly concerned about the custody and care of their children during their confinement. Children most frequently stay with maternal grandmothers, but other caretakers include the child's father or other relatives. Imprisoned women express the most satisfaction when children are placed with the maternal grandmother and when they have participated in the decision as to where their children will live. In placing children with the maternal grandmother, inmates feel relatively confident that they will receive minimal difficulties in taking the children back upon release. But children may also be placed in foster homes or put up for adoption if no other suitable alternatives are available. These latter placements make it much more difficult for mothers to reclaim their children after release.[83]

Imprisoned women are burdened with the knowledge that their own behavior

Box 17-4 Women Organize Themselves to Cope with the AIDS Crisis

A recent study showed that nearly 20 percent of the incoming women at the Bedford Hills Correctional Facility in New York state were HIV (AIDS) infected. In the period 1985 to 1987, the situation regarding AIDS at this facility was characterized by secrecy and denial, shame and fear, ignorance and ostracism, and inadequate medical care. As prisoners and staff became more aware of this epidemic, fear and stigma spread throughout the institution.

In December 1987, a group of six inmates submitted a proposal to the superintendent to create a peer counseling and education program, and 35 inmates attended the first meeting of what became known as ACE (AIDS Counseling and Education). Initiated and built by women prisoners and recognized by the prison administration, this prison program employs peer education, counseling, support, and health advocacy. In addition, ACE encourages group and individual self-respect and initiative. Even more broadly, ACE has as its goal the empowerment of the prison community in order to deal with all the ways that AIDS affects it.

Source: Judy Clark and Kathy Boudin, "Community of Women Organize Themselves to Cope with the AIDS Crisis: A Case Study from Bedford Hills Correctional Facility," *Social Justice* 17, (1989), pp. 90–109.

has caused their separation from children. This separation generates feelings of emptiness, helplessness, guilt, anger and bitterness, and fear of loss or rejection by the children. With prolonged separation, mothers fear that children might establish more bonds of affection with caretakers than with their mothers. Furthermore, mothers feel that teenage children staying with material grandparents may be arrested because of inadequate supervision.[84]

Even more problems await those women pregnant at the time they are imprisoned or who become pregnant while serving their sentences. Risks of pregnancy during imprisonment are high because of coed prisons, furloughs and work release, conjugal visits, and even the possibility of sexual intercourse with or rape by prison staff. On the one hand, the termination of prison pregnancy may not be possible even if the inmate desires it, but, on the other hand, inmates may be forced into an abortion by prison officials.[85]

California, which permits the mother to keep a child born in prison for up to two years, has the most liberal policy of keeping the child with the mother. In contrast, the Department of Corrections in Florida takes responsibility for the newborn child and arranges a custody hearing for the child's placement. Although other states fall in between these two extremes, the fact of the matter is that mothers stand a high risk of losing children they have in prison.[86]

Baunach explored attitudes of inmates toward allowing children to stay in the prison for short periods of time (i.e., all day or overnight) and found that women in prison, regardless of whether or not they had children of their own, tend to respond favorably to the presence of children. Many women responded that they try to "clean up their language and behavior" when children are present and enjoy watching or playing with them. No research, however, has been done on the effects on the children of being in prison with mothers for short or long periods of time.[87]

A way in which women with children might be given a chance to develop responsible decision-making skills is to involve them in dealing with their children on a routine basis prior to release. Mothers who plan to reunite with their children upon release clearly need this opportunity. A number of states, including California, Kentucky, Minnesota, Nebraska, New York, Tennessee, and Washington, now allow children to stay overnight with mothers in prison.[88]

CONCLUSIONS

The "forgotten criminal" is coming into her own. A few violent, sensationalized crimes by women in the mid-1970s generated considerable interest in the female offender. The law-and-order emphasis in the mid-1970s also resulted in greater numbers of women being incarcerated. Several states found it necessary to build new prisons to house the increasing number of female prisoners. The south has long been notorious for incarcerating large numbers of women, but other sections of the nation are now incarcerating large numbers of women. Indeed, California leads the way, with 6375 women inmates on June 30, 1990.

Still, very little is known about today's female prisoner. It appears that she is committing more crimes—chiefly drug-related property offenses, the largest category on the list of rising crimes by women. It also appears that the old codes of chivalry continue to exist in the courtroom, although their effect is diminishing at both the arrest and parole stages. Furthermore, it appears that the increase in number of women in prison is due more to the willingness to send women to prison than to increased crime among women. Moreover, it appears that women in prison are becoming more difficult to manage and that they are beginning to make demands on prison administrators through civil suits and inmate grievance procedures.

Women, like men, must learn how to cope with imprisonment. Whereas the prison for men is more like a jungle, where the strong survive at the expense of the weak, the prison for women is marked by small pockets of friendship and allegiance. Female prisoners must still guard against exploitation, both from other inmates and staff, but there is less reason to fear and more opportunity to create bonds of love.[89]

Before women's prisons can be improved, several questions must be considered: What effect does imprisonment have on women? What prison programs will be the most helpful for those who have a history of drug abuse? Why is the imprisoned female offender becoming more difficult to handle? What can be done to prepare women more effectively for release to the community? What can be done to better handle the problem of the confined female's separation from her children? What can be done to reduce the stigma of being processed through the criminal justice system? What correctional policy is needed to respond to confined women with understanding and respect? Confusion abounds, but the answers to these questions are crucial—both to the female offender and to society.

KEY TERMS

assault on personal identity

homosexuality

inmate code

kinship systems

pseudofamily

DISCUSSION TOPICS

17.1 Women are committing more crimes, but the real increase shows up in drug-related crimes against property rather than against people. Explain this pattern.

17.2 Who is the victim of the misdemeanor called prostitution? Why?

17.3 When a woman turns to violence, who is her victim most likely to be?

17.4 The typical female offender has children. How does motherhood affect her chances in court? How does motherhood affect her "doing time"?

17.5 Women's inmate society establishes a substitute group in which women can identify or construct family patterns similar to those in the free world. Describe the family structure in a women's prison.

17.6 Are the apparent differences between female and male offenders real? Using the facts provided in this chapter, construct and justify your argument.

17.7 What are the major differences between the subcultures of men's and women's prisons.

17.8 Do you support a separate yet equal women's criminal justice system?

ANNOTATED REFERENCES

Burkhart, Kathryn Watterson. *Women in Prison.* Lexington: Mass.: Heath/Lexington Books, 1976. *An investigative reporter's description of women's prisons in the United States.*

Giallombardo, Rose. *Society of Women.* New York: Wiley, 1966. *An interesting study of inmates at the Federal Correctional Prison for Women at Alderson, West Virginia.*

Heffernan, Esther. *Making It in Prison.* New York: Wiley/Wiley-Interscience, 1972. *This study of the District of Columbia Women's Reformatory at Occoquan, Virginia, identifies the three most dominant social roles in that institution.*

Pollock-Byrne, Joycelyn M. *Women, Prison and Crime.* Pacific Grove, Calif.: Brooks-Cole, 1990. *The most comprehensive and up-to-date book yet on women's prisons. It is especially helpful in identifying the inmate subculture in women's prisons.*

Ward, David A., and Gene G. Kassebaum. *Women's Prison: Sex and Social Structure.* Chicago: Aldine, 1965. *These authors, like Giallombardo, identify the specific roles women play in the prison family structure.*

NOTES

1. Bureau of Justice Statistics, *Prisoners in 1989* (Washington: U.S. Department of Justice, 1990), p. 4.
2. Joycelyn M. Pollock-Byrne, *Women, Prison and Crime* (Pacific Grove, Calif.: Brooks-Cole, 1990), p. 1.
3. Rita James Simon, *Women and Crime* (Lexington, Mass.: Heath, 1975), pp. 69–70.
4. E. Lekkerkerker, *Reformatories for Women in the U.S.* (Gronigen, Netherlands: J. B. Wolters, 1931).
5. R. Giallombardo, *Society of Women: A Study of a Women's Prison* (New York: Wiley, 1966); D. Ward and G. Kassebaum, *Women's Prison: Sex and Social Structure* (Chicago: Aldine, 1965).
6. Alice Propper, *Importation and Deprivation Perspectives on Homosexuality in Correctional Institutions: An Empirical Test of Their Relative Efficacy.* Ph.D. Diss., University of Michigan, Ann Arbor, 1976.
7. Esther Heffernan, *Making It in Prison: The Square, The Cool and The Life* (New York: Wiley, 1972); A. Mitchell, *Informal Inmate Social Structure in Prisons for Women: A Comparative Study* (San Francisco: R & E Research Associates, 1975).
8. E. Freedman, *Their Sisters' Keepers: Women's Prison Reforms in America, 1830–1930* (Ann Arbor: University of Michigan Press, 1981); N. Rafter, *Partial Justice: State Prisons and Their Inmates, 1800–1935* (Boston: Northeastern University Press, 1985).
9. Pollock-Byrne, *Women, Prison and Crime.*
10. Donald Clemmer, *The Prison Community* (New York: Holt, Rinehart & Winston, 1958).
11. Phyllis J. Baunach, "Critical Problems of Women in Prison." In Imogene L. Moyer, ed., *The Changing Roles of Women in the Criminal Justice System* (Prospect Heights, Ill.: Waveland Press, 1985), p. 96.
12. Pollock-Byrne, *Women, Prison and Crime*, p. 142.
13. R. Dobash, R. Dobash, and S. Gutteridge, *The Imprisonment of Women* (New York: Basic Blackwell, 1986); J. Crawford, "Tabulation of a Nationwide Survey of Female Offenders" (College Park, Md.: American Correctional Association, 1988).
14. Dobash et al., *The Imprisonment of Women.*
15. Simon, *Women and Crime.*
16. Ibid., p. 49.

17. Ibid., pp. 69–70.
18. D. Steffensmeir, "Assessing the Impact of the Women's Movement on Sex-Based Differences in the Handling of Adult Criminal Defendants." *Crime and Delinquency* 26, 1980: 344–357.
19. W. Wilbanks, "Are Female Felons Treated More Leniently by the Criminal Justice System?" *Justice Quarterly* 3, 1986: 517–529.
20. C. Kruttschnitt, "Women, Crime and Dependency." *Criminology* 19, 1982: 495–513.
21. P. C. Kratcoski and K. Scheuerman, "Incarcerated Male and Female Offenders: Perceptions of Their Experiences in the Criminal Justice System." *Journal of Criminal Justice* 2, Spring 1974: 73–78.
22. National Institute of Justice, *Drug Use Forecasting Program* (Washington: Department of Justice, 1990), p. 2.
23. U.S. Department of Justice, *Drug Use and Crime* (Washington: Bureau of Justice Statistics Special Report, 1988).
24. S. L. Weitzel and W. R. Blount, "Incarcerated Female Felons and Substance Abuse" (*Journal of Drug Issues*, Vol. 12, 1982), pp. 259–273.
25. Department of Justice, *Drug Use and Crime.*
26. E. DeCostanzo, "Women Behind Bars: Their Numbers Increase" *Corrections Today* 50, 1988: 104–108.
27. I. J. Silverman, M. Vega, and T. Danner, "The Female Murderer: A Literature Review." In A. Kuhl, ed., *The Dynamics of Victim-Offender Interaction* (Cincinnati: Anderson, 1990).
28. William R. Blount, Terry Danner, Manuel Vega, and Ira J. Silverman, "The Influence of Substance Use Among Adult Female Inmates." (Paper presented at the Annual Meeting of the American Society of Criminology, Reno, Nevada, November 1989), pp. 2, 9, 10, 11.
29. Marvin E. Wolfgang, Robert M. Figlio, and Thorsten Sellin, *Delinquency in a Birth Cohort* (Chicago: University of Chicago Press, 1972).
30. Ray V. Lewis, "Does There Exist an Adult Female Chronic Offender?" (Paper presented to the Annual Meeting of the American Society of Criminology, Reno, Nevada, November 1989), p. 4.
31. Ibid.
32. Freda Adler, *Sisters in Crime* (New York: McGraw-Hill, 1975), pp. 10–11.
33. Simon, *Women and Crime.*
34. Christopher A. Innes, *Violent State Prisoners and Their Victims* (Washington: Bureau of Justice Statistics, 1990), pp. 4–5.
35. Meda Chesney-Lind, "Girls' Crime and Woman's Place: Toward a Feminist Model of Female Delinquency" (Paper presented to the Annual Meeting of the American Society of Criminology, Montreal, 10–14 November 1987), p. 17.
36. Ibid.
37. Phyllis Jo Baunach, "Critical Problems of Women in Prison." In I. Moyer, ed., *The Changing Roles of Women in the Criminal Justice System* (Prospect Heights, Ill.: Waveland Press, 1985), p. 96.
38. I. Moyer, "Deceptions and Realities of Life in Women's Prisons." *The Prison Journal* 24, 1984: 45–56.
39. Richard Hawkins and Geoffrey P. Alpert, *American Prison Systems: Punishment and Justice* (Englewood Cliffs, N.J.: Prentice-Hall, 1989), p. 319.
40. Kathryn Watterson Burkhart, *Women in Prison* (New York: Popular Library edition, 1976), p. 129.
41. James G. Fox, "Women in Prison: A Case Study in the Social Reality of Stress." In Richard Johnson and Hans Toch, eds., *The Pains of Imprisonment* (Beverly Hills, Calif.: Sage, 1982), p. 214.
42. Baunach, "Critical Problems of Women in Prison," p. 96.

43. Phyllis Jo Baunach, *Mothers in Prison* (New Brunswick, N.J.: Transaction, 1984).
44. Ralph Weisheit and Sue Mahan, *Women, Crime, and Criminal Justice* (Cincinnati: Anderson Publishing Co., 1988), p. 71.
45. N. Shaw, "Female Patients and the Medical Profession in Jails and Prisons." In N. Rafter and E. Stanko, eds., *Judge, Lawyer, Victim, Thief* (Boston: Northeastern University Press, 1982), p. 265.
46. Bureau of Justice Statistics, *Prisoners in 1989* (Washington: Department of Justice, 1990), p. 4.
47. Russ Immarigeon and Meda Chesney-Lind, "Women's Prisons: Overcrowded and Overused." (Paper presented at the Annual Meeting of the American Society of Criminology, Baltimore, Maryland, 1990), p. 3.
48. Ibid., pp. 16–20.
49. K. Kruttschnitt, "Prison Codes, Inmate Solidarity and Women." In M. Warren, ed., *Comparing Female and Male Offenders* (Beverly Hills, Calif.: Sage, 1981), p. 125.
50. Heffernan, *Making It in Prison.*
51. Pollock-Byrne, *Women, Prison and Crime,* p. 131.
52. Ibid.
53. Candance Kruttschnitt, "Race Relations and the Female Inmate." *Crime and Delinquency* 29, 1983: 577–592.
54. See I. Moyer, "Leadership in a Women's Prison." *Journal of Criminal Justice* 24, 1984: 45–56, and K. Van Wormer and F. Bates, "A Study of Leadership Roles in an Alabama Prison for Women." *Human Relations* 32, 1979: pp. 793–801.
55. Giallombardo, *Society of Women.*
56. Heffernan, *Making It in Prison.*
57. Pollock-Byrne, *Women, Prison and Crime,* p. 137.
58. I. Simmons, *Interaction and Leadership Among Female Prisoners.* Ph.D. Diss., University of Missouri, Columbia, Missouri, 1975.
59. Moyer, "Leadership in a Women's Prison," pp. 233–241.
60. Heffernan, *Making It in Prison.*
61. J. Pollock, an interview conducted with a correctional officer, 1981.
62. Pollock, interviews, 1981.
63. Giallombardo, *Society of Women,* pp. 105–132.
64. Pollock-Byrne, *Women, Prison and Crime,* pp. 147–148.
65. James G. Fox, "Women in Prison." In *The Pains of Imprisonment,* pp. 209–210.
66. Giallombardo, *Society of Women*; Heffernan, *The Square, The Cool and The Life;* Ward and Kassebaum, *Women's Prisons.*
67. Lee H. Bowker, *Prisoner Subculture* (Lexington, Mass.: Heath, 1977), p. 82.
68. Pollock-Byrne, *Women, Prison and Crime,* p. 145.
69. Cited in Pollock-Byrne, *Women, Prison and Crime,* p. 150.
70. Burkhart, *Women in Prison.*
71. Interviewed in October 1978.
72. Charles A. Lindquist, "Female Violators of Prison Discipline: Backgrounds and Sanctions" (Paper presented at the Annual Meeting of the American Society of Criminology, Dallas, Texas, November 8–11, 1978), pp. 7–8.
73. Pollock-Byrne, *Women, Prison and Crime,* p. 153.
74. Information gained during interviews with administrators of prisoners during 1978 and 1979.
75. Sheila Balkan, Ronald J. Berger, and Janet Schmidt, *Crime and Deviance in America* (Belmont, Calif.: Wadsworth, 1980). See also Shaw, "Female Patients and the Medical Profession in Jails and Prisons."
76. Pollock's 1981 interview with correctional officers.
77. Pollock-Byrne, *Women, Prison and Crime,* p. 153.

78. A. Aylward and J. Thomas, "Quiescence in Women's Prisons Litigation: Some Exploratory Issues." *Justice Quarterly* 1, 1984: 253–276.
79. K. Gabel, *Legal Issues of Female Inmates* (Northampton, Mass.: Smith College School for Social Work, 1984).
80. Ibid.
81. J. Fox, "Women's Prison Policy, Prisoner Activism, and the Impact of the Contemporary Feminist Movement: A Case Study." *The Prison Journal* 64, 1984: 15–36.
82. Phyllis Jo Baunach, "You Can't Be a Mother and Be in Prison . . . Can You? Impacts of Mother–Child Separation." In B. R. Price and N. J. Sokoloff, eds., *The Criminal Justice System and Women* (New York: Clark Boardman, 1982).
83. Baunach, "Critical Problems of Women in Prison," pp. 97–98.
84. Ibid.
85. Karen E. Holt, "Nine Months to Life—the Law and the Pregnant Inmate" (*Journal of Family Law* 20, 1982), pp. 524–525.
86. Ibid., p. 537.
87. Baunach, *Mothers in Prison*.
88. Ibid., p. 105.
89. Pollock-Byrne, *Women, Prison and Crime*, p. 152.

Chapter 18

The Male Prisoner

CHAPTER OUTLINE

The male prisoner experiences many of the same feelings about and reactions to confinement as the female prisoner. Typically far from home with little or no contact with loved ones, both feel alienated. They also must learn to adapt to a world of deprivation. This adaptation requires doing without certain creature comforts and pleasures enjoyed in the free world, but, at other times, these pleasures—such as drugs—can be attained through illicit prison markets. Boredom is everpresent. The experienced male or female convict eventually learns to do time, but one has to fight against going "stir crazy." Furthermore, the total impact of incarceration, with one negative experience stacked on the next, hardens a person (see Box 18-1 for male prisoners' reactions to imprisonment). Male inmates, especially, learn that the best way to avoid being hurt is to repress one's emotions. An ex-offender talks about the consequences of repressing your emotions in prison: "It took me a long time after I got out before I could feel anything. I was so used to making sure that nobody 'messed' with me that I didn't trust nobody. I couldn't let anyone close to me. I didn't know what it felt like to love somebody. Man, I was dead."[1]

Box 18-1 Evaluations of Imprisonment

"The system has been fair to me. I got a lot of chances to make it, but I guess I am too hardheaded. I have been given a lot of opportunities, but I have f__ed them all up. For example, when I first got out of prison, the first time, my brother sent me a plane ticket to California so that I would get away from the dudes I was hangin' around with. You know what I did with that ticket? I cashed it in for money so I could buy me some 'coke.' If it wasn't for my wife and family who stuck by me for three prison terms, I would not have any hope at all."

—a 26-year-old black male who has been in prison on three occasions

"When you're in prison, the 'truth' is whatever people want it to be. Once other inmates see you in a certain way, you can't change their minds no matter what you do or how hard you try. Once labeled, always labeled."

—a 41-year-old black male who has served seven prison terms

"If you hold your own ground in prison, nothing serious will happen to you, but if you act like a 'punk,' look out, cause sooner or later, you will get f__ed over."

—a 24-year-old white male who has served one prison term

"It's the most disrespectful place I have ever seen. They take all your dignity away from you. It is people's lives they are dealing with, and until they realize this, it will stay the same old shit hole. I did come to the conclusion that I don't want to come back here. I talked with 10 to 20 inmates who will be getting out soon, and they expect to go right back in. They have no hope; it's a pitiful sight."

—a 26-year-old white male who has been in prison for eight months

"The whole [prison] environment is negative. It is dehumanizing, humiliating, and degrading. It is a punitive system. We need a boost in attitude. We need a positive atmosphere, rather than this negative attitude, which only makes us bitter toward the system."

—a 30-year-old white male who has been in prison for six years

Source: Interviewed in 1989 in Iowa prisons.

However, differences in imprisonment do exist for male and female prisoners. The male must learn to coexist with larger numbers of peers because men's prisons are several times the size of women's prisons. The issue of survival represents a more serious problem in men's prisons, and, accordingly, men are more likely to arm themselves for self-protection. In many state and federal prisons, male prisoners also must deal with inmate gangs. As a gang member in a midwestern prison noted, "In here you can't fly alone; you've to join an organization if you want to survive."[2] Moreover, racial conflicts are more acute in men's than in women's prisons. These racial tensions sometimes erupt in mass disturbances, in killings and assaults, and in sexual victimizations.

There are a few white-collar criminals "doing time," especially in federal prisons, and a few members of organized crime families—usually the lower-ranking ones—are locked up. But the typical male prisoner is a loser among losers, a marginal individual who has failed in one endeavor after another. He is usually no better at crime than he is at anything else. The typical male inmate is young, in his twenties. White males are arrested nearly three times as frequently as members of other racial groups, but nearly one-half of those sentenced to state and federal prisons are members of minority groups.[3] Moreover, the average male inmate is poor, uneducated, unemployed, drug- or alcohol-addicted, and beset with medical and psychological problems. He is also more likely to have been incarcerated for a violent offense than was the case in the past. For example, murder, nonnegligent manslaughter, rape, robbery, aggravated assault, and burglary—the most serious offenses—now account for approximately half of prison commitments from courts.[4]

Finally, the majority of prisoners released from prison are likely to be rearrested and nearly half of those rearrested will be returned to jail or prison. A study of the Bureau of Justice Statistics estimates that of the 108,580 persons released from prisons in 11 states in 1983, representing more than 50 percent of all released state inmates that year, 63.2 percent of the males were rearrested for a felony or serious misdemeanor, 47.3 percent of these offenders were reconvicted, and 41.9 percent were returned to prison or jail within three years. These rearrested ex-offenders were charged with more than 326,000 new felonies and serious misdemeanors, including approximately 50,000 violent offenses. Released prisoners were often rearrested for the same type of crime for which they had served time in prison.[5] Other findings of this survey on recidivism were as follows:

- Recidivism rates were highest in the first year—1 of 4 released prisoners were rearrested in the first 6 months and 2 of 5 within the first year after their release.
- Recidivism rates were higher among men, blacks, Hispanics, and persons who had not completed high school than among women, non-Hispanics, and high school graduates.
- Recidivism rates were higher among younger men. Indeed, the older the prisoner, the lower the rate of recidivism.
- Recidivism rates were higher among those with extensive prior records. In this regard, the more extensive a prisoner's prior arrest record, the higher the rate of recidivism.
- Recidivism rates were higher for some categories of violent crime. Released rapists were 10.5 times more likely than nonrapists to be rearrested for rape, and released murderers were about 5 times more likely than other offenders to be rearrested for homicide.[6]

This chapter discusses the inmate world, including gang activities, and a typical prison experience as seen in the case study of a male offender.

THE INMATE WORLD

John Irwin's division of the recent history of the prison into three eras—those of the Big House, the correctional institution, and the contemporary prison—provides a helpful outline in examining the inmate world.[7]

The Big House

The "**Big House**"—a term which conjures up an image of the prison that still prevails in the minds of many—dominated American corrections from the early twentieth century through the 1950s. In the Big House, prison populations showed considerable homogeneity. Inmates usually were white, were thieves (and not very good ones at that), and had spent several stints in prison during the course of their criminal careers.[8]

New prisoners were informed by both staff and other inmates that they could do "easy time" or "hard time." The staff assured prisoners that to disturb the order within the walls would bring them "hard time." Old "cons" reaffirmed the message that the "keepers" were in control and that prisoners had to make the best of it. To make their time easier in the Big House, convicts developed their own **social roles,** informal rules, and language.[9] Gresham Sykes created a typology of these social roles:

> Rats and center men, who hope to relieve their pains by betrayal of fellow prisoners.
>
> Gorillas and merchants, who relieve deprivation by preying on their fellow prisoners, taking their possessions by force or the threat of force.
>
> Wolves, punks, and fags, who engage in homosexual acts either voluntarily or under coercion to relieve the deprivation of heterosexuality.
>
> Real men, who endure the rigors of confinement with dignity, as opposed to ballbusters, who openly defy authority.
>
> Toughs, who are overtly violent and "won't take anything from anybody."
>
> Hipsters, who talk tough but are really "all wind and gumdrops."[10]

The social roles played by prisoners—other than the real man—are ways chosen to reduce the rigors of prison life at the expense of fellow prisoners, whereas real men are loyal and generous and try to minimize frictions among inmates. To the extent that they succeed, they achieve a social cohesion that is necessary to avoid a state of war among inmates. Quoting Thomas Hobbes's famous account of society in a state of war, "where every man is an enemy to every man. . . . and which is worst of all, [lives in] continual fear and danger of violent death." Sykes concludes that when cohesion is not achieved, and the rats, center men, gorillas, wolves, and toughs breach solidarity, prison life becomes "solitary, poor, nasty, brutish, and short."[11]

As described by Gresham M. Sykes and Sheldon L. Messinger, the informal code, or norms, was based on the following tenets:

1. Don't interfere with inmate interests.
2. Never rat on a con.
3. Do your own time.
4. Don't exploit fellow inmates.
5. Be tough; be a man; never back down from a fight.
6. Don't trust the hacks (guards) or the things they stand for.[12]

The **inmate code** had a special role in the system that developed, for it was ultimately functional to both prison administrators and to prisoners.[13] In the eyes of prison staff, the code promoted order, for it encouraged just doing one's time rather than creating problems. Disorder within the walls could mean that the informal arrangements between leaders and staff would be set aside, and prisoners would lose privileges it had sometimes taken years to obtain. But the code also protected the self-respect of inmates because the cons knew they were maintaining order not for the staff, but for themselves. "Hacks" or "screws" (guards) were the enemy, and a convict who was worthy of his role within the prison would make his animosity toward the enemy very clear.

Donald Clemmer, who studied the Big House in his seminal study of Menard Prison in southern Illinois, claimed that the solidarity of the inmate world caused prisoners to become more criminalized. Clemmer coined the concept of **prisonization,** defining it as the "taking on in greater or less degree of the folkways, customs, and general culture of the penitentiary."[14] "Prisonization," he added, "is a process of assimilation, in which prisoners adopt a subordinate status, learn prison argot (language), take on the habits of other prisoners, engage in various forms of deviant behavior such as homosexual behavior and gambling, develop antagonistic attitudes toward guards, and become acquainted with inmate dogmas and mores."[15]

Clemmer's emphasis was on the unique situation of the prison as a half-closed community composed of unwilling members under the coercive control of state

Inmate at Goodman Minimum-Security Prison, South Carolina, with produce from his garden. (*Source*: South Carolina Department of Corrections.)

employees. Many people still think of the prison as a completely closed institution, forgetting that the staff and the prisoners bring in the outside culture and its values. The culture that the prison experience creates consists of these outside values, to which are added the consequences of the humiliations, the fears, the deprivations, and the despair imposed on men and women in confinement. Clemmer thought that all convicts are prisonized to some extent and that possibly as many as 20 percent were completely prisonized. It appeared that upon release the highly prisonized offenders were likely to return to crime. Just as an immigrant coming to the United States would be "Americanized" to a greater or less extent, so would a convict entering prison be more or less prisonized.

The Correctional Institution

After World War II, **correctional institutions** replaced Big Houses in many states. The use of indeterminate sentencing, classification, and treatment represented the realization of the rehabilitative ideal in correctional institutions.[16] But as most staff knew and new prisoners quickly learned, the primary purpose of the correctional institution was to punish, control, and restrain prisoners, and treatment played only a minor role.

Michel Foucault has argued that the rehabilitative ideal is the ultimate means of promoting order within the correctional institution.[17] The fact that most prisoners were busy at work or at school, whether or not they believed in the rehabilitative ideal, promoted peace and stability. The indeterminate sentence and the parole board represented a more direct means of promoting order, or control, because they communicated the clear message to the inmate that conformity was necessary for release.

As black prisoners began to increase in numbers in the late 1950s, racial unrest and hostility became the major source of disruption within the correctional institution. Racial unrest followed the desegregation of housing units, jobs, classrooms, and recreational programs in the prison. Racial unrest toppled the social order in many prisons, but when it fell, inmates tried to stop the disintegration, mend the cracks, and pull the pieces back together.[18]

The social reintegration of prisoners began in the late 1960s, as inmates began to redefine the relationships with one another, the prison administration, the criminal justice system, and society in a more political fashion. The politicization of prisoners contributed to the outbreak of a series of prison riots totally different from those of past eras. The riots were more organized, supported from the outside, and led by prisoners who defined themselves as political activists and who intended to make far-reaching changes in the prison and justice system, if not in society itself.[19]

The inmate's response to imprisonment received some examination during the era of the correctional institution. Stanton Wheeler, in a study of the Washington State Reformatory, found strong support for Clemmer's concept of prisonization. But Wheeler found that the degree of prisonization varied according to the phase of an inmate's institutional stay; the inmate was most strongly influenced by the norms of the inmate subculture during the middle stage of his or her prison stay (with more than six months remaining).[20]

Further examination of the process of prisonization led to the development of the **deprivation model** and the **importation model.** The deprivation model, according to

Gresham Sykes, describes the prisoner's attempt to adapt to the deprivations imposed by incarceration.[21] But John Irwin and Donald R. Cressey, among others, contend that patterns of behavior are brought to, or imported into, the prison, rather than developed within the walls.[22] Charles W. Thomas, in a study of a maximum security prison in a southeastern state, concluded that an integration of both the deprivation and importation models was needed to understand the impact of the prison culture upon an inmate. Thomas found that the greater the degree of similarity between preprison activities and the norms of the prison subculture, the greater the receptivity to the influences of prisonization. He also found that those inmates who had the greatest degree of contact with the outside world had the lowest degree of prisonization.[23]

The Contemporary Prison

The setting of the 1990s inmate world remains one of violence, but now the mood is one of disillusionment. The hopelessness experienced by many inmates can be explained by the ever-increasing problem of idleness, by longer sentences, by tighter controls imposed by staff, by overcrowded institutions, by the decline of political ideology, by the reduced possibility of relief through the judicial process, and by problems with drug and alcohol abuse.

In the contemporary prison, the social order often verges on total collapse; in fact, at times, the social order does collapse, but over the long term, this fragmented, tense, and violent setting remains intact because inmates ultimately prefer order to disorder. Inmates feel they have too much to lose if the "lid" comes off the institution.[24]

Increased administrative controls and stiffer penalties for criminal behavior also have curbed some of the violence in prisons. The increased number of habitual offender statutes has led to the "greying" of the prison population (i.e., the average inmate is older now), and these offenders realize that they must make peace because they may be imprisoned for the rest of their lives.

Lynne Goodstein's study of three adult male state correctional institutions in two northeastern states provides a serious critique of this nation's policy of imprisonment. She found that the inmates who adjusted most successfully to a prison environment encountered more difficulty making the transition from institutional life to freedom. She concluded that the inmates who were least able to adjust to the formal institutional culture seemed to make the smoothest transition to community life. She adds that "it is ironic that . . . inmates who accepted the basic structure of the prison, who were well adjusted to the routine, and who held more desirable prison jobs . . . had the most difficulty adjusting to the outside world."[25]

THE WORLD OF GANGS

James B. Jacobs, a lawyer and a sociologist, published his extended observations of a maximum security prison in Illinois.[26] The prisoner solidarity that Sykes described was eroded by the increasing penetration of the prison by external forces. Militancy brought about a certain cohesion among black prisoners. The black population had increased from 47 percent in 1953 to 74 percent in 1974. Cohesion was complicated by competing **inmate gangs**—the Black P Stone Nations, the Black Gangster Disciple Nation, the Conservative Vice Lords, and the Latin Kings.[27] These gangs were—and are—very large, some of them with memberships numbering in the hundreds. To distinguish them from the old-fashioned street gang of a few dozen at the most, Jacobs refers to them as "supergangs." All of them originated in the slums of Chicago, and many of the leading figures were gang leaders in free society. Stateville became a recruiting ground for new members.

Formal agreements among the gang leaders assure members that they will not be molested by members of other gangs. Inmates who are not affiliated—around 50 percent of the Stateville population—are fair game for thievery, intimidation, blackmail, assault, and sexual pressure.

The solidarity brought about by the "real men" in New Jersey no longer exists at Stateville or at the many other prisons in which the supergangs have come into prominence. Instead, the supergangs have achieved among their members a kind of loyalty that is hard to match. One older gang member told Jacobs,

> The gang leaders have absolute control. T. could have told his men to tear it down and they would—a lot of these guys would die for their gang—dying doesn't mean anything to them. They'd rather die than let it be said that they wouldn't go all the way.[28]

An exaggeration, perhaps, but the willingness of gang members to engage in massive and violent confrontations with custodial staff armed with batons and shields was a new phenomenon in corrections. The results were the seizure of more and more power by the supergangs, the terrorization of white and unaffiliated blacks and Hispanics, and the demoralization of the guards, dozens of whom resigned rather than continue in their increasingly dangerous occupation. Eventually new administrators restored the state's authority, but it was a long and arduous process.

California and Texas are other states that have severe problems with supergangs (see Box 18-2). Table 18.1 on page 504 reveals that inmate gangs have spread to 32 states and the federal Bureau of Prisons. Prison officials in 29 jurisdictions, according to G. M. Camp and C. G. Camp's 1985 national inmate gang survey, have identified 114 gangs, with an estimated membership of 12,634. Overall, gangs are estimated to make up about 3 percent of the total state and federal prison populations.[29] In 1987, the Camps concluded that prison gangs account for at least one-half of all prison problems.[30]

FRED AND "DOING TIME": A CASE STUDY

What is it like to be sentenced to prison? Obviously, this question can be answered literally only by an offender who has "done time," but this section will attempt to capture a glimpse of what it feels like to be sentenced and imprisoned.[31]

Fred, a 19-year-old white youth with a juvenile record, became involved with a group he had met. One night he was driving three of them around in his car when one said, "Let's stop and get some liquor." Fred stayed in the car as they went into the liquor store. They came running out and said, "Let's go. We just robbed the store." But as they were making their getaway, they were stopped for speeding. All of them were charged with armed robbery.

Fred's attorney told Fred, "You're going to have to come up with a lot of cash to

Box 18-2 Organizational Structure of Prisons Gangs in Texas

Formed in 1975 by a group of prisoners who had previously served time in the California prison system, the Texas Syndicate, with a confirmed membership of 241, is the oldest and the second largest inmate gang in the Texas Department of Corrections. The Mexican Mafia or MEXIKANEMI (Soldiers of Azthan) is only two years old, but it has a confirmed membership of 304 and is the largest inmate gang in Texas.

Both gangs are organized along paramilitary lines. The Texas Syndicate is headed by a president and vice president who are elected by the entire membership. On the unit level, the Texas Syndicate is controlled by a chairman, who oversees the vice chairman, captain, lieutenant, sergeant-at-arms, and soldiers. The Mexican Mafia is composed of a president, vice president, regional generals, lieutenants, sergeants, and soldiers. All ranking positions in the Mexican Mafia organization, excluding the sergeants, are elected solely on individual's ability to deal harmoniously with people.

Both inmate gangs require their members, regardless of rank, to abide by a strict code of conduct known as the "constitution." For members of the Texas Syndicate, the constitution consists of eight rules:

1. Be a Texan.
2. Once a member, always a member.
3. The Texas Syndicate comes before anyone and anything.
4. Right or wrong, the Texas Syndicate is right at all times.
5. All members will wear the Texas Syndicate tattoo.
6. Never let a member down.
7. All members will respect each other.
8. Keep all gang information within the group.

For members of the Mexican Mafia, the constitution outlines 12 rules:

1. Membership is for life—"blood in, blood out."
2. Every member must be prepared to sacrifice his life or take a life at any time when necessary.
3. Every member shall strive to overcome his weakness to achieve discipline within the MEXIKANEMI brotherhood.
4. Never let a MEXIKANEMI down.
5. The sponsoring member is totally responsible for the behavior of the new recruit. If the new recruit turns out to be a traitor, it is the sponsoring member's responsibility to eliminate the recruit.
6. When disrespected by a stranger or a group, all members of the MEXIKANEMI will unite to destroy the person or the other group completely.
7. Always maintain a high level of integrity.

8. Never release the MEXIKANEMI business to others.
9. Every member has the right to express opinions, ideas, contradictions, and constructive criticisms.
10. Every member has the right to organize, educate, arm, and defend the MEXIKANEMI.
11. Every member has the right to wear the tattoo of the MEXIKANEMI symbol.
12. The MEXIKANEMI is a criminal organization and therefore will participate in all aspects of criminal interest for monetary benefits.

For both inmate gangs, the penalty for violating any of the established rules is death.

The Texas Syndicate practices a more comprehensive and lengthy recruiting process than does the Mexican Mafia. Both gangs require that every prospective member meet the "homeboy connection" requirement, which means that he is known by one of the active members as a childhood friend. The Texas Syndicate also conducts a thorough background investigation. If the investigation reveals that the prospective member is "clean," the entire membership must cast a unanimous vote before formal admittance is granted.

Both the Texas Syndicate and the Mexican Mafia operate in secretive ways in the prison setting. On the unit level, instructions and decisions are relayed through verbal communications. But for inter-unit communication, the most commonly known method is through the use of coded messages in the U.S. mail.

Released members of both gangs are required to stay in close contact with members in the prisons. In the free world, both gangs appear to be engaging heavily in drug trafficking from such countries as Mexico, with the assistance of nonmembers called "associates." For those released members who can generate independent income, the Texas Syndicate requires a 10 percent income contribution, while the Mexican Mafia takes a 15 percent income contribution. The failure to obey this rule supposedly will result in the death of the member.

Source: Robert S. Fong, "The Organizational Structure of Prison Gangs: A Texas Case Study," *Federal Probation*, March 1990, pp. 36–43.

be able to bond out. I'll try to get it as low as I can." Two days later, Fred was officially charged, in court, with armed robbery. He couldn't believe it when the assistant prosecutor asked for bond to be set at $100,000. Fred's attorney objected to the high bond. He argued that Fred had no prior record as an adult, his parents lived in town, and he had not actually been involved in the armed robbery. The judge called the attorney to the bench and, in a stern voice, said, "I'm aware that your last client in this court was given a low bond, and he skipped town. You better make sure Fred doesn't do the same. Bond will be lowered."

Fred's attorney talked to Fred prior to his return to jail. "It's important you do not jump bail. Don't be like John! They'll catch up with him one of these days and nail him twice as hard. Also," the attorney added, "if you jump bail there will be no way you can get probation."

Table 18.1 NUMBER OF GANGS AND GANG MEMBERS REPORTED BY CORRECTIONAL AGENCIES IN THE UNITED STATES, 1984

Jurisdiction	Prisoners 1-1-1984	Number of gangs	Total members	Year started	Percent gang members
Arizona	6,889	3	413	1975	6.0
Arkansas	4,089	3	184	1974	4.5
California	38,075	6	2,050	1957	5.5
Connecticut	5,042	2	—	—	—
Federal System	30,147	5	218	1977	0.7
Florida	26,260	3	—	—	—
Georgia	15,232	6	63	—	0.4
Idaho	1,095	3	—	—	—
Illinois	15,437	14	5,300	1969	34.3
Indiana	9,360	3	50	1983	0.5
Iowa	2,814	5	49	1973	1.7
Kentucky	4,754	4	82	1982	1.7
Maryland	12,003	1	100	—	0.8
Massachusetts	4,609	1	3	—	0.1
Michigan	14,972	2	250	—	1.7
Minnesota	2,228	2	87	—	3.9
Missouri	8,212	2	550	1981	6.7
Nevada	3,192	4	120	1973	3.8
New York	30,955	3	—	—	—
North Carolina	15,485	1	14	1974	0.1
Ohio	17,766	2	—	—	—
Oklahoma	7,076	5	—	—	—
Pennsylvania	11,798	15	2,400	1971	20.3
Texas	35,256	6	322	1975	0.9
Utah	1,328	5	90	1970	6.8
Virginia	10,093	2	65	1974	0.6
Washington	6,700	2	114	1950	1.7
West Virginia	1,628	1	50	1980	3.1
Wisconsin	4,894	3	60	1978	1.2
Average Totals		114	12,634		3.0

Source: G. M. Camp and C. G. Camp, *Prison Gangs: Their Extent, Nature, and Impact on Prisons.* Washington, DC: U.S. Department of Justice, 1985.

Fred quickly responded, "Probation! Can you really do it?"

Although the attorney knew it would be unlikely that Fred would be placed on probation because the high bond indicated that the prosecutor's office wanted him off the streets, the attorney wanted to be sure that Fred would not jump bond. "Yes, if you play your cards right, you won't do any time in the joint. Just don't jump bond."

Fred put up 10 percent of his bond and was released the next day. Three weeks after Fred's release from jail, his attorney informed him that the preliminary hearing was set for August 6. Fred was not sure of what happens at a preliminary hearing and was surprised to learn that this was just an early stage of his case in the court process.

His arraignment was held a month later. Fred pleaded not guilty, as his attorney had instructed him to do. The judge set the trial date for six weeks later. Outside the courtroom, Fred's attorney said, "Don't worry, the prosecution will never be ready for trial at that time. They will move for a continuance. A new date will be set, and then we will find a reason to move for a continuance."

Fred asked, "Why will we do that?"

His attorney answered, "Public anger toward you for the armed robbery and your other crimes will lessen the longer the case drags on. The prosecutor and the judge won't have so much public pressure on them and should be more inclined to be lenient. Finally, those involved will get tired of the case as time goes on and may be more willing to give better concessions if we plea bargain."

The continuances occurred as Fred's attorney predicted. In late March, three weeks before Fred's fourth trial date, a new prosecutor was assigned to his case. The new prosecutor informed Fred's attorney that one of the police officers who had investigated the case had quit the force and would not be available to testify. The bargaining session lasted an hour and a half, but the new prosecutor proposed that the charge be reduced to unarmed robbery if Fred would plead guilty. He also agreed to stand mute at the sentencing hearing, which meant that he would not ask for any specific kind of sentence.

When Fred's attorney told him about the deal, Fred accepted it and then asked, "How do we convince the judge to give me probation?" Fred's attorney answered, "We can have witnesses come into the court at your sentence hearing and make positive statements about you. We can use them and a good presentence investigation report to get you probation."

At the sentencing hearing Fred's attorney argued for the minimum sentence of three years, a suspended sentence, and probation. He explained that Fred had enrolled in group counseling at the mental-health clinic and that he was living with his parents. He emphasized that Fred had no prior convictions as an adult. School officials, in addition, testified that Fred could receive his diploma after one session of summer school.

The judge listened intently. He also read the presentence report, which described Fred's past accurately. Furthermore, the judge was aware of the past manipulations of Fred's attorney, and he was fed up with him. Pronouncement was scheduled for nine o'clock the next morning. Fred was confident that the sentence would be probation.

Fred braced himself the next morning and heard the judge's pronouncement: "You will be sentenced to the state penitentiary for no less than three and no more than eight years." The convicted offender waited, assuming the judge would then suspend the sentence. The words never came; instead, he became aware of a sinking feeling in the pit of his stomach as he felt the hand of the deputy sheriff on his shoulder and heard him say, "Come on, let's go."

Jail

Outside the courtroom two deputies handcuffed Fred and took him to the county jail, where he was placed in a cell with several inmates. Later that day as Fred walked around the day room, terrified about his trip to prison the next day, he was approached by an older black inmate who held out his hand and introduced himself: "My name is Sam Jones. Let's rap a little."

Sam then gave Fred a quick course on how to survive in prison. "Let me tell you a few things about life behind bars. First, never show weakness to nobody. Stay by yourself and do your own time. Second, never take anything from another con. When you're offered a candy bar, some cigarettes, or food lifted from the dining room, you better not take it because your new friend will come around in a few days and want the candy bar or cigarettes back right now. If you don't have them, he will want some other payment, and he usually has sex in mind. Third, never go into another con's cell when you are in quarantine [classification] or even when you get into the general population. One of the favorite tricks is to get a fish [new inmate] into a game of chess or checkers, but the fish is the only pawn that is jumped. Next, get yourself a shank [knife] as soon as you can."

"Where do I get a shank?" Fred interrupted.

"The best place," Sam answered, "would be to get a spoon in the dining room. Or if you get assigned to the metal shop or any of the other industries, you should be able to get hold of a piece of metal. You can always make connections to cop [buy] one. But if nothing else works, make it out of the metal of your bed."

"But where will I hide the shank after I get it?" Fred asked. "Don't they search you all the time in prison?"

"Yeah, but you can tape it to your chest or you can hide it in your crotch. But whatever you do, take that knife with you when you go to other parts of the institution unless you're going places where you might be stripped and searched." Sam paused to light a cigarette and then concluded, "Finally, don't trust nobody. Never relax; always be on guard. If you drop your bar of soap in the shower, leave it there. And don't trust the hacks [guards] to help you. They'd sell you out in a minute if it would make their jobs any easier."

Sam concluded his survival lesson with a request: "I don't get any commissary because I don't have any friends out there. How about some cigarettes and coffee?"

Fred quickly responded, "Let me ask a turnkey [correctional officer] to get me a couple of packs of my cigarettes and I'll give them to you. I don't have any coffee, but I'll give you some candy. I really appreciate your help."

The First Day in Prison

Fred was wakened around seven o'clock the next morning, ate breakfast, and mentally prepared himself for the trip to prison. Two sheriff's deputies arrived about ten o'clock. They gave him white overalls, told him to tag his clothes, and put him in leg irons and handcuffs. Fred and another prisoner were then transported to prison in the sheriff's van and, sitting together in the back seat, the two began to talk. It became clear to Fred that this kid was going to be a pushover for predatory inmates; he had long blond hair, fair skin, a beard, and feminine features. He also was conspicuously petrified and, like Fred, had never been in prison before. Fred told him not to let anyone mess over him, but he did not say any more because he was uncertain about how cool he himself would be when faced with the intimidation and violence of prison life.

The two offenders arrived at the state prison and went through the customary intake procedures. They were now part of a larger group that received an orientation lecture from a guard captain, who informed the new inmates that above all they should do their own time, as opposed to getting involved in somebody else's business. If they did this, he advised, they would be out before they knew it.

Fred received his prison clothing from an inmate storekeeper who stared at the neophyte for several moments and then asked, "Anything more I can do for you, sweetie?" Fred had decided that he was going to follow Sam's advice to the letter and not let any verbal or physical putdowns go unchallenged, so he looked the storekeeper in the eyes and, with anger choking his voice, said loudly, "My name is Fred Sterns. I'm no sweetie."

"Take it easy," the storekeeper replied with a grin.

Fred was taken to his new home on the third tier of the north cellhouse, where new inmates were isolated from the general population. Fred had seen movies of tier after tier stacked up, one on another, but he still was not prepared for the real thing.

The rest of the day was rather uneventful. Fred met his cellmate, had his first prison meal, which was at least better than jail food, and spent the recreational period in the yard with the other inmates in the reception unit.

Time to Turn Out

Fred noticed that every time he went through the cafeteria line one particular black inmate stared at him. After a couple days, this old con assigned to serve food to the newly admitted inmates approached Fred. "Hey, kid, when are you and me going to get together? You've got to ride with somebody. You better hook up with me, or the other animals in the penitentiary will get you."

Fred ignored him, but the next morning he saw another fish grabbed by three old cons, dragged into an open cell, and gang raped. Fred thought, "My God, that could have been me."

As Fred went through the lunch line that afternoon, he was greeted with the words, "I see my friends grabbed a punk today. It's your turn next unless you get over for me." He assured Fred that he would have him assigned to his cell following the three-week classification period and that he would take care of him. Specifically, this meant that he would keep him in cigarettes, candy, and food; most importantly, he would keep others away from him.

Fred's reply to this predator inmate was that they might rip him off, or physically assault him, but if they did, they had better watch out afterwards because he had a store-bought shank and he would get them one by one. Apparently, Fred made his point because he did not have any more problems until he reached the general population. This time he was approached by a white con who offered him a candy bar; Fred turned him down. Then, he offered Fred a pack of cigarettes; again Fred turned him down, even though he was dying for a cigarette and had run out that morning. The inmate then asked Fred for sex, warning that he would be gang raped if he did not cooperate. At that point Fred pushed him; the other inmate swung at Fred, and they began to scuffle. Eventually, a guard separated them, but Fred had established a reputation for strength, letting the other inmates know that they could not mess with him.

Programming

Fred was assigned to the license plate factory. The sergeant in charge left the inmates alone as long as they did a little work and minded their own business. In fact, they did well if they worked three hours a shift. But, after all, Fred reasoned, they were being paid only slave wages. Fred was disgusted when he thought about the pretense that prison industries provided rehabilitation programs, for he and all the other inmates knew that this was only rhetoric.

The only rehabilitation for Fred lay in the reading he was doing in the prison library. He read every book he could get his hands on. Most of the time he read randomly just to escape the deadening boredom of the prison environment. Occasionally, he came across a book on corrections, and he always found it amusing to read what people who had never experienced imprisonment had to say about it.

Life in the Yard

To Fred, life in the big yard was one of the most unforgettable experiences of the prison world. To the observer, the yard was simply the area in which prisoners exercised—lifting weights, playing basketball, running around a jogging track—or just stood around talking. But to the convict, the yard was more than an exercise area: It was a place in which racial groups had their own space and where gambling took place, as did negotiations for participation in the drug traffic. Fred was surprised to discover that drugs were easier to come by within the walls than they had ever been on the streets. The yard was also a place where some of the hits of prison life took place, where two or three inmates would slink up to an unsuspecting victim to honor the contract out on him.

Coping with Imprisonment

Doing time, according to the old-timers, was more difficult than it used to be. The inmate society used to have a clearly defined pecking order, with some at the top and some at the bottom. Formerly, inmate leaders ran the cellblock, receiving special privileges from guards for doing so. There also used to be a code of inmate behavior that specified what was acceptable and unacceptable. Inmates were supposed to do their own time, staying out of every other inmate's affairs, avoiding snitching, and resisting the people changers, or staff, at every opportunity.

Now, inmates divided themselves into racial groups, and within each group there was at least one leader. A racial war raged among the various groups. If an inmate was stabbed and the stabbing did not appear to have racial overtones, there were no problems. But if a black inmate was stabbed by a group of white inmates, retaliation usually followed. Racial conflicts and the greater availability of lethal weapons made it more difficult to stay alive from one day to the next, but Fred gradually became aware that there were at least six ways to make it in prison: aggressive reaction, collective reaction, self-satisfying reaction, legalistic reaction, withdrawal reaction, and positive reaction (see Table 18.2).[32]

Aggressive Reaction Fighting the system and not giving an inch was one way to deal with prison life. But the problem with this coping mechanism was that the convict who had a number of disciplinary reports, or tickets, could spend much of his time in segregation, and parole boards did not look very favorably upon poor conduct reports. Fred, who spent several days in segregation for fighting, had come to realize that personal defiance has no real impact on the system; it is self-destructive and results in a prolonged institutional stay.

Collective Reaction Other inmates, Fred observed, became radical and attempted through violent or nonviolent disturbances to achieve their demands. They

Table 18.2

Types of response	Characteristics	Outcome
Aggressive Reaction	Fights the system by disobeying the rules.	Prolonged imprisonment and considerable time in segregation.
Collective Reaction	Fights the system through rebellion and protest.	Prolonged imprisonment, perhaps brutality from staff, and some improvement in living conditions.
Self-satisfying Reaction	Makes the best of the prison experience by satisfying himself in every way possible.	Reduction of the pain of imprisonment.
Legalistic Reaction	Fights the system through the courts.	Possible reduction of time or even release from imprisonment.
Withdrawal Reaction	Escapes from the painfulness of prison life.	Depends on the withdrawal-coping mechanism.
Drug Use	Escapes through chemicals ranging from alcohol to hard drugs.	No negative outcome unless inmate is caught.
Protective Custody	Requests segregation.	Safety from prison violence, but if the choice is later made to return to the general population, increased vulnerability to victimization is possible.
Mental Disturbance	Escapes through mental illness.	May be permanently affected, which may result in transfer to hospital for the criminally insane.
Suicide	Choice is to end one's life because of the meaninglessness and pain of prison life.	Death.
Positive Reaction	Uses the prison experience for self-development.	Depends on the permanence of the positive reaction; if the offender can sustain it in the community, he may be able to turn his life around.

spoke of themselves as political prisoners who were victims of an oppressive social system and proclaimed that they were in prison because of their class and race rather than for their crimes. Yet Fred knew that they could not win. Even if they took hostages, the inmates would lose. All they would accomplish would be to bring brutality upon themselves and lengthen their prison stay.

Self-satisfying Reaction Instead of fighting the system, some inmates tried to make the best of prison life. They wanted to do "easy time." They could make up for the sexual deprivation of prison life by taking a kid under their wing. They could also steal food from the dining hall so that they would have food in their cells when they wanted a snack. They could have the inmates who worked in the laundry press their prison clothes, a small but satisfying luxury. Furthermore, they could fix up their cells to contain any such amenities as were permitted in prison.

Legalistic Reaction More and more, inmates tried to fight the system through the federal courts. Supported by the jailhouse lawyers and by the host of attorneys from the free community who swarmed through the prison gates, many inmates used all their energies to study criminal law, preparing civil suits and writing legal briefs to appeal their cases or to ask for new trials. Fred was aware that some inmates had been awarded damages by the courts. He also knew that some correctional systems had been charged by the federal courts to either institute major reforms or to close their facilities. Thus he could see why convicts serving long sentences became so involved with the law.

Withdrawal Reaction Ranging from voluntary activities as using narcotics and alcohol, invoking protective custody, and attempting suicide to involuntary activities as becoming mentally ill, withdrawal was a favorite coping mechanism for many prisoners. The use of narcotics was probably the most common method of withdrawing from the stresses and pressure of prison life, chiefly because of their easy availability and by the high percentage of inmates who had developed an appetite for them on the streets. Protective custody was the preference of more and more inmates. Fred was surprised by the inmates who chose this response, for they frequently were strong and quite capable of taking care of themselves. But, as one said to Fred, "I just don't want to put up with the hassles of prison life anymore." Other inmates became depressed and mentally ill; they simply psychologically withdrew into a world of their own. Finally, suicide was chosen by those inmates who would rather be dead than continue to live the hellish prison existence.

Positive Reaction The final way to make it in prison, as Fred saw it, was to use the prison experience to develop a strong mind. He was attracted to this coping mechanism, for it was an attempt to prevent the dehumanizing prison experience from permanently damaging an inmate's self-respect. Those who chose this response were determined to come out of prison better and stronger persons than when they went in. One prisoner, a leader of a Chicago gang, defined "strong mind" in this way:

> When we have a "strong mind," we have a feeling of self, a continuity to life, and an enhanced faculty of reasoning. Having a "strong mind" doesn't imply that one strives to be a paragon of information. It has more to do with one not having any feelings of inferiority and worthlessness. A strong mind will help us know who we are, what we are; it will help us to accept and respect who and what we are, and know that virtually everything and every situation we encounter in life offers us a valuable lesson, which, if fully understood, makes us wiser.[33]

To develop this strong mind, some Black Muslims, for example, subjected themselves to rigorous mental and physical discipline. They often slept on the floor and spent much of their time in meditation. Other inmates worked on developing a strong mind by making individual sacrifices, such as limiting the amount they ate, so they could purify their bodies. Still others used rigorous exercise, running marathon distances or lifting enormous weights. A few became involved in religion as a means of developing a strong mind. Other prisoners turned to working on creative projects, such as writing, painting or sculpting, designing jewelry, or working at handicrafts of some kind.

The strong mind, Fred reasoned, will help a person cope with life in mature ways. First, mature coping means "dealing with problems and meeting them head-on, using all resources legitimately at one's disposal."[34] Mature coping requires that you do the best you can with what is rightfully yours. Second, mature coping requires that an inmate address problems without resorting to deception or violence, except when necessary for self-survival. Deception, of course, "is the name of the game in prison."[35] Third, mature coping requires that prisoners be able to empathize with others, be able to make an effort to assist others in need, and be able to work together with others to create a more secure and gratifying community.[36]

Inmate self-help group in federal prison. (*Source*: Federal Prison System.)

Parole

Fred decided that he would do everything possible to ensure that he would make parole on his first time before the board. He received his high school diploma by passing the GED examination. He joined the Jaycees and even became an officer in this organization. He avoided any further appearances before the disciplinary committee, and several staff members wrote excellent letters to the parole board on his behalf. Fred did not see how he could miss, but he was turned down twice before he was paroled.

The release day finally came. Fred knew that the time he had spent in prison had taken its toll. He knew he had lost a lot of self-confidence, because he had difficulty making decisions now. To help him make a successful reentry into society, he was given a new suit—which he planned to dispose of as soon as possible—and $50. He did not know what the future had in store for him, but he hoped to make up for the wasted years of his life.

Fred found the initial impact of community life to be staggering. The slow, monotonous, familiar prison routine was replaced by a chaotic and foreign outside world. The impact of cars, buses, noises, lights, and building had not been experienced for a long time; some automatic reactions, such as answering the telephone, ordering a meal, or getting on a bus, were no longer automatic to him.

He soon discovered that parolees like himself encountered three major areas of danger: problems that arise immediately upon release, problems that arise after parolees have gotten on their feet, and problems that arise with the parole agency during supervision.[37] To make a successful adjustment in the community, the parolee must find immediate solutions to the problems of employment, residence, clothing, transportation, and money. Fred found this initial period difficult because he had so few resources for meeting these basic needs. Once he made it through the initial period, he wanted to do more than just get by, and this brought him to another set of problems. He had to develop new friends, find a good job, deal with the stigma of being an ex-con, establish meaningful relationships with women, and manage disappointment and failure. Meanwhile, he was having problems with his parole agent, for he felt that the agent was harassing him and would not get off his back. He sometimes thought that the system was set up to make him fail.

Fred considered drifting back into crime. He still had some contacts in the community who would help him if he chose, but he decided to stay clean. He had already given up nearly five years of his life to the state, and he simply made up his mind that it was time to settle down. He had found a good job. He was also planning to be married and did not want to lose his fiancée's respect. All these factors joined together to keep him from returning to crime.[38]

CONCLUSIONS

The many empirical studies of the male prisoner vary in their findings, but they consistently document the increased use of drugs, the dangerous nature of some prisoners, and the difficulty of reforming the career criminal. The street criminals who receive all the notoriety represent only a small part of the crime problem, for organized crime and white-collar crime are far more costly to the economy of the United States.

Charles E. Silberman's *Criminal Violence, Criminal Justice* demonstrates clearly that the criminal who persists in crime will eventually be caught because the law of averages is against him or her. Silberman claims not to have known or heard of anyone who had been a criminal for any length of time without having spent time in prison. Criminals are caught, according to Silberman, because most of them are not good at crime. He adds that the folk wisdom of criminal subcultures is that the police will eventually get you: "If you want to play, you have to pay"; "If you can't do the time, don't do the crime"; and "Everyone has to take a vacation now and then, I take mine at government expense."[39]

Other than death, the most severe punishment society can inflict on a criminal is to send him or her to prison. Under changing conditions of confinement, the inmate's last defense against the prison's reductive effects is crumbling. Today, prison time is hard time, and no one is the winner in the triangle of fear that develops between inmate and inmate and between inmate and staff. The male prisoner who is strong and knows the score is likely to survive prison life. But if he is not streetwise or is easily intimidated, then prison life can be a real hell, one in which he stands to lose everything, including his manhood. Many male prisoners are now choosing to lock up (accept protective custody) rather than deal with the tensions and conflicts of prison life.

Upon their return to the streets, parolees face new problems. The pressure is on them to find employment, manage their finances, locate a place to live, and keep the parole officers off their backs. Some parolees leave prison with every intention of returning to crime; others leave prison determined to stay away from crime but find themselves unable to handle the pressures. However, some do persevere and walk away from crime.

KEY TERMS

"Big House"

correctional institution

deprivation model

importation model

inmate code

inmate gangs

prisonization

social roles

DISCUSSION TOPICS

18.1 White-collar criminals, street punks, or Mafia—which category has filled this nation's prisons to overflowing? Why?

18.2 You are in prison. Which model of survival will you choose? Why?

ANNOTATED REFERENCES

Brady, Malcolm, *On the Yard.* Boston: Little Brown, 1967. *One of the best and most interesting accounts of inmate life.*

Clemmer, Donald. *The Prison Community.* New York: Holt, Rinehart & Winston, 1958. *A classic examination of prison culture and how it affects inmates.*

Fong, Robert S. "The Organizational Structure of Prison Gangs: A Texas Case Study." *Federal Probation,* March 1990: 36–43. *An interesting examination of the two largest gangs in the Texas prison system.*

Irwin, John. *Prisons in Turmoil.* Boston: Little Brown, 1980. *Irwin, an ex-con himself, traces the development of the twentieth-century prison to its present form.*

Silberman, Charles E. *Criminal Violence, Criminal Justice.* New York: Random House, 1978. *The first section of this book presents a fascinating account of the male offender.*

Sykes, Gresham M. *The Society of Captives.* Princeton, N.J.: Princeton University Press, 1971. *This analysis of life at the Trenton State Prison has become one of the most popular studies of the prison.*

Thomas, Piri. *Down These Mean Streets.* New York: Knopf, 1967. *A realistic description of the violence and exploitation of prison life.*

NOTES

1. Interviewed in April 1986.
2. Interviewed in June 1985.
3. U.S. Department of Justice, *Uniform Crime Reports* (Washington: Government Printing Office, 1989), pp. 178–79.
4. Bureau of Justice Statistics, *Prisoners in 1989* (Washington: U.S. Department of Justice, 1990), p. 7.
5. Allen J. Beck, *Recidivism of Prisoners Released in 1983* (Washington: Bureau of Justice Statistics, 1989), p. 1.
6. Ibid, pp. 1–2.
7. John Irwin, *Prisons in Turmoil* (Boston: Little Brown, 1980).
8. Ibid., p. 20.
9. Gresham Sykes, *Society of Captives* (Princeton, N.J.: Princeton University Press, 1958).
10. Ibid., pp. 64–108.
11. Ibid.
12. Adapted from Gresham M. Sykes and Sheldon L. Messinger, "The Inmate Social System." In Richard A. Cloward, et al., eds., *Theoretical Studies in the Social Organization of the Prison* (New York: Social Science Research Council, 1960), pp. 6–8.
13. Sykes, *Society of Captives,* Sykes and Messinger, "Inmate Social System."
14. Donald Clemmer, *The Prison Community* (New York: Holt, Rinehart & Winston, 1958), p. 299.
15. Ibid., pp. 299–300.
16. Irwin, *Prisons in Turmoil,* pp. 37, 40.
17. Michel Foucault, *Discipline and Punishment: The Birth of the Prison* (New York: Pantheon, 1977).
18. Irwin, *Prisons in Turmoil,* p. 75.
19. Ibid., pp. 76–77.
20. Stanton Wheeler, "Socialization in Correctional Communities." *American Sociological Review* 26, October 1961: 697–712.

21. Sykes, *Society of Captives.*
22. John Irwin and Donald R. Cressey, "Thieves, Convicts and the Inmate Culture." *Social Problem* 10, Fall 1962: 143.
23. Charles W. Thomas, "Prisonization or Resocialization: A Study of External Factors Associated with the Impact of Imprisonment." *Journal of Research in Crime and Delinquency* 10, January 1975: 13–21; Charles W. Thomas, "Toward a More Inclusive Model of the Inmate Contraculture." *Criminology* 8, November 1970: 251–262.
24. Gang leaders and members consistently make statements of this nature.
25. Lynne Goodstein, "Prisonization and the Transition to Community Life." *Journal of Research in Crime and Delinquency* 16, July 1979: 265–266.
26. James B. Jacobs, *Stateville: The Penitentiary in Mass Society* (Chicago: University of Chicago Press, 1977).
27. Ibid.
28. Ibid., p. 138.
29. G. M. Camp and C. G. Camp, *Prison Gangs: Their Extent, Nature and Impact on Prisons* (Washington: U.S. Department of Justice, 1985).
30. G. M. Camp and C. G. Camp, *The Correctional Yearbook* (South Salem, N.Y.: Criminal Justice Institute, 1987).
31. Reno Johnson developed the first half of this case study; Alfred Anderson, ex-offender, made many helpful observations about Fred's adjustment in prison.
32. See John Irwin, *The Felon* (Englewood Cliffs, N.J.: Prentice-Hall, 1970), for other adaptions to prison life.
33. Letter received from this inmate and quoted in Clemens Bartollas and Stuart J. Miller, *Correctional Administration: Theory and Practice* (New York: McGraw-Hill, 1978), p. 213.
34. Robert Johnson, *Hard Time: Understanding and Reforming the Prison* (Monterey, Calif.: Brooks/Cole, 1987), p. 56.
35. L. Empey, "Implications: A Game with No Winners." In A. J. Manocchio and J. Dunn, eds., *The Time Game: Two Views of a Prison* (Beverly Hills, Calif.: Sage, 1982), p. 251.
36. Ibid.
37. Ibid., pp. 86–173.
38. Thomas Meisenhelder, "An Exploratory Study of Exiting from Criminal Careers." *Criminology* 15, November 1977: 319–334.
39. Charles E. Silberman, *Criminal Justice, Criminal Violence* (New York: Random House, 1978), pp. 75–83.

PART SEVEN

Research and the Future

Chapter 19

Promise and Realities in Correctional Research

CHAPTER OUTLINE

Success in the management of industry, agriculture, education, and most governmental institutions in the United States depends on a partnership with research. Administrators in every field know that progress and often the very survival of their enterprises depend on the timely flow of reliable information. With modern computers functioning at full speed, unprecedented masses of information can be collected, analyzed for decision making, and stored for the study of trends. Administration in government and industry has benefited immensely from a revolution in our systems of collecting and analyzing information. For corrections, the revolution has made possible quantitative research projects that could never before have been attempted.

Efficient managers recognize that there is always room for improvement in their operations and that improvement is usually based on new ideas leading to the better performance of tasks and the profitable assumption of new tasks. For these reasons most large industrial corporations invest heavily in research and development. For generations the federal and state departments of agriculture conducted brilliant research to enable farmers to grow better and larger crops. Industrial concerns set aside large percentages of their revenues for research to improve products and increase productivity. The benefits have been many, and greatly admired throughout the world. American investment and application in research and development have been copied with enviable success in most modern industrial nations.

Not all managers are efficient. As we have seen in the preceding chapters, the history of correctional management has been studded with slovenly and lazy personalities, stubbornly resistant to change. These characteristics persist to the present day in some jurisdictions. The conviction that the old ways are the best ways prevails in too many high correctional places. It is encouraged by hardline pundits and public officials who see change in penology as so much soft-headed leniency toward criminals who deserve no improvement in their lot.

Like it or not, correctional officials have had to adjust to the requirements of research. Budget directors and appropriations committees in state legislatures disdain guesswork when estimates can be supported by information. Not only must corrections commissioners make room for the conduct of research, but they have also found themselves under pressure to make use of the not always welcome findings of the outsiders poking into the traditional ways of doing things.

In spite of those who want to retain the ways of the past, an increasing number of managers have discovered that research serves their interests as well as those of the budget analysts. Their cooperation with researchers has become almost enthusiastic. Most departments of correction now have well-established statistical units run by professional head counters. Their colleagues in management and administration have become insatiable consumers of the information produced.

Well-organized information of any kind will inspire thoughtful readers to ask "what if" questions. Such questions abound in correctional agencies. What if maximum custody were to be reserved for prisoners requiring maximum restraint, and all others were allowed cheaper accommodations and more freedom of movement? What if nonviolent offenders were kept under surveillance in the community instead of immured in prison cells? What if a concerted effort were to be made by management to require illiterate and semiliterate prisoners to attend classes until they were able to read and write at a level that would enable them to communicate and conduct business without difficulty?

The more we know about the realities of the enterprises in which we are engaged, the more we need to know, and the more possibilities we can see for doing our jobs better. New methods of organizing information and projecting future changes enable us to give tentative answers to these questions before new policies are adopted. As the tentative answers blossom into projects, the results can be tested with some rigor.

In this chapter we shall report on the slow and uncertain development of information capabilities in corrections. We shall dwell briefly on how research is done.

Our purpose is not to teach our readers to be researchers; that is an objective beyond the scope of this book. Rather, we hope to show the conditions that a professional requires to do his or her job, such as counting and classification, and why some of these conditions must, necessarily, inconvenience the routines of management. Finally, to prove our point, we shall offer examples of research that has changed corrections for the better.

The information revolution continues, and with it there is a revolution in research methods and opportunities. It is a continuing revolution; new techniques appear with bewildering frequency. Managers must be alert to innovations from which their agencies can benefit.

COUNTING

All correctional officials know that prisoners have to be counted every day, and, in some facilities, several times every 24 hours. Probationers and parolees for whom they are responsible must be accounted for at least every month. Escapes from prison and absences from supervision in the community are serious problems. The daily count of prisoners establishes whether all the convicts for whom the warden is responsible are present and accounted for. If the count does not clear, it is a signal that someone may have escaped. Determined efforts must be made to track down the convict and return him or her to custody. Likewise, though not so urgently, "missing" probationers and parolees must be located so that proceedings to decide on whether liberty should be revoked can begin. No one disputes these requirements.

The counting of clients also lays the groundwork for budget controls and research analysis of the effectiveness of the system in achieving its objectives. Budget analysts need to know how many mouths must be fed and how many bodies must be clothed. Researchers need a baseline of the prison population and its composition as to offense categories, the age groups of convicts, and other characteristics before they can plan their projects.

The count is only the beginning. Next in the process of control is the measurement of flow into and out of the system. This has always been essential information for budget control. It is especially important in the complex process of establishing trends in the increase, or, rarely in these times, the decrease of prison populations and supervision caseloads. We shall see that modern statistical techniques make it possible to predict future population totals with surprising accuracy. The usefulness of this achievement in preparing the correctional budget is obvious.

These are the easy counts. No one doubts that they must be done. But counts that attempt to gauge the prison climate are not so easy. An enlightened warden will need to know how many violent incidents take place during each month. But what is a violent incident, and what distinctions among them should be made? Obviously any assault that results in a fatality, whether of a staff member or of a prisoner, is the most serious type of violence. It is easy enough to decide that an assault that results in injuries requiring medical attention falls into a serious class. But what about an assault in which no one is injured, but only because the attacker was successfully restrained? How shall we distinguish that kind of incident from violence that looks serious but that the participants insist was only innocent horseplay? It's not impossible to draw these distinctions, but the individuals doing the counting must know what they are doing and why. Not only must the violence be classified by degrees of seriousness, but it is also useful to note where it happened: Trouble spots should be identified so that corrective measures can be taken.

In prisons where violence is frequent, there will often be weapons in use. They should be counted. What weapons were used? Where were they made? How many weapons were found in cell shakedowns? How many were found on prisoners in pat-downs or by metal detectors? Very few in the latter; not many prisoners are stupid enough to carry a shank through an electronic barrier, but that is hardly a valid reason for removing these devices.

For generations prison officials have been concerned with substance abuse. The manufacture of "pruno," or homemade booze, led to a cat-and-mouse game in which prisoners found ways to manufacture the stuff and store it while the captain and the custodial staff searched likely and unlikely places of concealment and often found it. It is agreed that pruno manufacture has to be stopped, but doing so is seldom the highest priority on the warden's agenda.

In the 1970s a much more serious concern began to preoccupy prison management: prisoners' use of various narcotic drugs. First it was marijuana, which made its way into prisons by all sorts of avenues. Marijuana was then followed by heroin, and most recently by cocaine. In many prisons the correction officials' database has had to be expanded to include information on the introduction, distribution, and use of illicit drugs. Today, the population has to be screened for persons with histories of drug use and addiction as well as for persons who have been known to be engaged in narcotics trafficking.

This kind of information must necessarily be incomplete. Felons don't always arrive at the prison gate with tags indicating whether they have a predilection for substance abuse. Usually, but not always, the presentence investigation accompanying the commitment papers will report whatever the police know about a convict's inclinations. It helps to know the likely people to suspect when contraband begins appearing. For researchers there are several paths of investigation open. What is the connection between drug use and trafficking and the incidence of various types of crime? What is the effectiveness of drug treatment programs in prison? What happens to drug users after their release on parole? To what extent can they be induced to accept clinical treatment for their addiction? Does intensive surveillance inhibit the parolee's return to substance abuse?

In some states, especially those with large inner-city populations consisting of minority groups, aggressive and violent gangs of young men and women create new and dangerous problems for law enforcement. Some of these gangs had their origins in prison, but most were formed on the disordered streets of urban slums. In prison and out, the traffic in narcotics has been a source of profit. The revenues from narcotics sales make possible the cohesion of prison "supergangs," of which we shall have more to say later in this chapter. The database must be expanded again to list the gangs represented in prison yards, their members, and the disciplinary incidents in which they have been involved.

These kinds of data are grist for the researcher who is trying to make sense out of the gang phenomenon. The individual gang members who can be identified may also be objects of study. The control of gangs in prison is a problem that is far from an effective solution, but the accumulation of information may lead to experimentation that will reduce the damage gangs inflict on the prison community.

All this information can be consolidated into a running index of the safety of the prison. Some administrators will see this sort of counting as needless fussing with figures. Apprehending the prisoner-thugs and deep-sixing them to "the Hole" should be enough. For more farsighted wardens, however, the study of continuities in violence, the circulation of dangerous contraband, and the formation of antisocial groups will allow the design and installation of preventive measures and the evaluation of their success.

That is by no means all the counting that should be done in a modern prison. Disciplinary infractions of all kinds, violent and nonviolent, must be counted and the disposition of the infractors recorded and tabulated. Prison education programs keep track of enrollment, attendance, course completion, dropouts, and failures. In a similar vein, prison industries count the number of prisoners employed, gauge their productivity and the wages paid, record employee turnover, and carry out the numerous measurements that any industrial operation must perform in order to know its prospects for profitability.

All these operations sound like low-level research far beneath the esoteric complexities of research in the natural sciences. Yet low-level research must go on even in the most difficult sciences if advances are to continue. Counting is essential for competent management, especially in times when money is scarce, as is almost always the case in correctional systems. Accurate and reliable counting is the foundation of serious research in any field. The single person or incident counted tells us little. The aggregation of similar persons and incidents tells us much about the effectiveness of operations at one particular point in time. When counts are systematically recorded over months and years, progress, regress, or static equilibrium can be inferred from an inspection of the trend lines. This is research, and it is of vital importance to the officials in charge and to the criminal justice system.

Before the advent of the computer, counting was a laborious undertaking, if it were to be done at all, requiring large staffs of statistical clerks. It was understandable that in many correctional systems a record of the daily count of prisoners was quite enough. With powerful computers available at comparatively modest cost, there is no excuse for not engaging in a comprehensive system of counting all the data we have mentioned and more.

The U.S. Bureau of Prisons began publishing an annual report of prison populations in 1950. The staff assigned to these reports was meager, and the reports were issued irregularly, usually with gaps for states that did not or could not submit summaries of prisoner numbers. The national census of prisoners was taken over by the National Criminal Justice Information and Statistical Service (NCJISS) in 1971. Federal grants-in-aid enabled states to modernize their counting procedures in accordance with uniform standards set by the NCJISS. Reliable and comprehensive data from all states and calculations of rates of incarceration, charts of past trends, and projections of future developments became available.

The NCJISS was given a less cumbersome title in 1978: the **Bureau of Justice Statistics** (BJS). As under its earlier name, the BJS publishes data on all phases of the criminal justice system in the United States from the sentencing of offenders, both adult and juvenile, to their final release from control.[1] To compile national data on prison populations, the BJS, in cooperation with the Bureau of the Census, publishes two reports every five to seven years: *The Survey of Inmates of Adult State Correctional Facilities* and the *Census of State Adult Correctional Facilities.*[2]

The counting process is complemented by the indispensable **rapsheets** collected by the Federal Bureau of Investigation (FBI), which include the arrests, judicial processing and disposition, and prison or jail receptions of each man or woman arrested for a felony or misdemeanor in the United States. The rapsheet is initiated with the first arrest and continues as long as the offender is known to criminal justice agencies—some rapsheets are many pages long. It is a basic document for correctional **classification** and is indispensable to many research projects. The information assembled is consolidated to produce the annual **Uniform Crime Reports** (UCR) published by the FBI.[3] This series has been published since 1930 with more than 16,000 agencies now participating.

Critics of the UCR argue that the agency's reliance on police reports seriously limits UCR's usefulness. Some police departments are simply not equipped to make accurate reports, others make honest mistakes, and it is at least possible that some do not tell the FBI all they know. (For several years the FBI has refused to include the data reported by the New York City police on the grounds that the statistics had for political reasons been deliberately falsified.) Further, many offenses are committed that are never reported to the police, or are reported but never cleared by an arrest. No one knows how much this "dark figure of crime" affects the official rates of crime and recidivism. Critics of the UCR are also concerned that the FBI definitions of the crimes to be reported will differ from local definitions, often resulting in distortions of the data.[4] Aware of these criticisms, the FBI is now engaged in a redesign of the UCR. It is expected that the full effect of the changes won't be known until the late 1990s.

As a needed complement to the UCR, the BJS and the Bureau of the Census have cooperated to produce the National Crime Survey, in which a sample consisting of 100,000 households across the nation is selected. Each member of the household is interviewed about his or her experiences, if any, with crime during the previous year. The results are published annually, providing a perspective on the prevalence of crime that amplifies the data of the UCR.[5]

CLASSIFICATION

The first cut at classification is easy. We have to know for what offenses prisoners are serving time. It's a simple matter for the prison records officer to compile from commitment documents a distribution of the convicts on hand by the principal offense for which each was convicted, and then to add the sentence of the court and the first eligible parole date. The determination of the status as to recidivism awaits the arrival of the rapsheet from the FBI. These data have administrative uses, but for researchers they are vitally important in distinguishing persistent offenders—"**career criminals**"—from mere dabblers in crime.

Something must be said about the rapsheet as a source of data. It is the only routine access we have to the individual offender's criminal career. That information may or may not be amplified in a presentence investigation report or by interviews at the time of reception. It is perfectly possible for an investigator to interview a significant number of offenders—especially if they are in custody—and obtain self-reported criminal histories. A wise researcher will cross-check the information obtained in this way with the official rapsheet. Sometimes memory will not have served the respondent well, and important events will have been honestly forgotten. Some offenders will embellish a history with fictitious offenses, and some will attempt to minimize their criminal histories. Often a self-reported criminal history will add to the list offenses that had been known to the police but not identified with the offender who reports them. The inadequacies of the rapsheet are well known and obvious to a regular user. The rapsheet remains the only routinely collected source of individual data on all offenders. It's all we have, and despite its limitations, it is much better than nothing at all.

The second cut will be the usual demographic data: age, race, county of commitment, marital status, occupation before arrest, claimed educational status, and so forth. Almost always the school achievement score will be lower than the last grade of school completed. At this point we begin to see what niche this fellow will fill, not only in the prison community but also, for example, in a study of prison adjustment or parole performance.

The third cut comes from the tests that will have been administered when the offender was received into the system. The IQ tests are not truly reliable instruments to administer to men and women who have just arrived in prison, many of them depressed, many of them unskilled at reading, and many quite unmotivated to do their best on the batteries of tests that are impersonally administered to the newly arrived "fish." Still, the results give a rough—very rough—idea of the intellectual capabilities of the new prisoner. It is another step in the classification process, another item for the researcher to take into account in future studies. We begin to be sure of the pigeonhole in which the new arrival belongs.

In most prison systems personality tests will also be administered. The results will provide a first look at the numbers of disturbed men and women within the

Reality of classification is often quite different from theory.

population. None of these tests make final diagnostic determinations, but they provide a basis for routing the troubled prisoner to professional help. Knowing how many there are will help determine the numbers of psychiatric personnel needed.

As Wright and colleagues have recently pointed out, classification that relates human and environmental variables can improve prisoner adjustment and prison management.[6] A number of classification instruments can make human–environmental matches in ecological terms and, therefore, permit staff to place inmates, especially crisis-prone inmates—in niches, or environments conducive to their needs.[7] These instruments provide "information on which inmates are in distress, what their needs are, what resources they see as available to satisfy needs, what settings best suit their needs, and how they fare in those settings."[8]

Another promising (and less ambitious and expensive) instrument is the Quay classification system. With this approach, inmates are classified into three groups: "heavies" who prey on others; "lights," who are anxious and dependent individuals who are readily victimized; and "moderates," who are able to "do their own time" and are willing to leave others alone. The Quay system offers the advantage of assigning inmates to housing and perhaps even program units that separate predator from prey.[9]

The assignment to functional units, used throughout the federal prison system and in several state systems, provides an opportunity to send inmates to units that differ according to inmate types, management styles, social norms, and programs. This decentralization approach to management has also helped produce "congenial units for tougher and more vulnerable inmates" and more "favorable climate ratings by inmates."[10]

The necessities of prison management call for the collection and classification of large amounts of information about convicts and their characteristics. This is convenient for the researcher, who must often work from the same information, organized in the same ways. For most research projects the raw administrative information found in the reports and files of the institution will be only the beginning of complexity. Usually he or she will need to amplify the information given, or make selections, or focus on a special class of prisoners, or obtain personal data by interviewing members of a class or classes. While the researcher can be a burden on prison personnel, whether the research to be done is needed or not by management, there are benefits to such work—first, something useful may be discovered, and second, all research has a beginning and an end.

PREDICTION

Criminal justice professionals yearn for a computerized crystal ball in which futures could be discerned. Judges and parole boards think they need a device with which they can predict with confidence which offenders would be dangerous to the public if and when they are released from custody. All they have now are tables that will predict with accuracy above 50 percent, but nowhere near the infallibility required for just sentencing policy. Later in this chapter we shall discuss at some length the **Selective Incapacitation** strategy, which uses **predictive methods** to identify repetitiously violent muggers and burglars for special attention by the courts. There is no chance that improvement approaching 100 percent accuracy will ever be achieved.

The Need for Prediction

Prison officials would like a device that would define the risk of escape for convicts. They will never get it: There is no statistical procedure for the reliable prediction of rare events. For judgments of dangerousness and escape risks, decision makers have to rely on examined experience, as they always have in the past. An offender who has committed more than one violent crime in the past is more dangerous than one who has never committed such a crime or one who has committed only one. The law accepts the assumptions implicit in these commonsense principles. Judges may impose longer sentences on violent repeaters, and in many jurisdictions more time is mandated by the penal code. Fairly or unfairly, correctional officials assume that young auto thieves are prime escape risks and necessary precautions are undertaken on that account.

Some progress has been made in the prediction of **recidivism** and the forecast of future prison population. These are the two crystal balls that statisticians have provided to corrections. There is reason to believe that they are the only reliable predictive devices we will ever have. Both have been developed from the analysis of large masses of data, and both can be adjusted with experience.

Base Expectancies

Drawing on the early work of Hermann Mannheim and Leslie T. Wilkins, published in 1964, on predicting the behavior of Borstal lads released on license,[11] a team of California researchers created a predictive scheme designated as the **base expectancy** system. Wilkins was brought from England to California to advise on the development of the system. Douglas Grant and Don Gottfredson, staff members of the new research division of the California Department of Corrections, led the team working on this innovation. By 1958 it was off and running, somewhat to the bewilderment of the Adult Authority, as the parole board was then designated in California. The members of the board were never quite sure what to do with the system, to which they gave a muted welcome at best.

The base expectancy system rested on the selection of **variables** found to be associated with success or failure on parole. These variables were identified from the prison and parole records of a large sample of paroled convicts. They included such items as a history of alcoholism and of narcotics use, length of time on the last job before commitment, prior convictions, marital status, and disciplinary record while in prison. Points were assigned to these variables in accordance with the degree to which they are found to be associated with success or failure. The sum of the points found in individual case records determined whether success or failure was to be expected. The highest base expectancy score would indicate virtually certain success; the lowest would predict an almost certain failure. In the middle would be the 60–40, 40–60, and the 50–50 risks.

The system was complex to develop but simple to administer, requiring only a clerical process to search case records and add up the points. Unfortunately, the high-scoring prisoners were obviously good risks, needing no statistical procedures for identification, and the same was true of those with low base expectancy scores. The majority of prisoners would fall into the middle range, leaving the decision maker with not much guidance for judgment.

For researchers, the base expectancy methods have provided a convenient classification of offenders by which treatment procedures can be evaluated. Does treatment X affect favorably the behavior or the recidivism of middle base expectancy offenders? Does treatment Y have anything to offer the low base expectancy offender? We know that high base expectancy offenders are probable successes after release, so they can be excluded from some evaluation procedures.

Sentencing authorities have done little with parole prediction methods in recent years, but the variables used in scoring base expectancies have been transferred for use as "salient factors" in the development of parole guidelines.[12] These instruments are very much alive, as we discussed in Chapter 6.

Selective Incapacitation

One important outgrowth of the prediction research was a system proposed by Peter Greenwood of the Rand Corporation, a private research conglomerate undertaking studies of public policy.[13] Greenwood noted that previous Rand research, particularly surveys of prisoners in California, Michigan, and Texas, had found that a relatively small number of offenders were responsible for a very large number of serious crimes. These surveys had collected self-report questionnaires from 2100 male prison and jail inmates. Greenwood reasoned that with prediction methods it should be possible to identify the "high-rate" robbers and burglars and provide for their long-term incarceration. Adapting the research strategies of Wilkins and Gottfredson, he produced a system for tagging them early in their careers.

A by-product of the system would be the identification of offenders guilty of the same crimes but who were not likely to go on to "high-rate" offending.[14] These offenders might receive shorter sentences and be sent back to the community, thereby freeing cell space for the protracted detention of the high-level types. This scale identified 43.4 percent of the tested sample as high rate, with an average offense rate of 30.8 robberies per year. Finally, Greenwood calculated that for California robbers a selective incapacitation strategy that "reduced terms for low- and medium-rate robbers while increasing terms for high-rate robbers could achieve a 15 percent reduction in the robbery rate, with only 95 percent of the current incarcerated population level for robbery."[15]

To identify the high-level offender, Greenwood chose seven variables:

1. Prior conviction for robbery.
2. Incarcerated more than 50 percent of two years preceding current commitment.
3. Conviction prior to sixteenth birthday.
4. Commitment to state juvenile authority.
5. Use of hard drugs in two years preceding current commitment.
6. Use of hard drugs as a juvenile.
7. Employed less than 50 percent of preceding two years (excluding time incarcerated).[16]

Positive scores on four or more of these items would identify a convict as a high-rate offender. Two or three positives would indicate a medium-rate offender, and those with one positive or none would be low rate.

Greenwood's proposal was favorably received by criminal justice conservatives. The blend of economy in the use of prison space with severity toward the truly repetitive offenders had an irresistible appeal for utilitarians who had given up on reformation of the criminal but devoutly believed that deterrence and incapacitation were realistic avenues to the reduction of crime.

Opposition to selective incapacitation was based on two ethical considerations. First, advocates of the Justice Model of sentencing argued that offenders should be punished by like sentences for like offenses. To add personal and criminal history, including crimes never brought to trial, into the balance in fixing a mugger's sentence is to consider factors not relevant to the crime itself. Doing so amounts to sentencing the high-rate offenders on the supposition that they may have committed crimes for which they have never been apprehended, tried, and found guilty. Selective incapacitation also calls for sentencing offenders for future crimes they are predicted to commit.

To these arguments, selective incapacitation advocates respond that in sentencing repetitively violent offenders judges and parole boards routinely use these considerations in decisions to increase terms to be imposed on persons they view as particularly dangerous. Further, most states had provisions in their penal codes allowing for prior offenses to be pled and proven by prosecutors to increase sentences.

The second objection had to do with **false positives**—those who are predicted to commit crime but do not. The Greenwood scale was admittedly not infallible, and it was certain that some offenders who were not in fact high-rate robbers would, due to a false positive, be selected for prolonged incapacitation. Greenwood's data indicated that these false positives might affect as much as 4 percent of the robber population, and 3 percent would be labeled low rate but would actually be high rate.[17] His Rand colleagues, Jan Chaiken and Marcia Chaiken, who conducted the most massive of the self-report surveys, showed that low-rate robbers were identified at a false negative rate of about 3 percent per street year—that is, they committed 10 or more robberies. At the high-rate end of this spectrum Chaiken and Chaiken found that 30 percent of those so identified committed no robberies per street year.[18]

That objection can be met by the reasoning that at least the selective incapacitation process is objective, whereas the judge and/or parole board member will arrive at sentencing decisions based on subjective criteria, which is at least equally faulty.

The debate has been inconclusive, but the selective incapacitation model has never been incorporated into a penal code.[19] The extent to which it may be used informally by police and district attorneys in choosing cases for priority in prosecution is not known. Greenwood's Selective Incapacitation proposal remains an impressive innovation based on laborious research, but yet to be tested in formal application.

Population Projections

The prediction of future prison populations is crucial for research staff. The preparation of a realistic budget for corrections and the planning of personnel recruitment and new facilities depend on reliable estimates of the population trends in years to come. To the newcomer to prison statistics it might seem that a trend line could be drawn for the prison population for the five years previous to the current year and extended for another five years. If the rate of incarceration, the number of prisoners per 100,000 population is stable, it might be assumed that this trend line would predict populations for the next five or more years. Wouldn't that be all that a budget analyst would require?

In fact it wouldn't. Experience demonstrates that prediction is not that simple. Changes in legislation may dramatically increase—or rarely, decrease—the population level predicted by the trendline. Alert statisticians will keep track of proposed changes in sentencing statutes and inform the legislature of the consequences for prison population changes. Other statistical trends to be factored into the predictions include information about changes in arrest rates in high-crime jurisdictions, what judges are doing when it comes to sentencing offenders, what parole boards are doing in setting release dates, and the rates of probation and parole revocation. A large and complex order, but competent statisticians have been able to make these computations with enough accuracy to keep surprise to a minimum.

It is especially difficult to predict criminal behavior. The difficulty is compounded by the constitutional requirement of due process of the law and by the imperfections of the predictive methods so far conceived.

THE DANGEROUS OFFENDER

Who Is Dangerous?

Almost everyone agrees that **dangerous offenders** should be incarcerated for at least as long as they are dangerous to the public. Immediately difficulties arise in making policy. What is meant by dangerous? How may a dangerous offender be identified? For how long a stretch of his or her life should such an offender be locked up?

Some men and women falling into this category serve life sentences without possibility of parole. Most sentences for violent crimes are for much shorter terms, even though many people believe that no sentence is too long for persons disposed to violence. Law and policy depend on a poorly defined concept and public anger. Society's experience with the actual careers of violent offenders has seldom been taken into account.

Approaches to Answers

In an effort to bring facts to bear on the concept, a team led by Simon Dinitz and John Conrad of the Academy for Contemporary Problems of Columbus, Ohio, undertook three lines of research.

The Career of the Violent Juvenile Offender This study was published under the title, *The Violent Few.*[20] Two questions were posed:

1. What are the social and criminal characteristics of juveniles who are arrested for violent crimes?
2. What relationship do these characteristics bear to identifiable violent career patterns?

To answer these questions, a **cohort** was created comprising all the boys and girls born during the years 1956 to 1960 who had been arrested at least once by the

Columbus police for a violent offense before 1978, the year when the study began.[21] There were 1222 individuals in the cohort, of whom 1031 were boys, and 191 were girls. Although blacks made up only 12.5 percent of the Columbus population, their share of the cohort was 54.2 percent.

The cohort members had been arrested for a total of 4481 occasions on charges ranging from homicide to curfew violations. There were 1469 violent offenses. In the cohort of 1222 there were 378 (30.9 percent) defined as **chronic offenders,** persons who had been arrested five or more times.

Forty-two committed two or more offenses in which serious harm was inflicted or threatened. Their careers were followed into adulthood (up to age 28 for the oldest). All had been incarcerated at least once while still juveniles. As adults only 21 had been arrested for serious, violent offenses. As of the conclusion of the study, 17 were doing time in a state prison.

It is impractical to summarize all the findings of this study. For the student of corrections, the significant conclusion was that although there had been early signals that much was wrong with most of the young people in the cohort before they came to the attention of the police, preventive services in the schools or social agencies had not reached them successfully. When they arrived in the juvenile court, the choice open to the judge was limited to commitment to the Ohio Youth Commission or placement on probation, a status that would ordinarily allow only nominal contact with helping services. The statistics suggested that for the youths subjected to this choice, neither disposition helped, and it was probable that both were damaging.

Dangerous Careers In a second study, the project undertook to chart the careers of adult male violent offenders.[22] The research design was unusual. Random samples of all males arrested for violent crimes during the period 1920–1976 were drawn. There were 967 men in the sample of persons charged with murder, assault, or rape, and 624 charged with armed robbery, making a total study group of 1591. The samples were then divided into age groups: persons born before 1920, of whom there were 234; persons born between 1920 and 1939, of whom there were 729; and persons born after 1939, of whom there were 630. Complete arrest histories were obtained from the Federal Bureau of Investigation, providing lists of arrests throughout the country. It was possible to determine the number and the **spacing of arrests** for violent and nonviolent offenses for each man in the study. The object was to determine the **persistence** of each individual's criminal activity and the time of his **desistance.** The study of spacing (the time elapsed between arrests, not counting time in confinement) enabled a determination of the **velocity of criminal recidivism.**

There were six principal findings:

1. Of the total of 1591 men, 420 (26.7 percent) committed only one offense, necessarily violent. The rest—1171 (73.3 percent)— were recidivists, committing both violent and nonviolent offenses. There was no indication that violent careerists specialized in violence or any other category of offense.
2. The chance that a recidivist will commit a second violent crime is about 50 percent. But the probability that he will commit another offense is about 80 percent.
3. So far as it could be determined from the accumulated data, the criminal justice system does not appear to deter recidivist violent offenders. The fact

that slightly more than a quarter of the sample committed one and only one offense suggested that if deterrence has any effect it is at the outset of a criminal career.

4. None of the available statistical variables, alone or in combination, were successful predictors of court dispositions. This suggested that discretion exercised by prosecutors and courts was wide and flexible.
5. High velocity at the start of a criminal career portends a long succession of arrests. A rapid increase in velocity at any point in an arrest history indicates increased seriousness as well as increased frequency of violations.
6. Criminal careers punctuated by violent episodes often continue past age 40. Final desistance from a criminal career cannot be assumed to occur in the mid-thirties.

The significance of these findings for correctional systems is the strong indication that recidivist violent offenders require prolonged supervision—either incarceration or intensive surveillance, and usually both.

The Effectiveness of Incapacitation In the third study, the project tested the assumption that if corrections cannot reliably deter or rehabilitate offenders, at least by incapacitating those who are dangerous, the rate of violent crime can be reduced.[23] In an unusual research design, the violent offenses reported to the Columbus police in 1973 were studied. There were 2892 homicides, assaults, rapes, and robberies. Of this number, 638 were **"cleared" by arrest**. The arrest histories of all these individuals were collected. The question addressed was: If at the time of the last felony arrest for any offense previous to the violent arrest of 1973 a five-year sentence had been imposed, how many of the violent crimes of 1973 would have been prevented? (In this study it was stipulated that *all* arrests would have resulted in a conviction in court.)

The answer was discouraging. By a complex analysis of the data and distributing, with liberal but not unreasonable assumptions, some of the uncleared crimes reported in 1973 to those arrested five years before, a maximum figure of crimes prevented was about 34 percent.[24]

The cost of this impractical and unjust sentencing policy would be enormous. Applied to the state of Ohio in 1973, the prison population would have increased from about 9000 to 33,000. Those were years of relatively moderate crime rates as compared to the 1980s and 1990s.

A similar study conducted in Denver, Colorado, by the Rand Corporation, arrived at similar results.[25] A sentencing policy similar to the one assumed in the Columbus hypothesis arrived at a theoretical reduction of violent crime of about 31 percent at the cost of increasing the Colorado prison population by about 450 percent.

The significance of these findings brings out the limits of crime reduction that can be expected from the controls of the criminal justice system. No one will argue that violent offenders should not be arrested, prosecuted, convicted, and incarcerated. Even if the sentences are long, violent crime reduction will be moderate. The intractability of the rates of violent crime for the last decade testify to the validity of this conclusion.

PROGRAM EVALUATION

Intensive parole and **intensive probation** have been two of the most significant innovations in corrections.

Intensive Parole: Ten Years of Experimentation and an Evaluation

During the decades following World War II, correctional agencies have engaged in hundreds of innovative programs. All of them have cost money, and some have been very costly. Public officials, especially those in charge of budgets, have great concern about how effective these projects have been in the achievement of their stated goals. Most of the innovations have been intended to reduce the recidivism of offenders released from custody. Has recidivism in fact been reduced by these adventures in corrections? Were the costs of corrections discernibly affected? These questions have spurred social scientists into action. It became routine for fiscal guardians to require an evaluation of new programs that were proposed and authorized. The glowing claims made for innovations were routinely deflated, though sometimes modest successes were reported.

The early evaluations were crude. The standard criterion was the reduction of recidivism for an undifferentiated experimental group of released prisoners—a task not unlike evaluating aspirin for its effect on headaches arising from all possible causes, whether nervous tension or brain tumors. Possible favorable effects for some were masked by ill effects or no effects on others. Some programs were subjected to evaluation by recidivism reduction when there was no theoretical or commonsense reason to believe that they could have the slightest effect on a convict's behavior after release from prison.[26] Later program evaluations have become more discriminating. A general loss of interest in rehabilitation programs has reduced the number of evaluations addressed to attempts to change antisocial behavior.

The 1950s saw an increase in prison populations that alarmed correctional officials and those state policymakers responsible for maintaining services while at the same time keeping the budget in balance. Prison overcrowding had led to expensive new construction; as soon as new prisons were built they became overcrowded and more construction would be required. In California the rapidly expanding general population had been accompanied by an equally rapid expansion of the prison population.

A solution was proposed: Prison populations could be reduced by increasing the use of parole. Convicts would be paroled three to six months earlier than their normal release dates. There was some apprehension about the risks of such a departure from established paroling policy; it was thought that early release of so many convicts might jeopardize public safety.

It was generally agreed that there was little reason to believe that an early release policy would be effective, given the large size of parole caseloads. Each parole officer was expected to supervise 90 or more parolees. It was not reasonable to suppose that he or she could be in significant contact with all these parolees or that work could be organized so that sufficient contact could be maintained with those who most needed attention, especially those who had been released in advance of their expected time.[27] Merely increasing the number of parole officers would keep surveillance of parolees at the prevailing low level of efficiency, while the parolee population would be increased by numbers of men who had not had the benefit of a normal prison term.

It was decided to amplify the experiment of reduced prison time by creating an experimental unit in the parole division consisting of 14–15-man caseloads. If this were to be an experiment, how would the outcome be determined? It was decided that a real experiment should be governed by the "classic" **research design,** modeled, so far as possible, after successful medical tests of new drugs and vaccines. That called for the creation of a **control group** of parolees. A pool of eligible parolees would be established from which random assignments would be made to the experimental caseloads, while the remainder, the control group, would be placed in the normal 90-man caseloads. Excluded from the eligible pool were narcotic addicts, chronic alcoholics, physically incapacitated men, non–English speakers, men with histories of psychosis, mentally retarded prisoners, those paroled out of state or to remote areas where frequent contact was impracticable, and those paroled to custody or out of state.

Each of the 14 district offices in the parole division would assign one officer to the experimental operation. A second element of the experiment was the assessment of the effect of advancing parole release. How would the extra months of freedom affect the recidivism rates? The Adult Authority kept its prerogative in making decisions about parole advancement, and these decisions were duly recorded. The parole staff distributed advance and regular releases as equitably as possible between the experimental and control groups.

The research design, such as it was, began with two **hypotheses:**

> H_1: Prisoners released on parole to reduce caseloads for periods of three months, followed by transfer to regular supervision will commit significantly fewer violations of parole than those in the 90-man, regular caseloads.
>
> H_2: Prisoners whose parole release has been advanced 3–6 months will not commit significantly more violations of parole than those whose parole was not advanced.

In the language of experimental science, the **independent variable** in H_1 was the assignment for three months to a 15-man caseload, followed by transfer to a "normal" 90-man unit. The **dependent variable** was recidivism, and measurement of the dependent variable would determine the success of the experiment. In H_2 the independent variable was the advanced release date, and recidivism was the dependent variable.

This was the Special Intensive Parole Unit (SIPU) project, an experiment that went through four different phases, lasting from 1954 through 1964. The size of the experimental caseloads was increased, and the time in these reduced caseloads was increased in each phase. In Phase IV the research design provided for six 15-man caseloads, six 30-man caseloads, and three 70-man caseloads, with time in caseloads varying between 1 and 2.5 years. Other complexities were introduced as variables to be measured: base expectancy scores, maturity level as scored by tests, and type of supervision (i.e., emphasis on surveillance for low maturity parolees and emphasis on casework service for those rated as high maturity). The overall results showed no significant differences in returns to prison or technical violations of parole among the three caseload sizes or the varying kinds of parole supervision.[28]

As to H_2, where the independent variable was the advance of parole for periods of three or more months, the outcome attracted less attention, but it was clear that, regardless of the size of the caseload to which they were assigned, those whose parole was advanced got into no more trouble than those who were not allowed this act of grace. The Adult Authority made the advance a permanent policy change, but no thought was given to a further test of the limit to the point at which advancement might increase recidivism.

With hindsight, several defects in the original concept and the research design can be identified. Some parole officers assigned to SIPU were genial and helpful, and saw their primary function as service based on a relationship of confidence. Others assigned so much priority to surveillance that they were unable to form such a relationship. Some were working in communities with high crime rates; others were assigned to caseloads located in more favorable districts. There was no special training or supervision to encourage a standard of treatment. The possibility that different supervision styles might result in different effects on recidivism was not studied until the last phase of SIPU, and then inconclusively. The independent variable of small caseloads was so confounded with differences in parole practice as to be incoherent.

The logic underlying H_1 was loose. Nobody constructed a theory of parole more complex than the notion that somehow men assigned for a period of time to small caseloads would be more likely to abstain from crime than those who enjoyed the freedom from control allowed in the normal 90-man caseload.

Flimsy ground for a rigorous test, but the "classical" research design was applied with commendable rigor. The outcome suggested that whatever parole may be and however it is administered, it makes little difference in the ability of released prisoners to survive in the community. Some make good adjustments, some squeak through without serious encounters with law enforcement, and some run into familiar opportunities leading to all-too-familiar trouble. The outcome of SIPU and similar experiments showed that the influence of parole is marginal at best. The reduction of time served before release on parole will save taxpayers some money, but not enough to create a demand for the systematic reduction of time in prison.

Intensive Probation: An Acceptable Alternative to Incarceration

Years later, the 1980s became another decade in which prison populations rose alarmingly. Many states invested heavily in new prisons to accommodate the unprecedented growth of prison populations. The reasons for this expansion need not detain us here. We will consider an innovative expedient—**intensive supervision programs** (ISP)—to reduce prison commitments that was adopted in several states unwilling or unable to invest millions of dollars in prison construction. Two such programs have been subjected to serious evaluation.

The first state to try ISP was Georgia, under the designation Intensive Probation Supervision (IPS). The year was 1982. The model created was a far cry from the routine, almost nominal probation still characteristic of so many jurisdictions. Eligibility was limited to men and women who had been convicted of a nonviolent offense and sentenced to prison. Before their removal to prison, their presentence investigations would be reviewed by the headquarters staff of the Department of Corrections. When in the judgment of the reviewer, there was some basis for belief that the convicted felon might respond favorably to intensive supervision, he or she was offered the choice of IPS or commitment to prison.

The IPS offer was almost always accepted. To most convicted felons, anything seemed better than a sojourn in one of Georgia's overcrowded prisons. The reality that then confronted the prospective IPS client was daunting. First, the offender and the probation officer would prepare a detailed plan for the term of probation, including residence, employment, community service, and other activities that might be indicated, such as drug treatment or mandatory attendance at Alcoholics Anonymous meetings. If restitution to a victim was required, the plan would show how and when payment would be made. Such a plan is frequently called for in ordinary probation but not necessarily carried out. IPS provides a credible structure for compliance. The court would then have to be convinced that with IPS the probation plan was realistic and that the probationer would make a serious effort to carry it out. If the court agreed to the plan, the standard requirements of IPS were as intrusive as ingenuity could devise:

- Five face-to-face contacts with an IPS officer each week, at least two of which will be in the client's home at night.
- Full-time employment.
- Eight hours a week of community service. If the probationer is between jobs this requirement is increased to 20 hours.
- Restitution payments must be kept up to date.
- An 8:00 P.M. curfew unless the probationer is working a night shift. Curfews to be randomly checked twice a month.
- All probationers to be listed with local police, who are asked to maintain surveillance.
- IPS personnel to make weekly checks of local arrest records to make sure that clients are not in violation of the terms of their probation contract.
- A monthly fee of $10 to $50, depending on ability to pay.[29]

To carry out the supervision of probationers assigned to this regime, 25-person caseloads were established, to each of which a probation officer and a surveillance officer were assigned. (Probation officers volunteering for the assignment were paid one step higher on the civil service scale than those carrying the ordinary caseloads.) The surveillance officers were former police or correctional officers. Later in the IPS development some caseloads were expanded to 40, and the supervisory team consisted of a probation officer and two surveillance officers. Implementation has been cautious, step by step, with much preparatory work in familiarizing judges, police, and the media with the program's objectives, eligibility rules, and general requirements.

Does this program work? From the first, the data have been organized to facilitate evaluation. There were and still are three principal questions to answer:

- Is recidivism lower than with regular probation and with prison releases?
- Is the state's prison population reduced?
- How much money does the program save the taxpayers?

To answer the first question, the evaluation established three groups for comparison. The program participants were matched with prison release cohorts and a cohort of high-risk probationers for age, race, sex, type of crime, risk score, and need score. These groups were tracked for 18 months for rearrests, reconvictions, and return to prison.[30]

As to recidivism reduction, the evaluator's data showed that probation for 16 percent of the IPS group was revoked. They were transferred to prison during the

18-month tracking period (1983–85), compared with 17 percent of the prison release cohort and 12 percent of the regular probation cohort. In 1989 a five-year followup showed that 36 percent of the IPS people had been sentenced to prison, compared to 42 percent of the prison releases.[31] These findings seem encouraging, but their interpretation is a matter of controversy, as we shall see.

The Georgia evaluation claimed a reduction in prison population by finding that whereas in 1982, 37 percent of all convicted felons were committed to prison, in 1985 only 27 percent were committed. Comparing IPS costs with prison costs, it was claimed that IPS saved about $6000 for each offender kept out of prison.

All these findings are encouraging to those who hope to reduce the use of incarceration in the punishment of offenders. But all are open to serious challenge. In a critique of the evaluation, Michael Tonry argues that it is most uncertain that the offenders committed to IPS would really have gone to prison had the IPS option not been available.[32] Although all IPS commitments were convicted felons, there was no way to show that they would really have been sent to prison if there had been no IPS. Tonry suspects that many judges handed down a prison sentence in the reasonable expectation that the offender so sentenced would be found eligible for IPS.

As for the claimed savings, the comparisons between IPS and prison are based on the per capita cost of the entire prison population. Per capita incarceration costs are calculated by dividing the cost of prison maintenance by the average daily population. In Georgia this calculation results in figures ranging from $28 to $73 a day, depending on the security level of the prison. The prisons range in population from about 300 to about 1800. The diversion of fewer than 300 saves only the cost of maintaining a single prisoner multiplied by the number diverted. The single-prisoner cost would amount to around $8 a day at the most.

The recidivism reduction is also questioned. The stringent requirements that IPS clients must observe cause a larger number of revocations that would not be imposed on regular probationers. This results in many "technical" violations that required his or her return to confinement, which would not have occurred had the IPS probationer been assigned to normal probation.

Most of Tonry's reservations about the Georgia program apply to the similar Intensive Supervision Program (ISP) service in New Jersey. The difference between the two programs is simple but not crucial. Georgia IPS clients are diverted from prison after conviction but before actual confinement. New Jersey ISP clients must serve at least three or four months in prison before they become eligible. About 500 clients are in the program at any one time. The preassignment review process is cumbersome and results in the rejection of about 7 percent of the cases recommended for ISP. One commentator has remarked that the screening "process can best be described as a program to remove from prison those who should not have been there at all."[33]

Although Georgia is experimenting with electronic bracelets to improve surveillance, New Jersey has gone farther with high-tech gadgetry. To reinforce the face-to-face surveillance, a programmed automatic telephone calling system summons participants randomly; participants are required to respond verbally. Their replies are recorded for review by ISP officers. The electronic bracelet is a second requirement for new participants and program violators. When the automatic telephone system calls, the participant must place his wrist bracelet in contact with a modem that transmits a code to a computer. Failure to make contact with the modem activates a nonresponse code. Other high-tech augmentations of surveillance are under test. The reactions of participants to all this quasi-Orwellian control have so far not been recorded.

The outcome was studied and reported by the Institute of Criminological Research of Rutgers University.[34] The special requirements imposed on participants were carried out with commendable fidelity. The recidivism experience was favorable to ISP. Between December 1985 and December 1988, 554 individuals had been assigned to ISP. These men and women were compared with 500 who were convicted and served ordinary terms of imprisonment and then served ordinary terms of parole. Of these 500, 132 were identified whose criminal histories and sociodemographic characteristics closely matched those of the ISP group. It was found that 12 percent of the ISP group had been arrested and convicted for a new offense at the end of two years, compared with 23 percent of the control group. The dollar savings were computed on a comparison of time served in prison plus time served on ISP with time served in prison and on parole by those in the control group. The average cost for the ISP group was $13,000, whereas for those serving ordinary sentences, the cost was $20,000 to $21,000. The ISP participants averaged incomes of $10,000 per year, compared with about $5000 for the convicts serving ordinary terms.

If there were no expectations of change or enlargement, the criticisms of these programs might raise some questions as to the wisdom of persisting with them. However, these are early times for ISP. With the general public heavily influenced by a crime rate that keeps rising in spite of all efforts to control it, the implementation of ISP has been cautious. One or two headline crimes committed by ISP probationers might well sink the program.

It would be difficult to find a prison system that is not confining considerable numbers of nonviolent offenders for whom a nonincarcerative sanction would have been more appropriate. It was an achievement to develop a program that kept these relatively harmless individuals out of prison without appearing to allow them undue leniency. For years these prisoners have been assigned as "trusties" or to minimum custody facilities. They have enlarged prison populations without thereby enhancing public safety.

At the same time, judges everywhere have been confronted with an unpleasant sentencing choice between a needlessly destructive prison sentence or assignment to nominal probation.[35] It is not at all difficult to understand the general approbation that ISP has received from the trial judiciary. Finally, the experience with ISP over the seven or eight years that it has been in existence will give both practitioners and the public confidence that it is a safe alternative to incarceration, worthy of extension to reduce the economic and social burdens of a constantly expanding prison system.

CONCLUSIONS

Research in corrections has taken many forms. As in any science, the phenomena have first to be identified and, as far as possible, quantified. Classification is the standard next step in the scientific method, and it is convenient that the necessities of correctional administration require the classification process. A primary criterion of the success of an endeavor in any science, natural or social, is the power to predict. Criminologists have had mixed success with predicting the behavior of offenders.

As in most sciences, experimentation to discover new controls of phenomena has been undertaken in correctional research. We have seen that some experiments have met with modest success, but no breakthroughs to new methods or new controls have been achieved.

The researcher's work is never done. Offenders must be counted and classified. Risks must be assessed. Programs must be evaluated, and by more accurate criteria than those we have described in this chapter. There is much more to be learned about the prison community and how the damage that incarceration does can be safely minimized without compromising public safety and security.[36]

The realities of today's prisons are grim. The promise of social science is modest. Prisons being what they are, they can never be perfected. But with understanding they will become safer and less destructive to the men and women in them. That understanding is the promise of research.

KEY TERMS

base expectancy

Bureau of Justice Statistics

career criminals

chronic offenders

classification

cleared by arrest

cohort

control group

dangerous offenders

dependent variable

desistance

false positives

hypotheses

independent variables

intensive parole

intensive probation

intensive supervision programs

persistence

predictive methods

rapsheets

recidivism

research design

Selective Incapacitation

spacing of arrests

Uniform Crime Reports

variables

velocity of criminal recidivism

DISCUSSION TOPICS

19.1 You are the warden of the only prison in your state. The Commissioner of Corrections requests that you submit with your budget for the next year, the total number of prisoners in your prison classified by age, race, and sex, and also by the length of the terms they are to serve. This is a heavy burden on your overworked staff. Should you protest or comply without complaint? Why?

19.2 As the warden of an old and not-well-maintained prison you are uneasy about the danger of prisoner escapes. You require the captain to identify the serious escape risks. What instructions on methods should you give him?

19.3 The state legislature has enacted a law providing for Selective Incapacitation. To carry it out, what will be your responsibilities as a warden?

19.4 You have been promoted to the office of Commissioner of Corrections. The governor, deeply concerned about the overcrowding in the prison, asks you for your opinion about Intensive Supervision Programs and whether they should be installed in the statewide system. Relying on research you have read, give your candid opinions, pro and con.

19.5 The new warden of the state prison reports to you that there are signs of ethnic gangs forming, and asks if a study could be done on measures to counteract their influence. This seems like a good idea to you, but what steps should he take to make such a study feasible?

Annotated References

Camp, George, and Camille Camp. *Corrections Yearbook.* South Salem, New York: Criminal Justice Institute. *Issued annually, this compendium of information organizes the current national data on corrections efficiently and economically.*

Conrad, John P. *The Dangerous and the Endangered.* Lexington, Mass.: Lexington Books, 1985. *A summary of the findings of the Dangerous Offender Project, with commentary on their significance.*

Goodstein, Lynne, and Doris Layton McKenzie, eds. *The American Prison: Issues in Research and Policy.* New York: Plenum, 1989. *A comprehensive review of the state of the art in correctional research and perspectives on future research.*

Gottfredson, Don M., Leslie T. Wilkins, and Peter B. Hoffman. *Guidelines for Parole and Sentencing.* Lexington, Mass.: Lexington Books, 1978. *The first cookbook on the preparation of sentencing guidelines. Technical, but an important landmark in the sentencing guidelines movement.*

Greenwood, Peter W., with Alan Abrahamse. *Selective Incapacitation.* Santa Monica, Cal.: Rand, 1982. *A highly controversial application of prediction research. Well worth study for a consideration of not only its validity but of its ethical status.*

Kassebaum, Gene, David Ward, and Daniel Wilner. *Prison Treatment and Parole Survival.* New York: Wiley, 1971. *A meticulous evaluation of group counseling in California prisons. Important not for its conclusions about the effectiveness of the program but rather for its demonstration of evaluation methodology.*

Petersilia, Joan, Peter W. Greenwood, and Marvin Lavin. *Criminal Careers of Habitual Felons.* Santa Monica, Calif.: Rand, 1977. *An excellent sourcebook on this important topic, with a full exposition of the methodology of collecting and organizing information.*

Petersilia, Joan, Susan Turner, and Joyce Peterson. *Prison versus Probation in California.* Santa Monica, Calif.: Rand, 1986. *An unsparing study of intensive probation in selected California counties, with a consideration of the implications for future implementation.*

NOTES

1. Students should also be familiar with the *Sourcebook of Criminal Justice Statistics,* edited by the Michael Hindelang Criminal Justice Center of the State University of New York at Albany and issued annually by the BJS. It covers the entire array of offenses and offenders, from traffic violations to homicides.
2. For a full account of these publications, see Phyllis Jo Baunach, "State Prisons and Inmates: The Census and Survey." In Doris L. MacKenzie, Phyllis Jo Baunach, and Roy R. Roberg, eds., *Measuring Crime: Long Range Efforts* (Albany: State University of New York Press, 1990), pp. 119–141. For a convenient reference to the essential data on population and expenditures of state and federal prison systems, see the *Corrections Yearbook,* published annually by the Criminal Justice Institute, South Salem, New York.
3. The formal title is *Crime in the U.S.,* prepared by the Uniform Crime Reporting Section of the FBI.
4. For a summary critique of the UCR, see Victoria W. Schneider and Brian Wiersema, "Limits and Use of the *Uniform Crime Reports.*" In MacKenzie, *Measuring Crime,* pp. 21–48.
5. For an account of the present status of the National Crime Survey, its uses, and its limitations, see James Garofalo, "The National Crime Survey, 1973–1986." In MacKenzie, *Measuring Crime,* pp. 75–96.
6. K. N. Wright with J. M. Harris and N. Woika, *Improving Correctional Classification Through a Study of the Placement of Inmates in Environmental Settings, Final Report,* NIJ Grant 83–IJ–CX–0011, 1985.
7. To measure stress, the SCL–90 or the more widely used MMPI have been used. Instruments to assess environmental needs include the Prison Preference Inventory, the Jail Preference Inventory, and the Smith Jail Preference Inventory. To examine environmental resources, the Environmental Quality Scale or any of a variety of the Moos correctional climate scales have been used.
8. J. J. Gibbs et al., *Street, Setting, and Satisfaction: The Final Report of the Man–Jail Transaction Project* (New Brunswick, N.J.: Rutgers University School of Criminal Justice, 1983), p. 561.
9. H. C. Quay, *Managing Adult Inmates: Classification for Housing and Program Assignments* (Rockville, Md.: American Correctional Association, 1984).
10. H. Toch, "A Revisionist View of Prison Reform" (*Federal Probation,* 1981), pp. 3–9.
11. Hermann Mannheim and Leslie T. Wilkins, *Prediction Methods in Relation to Borstal Training* (London: Her Majesty's Stationery Office, 1955). The technical literature on base expectancies as developed in California is out of print and mostly in typescript. A fairly adequate summary of the process, but lacking in details on the "criterion variables," is contained in Don M. Gottfredson, "Assessment and Prediction Methods in Crime and Delinquency," Appendix K of the *Task Force Report on Juvenile Delinquency and Youth Crime* of the President's Commission on Law Enforcement and Administration of Justice (Washington: Government Printing Office, 1967), pp. 171–185. The article ends with an excellent bibliography.
12. For a full technical account of the design and implementation of parole guidelines, see

Don M. Gottfredson, Leslie T. Wilkins, and Peter B. Hoffman, *Guidelines for Parole and Sentencing* (Lexington, Mass.: Lexington Books, 1978).

13. Joan Petersilia, Peter W. Greenwood, and Marvin Lavin, *Criminal Careers of Habitual Felons* (Santa Monica, Calif.: Rand, 1977).
14. Peter W. Greenwood with Alan Abrahamse, *Selective Incapacitation* (Santa Monica, Calif.: Rand, 1982).
15. Ibid., p. xix.
16. Ibid., p. 65.
17. Ibid., p. 60.
18. Jan M. Chaiken and Marcia R. Chaiken, *Varieties of Criminal Behavior* (Santa Monica, Calif.: Rand, 1982), pp. 179–180. For a summary of this massive account of the Chaikens' research, see their *Varieties of Criminal Behavior: Summary and Policy Implications* (Santa Monica, Calif.: Rand, 1982).
19. For a debate on the issues of selective incapacitation, see "Selective Incapacitation: Two Views on a Compelling Concept." *NIJ Research Reports,* January 1984: 5–8.
20. Donna Martin Hamparian, Richard Schuster, Simon Dinitz, and John P. Conrad. *The Violent Few* (Lexington, Mass.: Lexington Books, 1978). For a summary of this complex study, see John P. Conrad, *The Dangerous and the Endangered* (Lexington, Mass.: Lexington Books, 1985), pp. 29–55.
21. This study adopted some of the methodology of the landmark research of Wolfgang et al. See Marvin E. Wolfgang, Robert M. Figlio, and Thorsten Sellin, *Delinquency in a Birth Cohort* (Chicago: University of Chicago Press, 1972).
22. Stuart Miller, Simon Dinitz, and John P. Conrad, *Careers of the Violent* (Lexington, Mass.: Lexington Books, 1982). For a summary, see Conrad, op. cit., note 20, pp. 57–76.
23. Stephan Van Dine, John P. Conrad, and Simon Dinitz, *Restraining the Wicked* (Lexington, Mass.: Lexington Books, 1979). For a summary, see Conrad, op. cit., pp. 77–90.
24. For details of this analysis see Conrad, *The Dangerous and the Endangered,* pp. 83–88.
25. Joan Petersilia and Peter W. Greenwood, *Mandatory Prison Sentences: Their Projected Effect on Crime and Prison Population* (Santa Monica, Calif.: Rand, 1977).
26. An example of this misplaced optimism will be found in Gene Kassebaum, David Ward, and Daniel Wilner, *Prison Treatment and Parole Survival* (New York: Wiley, 1971). This was a needlessly complex evaluation of a group counseling program in a California prison, in which the program tested was a weekly session of group counseling conducted by minimally trained guards. The results should have surprised no one. The experimental groups showed no significant difference from the group in parole outcomes. Nor was there any difference found in the behavior of prisoners while still in prison.
27. In the discussion to follow, only male parole officers and male parolees were involved.
28. For a full analysis of the complex results of SIPU, see Douglas Lipton, Robert Martinson, and Judith Wilks, *The Effectiveness of Correctional Treatment: A Survey of Treatment Evaluation Studies* (New York: Praeger, 1975), pp. 115–138.
29. John P. Conrad, "The Penal Dilemma and Its Emerging Solution" (*Crime and Delinquency* 31, July 1985), pp. 411–422.
30. Billie S. Erwin, "Old and New Tools for the Modern Probation Officer." *Crime and Delinquency* 36, January 1990: 61–86. Erwin is the Chief of Evaluations of the Georgia Department of Corrections.
31. Ibid., pp. 63–64.
32. Michael Tonry, "Stated and Latent Functions of ISP." *Crime and Delinquency* 36, January 1990: 174–190.
33. James M. Byrne, Arthur J. Lurigio, and Christopher Baird, "The Effectiveness of the New Intensive Supervision Programs" (Monograph published by the National Institute of Justice, 1989), pp. 1–48.
34. We draw from the evaluation report prepared by Jackson Toby and Frank S. Pearson

(Rutgers University, 27 November 1987, in photocopy only). See also Frank S. Pearson and Alice Glasel Harper, "Contingent Intermediate Sentences: New Jersey's Intensive Supervision Program, *Crime and Delinquency*, 36 January 1990: 75–86.

35. Concern about the value of ordinary probation is supported by data on the recidivism of probationers. See Joan Petersilia, Susan Turner, and Joyce Peterson, *Prison versus Probation in California; Implications for Crime and Offender Recidivism* (Santa Monica, Calif.: Rand, 1986), pp. 16–21. These investigators found that in their study population of probationers there was a 35 percent rate of recidivism. Of these recidivists, 27 percent were charged with violent crimes.

36. For a review of the most important outstanding issues for correctional research, see Lynne Goodstein and Doris Layton MacKenzie, eds., *The American Prison. Issues in Research and Policy* (New York: Plenum, 1989).

Chapter 20

The Uncertain Future

CHAPTER OUTLINE

Penologists are painfully aware that expert predictions are too often no more accurate than calling heads or tails when a coin is flipped. The future of corrections has been wrongly predicted by optimists, pessimists, and statisticians. In this chapter we shall try to be realists. The past thrusts its way into the future, but unknowable forces and events can be expected to divert the course of criminal justice—for better or for worse—from the familiar channels of the present.

In the preceding chapters we have narrated the history of corrections and discussed at length the underlying principles that justify the array of controls imposed upon offenders. We have described the difficulties of reaching the objectives that society has expected of correctional agencies. As we watch the last years of the twentieth century and look ahead at the twenty-first, the difficulties remaining to be surmounted look even more formidable. If the policymakers of the future are more imaginative than their predecessors, they may find that their problems offer opportunities for economy and constructive innovation. Those who plod on with the policies of the past will drag criminal justice through endless crises.

THE NEW WAVE OF TOUGHNESS

In 1982 George Deukmejian, a lawyer, a former member of the legislature, and then attorney-general, was elected governor of California. His platform was simple, containing two pledges to the electorate: There would be budgetary parsimony, and there would be a tough, hard line on crime. The penal code would provide for longer sentences, so that good citizens would be protected from predators and the streets would become truly safe. More prisons would be built so that more criminals could be locked up. There can be no doubt that these promises held wide appeal for the California public. Deukmejian fulfilled his promises, and in 1986 he was reelected.

These are times when **toughness** on crime is an essential element of any politician's campaign plan. Criminal justice practitioners, criminologists, and informed observers will differ on how severe America's crime problem has become. Perhaps it has been exaggerated by the media, or perhaps it's even worse than stated. There is general agreement that however severe it is, it is a different problem both in its scope and in its nature than it was earlier in our history. There were plenty of thugs in the old days, but they were not armed with Uzis and AK-47's. The illicit sale of narcotics is nothing new, but distribution was never before so efficiently organized, and never before so lucrative. Under these circumstances, the hard line is a natural response. There is plenty to worry about, and the worst of it is that a hopeful solution isn't in plain sight.

How Much Toughness Can We Afford?

Is hope to be found in unrelenting toughness? Let's return to Governor Deukmejian's platform. California is not a representative state. It is the richest of all, and the most populous. Its crime problems are not those of the Midwest or the South. Still, it is often said that what's new in California will eventually catch on nationally. A case study of the California predicament is relevant for policymakers in more fortunate states.

As of May 1991, there were exactly 100,000 inmates in California's 20 state prison complexes. (That's about one-seventh of the total prison population in the United States.) The incarceration rate for 1989, the latest year for which it has been calculated, was 277 per 100,000, somewhat higher than the national average.

The total capacity of California prisons, as listed in the *1991 Directory of the American Correctional Association* is 58,310, of which 16,118 are beds in prisons built during the Deukmejian years. That total does not include new capacity built into prisons existing before 1981. Under construction are six new prisons, which will add 9250 beds. There are 18,189 new beds planned for six prisons still on the drawing board and not yet authorized. If they are financed, the bill will be about $4 billion. As planned, the system will have a capacity of 77,759 at an unspecifiable date in the future—22,241 short of the May 1991 count. The total population for 1996 is projected at 170,000, nearly twice the capacity planned for that time.

Except for the May 1991 total population, all these figures are soft. The **rated capacity of a prison** is a flexible statistic, depending on how many prisoners can be allowably crammed into a dormitory, how many school rooms and how much industrial space can be converted into additional housing, and how many prisoners the courts will allow to occupy one cell. The California Department of Corrections has conceded a tolerance of 25 percent of population above rated capacity.

Projections of population five years into the future often miss the mark, all too often falling short of realities. What is clear from all these data is that however they are counted, California's prisons will be seriously overcrowded for many years into the future. Even with well-trained staff, conservative classification, and the benefits of the highest possible technology, they will not be safe places for prisoners or staff.

The costs have been great and are increasing all the time. About $3 billion was spent on construction during the period 1981–90. The authorized expenditure for coming years, not including expenditures planned but not financed, will be $1.3 million. These huge amounts do not include operating expenses, which come to about $2 billion a year at present and are on the rise.

Until the 1990 election the voters routinely approved bond issues to fund new prisons. That changed in November 1990 when a $450 million issue was resoundingly defeated. It's doubtful that taxpayers have decided that criminal justice is now sufficiently tough, but it may be that the present level of toughness is all that they can afford. The over 100,000 men and women now confined is four times the 24,569 on hand on December 31, 1980.

Do We Need to Be So Tough?

In 1980, 210,290 violent crimes (homicide, rape, robbery, and aggravated assault) were reported by California police agencies to the FBI. The corresponding figure for 1988 was 261,912, an increase of 24.5 percent. During this period the population of California increased by about 19.6 percent. Whatever the new-found toughness has accomplished, it has not reduced the rate of violence.

In 1980, 13,608 male prisoners, 63.5 percent of the total, were serving time for violent offenses. The corresponding figure for 1991 is 37,993, or about 38 percent. As for property offenses, 6079 males, 29.5 percent of the total, were locked up in 1980 for burglary, forgery, and other forms of theft. In 1991 there were 25,681 property offenders, 26 percent of the population.[1] Narcotics offenders accounted for about 33 percent.

The question to which these data lead is simple: Does toughness pay? The easy answer is no. It may also be the correct answer. California presently locks up far more prisoners than in 1980, and the rate of violent crime is about the same. On the other hand, if the 37,993 violent offenders now doing time in California were not locked up, a good deal more violent crime might be taking place. Whatever the case, we can assume that men and women who kill, rob, rape, and assault ought to be in prison. For how long? About 8000 are serving sentences of 20 years or longer, including those who are lifers. The median time violent offenders serve before release on parole is about 2 years.

Narcotics offenders have been pouring into the system. In 1988 there were

16,684 persons serving time for drug offenses, which was an increase of 463.8 percent since 1983. In 1991 that number has almost doubled to a total of over 32,000. Although there is a vocal minority of opinion leaders who advocate the legalization of narcotics sale and use, they have made no impact on legislators or the enforcement of the laws. As there is no sign of a significant abatement of this element of the intake, it is certainly reasonable to expect the prison population to soar to ever dizzier heights.

What Is to Be Done?

This is a crisis, by any definition of the term. It is a desperate crisis in California, where the system is 73.7 percent overcrowded, and getting worse. Only 15 states were not affected at the outset of 1990. Twelve of these states were less than 5 percent *under* capacity. The federal system was at 68.2 percent over capacity. Connecticut was at 112.8 percent beyond capacity, and Massachusetts was not far behind at 89.5 percent. The national average worked out to 16.2 percent[2] (based on January 1, 1990 data). During 1991 there was very little improvement anywhere.

There are two and only two ways to abate **overcrowding** of our prisons. We can keep on building prisons, even though no end is in sight and the expense increases with every new one that is built. We can modify sentencing policy, recognizing that no society can sentence crime out of existence. The call for alternatives to incarceration was sounded on a muted trumpet for many years; those who sounded it were accused of being visionaries, soft on crime and criminals. The call is urgent now.

In previous chapters we have outlined changes that might be made—intensive probation and parole programs, electronic surveillance in house arrest, drug treatment programs, halfway houses, Victim-Offender Restitution Programming, day-fines,[3] community service, and so on.[4] It is reasonable to suppose that most property offenders and most drug retailers and users could be successfully managed in programs of these kinds. We may find that some women's prisons and some minimum custody facilities could be vacated with the imaginative use of such alternatives.

Toughness and the Root Causes of Crime

Neither massive investments in prison construction nor the adoption of the most efficient **alternatives to incarceration** will solve the crime problem or even relieve the overloaded system. The solution is the prevention of crime, and here the performance of this rich and progressive nation falls short of the rest of the world. No other nation, not the Soviet Union, not the Republic of South Africa, incarcerates so large a proportion of its citizens. No other nation experiences so high a level of criminal violence.[5] We must do better at tasks that have long been obvious.

The most tiresome of all criminological clichés is the call to search for the "root causes of crime." It is argued that until social scientists identify these roots, policy makers and practitioners will be at a great, if not insuperable, disadvantage in preventing crime.

There are enough causes that we can identify by watching the procession of convicted offenders from the courts to the prison reception centers. Most of them are poor men and women from inner-city ghettos. Too many of them have assuaged their deprivation with drugs. Too many of them were poorly educated in schools in which even the most eager students would be hard pressed to learn. Too many of them were armed with automatic or semiautomatic weapons for which only soldiers should have any use. Too many of them have never held a legitimate, full-time job, or a job of any kind. Too many of them are without skills to offer in an economy that has less and less use for the unskilled.

The existence of an **underclass**, inhabiting the squalor of our inner cities, has been the shame of America for too many generations. The underclass is now becoming not only a danger to life and limb but an increasing burden on the national economy as well. The condition of our metropolises deteriorates and is universally lamented. The application of remedies will be costly. The nation bickers about how any change can be paid for, and by which taxpayers—federal, state, or local. Meanwhile, middle-class citizens leave the cities if they can. The procession of inner-city convicts drags endlessly from the streets through the courts and into our bloated prisons—and back to those criminogenic streets.

In sum, this new wave of toughness has contributed to prison crowding, to the increased prison construction and the resulting fiscal difficulties, and to the tendency to punish rather than provide for the needs of the underclass. In Box 20-1, Janet A. Leban, executive director of the Pennsylvania Prison Society, predicts that the prospects for prison reform in the near future are not very encouraging.

FOUNDATIONS FOR THE CORRECTIONAL FUTURE

A major objective of this book is to portray the realism of the present, while, at the same time, pointing the way to a more hopeful future. The foundation for this more hopeful future depends upon low crime rates, the changing nature of mischief, the continuation of professional management, and humane conditions of confinement.

Crime Rates and the Correctional Population

In the 1960s and the 1970s, conventional wisdom had it that well before 1990 the crime rate would fall dramatically. The reasoning behind this was plausible. The baby boom of the 1950s had produced an unprecedented number of young men and women who at this time were between the ages of 15 and 30. This has always been—and still is—the age group most productive of serious offenders. Because there were so many youths during this period it was only to be expected that they would commit the large volume of crime that the country was experiencing.[6] Obviously the much smaller cohort of babies born in the 1960s and 1970s would be far less productive of crimes. The criminal justice system could relax. Some of our most ancient prisons could be closed, and the criminal justice budget could be reduced as dramatically as it had been raised.

This happy turn of events did not, of course, come to pass. Everyone knows why. A culture of hopelessness had permeated America's inner cities. Young men and women had turned to narcotics as the only means of gratification available to them. The sale of drugs opened up chances for riches for enterprising but reckless youth. Competition between drug-dealing gangs led to violence and murder. The police and the courts were hard pressed to arrest, try, and convict the numbers of young men and women who were neither deterred by law enforcement nor reformed by cor-

Box 20-1 Interview with Janet A. Leban

Question: Where is prison reform today?

Answer: From the perspective of the Prison Society, which has been in this business for over 200 years, it's hard to weigh the ups and downs. The pendulum swings. Having said this, let me predict that the last decade of this century is going to be a very tough time to be in the business of prison reform. I think the reasons are pretty obvious; the public does not want to hear about the need to address prison issues because they will eventually impact on them one way or the other. They do not want to hear that public safety is not improving by putting all these millions into construction and incarcerating more and more people. It's a difficult message to get through. It makes it more important that we keep on giving that message, whether it's with hopeful results or not. There are not too many agencies like ours in the country, and I think we're all laboring under the same difficulties. We are continually hammering home the question whether it is appropriate to spend all this money on corrections at the cost of other areas. We want people to be realistic about sentencing guidelines and mandatory sentences. We are also concerned about the kinds of things we're living with in Pennsylvania, where legislatures pass bills without any understanding of the impact, either in numbers or in dollars and cents, on the total system.

I don't know when the tide will turn, but I do think dollars-and-cents issues will be important in redirecting corrections. I think there's always a lot of lip service, which is certainly not limited to this year or last year, about the need to focus on community corrections. Not everybody that is currently incarcerated, which is about one-third to one-half of the inmates in state correctional institutions, needs to be there. We can start by giving more than lip service to restitution, to drug and alcohol treatment programs, to more use of work release, and to job training. These can happen in the community corrections setting rather than in the medium or maximum security prisons, which are very expensive to build and extremely expensive to operate. The time will come when people will have to see that what we're doing does not work. I would like to think that before the decade is out, we will pursue more community-oriented approaches.

Source: Interviewed in June 1990.

rections. The numbers of convicted felons increased by leaps and bounds. Rich states built new prisons to accommodate them but never supplied the number of cells required to meet the demand. Less affluent states turned to programs of surveillance—Intensive Probation Supervision, house arrest, electronic surveillance, and still other applications of high technology—as alternatives to the annually rising costs of incarceration.

The Changing Nature of Mischief

Dread of street crime, fury about the unprecedented costs of white-collar crime, and the demand that the nation's persisting indulgence in narcotics must all be resolved by criminal justice will keep the correctional caseload mounting for years to come.

For pessimists, this prospect is reason enough to expect the lapse of corrections into the cruelties of the past. We cannot be certain that the pessimists are wrong, but it is improbable that the most repulsive horrors of the not-too-distant past will be repeated. There may be horrors to come, but they will be different. They can be prevented by wise planners, competent administrators, a vigilant public, and a conscientious judiciary.

That is a modest reassurance, but it is supported by some firm realities. Correctional personnel, from top to bottom, were formerly uneducated and untrained men—with female staff limited to the small women's prisons—most of whom owed their employment to political patronage. There were exceptions, but very few. A career in corrections enjoyed little prestige. It was not an occupation that was a first choice for those who engaged in it.

Excesses of severity, corruption, and sheer incompetence in human relations were inevitable. Here and there remnants of the old nastiness and brutishness can still be found in American corrections, but the face of the system has been changed. It is not unreasonable to conclude that the change is irreversible.

Sweetness and light have not replaced the old ways. It is still a system that administers punishment—*mischief*, to resurrect Jeremy Bentham's word. Under our Constitution, punishment may not be cruel and unusual, but it is still unavoidably unpleasant, degrading, and humiliating to those who must submit to it. Those who administer punishment will find ways of rationalizing the particular form it takes. At best, criminal justice tries to keep the damage to a minimum while trying to reconcile the offender to the community he or she has offended. At the worst, the mischief is the relegation of the offender to a warehouse, where decay is inevitable, for a term of years—or for the rest of his or her life.

The Irreversible Innovations

What has happened is the installation of norms of conduct and standards of practice where neither existed in the bad old days. The rules no longer allow corporal punishment, even though those rules can still be breached with impunity in too many prisons. The same rules forbid filth and require adequate sanitation, but vermin can still be found in some kitchens, and disgusting conditions are still to be seen in shower rooms and toilets. There is no such thing as a utopian prison, but humane and aseptic housing is expected by the public that pays for corrections.

Nearly everywhere, professional management of the prisons is the norm. Correctional personnel must possess credentials for employment—for beginning guards, at least a high school education and no felony record. For promotion, many departments expect the completion of college courses in criminal justice. The standards for accreditation of correctional facilities call for a continuous curriculum of in-service training for all personnel.

It was once unthinkable that women would be employed in men's prisons except as nurses in the hospital or as secretaries and file clerks in the warden's office. Women are now to be found patrolling yards and as armed officers on the catwalks and in towers. Here and there a woman can be found in charge of an all-male prison as a warden. So far, no one has proved that the feminine touch softens the harshness of prison life, but the disasters predicted by old-timers have not occurred.

In addition to these internal changes, legislatures, courts, and civic organizations monitor the administration of correctional systems and the conditions of confinement. Correctional authorities have learned in this litigious age that they may be hauled into court for deficiencies for which their recent predecessors would never have been reproached.

The transition has been rapid. The prison was once a semifeudal organization ruled by a warden who was hardly accountable to anyone but a governor who was too busy or too indifferent to bother with a public institution in which there was negligible public interest. Since World War II, the correctional apparatus has evolved into a typical public bureaucracy. The way things are to be done is governed by administrative manuals, classification manuals, custodial manuals, and a ceaseless, voluminous paper flow from headquarters to wardens and from wardens to headquarters. The flow surges on to captains, lieutenants, and guards on the line. Computers clatter with inputs and outputs. Electronic technology provides surveillance of fences and cellblocks. There is a jacket (record) for each prisoner, sometimes a jacket of several bulky volumes. The contents of each jacket are distilled for computer printouts. Prison managers stick to their desks to keep their heads above the flood of information.

A Managerial Revolution

These changes have come thick and fast. What warning do they bring? On the positive side, the rules and regulations governing the conduct of staff and prisoners can be clear and unambiguous—decisions are no longer subject to a warden's whim. Information about each prisoner is readily accessible. If it has been conscientiously assembled, decision making about classification, work and housing assignments, disciplinary action, and release on parole can be made without reliance on wishful thinking or unreasonable prejudice.

The message of the courts has been clear so far as it goes: Overcrowding of the prisons beyond their capacity will not be tolerated. Reasonably humane conditions of confinement must be maintained. Prisoners are entitled to due process when decisions are made about their discipline and/or removal from the main body of the prison population. Rehabilitation cannot be coerced nor even required, yet prisoners must be allowed opportunities to improve themselves. In short, from a regime under which prisoners have no rights and could be considered civilly dead there has been a transition to the concept that prisoners enjoy all the rights of citizens in the community, except those that must be suspended because of the restrictions imposed by confinement. That the concept is still not honored in universal implementation does not negate its acceptance. The days of civil death appear to be over for good.

TWO SCENARIOS FOR THE FUTURE OF CORRECTIONS

The bureaucratization of corrections provides both the possibility of regression, leading to a gloomy scenario, and the possibility of enlightened leadership, leading to a hopeful scenario.

A Gloomy Scenario

The bureaucratization of corrections is not without ominous possibilities. Efficiency has been achieved, if only on paper. Efficiency in the conduct of human relations is not the same as effectiveness. From the standpoint of efficiency, the Holocaust perpetrated by the Nazi regime was an extraordinarily efficient operation. Millions of men, women, and children were expeditiously and with minimum resistance moved from their homes all over the territories controlled by Germany to the chambers in which they were asphyxiated or the ovens in which they were incinerated. This monstrous process was made possible by an efficient bureaucracy that was able to assemble its victims, transport them over long distances, hold them securely until their scheduled killing, and then dispose of their remains.

An efficient bureaucracy was aided by two additional factors. The relationship between the captors and the captives was highly impersonal. Ordinary men and women managing Auschwitz, Buchenwald, and Treblinka saw their victims not as individuals but as units in a mass of people who were to be destroyed. Very few of the Jews, gypsies, and other persons classified as undesirables were in human contact with the executioners. The occasions to create even a fragment of a relationship were rare to nonexistent.

The second condition favoring this terrible operation was secrecy. Nobody outside the Gestapo needed to know anything about what was going on in the death camps. Nobody was allowed to know. Some Germans were suspicious, but the facts were made as hard to come by as an efficient organization could contrive.

A holocaust is inconceivable in American prisons. What is conceivable is a gradual deterioration of the conditions of confinement through some of the same processes that made the Holocaust possible. An efficient bureaucracy can depersonalize the prisoner population into a mass of classified numbers easily manipulated on a computer. If the prison is overcrowded, the crowding will be seen as a percentage of capacity, not as the misery of hundreds of men and women jammed too closely together. Misery is not measurable as such, or, if it is seen, it can be translated into no more than a criminal's desert. The overcrowding factor may signal to a vigilant administrator that special care must be taken to prevent disturbances from turning into destructive riots. That measure of care need not call for interaction between the prison staff and the prisoners.

We do not suppose that the German people would have been moved to take steps against the Gestapo if they had known about the Holocaust. The Nazi regime had conditioned the public into unquestioning submission. There is no intentional secrecy about the management of American prisons, but the public in this country is not much concerned about corrections except when shocked into brief fascination by a riot, a dramatic escape, or a scandalous episode of violence. If conditions are worsening, only special segments of the public will take an active interest. Vigilance is not a completely effective prophylactic against the decay of correctional standards, but it is an assurance that indifference and mistreatment will not go without notice.

A Hopeful Scenario

We have dwelt on the most horrific possibilities because of the natural tendency of any bureaucracy to regress. Public agencies are managed by human beings, most of whom are creatures of habit. The culture of any bureaucracy is to leave well enough alone: "If it ain't broke, don't fix it." Change is resisted, even if the system is no longer well enough and is breaking down at crucial points. For some managers, the solution is to get tougher. If the crime wave continues to produce more offenders than can be housed in the existing prisons, then more prisons must be built, and hang the expense. For a sufficiently affluent jurisdiction, this response to the challenge of crime might be acceptable until the limits of affluence are tested.

Yet, as this book continually points out, there are individuals who are making a difference in corrections today (see Box 20-2). More enlightened managers, often faced with a budget that cannot be stretched to allow for enormous investments in new facilities, look for new policies instead. In the 1970s California led the way with a program to subsidize counties to intensify probation services.[7] The program succeeded for a few years in the significant reduction of prison populations. The end came when the subsidies to probation departments were eroded by inflation, and hardliners in the legislature refused to augment the subsidy formula. Prison building was resumed.

Budgets are tighter in most states. As prisons filled to overflowing, the attraction of alternatives to incarceration became irresistible to all but the intransigent. In Chapter 19 we described the Intensive Supervision Programs pioneered by Georgia

Box 20-2 Good People Make a Difference

One of the themes of this book is that good people make a difference. A study of correctional pioneers in this nation typically reveals several characteristics they have in common. They are persons of vision. They believe that a better way can be fashioned by men and women of good will. They are dedicated to working with offenders and going beyond the call of duty in countless ways. They are sensitive and understanding, able to perceive the problems and needs of offenders, and highly skilled in persuading both staff and offenders to develop more of their potential. Finally, they are not quitters. They believe that keeping everlastingly at a task will ensure success. John A. Thalacker, warden of the Men's Reformatory at Anamosa, Iowa, describes the values and knowledge that people who make a difference need to have:

> The values a person has acquired, whether it be in the family or through community and school activities, really is the guiding rudder for all subsequent decisions. Honesty, positive attitude in the face of adversity, flexibility, and openmindedness about others' perspective while being able to maintain their own value system are key ingredients.
>
> In correctional administration you deal with a wide range of personalities who do not share a common source of motivation. Extremes of highly motivated and those who seemingly have demonstrated no motivation in their life exist in the same families. Corrections workers also need to know how to emotionally accept disappointments of an offender reappearing at the prison door and recognize that it is that person's choice and not the correctional worker's lack of effort that brought him or her back. A high energy level is needed, as corrections workers can expect in their career a steady stream of young people who will be coming through the door.

Source: Warden John A. Thalacker was interviewed in August 1990.

and New Jersey and adapted in many other states. These programs have been criticized by some as mere "net wideners"—that is, they impose a needlessly severe sanction on offenders who could survive in the community with no more than a conviction and a reprimand by the judge. To the extent that this is the case, it is attributable to the caution of the innovators. Experience with ISP should eventually justify its adoption as the sanction of first choice for all property offenders, and eventually as a parole alternative allowing earlier releases for men and women serving sentences for more serious felonies. So long as the intensive surveillance programs require interaction between an officer and an offender, the depersonalization of corrections will be avoided.

Ultimately prison space should be reserved for violent felons, drug wholesalers, probation violators, and major white-collar criminals. Most felons will be serving longer terms than is the case now, but there will be fewer of them. Some prisons may become redundant; there is some reason to hope that the fortresses surviving from the nineteenth century may be vacated and demolished. There is no reason at all to expect that the deinstitutionalization of corrections, so ardently advocated by some altruists, will ever occur.

THINKING ABOUT MODELS

As the 1990s began, prison officials throughout the United States were preoccupied with the pressures of overcrowded cellblocks and dormitories, the violence of prisoners, the persistent problem of contraband drugs, and the mounting costs of meeting the requirements of the Constitution and the law. Out in the community, probation and parole officers are swamped with presentence investigations, large caseloads to monitor, dangerous neighborhoods to cover, and offenders to whom drug tests must be administered. There is no comfort in the statisticians' gloomy projections of rising numbers of convicted offenders. Few officials have the time or inclination to give thought to what the correctional system can and should accomplish.

The Obsolescence of the Medical Model

In the palmy days of the 1950s, when prisons were under better control and nominal probation and parole services were acceptable, it was reasonable to think of corrections as based on a **medical model.** Offenders were "sick," and the task of corrections was to diagnose their disabilities and prescribe "treatment." When the treatment was successfully completed, the offender could be released from the control of his or her indeterminate sentence. No one claimed that either diagnostic procedures or the treatments prescribed were as reliable as in the practice of medicine.

The assumption underlying the medical model was that criminals were objects to be molded into noncriminals. Advocates of the rehabilitative ideal readily admitted that the required "technology" for accomplishing this goal was rudimentary. Given time, experience, and research, all would be well.

Essential to the medical model as conceived by its theorists was the indeterminate sentence. Its practice allowed serious injustices to which we have referred in previous chapters. Liberal critics noted the disparities in time served for identical crimes. Conservatives argued that the indeterminate sentence led to unacceptable leniency in sentencing. Both liberals and conservatives agreed that the prospect was dim that the model would ever achieve its intended success.

The Justice Model Supplants the Medical Model

In the 1970s, the two sides joined to reject the medical model and the indeterminate sentence in favor of a more pragmatic **justice model.** The theme was that rehabilitation could not be coerced but at least justice could be done.

We believe that corrections cannot forever limit its goals to the administration of fairness. The justice model should be the foundation on which a **citizenship model** can be built. We contend that it is not enough for a correctional service to transform an offender into a nonrecidivist. The product should be a citizen.

Proposal for a Citizenship Model

Citizenship is fundamental to the achievement of a democratic society. Its essence is the recognition of the rights of the citizen, and the expectation that the enjoyment of those rights requires the citizen's acceptance of accompanying duties.

American prisoners are no longer consigned to a "civil death" as were their predecessors in the not very distant past. Nevertheless, they do not lead the lives of citizens. Their rights are limited and uncertain and their duties are enforced. While they are incarcerated some rights must be withheld, and some duties must be performed under duress if not voluntarily. Much could be changed. Many rights could be matters of course rather than grudgingly allowed as a federal court may mandate. We enumerate the rights and duties of the citizenship model here:

- *The right to personal safety.* Life in the contemporary prison is dangerous. Prisoners in custody cannot protect themselves in the human morass in which we hold them. Correctional officers cannot assume safety and sometimes they cannot protect themselves. The obligation of the state to provide safe custody is clear. Corresponding to this right is the prisoner's duty to do nothing that will increase the hazards of prison life. For assaults and threats of assaults the penalties should be swift and severe.
- *The right to care.* Decent, clean shelter, an adequate diet, enough clothing, and competent medical care when needed are basic rights of all citizens. When prisons are crowded, convicts cannot be expected to live like responsible citizens, nor will they be reconciled to society. Corresponding to these rights is the prisoner's duty to live decently, to assure that his actions do not make conditions worse for himself and others.
- *The right to personal dignity.* Whatever his origin in the community, the prisoner's sense of worth has been severely damaged by the humiliation of his or her sentence. The system must not damage it further. That responsibility also rests with all prisoners. The indignities and verbal abuse that some prisoners shower on one another should be vigorously discouraged.
- *The right to work.* No industrialized country does as badly as the United States in providing occupations for its prisoners. Like the poor, their redundancy is always explicit—society has no use for them. The right to work and

the right to a living wage for the work done make a pair of rights without which all the other rights of citizens lose meaning. A prisoner should work if he or she wants to and should be paid at the rate prevailing in the free labor market. Under this condition, prisoners should pay a reasonable amount for their room and board. Convicts should meet their responsibilities for their dependents like the rest of us, and save for their future if they can. They will need nest eggs more than most citizens ever will. Prisoners may choose not to work but will be treated as indigents, to be housed under less favorable conditions, provided all necessary services, but allowed no special privileges.

- *The right to self-improvement.* No convict should be coerced into enrollment in an educational or training program, but there must be opportunities to increase skills and understanding of the world. To close off opportunity is to foreclose hope—as cruel a punishment as can be devised.
- *The right to vote.* The electoral disabilities imposed on convicts are pointless. They serve only to add humiliation to the prisoner's plight. Participation in the democratic process should be encouraged so as to make civic responsibility a real and vital feature of the new citizen's life.
- *The right to a future.* Contacts with families and friends should be allowed as liberally as possible within the constraints of custody. A man or woman who is isolated from the outside world cannot plan realistically for the future. Too often prisoners are returned to the community only to live in the same degree of isolation that they experienced when locked up. Citizens must look ahead to meet their responsibilities. The prisoner has nothing to look to if the community is not in plain sight.

Many of these rights can be put into effect without special measures. Others will require significant changes in public attitudes and improvements in the economy. If we can set our sights on these rights and duties as goals to be achieved, we can begin to make sense of the American prison.

CONCLUSIONS

Corrections will enter the twenty-first century with a potential for humane management and humane programming. The leadership is no longer in the hands of semiliterate political hangers-on. Standards of personnel selection and promotion provide more intelligent and resourceful staff than has been available in the past. The intrusion of the courts has given some assurance that violators of decency will be held to account. The application of high technology can shift many of the property offenders and some of the narcotics offenders from prison to the community.

The enormous increase in the numbers of people under correctional control, both in the prisons and in the community, presents opportunities: Change can no longer be the option chosen by idealists; it is a necessity required by realism. The future of corrections in the hands of trained realists may be the successful test of American civilization.

Long ago, Winston Churchill wrote:

> The mood and temper of the public in regard to the treatment of crime and criminals is one of the most unfailing tests of the civilization of any country. A calm dispassionate

> recognition of the rights of the accused and even of the convicted criminal against the State; a constant heart-searching of all charged with the deed of punishment; tireless efforts toward the discovery of regenerative processes; unfailing faith that there is a treasure if you can find it, in the heart of every man. These are the symbols which in the treatment of crime and criminals make and measure the stored-up strength of a nation and are sign and proof of the living virtue in it.[8]

That was written when Churchill was Home Secretary in the British government in 1910, and in that capacity responsible for the prisons of Great Britain. It still stands as a challenge to the humanity of any nation claiming to be civilized. It is a challenge that can be met only by men and women of enlightened good will. Technology alone or in the hands of impersonal bureaucrats will never be enough.

KEY TERMS

alternatives to incarceration

citizenship model

justice model

medical model

overcrowding

rated capacity of a prison

toughness

underclass

DISCUSSION TOPICS

20.1 What "unknowable forces and events" invalidated the predictions made for corrections in the 1970s?

20.2 Under the regime of toughness, "narcotics offenders have been pouring into the prisons." What programs should be provided for them?

20.3 What criteria should be used in deciding on the length of an armed robber's term of incarceration? Or a murderer's? Or a rapist's?

20.4 Which scenario for the future of corrections is the more probable—the gloomy or the hopeful?

20.5 In the citizenship model of corrections, what rights should a prisoner enjoy when he chooses not to work?

NOTES

1. These data are extracted from *California Prisoners, 1980,* and from the January 1991 population report of the California Department of Corrections.
2. See *The Corrections Yearbook, 1990* (South Salem, N.Y.: The Criminal Justice Institute), pp. 28–29.

3. For an introduction to day-fines, see Sally T. Hillsman, "Day Fines, an Overview." In *Overcrowded Times* (Castine, Maine: Castine Research, 1990), pp. 4–6.
4. For an excellent review of the possibilities, see Kay Pranis and James Read, "Sentencing Our Way Out: Creative Alternatives to Incarceration." In *Blueprint for Social Justice* (Chicago: Institute of Human Relations, Loyola University). See also Marc Mauer, *Americans Behind Bars: A Comparison of International Rates of Incarceration* (Washington: The Sentencing Project, 1991).
5. For further details, see Mauer, op. cit., note 4.
6. For an account of the baby boom and its effects on American culture, with inferences that turned out to be too hopeful, see Daniel Patrick Moynihan, " 'Peace—' Some thoughts on the 1960's and the 1980's." *The Public Interest* 32, 1973: 3–10.
7. Edwin L. Lemert and Forrest Dill, *Offenders in the Community* (Lexington, Mass.: Lexington Books, 1978). This study describes the background and operation of the Probation Subsidy program, and assesses its effectiveness.
8. Quoted by Evelyn Ruggles-Brise, *Prison Reform at Home and Abroad* (London: Macmillan, 1924), p. 4.

Glossary

accreditation process Standards made for police and corrections that are supported by a separate Commission on Accreditation for the purpose of upgrading the police and correctional programs of nearly every state.

administrative regulations These pertain to such matters as laws and rulings made by federal, state, and local agencies to deal with such contemporary problems as wage and hour disputes, pollution, automobile traffic, industrial safety, and the purity of food and drugs.

arraignment hearing The step following a criminal charge in which the defendant or accused is read the charges and advised of his or her rights. At this step the accused may plead guilty, not guilty, no contest, or not guilty by reason of insanity.

arson Any willful or malicious burning or attempt to burn, with or without intent to defraud, a dwelling house, public building, motor vehicle or aircraft, or personal property of another.

autocratic style A management style in which one person makes all the decisions, is suspicious of the intentions of workers, and uses whatever measures are considered necessary to control behavior.

autocratic warden A warden who is clearly the boss and who uses negative and punitive means in an attempt to control staff and inmates.

bail hearing A hearing in which a monetary amount is set to ensure the return to court of the defendant.

behavior modification A technique in which rewards or punishment are used to alter or change one's behavior.

bench or unsupervised probation A type of probation in which probationers are not subject to supervision.

benefit of clergy The right to be tried in an ecclesiastical court, where punishments are less severe than those given out by civil courts.

beyond reasonable doubt The standard required to prove guilt and convict a defendant of a crime.

Bill of Rights Ten constitutional amendments whose purpose is to protect the individual against coercive government action, unless such action is permitted by the law.

building tenders Until the *Ruiz* decision, inmate "building tenders" in Texas were given authority by prison administration to discipline erring inmates who disturbed the social order.

bureaucracy A system with a clearly outlined organizational hierarchy.

bureaucratic warden A warden whose power is limited by government.

burglary The breaking and entering of a structure, usually for the purpose of committing a theft or an assault.

California Community Treatment Project Under this project, wards in Youth Authority institutions were randomly divided into control and experimental groups; those in the experimental group were immediately released to community supervision while those in the control group were released after serving normal sentences.

campus style An architectural style in which the units of a prison are housed in a complex of buildings surrounded by a fence.

capacity limitations The limited ability of the justice system to provide adequate protection for society.

capital punishment The sentence of death for an offense.

career criminal A person for whom crime is a way of life and who has repeated contacts with the criminal justice system.

case law Law based on judicial decisions that occurred previously.

case overload An excessive number of cases to be handled by the courts.

citation A written notice ordering a suspect to appear in a court of law to answer for a certain offense.

citation release Field citation allows an officer to release in the field with a signed promise to appear; station house citation allows for release after a suspect has been arrested and brought to the station house.

classification The process of assigning inmates to types of custody or treatment programs appropriate to their needs.

clearance rate The number of crimes solved expressed as a percentage of the total number of crimes reported to the police.

Code of Hammurabi Issued during the reign of King Hammurabi of Babylon, it was one of the first comprehensive views of the law. The law of talion makes its appearance in this code.

common law The basis for common law was custom and tradition; common law was judge-made law, in that the laws were molded, refined, examined, and changed as decision making took place from one period to the next.

community corrections acts Fifteen states passed community corrections acts in the 1970s and 1980s, in which states assumed some support for community-based corrections.

community service order Requires that an offender perform a certain number of work hours at a private nonprofit or governmental agency.

computer theft The most common technique of this white-collar crime involves the unauthorized modification, replacement, insertion, or deletion of data before or during their input to a computer system.

concurrent sentence Prison terms for more than one crime that are served simultaneously.

conflict perspective The organizing principles of this perspective are these: (1) at every point society is subject to change; (2) society displays at every point dissension and conflict;

conjugal visitation A policy under which prisoners can enjoy private visitation with their families.

(3) every element contributes to change; and (4) society is based on the coercion of some of its member by others.

constitutional order The order codified or laid down in criminal law.

continuance An order from the court continuing a case, usually for the purpose of gathering more information.

contraband Any unauthorized substance or material possessed by inmates.

corporate crime Organizational crime occurring in the context of the complex relationships among boards of directors, executives, and managers on the one hand, and among parent corporations, corporate divisions, and subsidiaries on the other hand.

corrections The programs, services, and institutions that are responsible for those individuals who are accused and convicted of criminal offenses.

corruption The misuse of authority by a corrections officer for personal gain.

counterfeiting A crime related to forgery in that it represents an alternative method of producing illegal tender.

crime Derived from the Latin *crimen*, meaning judgment, accusation, and offense. Crime is an intentional act in violation of criminal law (statutory and case law), committed without defense or justification, and sanctioned by the state as a felony or misdemeanor.

crime control model A model that emphasizes the protection of society and control of offenders. It calls for deterrents to crime, such as harsh punishments.

crisis in confidence Term currently used as descriptive of the present attitudes toward political and legal institutions of American society.

Declaration of Principles The 37 principles developed by the correctional congress that met in Cincinnati in 1870 to guide the reformation of this nation's prisons.

deferred sentence A sentence that delays conviction on a guilty plea until the sentenced offender has successfully served his or her probation term.

deinstitutionalization A crime strategy that focuses on keeping offenders in the community rather than placing them in long-term institutions.

determinate sentencing Its main forms are flat-time sentences, mandatory sentences, and presumptive sentences. In flat-time sentencing, the judge may choose between probation and imprisonment but has limited discretion in setting the length of any sentence to prison. The presumptive sentence is based upon the concept of "just deserts," which has been proposed by David Fogel, by Andrew von Hirsch, and by the Twentieth Century Fund in Fair and Certain Punishment. Mandatory sentencing sets a required number of years of incarceration for specific crimes.

deterrence A crime-control strategy that uses punishment to prevent others from committing similar crimes.

disorder A threatening lack of predictability in the behavior of others; disorganization, cultural conflict, normlessness or anomie, norm erosion, disconsensus, and entropy.

diversion Establishment of alternatives to the formal justice system such as deferred prosecution, resolution of citizen disputes, and Treatment Alternatives to Street Crime.

double jeopardy Contained in the Fifth Amendment, which states that a citizen cannot be punished more than once for the same offense.

due process Part of the Fourteenth Amendment, which guarantees citizens fair and proper treatment by government.

due process model The theoretical basis upon which the criminal justice system operates, it contends that the process of proving guilt or innocence must be slow in order to ensure that innocent defendants are not convicted.

Eighth Amendment States that excessive bail shall not be required, nor excessive fines imposed, nor cruel and unusual punishments inflicted.

electronic monitoring devices Through these devices, corrections staff can verify that an offender is at home or in a community correctional center during specified hours.

excessive use of force More force than is necessary either to control a situation or make an arrest.

FBI Federal Bureau of Investigation, whose duties include those of performing federal crime investigations.

Fifth Amendment Allows a person the right to be free from self-incrimination.

financial restitution Establishes a sum of money that an offender must pay either to the victim or to a public fund for victims of crime.

fiscal constraint Restriction of revenues.

flat-time sentence The offender will serve the entire sentence, no more or no less.

forcible rape Legally, the sexual penetration of a woman's body without her consent and with either the use or the threat of force.

formal system The rules, regulations, policies, and procedures.

Fourth Amendment Guarantees citizens the right against unreasonable searches and seizures by the government.

fragmentation The interdependence and cooperation of the components of the criminal justice system.

good time A deduction of time awarded to inmates for good behavior.

hands-off doctrine phase Prisoner had no rights when sentenced to prison.

hedonic calculus Beaccaria and Bentham presumed that people will choose pleasure rather than pain and, therefore, it is necessary for sanctions to be proportionate to the offense and to outweigh the rewards of crime.

house arrest A sentence imposed by the court whereby offenders are ordered to remain confined in their own residences for the length of the sentence.

immaturity (defense against responsibility) Can be used as a defense for children under the age of seven on the grounds that children under this age are immature and are not responsible for their actions.

incapacitation Isolating offenders to protect society.

indefensible space Certain space within a prison that staff are unable to control.

indeterminate sentencing Permits early release of a prisoner from a correctional institution after the individual has served a portion of his or her sentence.

informal codes The values of the inmates or staff cultures that are found in unwritten procedures not covered in the formal system.

informal probation Supervising an offender without placing him or her under the jurisdiction of the formal justice system.

informal system Provides both status and social satisfaction, which frequently are not found in the formal system.

initial hearing A hearing shortly after arrest in which a defendant is informed by a judge or magistrate of the crime he or she has been charged with by the police and is then informed of such constitutional rights as the right to remain silent and to have an attorney appointed.

intensive supervision Supervision based on the belief that increased contact and referral result in more positive adjustments to society, such as higher employment rate and a lower rate of involvement in crime.

intermediate sanctions Punishments that are more restrictive than traditional probation but less so than incarceration.

involved-hands doctrine phase States that due process rights must be accorded to all groups within a correctional facility.

jex talionis Law of retaliation; that is, an eye for an eye and a tooth for a tooth.

just deserts A system under which a criminal is punished proportionately to the damage that the crime inflicted on society; that is, the seriousness of punishment should be commensurate with the seriousness of the harm.

justice model David Fogel and Andrew von Hirsch, the two main proponents of this model, advocate that offenders should be sentenced according to their just deserts.

larceny Unlawful taking, carrying, or leading away of property that belongs to another, without the use of force or fear.

Laws of Solon Solon, in repealing the cruel laws of Drakon in ancient Athens, attempted to make laws that applied equally to all citizens.

LEAA Law Enforcement Assistance Administration, created to distribute funds to local governments for improved crime control.

management style The style used by managers in making decisions and handling subordinates in an organization.

mandatory sentence A required period of incarceration for specific crimes.

Marxist perspective Views the state and the law as tools of the ownership class that reflect the economic interests of that class.

master An individual appointed by a court to administer a correctional system as an institution under judicial direction.

medicalization of deviance The process by which certain categories of deviant or criminal behavior became defined as medical rather than moral problems.

medical model Regards the criminal as one who is sick with the disease of criminality and who must be cured through psychological intervention.

mens rea Refers to the state of mind that must be in existence at the time the crime occurred so as to establish criminal conduct.

Minnesota Community Corrections Act (CCA) The CCA had four major purposes: (1) reduction of commitments to state prisons; (2) encouragement of local units of government to maintain responsibility for offenders whose crimes are not serious (those who would receive a sentence of less than five years in a state facility); (3) promotion of community corrections planning at the local level; and (4) improved coordination among local components of the criminal justice system.

minority hiring Hiring women and members of underrepresented groups as corrections staff.

M'Naughten Rule Stipulates that a person cannot be found guilty if at the time of committing the wrongful act he or she was suffering from a disease of the mind so as to not know the nature and quality of the act he or she was engaged in.

motor vehicle theft The theft or attempted theft of a motor vehicle.

murder The unlawful killing of a human being.

mutual welfare league An approach to prisoner self-government that Thomas Matt Osborne developed at Auburn prison in New York state.

New Generation Jail A popular architectural design facility that emphasizes interaction of inmates and staff.

occupational stress Comes from a number of areas: department pressures for allegiance to the formal rules and regulations, boredom from doing the same unexciting activity, isolation, problems in marital relationship, and family.

order A condition in which every part or unit is in its right place or in a normal or efficient state; the condition brought about by good and firm government and obedience to the laws.

organizational chart A graphic chart showing the organizational structure.

organized crime The two basic approaches to dealing with organized crime are the structural view and the process view. The structural approach usually argues that the criminal syndicate is a highly structured network of sustained relationships. The process view argues that group relation networks labeled "Mafia" are best understood as an extension of the interaction and exchange processes inherent in social life.

panacea A remedy or cure for any disease or illness.

panopticon A prison designed by Jeremy Bentham, in which guards could keep prisoners under constant observation.

parens patriae A medieval English doctrine that sanctioned the right of the crown to intervene into family relations whenever a child's welfare was threatened.

parole guidelines A three-step process is typically involved: First, upon reviewing a prisoner's case, the examiner panel gives the case a salient factor score, ranging from 0 to 11. Second, the case is then given an offense severity rating on a scale of 1 to 8. Finally, equipped with the salient factor score and the offense severity rating, the examiners refer to another chart, which reveals the amount of time a prisoner should serve, assuming good prison performance.

participatory management A management style based on developing a team approach and on sharing the decision-making responsibilities throughout the organization.

penitentiary Also known as prison or reformatory, used to isolate from normal society persons found guilty of a felony.

penitentiary model A model that provides offenders with a properly structured environment to enable them to repent their wrongdoings and become useful citizens upon their return to the community.

plea bargaining A process by which the defendant in a criminal case relinquishes his or her right to go to trial in exchange for a reduction in charge and/or sentence.

politicalization of crime Under this phenomenon, politicians blame crime for the social disorder perceived to be apparent in the larger society.

popular justice A system of justice under which the politically powerful imposes its notions of what constitutes a good community and often takes the lead in vigilante movements.

positivism The belief that human behavior is caused by specific factors and that it is possible to know what these factors are.

preliminary hearing Usually occurs within seven to ten days after arrest. The charges are read to the accused at the initial appearance, and he or she is reminded of the right to remain silent and to have an attorney appointed by the court if he or she cannot afford to retain one.

presentence investigation (PSI) The primary purpose of the PSI is to help the court decide whether or not to grant probation, to determine the condition of probation, to determine the length of the sentence, and to decide upon community-based or institutional placement for the defendant.

presumptive sentence A form of determinate sentencing in which the legislature sets the penalties for criminal acts.

pretrial detention The detention or holding of a defendant prior to the time of trial.

pretrial release Permits a person to be released from jail or pretrial detention centers pending adjudication of the case.

preventive detention Statutes passed in many states for stricter bail practices to help decrease crime and pretrial flight of defendants.

prison abolition Doing away with or deletion of confinement for convicted criminals.

prison democracy The principle of equality of rights for convicted criminals.

prison gangs Inmates have organized themselves in gangs in 32 states and the Federal Bureau of Prisons.

prisonization The process by which inmates learn and internalize the prison culture.

probation Permits the convicted offender to remain in the community, under the supervision of a probation officer and certain conditions set by the court.

Probation Subsidy Statute Passed in California in the 1960s, through which counties would be subsidized by the state to organize 50-person probation caseloads for felony offenders who would ordinarily be sentenced to prison.

procedural criminal law Concerned with criminal conduct and the necessary punishment for such conduct.

professionalism Establishes standards of behavior based on education, a code of ethics, pride, and dignity.

protective custody (PC) A specific area of the prison in which vulnerable inmates are isolated from the population.

psychological positivism Focuses on understanding the differences between the personality traits of criminals and noncriminals.

psychopathy The psychopath or sociopath generally is not delusional or irrational and does not exhibit nervousness or psychoneurotic manifestations; he or she is unreliable, lacking in either shame or remorse, willing to commit all kinds of misdeeds for astonishingly small stakes, and characterized by poor judgment.

psychotherapy The treatment of a mental disorder that involves any means of communication between a patient and a trained person.

reality theory The theory that an individual's mental activity can be adjusted to meet the demands of his environment.

reformatory model A reformatory for youthful offenders consisting of indeterminate sentencing and parole, classification of prisoners, educational and vocational training, and increased privileges for positive behavior.

rehabilitation To change an offender's character, attitudes, or behavior patterns so as to diminish his or her criminal propensities.

reintegration model A model whose task is to keep offenders in the community and help them readjust to community life.

release on own recognizance (ROR) The release without bail of defendants who appear to have stable ties in the community and are a good risk to appear for trial.

reparation Requires the offender to make amends for a wrong or an injury and the defendant must pay compensation to the victim or society for the harm resulting from the criminal offense.

residential programs Probation centers, work release centers, restitution centers, prerelease centers, and halfway houses are the main residential programs for adult offenders.

restrained-hands doctrine phase A balance between prisoners' rights and legitimate institutional interests.

retribution Justification for punishment that it is society's moral duty to punish the criminal for the wrong he or she has done.

revocation of probation A judicial procedure that takes place when a probation officer recommends to the court that probation should be revoked because a probationer has committed a new crime or violated the conditions of probation.

right to jury trial If it appears the suspect will be sentenced to jail for more than a short period (six months) the jury trial must be offered.

robbery The taking of property or something of value from a person or near a person through means of force or the threat of force. The use of a deadly weapon makes the offense more serious and elevates it to armed robbery.

role variations Various roles performed by individual correctional officers.

selective incapacitation Researchers have discovered that individual offending rates are highly skewed, with a small number of offenders responsible for a large portion of crimes or arrests. Therefore, the potential exists to realize major crime-reduction benefits from incarceration by selective imprisonment of high-rate offenders.

self-defense (defense against responsibility) The legal right to ward off an attack from another, if a person thinks that he or she is in immediate danger of being harmed.

self-growth programs Programs developed to promote personal gain and improvement.

self-report studies Studies that ask juveniles or adults to tell about the crimes they have committed in a previous period of time.

sentencing guidelines The length of sentence is determined by decision rules that apply to all sentences.

sentencing hearing For those defendants who have either pled guilty or been found guilty during a trial, the judge must decide upon the appropriate sentence during a sentencing hearing.

serial killers Murderers of more than one person who kill their victims on different occasions.

shared-powers model A movement in the 1970s aimed at the democratization of the prison, in which staff and inmates were brought into the prison.

shock incarceration Requires participation in drills and physical training in "boot camp" prison settings.

shock probation The offender, his or her attorney, or the sentencing judge can submit a motion to suspend the remainder of a sentence after a felon has served a period of time in prison.

Sixth Amendment States that in all criminal prosecutions, the accused shall enjoy the right to a speedy and public trial, by an impartial jury of the state and district wherein the crime shall have been committed, which district shall have been previously ascertained by law, and to be informed of the nature and cause of the accusation; to be confronted with the witness against him; to have compulsory process for obtaining witnesses in his favor; and to have the assistance of counsel for his defense.

skill development Improving or becoming proficient at an art, craft, or science.

social injustice The thrust of the perspective is that the criminal justice system is biased to weed out the middle and ruling classes so that the vast majority of those found in the system come from the lower classes.

state appellate courts Approximately 207 state-administered courts whose main task is to hear appeals from lower state courts.

statutory law Laws passed by state legislators.

substantial criminal law Concerned with criminal conduct and the necessary punishment for such conduct.

therapeutic community A privately administered community treatment group designed to divert drug abusers from the criminal justice system.

Transactional Analysis (TA) A form of psychotherapy that brings into balance the three states of the ego: parent, adult, and child.

treatment technologies Rehabilitative programs used in correctional institutions.

Uniform Crime Report A national compilation of crime statistics based on information provided the FBI by local and state police agencies.

U.S. Courts of Appeals The 11 federal courts of appeals hear all appeals from federal district courts and the decisions of specified administrative and regulatory agencies.

U.S. District Courts Criminal matters involving the violation of a federal law are brought to these courts.

U.S. Supreme Court The final court of appeals. Cases reach this final court of appeals from a variety of routes: from federal courts of appeals, from the special three-judge federal courts, from petition from paupers (generally state and federal prisoners), and from a small number of cases involving disputes between states.

utilitarianism An effort to derive some socially beneficial outcome from punishment.

utilitarian punishment philosophy A conservative response that arose to crime in the 1970s.

victimization surveys Surveys that measure the extent of criminal behavior by focusing on its targets, the victims.

victims' rights movement During the 1980s, a number of grassroots groups propelled the needs and rights of victims.

vigilante justice A type of "justice" wherein individuals take the law into their own hands because the official agencies were too weak or simply did not exist.

war on crime A "get tough" response to crime that began in the 1970s and continues to the present.

white-collar crime Crime committed by a person of respectability and high social status in the course of his or her occupation.

Wisconsin system (NIC Model Probation Client Classification and Case Management System) Under the Wisconsin system a risk/needs assessment instrument is completed on each probationer at regular intervals. The scores derived from the assessment are used to classify probationers by required level of supervision: intensive, medium, minimum.

work release Release of an inmate from a prison or jail during the day so that he or she can work in the community.

Name Index

Subject Index